CHINA
A Geographical Survey

A HALSTEAD PRESS BOOK
JOHN WILEY & SONS
NEW YORK

CHINA
A Geographical Survey

T. R. Tregear

Acknowledgments

The author and publisher wish to thank the following for permission to reproduce the illustrations in this book; the Anglo-Chinese Educational Institute 7, 11, 12, 13, 14, 17, 18, 24, 29; Hsinhua News Agency, 3, 5, 6, 8, 10, 15, 16, 19, 20, 21, 22, 23, 25, 27; the Society for Anglo-Chinese Understanding, 1, 2, 4, 9, 28.

Acknowledgment is also made to the publishers of *A Geography of China* (University of London Press Ltd) and *An Economic Geography of China* (Butterworth) in which some of the material in this book first appeared.

ISBN 0–470–26925–1 Boards
ISBN 0–470–26926–X Paperbacks

Published in the USA by Halsted Press
a division of John Wiley & Sons Inc. New York

First published 1980
Copyright © 1980 T. R. Tregear
Maps and diagrams copyright © 1980 Hodder and Stoughton

Printed in Great Britain

Contents

Plates

Maps and Diagrams

Introduction

Much water has flowed under the Chinese bridge since my *Geography of China* was published in 1965. As the time has approached for the production of a new edition I have thought it right to produce a larger, fuller work in place of the old, augmenting the original by the inclusion of new material, by incorporating much of the matter in my *Economic Geography of China* (1970 – now out of print) and by bringing the whole up to date as far as possible. It is my hope that this book will fulfil the dual purpose of providing the geography student with material on which he can build further studies and also provide the general reader with basic information on a country which receives less attention than its size and importance should command.

It has been my aim to present, wherever the subject matter permits, a picture of geographical growth and to show the interaction of geographical environment and human activity. If the rapid political, economic and social changes of the last three decades are to be properly understood, they need to be seen against their geographical and historical background; hence the inclusion of a historical section. There is such a wealth of Chinese history that I have allowed myself to consider only a few aspects which have geographical significance. These have been supported by ample quotations which I hope will convey in some small degree a sense of the great heritage which the Chinese people of today enjoy and wish

to preserve, notwithstanding their revolutionary fervour and their break with the past.

In China today politics impinge at every point. There is constant emphasis in every aspect of life, on the farm, in the factory, school, hospital, office, and in sport, on political – i.e. ideological – correctness as the *sine qua non* of success, as expressed in Mao's dictum 'Put politics in command!' It is held that correct thought will determine correct action in all fields, political, economic, social, military, cultural, recreational, even geographical. While thought cannot materially affect basic geographical phenomena such as relief, climate, mineral resources, it can and does vitally affect man's use of his environment. This is a fact that communists in general – and Chinese communists in particular – have seized on, and it is the reason why, in season and out of season, they seek to mould men's minds with all means in their power. The objective is to build a modern industrial socialist state, and if this is to be achieved a socialistically-minded people must be created. This is a colossal task, involving the conversion of 800 million people, 80 per cent of whom are of conservative peasant stock, from an individualistic and clannish outlook to a national and international outlook, in which the main incentive to effort shall be service of the people. Mao has repeatedly emphasized that this cannot but be a long and arduous struggle. The years ahead alone will demonstrate the success or failure of this endeavour.

The subject of China is charged with emotions – and consequently with much inaccurate information – for all. Accounts of developments in China since 1949, especially during times of tension such as The Great Leap Forward and the Cultural Revolution, whether emanating from China itself or from the West, have often been written with so much bias and sometimes with deliberate intent to mislead, that, the formation of accurate conclusions becomes elusive. When matters of individual freedom and standards of living arise it is difficult not to project western values and standards onto situations to which they are not very relevant. The more enlightening comparisons, political and economic, are those between pre-1949 and post-1949 China rather than between China and the West.

The western student studying Chinese geography is faced with difficulty regarding place names, which are presented in differing forms of romanization. The Chinese are free of this problem since place names are depicted in ideographs, understood by all. Further, cities, large and small, throughout history, have changed their names many times. This habit continues. For example, Anlu, a city on the Han river where I lived and worked in 1923, is now known as Chungsiang, whilst its nearest neighbour 100 km to the east, which was then known as Teinan, has now assumed the name of Anlu. This can be very confusing. In order to meet this difficulty, place names used in the text have been plotted, as far as possible, on the accompanying sketch maps and have followed those used in the 1957 edition of the *Times Atlas of the World* rather than the *Times Atlas of China* (1974) to which few readers will have access and which uses the as-yet unfamiliar 'pin yin' romanization.

The Chinese have kept records of various aspects of life and economy from very early days, mainly on a provincial level. There are statistics of flood and drought reaching back to early Han times. These early records need to be read with care since they usually rest on the subjective judgment of district or provincial officials. Statistical material in all fields, except Customs, before 1949 is very patchy: some is excellent for small areas but, on the whole, figures lie in the realm of estimates. When the Chinese People's government came into power, the State Statistical Bureau was formed and the slow, laborious process of building a reliable, objective service progressed.

Fairly dependable figures for population were forthcoming in 1954, and in 1960 the Bureau published *Ten Great Years: Statistics of the Economic and Cultural Achievements of the People's Republic of China*. Unhappily, during the enthusiasm and fanaticism of the Great Leap Forward in 1958–9, returns of production were wildly exaggerated and had to be repudiated and the work of the Bureau was shattered. Since 1960 very few precise and reliable statistics have been published, progress being normally reported in percentages of change. Recently, however, there have been signs of a return to firm statistics. The reader will note that a number of economic (dot) maps are included in the text. These give a verisimilitude which may be misleading. They have not the statistical exactness with which they are usually associated. Nevertheless they do give a fairly accurate picture of relative distributions.

Taiwan, Hong Kong and Macau have been included in the text as though they were legally integral parts of China. It would be ludicrous to exclude them on the ground that at the moment they are politically administered by governments other than that of the People's Republic. Geographically and ethnically they are parts of the same whole and it is virtually certain that, sooner rather than later, they will come under the jurisdiction of the Chinese government.

The country is immense. It stretches from latitude 54° N (Dzhalinda) to 18° N (Hainan) and from longitude 74° E (West Sinkiang) to 135° E (Khabarovsk), but a recital of latitude and longitude is rather sterile. A superimposition of the map of China on those of other parts of the world is perhaps more helpful. For example, if the People's Republic of China were superimposed on North America, its northernmost point, Dzhalinda in the Northeast (Manchuria) would lie in the vicinity of James Bay, while the southernmost point, Hainan, would coincide with Jamaica. The western border of Sinkiang would lie off the coast of California and Khabarovsk at the confluence of the Ussuri and the Amur would coincide with Cape Breton Island. For those who are more familiar with Europe a similar superimposition would show China covering the Mediterranean from end to end with Dzhalinda in the vicinity of Moscow and Hainan near Khartoum.

The area of the People's Republic of China is 9 473 611 sq km. This is some 1 607 320 sq km less than under the Manchu regime, owing to the secession of Outer Mongolia in 1921, prior to which the estimated areas were:

China Proper	3 969 950 sq km
Manchuria	941 983
Mongolia	3 543 998
Chinese Turkestan (Sinkiang)	1 426 000
Tibet	1 200 000
	11 080 931

Outer Mongolia is a vast area and, although economically it seems of comparatively small importance, since it consists largely of desert, semi-desert and poor steppeland, politically and strategically its loss may have far-reaching implications.

For at least the last 2000 years there has been a distinction in Chinese eyes between what is termed China Proper and the dependencies or colonies of Imperial China. China Proper embraces the eighteen provinces which lie between the Pacific coast and the Tibetan highlands in the west and the series of ranges forming the edge of Inner Mongolia in the north. Within these limits was developed the civilization which has had a continuous existence from ancient times until today. Beyond these boundaries have been the lands of the 'barbarians' from whom, in times of Chinese ascendancy, tribute was received. Owing to its encirclement by great upland wastes on the west and mountain ranges and desert on the north and northwest, China Proper has been singularly cut off by land from the intimate influence of other civilizations. The dependencies of Tibet and Mongolia have acted as effective buffers, and the only invasions experienced were from the nomadic peoples occupying the steppelands who were, eventually, either absorbed or expelled.

Similarly, the vast expanse of the Pacific Ocean for long militated against intercourse with the Americas to the east, regions which, in any case, were undeveloped until recent centuries. True, there was appreciable trading with the Arabs, Persians and Indians in early medieval times but this had little impact on so vast a land as China and there was no danger of invasion from this direction. Since any such attack would have entailed far greater accumulation of capital and military 'know-how' than then existed, such penetration had to wait until the industrial revolution in the West had come to full fruition.

Thus it was that China remained in virtual isolation. Even in time of its greatest expansion its contacts with Europe and even with India were seldom, if ever, direct. Meanwhile it cultivated a rich civilization of its own, conservative and complaisant in its own self-sufficiency. The stirring intellectual and spiritual revolution of the Renaissance, which so rocked Western thought, left China unmoved. The industrial and technical revolution of the eighteenth and nineteenth centuries made no appreciable impact on China until the twentieth century. In spite of her great culture and early scientific inventiveness, China remained essentially medieval and rural in essence until very recently. The explosiveness of the sudden intrusion of Western ideas and techniques has therefore been all the greater. The rapid changes that have taken place in the last hundred years have been attended by constant wars, unrest and internal disorder, which were resolved only by the Communist revolution in 1949.

During the early years of Liberation little interest was shown in happenings abroad, which perhaps was not surprising in view of the colossal task confronting them. Today, even though much more weight is given to the international scene, the influence of their long isolation would seem to be with them still: the Chinese still regard their country as Chung Kuo, the Central Kingdom.

I would like to thank Dr. R. P. Beckinsale and Dr. A. S. Goudie for their help on the Physical section.

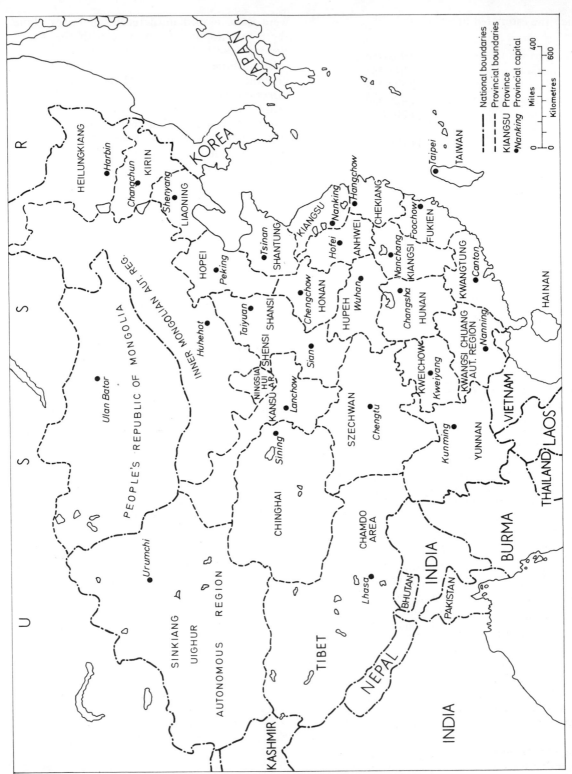

Fig. 1 Political divisions of China

1   Physical Geography

The physical features of a country represent the sum total of the constructive, deformative and erosive processes that have operated in that country throughout geological time.

J. S. Lee

STRUCTURE AND RELIEF

The physical physiognomy of a country, its mineral resources, its vegetational cover and even, to some extent, the character of its people, are determined, in greater or less measure, by its geology and its structural history. It behoves us, therefore, to turn our attention at this early stage to the evolution which the topography of present-day China has undergone, to pass in rapid review the main geological successions and to observe the effect of the chief periods of revolution.

Much of the vast country is still unexplored or quite inadequately surveyed. A great deal of work is now being done in the field in China but, until this has been properly plotted, analysed and published, we must continue to rely on the work of such pioneers as Richthofen, Willis and Grabau, and of their successors, such as Andersson, Pierre Teilhard de Chardin, Young and Lee. It is to be hoped that in a few years' time many of the problems and uncertainties that now exist will be cleared up.

The ancient floor

Underlying the whole of China, from east to west and north to south, is a floor of ancient rock.

Cores of pre-Cambrian rocks lie exposed in many parts, mainly in ranges to the north of the Yangtze, in Inner Mongolia, Shensi, Shansi, Shantung and Liaoning. They are of two systems: the *Wutai*, named after the Wutai Shan in the Peking Grid, which is composed of highly metamorphosed sedimentaries (gneiss and schist), together with acid and igneous rocks; and the *Sinian*, first named by Richthofen and included in the Palaeozoic by Grabau, which is also sedimentary but much less metamorphosed.

Rising from this ancient floor are three massifs, none of which has been completely submerged by subsequent transgressions. The largest and most stable of these is Tibetia, whose pre-Cambrian ranges rise through thin layers of gravel, loess and sand. Gobia, although covered in parts during Tertiary times by seas which laid down clays and sands, has also been generally above sea-level. The third, named by Grabau as Cathaysia, is the southeastern area of China and is the western remnant of a massif, which was raised by folding in the Sinian and existed throughout Palaeozoic times. The eastern part of Cathaysia, through violent folding and downfaulting in recent geological time, has been submerged, leaving Japan, the Philippines and festoons of islands marking its eastern rim.

Palaeozoic

A geosyncline, known as the Cathaysian geosyncline, running from the northeast in present Manchuria to the present mouth of the Ganges and thence westward in the Sea of Tethys, existed almost continuously throughout the Palaeozoic. During the Cambrian this geosyncline underwent considerable subsidence, while the surrounding land was peneplained. Even Shantung was partially submerged.

In Middle and Late Ordovician times, this geosyncline was interrupted by the raising of a land barrier running east to west along the line of the present Chinling (Tsinling) in a movement known as the Hsiayuan. This east–west axis has been maintained to the present day and is one of the great geographical divides of China. In these same Ordovician times there was a general subsidence to the south, accompanied by intense folding in Indo-China. The area to the north of the east–west Chinling (Tsinling) axis, which had previously been subjected to repeated submergence, was now uplifted and so remained until late Carboniferous and Permian times, subject to a long period of erosion. In fact, this northern area has never again been deeply submerged.

Owing to this uplift and consequent absence of sedimentary rocks of the period, there is a lack of evidence of the Caledonian movement north of the Chinling (Tsinling). In the far north, the fold mountains of Sayan and Irkutsk on the east and west of lake Baikal were raised. There was also considerable folding in the southwest, and in the southeast the Nanling and southeast highlands were raised.

During Permo–Carboniferous times the sea (Chinese Tethys) spread northward, and great stretches of the north oscillated between land and sea, forming at times a broad, shallow continental shelf. It was in this period that the main coalfields of the north and centre were formed.

Towards the end of the Permian, the Tungwu orogeny occurred. It was a period of intense folding, corresponding to the Hercynian in the

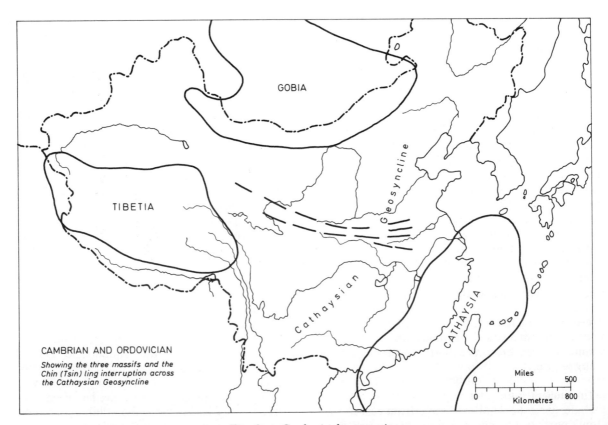

Fig. 2a   Geological succession

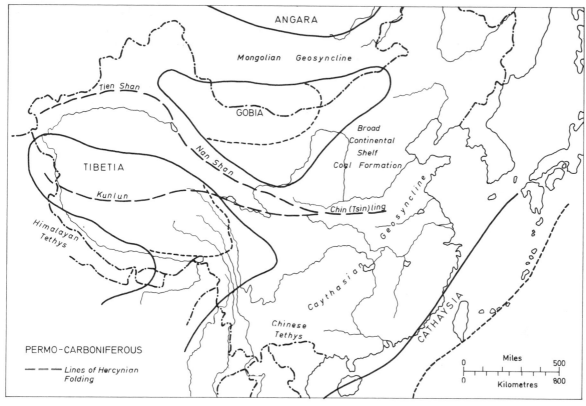

Fig. 2b   Geological succession

West. The great systems, comprising the Tien Shan, Kunlun, Altyn Tagh, Nan Shan and Chinling (Tsinling) were formed at this time, and their line continued through Shantung and the East Manchurian Mountains. The coal measures, previously laid down in the Carboniferous and Lower Permian, were greatly disturbed. During this revolution Tibetia remained firm and most of north China remained above sea-level, but considerable areas of Gobia were temporarily submerged. Most of southern China and Kweichow were also below sea-level.

Mesozoic
During the Early and Middle Triassic, southwest China, the Red Basin of Szechwan and the lower Yangtze valley lay below the sea. Thin bedded limestones, which are oil-bearing, were laid down at this time. During later Triassic times the greater part of Burma, Thailand and Indonesia were submerged as the Chinese Tethys rejoined the Himalayan Tethys from which it had been cut off during the Permian.

Subsequently, in the Jurassic, coal-bearing shales and sandstones, in widely distributed basins of greatly varying size, were deposited.[1] One of these was the present Red Basin of Szechwan. North China for the most part remained above sea-level and was eroded to a peneplain, while the geosyncline to the south of the Chinling (Tsinling) continued to develop and deepen. In late Jurassic or early Cretaceous, the Yenshan or Ningchinian movement occurred. This again was a period of extensive and powerful folding. Its main lines were along the former Hercynian lines of compression, i.e. Tien Shan, Kunlun, Nan Shan and Chinling (Tsinling) and were continued north and northeast through the Ala Shan and In Shan on the one hand and the Taihang Shan and Luliang Shan on the other to the Ta Hingan and Siao Hingan. Farther east and south it effected the shattering of the Shantung–Liaoning platform and heavily folded

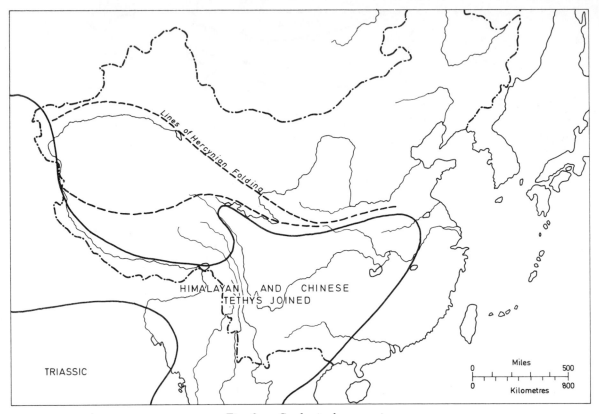

Fig. 2c   Geological succession

the land of southeast China (Cathaysia), Indo-China and North Borneo. A new geosyncline, known as the Hong Kong and Nippon Bays, was formed to the southeast extending from south Japan to Hainan.

Following this powerful revolution came a period of quiet sedimentation in continental basins, probably undergoing continual subsidence. The most notable and extensive of these basins were in Mongolia, where dinosaur eggs of Middle and Upper Cretaceous were found by P. Chapman Andrews, and in the Red Basin, where clays, sandstones and limestones to a thickness of over 3000 metres were laid down on the Jurassic coal measures. In northwest Shansi, north Shensi and Kansu beds of red sandstone were deposited. Lee comments on the oil-bearing potentialities of these Szechwan and northern deposits, potentialities which have been amply fulfilled by recent discoveries.[2]

This period of quiescence was followed by one of great volcanic activity everywhere outside the Cretaceous basins. The igneous intrusions of granite, granodiorite and porphyry at this time are largely responsible for the rich deposits of wolfram, tin, antimony, lead, zinc and copper, which occur especially in the southern half of the country.

The final phase of this Yenshan movement consisted of further folding and volcanic intrusion in Upper Cretaceous times, known as the Chinganian movement corresponding to the Laramide of North America, when the Rocky Mountains were formed.

Cainozoic

In mid-Tertiary times there was some marked folding in Sikang (Chamdo Area) but China, as a whole, bears few marks of the Alpine revolution which is so outstanding in Europe, western Asia and northern India. Apparently it affected only the extreme western margins of Yunnan and Szechwan.

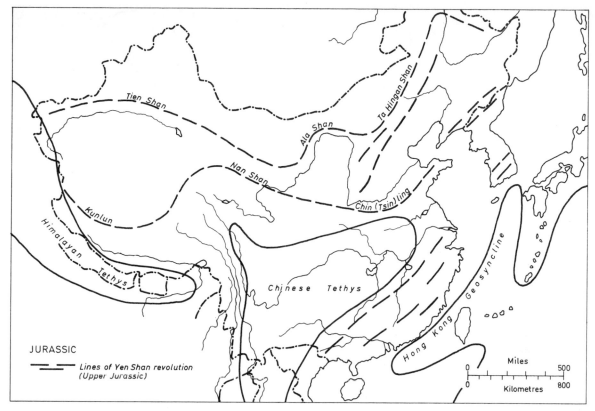

Fig. 2d   Geological succession

In Pleistocene times at a period equivalent to the Würm glaciations the main deposits of loess from the northwest were laid down in Shensi and Shansi. The extent and nature of this fine, wind-borne soil are dealt with fully in a later chapter. Suffice it here to say that deposition is still going on, although apparently at a slower rate than formerly.

Quaternary

It is generally agreed that there has been a considerable uplift in the west during quaternary times, a movement which is continuing in the present day. In support of this contention Lee says: 'A striking case . . . In the neighbourhood of Tatsinlu and on the eastern side of the Minyu Gongkai, Heim has actually observed the fluvio-glacial water cutting its own deposit formed in the glacial age to a depth of 100 metres. There is clear evidence that the glaciers in the high mountains have retreated in recent geological time. The argument that such stream erosion might be due to

increased precipitation in post-glacial time can, therefore, be safely ruled out.'[3] Further evidence of this recent uplift is seen in the physiographical history of the Yangtze (see p. 285 ff.).

Glacial action

Until recently the view that China was left untouched by the glacial epoch was firmly held. Andersson, in referring to the loess deposits, says that in north China and Mongolia everything indicates that the climate in those parts was too dry to permit the existence of an ice cover.[4] However, in the Tatung Basin and the Taihang Shan of Shansi, there are indications of glacial action such as erratics on the tops of high hills, striated boulders and U-shaped valleys. Lee suggests that local glaciers may have been formed towards the end of the Sanmen period when there was a fall in temperature and a rise in humidity.

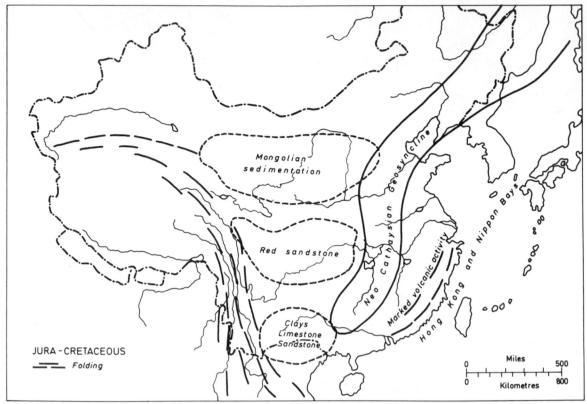

Fig. 2e   Geological succession

Similar evidence of grooved rocks, parallel striation of rocks in both mountain and plain, cirque formations, boulder clay and U-shaped valleys in the Yangtze valley, notably in the Lushan Hills, Kiangsi, have, for many years, suggested that there was considerable glacial action in this area.[5] Doubt was cast on the validity of evidence in the form of parallel scratches since it was contended that, in view of the heavy weathering to which the rocks have been subjected, the scratches could not have survived. However, in 1936, the occurrence of unusually low water around lake Poyang provided a unique opportunity for observations of formations, and it is now considered as conclusively established that there was widespread glacial action in this area.[6] Russian geographers have no doubt that the western part of China was heavily glaciated in quaternary times and state that it is a natural assumption that, given the great differences of relief and climate throughout the country, glaciation and its stages will also vary greatly, adding

that the solution of these questions must await further research.[7]

Topography

With this geological background in mind, it is now possible to take a general view of the relief and drainage of China. No attempt will be made to describe this in any detail, which would be a long and tedious undertaking. A more intimate treatment will be made in the regional section.

1. PLATEAUS AND BASINS

Western and northwestern China consists largely of great upland regions, separated from each other by massive mountain systems. While these basins vary greatly in height from below sea-level to over 3500 m, they have one common characteristic. They are all inland drainage basins.

(*a*) *The Tibetan Plateau.* This great massif stands today at a general level of over 3500 m. Its boundaries are everywhere considerably higher than the interior: on the south the Himalayan ranges;

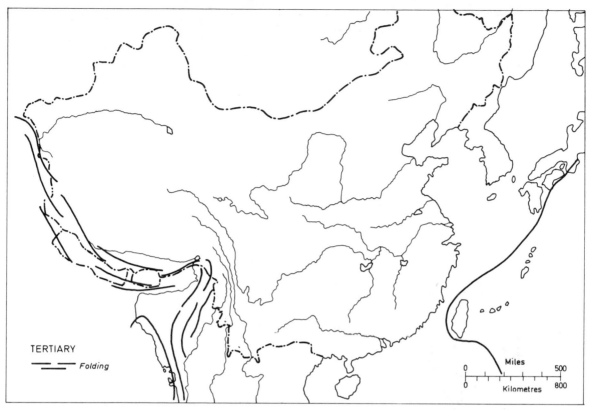

TERTIARY

—— —— Folding

Miles
0 ———————— 500
0 ———————— 800
Kilometres

Fig. 2f Geological succession

on the west the Hindu Kush, which extend into the plateau itself in the Karakorams; on the north the Kunlun and Astin Tagh (Altyn Tagh); and on the east the north–south folds of the mountains of Sikang. In its southern and eastern periphery great rivers find their sources and their way to the sea: the Indus and Brahmaputra; the Mekong, Yangtze and Hwang-ho. Most of the precipitation on the interior side of the boundary ranges flows inward and terminates in the many brackish lakes which stud the plateau. Innumerable east–west ranges, rising through thin layers of sand, gravel and clay, push their ancient cores to heights of over 5500 m.

(*b*) *The Tsaidam.* Northeast of the Tibetan plateau is a smaller basin, The Tsaidam, which stands at a general height of about 3000 m. This is bounded on the northwest by the Astin Tagh (Altyn Tagh); on the northeast by the Nan Shan and on the south by the Kunlun. This, again, is an inland drainage area.[8]

(*c*) *The Tarim Basin.* North of the Tibetan plateau and at the much lower general level of 1000 m lies the Tarim Basin. It is hemmed in by great mountain ranges; the Tien Shan on the north, the Pamir Knot on the west and the Astin Tagh (Altyn Tagh) on the south. From these heights, glacier-fed streams descend, only to lose themselves in the sands and gravels of the Takla Makan desert, which occupies the centre of the basin and which is one of the most barren of the world's deserts. This area figures prominently in Chinese history, for it was along the line of oases which fringe the north and south edges of the desert, that the earliest contacts with the West were made.

To the northeast of the Tarim Basin and included within the same bounds is the smaller Turfan Basin, which is 154 m below sea-level.

(*d*) *Dzungaria.* North of the Tarim Basin is yet another inland drainage area, Dzungaria. The heart of this basin descends to heights of less than 300 m above sea-level. Thus we find three clear

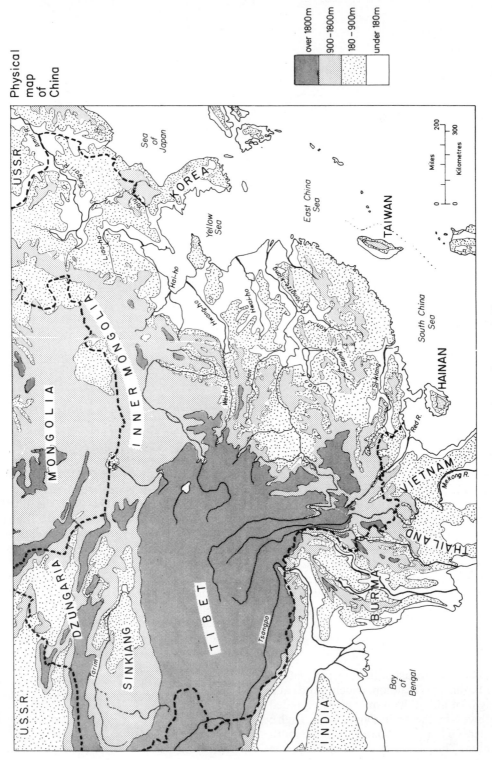

Fig. 3   Physical map of China

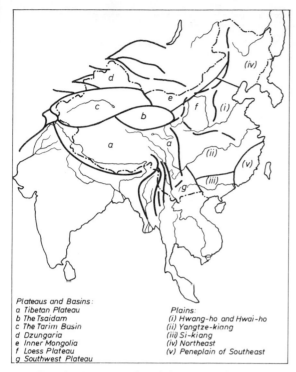

Plateaus and Basins:
a Tibetan Plateau
b The Tsaidam
c The Tarim Basin
d Dzungaria
e Inner Mongolia
f Loess Plateau
g Southwest Plateau

Plains:
(i) Hwang-ho and Hwai-ho
(ii) Yangtze-kiang
(iii) Si-kiang
(iv) Northeast
(v) Peneplain of Southeast

Fig. 4   Topographical divisions of China

downward steps as we pass northward from Tibet to the border of the U.S.S.R. Dzungaria is enclosed by the Tien Shan on the south; the Altai Mountains on the northeast, cutting it off from Outer Mongolia; and the Tarbagatai Mountains on the northwest, forming the frontier between China and the U.S.S.R.

Like the Tarim Basin, this area figures prominently in early East–West contacts, for one branch of the Silk Route passed along the northern edge of the Tien Shan.

It should be noted that, while formerly Sinkiang and the Tarim were often used as synonymous terms, today Sinkiang is officially the political district embracing both the Tarim Basin and Dzungaria.

(*e*) *Inner Mongolia.* Inner Mongolia is the southern half of the Gobi, which geographically embraces both Inner and Outer Mongolia and is the great shallow, inland drainage basin enclosed by the Khangai, Altai and Nan Shan in the west; the Ala Shan and In Shan in the south; the Ta Hingan in the east; and the Sayan and Irkutsk Mountains in the north. It descends to about 450 m in the centre. A number of streams, the

greatest of which is the Estin Gol, descend from the Nan Shan, across the 'pan handle' of Kansu, to be lost in the heart of the desert.

(*f*) *Southwest Plateau.* This plateau, which comprises the whole of Yunnan and the western part of Kweichow, is highly dissected. It is the only one of our classified plateaus whose drainage is entirely seaward.

2. THE GREAT PLAINS
The three east–west axes, along the In Shan, Tsinling and Nanling, noted by Lee,[9] have had marked influence on the three great rivers of China, determining their direction of flow.

(*a*) *The Hwang-ho* is confined between the northern axis of the In Shan and the central axis of the Tsinling. After it descends from the Tibetan massif, it meanders between these two until it finds an outlet of its own making across the North China Plain to the Gulf of Pohai. After cutting through the Nan Shan at the Liuchia gorge, it turns north in a great loop and flows in a wide, shallow stream through the Ordos Desert. Turning south just north of Hokow, it cuts deeply through the loess, and passes through the region which cradled Chinese civilization, where it turns abruptly eastward at the confluence of the Wei river by way of the Tung Kwan gorge. Thence it emerges onto the wide alluvial floodplain, which, although so subject to disaster, is yet so heavily populated.

(*b*) *The Yangtze Basin* lies between the Tsinling and the Nanling axes. Nearly one-third of the great river's upper course lies in the highlands of Sikang. After cutting its way through the Taliang Shan, it flows eastward through a series of former lake basins: first the Red Basin of Szechwan, with its four left-bank tributaries; then the lake-studded Central Basin of Hunan, Hupeh and Kiangsi, drained by the Han, Yuan, Siang and Kan rivers; and finally the 'delta' region of Anhwei and Kiangsu. These three basins form the most productive and most densely populated region in China.

(*c*) *The Si-kiang Basin.* Rising in the Yunnan plateau, the Si-kiang pursues an eastward course, south of the Nanling through Kwangsi and Kwangtung and enters the sea by an extensive delta at Canton. While not as extensive a plain as either the Hwang-ho or the Yangtze, it is important in that it has a subtropical climate and consequently is a double-cropping rice area.

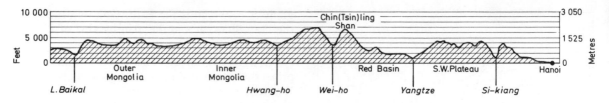

Fig. 5a   Section from Dzungaria to Bay of Bengal

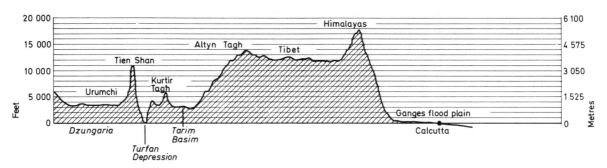

Fig. 5b   Section from Lake Baikal to Gulf of Tongking

(d) The Northeast (Manchurian) Plain. This great undulating plain lies in the extreme northeast and is comprised of the three provinces of Heilungkiang, Kirin and Liaoning. It is bounded on the west by the Ta Hingan Mountains and on the north by the Siao Hingan Mountains. The Eastern Manchurian Mountains form a considerable part of its eastern boundary, separating it from Korea. On the south the Jehol Mountains and the sea form the boundary. The plain is split into northern and southern halves by a low divide, the northern half being drained by the Sungari river and its tributaries, which empty into the Amur or Heilung Kiang, and the southern half by the Liao river.

3. THE SOUTHEAST

Lying between the lower Yangtze and the lower Si-kiang basins is a region of much-folded mountains, having a northeast, southwest trend, the main ranges of which are the Wuyi Shan. Rivers are comparatively short and fast-flowing in steep-sided valleys down to the rugged southeast coast. It is a land which long resisted incorporation into the Chinese Empire and, even today, it remains distinct, particularly in its dialects. Its people look largely to the sea for their livelihood.

CLIMATE

It is not surprising to find, in a country so vast as China, covering as it does so great a range in both latitude and longitude and including peaks of nearly 7500 m in height and basins below sea-level, that one encounters not one climate but a variety of climates. Here, in this vast subcontinent, are found hot desert climate in the Tarim Basin; cold desert in the Tibetan plateau; temperate continental climate in the northeast; the unique temperate Szechwanese climate of the Red Basin; and the tropical and subtropical in Kwangtung, to mention only a few. Yet, in spite of all these differences, close analysis will show that they are all variations on one basic theme of causation.

The theme is provided by the monsoon rhythm arising from the continentality of the huge land-mass of Asia. The variations on the theme, played on the instruments of varying altitude, contrasting ranges of seasonal and diurnal temperature, contrasting types of seasonal rainfall and precipitation and of quietude and storminess – all reveal in greater or less degree their causal relationship to this basic continentality, to a rhythmic seasonal change from a dense high-pressure centre over the land in winter to a low-pressure area in summer.

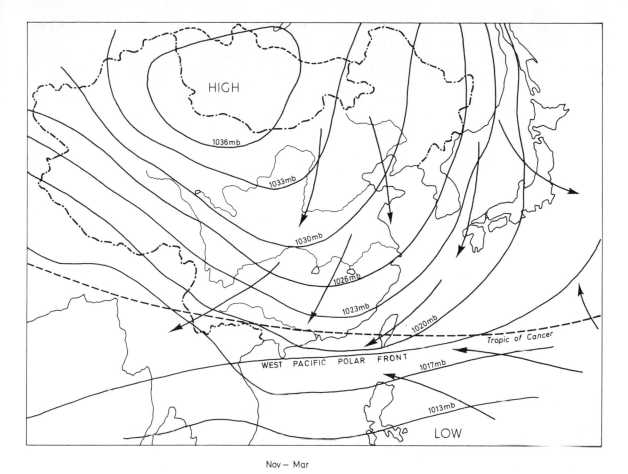

Nov — Mar

Fig. 6   Pressure and winds: winter

The monsoon

The term *monsoon* is used in everyday conversation to connote a particular type of weather experienced in Southeast Asia. Usually what is in mind is the onset of a summer season of heavy rain. It is true that this is a marked phenomenon of the monsoon, but it is the result of the monsoon rather than the monsoon itself, which technically is a wind system with a clear seasonal change in direction. In India this change is from southwest in summer to northeast in winter. In China the change is from southeast in summer to north and northeast in winter. To a less marked degree there is a similar seasonal change in eastern North America with an inflowing southeast wind in summer and an outflowing north and northwest wind in winter. However, owing to the fact that the landmass of North America is not nearly so great as that of Asia, the seasonal reversal of the winds is less marked. Moreover the general trend of highland is north–south in North America, admitting an easier flow of warm and cold air than in East Asia, where the mountain trend is rather east–west.[10]

The winter monsoon

Asia is the greatest of the world's landmasses and, in consequence of this, its heart experiences greater variations in temperature between summer and winter than any other part of the world. As autumn progresses, the landmass quickly cools in marked contrast to the slower cooling ocean along its southern and eastern borders. A great pool or mass of cold air settles in the large, shallow basins of Siberia and Mongolia, forming an anticyclone or centre of high pressure, which rises to 1035 mm. By November this cold airmass is fully established: its centre covers the whole of Inner and Outer Mongolia, and spreads steadily southward until it meets the warm airmass of the North Pacific Trades along a front rather to the south of the China coast and Taiwan in what is now known as the *West Pacific Polar Front*. This airmass is a fairly shallow layer of 3000–4000 m. It remains stationary over East Siberia and Mongolia from November to March and is generally in undisputed control.

From this great anticyclone there is an outflow of dry northerly and northeasterly winds over China bringing prolonged and bitter winters to the northern part of the country and really cold weather as far south as the Central and Lower Yangtze Basins. The barometric gradient between high pressure and low pressure is steep, and the resulting winds are strong.

Occasionally this bitter weather is interrupted by a welcome warm spell brought about, apparently, by depressions moving in from the west in the upper layers of the atmosphere. At 4000 metres the circumpolar westerlies move freely above the lower colder layers shown in figure 6. Farther south the vertical thickness of the winter monsoon drops. At Nanking it is 2000 metres and in North Vietnam only 1500–1000 metres. F. K. Hare says of these disturbances: 'Though they invariably weaken as they cross the continent, not a few of these European or Atlantic storms actually penetrate to Manchuria or North China every winter. At such times the Siberian high, usually regarded as permanent, is displaced far to the northeast, or may even be absent ... During the lull it is common for warm moist air (either mT or modified cP) to spread far northward across China and Japan, giving a welcome relief from the cold of the monsoon.'

These lulls are of short duration and, as the cold air moves southward once more with the re-establishment of the high, further cyclones are developed along the cold front and travel from west to east across China, continuing over Japan, often with increased intensity. These disturbances may arise on latitudes as far north as Dzungaria and Inner Mongolia. Pressure may rise very rapidly by as much as 25 millibars per day, giving rise in North China to dust storms, since the dried soil of the north is not only virtually devoid of vegetation but also has very little snow cover.[12] Their main development is along the Yangtze valley, where the increased humidity may cause heavy snowfalls, hail and glazed frosts.

There is, however, a marked difference between the weather of north and south China at this time. Whereas the north experiences generally clear, bright days with deep frost and occasional light snowfalls, there is more cloudiness and precipitation south of Tsinling Shan.

TRANSITION FROM WINTER TO SUMMER MONSOON
As spring (April) approaches the passage of cyclones increases both in number and intensity. The cold, heavy airmass over the heart of the continent begins to warm up, at first very gradually, giving place to a continental low, while a high pressure centre is slowly established over the eastern Pacific. Wind direction is slowly reversed, northerly and northwesterly winds give way to

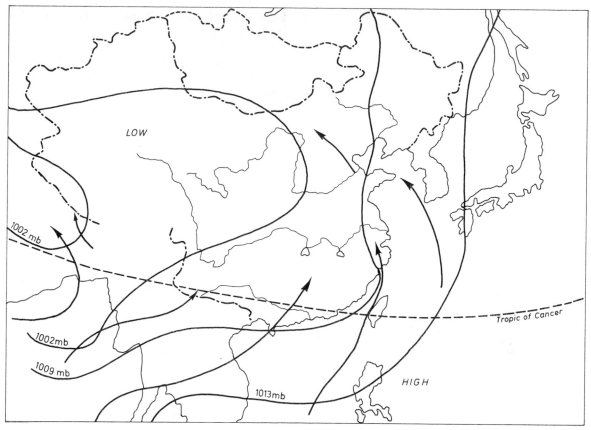

April – October

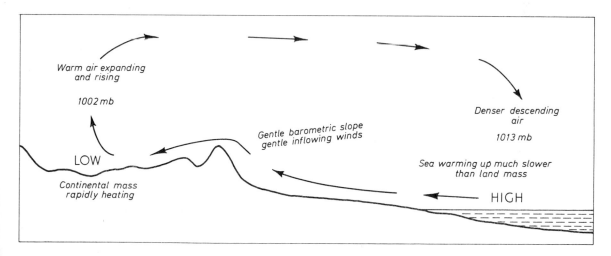

Fig. 7   Pressure and winds: summer

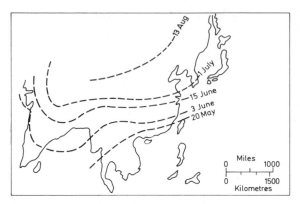

Fig. 8   Mean date of commencement of summer monsoon

those from the south and southeast, and a great current of warm, humid air moves in from the south. Its onset is felt earliest in the south and southeast. By May much of South China experiences mainly south and southeast winds and an increase in rainfall along the West Pacific Polar Front, which steadily retreats northward.[13] T'u Chang-wang comments on the gradualness of the onset: 'In India the "burst of the monsoon" can be followed pretty easily, but in China we have only a "burst of the cold waves", that is the winter monsoon, whereas the advance of the summer monsoon is very gradual and inconspicuous, hence the task of following its advance or retreat is more complicated.'[14]

By June the West Pacific Polar Front is over the Yangtze valley, and by July it lies somewhere across the loess region and the Ordos, bringing occasional heavy rainfall to this dry region. Winds are now southeasterly over the North China Plain and southerly over Central and South China. The summer monsoon has now arrived. As can be seen from the map (fig. 7) the barometric gradient between high and low is much gentler than in winter and consequently winds are lighter. The characteristic weather of the summer monsoon over much of China is hot, calm days of high relative humidity, which are very oppressive.

Exasperatingly, any slight breeze which may have been blowing during the day so often fails in the evening, giving long, breathless nights. Coastal regions, especially in the south and southeast, are periodic victims of disastrous typhoon winds. Further inland very strong winds, known as *feng pao*, occasionally disturb the prevailing calm.

The duration of the summer monsoon varies between north and south, being shorter in the north on account of the lateness of onset. T'u Chang-wang and Hwang Sze-sung make a general estimate:

Temperature

All three of the major influences on temperature namely altitude, latitude and landmass play very outstanding parts in China. There is a difference of over 9000 m between Everest and the Turfan basin. There is a difference of nearly 40° in latitude between Hainan (18° N) and Moho (53° 33′ N) on the Amur in Heilungkiang. China has an area of nearly 9·5 million sq km and lies on the eastern side of the greatest landmass in the world into which it penetrates some 4500 km. Small wonder therefore that we find vast differences both in range and level of temperatures from place to place and from season to season. There is a difference of more than 30 degrees of latitude between north and south China resulting in a marked difference in length of day and solar radiation. In mid-winter Canton receives double Harbin's radiation because of the greater angle of the sun's rays and 3 hours' longer daylight. Harbin at this time has a negative radiation balance. In summer the two cities receive about the same radiation, Harbin's 3 hours' longer daylight compensating for the lesser angle of the sun's rays.

In winter there is a large and steady fall in temperature from south to north. Hong Kong has a January temperature of 15°C, Harbin − 19°C. It will be noticed that the isotherms are remarkably regular in their alignment east–west. The isotherms bend slightly northward over the China Sea, but the ocean has very little moderating effect

			Rainfall
S. of Nanling Hills	mid April–end October	6½ months	75–90%
S. of Yangtze	May–mid October	5½	60–80%
N. China and N.E.	June–end August	3	60–75%
Kansu and Inner Mongolia	June–end August	3	less than 60%

Jen-hu Chang in his 'The Chinese monsoon' (*Geographical Review*, **51**, 1971) deals with the subject in detail.

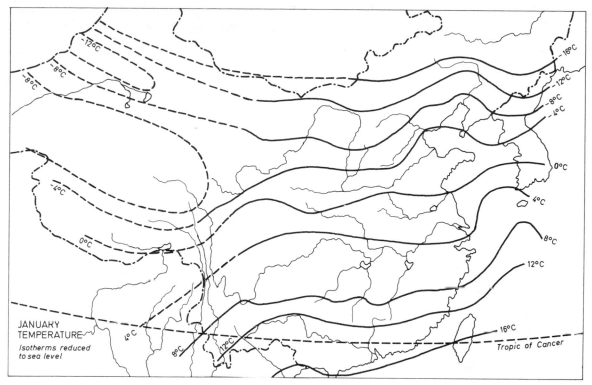

Fig. 9   Temperature: January isotherms

on winter temperatures since the winds are out-flowing from the central low pressure and the cold Kamchatka current hugs the coast in its southward flow. Chefoo, on the Shantung coast, is as cold as Peking, both having an average January temperature of − 5°C. Shanghai, on the coast, is as cold as Hankow, which is 1000 km inland.

In summer the isotherms run north–south and reflect the influence of the inflowing winds of the summer monsoon. There is a remarkable uniformity of temperature in summer, there being a difference of only 8° C between places in China proper as compared with some 33° C in winter. Everywhere it is hot and humid until one passes northwestward into the desert and semi-desert regions of Sinkiang, Mongolia and Dzungaria. Here annual temperature ranges are very great indeed. Luchun, which is in the Turfan basin and is 17 m below sea-level, has an annual range of 42° C. Compare this with Hong Kong, on the coast and in the tropics, which has an annual range of only 12° C.

As a result of continentality the cold pole of the northern hemisphere lies in the heart of Siberia,

over Irkutsk and results in the 0° C isotherm extending farther south in China than in any other region in the northern hemisphere. In China it reaches approximately 33° N; in Europe 43° N and in North America 38° N. The following are average temperatures for January of places of the same latitude:

Chefoo	− 5°C	—	Algiers	12·2° C
Mukden	− 13·4°C	—	Rome	7·0° C
Shanghai	3·3°C	—	Port Said	13·3° C

Rainfall

Excluding the small southwest corner of Sikang, which shares the phenomenal precipitation of Assam, rainfall in China shows a general decrease from southeast to northwest, ranging from 2156 mm in Hong Kong to 10 mm in Kashgar. A large part of south China receives over 1500 mm per annum; the Yangtze basin between 1500 mm and 750 mm. There is a marked decrease in rainfall on crossing northward the Tsinling Shan, the most significant physical divide in China.

Mean Monthly Average Temperature (in °C) and Mean Monthly Rainfall (in mm)

Town	Altitude (in m)	Jan	Feb	March	Apr	May	June	July	Aug	Sept	Oct	Nov	Dec	Total Rainfall (mm)
Hong Kong		15·6	14·4	17·2	21·7	25·0	27·2	**27·8**	27·2	26·7	24·4	20·6	17·2	
	31	*33*	*46*	*68*	*135*	*305*	*401*	*366*	*356*	*246*	*129*	*43*	*28*	*2156*
Canton		13·3	13·9	17·2	21·7	26·7	27·2	**28·3**	**28·3**	26·7	23·9	19·4	15·6	
	15	*23*	*48*	*107*	*173*	*269*	*269*	*205*	*219*	*165*	*86*	*31*	*23*	*1618*
Swaton		15·0	13·9	16·7	21·1	25·0	27·8	**28·9**	28·3	27·8	24·4	20·0	16·7	
	4	*36*	*63*	*79*	*145*	*229*	*267*	*198*	*213*	*142*	*71*	*41*	*38*	*1522*
Foochow		11·7	11·1	13·3	17·8	22·2	26·7	**28·9**	**28·9**	24·4	19·4	15·0	10·0	
	20·4	*46*	*96*	*114*	*122*	*150*	*207*	*160*	*183*	*213*	*51*	*41*	*48*	*1431*
Kweiyang		2·8	5·6	11·7	17·2	21·7	22·2	24·4	**25·0**	20·0	13·9	11·7	8·3	
	1390	*25*	*28*	*23*	*74*	*178*	*209*	*229*	*104*	*138*	*107*	*51*	*15*	*1181*
Kunming		8·9	10·6	15·6	18·9	21·1	**22·2**	21·1	21·1	18·9	17·2	13·3	9·4	
	1805	*13*	*13*	*15*	*18*	*96*	*155*	*249*	*208*	*137*	*91*	*43*	*15*	*1053*
Shanghai		3·3	3·9	7·8	13·3	18·3	22·8	**26·7**	**26·7**	22·8	17·2	11·1	5·6	
	10	*51*	*57*	*91*	*94*	*92*	*188*	*150*	*145*	*119*	*79*	*51*	*33*	*1142*
Kiukiang		4·4	5·6	10·0	16·7	21·7	26·1	**30·0**	28·9	25·0	18·9	12·8	7·2	
	33	*63*	*84*	*150*	*180*	*173*	*244*	*142*	*132*	*89*	*97*	*68*	*43*	*1465*
Hankow		4·4	6·1	10·0	16·7	21·7	26·7	**29·4**	**29·4**	25·0	19·4	12·8	7·2	
	36	*48*	*48*	*97*	*152*	*165*	*244*	*180*	*97*	*71*	*81*	*48*	*28*	*1259*
Changsha		6·1	7·8	10·6	17·2	21·7	26·1	**30·0**	**30·0**	25·0	18·9	12·8	6·1	
	92	*46*	*97*	*147*	*155*	*198*	*224*	*121*	*132*	*86*	*91*	*79*	*46*	*1422*
Ichang		5·6	7·2	11·7	17·8	22·2	26·1	**28·9**	**28·9**	24·4	19·4	13·3	7·8	
	50	*20*	*31*	*53*	*102*	*122*	*155*	*211*	*170*	*102*	*84*	*35*	*15*	*1100*
Chungking		8·3	10·0	14·4	19·4	23·3	26·1	27·8	**28·9**	24·4	19·4	15·0	10·0	
	230	*15*	*20*	*36*	*102*	*140*	*180*	*142*	*129*	*147*	*117*	*51*	*23*	*1102*
Chengtu	6·7	7·8	12·8	17·2	21·1	20·4	**25·6**	**25·6**	21·7		17·8	13·3	7·8	
	475	*5*	*10*	*15*	*43*	*71*	*104*	*145*	*246*	*46*	*104*	*10*	*3*	*802*
Tientsin		−2·2	0·0	6·1	13·3	19·4	20·4	**27·2**	25·6	22·2	14·4	5·0	0·0	
	2	*5*	*3*	*10*	*15*	*28*	*61*	*173*	*129*	*71*	*15*	*10*	*2*	*522*
Peking		−5·1	−1·7	5·0	13·9	20·0	24·4	**26·1**	24·4	20·0	12·2	3·3	−2·8	
	39	*3*	*5*	*5*	*15*	*36*	*76*	*239*	*160*	*66*	*19*	*8*	*2*	*630*
Chefoo		−5·1	−0·6	4·4	11·7	18·3	22·8	**25·6**	**25·6**	21·7	15·6	8·3	1·7	
	0	*13*	*10*	*15*	*25*	*36*	*61*	*173*	*155*	*66*	*25*	*31*	*15*	*625*
Taiyuan		−8·4	−3·3	3·9	12·2	18·3	22·8	**25·0**	22·8	17·2	10·6	2·2	−5·7	
	788	*8*	*0*	*10*	*8*	*15*	*43*	*125*	*86*	*41*	*15*	*0*	*3*	*354*
Sian		0·6	3·9	10·0	17·2	23·9	27·8	**30·0**	27·8	22·2	17·2	6·7	1·7	
	334	*10*	*8*	*15*	*43*	*51*	*71*	*84*	*127*	*41*	*41*	*8*	*10*	*509*
Saratsi		−15·2	−9·5	0·0	8·3	7·8	20·6	**22·8**	21·1	13·9	6·7	−4·5	−15·2	
	933	*3*	*5*	*8*	*8*	*23*	*46*	*99*	*74*	*51*	*15*	*3*	*3*	*338*
Lu-ta Dairen		−3·9	−3·9	2·2	8·9	15·0	20·0	22·8	**24·4**	20·6	14·4	6·1	−1·1	
	10	*13*	*8*	*18*	*23*	*43*	*46*	*163*	*130*	*102*	*28*	*25*	*13*	*612*
Shenyang Murden	*34*	−12·8	−10·6	−2·2	7·8	15·6	21·1	**24·4**	23·3	16·7	8·9	−1·7	−10·0	
		5	*5*	*20*	*28*	*56*	*86*	*160*	*155*	*84*	*41*	*28*	*5*	*673*
Harbin		−19·4	−15·2	−4·5	5·6	13·3	18·9	**22·2**	20·6	10·6	4·4	−6·2	−16·4	
	159	*5*	*5*	*10*	*23*	*43*	*104*	*147*	*107*	*56*	*31*	*10*	*5*	*546*
Urumchi		−15·2	−13·4	−7·3	8·9	16·7	20·0	**22·8**	21·1	15·6	4·4	−4·5	−11·1	
	903	*5*	*3*	*5*	*10*	*13*	*15*	*5*	*8*	*10*	*15*	*5*	*5*	*99*
Luchun		−10·0	−2·8	7·8	18·9	24·4	29·4	**32·2**	30·0	23·3	12·8	0·6	−7·8	
	− 17													
Kashgar		−5·7	0·0	8·3	17·8	19·4	20·4	**27·8**	25·6	19·4	12·2	3·9	−2·2	
	1218	*5*	*5*	*5*	*15*	*20*	*25*	*5*	*5*	*0*	*15*	*0*	*0*	*100*
Uliassutai		−26	−17·6	−6·6	2·8	8·9	19·4	18·9	16·7	9·4	−0·6	−12·3	−15·2	

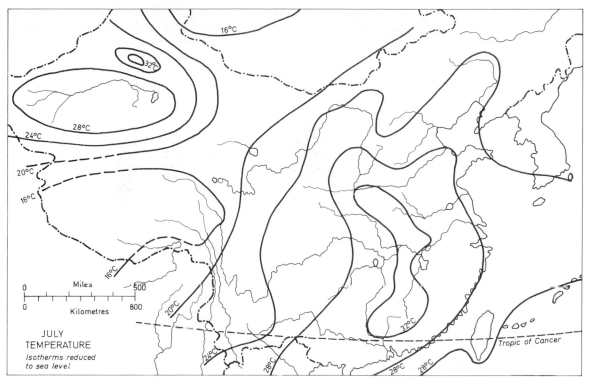

Fig. 10   Temperature: July isotherms

Everywhere the same seasonal distribution of a summer maximum and winter minimum is reflected. This is true even in remote Sinkiang, where rainfall is seldom over 130 mm a year. The lower Yangtze valley has a more even distribution of rainfall throughout the year than any other part, due to the passage of cyclones between the cold Polar and warm Tropical fronts but, nonetheless, a very clear maximum is maintained.

The basic cause of this seasonal variation is clearly the monsoon rhythm with warm, moist, inflowing winds in summer and cold, dry, outflowing winds in winter. However, this phenomenon by itself is not enough to account for the heavy summer rains. Rain does not always accompany the movement of humid air from sea to land. The increased temperature of the land in summer increases the air's capacity to hold moisture. In order that condensation shall take place, this warm, moist air must be cooled to saturation point. While in China this cooling is to some extent effected by the mountains, resulting in relief rain, the main cooling agent is the cyclone.

Coching Chu comments strongly on this: 'It has always been taken for granted that the southeast monsoon in China, like the southwest monsoon in India is a rainbearing wind. Yet the southeast wind in the eastern part of China is a dry wind in summer as well as in winter; and in the Yangtze valley, when it blows consistently, drought is imminent. These facts were known to the ancient Chinese philosophers and one famous poet of the Sung dynasty wrote to the effect that, when the southeast wind blows, the rainy season is at an end. Recent observations confirm this statement. The apparent paradox is explained by the fact that the rainfall in China is mostly cyclonic in origin and not orographic as in India; and that most of the precipitation is in the cold sector. It is necessary to have a northerly or northeast cold air-current to lift the southeast monsoon to sufficient height for it to yield its quota of moisture.'[15] There is a tendency for depressions to form over southwest China during the summer months. They move slowly along the Yangtze valley and it is these which bring torrential rains, known as

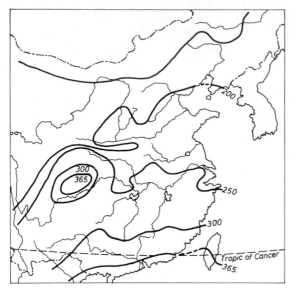

Fig. 11   Number of frostless days per year in the lowlands

'plum rains' (*mei yu*) when plums are ripening in mid-July and August and when temperature is high and relative humidity well-nigh intolerable. These rains, however, are not consistent, some years bringing flood and others failure and drought in the middle and lower Yangtze valley.

| | % of total area suffering from[16] | |
	1931 flood	1934 drought
Anhwei	37	69
Hupeh	29	32
Hunan	25	53
Kiangsi	6	48
Kiangsu	43	54

It was the passage of a series of seven cyclones in July which caused the disastrous floods in the Yangtze valley in 1931. The nature and course of these temperate cyclones has been examined and plotted by Sung Shio-Wang.[17]

A further cause of rainfall is the typhoons or tropical cyclones which originate in the Pacific Ocean somewhere east of the Philippines generally between 5°–25° N latitude and 120°–140° E longitude. These typhoons move generally, but uncertainly, westward over the Philippines and northwest to the coast of southeast China. On an average there are eight typhoons a year, 80 per cent of which occur between July and November. They bring with them winds of over 160 kph and torrential rains, sometimes of over 500 mm in 24 hours. However, an examination of Hong Kong's rainfall records reveals the curious fact that years of serious typhoons do not coincide with the years of heaviest rainfall. These disturbances bring with them havoc and disaster to the coastlands where they strike. Happily they die out rapidly as they penetrate inland and thus they have little effect on the mainland as a whole. Considerable research on typhoons has been carried out since 1949.

Perhaps more important to mankind than the amount of rain that falls is the reliance that can be placed on the regularity of its fall. Variability of the annual precipitation from the mean increases in China from southeast to northwest,

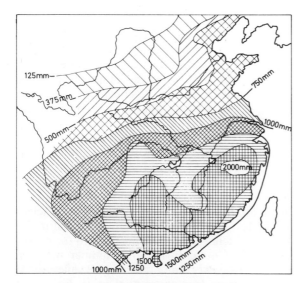

Fig. 12   Mean annual rainfall

No. of typhoons noted on Taiwan from 1897 to 1952

May	June	July	Aug	Sept	Oct	Nov	Total
9	11	54	64	45	18	3	204

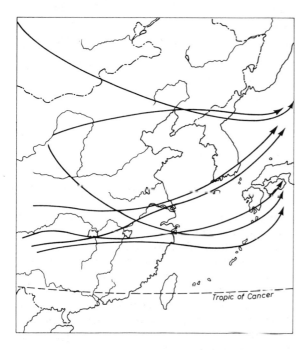

Fig. 13   Courses of cyclones

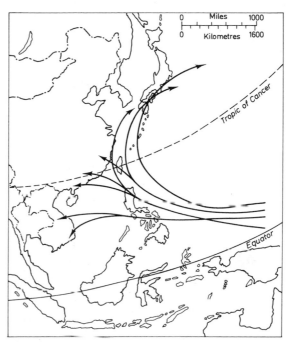

Fig. 14   Tracks of typhoons

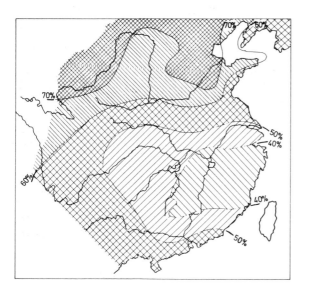

Fig. 15   Percentage of annual precipitation: June
to August

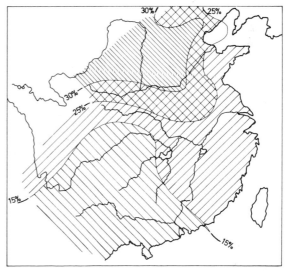

Fig. 16   Percentage variability of annual
precipitation

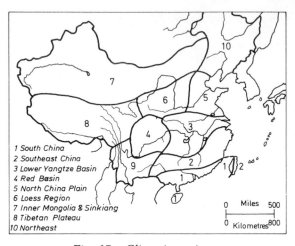

1 South China
2 Southeast China
3 Lower Yangtze Basin
4 Red Basin
5 North China Plain
6 Loess Region
7 Inner Mongolia & Sinkiang
8 Tibetan Plateau
10 Northeast

Fig. 17   Climatic regions

Pakistan. In consequence there is a fair balance in evapotranspiration. Imbalance begins to show itself north of the Yangtze basin and becomes really serious only in the northwest.

Place	Rainfall (in cm)	Evapotranspiration (in cm)
Peking	63	107
Shanghai	114	119
Canton	162	142

Farther north in the Yangtze valley the yearly variation is more marked as these figures of Hankow show:[19]

1916	1917	1918	1919	1920	1921
1280	813	1067	1244	948	1292

1922	1923	1924	1925
759	1011	860	828 mm

Climatic regions

Although the amount of published meteorological data is very limited for so large a country, there are enough stations of sufficiently long standing to warrant an attempt to divide China into broad climatic regions. Since 1949 large numbers of weather stations have been opened. It is to be hoped that, in due course, their records will be published, when a more accurate and more detailed division will be possible than heretofore. The following is a general regional division:

that is, in inverse ratio to the amount that falls. The area with least rainfall, i.e. the northwest, has a variability from the mean of 30 per cent; consequently this is the region notorious for famine. Even in the much more reliable south there is considerable variation, although, on account of the greater rainfall, its effects are not so serious. Rainfall in China as a whole is more evenly distributed throughout the year than in India and

1. HAINAN, SOUTH KWANGSI AND SOUTH
      KWANGTUNG AND THE WESTERN HALF OF
      TAIWAN

This region has an essentially tropical climate. The long summers are hot and the relative humidity is high, but there is a cooler, drier winter season,

which brings some relief. Frost is known only occasionally on the highlands. The average temperature for January is over 12° C. The annual rainfall is between 1500 mm and 2000 mm with a very marked summer maximum. There is a twelve-month growing period.

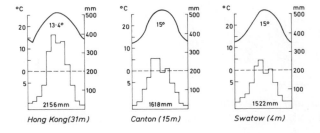

Hong Kong(31m)   Canton (15m)   Swatow (4m)

2. SOUTH CHINA; NORTH KWANGSI, NORTH KWANGTUNG, FUKIEN AND SOUTH CHEKIANG

This is a subtropical area. The summers are as hot as farther south and nearly as wet, but the winters are somewhat cooler. The coastal areas have a secondary maximum of rainfall in the early autumn, which is accounted for mainly by typhoons. The growing period is rather shorter, of about ten months. This is long enough for double cropping of rice but usually without a catch crop between, which is possible in 1.

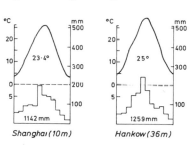

Foochow (20 m)

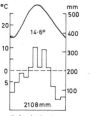

Taipei (9 m)

3. THE YANGTZE BASIN BELOW THE GORGES

This region has as hot a summer as 1 and 2 with a marked summer maximum of rainfall. Winters are much colder; heavy frost and some snow are brought with the bitter north winds which blow in January and February. The summers are oppressive, having both high temperature and high relative humidity. An unpleasant characteristic of the whole of the lower Yangtze basin is the consistent absence in summer of the evening breeze just when it would be most acceptable. The growing period is about nine months. Rice is grown in the south and central parts, but it faces competition by wheat and barley in the north.

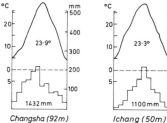

Shanghai (10 m)   Hankow (36 m)   Changsha (92 m)   Ichang (50 m)

4. THE RED BASIN OF SZECHWAN

This is a region with a unique climate. Situated in the heart of China as it is, one would expect it to have a climate of greater extremes than 3, but the reverse is the case. Chengtu, which is 1600 km inland from Shanghai, has an average minimum (January) temperature of 7° C and an average maximum (July and August) temperature of 25° C as compared with Shanghai, which has average temperatures of 3° C and 27° C for the same periods. The Red Basin is sheltered by the Tsinling and Ta Pa Shan from the bitter north winds and this accounts for the mild winter. The region is renowned for its humidity and mistiness. There is a Szechwan saying that 'when the sun shines, the dogs bark'. Rainfall is usually gentler than farther east and is ample for the temperature at various seasons. In consequence, there is a growing period of eleven months. It is a most productive region, having a greater variety of agricultural products than any other part of China.

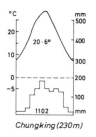

Chungking (230 m)

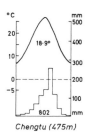

Chengtu (475 m)

5. THE NORTH CHINA PLAIN

This also includes the peninsula of Shantung. Here the range of temperature between summer and winter is considerable, being at Peking 31° C as compared with Hong Kong's 13° C. Summers are as hot as, sometimes hotter than 1 and 2, although not nearly as wet. Summer rains are often torrential and therefore of less value than they might be. Winters are long, cold and dry. The biting north and northwest winds descend onto the plain from the loess region and are often heavily dust-laden. The growing period here is not more than eight months.

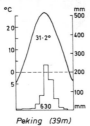
Peking (39m)

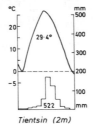
Tientsin (2m)

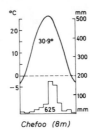
Chefoo (8m)

6. THE LOESS REGION

As one moves northwest, so the continental nature of the climate becomes more marked. This is so in the Loess region. The range of average monthly temperature between summer and winter is, for most places, between 37° C and 40° C. The winters are long and strong, bitter northwest winds sweep over the hills, whipping up heavy dust storms. There is a marked summer maximum of rainfall but it is sparse (250–380 mm), and what is worse, it is very variable and even more subject to cloud-burst than 5. Hail storms can be very destructive. In years of drought the dust storms in summer are worse even than those of winter.

The sheltered valley of the Wei in this region is more favoured than the rest, having, as the graph of Sian shows, rather more rain and a more equable temperature.

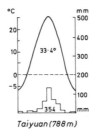
Taiyuan (788m)

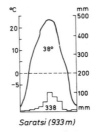
Saratsi (933m)

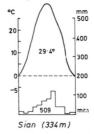
Sian (334m)

7. INNER MONGOLIA AND SINKIANG

These areas have temperate desert or semi-desert climates. The whole region, which is a series of basins in the heart of a landmass, is subject to great contrasts in temperature between summer (27°–33°C) and winter (− 5°C to − 15°C). There are also big diurnal ranges. Rainfall is very sparse and seldom more than 10–13 mm per annum on the lowlands, and moreover is very uncertain. In spring the entire arid north and northwest is marked by dust storms. These are of two kinds: *yaman* or *kara-buran* (evil or black storms) are rare and short-lived, usually lasting less than 24 hours. The commoner *kyzyl buran* (red storms) last 2–3 days and cover everything with yellow dust. Sinkiang folk, at this time, talk of 'it is dusting' instead of raining, the rain drops being cemented with loess.[20]

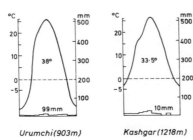

Urumchi(903m)   *Kashgar(1218m)*

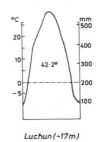
Luchun (~17m)

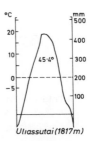
Uliassutai(1817m)

8. THE GREAT HIGHLAND PLATEAU OF TIBET

This forms a separate division. A great deal of it lies at over 4500 m. In consequence the density of the air is much less than on the lowlands. The air is dry and clear, with resulting rapid insolation and radiation. Both seasonal and diurnal ranges of temperature are great. Rainfall for most of the region is negligible. The southeast corner of Tibet in which Lhasa is situated and the only part for which any reliable meteorological statistics exist, shares the monsoon climate of northeast India, as the accompanying graph shows, and is in no way typical of the climate of the plateau.

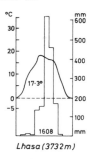

Lhasa (3732m)

9. THE YUNNAN–KWEICHOW PLATEAU

This plateau is between 1250 and 2500 m in height. Its summer, in consequence, is not as hot as the regions 2 and 3 to the east. Its winter is not influenced by the out-flowing north winds from the continental high. There is a summer maximum of rainfall, which is ample for the latitude and temperature. The resulting climate is described, by those who have experienced it, as delightful and almost ideal. The deep north–south valleys of the headwaters of the Yangtze, Mekong and Salween, which lie to the west, however, are unhealthy and malaria-infested.

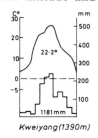

Kweiyang (1390m)

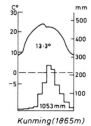

Kunming (1865m)

10. THE NORTHEAST OR MANCHURIA

This region has an east coast continental type of climate. Temperatures increase in seasonal range the farther northeast one goes. As a result, the growing period is shorter in Heilungkiang than it is in Liaoning. Rainfall also decreases to the northeast but is everywhere adequate for the growth of wheat and kaoliang.

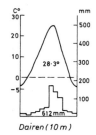

Dairen (10 m)

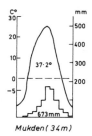

Mukden (34 m)

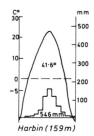

Harbin (159m)

SOILS

While the rocks of a region are the original basic source of all soil, it is the climate of that region, which, in the long run, determines the nature of its soil, aided by the organic agents, the flora and the fauna, which are themselves both cause and effect, and aided also by the action of human beings.

It is estimated that only about one tenth of

Chinese soil is residual and that 90 per cent has been transported either by wind – witness the great deposits of loess in Shensi and Shansi – or by water in the great alluvial plains of north China, the Yangtze and Si-kiang. There is little or no evidence of glacial transportation on any large scale – certainly nothing comparable to that of the North German Plain or Canada. Human beings in China throughout the centuries have been no mean transporters: terracing, carrying soil from field to field and from river bed to field. Today the process is being accelerated.

Soil formation depends less on the method of its origin and the nature of the parent rock than on the type of climate to which it is exposed. Both temperature and rainfall play leading parts and therefore it is not surprising to find that there are marked differences between north and south China. The north, being both colder and drier, tends to form its soils mainly by mechanical action, i.e. by frost and exfoliation. Because the climate is cold, chemical action is weak and soil formation slow. Because it is dry, there is little leaching of the soil. Thus the soils of the north are generally slow to come to maturity but tend to retain their fertility for a much longer period than the lands of the south, where macro-climatic conditions are reversed. In tropical and sub-tropical regions, where temperatures are much higher and rainfall much heavier, chemical decomposition of the rocks is much quicker. Through the combination of these two, the higher temperature and heavier rainfall, granites of Kwangtung and Hong Kong break down remarkably quickly and to astonishing depths. The heavy rainfall causes rapid and severe leaching. Thus the soils of the south tend to come to maturity quickly but are liable to lose their fertility very rapidly. This difference between north and south, and particularly the ease with which the soils of the south lose their fertility, is of the highest importance in considering the planning of the economic development of the country. We therefore must look more fully into the subject.

Gourou, in his admirable little book, *The Tropical World*, points out that 'tropical soils are poorer and more fragile than those of temperate regions. Great care is needed in using them if their further impoverishment and destruction are to be avoided.'[21] The luxuriant forests of the tropics and subtropics give the impression of great fertility. The use of migratory *ladang* cultivation of forest clearings in the tropics by primitive tribes

and the fact that these clearings lose their fertility in about a couple of years is enough in itself to make us distrust such an impression. The fact is that these forests are just able to maintain a state of soil equilibrium. The leaf fall is just sufficient to maintain a supply of humus, and the leaf cover provides the very necessary protection of that humus against rapid destruction by the sun. Then, too, the forest cover helps to prevent rapid leaching and if this cover is removed the soil loses its fertility very rapidly. Any fertile soil met with in tropical or subtropical conditions will be found to be either one of recent origin, such as newly laid-down river or marine alluvium, or basic volcanic ash, or one which is receiving constant renewal by human action. The writer remembers vividly learning this lesson when he tried to demonstrate in Central China the superiority of the temperate western method of digging in manure over the local Chinese method of almost daily top feeding with very weak maturized liquid night-soil. He found that his own plots maintained their fertility for only three or four months instead of the two years he had expected, while the top-fed plots continued to yield as long as the feeding was maintained. Manure, which in England would suffice for two or three years, may be leached away in a matter of months. The infertility of tropical and subtropical soils, unless constantly fed (as they are generally in south and central China) is reflected in the figures below:[22]

Average yield of rice 1926/27–1930/31

	Hectolitres per hectare
Temperate countries	
Spain	168
Italy	110
Japan	96
U.S.A.	60
Korea	50
Tropical countries	
Sierra Leone	59
Siam	45
Indonesia	42
Brazil	40
India	37
Philippines	32
Malaya	32
Madagascar	32
French Indo-China	28

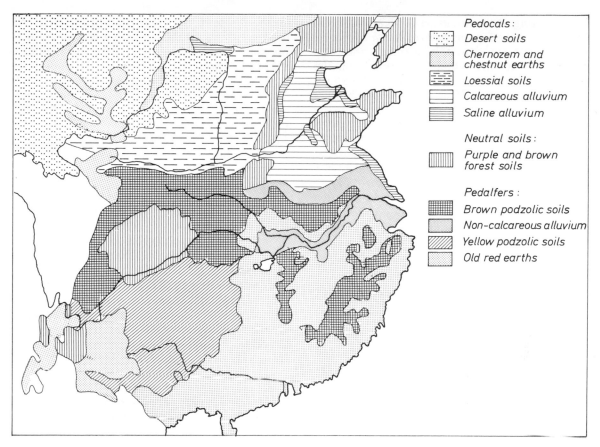

Fig. 18   Soils

As a result of the difference of climatic conditions between north and south, of the drier, cooler north and the wetter, hotter south, there is a twofold major classification of soils. Generally speaking the soils north of the line of the Nan Shan, Chinling (Tsinling) Shan, Funiu Shan are pedocals – calcium soils from which the lime has not been leached – whilst south of this line are the pedalfers from which the lime has been leached, leaving much iron and aluminium and increasing in acidity as the tropics are approached.

Pedocals
These can be given a wide five-fold division:

1. *Desert soils*, which are generally grey or yellow–grey in colour, are found in the northwest, Kansu, Inner Mongolia and Sinkiang. They are light in texture and liable to be blown away. It is probable that the loess farther east has been

derived from this region. Generally the soil is thin, but given sufficient depth and adequate water supply by irrigation, it can be farmed. Considerable effort has been made to develop these soils in Sinkiang in the last decade. Great care has to be taken to meet the danger of alkali accumulation.

2. Lying roughly between the desert soils and the loess is a belt of *chernozem*, *chestnut* and *black earths*. These are light soils, developed in semi-arid areas and under natural grass. They are potentially very productive and have been a constant temptation to the Chinese colonist, luring him northwestward only to send him back once more after experiencing the short growing season and the variable rainfall. After a series of dry summers he can watch his fields, denuded of their natural grass cover by cultivation, whipped away eastward by the wind. Today irrigation and afforestation are helping to anchor the soil.

3. Covering an enormous area of Kansu, Shensi and Shansi is the famous *loess of North China*, by far the biggest deposit of its kind in the world. This fine, windborne soil has been transported from the desert soils and deposited in beds of thickness, varying from 30 m to 75 m, masking much of the former relief.[23] The process is still going on. Being wind-borne, loess is generally unstratified and is laid down without the horizontal bedding planes of water-borne deposits. It is so fine a texture that it holds moisture easily, which is drawn to the surface by capillary attraction. A further characteristic is its vertical cleavage, giving steep, often sheer, valley sides. Given adequate water supply, loess is very fertile indeed. It is easy to work and it thus enabled Neolithic Man of China to move forward from hunting and fishing into the primitive agricultural stage.

4. Spread out over the whole of the North China Plain are the deep *alluvial deposits of the Hwang-ho floodplain*. An artesian well, bored to a depth of 865 m in 1936, revealed that the shells of the same small bivalved *Lutraria* and of small snails were present at the greatest depths as are present in the deposits being laid down today.

> The sand in which they were discovered had once been the top layer of the Yellow river delta ... The digging of this well demonstrated, as no previous excavation had done, how much the rock floor of this part of the Asiatic continent has sunk and what an immense load of silt and sand the Hwang-ho has carried down and spread over the sinking plain in order to keep the ancient home of the Chinese above sea level.[24]

The alluvial soils are generally light in texture and easily worked. They are mainly yellow or grey in colour. This is by far the most productive of the calcium soils, having both sufficient supplies of mineral foods and an adequate and reasonably reliable rainfall. Consequently there is a very dense population over the whole area. The soil has been worked and worked again over the centuries and has been most carefully tended, fed and replenished by the farmer. It is in regions such as this that it is difficult to determine whether nature or man is the chief soil-maker.

5. Scattered widely over north China are patches of *saline* and *alkaline soil*. The most extensive of these are (i) a long strip along the coast of Kiangsu, (ii) a considerable area around the mouth of the Hwang-ho, and (iii) patches in the floodplain of the river itself, and along the northern side of the great bend of the river. All these areas are associated with a combination of poor drainage and aridity, where the rainfall is insufficient both to dissolve and carry away the salts in solution. Sodium chloride, sodium sulphate and sodium carbonate are all present, but happily the latter is not very prevalent. The People's Government has devoted a good deal of research to these saline areas and large tracts have been reclaimed and are now productive.

Neutral soils

6. *Purple and brown forest soils.* Between the pedocals of the north and the pedalfers of the south lie, not unnaturally, soils which are neutral, i.e. where soil formation and leaching are approximately in balance. The purple and brown forest soils of the Red Basin of Szechwan come within this category. This is the land where 'the dogs bark when the sun shines', a land of mists and light rains, which do not cause rapid leaching. This balance between alkalinity and acidity is maintained in the higher lands of Honan, Hopei and Shantung, where purple forest soils also occur.

Pedalfers

Once south of the Tsinling–Funiu Shan line we are in the region of podzolic soils.

> Podzolization is understood to be a process by which soils are first leached of their easily soluble components and then the iron and manganese family are preferentially mobilized from the upper horizon. Laterization is thought of as the opposite process. The silica is preferentially mobilized and the iron and aluminium accumulate in the surface horizon as a residual concentration.[25]

1. *Brown podzolic soils.* This reddish-brown soil is distributed widely over the highlands surrounding the west, north and east sides of the Red Basin and over the mountainous areas of Hupeh, Hunan, Chekiang and Fukien. It is less severely leached than the soils farther south and is therefore less acid. Formerly under forest, much of this has been stripped, with the result that the hill slopes have been eroded and the rice–wheat lands of the plains covered with a sterile clay. Over-enthusiasm to increase cultivation in recent years has led to unwise development of these soils, which are better kept under forest.

2. *Non-calcareous alluvium.* The floodplain of the Yangtze below the Gorges, i.e. from Ichang to the sea, is overlain with a thick cover of non-calcereous alluvium, as also is the greater part of the Hwai

basin. These soils are largely neutral, being neither calcereous nor acidic and for the most part are exceedingly fertile and of good texture.

3. *Yellow podzolic soils.* The plateau lands of Yunnan and Kweichow are characterized by strongly podzolized yellow soils of many types, all of which are strongly acid. The highland valleys are reasonably fertile but require constant feeding. The hillslopes, like all the southern regions, are best kept as forest lands.

4. *Old red earths.* These are the preponderating soils of southern China. They are increasingly acidic as the Tropic of Cancer is approached, when a distinct tendency to become lateritic can be detected. The only true laterite in China is found in Hainan. However, over large areas of Kwangtung and Kwangsi much of the hillsides are covered with a hard crust, an 'iron pan'. this may be only a few millimetres in thickness, but it is highly resistant. This iron pan, so essential in the paddy field when it is found some 300–450 mm below the surface, is fatal to cultivation when it appears on the surface. Gourou describes it as a 'pedological leprosy'. The old red earths, like the yellow podzolic soils, are best left to their natural forest cover. The alluvial valley bottoms are cultivated, but because of heavy leaching they need constant feeding.

Soil erosion

In view of his long attachment to the soil and his veneration for his ancestral lands, it is rather surprising to find how careless the Chinese peasant has been in preventing the loss of soil through erosion. Largely through ignorance he has 'left undone those things which he ought to have done and done those which he ought not to have done' and so imperilled the very thing on which his life depends. He has had a false sense of security. 'Land is there. You can see it every day. Robbers cannot take it away. Thieves cannot steal it. Men die but land remains.'[26] He has not been quick to recognize the many robbers, some of his own creation, that are ever ready to filch his land from him. Happily there has been considerable education in this field during the last two decades and the peasant today is much more alive to the causes and the means of prevention of soil erosion.

Soil erosion in all its forms can be found within Chinese borders, in some places to a disastrous extent. The sequence is the same no matter what the location. First the natural cover of the land is lost. The causes of this loss may be deforestation, unwise cultivation, overgrazing, cutting and burning off the grass and scrub, or desiccation from natural causes. Each and all these will lead to a loss of organic matter and with it the loss of structural stability. The valuable crumb structure breaks down, porosity is lost and the stage is set for rain to wash away the top soil by sheet and gully erosion or, in drier regions, for the wind to whip it away.

Of all the regions of China, the loess region is the most vulnerable since it is subject to the action of both rain and wind. Its natural vegetational cover is grass and scrub, although it is maintained that formerly much was covered by forest. The most insidious form of attack is sheet erosion. During the wet summer when the ground is saturated, the soil is carried down even gentle hillslopes in innumerable tiny gullies or channels. The immediate effect is not easily noticeable and is masked by the next ploughing. Nevertheless there is a tendency for a steady downward movement. An attempt has been made over many centuries to meet this danger by terracing, and the whole of the cultivated countryside presents a picture of large terraced fields on more or less gently sloping hills, each field being divided from the next by a low wall of sods. The method has been generally successful in preventing wholesale erosion, but neglect over even a short period, perhaps due to political unrest or to famine, will result in gullying from which recovery is well nigh impossible. The formation of communes has made the mobilization of labour possible with the result that terracing, particularly in the loess region, has been greatly developed. Terracing here needs to be reinforced by scientific contour ploughing to make arable farming secure from erosion. In recent years the Puerto Rican method of digging pits 600 mm deep all over the field and cultivating around them has been successfully practised in a few places. The pits serve to hold and conserve any heavy rainfall and prevent both sheet and gully erosion. It is not, however, a method which commends itself to large-scale farming.

Loess is very prone to gullying. The smallest depression, the slightest channel or footpath may be sufficient to set in train disastrous erosion. We have noted that loess has a marked vertical cleavage and also that it has a high lime content. We have seen also that, although this is a region of sparse rainfall, the rain often falls in very heavy storms or cloudbursts. These three factors combine to produce very steep-sided, often vertical gullies or gorges, which may be deeper than their width and produce the characteristic dissected landscape of the loess.

Andersson describes yet another type of erosion in the loess:[27]

> During the great summer rains, it is true, the water rushes in cascades from the fields down into the depths, but the essential process is of quite a different kind. In order to understand the manner of form tion of the loess ravines we must examine the yellow earth a little more closely. The typical *huang-t'u* is a greyish, yellow dust, which does not as a rule show any stratification, but shows on the other hand a remarkable capacity for adhering to perpendicular cliffs. This fine, porous earth easily lets through water which falls upon its surface. Consequently only part of the summer rains drains off its surface. For a large part of the rainfall it acts as a sponge, or, perhaps better, like a gigantic filter, through which the water sinks to the bedrock of the loess deposits, consisting of gravel, Tertiary clay and solid rock. The lower part of the loess soil in this way often becomes saturated with water and assumes a consistency like that of a thin porridge or gruel. This bottom layer then slowly begins to move and slides down any slope and in proportion as the saturated bottom slides away towards the open valley, the superimposed, relatively dry mass of loess sinks down perpendicularly. This vertical movement may be studied everywhere in the ravines, in which one sees large and small blocks of the old vegetation-covered surface in all sorts of more or less inclined positions halfway or more down to the bottom of the ravine.

It is the erosion of this loess, this *huang-t'u*, that is the main reason for the constant flooding of the lower Hwang-ho, the floodplain of which is built largely of loess silt. Nothing short of a gigantic afforestation of large areas and reversion to pasture of much of the rest will suffice to anchor this fine, light soil.

In south and central China the contrast between the meticulous care lavished on cultivated fields and the almost contemptuous disregard of the welfare of the hillsides and the rough land, has been most striking. So much of the countryside has been denuded of its natural forest cover to make room for cultivation in the valleys and lower hillslopes. Happily the careful terracing and cultivation of the ricefields has, to a large extent, afforded protection against erosion. However, nearly everywhere the higher hillslopes have suffered from severe sheet and gully erosion. This is the result of generations of disregard of the elementary rules of soil conservation. The hill

have been stripped not only of their trees but also of the grass which is cut annually and the very roots grubbed up for fuel, thereby constantly exposing the soil surface. The cooking stove of south China is designed to burn grass and wood. If an acceptable coal-burning stove could be designed and communications improved sufficiently to distribute the coal, which even in the centre and south is abundant, this would probably do more than any other measure to check erosion.

There was until recently an almost universal custom of burning off the hillsides in the autumn each year. Apparently there were many reasons for this. One undoubtedly was the historical fact that the Chinese farmer was an agriculturalist, that in earlier times the land was forested, and to clear this obstacle he felled and burned. The idea still holds. Other reasons put forward were that the clearance of the hillsides gave protection as it deprived bandits and wild animals of cover. There is still quite a lot of wild game – deer, wild pigs and even some leopards and tigers – in the uplands of China, which cause a lot of damage to crops.[28] During the unstable political conditions which were prevalent throughout the whole of the first half of this century danger from robbers and bandits was real. Two other reasons are given for the burning. One has a pseudo-scientific flavour, i.e. that potash from the burnt grass and brush is washed down and replenishes the rice fields below and also that the subsequent young grass on the hillsides is better grazing. Lastly, there is some truth in the statement that the peasants like to see the hillsides lit up at night. Whatever the reasons may be, there is no doubt that the practice of burning off the hillsides has contributed to the dangers of erosion. Happily burning off has now ceased in most regions of mainland China.

NATURAL VEGETATION

So much of China Proper has been so densely populated and subjected to the action of agricultural man so long, that it is difficult to know, in some parts, exactly what would grow if the land were left untouched. For example, most of the great North China Plain would probably be covered by deciduous woodland if uninhabited. As it is, it is now one vast patchwork of cultivated fields in which trees are a luxury.

Being itself largely the outcome of climate and soils, there is a close correspondence in distribution between these and the various types of natural

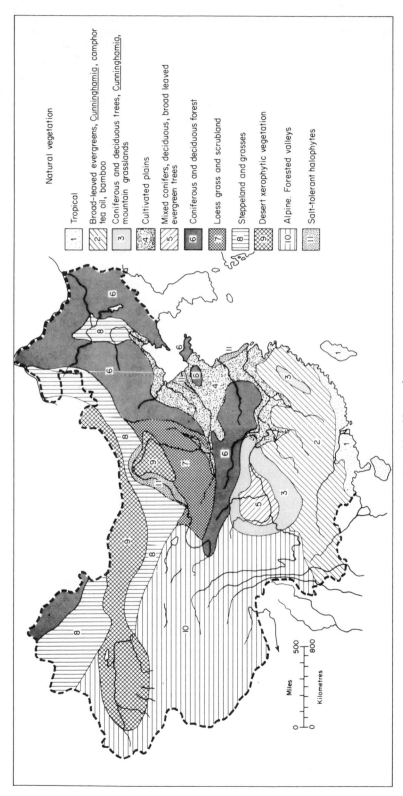

Natural vegetation

1	Tropical
2	Broad-leaved evergreens, <u>Cunninghamia</u>, camphor tea oil, bamboo
3	Coniferous and deciduous trees, <u>Cunninghamia</u>, mountain grasslands
4	Cultivated plains
5	Mixed conifers, deciduous, broad leaved evergreen trees
6	Coniferous and deciduous forest
7	Loess grass and scrubland
8	Steppeland and grasses
9	Desert xerophytic vegetation
10	Alpine. Forested valleys
11	Salt-tolerant halophytes

Fig. 19 Natural vegetation

vegetation. Before embarking on a brief survey of the distribution of vegetational types, mention should be made of the differentiation of growth on the north-facing and south-facing mountain slopes which is noticeable throughout the whole country. The north-facing slopes tend to be more generously covered than the south. If the south-facing slopes have short grasses, those facing north are likely to have long and more abundant grass or scrub. If there is grass and scrub facing south, we may look for woodland on the north-facing slopes. This differentiation is due to the difference in insolation, particularly in the dry winter months when the south-facing slopes are subject to great evaporation.

In the northwest, where there is not true desert, there are vast areas of very sparse xerophytic (drought-resisting) vegetation, within which, in the lower lying land and depressions, are patches of halophytes (salt-tolerant plants), notably in the Tarim Basin, the Ordos, the Tsaidam and the Gobi. Skirting the southern edge of the Gobi is a wide belt of grasses of many kinds and of varying abundance, the main home of Mongolian nomads. The natural covering of the loess region is mainly grass and scrub, although there is some forest land on the higher hills, particularly where these penetrate above the loess deposits.

Spread out over the whole of the North China Plain, the Wei Valley, the lower Fen, the flood-plain of the Yangtze below the Gorges and the floodplain of the Hwai, are the farmlands of China, which allow of little or no natural vegetation. A strip of salt-tolerant vegetation should be noted dividing the cultivated Hwai plain from the sea.

Stretching in a broad belt from the Nan Shan in the west, through the Tsinling and Funiu Shan, is a broad belt of coniferous and deciduous forest, the broad-leafed trees increasing to the east and south. These forests continue in the Shansi high-lands, which form the western border of the North China Plain and which in earlier days provided the hunting forests of the Shang nobility. The high-lands of Shantung also have a similar forest cover.

From this belt southward to the sea the natural vegetation of China is forest of one kind or another. China enjoys a great variety of trees. There are twenty-six species of conifers in the country and a great variety of broad-leafed trees, including the *Eucommia*, the camphor, the nanmu (Phoebe), the sassafras, the t'ung yu (wood oil),

tea oil, Chinese tallow and varnish tree. In the more populous south and east most of this forest has been stripped. A pre-Liberation Russian survey estimated that, whereas China should have a forest cover of 30 per cent in order to give adequate control of flood and drought, it had, in fact, only about 5 per cent, which gives some measure of the deforestation which has taken place.

The southern forest lands can be divided generally into the following categories:

(*a*) Very mixed tree growth of the Szechwan Red Basin, which includes conifers and deciduous, broad-leafed evergreens, t'ung yu, cypress and bamboo.

(*b*) Surrounding the woodland of the Red Basin is a broad forest belt of more uniform character, consisting of conifers and deciduous trees, interspersed with mountain grasslands. A similar belt along the highlands of the south-east contains a great deal of *Cunninghamia*, as also do the highlands of Taiwan.

(*c*) The natural cover of the greater part of Hupeh, Hunan, Kiangsi, Kweichow, Che-kiang and Fukien is broad-leafed evergreen forest, a great deal of *Cunninghamia*, pine, camphor, tea-oil and bamboo.

(*d*) Kwangsi, the coastal regions of Kwangtung and the island of Hainan have tropical vegetation in considerable variety and, where untouched, in abundance. Evergreens of all kinds, pines, bamboos and large fleshy grasses, such as wild pineapple, all flourish.

(*e*) The valleys of the deep-cut ravines of West Szechwan and the Chamdo Area are densely forested with deciduous and coniferous trees, while the tops of the mountain ranges and the plateaus are covered with grasses of the *Aveneae* and *Festuceae* tribes.

FAUNA

Archaeologists, notably Teilhard de Chardin, and ancient historians, such as Ssu-ma Ch'ien, have drawn for us a picture of the animal and bird life that existed in China in Pliocene and Pleistocene times. The northern forests were inhabited by the rhinoceros, stegadon (primitive short-tusked elephant), sabre-toothed tiger, wolf, hyena; deer, gazelle, hipperion (horse-like Perissodactyl), onager or wild ass and ostrich roamed the steppe-lands.

Subsequent climatic changes led to the disappearance of most of those cited and the appearance and rapid increase of *Homo sapiens* restricted the whereabouts of others. The stegadon became extinct and the hipperion faded from the scene in the Pleistocene. Although the horse figures so prominently in Chinese art and sculpture, it is no Chinese animal that is depicted but rather the 'heavenly horses' from Ferghana.[29]

Nevertheless there is no dearth of animal and bird life in modern China but rather the reverse. It is calculated that, of the world's species, 11·1 per cent of animal species and 13·4 per cent of bird species are to be found in China today.[30] Given this abundance, all that can be done here is to make a brief catalogue of the main groups, classifying them in wide natural regions. There is a marked difference in species between the fauna found north and south of the Nan Shan–Tsinling line. Owing to the dense population and intensive cultivation of the low-lying plains wild life there is sparse and confined mainly to the surrounding uplands. Rodents, however, are found everywhere.

1. *The Tibetan Plateau.* All life here must adapt itself to the meagre food that will grow in the hard, cold, dry conditions. Consequently animal and bird life is sparse. The yak and Tibetan antelope are notable ungulates. The yak, when domesticated, is virtually the only means of transport. Asian big-horned sheep and some carnivores – snow leopard and Tibetan sand fox – are found. Rodents, such as the marmot, woolly hare and Ladak pika, are fairly numerous. Snow cock, sand grouse, snow finches and Himalayan griffon make up the main bird population.

2. *Desert and Steppeland of North and Northwest.* As might be expected, the commonest animals in these sparse grasslands are the Mongolian gazelle and the saiga antelope, the latter being found mainly in the north of Dzungaria, where it is hunted for its horns, which are used in Chinese medicine. The onager (wild ass) is still extant in the region, as also is the tarpan or wild horse. The Bactrian camel is common to the whole region, and was, until recently, the main means of transport. In this sandy environment rodents (marmots, squirrel, gerbil, hare) abound and are destructive of pasture. The chief carnivores are the grey wolf and fox. Bird life is well adapted to the environment and consists mainly of bustard, sand grouse, sand lark and blue-eared pheasant.

3. *The Northeast.* The forested slopes of the Ta Hingan–Siao Hingan Shan abound in animal life. Hunters and trappers seek the pelts of the wealth of fur-bearing life from rodents such as squirrel and chipmunk to moose, deer of many kinds (red-wapiti, sika and roe) and the carnivores (tiger, leopard, red fox and sable martin). The domestication and farming of some of these animals for their fur is increasing and replacing hunting to some extent. The commonest birds are the hazel grouse, ring-necked pheasant and Daurian partridge.

4. *The Southwest Plateau.* This mountainous plateau is rich in its great variety of fauna. In the higher altitudes there are marmots, musk deer and pika together with the takin or horned mountain sheep. On the lower slopes there are many species of monkey, including the rhesus and golden-haired: giant and red pandas live in the bamboo groves between 2000 and 3000 metres above sea-level. Asiatic elephants are located in the southern plateau of Yunnan. Bird life is particularly abundant and includes parakeets, sunbirds, many kinds of pheasants and babblers (laughing thrushes).

5. *The Yangtze Basin.* Because of the high density of human settlement, wild life is confined mainly to the hill land and enclosing mountains. Deer inhabit the hills and a few tigers are still to be found. Mention should be made of the water-buffalo, which, though now entirely domesticated, has continued uninterrupted existence since Pleistocene times. Fox and hare were numerous. After Liberation when water conservancy and flood control were undertaken seriously a determined campaign to exterminate foxes was carried out, particularly in the lower Hwang-ho and Hwai valleys, since their burrowings threatened to weaken the dykes. Bird life is abundant and includes the golden pheasant, partridge, golden oriole and the ubiquitous blue magpie. One of the world's rare animals, the Yangtze alligator, lives in the river near Wuhu. It is less than two metres long and lives mainly on fish. The central and lower Yangtze basins are lake-studded and form the wintering ground of a vast waterfowl population. In its lower reaches the river is a prolific fishing ground of big head and carp of many kinds.

6. *South China.* Within the tropical south of China there is a different range and a greater variety of species. The larger carnivores include the South China tiger, clouded leopard and large Indian civet. There is a wealth of arboreal animals, most

notable of which are the fruit bat (flying fox), tree shrew, slow loris and the gibbon. Taiwan has its own specialities – the black bear, Taiwan monkey and long-tailed pheasant.

Since the establishment of the People's Republic in 1949 serious attention has been given to the protection and preservation of wild life. Hitherto this had been mainly aimed at furthering economic production.

References

1 J. S. Lee, *Geology of China* (London, 1939). pp. 155–61.
2 J. S. Lee, op. cit., pp. 183–4.
3 J. S. Lee, op. cit., p. 207.
4 J. G. Andersson, *Children of the Yellow Earth* (London, 1934), p. 130.
5 J. S. Lee, op. cit., p. 395.
6 ibid., pp. 398–9.
7 U.S.S.R. Academy of Sciences, *The Physical Geography of China*, Vol. I, pp. 26–7.
8 P. Fleming, *News from Tartary* (London, 1938).
9 J. S. Lee, op. cit.
10 See F. K. Hare, *The Restless Atmosphere* (London, 1953), chapter 12.
11 ibid., p. 144.
12 U.S.S.R. Academy of Sciences, op. cit., Vol. I, p. 20.
13 Tao Shih-yen, 'Surface air mean circulation over China', *Academia Sinica*, **15**, no. 4 (1948).
14 T'u Chang-wang and Hwang Sze-sung, 'The advance and retreat of the summer monsoon in China', *Meteorological Magazine*, **18** (1944).
15 Coching Chu, *Journal of the Geographical Society of China*, **1**, no. 1 (1934).
16 U.S.S.R. Academy of Sciences, op. cit., Vol. I, p. 38.
17 Sung Shio-wang, 'The extratropical cyclones of East China', *Memoirs of the National Research Institute of Meteorology*, **3** (1931).
18 U.S.S.R. Academy of Sciences, op. cit., Vol. I, p. 44.
19 S. V. Boxer, *Hankow Weather Guide* (Hankow, 1926).
20 U.S.S.R. Academy of Sciences, op. cit., Vol. I, p. 28.
21 P. Gourou, *The Tropical World* (London, 1953).
22 P. Gourou, op. cit.
23 G. B. Cressey, 'The Ordos Desert of Inner Mongolia', *Dennison University Bulletin*, **33**, no. 8.
24 N. Carrington Goodrich, *China* (Berkeley, California, 1946), p. 42.
25 Carter and Pendleton, *Geographical Review*, October 1956.
26 Fei Hsiao-tung, *Peasant Life in China* (London, 1947), p. 182.
27 J. G. Andersson, op. cit., p. 129.
28 G. Fenzel, 'On the natural conditions affecting the introduction of forestry in the province of Kwang-tung', *Lingnan Science Journal*, no. 7 (June 1929).
29 A. Houghton Brodrick (ed.), *Animals in Archaeology*, chapter 7 'Animals in China' (M. Tregear) (London, 1972).
30 *China Reconstructs*, **21**, no. 7 (July 1972).

2   Historical Geography

Mature historical understanding requires full recognition of the factors of physical geography, climatic stimulus (where it can be proved) and the character of the environment as a whole; but it also demands an appreciation of the dynamics of social groups.

Owen Lattimore

It has been said that the trouble with Chinese history is that there is so much of it. Authentic written records carry us back well into the first millennium BC, and archaeological research of the last fifty years has reached back already into the deep recesses of the second millennium and is giving us an increasingly full and accurate picture of life in that remote period. The rapid and widespread industrial development of the last two decades involving extensive excavation, has brought to light so great a mass of artefacts of ancient Chinese civilization that many years will be required for their adequate examination, classification and interpretation.

In face of this great wealth of historical material, all that is attempted in the following pages is to select a few topics to demonstrate the influence which geography has had upon them. This will give a geographical background to some of the outstanding developments in Chinese history.

CHINESE ORIGINS

The Neolithic age, disdained by pre-historians because it is too young, neglected by historians because its phases cannot be exactly dated, was nevertheless a critical age and one of solemn importance among all epochs of the past, for in it Civilization was born. . . . In a matter of ten or twenty thousand years man divided up the earth and struck his roots in it.

(Pierre Teilhard de Chardin, *The Phenomenon of Man*)

Whence has sprung the great Chinese people, who today number nearly one quarter of the people of the earth? Who are they? Did their great and continuous civilization develop *in situ* or does it owe most of it to importation and invasion from surrounding lands? If it is indigenous, what natural factors have influenced that development? These are some of the questions which have engaged the attention of Chinese scholars through the centuries and Western scholars in more recent years.

Until quite recently, when modern Western scholarship introduced the concept that earliest civilization had its birth in a common centre in the Near East from which it has radiated, the Chinese accepted as valid their classical mythology, which attributed their beginnings to legendary heroes, beginning with the creator, P'an Ku, followed by the pastoral age under Fu Hsi the agricultural genius of Shen-nang in 2953 BC. These myths fell into disrepute and gave place to the Western theory that nomadic tribes of Turko extraction spread out eastward from Turkestan and gradually, in the course of many generations, migrated into the Tarim Basin and Dzungaria, across the southern borders of the Gobi, and, following the grass-covered slopes of the Nan Shan, crossed the Hwang-ho, descended into the basin of the Wei-ho, a land flowing with milk and honey, and there settled to become the Chinese people. It was not until the third decade of this century that this theory, in its turn, was seriously challenged. The questioning arose from the growth and spread of archaeological survey and research in north China. The work of a group of devoted and eminent pioneers, including J. G. Andersson, Davidson Black, Pierre Teilhard de Chardin, C. C. Young, V. K. King, W. H. Wong and C. D. Wu, has revealed evidence which suggests that Chinese origins are to a large extent indigenous; which evidence largely, though not entirely, discredits both Chinese mythology and Western migration theories.

In 1921 and 1926 the remains of very early man, *Sinanthropus pekinensis* – Peking man were found in a cave at Chou Kou Tien to the south of Peking, giving proof of the presence of very primitive man in China some 500 000 years ago. He was probably later than *Pithicanthropus erectus* and earlier than Neanderthal man. It is contended that the jaw and skull present affinities with those of the modern Mongol.[1] Then comes a long gap in our knowledge. The next trace of human beings in this area was found at Chou Tong K'ou, about 13 km east of Ninghsia, where remains of Palaeolithic man, probably about 50 000 years old, were found. Andersson suggests that he lived there at the end of the wet Pleistocene period and at the beginning of the dry period which followed when the thick deposits of loess were laid down.[2] This was the period equivalent to the Würm glaciation in Europe when, in China, the bitter, dry wind carrying the loess was inimical to both vegetation and animal life.[3] A further long blank period follows. Then, evidence appears of a mongoloid hunter-fisher people, widely spread through Sinkiang, Inner Mongolia and Manchuria in Mesolithic times. These 'hunter–fishers of the North began to cultivate plants and to domesticate animals, entering the food-producing stage in cultural history and laying a foundation for the North China Neolithic and post-Neolithic cultures to appear and prosper'.[4]

At Yang Shao Tsun, not far from modern Loyang, extensive finds were made in 1922 by Andersson of neolithic artifacts – polished stone tools, axes, adzes and hoes, bone ornaments and fine painted pottery, great round-bottomed burial urns and domestic pottery with bold and flowing designs in red and black. Further finds of a similar but not identical character were made in the upper Hwang-ho in Kansu at Ma Chia Yao, at Pan Shan and in the Koko Nor area at Ma Ch'ang. This pottery, known as Yang Shao, is not unlike neolithic pottery of both western and central Asia, and points to there having been considerable inter-communication at that early time (3000 BC). Since then many more such sites have been discovered in north China, emphasizing how widely Neolithic man was spread. Nevertheless, Yang Shao pottery has several unique shapes, which re-appear in subsequent cultures of north China and are found nowhere else. These support the belief that Chinese civilization rises from an indigenous culture. The unique shapes are the *li*, a very efficient tripod cooking-vessel with hollow legs, shaped rather like goat's udders, sometimes large enough to cook, say, a goose in one leg, an antelope in another and vegetables in a third.[5] A second unique shape, the *hsien*, a kind of sieve or steamer, is fitted above the *li*, the two together forming the *hsien*.

Yang Shao man lived on the loess plateau at a time when the water-table must have been much higher than it is today, and before the countryside was cut up by deep ravines, as this section (after Andersson) shows:

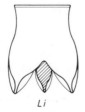

Fig. 20 Characteristic Yang Shao pottery-shapes

While he certainly was a hunter, as his arrow-heads and scrapers indicate, his large limestone hoes and adzes also point to his practising primitive agriculture. 'In one coarse, thick fragment [of pottery] we observed imprints, which have been shown to be husks of rice (*Oryza sativa L.*), which was thus cultivated at Yang Shao Tsun by the people of the late Stone Age.'[6]

In 1929 further discoveries were made, this time at Cheng Tzu Yai, east of Tsinian in Shantung. The finds were of Black Pottery, hard and highly polished, wheel-made and of very fine texture. This culture is known as the Lung Shan. It continues the shapes of the Yang Shao, notably the *li* and the *hsien* and apparently is unconnected with anything found in the West. Wherever Black Pottery is found in conjunction with Yang Shao Pottery, it is found lying above it, indicating that it is later in origin. Lung Shan culture shows considerable advance in complexity over Yang Shao and was much more widespread. Yang Shao was confined largely to the North China Nuclear Area, i.e. the valleys of mid-Hwang-ho and Wei-ho. Lung Shan extended east, north and south over the coastal plain, Manchuria and Central China. Yang Shao cultivation was of the primitive *ladung* or slash and burn type with its shifting or rotating settlement whereas Lung Shan people lived in permanent villages, surrounded by *hang-t'u* (stamped earth) walls. They had developed a much higher grade of farming with some suggestion of irrigation, well digging and the use of fertilizer in the cultivation of rice, wheat and millet. The sheep and the horse were added to the domesticated pig, dog and horse of Yang Shao. Lung Shan's tools (hoes, spades, sickles, axes and arrowheads) were more refined as was their pottery, which was wheelturned and included ceremonial as well as utility wares. There are indications of the practice of ancestor worship, of scapulimancy and of growing specialization and some class differentiation. In some degree the two cultures can respectively be identified with the legendary age of Shen-nung, China's mythological agricultural genius, and emerging urban life of the age of Hwang-ti (Yellow Emperor).[7]

In 1934–5 extensive and careful excavations were carried out near Anyang. This work led to exciting discoveries. The site of the ancient capital city of the Shang or Yin dynasty was uncovered close to the modern Anyang, revealing a highly organized society and an advanced civilization, the emergence of which marks a fusion of arch-aeology and history. In spite of certain differences, such as the rather sudden appearance of metallurgy and the warlike characteristics of the Shang people, K. C. Chang is certain that Lungshanoid culture is of Shang civilization.[8]

The excavations at Anyang and the extensive work done since Liberation show a firmly settled people in planned towns, developed forms of government and marked class differentiation.

Quite elaborate houses with pounded earth walls and floors and gable roofs at least for the ruling class had replaced the neolithic beehive shaped huts. While stone and bone tools and implements were still in general use, elaborate and exquisitely shaped bronze vessels, mainly for sacrificial and ceremonial purposes, are found in the tombs of royalty and the aristocracy. Significantly, some of these bronzes are cast in the same unique shapes that we noted in the Yang Shao and Black Pottery. The tombs, too, yield evidence of clothing, of handicrafts, of painting and music. There was highly developed ceremonial worship and an extension of scapulimancy in which writing in the form of pictograph on oracle bones made its appearance.

We must pause at this point for some explanation of oracle bones, which are important in throwing light on the origins of the Chinese people. They are, in fact, the main source book of history before 1122 BC. Country folk of north China have, for centuries, found pieces of bone on which they noticed curious markings. These were termed 'dragon bones' and were sold to the medicine shops as being specially efficacious. A big sale of these in the late nineteenth century led Chinese scholars to take note of them. Early in this century these markings were recognized as very early writing, but it was not until later that scholars, notably Tung Tso Ping, were able to decipher them. Then, and only then, were the oracle bones recognized for what they were and their true importance realized. From them Tung Tso Ping was able to establish that the Shang moved their capital to Anyang in 1384 BC.

The bones were scapulae (shoulder blades) or leg bones of cattle, or carapaces of the tortoise. Prayers or advice asked of the gods were incised on them. Unincised bones had been used in Black Pottery times, but by mid-Shang writing had appeared. Oval holes were cut on the surface of the bone and a hot iron placed to one side of these holes. This resulted in a crack appearing on the other side of the bone. The cracks were always

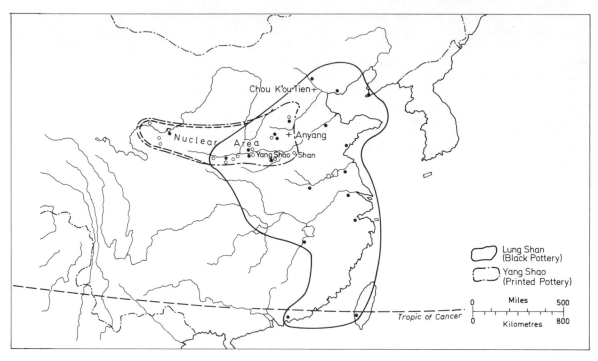

Fig. 21   Neolithic sites of the Yang Shao and Lung Shan cultures

along the length of the hole and then to one side ⚹ ⚹ ⚹, the simple answer 'yes' or 'no' being divined from this angle. The system by which this was done has not been worked out. The questions were on all sorts of everyday subjects, very largely of an agricultural nature, asking, for example: 'Will there be enough rain for the crops?' 'Will the harvest be good?' or making a request such as: 'We pray for rain.' Wheat and millet figure frequently, and hemp and even rice are mentioned. This mention of rice might indicate that in Shang times the climate was wetter than today, and the constant concern about rain an indication that desiccation was taking place. What is of significance is the almost exclusive concern in these oracle bone inscriptions for agriculture: for the crops, for rain, for the harvest. Sheep are rarely mentioned, indicating that we are dealing with a settled agricultural people. Just as the Hebrew imagery of the Old Testament (e.g. the twenty-third psalm) is cast in a pastoral mould, so that of the Shang is essentially agricultural, as one or two examples will show:[9]

> 'If, the father having broken up the ground, his son is unwilling to sow the seed, how much less will he be

willing to reap the grain.' 'Heaven in destroying Yin is doing husbandman's work – how dare I but complete the business of my fields.'

In the early stages of development of any society, environment exercises its influence much more powerfully than it does in later stages. We are justified in looking for the development of a settled stable society from a primitive nomadic society only in very favourable environments in which its peculiar advantages can be put to specialized use.

There are good geographical reasons for believing that a differentiation in economy into pastoralists and agriculturalists in north China was taking place in Neolithic times. The region at the confluence of the Hwang-ho and the Wei-ho provided an environment in which this could occur. The rivers themselves and some of their tributaries in this area were less liable to flood than lower down the course. Here was a light, fertile loess soil, which could be easily worked with the crude stone implements of Neolithic man. The natural vegetation was mainly grassland, thus eliminating the heavy work of forest clearing, although probably there was also considerable woodland since heavier rainfall was experienced then than now. The presence of some woodland would enable the primitive agriculturalist to supplement his food supply by hunting – the way of life from which he was emerging. This, too, is an area where variability of rainfall is beginning to be marked but not serious, and this factor would tend to make man thoughtful and forward-looking, a necessary quality in the development of civilization. From this the art of irrigation and water control eventually developed and with it the cooperation and organization that it implies. Neolithic man availed himself, as does the modern Chinese in this area, of the peculiar vertical cleavage and ease of working of the loess for housing. Caves, which are dry and cool in summer and warm in winter, can be cut with comparative ease. These are some of the geographical factors which led to early settlement in this region.

Farther north and northwest climatic conditions were too hostile for agricultural development; rainfall is sparse (less than 375 mm per annum), the seasonal range of temperature increases and the growing period becomes very short. To the east the lower reaches of the Hwang-ho were subject to such constant flooding that they were unusable in the state of knowledge of those times. The Yangtze valley to the south and west at that time was a region of dense forest and marshland, occupied by thinly distributed aboriginal tribes, relying mainly on hunting and migratory *ladang* agriculture.

As we shall see later when discussing Chinese growth outward from its primary focus in the Wei–Hwang-ho bend, while expansion was comparatively easy, rapid and permanent, southward and eastward, no such movement was possible northwestward. To the south and east the same agricultural economy as that of the focal centre, with modifications occasioned by local differences, could be established. Dry agriculture had to give place to wet agriculture in the south, but agriculture it remained. To the north and northwest this was not so. The increasing aridity northwestward dictates, at least to a primitive culture, a pastoral way of life. Attempted agricultural expansion northwestwards met with increasingly adverse conditions. More and more reliance had to be placed on rearing livestock on the steppe grassland until a region is reached where dependence on grazing is complete and a true pastoral economy is established.

There thus grew up two ways of life, which were mutually exclusive and which were hostile to each other: the Chinese (Shang) retained their hunting habits but developed more and more their agricultural activities, while the Mongols placed more and more reliance on their sheep, goats, camels and horses. Lattimore suggests that the two ways of life did not become finally exclusive until the 'barbarians' of the north developed horse riding and the use of a bow on horseback, while the Chinese continued to use the horse harnessed to chariots.[11] Between the true agriculturalist (Chinese) and the true pastoralist (Mongol) there has lain a transitional zone, which throughout history has been contended for and which is marked geographically by the 375 mm isohyet and historically by the Great Wall.

THE GREAT WALL AND ITS FUNCTIONS

Obviously a line of cleavage existed somewhere between the territories and peoples that could advantageously be included in the Chinese Empire and those that could not. This was the line that the Great Wall was intended to define.

Owen Lattimore

We have seen how, out of the Lung Shan culture, there emerged a highly organized people based on the Great City *Shang* or *Yin*, having a king or *Ti* and an elaborate hierarchy of classes. However, they were not yet fully sinicized. For example, theirs was largely a matriarchal system. This, the first dynasty (Shang 1450–1054 BC), was eventually conquered by a small kingdom, Chou, under the leadership of Wu Wang. The Chou people were probably of Turkish stock and occupied the land lying to the west of Shang. The Chou introduced a patriarchal system and the worship of Heaven by the Emperor, and ancestor worship, all of which played so important a role in Chinese history from then until the fall of the Manchu dynasty and the rise of the Republic in 1911.

When the Chou defeated and overran Shang lands, the only way of governing this newly acquired and comparatively vast area was to divide it up and distribute it as fiefs to the lords and tribal leaders, who had been instrumental in achieving victory. Thus it came about that China

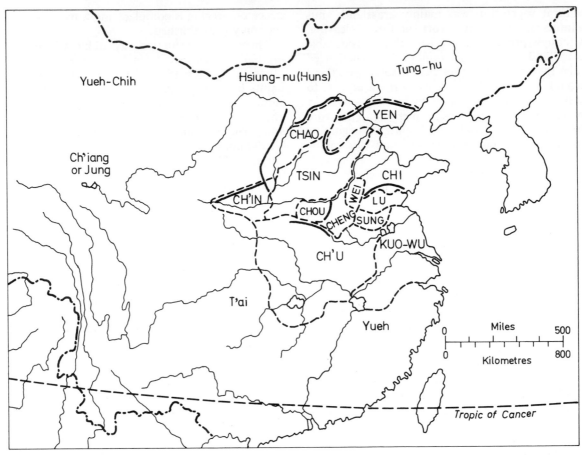

Fig. 22   Inter-state walls c. *350 BC*

entered a long feudal period (1054–256 BC). Chou territory proper, i.e. the royal domain, was sited in two areas, the original home in the west, having Hao (Sian) as its capital and a newly acquired realm in the heart of the kingdom, with Loyang as its centre.

The Chou were never a very big tribe themselves; nevertheless the first emperors of the Chou dynasty exerted a strong central control. However, as time went on, the various fiefs and dukedoms became virtually independent kingdoms, vying with the centre and each other for power. After establishing themselves, the Chou were constantly engaged in subduing and controlling the Yueh Chih, Mongols (Hsiung-nu) and Tibetans (Ch'iang) on their northern and western borders. Eventually their western domain was overrun and the Chou prince had to flee to Loyang. The territory was regained by the prince

of Ch'in, who retained it for himself. Thus the Chou prince became merely the nominal head but continued to carry out the sacrifices which were considered so essential for securing harmony between heaven and earth, without which there could be no general well-being.

From now on (c. 770 BC) there was a constant struggle between the feudal princes and lords for power. This is the period of the 'Warring States' when Confucius and Mencius expounded their theories of good government and the right relationship of heaven to prince, and prince to subject. The farther the fief was from the centre, the less it was subject to control. Moreover, the nearer it was to the 'frontier' and the steppelands, the more it was subject to nomadic influence. There was a persistent danger that those lords holding lands on the northern periphery would throw off their Chinese allegiance and culture and

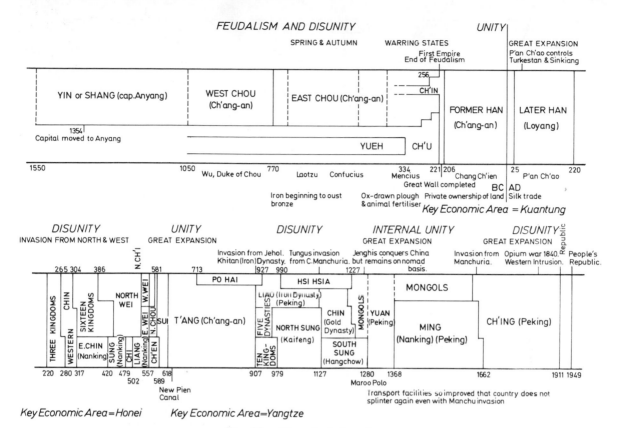

Fig. 23 Historical timechart

go over to a pastoral way of life, thus adding weight to the constant steppeland pressure on the Chinese intensive agricultural way of life, centred on the walled city.

We have seen how, in 771 BC, the feudal prince of Ch'in rescued the Chou emperor in the west and took over his domain there. In 256 BC the Chou dynasty came to an end, abdicating to a later head of this same state of Ch'in. By 222 BC the young Ch'in prince, Ch'in Shih Hwang Ti, had subdued all the other feudal states. He then proceeded to create the first unitary state of China. He centralized control in every sphere. He set up military and civil governors in all districts, making them directly responsible to the emperor. He attempted to formulate a universal language and writing. He standardized the length of cart axles – a very necessary measure as the varying lengths rendered the dirt roads unusable. He nearly succeeded in destroying all Confucian literature, since Confucius was the great upholder of the feudal tradition that the Emperor was attempting to destroy.[13]

Ch'in Shih Hwang Ti further tried to unify the state by stabilizing its northern frontiers. As we have seen, this frontier posed an eternal problem, not only of resistance to invasion from the surrounding tribes but also of loss of the frontiersman to the pastoralist way of life. It was to solve this problem that Ch'in Shih Hwang Ti built the Great Wall. In feudal times, the various princes had built many walls along their borders to secure them against the inroads of their neighbours, both Chinese and barbarian (see fig. 21). Ch'in Shih Hwang Ti, by means of immense forced labour, untold misery, blood and sweat, set to work and connected all the individual walls of the feudal princes on the north and extended them right round the great northward bend of the Hwang-ho as far as Ninghsia. Later, under the Han emperors, this wall was extended far into the west to Tun Huang and Yumen (Jade Gate) to protect the Imperial Silk Route against the Hsiung-nu (Huns) of the north. Ch'in Shih Hwang Ti thus occupied and attempted to hold the whole of the Ordos by settling some 30 000 Chinese families in

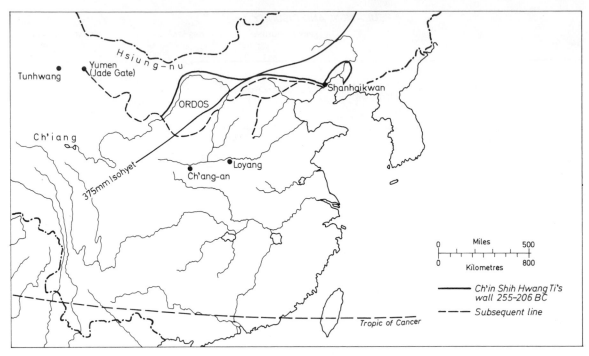

Fig. 24   The Great Wall of Ch'in Shih Hwang Ti

this semi-desert region. However, the attempt was doomed to failure. Within a century the Hsiung-nu, who had been driven out, were back in full occupation of the Ordos.

From Shanhaikwan on the shores of the Gulf of Liao-tung to the Hwang-ho, Ch'in Shih Hwang Ti's Great Wall followed the highlands of the southern rim of the Mongolian basin and thus had some physical justification. However, in its continuation westward along the north bank of the Hwang-ho the Wall ceases to conform to a natural region, for it crosses the 375 mm isohyet and embraces a large area of sparse and variable rainfall, the Ordos, which is far more suited to pastoral economy than intensive agriculture. Thus, in disregarding geographical factors and attempting to include permanently within his domains essentially pastoral lands, Ch'in Shih Hwang Ti defeated his own ends and the main purpose of the Wall, i.e. the separation of these two economies.

Often there were large numbers of nomads living within the Great Wall while it was sited so far north. Nineteen Hsiung-nu tribes occupied all the Ordos region at the time of the Three Kingdoms (AD 220–65). While the Han emperors remained powerful and energetic, they were able to keep the northern pastoralists under control, but immediately there was a weakening of imperial power, the old forces reasserted themselves and the struggle between the two ways of life was renewed. Ch'in Shih Hwang Ti's wall to the north of the Ordos was eventually abandoned, and one to the south, conforming closely to the 375 mm isohyet, was built.

For more than two millennia there has been an ebb and flow across a zone of transition between these two ways of life. It has fluctuated as first the agriculturalist and then the pastoralist has had an accession of power and an urge to energetic action. Particularly in recent centuries, as population in China has rapidly increased, there has been an outward pressure by the agriculturalist to colonize the more arid regions beyond the Wall, but until today, the 375 mm isohyet has been the inexorable controller, and the Chinese farmer, on the whole, has remained within the confines of the Wall.

Now, once again, a strong central government in China is pushing its culture far beyond the Great Wall and the 375 mm isohyet into the lands

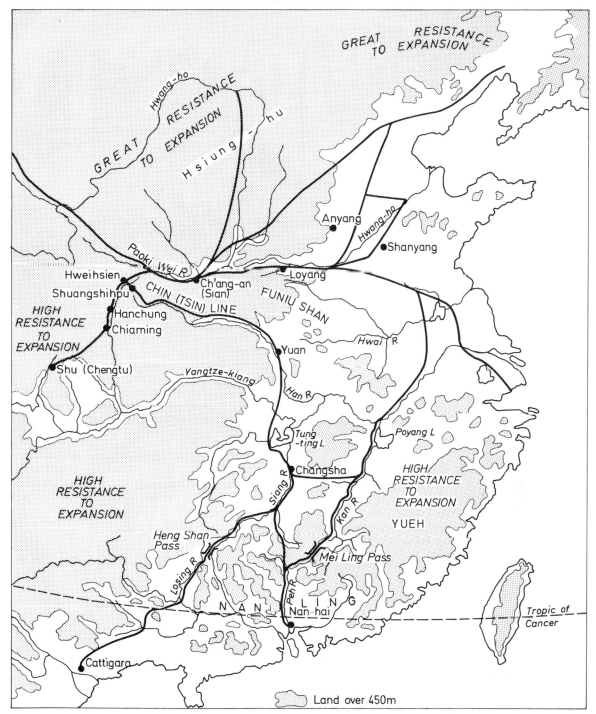

Fig. 25 Main routes of southward penetration in Ch'in and Han Dynasties

of the northern pastoralist, imposing its own intensive methods of agriculture on the steppeland people. This modern attempt, however, differs from all such movements in the past in that it is today fortified by all the techniques of modern science as applied to irrigation and power, which may be able to defy the old dictation of climate.

CHINESE EXPANSION AND DEVELOPMENT

We have seen how the natural advantages offered by the loess region enabled Neolithic man to develop a primitive specialized agriculture from general undifferentiated Neolithic culture. Later, early Chinese under Shang and Chou leadership developed intensive agriculture and were able to establish stable government and a settled community in the valleys of the lower Wei and middle Hwang-ho, a district known as Kuan-chung. Ssu-ma Ch'ien, writing of it, claimed that it 'occupied one third of the territory under heaven with a population of three-tenths of the total; but its wealth constitutes six-tenths of all the wealth under heaven'.[14] We have seen also that the extension of agricultural economy and way of life towards the north and northwest was fraught with great difficulty. The high Tibetan plateau in the west held out no invitation. If expansion was to take place, therefore, it had to be to the east and the south.

It was to the east, out over the alluvial plain of the lower Hwang-ho, into the region known as Honei, that Kuan-chung first naturally expanded. As Pan Ku, extolling the natural strength and advantages of Kuan-chung, put it, 'the abundance of Shu and Pa [Szechwan] on the south, the nomadic herds of the Hu on the north, and with natural barriers on three sides, it can easily be defended; with one side opening to the east it is an excellent base for the subjugation of the feudal lords'.[15] By the end of the Chou dynasty the whole of the North China Plain as far north as the walls of Yen and Chao (present Shansi, Hopei and Shantung) was occupied by Chinese princedoms and kingdoms. The Ch'in and Han dynasties, which followed, marked a period of great development and change politically, socially and economically. China was united under one ruler and government; feudalism was abolished and the peasant was no longer bound to the soil. It entered the Iron Age, the plough and animal fertilizer were

introduced and great water conservancy works were carried out.

Routes south

It was not until the great conquests under Ch'in Shih Hwang Ti and the Former Han that any considerable expansion south of the Tsinling was made. Penetration southward followed five comparatively easy topographical lines.

The easiest way was that southeastward over the almost imperceptible divide between the lower Hwang-ho and the Hwai basin. This route, more restricted in width then than now on account of marshland and poor drainage, was destined to become of great strategic importance once the Yangtze basin had been developed and incorporated in the Middle Kingdom. It formed a bottleneck between north and south. Writing in the Sung period (AD 960–1280), when threatened by invasion from the north, Shu Tsung-yen says, 'Shanyang is a place over which north and south must fight. If we hold it, we can advance to capture Shantung, but if the enemy get it, the south of the Hwai can be lost in the next morning or evening.' This Hwai route forks farther south, the eastern prong leading to the mouth of the Yangtse and the Hangchow, and the western prong up the Yangtze to the Poyang lake, thence southward via the Kan river, over the Mei Ling Pass and down the Pei-kiang to Nan-hai (Canton) at the mouth of the Pearl river. East of this route is the very dissected, rugged highland of southeast China. This is the country which the Yueh tribes occupied and which resisted the arms of both the Ch'in and the Han.

A second route southward had two starting points, Ch'ang-an and Loyang. That from Ch'ang-an crossed the Tsinling by the Wu-ling Pass and descended to the Han valley at Yuan. It was here that the route from Loyang joined it after crossing the Funiu Shan. From Yuan it went south via the Tung Ting lake and the Siang river to Ch'ang-sha, over Heng Shan and Nan Ling, forking east to Nan-hai (Canton) and west to Cattigara (Tongking).

A third route was more difficult. It ran west from Ch'ang-an to Paoki, thence south over the high passes and very difficult terrain of the Tsinling at Shuangshihpu. There it divided, one branch going eastward down to the source waters of the Han at Han-chung and continuing, joined the second route, described above, at Yuan. The main route, however, at that time branched southwest via Hweihsien and Chia Ming to Shu (present day Chengtu) and so into the heart of the State of Shu-Oa (Szechwan). This was the route followed by Ch'in Hwang Ti when he subdued Shu in 220 BC and also by Kublai Khan about AD 1280 as a means of outflanking the Middle Yangtze.

Reasons for southern expansion

Movement southward along one or other of these routes was occasioned, as may be expected, by many causes. Under Ch'in Shih Hwang Ti and the early Han emperors there was a rapid and vast expansion of imperial territory south, extending to the Pearl river and to Tongking. This expansion was due in large measure to the perennial ambition and the desire for prestige of the emperors themselves and their generals. However, one must not be misled by the maps into imagining that this vast new area was very much under central control or that the land was closely settled by immigrants from the north; in fact it was held for centuries only by widely dispersed garrisons, often giving a very doubtful loyalty.

Population pressures appear to have had little to do with southward movement if the following figures are any guide:[16]

which are known as 'panics' and each has been the result of invasion and internal disorder. Between AD 299 and 317 the Western Ch'in dynasty broke up as a result of intrigue and misrule, coupled with a series of droughts. Subordinate princes in alliance with strong frontier tribes, notably Hsiung-nu, invaded the country, which resulted in mass migration of the Han Chinese from Kuanchung and Honei southward into Szechwan, Hupeh and Hunan.[18] A Ch'in prince, Yuan Ti, formed the Eastern Ch'in dynasty in the south with its capital at Nanking. 'Countless members of the Chinese gentry had fled from the Huns at that time and had come into the southern empire. They had not done so out of loyalty to the Chinese dynasty, or out of national feeling, but because they saw little prospect of attaining rank and influence at the courts of the alien rulers, and because it was to be feared that the aliens would turn the fields into pasturage.'[19]

There have been three other such 'panics'; one when the Toba (Turks) conquered the north at the end of the eleventh century; another when Jenghis Khan and his Tartars swept into northern China at the beginning of the thirteenth century; and lastly when the Japanese invaded China in

Period	Year AD	Population	
Western Han	2	59 595 000	
Eastern Han	156	56 487 000	
T'ang	755	52 919 000	probably an under-estimate in order to avoid taxation
Northern Sung	1102	43 822 000	
Yuan (Mongol)	1209	59 847 000	
Ming	1578	60 693 000	
Ch'ing (Manchu)	1783	284 033 000	probably an over-estimate in order to flatter the court. Also tribes not before included
Ch'ing (Manchu)	1851	432 140 000	
Communist	1951	563 000 000	
Communist	1953	582 603 417	first reliable census
Communist	1971	780 000 000	estimate[17]

The figures show a more or less static population over nearly 1600 years. Nevertheless there have been periods of mass migration southward caused by invasion from the northwest by the Hsiung-nu or Mongols and, to a lesser extent, when natural disasters of flood or drought have occurred. Wiens quotes four such occasions,

1937, followed shortly after, in 1949, by the sweeping victory of the Chinese Communist armies.

A further reason for migration southward and subsequent colonization was the promise which the fertile lowlands of the Yangtze basin held out. Although a great deal of it was heavily forest clad, the potentialities of the Yangtze valley as a granary were not lost on the early settlers, and it became, in due course, the economic heart of the Middle Kingdom. Wiens comments:

> No doubt the psychological appeal of the southern rice regions has had its influence in effecting a continuous migration southward. Since the earliest days the south has been regarded as a granary for the north, and in this manner, the north early became a parasite upon the south. First the grain of Ssu-ch'uan was drawn upon to support northern political and military power. This became especially significant after the construction of the Grand Canal.[20]

When the Han Chinese moved into the Yangtze valley and Szechwan, they found it far from unoccupied. Eberhard estimates that of the 800 or so tribes and folk groups in China at this time, 345 were on the southwest and west, 290 in south China and only 80 in north China. In the west and southwest outstanding tribes were the Ch'iang (62), Lolo (93) and Fan (32), while in the centre and south were the Miao (65), Pai Man (44) and Yao (32). Many of these tribes were known collectively as the T'ai people and formed the state of Ch'u, which long resisted intrusion from the north until conquered by Ch'in Shih Hwang Ti in 222 BC. Wiens says:

> The political fall of the T'ai in the Yangtze valley, Szechwan, southeastern China and Lingnan occurred under the onslaught of the other mighty barbarian state, pressing upon the crumbling Chou Empire from the northwest. Fortunate it was for the Ch'in that the various semi-sinicized T'ai states were not united, for such a comity of states would certainly have thwarted his ambitious schemes to seize supreme power. All of south China at this time was dominated by the T'ai. In fact, as Eickstedt points out, most historians talk about a 'China' existing prior to the victory of the Ch'in that not only never existed but was actually a T'ai empire (Eickstedt, pp. 115–30). This, he rightly asserts, ought to be recognized once and for all.[21]

While the Miao, Yao, Lolo and many other groups of tribes were hill rovers, existing on gathering and hunting almost entirely, the T'ai were the primitive agriculturalists of the south, who, using *milpa* or *ladang* methods, practised wet rice cultivation. 'The custom was to fertilize the land by burning the vegetable overgrowth and, as the seeds were planted, flood the fields with water.[22] It was from the south, too, that the Shang and Chou dynasties obtained the copper and tin for their magnificent bronze work, and it is contended that they also learned their earliest

techniques from the south. The *Tribute of Yu* in the Shu Ching written in the Chou dynasty, lists also gold and silver, feathers, hair, ivory, hides, woods, silken fabrics, pearls, large tortoises and cinnabar as coming from the southern regions.[23]

Ssu-ma Ch'ien[24] describes Ch'u and Yueh, i.e. Lower Yangtze, as 'a large territory, sparsely populated, where people eat rice and drink fish soup; where land is tilled with fire and hoed with water; where people collect fruits and shellfish for food; where people enjoy self-sufficiency without commerce. The place is fertile and suffers no famine and hunger. Hence the people are lazy and poor and do not bother to accumulate wealth. Hence in the south of the Yangtze and the Hwai, there are neither hungry nor frozen people, nor a family which owns a thousand gold.'

The southern penetration under Ch'in Shih Hwang Ti met with strenuous resistance. Although the T'ai were defeated in the Yangtze valley, they continued to hold Yunnan and Kweichow. This region remained in T'ai hands as the Kun-chou or Nan-chou Kingdom until about AD 1000. The Yueh also resisted strongly, and, retreating into the forested hills of the southeast, were not subdued by either the Ch'in or Han dynasties. Szechwan, known then as Shu-pa, proved a hard nut for the early expansionists from the north to crack – and not only for these but for many succeeding invaders, not excluding the Japanese in the Sino–Japanese war of 1937–45, who never succeeded in cracking it. Liang Ch'i-ch'ao says of Szechwan 'Whenever there were disturbances under heaven [i.e. in China], Szechwan was held by an independent ruler, and it was always the last to lose its independence.'[25] The physique of Szechwan with its very difficult mountainous borders on all sides is sufficient explanation of this phenomenon.

The method of colonization used by the early conquerors as they pushed south was that of planting the invading armies as agricultural settlers under the leadership of their generals, who were appointed as governors. In spite of the fact that Ch'in Shih Hwang Ti attempted to plant half a million such settlers they were thinly distributed over a large area and, through intermarriage with the native population, they were strongly influenced by the 'barbarian' culture. As has so often been the pattern in history, the generals or leaders who have been instrumental in conquering new lands and who, as a reward, have been given control of the peripheral areas,

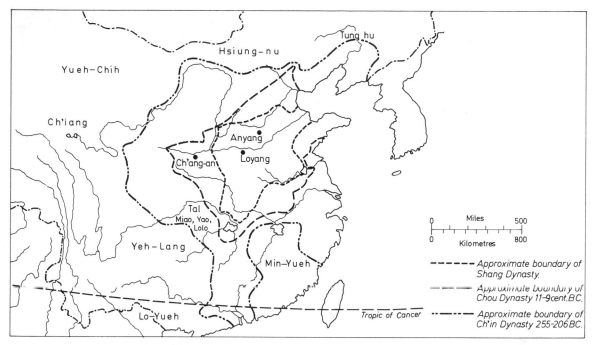

Fig. 26   Chinese expansion in Shang, Chou and Ch'in Dynasties

soon asserted their independence. For example, Chao T'o, Ch'in Shih Hwang Ti's most successful general, proclaimed himself King of Nan Yueh, although he continued to give nominal allegiance to the central power. He took to himself a Yueh wife and to some degree identified himself with the Yueh culture.

Defecting generals and chieftains were loath to sever entirely their ties with imperial authority as they valued very highly their identification with the 'civilized' culture of the north as against the 'barbarian'. We should remind ourselves that the distinction between 'civilized' and 'barbarian' in Chinese eyes, until quite recent years, has been 'our' culture as against all others. China did not call herself 'the Central Kingdom' for nothing. The high value set on maintaining this connection with the northern culture is reflected in the fact that the king or prince would be willing to concede vassalage to the emperor. This willingness played an important part in imperial expansion. The great prestige of Han culture and the desire to be included in its aurora was certainly as potent a factor as its military prowess in extension of its imperial rule.

However real conquest of the south did not come until T'ang and Sung times. To this day the

people of China living south of the Nan-Ling in Kwangsi and Kwangtung refer to themselves as T'ang Jen (Men of T'ang) while those to the north and centre call themselves Han Jen (Men of Han). While the maps (figs. 25 and 26a) of the Ch'in and Han periods show large areas of present-day China as under central sway, we have seen that much of it was held nominally only and was by no means fully sinicized. This was particularly true of all that area south of the Nan-Ling, known as Lingnan (Kwangsi and Kwangtung) and, of course, Yueh (Fukien and Chekiang), which did not give even nominal allegiance to the north. With the fall of Han and later the Three Kingdoms, connection with imperial power either at Ch'ang-an (Sian) and Loyang was even more tenuous and for long periods was entirely severed, for China was divided into hostile states and was not reunited until the Sui dynasty.

There were geographical reasons for the slow assimilation of Lingnan into the imperial fold. The hot, wet valleys of Kwangtung and Kwangsi were malaria-infested and certainly held little attraction for the Han Jen from the cooler, drier north. Curiously, the area of the upper reaches of the West river in Kiangsi apparently were settled earlier than the lower reaches and wider valley

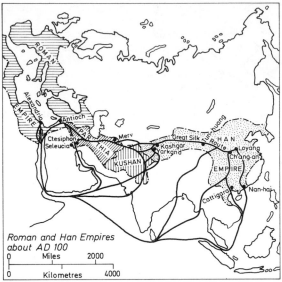

Fig. 27a   *Boundaries under the Roman and Han Empires*

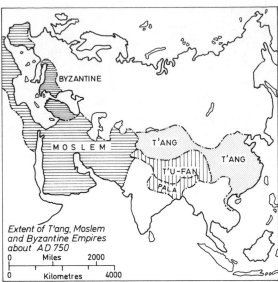

Fig. 27b   *Boundaries under the T'ang, Moslem and Byzantine Empires*

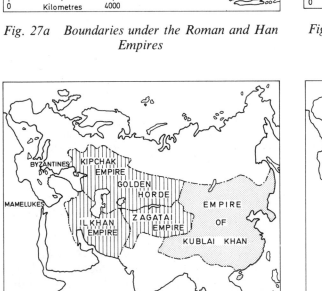

Fig. 27c   *Boundaries under the Mongol Empire*

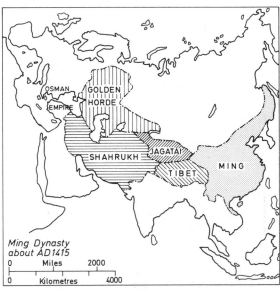

Fig. 27d   *Boundaries under the Ming Empire*

in Kwangtung. This was probably due to the more frequented use of the Siang river – Lotsing river route, leading to Cattigara (Tongking) than that of the Kan river – Peh river, leading down to the mouth of the West river at Nan-hai (Canton). The resurgence of imperial power and expansion which followed the reunification of the country

under the glorious T'ang dynasty (AD 618–906) led once more to the active planting of more military farm colonies in the south, and when, after the fall of T'ang, the succeeding Sung emperors (AD 960–1279) were forced south from their capitals in Ch'ang-an, Loyang and Kaifeng and established their headquarters at Nanking

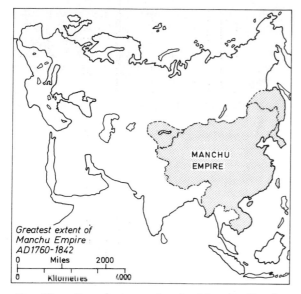

Fig. 27e Boundaries under the Manchu Empire

transport; a boat for water transport; a kind of basket for crossing marshes and crampons for crossing the mountains. He followed the mountains in separating the nine provinces; he deepened the river beds; he fixed tribute according to soil capacity; he made the nine roads usable; he dammed the nine marshes and surveyed the nine mountains.[26]

Amid the overflowing of inundating waters, Yu divided, arranged and reduced to order the land of the nine provinces.

This is the earliest recorded regional geography of the country. Legge says of it It may be regarded as a domesday book of China in the twenty-third century before Christ.[27]

To cope with the flood Yu used many methods. He is said to have divided the lower course of the Hwang-ho into nine channels, a method which, as we shall see, was carried out so successfully by Li Ping in the Cheng-tu region in Szechwan in 221 BC. Already, at this early time, the raised bed of the Hwang-ho (referred to as 'The Ho') was causing difficulty.

Then Yu, taking account of the fact that the Ho's bed was raised, that its waters were rapid and violent and that in crossing the plain they caused much damage, he drew off two canals in order to control its course.

In the north he carried the Ho on raised terrain beyond the R. Kiang to Tu-lou. He divided it into nine rivers, which he re-united to form the Ni-ho and emptied into the Po-ho.

When the nine courses had been well cut and the nine marshes cleaned [i.e. drained], the whole empire was orderly and at peace. This meritorious work was beneficial throughout three dynasties.[28]

Yu further used the obvious but much less satisfactory method of containment by building dykes along the river banks, a method continuously practised to the present day and equally continuously the source of disaster following the inevitable periodical breaking of the banks.

Ssu-ma Ch'ien records one such breakage in the early days (168 BC) of the Han Dynasty and another some thirty-six years later:

The Ho overflowed at Hou-tzu, spread out over the swamps of Chiu-yi and linked up with the Hwai and Szu. Then the Son of Heaven [i.e. the Emperor] sent Chi Yen and Ch'eng Tseng-chi to recruit men to close the breach but it suddenly broke through again.

The river then flowed out south of the Shantung Peninsula. There is an interesting little comment

and Hangchow, the whole of the south was fully occupied and completely sinicized. So it has remained ever since an integral part of 'China Proper' inhabited by Han or T'ang Jen as distinct from those wide alien areas which have been incorporated into the Middle Kingdom at times of imperial exuberance and ambition, and which have fallen away as soon as that energy has expended itself.

HISTORICAL DEVELOPMENT OF WATER CONSERVANCY AND COMMUNICATIONS

When water benefits are developed there will be good results in agriculture, and when there are good results in agriculture the State's treasury will be enriched.
Gazetteer of the Prefecture of Suchow

The Legend of Yu has it that there was a Golden Age in China between 2357 and 2205 BC. The Emperor Yao reigned from 2357 to 2255 and during this time he called on his minister Yu to cope with the floods, which were devastating the country. This Yu did with great energy, fidelity and self-abnegation.

Yu checked the overflowing waters. During thirteen years, whenever he passed before his home, not once did he cross the threshold. He used a chariot for land

in the same record showing that care and repair of dykes was not always pursued with enthusiasm or viewed with an altruistic eye.

> At that time T'ien Fen, Marquis of Wu-nan, was Prime Minister and was in receipt of the revenues of the city of Chow, which lay to the north of the Ho. After the breach in the Ho, the waters flowed south; the city no longer suffered from flooding and its revenues increased. Therefore T'ien Fen addressed the Emperor in these terms: 'The breaches of the Kiang and the Ho are of heaven's ordaining; trusting to human power it is not easy to close them; moreover, it is by no means certain that to do so is the will of heaven.' The necromancers gave the same advice and so, for a long time, the Son of Heaven made no effort to close the breach.[30]

However, after a lapse of twenty years, during which time, as a result of the breach, there had been a series of bad harvests, capped by a severe drought, the Son of Heaven was forced to take some action. So, in 110 BC we find him issuing orders for the mobilization of a vast labour force of several hundred thousand workers to close the breach. He visited the site in person where he propitiated the River God by throwing into the river a white horse and a jade ring and, having performed the necessary rites and sacrifices,

> He ordered all his subjects and officials, from the grade of general down, to carry faggots to fill the breach. At that time the brushwood had been burnt off and small wood was consequently scarce. Bamboo from the Ch'i woodlands was therefore cut and used for barrage stakes. The Son of Heaven, approaching the breach of the River, was grieved that the work was not finished and sang this song:
>
> There is a breach at Hou-tzu – what should be done?
> It is an inundation, an immensity – there, where hamlets stood, there is naught but the River.
> Since there is naught but River, the country can enjoy no peace.
> This is not the time to relax effort – our mountains are breaking down.
> Our mountains are breaking down and the Kin-yi swamp overflows.
> The fish are agitated and ill at ease, tortured by the approach of winter.
> The whole length of the river's bed is damaged: the River has abandoned its regular course.
> Alligators and dragons dart forth: they wander afar in complete liberty.
> When the River returns to its ancient bed, 'twill be the blessing of the God.
> How should I have known what was happening outside the capital had I not performed the *feng* and *chan* sacrifices?

> 'Tell me, Lord of the River, why are you so hostile?
> Your inundations cease not and you desolate my people.
> Yi-sang is submerged; the Hwai and Szu overflow.
> Long have you left your bed: the rules governing the waters are spurned.'

Evidently either the sacrifices or the hundreds of thousands of workers were successful, for a further verse runs:

> The bubbling waters rush along their courses.
> Turning towards the north, they return to their bed.
> Alert, they flow over all obstacles.
> Take up long poles: cast on the beautiful jade.
> The Lord of the River is answering our prayers.
> But the wood is insufficient. Why? The fault lies with the men of Wei.
> Fire has laid the land waste.
> Alas, how shall we stop the waters?
> Cut down the bamboo forest: drive in the stakes and place the stones.
> Ten thousand congratulations – at Suen-fang the barrage is secured.

The Hwang-ho was thus turned northward once more and resumed its old course, traced by the legendary Yu.

While the purpose of dyke building was primarily to prevent flooding, it was sometimes used as a weapon in the quarrelsome feudal days of the Chou dynasty (the fifth and fourth centuries BC). Feudal lords would construct dykes in such a way as to direct flood waters into their neighbour's country with the express purpose of embarrassing them.

> Those who were anxious to avoid the danger of floods also constructed dykes to force water into their neighbour's country, regarding the latter as a reservoir for surplus water. Thus more and more dykes were built day by day and they encroached so much upon the natural channel of the river that the dykes were burst and floods became frequent.[31]

Ssu-ma Ch'ien tells a typical Chinese story of an attempt by the head of the State of Han to use canal building to weaken its western rival, the State of Ch'in. This attempt was singularly unsuccessful: it recoiled on its instigator and helped materially towards the ultimate conquest by Ch'in of all the feudal states, and the formation of the first unitary government of China.

> Then the Prince of Han, learning of the success of the state of Ch'in, wished to exhaust it and to oppose

its attacks to the east. He therefore sent a hydro-graphic engineer, named Ch'eng Kou to the Prince of Ch'in and treacherously persuaded him to undertake the construction of a canal, which would lead the waters of the river King from Ch'ung Shan west to Hou-kou along the whole length of mountains to the north, emptying into the river Lo. The canal would be 300 *li* long and would be used for irrigation. The work was half finished when the ruse was discovered. When Ch'in would have killed Ch'eng, the latter said: 'True, at first I deceived you; however, if the canal is finished, it will be of great benefit to Ch'in'. The Prince of Ch'in agreed and ordered the completion of the canal. When finished it irrigated 40 000 *ch'ing* of alkaline land and production rose by one *ch'ong* per *mow*. Thus, the interior became a fertile plain without bad years and Ch'in became rich and powerful conquering other feudal lords. This is how the canal came to be named the Ch'eng Kou Canal.[32]

However, throughout the Chou dynasty, i.e. until 221 BC, water conservancy was on a relatively small scale. The whole economy was feudal and based on the well-field system, by which each square *li* of land was divided into nine squares each of 100 *mow*. The central square was a public field, the produce of which belonged to the lord. The other eight squares were occupied and cultivated by eight peasant families, who were bound to their holdings, and who paid a tenth part of their produce as tax. Moreover, work on their lord's square had to be completed before they could turn to their own. As long as this feudal system held sway no large-scale water conservancy work could be done since no large labour force, bound as it was to its feudal farm routine, could be organized. The breakdown of this system came when first the shortlived Ch'in dynasty (221–206 BC) broke the power of the feudal lords, and then the institution of private ownership of land under the Han emperors freed the peasant from his feudal bondage. At much the same time great technical changes in the use of the land were taking place. The use of iron was replacing bronze and stone, oxen were being used for ploughing and animal fertilizer was applied to increase the productivity of the land.

One of the effects of this agricultural and social revolution was to set free an army of peasants and serfs, who could be gathered into a labour force such as we have seen used in dealing with the breach in the Hwang-ho. This ability to mobilize large numbers was the necessary condition for ushering in a great era of canal building and irrigation, two aspects of water control which went

hand in hand and which were essential to the development and the expansion of China outlined in the previous chapter. Irrigation was necessary if the production of grain and foodstuffs was to keep pace with the growing population and the ever-increasing demands of the court and central government. Canals and navigable rivers were necessary for the transport of tribute grain to the capital, 'road' transport being hopelessly uneconomic. Once central government by the Emperor was established under the Ch'in and Han dynasties, tribute grain became of great importance and retained its importance until well into the nineteenth century. The functions of tribute grain were threefold: it formed the main supply for the maintenance of the emperor and his court in the capital, which was synonymous with the government; furthermore, it maintained the army on which the government relied to carry out expansion of its territories, to defend it against invasion and possible rebellion; and part of the tribute grain was stored in the Imperial granaries against times of famine. The efficient functioning of these granaries was a mark of able and stable government.

We have seen how Ch'eng Kou's Canal came to be built as a result of a ruse by the Prince of Han in the feudal times of Chou. In Ch'in and Han times this canal continued to be of local use in the heart of Kuanchung, transporting grain of the Wei valley to the capital, Ch'ang-an, and irrigating the alkaline land lying between the left-bank tributaries of Ch'ing and Lo. However, with the extension of government jurisdiction farther and farther eastward into the lower Hwang-ho district of Honei, the need for easier communication and transport to the capital along the line of the Hwang-ho and Wei became more pressing. Ssu-ma Ch'ien records the building of a further canal in these words:

At that time [approx. 132 BC] Ch'eng Tang-che was Minister of Agriculture. He observed 'Formerly transport of grain came by the passes up the course of the river Wei and required six months for its accomplishment. The route by water was about 900 *li* and sometimes was very difficult. If the waters of the Wei were led by a canal, which could be cut from Ch'ang-an, skirting the mountains on the south, to reach the Ho, the passage would be a mere 300 *li* and direct. Transport would be easy and a matter of only three months. Moreover, more than ten thousand *k'ing* of cultivable land below the canal could thus be irrigated. By this means, on the one hand

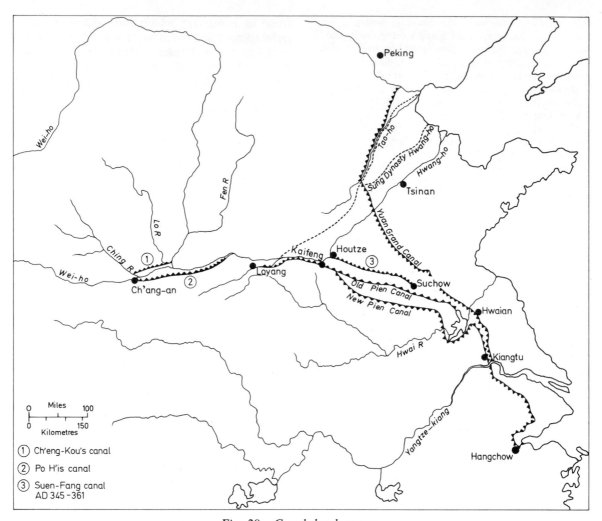

Fig. 28   Canal development

water transport would be shortened and the numbers engaged reduced and on the other hand, the fertility of the land above the passes would be increased and greater harvests obtained.' The Son of Heaven approved this project. He ordered the hydraulic engineer, Sui Po, native of Ts'i, to plan the canal and to recruit all available manpower to carry it out. The work was finished in three years and proved most beneficial. As a result, water transport gradually increased and the people who lived below the canal often used its waters for irrigation.

Later P'o Hi, administrator of Ho-tung, said: 'The amount of grain that is transported by water each year from east of the mountains to the west is about a million *che*. Passage of Ti-chou has lost much of its difficulty, fatigue and expense.'[33]

A great deal of irrigation work was carried out in Kuanchung and Honei under the early Han emperors. The great Emperor Wu Ti, in 111 BC was most energetic. He issued an edict laying the duty of irrigation on his government in these terms:

Agriculture is the basic [occupation] of the world. Springs and rivers make possible the cultivation of the five grains.... There are numerous mountains and rivers in the domain, with whose use the ordinary people are not acquainted. Hence [the government] must cut canals and ditches, drain the rivers and build dykes and water tanks to prevent drought.[34]

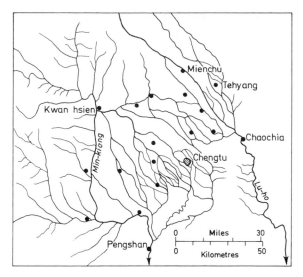

Fig. 29   Chengtu irrigation system

Big irrigation works were carried out in Ninghsia and Suiyuan. Ch'eng Kuo's canal was extended and supplemented by subsidiary canals between the rivers Ch'ing and Lo. However, some of the work lower down the river was rendered useless by one of the Hwang-ho's periodic changes of course. P'o Hi comments:

> When the canals carrying the waters of the Fen for irrigation of the land below P'i-che and Fen-yin and the waters of the Ho for the land below P'ou-fan are pierced, I estimate that five thousand *k'ing* of cultivable land will have been gained: land which until now has been only waste land beside the Ho, where people cut their hay and tended their herds. Now, if they irrigate the land, I reckon they will be able to reap more than two million *che* of grain. This grain will go up the river Wei and will be similar to that of the interior of the passes. Undoubtedly, one would not provide transport for grain coming from east of Ticheu. The Son of Heaven approved this project and great numbers of workers were recruited to make the canals and fields. After several years the Ho changed its course and the canals were of no use; the farmers reaped no harvest. In the end the canals and fields to the east of the Ho were abandoned. The land was given to the men of Yu and the *chao-fu* was ordered to be gentle in his tax collection.[35]

About 100 years before these big irrigation and transport schemes were being carried through by Emperor Wu Ti (141–86 BC), the first governor of Chengtu (Shu), Li Ping (255–206 BC) planned and executed one of the world's most remarkable

hydraulic engineering achievements. The plain of Chengtu, measuring approximately 110 km from northeast to southwest and 65 km northwest to southeast, was at that time an old lake bed, with stony desert in the north and rank marshland in the south. It was the recipient of many mountain torrents issuing from the steep edge of the Azure Wall range, which marks the western border of the Red Basin. These mountain torrents spread over the area in constantly changing courses. Li Ping began to convert this unpromising region into cultivable land. The work was completed by his son, Li Erh-lang.

The main river descending to the Chengtu plain is the Min. It cuts through the Azure Wall mountains at Kwan-hsien. In summer it is a torrent, flowing over a bed a kilometre wide. Even in winter, when the water is at its lowest and quietest, it flows in a stream 45 metres wide and 2 metres deep. Acting on the principle of divide and rule, Li Ping split the river at Kwan-hsien, leaving one half to flow southward in its old bed and turning the other in a new course eastward. He then proceeded to subdivide these two main streams into innumerable channels, covering the whole area with a net-work, which irrigated and indeed still irrigates the plain, turning it into probably the most densely populated, the most fertile and the most productive rural area in the world. In order to effect these divisions, Li Ping built 'arrowheads' of faced stone in mid-stream and supported these and the banks with enormous 'sausages' gabions 7 metres long and half a metre in diameter, of boulders, bound together in a net-work made of bamboo strips. This method is still used today, having been used continuously for more than twenty centuries. Moreover, Li Ping coined a maxim, a guiding rule, which is cut in the granite of the gorge at Kwan-hsien and which reads: 'Shen t'ao t'an, ti tso yen' (深淘灘低作堰) meaning 'Dig the beds deep; keep the dykes low.' This rule the farmers of Szechwan have religiously observed through the centuries to their profit and so have avoided the disasters which have attended the dyke building of the north.

There were no major additions to the work of the Lis, father and son, for more than one thousand years. During Yuan (Mongol) times the channels were increased, the dykes lined with faced stone, cemented with lime and wood oil (t'ung yu) and the banks planted profusely with willows.[37]

For more than 350 years after the fall of the

Later Han dynasty China was a disunited country. At first it was divided into the Three Kingdoms, which occupied three natural regions: Wei in the north occupied the middle Yellow river area; Shu in the west held the Red Basin, and Wu in the east held the middle and lower Yangtze. These broke up and were replaced successively by the West and East Chin, the Sixteen Kingdoms and the Wei Kingdoms. The Wei period (AD 386–535) was one of considerable Buddhist and Indian influence religious, social and political. The Lattimores write:

> Its monastic communities were important in advancing the techniques of a collective economy. Although they did not have the family type of heredity, from father to son, they did have corporate continuity. They made possible the pooling of individual knowledge and skill; they held large tracts of land; their farming was prosperous and progressive, and they carried on the great Chinese engineering techniques of irrigation, drainage, the prevention of floods and the building of transport canals.[38]

In spite of the turbulence and disunity of this long period, quite a lot of water conservancy work, some of it of a complex character as in the Hwai valley, was carried out. However, it was localized and on a comparatively small scale.

The country was once again brought under one government when the Sui swept in from the northwest in AD 581. Both the first emperor, Sui Wen-ti and the second, Sui Tang-ti, set about the work of unification with vigour. The problem was to draw together the political centre of gravity in the north and the economic centre of gravity, which was shifting rapidly to the rice lands of the Yangtze valley. To do this it was essential that good water communication be established between the granary in the south and the capitals of Ch'ang-an and Loyang in the north.

There already existed a fragmentary old route. In the north Ch'eng Kuo's and P'o Hi's canals, running from east to west, linked Honei with Kuantung. Loyang was linked with the Hwai valley by a canal (the Old Pien Canal) which ran via Kaifeng, along the Ssu river via Hsuchou to Hwai-an. A further canal ran south from Hwai-an to Kiang-tu (present day Yangchow) and so to the Yangtze. However, neither of these two last-named canals was in good repair or of adequate size. Accordingly, Sui Yang-ti embarked on the ambitious plan of cutting a new waterway, known variously as the New Pien, the T'ung Ch'i or the Grand Canal, from Kaifeng to Hwai-an. It ran south of the Old Pien, following close to the Kwei and Hwai rivers and so to Hwai-an. The section from Hwai-an to Kiang-tu, which had been both shallow and narrow, was greatly improved, being widened to forty paces and tree-lined throughout. The whole canal from Ch'ang-an to Kiang-tu was liberally equipped with post stations and imperial resting places. The work was carried through, as were all such large-scale projects, by dictatorial forced-labour methods. It is recorded that more than five million men were pressed into service and that there was great loss of life owing to the great hardships and also the cruelty of the administrators. The resulting unpopularity did not a little to bring about the fall of the Sui dynasty. Sui Yang-ti 'shortened the life of his dynasty by a number of years but benefited posterity to ten thousand generations. He ruled without benevolence but his rule is to be credited with enduring accomplishments.'[39]

During the T'ang dynasty (AD 618–907) the Yangtze valley became established as the key economic region of the Empire and has remained so until the present time. This New Pien Canal from Sui and T'ang times until the Mongol conquest in AD 1279 was of vital political and economic importance in holding together north and south.

Their vast conquests made it inevitable that the Mongol conquerors of 1279 should be greatly concerned with communications. Kublai Khan chose to regard China rather in the nature of a separate dominion, but still he could not afford to ignore the remainder of his great empire. Therefore, in order to be in touch with both China and the lands to the north and west, the capital was moved north from Loyang to Peking. Thus the political centre was even farther removed from the key economic area of the Yangtze. For this reason the route of the Grand Canal was changed. Instead of turning at Hwai-an in the northward journey, it followed the Ssu valley as far as Hsuchou, and then, turning north, picked up an old discarded (Sui Dynasty) bed of the Hwang-ho, thence to Peking. This enormous engineering feat was again carried out by means of massed forced labour with its usual accompanying cruelty, hardship and discontents.

With the fall of the Yuan and the rise of the Ming dynasty (1368) the capital was moved for a short while to Nanking but was very soon transferred back to Peking. There it remained until the fall of the Manchus in 1911. The need, throughout this long period was the same as during the time of Kublai Khan, i.e. the maintenance of good communications between the political north and economic south. The story, too, was the same in both dynasties – an energetic beginning during which time the Grand Canal was repaired and improved and then, as the dynasty waned and became decadent, it fell into disrepair and largely into disuse.

CHINA'S TRADE ROUTES

From very early times Imperial China has regarded trade with the barbarian without its walls with a certain superiority and aloofness. It has held that China produces all that is necessary for good living within its own borders and its rulers have said so in no uncertain terms on more than one occasion. For example, Emperor Ch'ien Lung in an edict addressed to George III on the occasion of Lord Macartney's embassy to Peking in 1793 said ... 'nor do we have the slightest need of your country's manufactures'. Even in China itself trade and the merchant were graded low in the social scale. The scholar-landlord-administrator was ever vigilant to see that the trader was kept in his place and excluded from governmental office.

Nevertheless, the emperor and his court were not averse from receiving what the outside world had to offer and a good deal of interprovincial and foreign trade was carried on under the guise of 'tribute'. The 'barbarian' envoy, paying court to the emperor, presented his tribute and in return was laden with gifts, which were at least to some extent a *quid pro quo*. Far more, however, passed through the hands of merchants.

There is a description in the *Book of Records* of what is known as 'The Tribute of Yu' (*Yu Kang*), being the movement of goods from the Nine *chou* or provinces to the Imperial Residence at Anyang about 1125 BC. The very varied produce which travelled to the capital is shown on the accompanying map.

In early times (Han dynasty) by far the most important and desired commodity which China had to offer was silk. This was in very great demand in imperial Rome; so much so that, it is said, a pound of silk was worth a pound of gold. Curiously, it was not the finely woven Chinese brocades and damasks that were wanted in Rome, for when they arrived they were unravelled and re-woven into lighter, flimsier silk gauzes. Other Chinese exports were cinnamon and such medicinal roots as rhubarb. Rome paid for these largely in gold and silver but also in dyes, woollen textiles and glass, which, before China learned to make it herself, was looked on as precious as jade.

The Chinese have never been an outstandingly maritime people. The rugged southeast coast has produced some redoubtable sailors – and pirates – but on the whole the Chinese have looked landward rather than seaward.

Land Routes

The Silk Route. China's east–west communications have been very largely dictated by physical geography.

Between China and Burma lie heavily folded mountains, giving rise to a series of deep valleys and high ranges, running north and south, which are particularly difficult to cross, the more so as the hot, damp river valleys are malaria-infested and the mountain sides are heavily forested. Thus, although the natural barriers are not impassable, this region has not lent itself to easy communication.

Tibet lies to the west. The high mountain ranges which form its eastern borders lead to a vast plateau, barren of anything that would attract the merchant.

There is, however, a route to the north which leads along the northern slopes of the Nan Shan, through the Jade Gate (Yumen) to the Tarim Basin, over the Pamirs at Kashgar to Afghanistan and Turkestan, thence to Persia and down into the Tigris–Euphrates basin and so to the Mediterranean. It was along this route that most of the merchandise between China and Rome in Han times flowed. From Ch'ang-an to Rome was a matter of some 11 000 km. When it is remembered that the only means of transport available were camel, pack mule and horse, yaks, sheep and human beings, it will be realized that only luxury goods of very high value in proportion to their bulk would pass along this route. Thus it was that silk was the principal commodity going westward, and gold, silver, glass, amber and precious stones eastward.

In Han times there was no direct contact along this route between Rome and the Seres, as the Chinese were called by the Romans. It may be that very occasionally a Roman merchant made the whole journey, but it was not until Marco Polo that we find any account of such an achievement. Trade passed between merchant and mer-

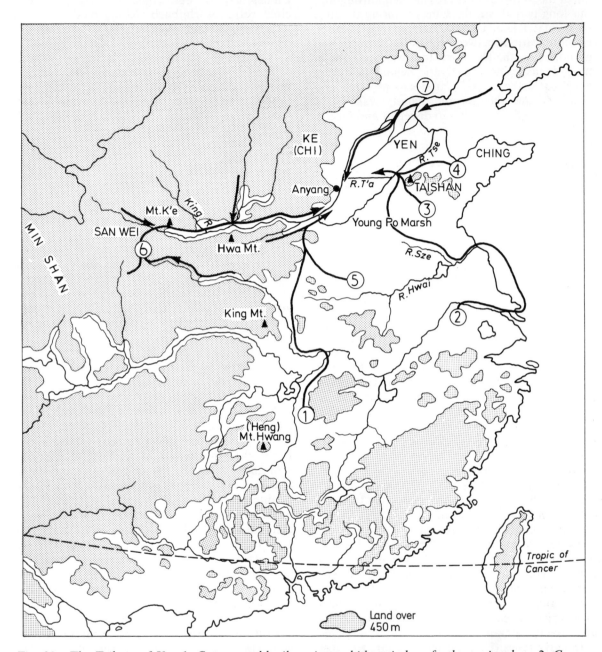

Fig. 30   The Tribute of Yu: 1. Copper, gold, silver, ivory, hides, timber, feathers, cinnabar; 2. Copper, gold, silver, bamboo, precious stones; 3. Silk, pearls, fish, feathers, varnish; 4. Salt, timber, silk, hemp, precious stones, varnish; 5. Silk, hemp, tung yu; 6. Furs, wild animals, silver, precious stones; 7. Mulberry, silk, varnish

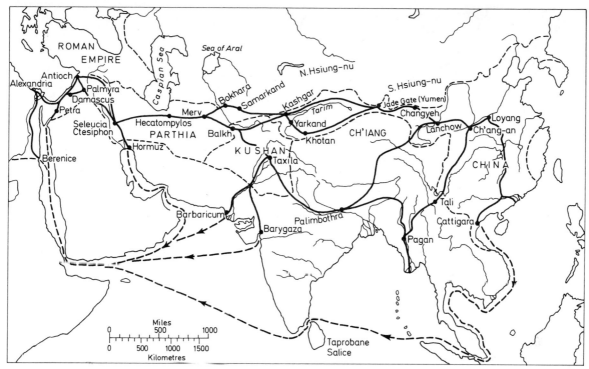

Fig. 31   East–West communications AD *100*

chant through the various stages of the route
and these stages were determined by the changing
political authority exercised in the region, which,
in its turn, was greatly influenced by physical
geography.

The route may be divided into four main
stages[40] and the first stage ran from Ch'ang-an
to Kashgar. Starting from the capital, Ch'ang-an
or Loyang, it crosses the Hwang-ho at Lanchow
and, utilizing the narrow but generous strip of
steppeland lying between the high ranges of the
Nan Shan on the south and the Gobi on the north,
reaches Yumen (Jade Gate). The Great Wall was
extended as far as Changyeh (Kanchow) in order
to protect the northern flank of the 'road' against
the Hsiung-nu (Huns). This was a very vulnerable part of the route owing to the presence
of the Hsiung-nu on the north and the Ch'iang
(Tibetans) on the south and was under Chinese
control only when there was a strong central
government, as under the Han, T'ang, Yuan and
Ch'ing (Manchu) dynasties.

Passing west of the Jade Gate, the traveller
meets one of the most difficult sections of this
stage. The road divides north and south as it
begins to skirt the eastern end of the Takla

Makan. Both roads have to traverse 250 km of the
most hostile desert. It is practically rainless, has
few depressions or wells and no grazing for camels.
The Imperial Silk Road is the southern of these
two roads. Chinese travellers and merchants,
more often than not, were obliged to use this
southern and more difficult route because the
Hami region was usually a Hsiung-nu centre.
Both the southern road, which follows the foot
of the Astin Tagh (Altyn Tagh), and the northern
road, which keeps to the southern slopes of the
Tien Shan, are true routes as distinct from
nomadic lines of march.[41] They are trade routes,
linking oasis with oasis in true desert. In the
nomad occupied semi-desert the needs of the
flocks and herds are paramount, and trade is subsidiary. Movement is over a wide 'fairway'. The
two north and south trade routes round the Takla
Makan desert meet again at Kashgar at the
western end of the Tarim basin, whence the road
crosses the Pamirs. However, before following the
Silk Route to its second stage we must note two
southern branches from this route, both leading
to India.

One route, little used but interesting because its
line is followed approximately by the newly built

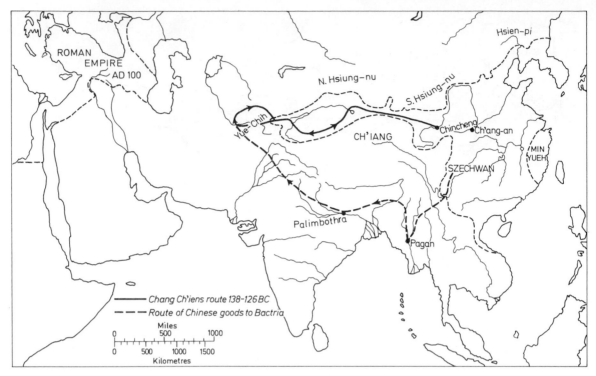

Fig. 32   Chang Ch'ien's route 138–126 BC

motor road to Lhasa, runs through the Ts'aidam and then south across the Tibet plateau to the Brahmaputra, and so on to the Ganges plain at Palimbothra (Patna), thence by sea westward to Rome. The second branch left the Silk Route at Khotan and entered India either by the Karakoram Pass or Khyber Pass and so to the coast either at Barbaricum or Barygaza. This was the road so well trodden by Buddhists making their way to and from China to India.

The second stage carried the road from Kashgar over the Pamirs, down the valley of the Alai, into the lowland of Bactria (Turkestan), through Samarkand to Merv. This region first came into Chinese ken in the reign of the great Han emperor, Wu Ti. The Hsiung-nu were constantly harrying the northern Han border and had also defeated another large nomad group, the Yueh Chih and driven them away westward. Wu Ti conceived the idea of searching out this tribe and supporting them against the Hsiung-nu. Accordingly he sent an envoy, Chang Ch'ien, in 140 BC to find this tribe and form an alliance. The misfortunes and adventures of Chang Ch'ien in his search make a classic Chinese epic. He eventually found the Yueh Chih in Bactria, where they had

defeated the Greeks and settled down comfortably. They showed no disposition to renew their struggle with the Huns. Chang Ch'ien was surprised to find some Chinese goods – cloth and bamboo – already in Bactria and discovered that they had come via India. The significance of Chang Ch'ien's mission is that it eventually led to two Chinese military expeditions against the King of Ferghana in Bactria, the second of which was successful and led to considerable increase in trade and intercommunication.

The Persian plateau between Merv and Seleucia formed the third stage. Both this and the second stage had the advantage of remaining in the hands of one ruler over longer periods than either the first or fourth stages and therefore enjoyed more security for trade. The fourth stage from Seleucia to the Mediterranean coast went either to Palmyra or Damascus, mainly along 'the Way', notorious for contenders for its use and control.

Serious interruption in communication along this east–west line came with the decline and fall of the Han dynasty. China lost control of the Tarim basin; silk became more difficult to obtain in the west and prices soared. It is not surprising, therefore, that the secret of sericulture, religiously

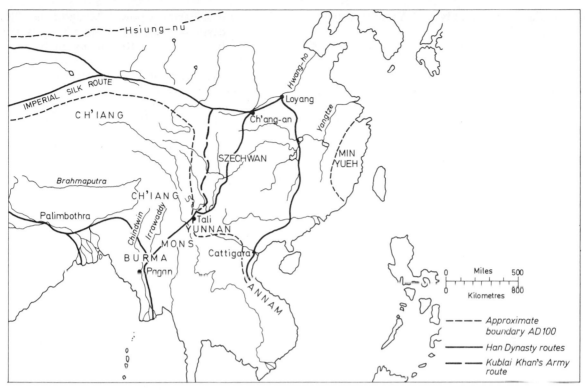

Fig. 33   Burma, Indo-China, Yunnan routes

guarded by China for so long, was lost. Eggs, moth and knowledge of silk processes were smuggled out. Various tales are told of how this was done: a Chinese princess was betrothed to a King of Ferghana and brought them with her in her trousseau; Buddhist monks on pilgrimage smuggled them out; merchants brought them in the hollow of bamboos. Be that as it may, sericulture began to flourish first in Syria, then in Italy and Spain and by the end of the sixth century AD Europe was virtually self-sufficient in silk. As a result trade, contacts and interest in the Far East decreased.

European interest was rekindled in the seventh and eighth centuries when Christendom looked hopefully but unsuccessfully to the powerful China of the T'ang dynasty as an ally on the eastern flank against militant Islam. Again later, for a short period there was considerable east–west overland trade during the Mongol regime (AD 1280–1368) when, in addition to the Silk Route, the nomadic lines of march across the Gobi and Dzungaria, farther north, were much used.

Burma, Indo-China and Yunnan. There are no formidable physical barriers between China and Indo-China. Early Chinese expansion under Ch'in Shih Hwang Ti reached out into Annam (214 BC) before penetrating into Lingnan, i.e. Kwangtung. Even the high parallel ranges to the west, though very difficult, are not impassable. The Mons, Khmers and Shan, remnants of which tribes are still in the highland borders, probably originated in southwest China and moved over into Burma as Chinese pressure from the north increased.

We have already seen how Chang Ch'ien noted that Szechwanese goods were being sold in Bactria and that they had come via Burma and India. On his return home he urged Emperor Wu Ti to develop this route, and this the emperor attempted to do. Silk and medicinal herbs moved up the Yangtze from Szechwan to Tali on the Yunnan plateau, thence down the Irrawaddy to Pagan, which became the trade centre. From Pagan, goods moved either down-river to Pegu or up the Chindwin and across the Naga Hills into Assam. Two Buddhist priests are said to have reached

China via the Irrawaddy and Yunnan between AD 58 and 75.[42]

The Mons constantly blocked this route. A campaign was led against them in the Three Kingdoms period (*c.* AD 230). The Mons chieftain was captured seven times, released and told to come back with his men, until at last the Mons gratefully laid down their arms and remained true to their promise never to block the route. However, later the Tibetans, who subsequently occupied the region, were not so cooperative and we find the Governor of Szechwan, Chang Chienchih, petitioning the Emperor in AD 698 in these terms:[43]

> Yunnan was kept open in earlier dynasties because through Yunnan China was connected in the West with Ta-tsin [e.g. India or the Roman Empire] and in the south with Indo-China. Tax receipts in cloth and salt are now declining and precious tributes fail to come. We press our people to garrison the territories of the tribes to no purpose. I therefore suggest that we withdraw from Yaochow [midway between Kumming and Tali] and leave the tribes south of the Lu river [Yangtze] as vassal states and prohibit all traffic except by special permission.

and the road was officially closed by the Emperor.

After the fall of T'ang the Turks and Tartars blocked the Imperial Silk Route in the north and for a while the route was used unofficially. It was not until Kublai Khan sent his armies into Burma that it was opened officially again and then only for a matter of forty to fifty years. It is interesting to note that Kublai Khan's army came south via Sikang to Yali and not through Szechwan, and used much the same route as that used by the Red Army in their Long March northward in 1934. With the fall of the Yuan dynasty the route again fell into disuse and was not revived until the Second World War, when the Burma Road was constructed.

Sea routes

Westerners did not sail the China Seas via Malaya until after AD 47 when Hippalus discovered the use of the monsoons. The Arabs had a virtual monopoly of sailing between the Red Sea and Malaya, and the Chinese a monopoly east of Malay. China was quite a considerable maritime power in Han times. A large fleet of 2000 naval junks was used to suppress a revolt in Indo-China and secure control of that area. Sea traffic was increased when the Imperial Silk Route was virtually blocked at the fall of the Han dynasty

and the rise of Parthian power. Much of the silk trade was carried all the way from China to Ta Ts'in (Arabia Felix) and Roman Egypt by sea, although probably never in the same bottoms all the way. Transhipment took place probably at Taprobane Salice (Ceylon).

First contacts with Japan were probably made after the conquest of Manchuria and Korea by Wu Ti (109–108 BC). *The History of the Later Han* records the first Japanese envoy to China in AD 57. By T'ang times there was a considerable sea trade with Japan and Korea. Entry into China was by way of either the mouth of the Hwai or Yangtze at Kiang-tu or modern Hangchow, thence by canal to the capital, Ch'ang-an. No use was made of the Hwang-ho, which was unnavigable. The normal crossing from Japan to China took from five to ten days. There was a considerable traffic of Buddhist monks and pilgrims. Incense and medicines were carried from China to Japan.[44] In addition to this Japanese trade there was considerable Arab and Persian trade in T'ang times. Kiang-tu (Hangchow) was the chief port. Some idea of the volume of trade and the importance of Kiang-tu can be gathered from the report that several thousand Arab and Persian traders were killed there during antiforeign riots in AD 760.

We have seen how the transfer of the imperial capital from Ch'ang-an to Peking in Yuan (Mongol) times drove Kublai Khan to build a new Grand Canal from the granary of the Yangtze to the north. This transference had its influence also on Mongol shipping. A speedy and safe sea route for the transport of grain was needed. Two former salt smugglers and pirates of the Yangtze delta, Chu Chin and Chang Hsuan, were given the office of superintendents of navigation and entrusted with the job of sea transport. Between 1282 and 1391 ships laid a course closely following the coast, taking more than two months to reach Taiku (now Tientsin). Delays were caused by the sandy inshore shoals, by the strong offshore winter north wind and the southward flowing current (East China Cold Current). Later the transport fleet, consisting of 6-masted junks, sailed only between April and September each year, making two return trips. In so doing the adverse winter winds were avoided, and by sailing out almost due east from Liu-chia-kang, the southern terminus at the mouth of the Yangtze, and then turning northwest, the fleet was able to utilize to the full both the southeast monsoon and the northward flowing Kuro–Siwo, thereby reducing the northward trip to a mere ten days.[45]

Although the Mongols were not natural sailors they nevertheless used sea transport to great effect in developing the spice trade between the Indies and Europe, via Persia and Egypt, during the short time they were in power. Ibn Battuta (1304–78), the great Moslem traveller from Tangiers, reckoned Zaiton (Amoy) to be the greatest port of the world and was lost in wonder at the huge cargoes of the great four and six-masted vessels, which sailed south carrying silk, porcelain, tea and camphor to the Malay Straits, where they picked up spices for their journey farther west to the Persian Gulf. When Marco Polo returned home, he used this route, landing at Hormuz, thence by land to Trebizond on the Black Sea. This trade undoubtedly had some influence in spurring on Portuguese sailors to their voyages of discovery later. The Venetians and Genoese, who were the principal European spice traders, carried spices from the Syrian and Egyptian ports to the rest of Europe. When Persia was converted to Islam and closed that door, Egypt remained the sole route of supply and, together with Venice and Genoa, foolishly used their monopoly to raise prices too high with a result that Portugal and Spain, and later England, France and Holland sought other routes.

Thus it was that eventually Portuguese sailors found their way to China and in 1557 were permitted to erect factories, i.e. small compounds containing offices, living quarters and warehouses on the isthmus of Macau. This was the beginning of a new era, which led to the invasion of the China seas by Western mercantile fleets, to the breakdown of Chinese isolation and with it the eventual crumbling of Confucian philosophy and the collapse of the last Imperial dynasty, the Ch'ing, in 1911.

CHINA'S CAPITALS

Probably no other country in the world, except perhaps India, has moved its seat of government so often or so far as China. The movement has generally been logical and the siting has usually shown an attempt to resolve a tension between the rival claims of production and defence. There have naturally been many periods in Chinese history when the country has been divided and in consequence has had several capitals simultaneously.

In early post-neolithic times, when Chinese civilization was just developing, states and principalities of north China were small and isolated. Communications were poor and there was very little consciousness of, or contact with, neighbours. The focal centres or capitals of these small communities were based on local factors and had only local significance. Their armies were small and their resources for campaigning were not large enough to allow anything but very limited scope. As the population grew and states expanded they began to impinge on one another. It was not till late Shang times, when Chou began to encroach from the west, that the siting of a capital began to have really wide significance.

According to the *Shu Ching*, the Shang or Yin capital, when T'ang ascended the throne in 1766 BC, was at Po, but it was removed to Anyang in 1384 BC by P'an King. Tradition and classical writing attribute a jurisdiction to Shang rulers extending to the Yangtze, but it is probable that effective rule was very much more limited.

As we have seen, early Chinese civilization was fostered in the loess foothills and on the surrounding loess plain of Shansi. Anyang itself was on the loess plain in a bend of the river. Lying on the plain gave it the necessary protection against sudden attack and yet it was within reach of the wooded foothills for hunting. Hunting was then still an integral part of the people's livelihood, whilst later and for many centuries it remained the sport of the privileged classes.

The Chou, who were at that time barbarians occupying the Wei valley, issued through the Tungkwan gate and conquered Shang in 1122 BC. They destroyed the Shang capital at Anyang and removed the seat of government to Ch'ang-an, Shensi, on the right bank of the Wei-ho, whence they were better able to meet the threat of others rather similar to themselves farther west. Ch'ang-an stands athwart the easy entry from the west, which was later to become the Imperial Silk Route. However, the Chou dynasty ushered in the classical feudal era and it was not long before the rulers found it necessary to build a new capital which was more central for internal control. This they did at Loyang, which lies to the south of the Hwang-ho (Honan), above the floodplain. From here there is easy access to the Hwai basin and comparatively easy entry into the Han basin and so to the Yangtze, where the strong state of Ch'u was situated. The capital remained at Loyang until 220 BC.

The feudal period of Chou came to an end again as the result of western invasion. Chou had shrunk to a small state centred on Loyang, to which nominal allegiance was given even by the two most powerful feudal states, Ch'in and Ch'u. Ch'in which had succeeded Chou in the Wei valley, first conquered Ch'u and then all the other smaller fry, and in 256 BC brought the whole country under one rule for the first time. Ch'in Shih Hwang Ti preferred to maintain his own former capital at Ch'ang-an. When his short but very momentous reign ended, his conquerors, the Han, reverted to Loyang as capital but very soon transferred their seat of government once more to Ch'ang-an, and there it remained from 220 BC to AD 25. This vacillation of capital between Ch'ang-an and Loyang reveals the tension between the rival strategic and economic claims of a capital. Whilst, as China grew in size and prosperity, the threat from the nomads of the north and northwest was increasing, at the same time the economic centre of the country was shifting steadily to the east and south. This tension increased with the rise of the Later Han (AD 25–220), when Chinese rule extended into Sinkiang and beyond the Pamirs. Trade along the Silk Route was most active. One would therefore expect that Ch'ang-an would continue as the imperial seat but expansion southward was of even greater significance and once again Loyang became the governmental centre.

With the fall of the Later Han in AD 220 there follows a long period of disunity (AD 220–581). The empire was first divided into three kingdoms. The northern and central provinces, under the King of Wei, had Loyang as capital. The King of Wu governed the southern provinces of the Yangtze valley from Nanking, and the King of Shu, the western provinces (Szechwan) from Chengtu. At one time there were as many as sixteen states, each with its own capital city. From 317 to 589 a succession of small independent kingdoms Eastern Chin, Sung, Ch'i and Liang) had Nanking (then known as Chien Kan) as capital. It was not until the Sui (589) and T'ang dynasties (618) that the country was once again united. T'ang came down from Shansi to conquer the land. Their capital had been at Taiyuan, but they followed the lead of Sui and moved to Ch'ang-an. They also maintained an eastern court at Loyang and built the New Pien Canal to link the two cities with the Yangtze valley.

China enjoyed united rule for 680 years between the end of Chou (220 BC) and the fall of T'ang (907). During this time Ch'ang-an was capital of the Empire for 530 years, thus emphasizing the importance of the western gate during those earlier years. It was not until the economic heart of the country shifted into the Hwai and Yangtze valleys that Ch'ang-an lost its ascendancy. It is instructive to note that at no time was the capital sited farther west than Ch'ang-an, even when in Han and T'ang times Chinese rule extended into Sinkiang and Turkestan. The 375 mm isohyet lies not far west of Ch'ang-an, and one quickly passes from true Chinese agricultural economy into nomadic pastoral way of life as one goes westward.

We have seen that it was not until the T'ang dynasty that the Yangtze valley and Nanling (South China) were fully incorporated into China, and the Yangtze valley became the key economic area. Towards the end of the T'ang era, threat of nomadic invasion shifted from the northwest to the northeast and in 907 the dynasty fell to the Kitan attacks from Manchuria. Then followed a further long period of disunity (907–1227). The Kitan kingdom of Liao was established in the north, having Yenching (Peking) for a capital, while the true Chinese kingdom of Northern Sung moved to Kaifeng to hold the gate to the south. Later, under Mongol threat from the north, Southern Sung emperors fled south and made Hangchow their centre, Nanking being too vulnerable. Until AD 591 Hangchow had been only a small fishing village, but after that date it developed rapidly as a trade centre and eventually became a great city of 2 million people with a wall which was 40 km in length. Hangchow suffered temporarily when the Mongols under Kublai Khan defeated Sung but it quickly rose again although never as a capital. It was Hangchow which so excited the admiration of Marco Polo. In 1852 it suffered very severely at the hands of the Taiping.

In 1280 China was once again a united country under the alien rule of the Mongols (Yuan Dynasty). Jenghis Khan defeated the Kitans and captured Yenching in 1234. It was raised to the status of imperial capital in 1271 when Kublai Khan rebuilt it, naming it Cambaluc. When the Ming drove out the Mongols in 1368 they favoured Nanking as their centre for thirty-four years, but in 1402 they moved to Peking. The capital remained there throughout the rest of the Ming and the whole of the Ch'ing (Manchu)

Fig. 34   China's imperial capitals

China's capitals

Ch'ang-an (Sian)

1122–255 BC	Chou Dynasty. Known as Haoking	
221–206 BC	Ch'in Shih Hwang Ti	Imperial
206 BC–AD 25	Former Han	Imperial
AD 316–29	Former Tsiao	
352–83	Former Tsin	
384–417	Later Chin	
534–44	Western Wei	
577–81	Northern Chou	
581–619	Sui	Imperial
619–907	T'ang	Imperial

Loyang (Honan)

770–249 BC	Eastern Chou	
AD 25–196	Later Han	Imperial
220–65	Wei	
265–311	Western Chin	
413–534	Later Wei	
924–38	Later T'ang	

Kaifeng (Pienliang; Pienking)
With the fall of T'ang there followed five dynasties of five military despots:

907–24	Later Liang	
924–38	Later T'ang	
938–47	Later Chin	
947–51	Later Han	
960–1127	Northern Sung	Imperial

Hangchow (Linan)

1127–1280	Southern Sung	Imperial

Nanking (Chienyi; Yintien)

229–80	Wu	
316–420	East Ching	
420–79	Lu Sung	
479–520	Tsi	
520–57	Liang	
557–89	Chen	
942–65	Southern T'ang	
1368–1402	Ming	Imperial
1850–61	Taiping	
1927–49	Kuomintang	

Peking (Yenching; Cambaluc)

937–1123	Liao	
1150–1234	Chin	
1271–1369	Yuan	Imperial
1402–1637	Ming	Imperial
1646–1911	Ch'ing	Imperial
1911–27	Republic	Imperial
1949–	People's Republic	Imperial

dynasties and to the present day, except for the twenty-two years of Kuomintang rule between 1927 and 1949, when Nanking and Chungking shared the honours.

Peking served well the needs of the three dynasties Yuan, Ming and Ch'ing. Standing near the Nankow Pass, it proved a good centre from which Kublai Khan could govern China itself and from which, at the same time, he could keep in touch with his vast steppeland territories to the west. For the Mings, although they drove out the Mongols from China but never subdued them in their own lands to the north, Peking served to hold the gate against them. The Manchus entered and conquered China mainly through the narrow coastal plain of Jehol at Shankaikwan. Again Peking was admirably situated for the simultaneous government by the Ch'ing emperors both of China and their own home territories in Manchuria.

THE IMPACT OF THE WEST

Before embarking on the economic and social development of China it is necessary, as a background to that development, to follow the course of the geopolitical revolution which has rent China during the last hundred years and to examine some of its ingredients.

To all intents and purposes China has rested in self-sufficient isolation over the past three thousand years. There have been invasions from the north, but the conquerors have quickly been assimilated. It is also true that Buddhism infiltrated, mainly over the land routes via Khyber and Karakoram through Sinkiang to China, but Buddhism was also absorbed, adapted and transmuted to become an integral part of Chinese civilization. Although Chinese rulers have seldom favoured Buddhism at the expense of Confucianism, this integration is the main reason why Buddhism has suffered less interference and persecution at the hands of the present Communist government than the two religions of Islam and Christianity, which have remained alien.

The Christian religion made its first entry in its Nestorian dress, carried by Syrian monks in the seventh century, but it made no deep or lasting impression. There was some contact with Rome during the Yuan dynasty through such travellers as William Rubruck, Friar John and Marco Polo. Kublai Khan ordered a great conference of religious leaders, Hindu, Buddhist, Christian and Moslem, in an endeavour to find a faith for his people. He sent a request to the Pope in 1269, asking for a deputation of one hundred learned men who would expound the Christian faith. This request was never answered, which is the more surprising since Christendom at that time had hopes of Mongol assistance against Moslem aggression on Europe's eastern borders. It is interesting, although perhaps not very profitable, to speculate on the course of history had these men been sent.

The first real impact of Christianity on China was made by the Jesuits in the seventeenth and eighteenth centuries. Led by such men as Xavier (1549) and Ricci (1601), the Jesuits were a body of learned and dedicated men, who set out to convert the intelligentsia, the fountainhead rather than the masses, to Christianity. They achieved a great measure of understanding of Chinese culture and scholarship and attempted an integration of Confucianism and Christianity. Their learning, especially their science, earned them respect and favour in court and scholarly circles, and for a long time they enjoyed a monopoly of the missionary field. It is doubtful, however, how deep an impression they really made. The Manchus were ready enough to accept their scientific contribution, which was very considerable. Much more doubtful was their acceptance of religion. In fact, Emperor K'ang Hsi repudiated it in no uncertain terms: 'As to the Western doctrine, which exalts the Lord of Heaven, it is opposed to our traditional teaching. It is solely because its apostles have a thorough knowledge of mathematical sciences that they are employed by the State. Be careful to keep this in mind.' Later the appearance of Dominican missionaries, who came with the idea of the conversion of the masses and an overthrow of a 'heathen' culture, diametrically opposed to the Jesuit idea of integration, led to bitter strife between them. K'ang Hsi sarcastically remarked: 'You Christians go to a lot of trouble, coming from afar to preach opinions about which you seem anxious to slit each others throats.' The Pope in 1742 joined in condemnation of the Jesuits' attempt at integration of Confucianism and Christianity. It was not until 200 years later that a papal edict rescinded this and stated that Confucian rites and Roman Catholic doctrine were not mutually exclusive.[46] Manchu patience was exhausted by this strife in the eighteenth century and Christian missionary work was prohibited.

For nearly a century and a half China was ruled by two of its ablest emperors, K'ang Hsi (1661–1722) and Ch'ien Lung (1736–96) and enjoyed one of is most glorious periods. The bounds of its empire were wider than at any previous time except that of the Yuan dynasty. Its culture, art, literature and crafts were both admired and envied by the West. Nevertheless, that civilization was static and petrified and was already showing signs of crumbling. At the turn of the eighteenth and the beginning of the nineteenth centuries Western traders, mainly British, were increasingly pressing for more trade with China. The official Chinese attitude was to discourage external trade on the grounds that China herself had all things needful within her borders. Trade was therefore confined with very narrow limits. Canton alone was the port of entry. There, a few 'factories', i.e. combined warehouses, offices and living quarters, were permitted to foreign merchants under strict control and as a result smuggling became prevalent. Western truculence and Chinese arrogance clashed. Chinese prohibition of the importation of opium, the most lucrative article of trade, led to wars which resulted in Chinese defeat in 1840.[47]

This date marks the beginning of the western 'break-in' and the beginning of a century in which western individualism, nationalism and capitalism imposed themselves on the autocracy and universalism of Confucian China. For one hundred years the western powers with their vast superiority in military and economic strength forced open Chinese ports, claimed extra-territorial rights, schemed for spheres of influence and concessions in which to invest their capital, and generally rode rough-shod over a decadent and impotent China to its mortification and humiliation.

With the opening of Chinese ports, Christian missions, both Catholic and Protestant, again moved in. In contrast to the earlier Jesuit attempt at Christianization, their efforts were directed almost entirely to the common people, the *peh hsing* and at first they made very little impact on the intelligentsia. While their early work was in the field of evangelism, they moved increasingly into first medicine and then education. Their influence in these fields has been far-reaching and revolutionary. The work of mission hospitals, doctors and nurses gave birth to the present vast and ever-growing medical services, which, while bestowing many benefits, are not a little responsible for the present population problems. Early evangelists, intent on the spread of the Gospel to the masses, translated the Bible into *kwan hwa*, i.e. writing which followed closely the spoken word in contrast to the abstruse literary *wen hwa*, intelligible only to the literati. Mission schools introduced western learning, Western democratic ideas, Western history and Western science. Large numbers of students have gone abroad to Europe and America for further education. The inevitable result has been a surge of revolutionary ideas in many fields.

In spite of the enormous amount of altruistic and self-sacrificing work done by Western missionaries and in spite of the vast amount of capital expended in this work, the final result has been a discrediting of Christianity in the eyes of the Chinese people. Christianity has come to be identified in the Chinese mind with Western culture and so with Western imperialism. So often the Christian missionary was made use of in the political game, although seldom so consciously and so cynically as did Napoleon, who is reported to have said: 'Religious missions may be very useful to me in Asia, Africa and America, as I shall make them reconnoitre all the lands they

visit. The sanctity of their dress will not only protect them but will serve to conceal their political and commercial investigations.'[48] Throughout the nineteenth century the expanding field of trade went hand in hand with the expanding mission field, sometimes preceding it but often following in its wake and making use of some incident, maybe the murder of a missionary or an arrogant action by the Chinese, as a pretext to exact further concessions.

Physical intrusion in the nineteenth century by the west, with which we must also associate Japanese aggression against China, was marked by two wars of 1840–2 and 1856–60 between Great Britain and China, which opened the land to trade and to missions; by a civil war, the Taiping Rebellion, which had its roots in peasant discontent combined with obscure fanatical Christian beliefs; by a war in 1894 between Japan and China; and finally by the Boxer Uprising, fostered by the reactionary Dowager Empress, Tz'u Hsi ('Old Buddha') in a bloody and foolish attempt to oust the foreigner and all his ways. All these opened the way for Westerners (British, French, Germans, Russians, Americans, Scandinavians) and Japanese to trade, to develop by investing capital and to exploit.[49]

Significant and far-reaching as were these events, even deeper was the spiritual and intellectual impact made by this entry. During this same period, Japan had had to face this same virile, self-confident individualism from the West with its new techniques and democratic ideas, but she was strong enough to meet the challenge. In judo fashion she accepted and adapted the new forces to suit her old religion and philosophy without significantly changing their essence. China, on the other hand, was too weak and decadent to do more than acquiesce or to resist passively. The philosophy of individualism, laissez-faire, nationalism and natural science of Hume, Bentham and Descartes entered through all channels. The old Confucianism was for a while discarded in favour of this new philosophy, which commended itself by the very power, wealth and vitality of its exponents, but not for long. It could not satisfy the innate Chinese desire for universalism and collectivism, which has supported their civilization for three thousand years. Moreover, Russia's defeat at the hands of Japan in 1904; and the spectacle of the First World War revealing a moral bankruptcy which could not but discredit the West; and the cynical failure of the

Allies at Versailles in 1919 to implement their promises to China regarding the Unequal Treaties brought great disillusionment. Add to this the intense hatred that was felt by most of the intelligentsia for that Western imperialism, which had so humiliated their country, and it is not surprising that Chinese thinkers of the early twentieth century turned to German philosophers for satisfaction. This they found in the writings of Hegel, which appealed at once to their universalism and to their sense of history. It further enabled them to retain Western science and industrialism while repudiating the rest. In needed only Lenin's adaptation of Marxism to the needs of the Orient under the banner of 'Marxism of the Era of Imperialism' for Marxist–Leninist dialectical materialism to be embraced by the revolutionaries and for it to become the creed under which the Communist Party eventually secured control of the country.

GEOPOLITICAL

China's present frontiers

EXTENT

Figure 26 shows the various stages of early Chinese expansion from the ancient Hwang-ho/ Wei core area. By mid-Han times it had virtually reached its southern limits in northern Vietnam and northern Annam but its northern boundaries, during two millennia, underwent great fluctuations according to the changes in strength and weakness of the centre, as subsequent maps show. The northern regions, lacking clear relief barriers like those of the west and south, have always been vulnerable spots, inviting invasion and expansion. 'Tribute'-bearing states flanking China proper have had the function of buffer states. Their tribute was usually a kind of camouflaged trade, being matched by gifts from the emperor. Often this was frankly a subsidy from China in return for the buffer service, the subsidy increasing in proportion to China's weakness at the time. Sea frontiers, until the nineteenth century, have been of comparatively little importance.

China's present boundaries measure about 36 000 km of which approximately 23 000 km are land and 13 000 km are maritime. Of the land frontiers, about half the total length lies along the northern region, some 7 000 km adjoining the U.S.S.R., 3800 km Outer Mongolia and 800 km North Korea. In the northeast China faces the U.S.S.R. along the Amur and Ussuri rivers for

about 4000 km and in the northwest on the borders of Altai, Kazakhstan and Kirghiz for 3000 km. Outer Mongolia lies between these two. In the west a narrow corridor of Afghanistan stretches eastward to the Pamirs to give it a border with China of about 100 km. Thence southward and eastward the Karakoram and Himalayan ranges form the boundary between Tibet and Kashmir, India, Nepal, Sikkim, and Bhutan. On the south the frontiers of Burma and Vietnam wind for about 2500 km through the mountains and the deep valleys of the Salween, Mekong and Red rivers.

Disputed boundaries

By no means all of this great extent of linear boundary, as distinct from frontier zones or regions lying between two or more countries, is accepted by the states concerned. Lines drawn as the result of negotiations arising from undue pressure or wars, particularly during China's weakness in the nineteenth century, carry no sanctity in Chinese eyes, and the related treaties are dubbed 'unequal'. In July 1929 the Soviet Russian government issued a declaration renouncing all concessions and territories which had been taken from China by the Tsarist governments and the Russian bourgeoisie.[50] In the light of this renunciation and the period of close friendship between the two countries until 1960 some credence was given to the possibility of their united control of the heartland of Asia and so to Mackinder's conception of rule over the World Island.[51]

> Who rules East Europe commands the Heart-land,
> Who rules the Heartland commands the World Island,
> Who rules the World Island commands the World.

In 1960 this friendship broke up and turned to antagonism and so the vision (nightmare) of a united power controlling the Heartland faded. Even before this friendship dissolved there were claims by China, sometimes wild and unofficial, to territories which it had lost, stretching even to the widest limits of the Ch'ing empire.

Sino–Russian frontiers

1. *Amur–Ussuri.* Russian expansion eastward towards the end of the seventeenth century led to collision with the Chinese on the Amur river.

40 G. F. Hudson, *China and Europe* (London, 1931), gives a full treatment.

41 O. Lattimore, 'Caravan routes in Inner Asia', *Geographical Journal*, **72** (1928), pp. 497–531.

42 Kuo Ts'ung-fei, 'A brief history of the trade routes between Burma, Indo-China and Yunnan', *T'ien Hsia*, **12**, no. 1 (1941).

43 ibid.

44 E. O. Reischauer, 'Notes on T'ang Dynasty sea routes', *Harvard Journal of Asiatic Studies*, **5** (1940–1), pp. 142–64.

45 Chang Sun, 'The sea routes of the Yuan Dynasty, 1260–1342', *Acta Geographica Sinica*, **23**, no. 1 (1957).

46 For a full discussion of the spiritual and intellectual impact of the West see A. De Riencourt, *The Soul of China* (London, 1959), chapters 8–11.

47 See the section on Foreign Trade on p. 257.

48 H. G. Wells, *An Outline of History* (London, 1920), p. 793.

49 For a full history of these events see K. S. Latourette, *The Chinese: Their History and Culture* (London, 1956).

50 A. Lamb, *Asian Frontiers* (London, 1968), pp. 209–10.

51 H. J. Mackinder, *Democratic Ideals and Reality* (Pelican ed.) p. 113.

52 *Peking Review*, no. 50 (12 December 1975). *China Quarterly*, no. 65, (January 1976), pp. 184–93.

3   The Economic Growth of China

The agrarian problem, of primary importance in any agricultural society, has always been China's major problem. Its solution determined the well-being of the peasant masses and of the ruling minority, the fate of governments and, in the last analysis, the rise and fall of dynasties.

E. Balazs

THE EARLY DEVELOPMENT OF AGRICULTURE

The remarkable coincidence between the 375 mm isohyet and the line of the Great Wall, constructed by Chin Shih Hwang Ti (221–210 BC), has been noted (Chapter 2, p. 44). Originally it extended westward along the great northern bend to include the Ordos within its bounds. But within one hundred years this section had been rebuilt to exclude the desert, for the Great Wall had a double purpose. Its primary function was to act as a barrier against the encroaching nomad, but it was also intended as a restraint on the agriculturalist within its bounds from pushing too far north and so becoming infected by the frontier spirit and estranged from the settled Chinese way of life.

Within the confines of this settled agricultural economy a fusion of the Yang Shao and Painted Pottery peoples probably took place and from that fusion Chinese civilization emerged. By the middle of the second millennium BC the Wei valley and part of the North China Plain were occupied by quite highly organized tribes under the leadership of the Shang (Yin) kings, living in planned, walled cities[1] and forming the first authentic Chinese dynasty. The governing classes, at least, lived in well-constructed houses.[2] Evidence of excavated tombs clearly shows that this was a society based on slavery, but, together with inscriptions on oracle bones, it also shows an advanced agrarian society.

With the decline of the Shang dynasty and rise of the Chou (1030–221 BC) this slave-based society gradually gave place to a feudal age to which Chinese reformers, through the centuries, have looked back as the 'golden age'. As explained in chapter 2, land was held on the well-field, *ching-t'ien* (ching = well; t'ien = field) system. Ideally the estate was divided into nine fields, as in the *ching* character, the central field belonging to the lord and the other eight to the serfs or peasants, who were bound to the soil and who were responsible for the cultivation of the lord's land. Each field was 100 *mow* in extent, an area considered sufficient for the needs of the ideal family of five and thus regarded as an equitable and equal distribution of land.

The Chou dynasty was overthrown by Ch'in Shih Hwang Ti (221–207 BC), who broke the power of the feudal lords and brought together many feudal states under unified, central rule for the first time. This constitutes one of the most significant periods in China's long history. Among the many changes wrought by Ch'in Shih Hwang Ti, and developed during the long Han dynasty, was the freeing of the peasant from his bondage to the soil. This brought with it a certain loss of security; serfdom, in one form or another, re-appeared right up to the twentieth century. Another change was the creation of a mobile labour force, non-existent under the *ching-t'ien* system. It was the presence of this force which enabled Ch'in Shih Hwang Ti to carry out the building of the Great Wall, and later emperors, the great canal and irrigation schemes.

Inevitably, with the break up of the *ching-t'ien* system, there came a redistribution of the land, the development of large estates and a landowning class, from which has stemmed the cause of the ever-recurring peasant revolts through the centuries.

> During the course of Chinese history, the free peasant was frequently reduced to servitude as a result of the formation of large estates and whenever this threatened to occur, voices were raised warning the government against the fatal consequences of the latifundia and demanding a return to the *ching-t'ien* system.[3]

Laws attempting to restrict the size of land holdings were periodically passed but were never really effective. Officials, i.e. nobles and scholar–administrators, who were exempt from taxes and corvée, were allowed by law estates varying between 5000 and 1000 *mow* according to rank, but, since it was they who administered the law, the restriction was seldom kept. The peasant, time and time again, through natural disaster, taxation, debt, forced labour, slipped into tenancy and then back into serfdom. Then, when conditions became intolerable, bloody revolt ensued, often leading to the fall of a dynasty. The land reform carried out since 1949 by the People's Government, with which we shall attempt to deal fully later, is one of a succession of attempts to deal with this agrarian problem. For example, in the Later Wei (386–534) laws were passed for the equal distribution of land, each individual receiving some arable land to be worked until the age of 60, when it was handed back to the state. These strivings towards the equalization of land were short-lived.

The pattern and structure of Chinese society remained unchanged from Han times right down to the twentieth century. The great peasant mass, living on a subsistence economy, holding their small plots of land either in ownership or on precarious tenancy, formed the broad base. There was a comparatively small class of merchants, artisans and handicraftsmen. Above all these was a very small but all-powerful oligarchy of land-owning scholar-officials, which, through its control of education – the only channel of admission to its ranks – and by its extolling of the Confucian virtues of respect, submission, humility and filial piety, governed practically all walks of public and private life.

The plight of the peasant

Although the peasant figured high in the social scale and although he formed the base of the country's well-being, this did not prevent his being exploited. For the most part he was very poor and lived near the level of subsistence. When conditions became intolerable, whether through natural calamity or bad government, he rebelled. He was organized in secret societies, which, at times, were powerful, and peasant revolt has resulted not infrequently throughout the centuries in the fall of dynasties. Consequently wise government has taken care to see that his lot was not too oppressive. Provincial granaries were kept stocked to insure against drought and famine; river dykes were kept repaired against flood, and, as we have seen, some attempt was made to protect him against oppressive landlordism.

Early in the nineteenth century the Ch'ing (Manchu) dynasty was showing signs of decay and demoralization; the state of the peasantry was deteriorating rapidly and unrest was widespread. In 1850 the Taiping rebellion broke out under the leadership of Hung Hsiu-ch'uan, the son of a Hakka farmer. This rebellion, which lasted 14 years, was a strange mixture of peasant revolt and religious crusade. Its early promise of great social reform degenerated later into a terrorist regime, attended by great devastation and loss of life, until it was finally quelled, largely by foreign forces under General Gordon in 1864.

From this time on, the plight of agriculture and the farmer grew steadily worse. Famine, in one part or another, as a result of natural calamity or political disorder, was endemic, highlighted by such catastrophes as the famines of 1878–9 and 1920–1 and the floods of 1931, each of which was attended by the loss of millions of lives. In spite of this, population has risen rapidly in the last hundred years, resulting in the further fragmentation of the already pitifully small peasant holdings and a great land hunger. Conditions of tenure varied throughout the land. In the north, with its larger farms (3–4 ha), about two-thirds of the farmers were occupying owners, while in the south more than half were tenants, although some owned part of the land. Rents, whether of the share or crop variety, were very heavy, usually amounting to about 50 per cent of the crop. Absentee landlordism, with all its attendant disabilities, increased very rapidly during the first half of the twentieth century.

Although the farmer was so industrious and so meticulous in the care of his fields, he worked within a very narrow compass of technique and knowledge. He reaped and sowed according to his agricultural calendar; his tools were few and primitive; his seed selection, if any, poor; his fertilization of the fields by night soil, careful but inadequate; his loss from pests and plant disease enormous. The result was a low output per hectare.

While the peasant was, to a large extent, self-sufficient, such surplus or cash crop that he produced found only a very confined and restricted market and he was largely at the mercy of the merchant. Communications were poor and transport, mainly by coolie pole, wheelbarrow or mule cart, very expensive – forty times as costly as by rail even though the coolie received a mere pittance for his toil.[4]

Agriculturalists the world over are at a disadvantage, vis-à-vis the industrialists, in that most of their products are slow to mature and therefore their turnover is slow. Their need for credit is thus urgent. Cooperation and cooperative banks would seem to be the obvious remedy, but until 1949, little use was made of these means by the peasant. It is estimated that in 1932 in the whole of China there were 1500 societies with 100,000 members. Instead, the peasant had recourse to the traditional means, the moneylender, who might be his own landlord, the pawn shop, the bank or the merchant. Two per cent per month was a recognized rate of interest, but often it was four times as high.

The peasant was tightly bound by rural custom, which demanded of him that he mark the three great events of life, birth, marriage and death, with appropriate ceremony. This always involved him in heavy expenses and almost invariably landed him in the hands of the moneylender from whose clutches he might never escape except by forfeiting his lands. (See Appendix, p. 354.)* In order to secure ready cash he often sold his main crop of rice, wheat or millet as soon as it was reaped, i.e. he sold on a buyer's market when prices were low, only to find that he had to buy grain for his family's use in the spring when prices were high.

These were the normal hazards of peasant life, but they were greatly aggravated by political events during the first half of the twentieth century, which were years of continual political unrest. As the nineteenth century closed, Japan defeated China in 1894; then followed the disorder of the Boxer Riots. The Manchu dynasty fell in 1911 and the Republic of China was proclaimed, only to be followed by fifteen years of disunity under contending war-lords, who despoiled all and sundry. The revolution of 1927, which promised relief to the peasant, turned out to be the prelude to twenty-two years of civil war or war with Japan, which are described in some detail below (Rise to Communism). These years brought havoc and distress to most Chinese, but it was the peasant who felt the full brunt. Despoiled alike by war-lord, bandit, landlord, government troops and the Japanese, his plight was desperate.

Tawney[4], writing in 1932, struck a warning and prophetic note:

> Much that the press ascribes to communist machinations seems, indeed, to the western observer to have as much, or as little, connection with theoretical communism as the Peasants' Revolt of 1381 in England or the *Jacquerie* in France. What is called the communist question is in reality, in most parts of the country, either a land question or a question of banditry provoked by lack of employment.... The revolution of 1911 was a bourgeois affair. The revolution of the peasants has still to come. If their rulers continue to exploit them, or to permit them to be exploited, as remorselessly as hitherto, it is likely to be unpleasant. It will not, perhaps, be undeserved.

THE EARLY DEVELOPMENT OF INDUSTRY

> The world owes far more to the relatively silent craftsmen of ancient and medieval China than to the Alexandrian mechanics, articulate theoreticians though they were. Needham[5]

Archaeology testifies to the advanced state of Chinese craftsmanship in very early times and history contains a long record of the inventiveness and ingenuity of the Chinese people. A glance at the bronze castings of ceremonial vessels of the Shang (Yin) and Chou dynasties reveals at once the great skill of those early workmen. The metal was precious and used almost exclusively for ceremonial purposes.

Iron was introduced in *c.* 6 BC and by *c.* 3 BC wrought iron was being produced. The already

*D. Y. Lin's figures for Hong Kong.

existing bronze-casting skills were applied to iron, which largely replaced the bronze. Iron ore being in much readier supply, its use was much wider spread. Weapons, notably swords and axes, agricultural implements (ploughshares, hoes and adzes), cast-iron evaporation pans for the production of salt and the like were made. Iron was also used in the casting of large statues and animal figures. A still extant 13-storey pagoda in Hupeh was built entirely of cast iron in AD 1061. The use of iron chains for suspension bridges was general as early as the Sung dynasty (AD 960–1279). Production was carried out in small units and foundries, and from a very early date was kept under the control of the scholar–administrator bureaucracy, which, in this and all other industry, deliberately restricted its commercialization throughout the centuries. Needham[5] writes: 'About 120 BC all iron production was carried on in forty-nine government factories, scattered throughout the empire.'

Chinese inventiveness was by no means confined to metallurgy but extended over a very wide field. Engineers of the Earlier Han dynasty (202 BC to AD 9) were already exploiting the great underground natural brine resources of Szechwan and quite early were sinking wells to a depth of 300 m to 600 m by means of bamboo shafts and steel bits[9]. Chinese bridge-building skill is epitomized by the beautiful segmental stone arch bridge, which was built by Li Ch'un in the Sui dynasty (AD 581–618) at Chao-Hsien, Hopei over the Tzeya-ho and which still stands. In other fields are Chinese early knowledge of magnetism; they had some knowledge of polarity even in Han times. The invention of gunpowder occurred in T'ang times (AD 618–906); happily the Chinese did not exploit it for warlike purposes. Movable block-type printing was in use in China centuries before Europe. These are but a few of the many innovations and serve to show how advanced scientifically the Chinese were in the early centuries. They will also serve to curb a Westerner's too-easily assumed superiority in the scientific world and to check too-great surprise at the ingenuity and inventiveness in the technical sphere, which has been evinced in so many walks of life in China since 1949.

In view of all this knowledge and invention over so many centuries in China, while the West remained in relative ignorance, it is legitimate to ask why it was that China did not develop into an industrial nation at an early age and why it did not undergo an industrial and technical revolution such as that experienced by Europe at the great breakthrough of the Renaissance and after. There are many factors contributing to the answer to that question but, undoubtedly, the basic one is to be found in the stable and static, self-recruiting scholar–civil servant administration, which controlled life, directly or indirectly, throughout the country for twenty centuries and which was able to absorb and bend to its own purposes each succeeding innovation. On the subject of iron, Professor Needham[5] writes: 'Like the legendary ostrich, China could digest cast-iron and remain unperturbed thereby: Europe's indigestion amounted to a metamorphosis'.

This bureaucracy assisted in and, indeed, to a large extent, initiated invention but, whenever development moved in the direction of private commercialization, it was taken over by the administration and, insofar as it was exploited at all, this was done as a state monopoly. For example, the production and distribution of salt, from early times, was a state monopoly, the control of which was in the hands of the scholar-officials who farmed it out to the merchant classes. Officials were prohibited from taking part directly in business and commerce, although this was indulged in secretly. It must be remembered that the merchant class, although wealthy, was scorned by the gentry. It stood low in the social scale, which descended from scholar–administrator, through peasant and craftsman, to merchant and soldier, and the governing class was always alive to prevent the merchant from becoming powerful. Both peasant and merchant looked up to the scholar–administrator and it was the ambition of all to enter his ranks. The only real gate of entry was through scholastic success in the civil service examination, but possession of land and rank did help in the rise. Thus capital tended to go to the purchase of land rather than into industrial enterprise.

Throughout the centuries, industrial production continued at the cottage industry–workshop–handicraft stage, using some form of apprenticeship for recruiting labour and operating, on the whole, on quite small capital. The merchant's sphere was largely that of middleman in the local district, centred on the walled city of the *hsien* or county. There he made his profit, often considerable, by buying cheap from the peasant, who had access to only a very restricted market, and selling dear in the centre.

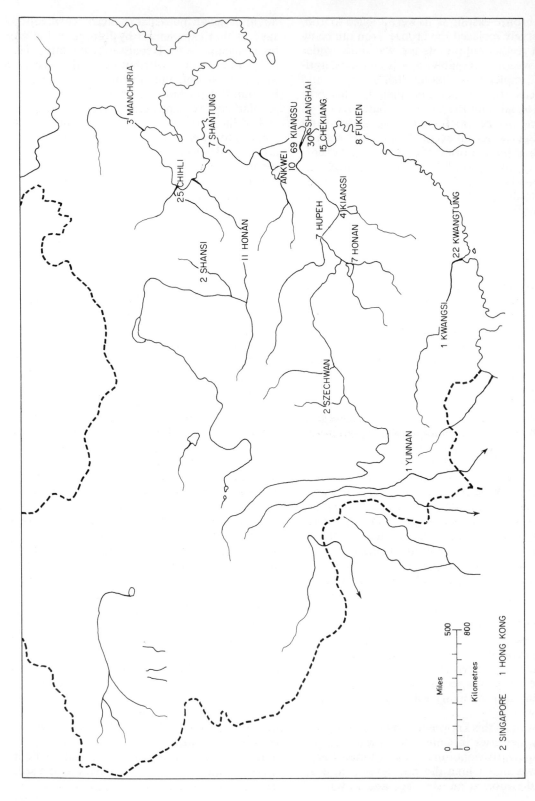

Fig. 37 Location of Chinese-owned companies registered with the Ministry of Agriculture, Industry and Commerce 1904–8; (Compiled from A. Feuerwerker, China's Early Industrialization) Figures indicate the number of companies in each town

This was the situation in which the Chinese reformers of the later half of the nineteenth century tried to act, in following the Japanese Meiji example of national industrialization, but before describing their activities we must look very briefly at the events which began to shake China out of its old complacency and stability.

Although signs of imperial decadence and decay were evident in the eighteenth century, it was the impact of the West on China in the nineteenth century that hastened the process and which eventually led to the revolutionary changes of the twentieth century. On the whole, any direct contact with Europe in early times was made by Chinese initiative by such travellers as Chang Ch'ien (138–126 BC). In the seventh century AD Syrian monks introduced Nestorian Christianity to China. Notable western travellers, such as William Rubruch, Friar John and Marco Polo, followed in the thirteenth and fourteenth centuries and Jesuit missionaries in the seventeenth and eighteenth centuries enjoyed a measure of popularity with the Chinese Court and intelligentsia on account of their scientific learning but, in total, this contact amounted to very little indeed. China, over the centuries, remained self-contained, self-sufficient and self-satisfied. In so far as it was known, it inspired the envy and admiration of the outside world for its stability, wealth and learning, especially by the West.

With the awakening of the West in the seventeenth and eighteenth centuries, expressed in part by its feverish exploration of the world for trade and markets, this vision of China naturally attracted first the Portuguese and then the Spanish, British and Dutch traders. But China, feeling no need for the goods of barbarians, showed no enthusiasm and confined trade through a government foreign trade monopoly to one port, Canton. Exports from China far exceeded imports, with a result that western traders had to meet the balance in cash (silver). To overcome this they sought a commodity desired by the Chinese and this they found in opium from India. The opium habit and demand for the drug grew very rapidly, resulting in a great increase in its importation and a consequent reversal of the flow of silver. The attempted suppression by the Chinese government of the opium trade, both for this reason and for the demoralization which the drug habit was causing, resulted in clashes between traders and officials in Canton and was the direct cause of war in 1840 between China and Great Britain.

China's defeat in that war marks the beginning of a century of constant, persistent imposition of western political, economic, religious and educational ideas, disrupting the old stability and hastening the downfall of the decadent and discredited Ch'ing dynasty. With each succeeding war and defeat more and more Chinese ports, known as Treaty Ports, were thrown open to foreign trade, concessions, i.e. areas of land under foreign jurisdiction, were leased to foreign powers and extra-territorial status granted. Christian missions extended their work beyond the evangelical into the medical and educational fields. The West, in which Japan must be included, with its superior military and economic power, imposed its will on China at every turn.

It was in this turmoil that the Chinese reformers in high circles sought, in the later half of the nineteenth century, to introduce into China some adaptation to modern industrial and commercial conditions similar to that which had occurred in Meiji Japan and to secure for China the economic benefits enjoyed almost exclusively by foreigners at that time. Their efforts met with opposition from many sides, not least being the conservative Court itself.

The first attempts at modern industry were in the military field. The ease with which the British had defeated the Chinese forces in the two wars of 1840 and 1856 emphasized the need for China to modernize her armaments. Small arsenals and shipyards were established in Kiangsi and Anhwei by Governor-General Li Hung-chang (1823–1901) and, in spite of Court opposition, one hundred and twenty students were sent to the U.S.A. and Europe to study western engineering, technology and science. But it was quickly realized by a few that there were many more things involved than the mere production of arms if China was to meet the challenge. Modern communications (rail, telegraph and steamship) had to be established and these entailed the production of coal and iron on a much larger scale than hitherto.

Working under the protection of Li Hung-chang, Governor-General of Chihli and Chang Chih-tung, Governor-General of Hu-Kwang (Hupeh and Hunan), it was Sheng Hsuan-huai (1844–1916) who spearheaded the late nineteenth-century attempts at the promotion of modern industry. He came of a long-established offical family in Hupeh. Although his methods were by no means always above suspicion, he was responsible for the initiation and management of most

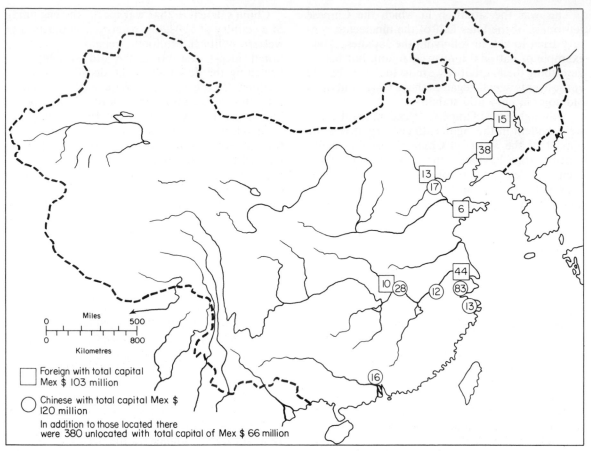

Fig. 38   Distribution of Chinese and foreign-owned firms inaugurated between 1895 and 1913. (Compiled from The Economic Development of China and Japan, *ed. C. D. Cowan and Edgar Allen, 1964; and Feuerwerker.* China's Nineteenth-Century Industrialization: The Case of Hanyehping Coal and Iron Co. Ltd.)

of the outstanding enterprises of the time. The earlier enterprises were entirely government owned and supervised (arsenals, railways) or joint official–merchant concerns (*kwan-tu, shang-pan*, meaning government supervised, merchant managed), which drew their capital from official funds, plus contributions from official–administrators and merchants. True joint-stock companies were not permitted until the end of the century. Some idea of the rate of progress in the development of these joint official–merchant concerns can be gathered from the following list: China Merchant Steam Navigation Company (C.M.S.N.C.) 1872; K'ai-p'ing Coal Mines, 1877; Shanghai Cotton Cloth Mill, 1878; Imperial Telegraph Administration, 1881; Mo-ho Gold Mines, 1887; Hanyang Iron Works, 1896; Imperial Bank of China, 1896; P'ing-hsiang Coal Mines, 1898[6]; Some of these

were later converted into joint-stock companies, notably the C.M.S.N.C. and also the Hanyang Iron Works, Tayeh Iron Mines and P'ing-hsiang Coal Mines, which became the Hanyehping Coal and Iron Co. Ltd in 1908. Official supervisors and often the merchants themselves were ignorant of modern practice and thus there was incompetence in planning and in poor regulations. Enterprises were subject to official exactions and levies and there was much graft and malpractice. The Government attempted to relieve its embarrassed finances, which were strained by the additional burdens of indemnity following the Sino–Japanese War (1894) and the Boxer Rebellion (1902) by levies on industry. One such was the institution of *Likin*, a transit tax, imposed in the first instance on goods passing through the Grand Canal, and later on goods in transit in all provinces. It further became a production tax at source and a sales tax at destination, proving a great millstone about the neck of all enterprise. On this subject Feuerwerker[6] quotes Cheng Kuan-ying, who, in these words, bemoans the lack of competent and honest men who will devote themselves to commerce:

> The officials do not protect the merchants, on the contrary they do them harm by regarding the merchants' wealth in the same way as Ch'in looked at Ch'u's prosperity. Although they fill their private purses, the sources of general wealth (*li-yuan*) are blocked up. This is the evil from above.
>
> As for the merchants, there are many who are ignorant and few with knowledge; many that are false and few that are truthful ... Therefore shares are collected [to start companies], but there are losses of capital; joint-stock enterprises are inaugurated, but they fail. This is the evil attributable to those below.

This failure on the part of the Ch'ing government to comprehend or to cooperate in the efforts at industrialization contrasts strongly with the attitude of the Japanese Meiji government, which worked in close cooperation with industrial managers and contributed considerably in capital investment in industry.

Likin was all the more hated in that the goods of foreign merchants were exempt under treaty and were shipped throughout China under 'transit pass', enabling Westerners to move all goods, even local Chinese produce, at a much lower cost than the Chinese themselves. It enabled foreign merchants and companies to compete on very unequal terms with the Chinese merchants dealing in cotton, timber, vegetable oil, tobacco, opium, etc. and drove large numbers of them either into bankruptcy or into dealing in foreign imported goods under foreign direction. This was not the least of the grievances which fanned the fire of a growing nationalism and anti-imperialism at the turn of the century and which flared eventually into revolution, overthrowing the Manchu dynasty in 1911[8].

A noticeable change, occurring in the later part of the nineteenth century, was the movement of governmental power away from the centre at Peking into the hands of powerful governor-generals, such as Li Hung-chang in Chihli and Chang Chih-tung in Hupeh. The latter was the initiator of the Hanyang Iron Works (1896) and No. 1 Cotton Mill, Wuchang.

Joint-stock companies began to make some progress in the first decade of the twentieth century after foreigners had gained the right to engage in manufacturing in China as a result of the Treaty of Shimoseski in 1895 at the close of the Sino–Japanese War. The Ministry of Agriculture, Industry and Commerce reported that between 1904 and 1908 there were 227 registered joint-stock companies. However, of these only 54 had a capital of over Taels 100,000 and only five of over Taels 2 million. (1 tael = 583·3 grains silver.) Commenting on the industrial situation, Feuerwerker[6] says: 'It has been estimated that in 1912 there were 20,749 "factories" in China, a term left undefined but one whose scope becomes quite clear when we note that only 363 of this huge total employed mechanical power, while the remaining 20,386 were operated with human or animal power only.'

Cheng Chu-yuan estimates that in 1933 only 250 units could be registered as modern factories and even so commanded comparatively little capital. Only about 28 per cent of the total industrial production was carried out by private modern factories. The remainder was produced in workshops and by handicraft workers.

Foreign investment rose from 789·9 million dollars in 1902 to 3242·5 million in 1931 and 3671·4 million in 1936 and controlled 39 per cent coal, 82·5 per cent pig iron, 48·2 per cent shipbuilding, 29·1 per cent cotton yarn and 61·5 per cent cotton cloth production[6].

Foreign industrial development was confined to the Treaty Ports and thus distributed along the littoral and the middle and lower Yangtze. Much of Chinese industry was initiated by compradors, who, having gained their experience in the employment of foreigners, later set up business on their own account. Their geographical distribution tended to follow closely that of the foreigners (see fig. 38)

THE RISE OF NATIONALISM

The intrusion of Westerners into China in the second half of the nineteenth century, the vice-like grip over industry and the privileged position which foreigners enjoyed, was a constant and growing offence to all Chinese. It needs very little imagination to realize the deep resentment felt at the existence of concessions, pockets of foreign territory, often right in the heart of the country, such as Hankow, Kiukiang and Nanking, in which foreign rule held sway and into which Chinese were allowed only on sufferance and not by right. This resentment was further deepened by extra-territorial rights by which foreign nationals in China lived under their own laws and were tried by their own courts even though plaintiff or defendant were Chinese. This right was, to some extent, extended to Chinese converts to Christianity and was one of the reasons why Christian missions were regarded as an integral part of the imperialist invasion and why, subsequently, under Communism the Chinese Christian Church was regarded with suspicion. Hostility to Christianity was particularly strong amongst the scholar–gentry class, with its deep-rooted Confucian ancestral tradition and strict code of conduct and personal behaviour. 'To eat Christianity', i.e. to embrace the Christian religion in these circles involved disownment. The 'barbaric' manners of Westerners were a further cause of Chinese dislike and disdain. Their arrogance, superiority, loudness and forthrightness of speech, lacking Chinese finesse and innuendo, were an offence, as were, also, their table manners, which even involved the use of a knife at table!

This was a fertile emotional field, always ready at hand, when the effete, corrupt Court of the failing Manchu (Ch'ing) dynasty wished to divert the attention of the oppressed peasantry from its own shortcomings, as it did in the days of the Boxer riots. But it was also a ready tool at the hand of the group of reformers and nationalists, who began to try to create a national consciousness out of a deep-rooted and universal clannishness.

Growing hatred of the alien dynasty, which, as it became progressively more decadent and corrupt in the nineteenth century, became also more oppressive, was evinced in the Taiping Rebellion (1851–64), largely a peasant uprising, which came very near to success. The Manchu Court was saved only by the intervention and help of the foreign powers, who feared the probable chaos and loss of trade that would follow the fall of the tottering dynasty. Working underground, largely through secret societies, a national leader emerged in the person of Sun Yat Sen. He was born in 1866, soon after the end of the Taiping Rebellion. At 13 years of age he went to Honolulu to live with his brother, who kept a general store. While there he attended the English Mission School until he returned to his native Kwang-tung. He was converted to Christianity and spent the years 1887 to 1892 studying at the College of Medicine, Hong Kong, from which he graduated with a doctor's degree. However, he turned his attention from medicine to politics and devoted the rest of his life to the task of overthrowing the Manchu dynasty and to the establishment of a democratic republic. He was proscribed and spent many years in exile in Japan and England, whence he planned several abortive revolutionary attempts. At first he was rejected by scholars 'because he was not of the literati; nor did he hold a degree under the old civil service examinations', but later they recognized his leadership. He also received much support from Overseas Chinese, especially those in North America and Malaya. Success came rather suddenly and unexpectedly in 1911, when a revolutionist's bomb was unintentionally exploded in the Russian Concession in Hankow and so sparked off an uprising which quickly spread throughout the whole country and toppled the Manchus. The Chinese Republic was declared with Sun Yat Sen as its first president.

However, hope and elation were quickly followed by disillusionment. Sun Yat Sen was ousted and forced again into exile by Yuan Shih-kai, the powerful military commander, who had ambition to found a new dynasty and become the next emperor. His death in 1916 marked the beginning of the disastrous and chaotic period of 'warlordism', which continued unabated until 1927. Military governors in the various provinces or groups of provinces seized power and fought each other to extend their control; the central government's writ ceased to run. Powerful war-lords, such as Wu Pei-fu (central China), Chang Tso-lin (north China and Manchuria) and Feng Yu-hsiang (the 'Christian' general of the northwest) emerged and under them hundreds of smaller tyrants operated. The miserable years that followed were marked by continuous civil war, widespread banditry, extortion by the armies, corruption and oppression. To raise funds for their wars, the war-lords taxed the countryside unmercifully and, as usual, the peasantry were the main sufferers. Able-bodied men in the fields were conscripted into the armies or pressed into forced-labour gangs; heavy taxes were collected years in advance; farmers were forced to grow opium, a great revenue raiser, to the detriment of food crops, and the armies lived like locusts off the countryside wherever they happened to be.

Realizing that if he was to halt this tyranny and build a unified, strong, democratic China, he must create a mass party with popular support and must back it with its own army, Sun Yat Sen returned to Canton and proceeded to form the

Kuomintang (KMT) – the Nationalist Party. He looked to the West for help, but the Great Powers, either because they were too exhausted by the struggles of World War I or because they looked with suspicion on an emerging radical China, turned a deaf ear to his appeals. Frustrated and disillusioned, it was then that Sun Yat Sen repudiated western democracy and turned to young, revolutionary Soviet Russia.

Believing that his newly-formed KMT and the Communists could cooperate and that the latter would submit to his leadership, he set about a big reorganization of his party. The army, assisted by Russian advisers, was built up under the young General Chiang Kai-shek, who was to lead the victorious Northern Expedition in 1926 and overthrew the power of the war-lords. But Sun Yat Sen was a sick man and in 1925 he died with his mission unfulfilled. As a man of action he had not been a conspicuous success, but he had been the honest and disinterested inspirer and mouthpiece of the emerging patriotism and nationalism, which eventually was to unite China. In his opening chapters of his *San Min Chu Ih*, which had great influence at the time, he exhorts the people to get rid of their old overriding loyalties to clan and family and to think and act in terms of a nation.

We have seen the desperate state of the peasantry at this time, clearly ripe for drastic reform or revolution. It was this rural situation which, in 1926, made the progress of the army of the united KMT and Communists from Canton into the Yangtze valley so easy and triumphant. The well-disciplined army, which was preceded by widespread propaganda promising agrarian redress and reform, was received by the peasantry with open arms. Wu Pei-fu's forces disintegrated and the whole of the Yangtze valley quickly fell to Chiang Kai-shek in late 1926. Scarcely had the victorious army reached Nanking than a rift between KMT based in Nanking and the Communists in Wuhan, arose. It quickly grew into open conflict and civil war, which was not to be resolved finally until 1949.

THE RISE OF COMMUNISM

Phase I (1921–7)

During and after the 1911 Revolution various socialist groups came into existence and out of these the Chinese Communist Party (CCP) emerged. In the spring of 1921, a group of twelve met in Shanghai under the leadership of Ch'en

Tu-hsiu and Li Ta-chao and formally inaugurated the Party. Mao Tse-tung was present. It became a member of the Third International and naturally was under Russian tutelage. In October 1921 a first Provincial branch was formed in Hunan under Mao Tse-tung's leadership.

At the Third Conference of the CCP, under the directive of the Comintern, they took the momentous decision to cooperate with the KMT and in 1924 the First National Congress of the KMT, under Sun Yat Sen's leadership, inaugurated the KMT–CCP with the avowed object of ridding China of its pestilential war-lords and its imperial overlords, and of establishing a national government. As we have seen, the building of an army was undertaken under the young general Chiang Kai-shek and his Russian advisers. A Peasants' Department was established in Canton. This was an institute for training cadres to go out into the countryside and to spread revolutionary propaganda amongst the peasants. It was markedly communist in emphasis – Mao Tse-tung was one of its lecturers – and its trainees did their work with enthusiasm. Already there were many shades of opinion and doctrine in the KMT and CCP, leading to the formation of cliques. It was activities, such as those of the Peasants' Department, that tended to accentuate them.

In November 1924, whilst Sun Yat Sen was in Peking taking part in a National Convention, Chen Chiung-ming, military governor in East Kwangtung, revolted against Sun Yat Sen and the KMT. This resulted in two 'Eastern Expeditions' and the final defeat of Chen; it also marked the remarkable rise to power of the newly-formed peasants' unions, under P'eng P'ai, who, in a matter of months had succeeded in securing a membership, mainly agrarian, of 210 000 in 22 *hsien*. These unions, centred in Hai-feng, took over control of the countryside and established soviets. This accession to power was accompanied by excesses and the ruthless liquidation of the landlords and 'rascals'; rents were drastically reduced or abolished entirely; directives from the KMT in Canton urging moderation were disregarded.

Communist thinking in these early days was tied very closely to Russian orthodox ideology and looked to the factory worker in the city as the spearhead of revolution. How little faith was placed in the peasantry is shown by Chen Tu-hsiu's statement in 1923: 'In such a country as China, over half the farmers are petit-bourgeois landed farmers, who adhere firmly to private-

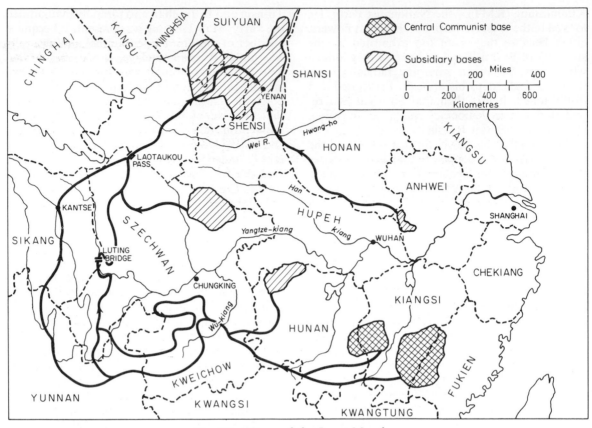

Fig. 39   Lines of the Long March

property consciousness. How can they accept Communism?'[9] Even in the heart of the country in east Kwangtung where the soviets were actually being established, mainly by the initiative of the peasants and where industry was confined entirely to small factories and workshops engaged in weaving, food-processing, papermaking and the like, we find this same adherence to orthodox ideology that the leadership resides in the urban proletariat. The Draft Resolution of the First Peasant Congress of Kwangtung soviet stated: 'Our struggle must be concentrated in the city because the political centre is located in the city, therefore the working class must strive to lead the peasants to participation in this struggle'[10].

However, the main interest and effort of KMT and CCP between 1924 and 1926 was concentrated on preparations for the Northern Expedition, which was started in the summer of 1926 and attended with such success. By autumn the whole of the Yangtze valley below the Gorges was in

the hands of the combined forces, with Chiang Kai-shek established in Nanking, and the CCP and their Russian advisers, led by Borodin, in Wuhan. As the combined forces swept northward many rural districts, especially in Hunan, encouraged by Mao Tse-tung, copied the Hai-feng example and established soviets. The difference in objective of the KMT and CCP became more and more marked and rifts began to be obvious. However, Russia was anxious to hold the alliance together and the Comintern issued a directive late in 1926 ordering that there should be no split with the KMT, that peasant demands should be boldly met and that the time was not yet ripe for the establishment of soviets. The first two of these directives were incompatible and mutually exclusive for the orthodox and right-wing members of the KMT were firmly opposed to any far-reaching land reform. The inevitable rupture came, although the left wing of the KMT and the CCP held together for some time. From this time

(1927) on, the CCP has been virtually independent of Moscow in making its major policy decisions, although, until 1960, it continued to regard the U.S.S.R. as the Father of Communism.

Phase II (1927–36)

The split between the KMT and CCP marks the beginning of a bloody and bitter civil war. Chiang Kai-shek made the extermination of the Communists his major objective, which he pursued unrelentingly until the outbreak of the Sino–Japanese War in 1937. The CCP was weak and divided in leadership and policy. Chen Tu-hsiu held to the Russian line of revolution through the worker in the city. Mao Tse-tung disagreed with him violently, regarding him as half-hearted and far too moderate. Mao placed his reliance on the peasant masses, a faith he maintained unswervingly to his death. His Report of 'an Investigation into the Peasant Movement in Hunan, March 1927', presented to and rejected by the Party, clearly revealed the direction in which his mind was moving. It strongly urged the full development of a peasant movement, and nearly led to his expulsion from the CCP.

Communist efforts at revolution and uprisings in cities were all failures and were suppressed most violently. However, between 1928 and 1934, in the mountainous countryside of Hunan and Kiangsi very considerable areas came under Communist control and were governed by peasant soviets[11]. Here in the mountain fastness of Ching Kan Shan, under the leadership of Mao Tse-tung, Chu Teh, Lin Piao, Chou En-lai, P'eng Teh-huai and other names well-known today, a military force was built up and the early strict puritanical disciplines, which later characterized the PLA (People's Liberation Army) and the CCP, were learnt, as were also the military tactics, which were practised with success here against the KMT and later against the Japanese. 'When the enemy advances, we retire; when he halts, we harass; when he retires or weakens, we attack'.

Chiang Kai-shek, in all, carried out five big campaigns against this central China large enclave of communism, all of which were accompanied by terrible loss of life, destruction of livelihood and consequent famine. It was only in the last, the fifth campaign, with German military staff assistance, that the Red Army was dislodged and then mainly because it failed to adhere to its well-tried guerrilla tactics of retreat and harass-

ment and instead engaged in a war of confrontation.

Although defeated, the Red Army of about 90 000 men was able to extricate itself and then, in October 1934, began the now famous 'Long March', a retreat of thousands of miles, which carried them west through Kweichow and Szechwan into the high mountains and deep valleys of the eastern edge of the Tibetan plateau and so north, and then east again into the dry, loess lands of Shensi. It was during this march that Mao Tsetung's leadership was finally established and it was out of its bitter hardships that the hard core was forged which, in 1949, was to form the new central government and which held together so long. Another far-reaching effect of the 'Long March' was the amount of indoctrination and education in communism that this retreating army was able to carry out in the districts through which it passed and sojourned[12]. The strict discipline of the Red Army, so much in contrast to that of the KMT or remote war-lords' troops, and its immediate application of land reform in favour of the poor peasant, ensured considerable rural support when it came into power later. The eight rules the Red Army was taught to obey were:

1. Replace all doors (used as beds) when leaving a house.
2. Return and roll up the straw matting on which you sleep
3. Be courteous and polite to the people and help them when you can
4. Return all borrowed articles
5. Replace all damaged articles
6. Be honest in all transactions with the peasants
7. Pay for all articles purchased
8. Be sanitary and especially establish latrines a safe distance from people's houses[11]

Of the 90 000 who set out on this retreat, a mere 30 000 reached Yenan, Shensi, which was to be the base of Communist activity for the next ten years or so. Here they were less vulnerable to Chiang's continuing attacks than they had been in Central China.

Phase III (1936–45)

This was a period of recovery, reconstruction and expansion in spite of the fact that the Communist armies were locked in continuous war with Japan during this period. Some idea of that expansion can be gleaned from the fact that, in 1937, the

Plate 1   Typical Hunan–Kiangsi border country
It was here that the Red Army under Mao Tse-tung held out from 1930 to 1935 against Chiang Kai-shek

CCP, from its drought-stricken loess base in Shensi, controlled a population of about $1\frac{1}{2}$ million. In 1945 the Party alone numbered 1·2 million members, had an army of 900 000 and controlled nineteen Communist-organized bases or soviets with a population of over 90 million[13].

One of the results of the revolution of 1927 was the surrender of concessions and some extra-territorial rights by western nations, but Japan took the opportunity of China's continued civil strife and weakness, first to annex Manchuria (Manchukuo) in 1930 in the face of League of Nations' condemnation and then progressively to make further inroads into China's sovereignty to the growing chagrin of all patriotically-minded Chinese. In December 1935 strikes occurred in Peking and throughout the country demanding a cessation of civil war between the KMT and CCP and calling for national unity to meet Japanese aggression. This agitation was largely at

the instigation of the Communists and was strenuously opposed by Chiang Kai-shek, who was bent on the extermination of communism as a *sine qua non* of unity. Dissident troops under Chang Hsueh-liang, who had been ousted from the northeast and who were clamouring for action against Japan, kidnapped Chiang in December 1936 while he was in Sian organizing a sixth campaign against the Communists. For a while he was in danger of his life; curiously it was Chou En-lai who was mainly instrumental in Chiang's release, after he had agreed to the formation of a united front against Japan[11]. Barely six months later (7 July 1937) the 'incident' of Marco Polo Bridge in Peking sparked off the Sino–Japanese War.

Chiang Kai-shek was the recognized Commander-in-Chief but he continued to look in two directions; the war was pursued with far greater vigour and determination by the CCP than by the

KMT. Mainly by guerrilla tactics, the CCP penetrated the areas occupied by the Japanese and in this way kept in touch with the peasantry and stimulated them to greater resistance. Thus the CCP came to be regarded by the masses as the patriotic and national party. In the regions which were under the Communist control, moderate policies were pursued with a view to uniting the landless, the peasants and the landlords to form a united resistance front. Mao Tse-tung declared 'For a people being deprived of its national freedom, the revolutionary task is not immediate socialism, but the struggle for independence. We cannot even discuss Communism if we are robbed of a country in which to practise it.'[11] This fight for freedom gave Chinese Communism the very strong flavour of patriotic nationalism, which it still retains in a very high degree.

It was during these eight years of warfare against Japan that much of Chinese Communist thought was hammered out. It is not the purpose of this book to discuss the development of Communist thought in any detail, but it is absolutely essential to an understanding of China today in any field, not least the economic and geographic, that the salient points should be appreciated. The planning and the activities of the whole nation are consciously geared to and directed by that thought and ideology. Everyone in the country is caught up in Communist ideology, which permeates every walk of life, from the highest powered research worker to the humblest peasant. That ideology is presented as stemming from the thought of Chairman Mao. Practically every article, report and statement, no matter in what subject, is prefaced with such words as 'Guided by the thought of Mao Tse-tung and the leadership of the CCP ...'. It is necessary, therefore, to pause and examine the main aspects of Mao's thought[13].

Mao Tse-tung was born in 1893 in Shao Shan, Hunan of lowly stock. His father was a poor peasant, who, by hard work and parsimony, rose to the ranks of the rich peasant. He was hard, grasping and avaricious and was hated by his children. Mao ran away from home and spent many years as an impecunious student. His life was one of hardship, adventure and peril. One of his earliest interests was in physical fitness, an 'advanced' subject in those days and his first published article, in *New Youth*, 1917, was on this topic. It is interesting to note that he retained his physical fitness through the years. Payne[14], writing of him in 1946, says: 'Then Mao came into

the room. He came so quietly that we were hardly aware of his presence ... Today he looked like a surprisingly young student. ... He was fifty-three and he looked twenty.'

Through reading, study and contact with 'advanced' associates at the Normal College, Changsha, and under Li Ta-chao in the Peking University Library where he worked for a while, he progressed through the liberalism of J. S. Mill, Adam Smith and Bentham to arrive in the Communist fold at a time when it was dangerous to be known even as a liberal. His brothers, his sister and his wife, who were akin to him in thought, were all killed or executed.

Mao was a strict Marxist–Leninist, holding firmly to dialectical materialism and repudiating all shades of the metaphysical approach and of determinism, as being static and lifeless. Dynamic development, he contended, was found in dialectical materialism and this he expounded in his *On Contradiction*, delivered first as a lecture in 1937 in Yenan to combat doctrinairism, which already was a serious problem within the Party, and later revised as an essay. This was probably Mao's main contribution to Communist thought. In it he maintained that within everything there are contending forces, which constitute the very essence of life. 'There is nothing that does not contain contradiction; without contradiction there would be no world' and again 'Contradiction is universal, absolute, existing in all processes of the development of things and running through all processes from beginning to end.'[15] Thus struggle is the stuff of life: every thing, every idea, every movement, every problem, contains within itself opposites, which strive together until resolution leads on to a unity in which new opposites are present and in which the process is repeated on a higher plane. Speaking to the Red Army in 1937 and urging them to greater efforts, he said 'It is a good thing, not a bad thing, to be opposed by an enemy.' The presence of the enemy reveals clearly the contradictions, shows clearly what is to be done and stimulates to action and to struggle. This thesis is universal and is applied not only to military enemies but to each and every activity. The peasant must look for and understand the contradictions, the contending claims as between the crops in his fields, water supply and the one thousand and one things that come within his purview. The worker in the factory must meet his problems in the same spirit. The planner must adjust continually the contending claims of the productive and distributive forces to the right use of transport and communication and so on throughout society. This stress or emphasis on struggle accords well with the characteristic trait of the Chinese peasant's perseverance, born of centuries of contending with hostile natural forces and calamities.

For all his strict adherence to the Marxist–Leninist line, Mao had a deep distrust of dogma and bookishness from early years. This comes out clearly in both essays, *On Contradiction* and *On Practice*. In the former he says, 'Our doctrinaires are lazy; they refuse to make any painstaking study of specific things, but regard general truths as something emerging out of the void, and turn them into purely abstract and utterly incomprehensible formulae, thereby completely denying, as well as reversing, the normal sequence in which man comes to know truth.'[15] Each and every particular contradiction must be examined and treated on its merits and its own particular solution found. He asserts that man's knowledge depends mainly on his activity in material production[16] and knowledge grows in the normal sequence by practice, i.e. actual experience (induction) leading to thought (deduction) on the experience gained, which, in its turn, leads to further action or corrected practice based on that thought[16]. He is conscious of the need to create confidence and initiative in the great mass of people and exhorts them to have courage and not be afraid of making mistakes. To the man who says 'I am not sure I can handle it' he says, 'In many instances, failures have to be repeated many times before errors in knowledge can be corrected and correspondence with the laws of the objective process achieved.'[16] This advice has been acted on very widely and has released a great deal of ingenuity and inventiveness in agriculture and industry. It has also brought its heavy crop of mistakes, witness the Great Leap Forward itself in 1958.

Although Mao was presented as theoretician, he was probably even more a practitioner and innovator. He was fearless and resolute in applying his theories. His refusal to be bound by dogma was nowhere more clearly demonstrated than in his reliance on the peasant masses as the basis of the Chinese revolution, as we have already seen. It is this faith in the peasantry, which, more than anything else, distinguishes Chinese Communism from Russian, which has been based firmly from its inception on the industrial proletariat. 'Mao Tse-tung has stood out as one of the very few national leaders in twentieth-century China who has shown sustained concern with the hardships, brutality and grinding want which characterized the lot of the poorer peasants.'[13] He also recognized 'that a major source of potential political energy rested in the Chinese peasants, and that the leader able to exploit and mobilize that energy source was destined to triumph in China in the long run.' Mao insisted that there must never be an alienation of the masses, as there was in Russia and which he suggested was Stalin's great mistake, i.e. that he went against history[17]. In assessing the respective contributions of peasant and worker to the revolution in China, he attributed 70 per cent to the peasantry: 'The people are the sea: the government is the fish.'

It is interesting to note another difference between Russia and Chinese revolutionary experience. Russia, from the start, was faced with the problem of the integration of the army. The CCP grew very largely out of its army, which was a missionary force carrying the doctrine wherever it went. China's problem was and still is to some degree the integration of its intellectuals, through whom runs a marked element of anarchism, of *tze chi kai kao*, meaning self-reform and personal purification and of deep distrust of government and thus runs counter to the massive and complex organization of Communism.

Finally, Mao and his colleagues have evinced a steadfast faith in the ultimate victory of their cause. They have maintained that all jobs are conquerable, however great the obstacles may appear to be. 'All reactionaries are paper tigers. In appearance the reactionaries are formidable, but in reality they are not so powerful. From a long-term point of view, it is the people who are powerful.' Chinese Communism is infused with a sense of world mission to spread its gospel and it sees itself as the liberator of all oppressed peoples.

Phase IV (1945–9)

On the defeat of Japan in 1945, the Japanese army was ordered to surrender to the Chinese C-in-C, Chiang Kai-shek, whose troops were mainly in the west, and in order to take this surrender there had to be a rapid transport of Chinese troops eastward. This was accomplished largely with the aid of the U.S. Air Force. Chinese Communist forces occupied a considerable area of north China. Soviet forces had moved into the northeast (Manchuria) and stripped that industrial region of most

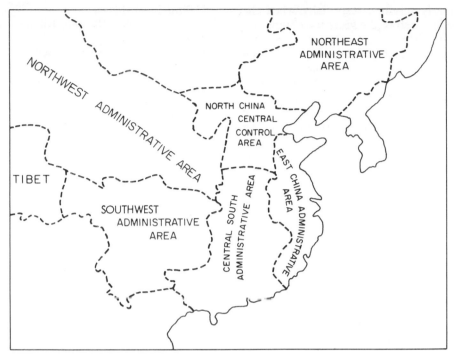

Fig. 40   Administrative districts 1949–54

of its Japanese-made plant.

With the elimination of an external enemy, the old enmity between the KMT and CCP, which had scarcely been hidden during the war years, once more came clearly to the surface. Attempts at forming a coalition government on a democratic basis were made in October 1945 and January 1946, but, to the dismay and disappointment of the mass of the people, ended in failure and were followed by a renewal of bloody civil war.

The KMT (Nationalist) army was, at first, very strong, far outnumbering the PLA (People's Liberation Army) and far better equipped, receiving from the U.S. larger quantities of surplus war stores. But corruption and indiscipline, which were already present, grew rapidly and defeat in the field in many places was followed by demoralization. The PLA, on the other hand, although outnumbered, was disciplined and schooled to a conscious purpose; morale was high. It pursued the same tactics as it had used against the Japanese, i.e. holding the countryside and leaving the towns to the enemy. The KMT, attacking Yenan and the northwest, 'found themselves in a position not dissimilar to that of the Japanese during their war with China', while the PLA 'succeeded in keeping their own units intact and mobile for eventual concentration and use at points of their own choosing.'[18] These evasive and harassing tactics led to great dissatisfaction and exhaustion in KMT ranks, resulting in large-scale surrender of men and equipment. The growing demoralization of the army is shown in the U.S. report: 'the exhaustion of the Nationalists, their growing indignation over the disparity between officers' enrichment and soldiers' low pay and their lack of interest in fighting far from home among an unfriendly populace, whereas the Communists are in the position of fighting for native soil'.[18]

While the civil war was being pursued with great intensity, the state of the country was deteriorating rapidly. Production steadily decreased to reach its lowest point in 1949. Nationalist rule became more and more repressive; a police state, albeit an inefficient one, came into being, with its usual accompaniment of spying, executions, assassinations, which bore especially severely on workers' associations, trade unions and on the student and academic world. Conscription and forced labour of the peasantry were particularly resented, especially when the farmers were required to dig great tank traps and trenches across their paddy fields, thus playing havoc with the irrigation systems. The falling production, which huge relief supplies from UNNRA did little to alleviate, and the great military expenditure led inevitably to two periods of galloping inflation. During the Sino–Japanese War there had already been serious inflation. The volume of banknotes in 1945 was 465 times greater than that in 1937[7], but what followed was disastrous. The last 'currency reform' occurred in September 1948, when all Mexican silver dollars, the only viable currency, were called in by the KMT on threat of death. At that time the price index stood at 5482 as compared with 100 in 1937. For each Mexican dollar 2 paper Gold Yuan were issued; by May 1949 the equivalent exchange had fallen to 2 million and more. This inflation, probably more than any other factor, led to the utter collapse of the KMT in 1949.

'Liberation', the name given to the 1949 Revolution, came with a suddenness unforeseen either by victor or vanquished. By November 1948 the whole of the Northeast (Manchuria) was in CCP hands; Peking and Tientsin fell in January 1949; the PLA crossed the Yangtze in April and the entire country was in its hands by the end of the year. Chiang Kai-shek and the remnants of his army retired to Taiwan, having left behind them a trail of desolation and destroyed communications.

The suddenness of this collapse presented the CCP with great administrative problems. Although the mass of people was apprehensive of what the future might hold, it was thoroughly disillusioned by the incompetence and venality of the KMT. A wave of patriotism swept the country and this, together with the exemplary behaviour of the PLA wherever it penetrated, gave reassurance generally and paved the way for immediate changes.

North China Control Area
Hopei, Shansi, Chahai, Pingyuan, Suiyuan
Municipalities: Peking, Tientsin
Northeast Administrative
Liaotung, Liashsi, Jehol, Kirin, Sungkiang, Heilung-kiang
Municipalities: Mukden, Fushun, Penhsi, Pt A-Dairen, Anshan
East China Administrative
Shantung, Chekiang, Fukien, N. & S. Kiangsu, Wanpei (Anhwei), Wannan
Municipalities: Shanghai, Nanking

Central South Administrative
Hupei, Honan, Hunan, Kiangsi, Kwangtung, Kwangsi
Municipalities: Hankow, Canton
Northwest Administrative
Shensi, Kansu, Ninghsia, Chinghai, Sinkiang
Municipalities: Sian
Southwest Administrative
Yunnan, Kweichow, Sikang
Municipalities: Chungking, Szechwan

The country was divided into six administrative areas (see fig. 40) under central control from Peking. From these the country was governed until 1954, when they were abolished and the present provincial divisions and autonomous regions substituted (see fig. 1). Considerable difficulty was encountered in early years in recruiting adequate personnel for the civil service.

To the surprise of most people, the chaotic monetary situation was brought to a state of reasonable stability and the budget balanced within a year. This was achieved by a number of measures. A unified, efficient tax collection, free from bribery and corruption, was initiated and its proceeds found their way into the national treasury. With land reform and the abolition of heavy rents, the grain tax yielded a heavy return without bearing oppressively on the peasantry. In so far as communications allowed, grain and goods were shuttled from surplus to deficiency areas. This helped to stop hoarding and speculation, which had been rife and also to steady prices. It is reported that in that year (1950) 1·03 million tons of grain were sent from the Northeast to east China; 110 000 tons from the southwest to Hankow and 339 000 tons from south to east and north[19]. Vast stores of valuable goods in KMT warehouses were confiscated and sold, thus enabling the Government to cut expenditure. In this way the monetary situation was stabilized. Interest rates, which at the height of inflation in early 1949, were sometimes as high as 100 per cent per day, fell from around 50 per cent p.a. in February 1950 to 3–5 per cent in May 1950. Prices were tied to a grain–cotton index and have remained remarkably steady ever since. The wholesale price index of 1952 was 100, that of 1958, 92·7[20].

First steps towards socialization were taken immediately. In agriculture, land reform and distribution of 'land to the tiller' were put in hand. In industry, the first steps towards public ownership of productive and distributive forces were taken. These are given full treatment later.

Perhaps the most remarkable immediate changes were in the social sphere. Backed by an intense patriotic fervour, Communist puritanism made its appearance almost overnight. Gambling, thieving and prostitution disappeared. Beggars were brought into productive employment or returned to their villages for rehabilitation.

Women were given equal status with men and the marriage laws radically revised. Public hygiene, street cleanliness and care of public property became the responsibility and the care of all.

This was the setting in which the Communist programme of building a modern industrial, socialist state began to take shape.

References

1 G. H. Creel, op. cit.

2 Leonard Cottrell, op. cit.

3 E. Balazs, *Chinese Civilization and Bureaucracy* (New Haven, Connecticut, 1964).

4 R. H. Tawney, *Land and Labour in China* (London, 1932), pp. 87, 74.

5 J. Needham, 'Science and China's influence in the world', in R. Dawson (ed.), *The Legacy of China* (London, 1964), pp. 238–9, 290–1, 293.

6 A. Feurwerker, *China's Early Industrialization: Sheng Hsuan-huai and Mandarin Enterprise*, 'Harvard East Asian Studies', 1958, pp. 9, 33, 5.

7 Cheng Chu-yuan, *Communist China's Economy 1949–62* (1963).

8 Han Su-yin, *The Crippled Tree* (London, 1965).

9 Shinkichi Eto, 'Hai-lu-feng: the first Chinese Soviet Government' (Part I), *China Quarterly*, no. 8 (October 1961), p. 177.

10 Shinkichi Eto, 'Hai-lu-feng: the first Chinese Soviet Government' (Part II), *China Quarterly*, no. 9 (January 1962), p. 155.

11 E. Snow, *Red Star over China* (New York, 1938), pp. 164–88, 431–71.

12 Tsai Shun-li, 'The Long March', *China Reconstructs*, **14**, no. 10.

13 H. L. Boorman, 'Mao Tse-tung: the lacquered image', *China Quarterly*, no. 16 (October 1963), pp. 33, 50.

14 R. Payne, *Portrait of a Revolutionary: Mao Tse-tung* (New York, 1961), p. 222.

15 Mao Tse-tung, *On Contradiction* (Peking, 1960), pp. 2–4.

16 Mao Tse-tung, *On Practice* (Peking, 1964), pp. 1–4.

17 Karl A. Wittfogel and Benjamin Schwartz, 'The legend of Maoism', *China Quarterly*, nos 1 and 2 (January and April 1960).

18 *United States' Relations with China* (Washington, 1949), pp. 314, 316.

19 Yang Pei-hsin, 'How China conquered inflation', *People's China*, 16 June 1950.

20 *Far East Trade* **20**, no. 4 (April 1965).

4   Contemporary Agricultural Development

If, in a period of roughly three five-year plans, we cannot fundamentally solve the problem of agricultural cooperation, if we cannot jump from small-scale farming with animal-drawn farm implements to large-scale farming with machinery – which includes state-sponsored land reclamation carried out on a large scale by settlers using machinery (the plan being to bring under cultivation 400–500 million mow of virgin land in the course of three five-year plans) – we shall fail to resolve the contradiction between ever-increasing demand for marketable grain and industrial raw materials and the present generally poor yield of staple crops. In that case our socialist industrialization will run into formidable difficulties: we shall not be able to complete socialist industrialization.

Mao Tse-tung

ORGANIZATION

We have recorded the warning given by R. H. Tawney in 1932 as he reviewed the miserable and parlous state to which the peasantry had been reduced during the decades of unrest in the twentieth century. Land reform, the return of 'the land to the tiller', had been one of the main planks of Sun Yat Sen's platform as he built up his Nationalist Party, the Kuomintang (KMT) in the early twenties. This and the redress of the peasants' grievances figured prominently in the propaganda which preceded the victorious march of the KMT and Communist armies of the Northern Expedition in 1926 and it was this promise and expectation which did much to gain the support of the land-hungry peasantry in the overthrow of the war-lords. Failure in succeeding years to implement this promise of land reform was one of the deep causes of the eventual collapse of the KMT.

Land reform

The CCP, after their expulsion from central China and after their Long March, found a compara-

tively secure centre in the northwest in Yenan, Shensi. From this centre they ruled a wide area of loess land in which they experimented and developed theory and practice in the change from private land ownership and individual cultivation to cooperation and socialization. After three years of bitter civil war the Communists swept southward in 1949 and within twelve months were masters of the whole country. The invading armies were preceded by propaganda almost identical with that used in the Northern Expedition of 1926 and again the peasantry clutched at the chance of escape from their poverty and oppression. This time they were not disappointed. The CCP set about land reform, but the process was not completed until the end of 1952 or beginning of 1953.

Land reform, the dispossession of the landlord class and the redistribution of land among the tillers, must be regarded as a deliberate and integral first step in a progression towards communal ownership of the land. The CCP made no secret that this was their intention, although, in the early stages, it is doubtful if this was appreciated by any but a very small minority of the peasantry. On the political side of the CCP intention was, at one and the same time, to create a lively sense of class consciousness and hatred in the peasantry, a hatred which at times and places ran beyond the power of the central government to control, and also to secure the loyalty and support of the poorer peasantry, which formed, by far, the greater proportion and on which the Communists have throughout placed their main reliance. The overthrow of the landlord class from which, throughout the centuries, the scholar–administrators have been drawn, was a central objective in the communist revolution – and with some reason. Chinese history abounds with examples of peasant revolts against intolerable conditions, resulting in the overthrow of an oppressive government or dynasty only to find the old scholar–administrator, because of his monopoly in government know-how, quickly back in the saddle.

For purposes of land redistribution the rural population was divided into six classes: landlords, rich peasants, middle peasants, lower-middle peasants, poor peasants and labourers or landless. In China there were few, if any, landlords owning large estates comparable with those of the big Russian landowners. Nevertheless, landlords were stripped of all land that they were renting out. Rich and middle peasants had to surrender any land which they were not farming directly themselves. The central authorities ruled that, in certain circumstances, land which was worked by hired labour might be retained, but more often than not, rich peasants were dispossessed of this surplus at village meetings. The confiscated land was then redistributed to the middle and poor peasants and the landless on a *per capita* family basis and title deeds issued. This distribution, which was completed earlier in the northern regions than the south, was carried through with a great deal of bitterness and vindictiveness and not a little loss of life. Public denunciation meetings fanned class hatred to a pitch difficult to control at times.

Mutual aid teams
At this time the CCP was trying to do two things which were mutually contradictory. While land reform, the distribution of 'land to the tillers' was absolutely obligatory if the loyalty of the peasantry was to be secured, it was, by its very nature, inimical to the second essential which was the immediate, rapid increase of food. The immediate effect of land reform was to increase

fragmentation of holdings, which already were minute. Moreover, the new landowners, although enthusiastic and proud of their property, were, on the whole, less experienced and less competent cultivators. In consequence there was a decline rather than an increase in agricultural production.

To meet this situation the CCP drew on the experience they had gained in the liberated regions of the northwest[2]. Mutual aid teams were quickly instituted. Three to six households came together to work on common tasks on each other's lands during the busy seasons – the simplest form of cooperation. This was no real innovation as it had been practised in an attenuated form in China throughout the centuries. The mutual advantages were obvious and, since it in no way challenged the newly acquired title to ownership, it quickly received fairly universal acquiescence and practice. Between 1949 and 1952 the functions of the mutual aid teams were expanded. Teams were extended to include a larger number of households and were formed for the whole year; some tools and animals were owned jointly. Any reclaimed land became common property and was cultivated by the whole team. Thus the embryo of socialization was introduced, but so small a degree of cooperation was quite inadequate to achieve the necessary increase in food production and was only the first small step towards the full collective ownership of land and means of production.

Elementary producers' cooperatives
In 1953 experiments were made in the formation of what came to be known as elementary or semi-socialist producers' cooperatives in which members contributed their land, animals and tools for joint cultivation by the whole. Because this involved some encroachment of the newly acquired rights of ownership, the CCP Central Committee was very conscious of possible opposition and therefore moved very cautiously. To soften the transition, it laid down certain requisites and directives to cadres involved. Entry by the peasant was voluntary and undertaken only when the whole scheme was fully understood. Each cooperative was economically independent; profit and loss its own concern[3]. The mutual benefits of cooperation were emphasized; the rich and middle peasants were assured that at least there would be no fall in income and the poor peasant could look to a rise. Withdrawal from the cooperative was optional, although, as might be expected, this was a difficult and socially un-

popular step. Nevertheless, at a later stage, in some regions where returns to rich and middle peasants fell below their former receipts, there were wholesale withdrawals for a time.

Although there was no universal standard or blue print laid down for these early cooperatives, they were expected to conform to a general pattern[4]. Central Committee directives required that they should be democratically based on annually elected management committees. Theoretically this placed management in the hands of the members, but in fact, in the vast number of instances leadership and control fell into the hands of Party-appointed cadres and keen Party members.

Remuneration to cooperative members was calculated partly on the amount of capital in the form of land, animals and tools contributed, and partly on the amount and quality of labour performed for which 'work points' were awarded. Work was organized on the basis of 'production terms' of 7 to 10 households. The intention was that there should be a gradual change in the proportion of return from land and from labour, starting from 60 per cent from land and 40 per cent from labour, moving to 50 per cent each, then to 30 per cent and 70 per cent respectively, until eventually no rent at all should be paid. It was pointed out that, if production increased sufficiently, the return to, say, a middle peasant from labour alone could be greater than his original receipts from both land and labour. All members kept their own small holdings for private cultivation[5].

Urged on by periodic speeches by Mao Tsetung, these elementary producers' cooperatives increased more rapidly than had been anticipated, nearly doubling their numbers between April and August 1954, from 58 000 to 100 000 and having 1·7 million members. At this time the size of cooperatives varied between 20 and 50 households. By May 1956 it is estimated that 110 million families, comprising 91 per cent of the rural population were organized into a million or so elementary producers' cooperatives. By the end of the year this figure had risen to nearly 2 million[6]. Doubtless, the ease and rapidity of growth was fostered by obvious advantages to the members. The larger fields made ploughing easier and the use of better techniques possible. Also, the underemployed farm labour in the off-seasons was put to better use in such small works as local road-building and irrigation works with clear advantage to the whole village. From the point of view of the central government, the bigger units made control and direction of agricultural output more feasible.

Advanced producers' cooperatives

Although these semi-socialist cooperatives had achieved considerable increase in agricultural production, politics and economics demanded further advances. Politics required a further move towards the ultimate objective of communism. Economics required still more rapid production since it was almost entirely on the surplus – the savings – of agriculture that the capital needed for vast industrial development depended. Thus it was that early in 1956 elementary producers' cooperatives began to be converted into advanced or socialist producers' cooperatives, which were, in effect, collective farms. Individual title to land, which had been upheld till now, was forfeited, together with ownership of draught animals and farm implements. The individual farmer received some compensation for his capital contribution, but his income henceforth was based entirely on the labour he contributed. Private ownership of smallholdings and the family holding of hog and chicken alone were permitted. The size of these new units was considerably larger than the elementary cooperatives, embracing between 100 and 200 families, who were organized into production brigades and production teams. It should be noted that the transition from one form to the other was uneven throughout the country. As might be expected, it was quicker and more complete in the north and northeast and slower in the southwest among the minority groups.

The loss of ownership rights brought considerable initial unrest and opposition to the formation of advanced cooperatives, but this melted surprisingly quickly and their inauguration was very rapid. It is estimated that by the end of June 1956, 75 million rural households (62·5 per cent) out of a total of 120 million were members of advanced cooperatives and that by the end of the year over 105 million households had joined. More serious and deep-seated criticism emerged later in 1957 due largely to the growth of bureaucracy consequent on the increased size of units. Officious and often ignorant direction from cadres led to much discontent among the peasants and to some fall in production. Government decisions to reduce the size of cooperatives and so ensure the placing of greater responsibility and power in the hands of the actual cultivator were taken but, before they could be implemented, a greater change in a diametrically opposite direction took place.

The commune

The precise manner by which communes came into existence is somewhat obscure, but what is certain is that some 25 to 30 advanced co-operatives in Honan in April 1958 amalgamated to form one single unit, the first commune. This took place at the beginning of the period of fanatical enthusiasm and energy, which came to be known as 'The Great Leap Forward' and marked a spate of such amalgamations. After Mao Tse-tung had visited the Honan commune and given it his approval, the movement swept the country. Before the year was out 99 per cent of the rural population was organized into these large units, reducing the 700 000 or so advanced cooperatives to 26 500 communes, averaging 4750 households apiece.

From their first formation they have been by no means uniform either in size, management or function, although they all conform to a general pattern. Northern farms in the past generally have been larger than those in the south and therefore one would expect the same to be true of northern communes. On the whole this is so, but there are notable exceptions. For example, the Fwah Tung People's Commune, 70 km from Canton, has a population of 51 050, covers 388 sq km and has 365 production teams, each having about 80 families[7], while the Yangtan People's Commune in south Shansi numbers only 11 000 persons, has only 61 production teams and covers only 150 sq km[8].

The communes took over all the local government functions previously performed by the *hsiang* and much more besides, but they still remain integral parts of the *hsien* or county. They became responsible for the organization of all the activities of the people within their compass – for agriculture, rural industry, water conservancy, afforestation, communications, education, civil defence, health and public hygiene, cultural and recreational activities.

Such an all-embracing local authority has required a vast reorganization. It is remarkable that, considering the inexperience of the majority of administrators – the emphasis placed on class struggle and giving authority to the poor and lower-middle peasantry as far as possible – the transition took place without utter chaos and catastrophe.

The structure of the commune is clear and straightforward. At the head is the commune, under which are the production brigades and the production teams. Once every two years commune members elect delegates to a commune delegates' conference. Election and representation is indirect, from production team through production brigade. An endeavour is made in a well-run commune to see that the various facets of its life are properly represented. The delegates' conference is responsible for the general policy and direction of the commune and usually meets about twice a year. From its members it elects its administrative and executive body, the commune management committee, which invariably will include the local CCP secretary and the Communist Youth League secretary. Subcommittees are then appointed to take care of the various aspects of the commune's activities, production, finance, trade, education, health, militia, etc. After the Cultural Revolution the communes generally were relieved of some of their functions and the composition of their management committees somewhat changed but the general pattern remains.

Apart from its general coordinating functions, the commune is required 'to organize its activities with high militancy and improve its productive efficiency and labour discipline'. The commune management committee periodically receives from the State Planning Organization the production targets proposed for the commune for the year. These proposals are sent down to the production brigades for discussion, amendment and approval and the brigades, in their turn, refer them to their respective production teams. The success or failure of commune production is closely bound up with these discussions and decisions and a great deal depends on the quality of brigade and team leadership, which is most onerous. It has been found by experience that the full consent of production teams must be secured if fulfilment is to be assured. In the early stages, ignorant and officious direction from above, without sufficient regard for local conditions, led to much discontent and a campaign for the relegation of local decisions to 'the tillers', i.e. the production teams, who will best know the local conditions. The following newspaper article voiced this complaint at the time:

What are the characteristics of a particular plot? What is the quality of the soil? What are the crops suited to the land? How should sowing be arranged? Over these questions, only those team members and cadres who are most familiar with local conditions have the right to speak. Under no circumstances may other people, regardless of the concrete circumstances, require production teams to plant crops that are not suited to the concrete conditions, though such people may have good intentions. If they do so, even high-yield crops will frequently be turned into low-yield ones.

If such powers of production administration are not delegated to the production teams, if their rights are not respected, if they are not allowed to make their own decisions, and if everything is managed from the production brigade level, it will be impossible to arrange production according to the land, the seasons, crops and manpower. It will do great harm to agricultural production.[9]

We have indicated above that the inception of the commune was one manifestation of the Great Leap Forward, that fanatical upsurge of enthusiasm, which had as its objective the attainment of 'communism in our time', a call to all to implement at once the ideal of 'from each according to his ability, to each according to his need'. All things, with the exception of intimate personal belongings, were to be held in common. Private plots held by individual members of cooperatives became commune property; all houses and house sites, tree holdings and livestock came under public ownership. Food at communal halls and kitchens was to be free to all regardless of work performed. Collective living, under the slogan 'Five-together' (working, eating, living, studying and drilling together) was the order of the day.

It required no great length of time to demonstrate clearly that the peasantry was in no way ready for so great an innovation. Where it was attempted there was great resentment at the loss of private plots and a marked fall in production followed. Therefore, they were restored quite soon to private ownership with the proviso that they should not exceed 5 per cent of the commune's holding of agricultural land.

Communal feeding, which apparently never attained great proportions, also quickly reverted to the normal family pattern and the system of payment according to work done, i.e. work points, which had been in force under the advanced cooperatives was restored. However, the more complex the organization becomes, the more complicated the assessing of services rendered and of

work points becomes. Members engaged in the commune's workshops, industries, schools and administration are paid wages and not according to work points.[10] The problem of equating the value of the thousand and one jobs, from agricultural and forestry work, through the numerous workshops to transport and educational services is most exacting, especially when one remembers the lack of workers with any degree of experience in accountancy in virtually all districts. In early days the situation in Yangtan is fairly typical:

> The young accountant was busy with his abacus totting up the work points earned by [production] team members last month. We were introduced and learnt that he had had a full primary school education, and had been elected accountant in 1964 when he was 17. He did this work part-time and also worked in the fields.[11]

Jan Myrdal[2] discusses intimately these difficulties and problems.

The basic accounting unit in a commune may be either the production brigades or the individual production teams. Whichever it is, it is responsible for gain and loss and is the owner of the means of production – land, draught animals, tools, etc. – within its jurisdiction, and its management committee is responsible for the working out and implementing the production plans and targets agreed upon, and for the distribution of income. The following table shows the income of the second team of the Paching brigade in 1964 and gives a general idea of its distribution.[11]

Expenditure	Amount in yuan	Percentage of expenditure
Production expenses	13 124	38·6
Agricultural tax	2 207	6·5
Reserve fund	1 697	5·0
Welfare fund	330	1·0
Reserve grain	1 488	4·4
Distributed to members	15 104	44·5
Total	33 950	100·0

The production expenses included seed, fertilizer, insecticide and the hiring of tractors, etc. 38·6 per cent is a higher figure than is general (25–30 per cent) and was accounted for by heavy rain and hail storms, necessitating the replanting and fertilizing of the crop. The reserve fund is, in fact, used mainly for capital expenditure on buying new tools, buying livestock, afforestation

Brigade	State taxes %	Cost of prod. and management %	Communal reserve fund %	Communal welfare fund %	Consumption fund %
Better production	7	21	21	3	48
Ordinary production	7	21	18	3	51
Inferior production	7	21	15	3	54

and land improvement. The welfare fund (1 per cent is below what is generally allocated for this purpose) is used in cases of accident, sickness and old age and is intended mainly for those who have no one in the family to depend on. All old people in China are supposed to enjoy security under the 'Five Guarantees' – enough to eat, adequate housing, clothing, day-to-day necessities and a decent burial. The reserve grain, required of all communes against natural disaster, is eventually distributed to members. Virtually all communes in 1974 held a full year's reserve grain.

The 44·5 per cent for distribution to members is below the norm of about 50 per cent on account of bad weather. This is not a high percentage, but it is considerably higher than the poorer peasant could expect from his labours before 1949 when his rent usually took half his produce and he was liable to unpredictable taxation, to say nothing of his endemic indebtedness at exorbitant rates of interest. His present income is fairly assured and, in most instances, is enough for him to save a little privately, enabling him, in due course, to buy such things as a bicycle, sewing machine and radio. In addition he works his recovered private plot assiduously – too assiduously for the approval of the more communistically minded. The following report from the Peng-pu Commune, near Shanghai gives some idea of the rise in income during the first decade of communist rule:[12]

	yuan
1949 (before Land Reform)	115
1952 (after Land Reform)	130
1954 (elementary coop.)	169
1956 (advanced coop.)	190
1958 (early commune)	332

Although the great discrepancy between the wealth of landlord and landless peasant no longer exists, there is still considerable difference of income between brigade and brigade, production team and production team owing to differences in natural conditions of soil, water availability, etc., and also to differences in skill in management. A good deal of prominence has been given to efforts to redress this imbalance. A slogan much used in industry and agriculture is 'Compare with, learn from, catch up with and overtake the advanced and help the less advanced'. To this end communes are directed to group their brigades into three categories and exhort the better-off to contribute a higher percentage of their income to the communal reserve fund than the poorer. In this connection Richard Hughes has produced the table below[13]:

He points out that, although the percentage allotted to the consumption fund of the better production brigades is less than the others, the actual income they receive is higher because of their higher production.

Crop (average yield (per mow)	Period of individual farming 1951 (catties)	Period of advanced coop. 1955 (catties)	Per cent increase	Under the people's commune 1965 (catties)	Per cent increase c.f. 1956
Wheat	104·2	168·9	62·1	303	79·4
Cotton	30·2	45·3	50·0	71	56·7

The advantages accruing to this larger unit, the commune, are not difficult to see. Soon after their establishment, a United Nations report (March 1959) stated that 'the people's communes appear to possess marked advantages from the point of view of technical organization of production'. Specialization and division of labour are possible to a degree denied to the largest of advanced cooperatives. The many departments of agriculture contained within the commune – arable, animal husbandry, market gardening, orchards, afforestation – can be developed and given specialized attention. It has made possible quite simple and obvious techniques, which formerly could not be practised.

The peasants of Yinhsi [Fukien] had always known that yields could be increased by rotating paddy rice with dry-land crops such as sweet potatoes, peanuts and beans; but, when plots were owned by individual peasants, cultivation of a wet crop next to a dry one led to disagreements between neighbours.... Yinhsi brigade now practises a four-year rotation:
1st year – early rice, late rice, then barley
2nd year – beans, then sweet potatoes and peas
3rd year – early rice, late rice, wheat
4th year – peanuts, late rice, legumes (to be ploughed in)[14]

As a result of improved techniques, big increases in production are claimed, as reflected in the Yangtan report[7]:

The local industries and handicrafts can be rationalized and speeded up to serve agricultural needs. Labour, so often unemployed or under-employed between peaks of agricultural activity, can be mobilized and productively employed. This factor, more than any other, has enabled the communes to carry out much greater water conservancy works of irrigation and drainage than could be contemplated by the smaller units, although, as will be seen below, this ability to mobilize was carried to impossible lengths in the early stages. This coordination of effort, made possible by the bigger unit, has already done much to give greater security to the community in times of natural disaster, the meeting of the threat of flood by dyke raising and strengthening, the care of and replanting of crops in time of drought. The failure of harvests during the years 1959 to 1961 would have resulted in disastrous famine and the loss of millions of lives, as in 1928, had it not been for the cooperation made possible by the communes. As it was, the people escaped with hardship and malnutrition only.

Further virtues of the larger unit are the improvement in communications and the increased opportunities for the mechanization of agriculture which it offers, but one must beware of exaggerating the achievements in these spheres if the Yangtan Commune can be taken as at all typical.

We have 10 production brigades, but when we started, 4 of them could not be reached by lorry. 6 brigades moved their goods mostly by shoulder pole. The commune repaired the old roads, built new ones, and put all the field paths in order. We laid 38 kilometres of motor road to link up the brigades. We arranged the fields so that 80 per cent of all the commune's land can be worked with tractors.
There are 42 engines, steam, gasoline and diesel in the commune. Every brigade has a fleet of small carts running on two cycle wheels, 640 of them all told, versatile little things that carry manure, fuel, water, cotton and what not; 68 pneumatic-tyred carts pulled by horses, mules or oxen. The Yangtan Brigade has 3 lorries. The back-breaking work of carrying heavy loads on men's backs has ended.[8]

Better credit facilities and marketing have resulted. Also, there has been greater capital accumulation – a very welcome fact from the central authority's point of view. With increase in production there has been increased individual saving and a willingness to plough back profits into the team's or brigade's holding.

The advent of the commune has enabled big changes to be made in the social field. Amongst these are the public health and hygiene services, which have been greatly expanded; serious attack has been possible on such diseases as malaria, hookworm, and schistosomiasis, which have been so debilitating and a constant cause of low production[15].

It has already been indicated above that, in spite of – and to some measure, because of – the extravagant enthusiasm which accompanied the launching of the rural people's communes that were supposed to be like 'a fine horse, which having shaken off its bridle, is galloping courageously directly towards the highway of Communism'[16], their early history is full of problems and shortcomings. Egged on by local party cadres, in their initial enthusiasm, commune management committees, brigades and teams vied with each other in setting production targets, which became impossibly high. Rather than admit failure or inadequacy, returns were falsified, resulting quickly in confusion and a breakdown in the

Plate 2   Production teams reaping and threshing the late rice crop in Haiyen, Chekiang
Note the size of field made possible by common ownership of the land and also the absence of mechanization

State Statistical Bureau, which was just attaining a professional basis and status. This upsurge was not confined to agriculture. The Great Leap Forward called for immediate and immense increases in industrial production, particularly in iron and steel. In 1958–9 there was an outburst of rural iron production in hundreds of thousands of tiny mud-brick blast furnaces in backyards, which drew much-needed agricultural workers away from their fields just when they were most needed to reap a bumper harvest. In the ensuing confusion the central government was slow to recognize the imminent agricultural crisis and to diagnose its true causes. 'The leadership was also unable to ascertain fully the true causes of the crisis. To accomplish this latter objective they would have had to require detailed seasonal and area breakdowns in data so that they could separate out

the effects of poor organization from the effects of the bad weather that affected most of China between 1959 and 1961.'[6]

Disillusionment accompanied these bad harvests. There had been wide discontent with the loss of private plots and a discernible fall in production followed. Their restoration to private ownership was essential, but higher authority was reluctant to do so as it was a retreat in the march towards Communism. An attempt was made to hedge their return with restrictions. Not more than 5 per cent of the cultivated land of the commune may be held in private plots and some attempt was made to limit the time and fertilizer that individuals might expend upon them. Free markets in towns at which cooperative members were able to sell their surplus produce had been discontinued on the formation of communes. During the acute shortages between 1959 and 1962 these markets were reopened but, with the better harvests of succeeding years, they have largely faded out since 'commune members found it uneconomic to peddle their produce in towns, as had been done during the period of shortage. Consequently they sold their surplus to producers and consumers' cooperatives where the price was at par with the government-operated markets.'[17]

During the first years of the communes there was a great deal of regimentation of labour. Millions of men and women were organized on a military basis, formed into battalions, brigades and companies, assembled at bugle call and marched with banners flying to whatever was the assigned task. Many of the tasks were enormous and, in most instances, were tackled with great patriotic zeal. The report of the famous Hua Mu-lan women's battalion reads like an emulation of the legendary Yu, who, whilst quelling the floods, never once entered his home although he frequently passed his door[18].

They were just like men, acting as if fighting a battle. They ate and slept right in the field. After the establishment of the battalion not a single member left her post for ten days and nights. Continually, during this period of combat labour, they passed the doors of their homes without entering or requesting permission to visit the premises even briefly.

    This initial outburst of energy was too exhausting. It could not be maintained, even by so tough a people as the Chinese, and had to give way to a more reasonable approach and more reasonable hours of work. After six or seven years of experiment and adjustment the communes have settled to an accepted general pattern. They have proved their worth as organizations for carrying out the necessary larger works, such as water conservation, irrigation and drainage, and have surrendered much of their original bureaucratic powers to the production brigades and production teams. The development of the commune in China has had a transforming effect on the landscape in a way somewhat similar to that in England during the last fifty years where hedges have been removed and fields extended. With the abolition of private ownership of land the minuscule fields, especially in south and central China, have been amalgamated to allow a more cooperative use of manpower and the freer use of machines; terracing in the north has been greatly developed; communal afforestation campaigns have resulted in very extensive windbreak belts, wooded hillsides and tree-lined highways, changing the face of the countryside.

State farms

In 1949 China was in urgent need of greater food production. Any development from traditional individual peasant farming to large socialized units was bound to take time. Therefore the Government embarked immediately on what, for China, was an entirely new departure – state farming. Once started, the growth of state farms has been very rapid. In 1952 there were 52 relatively large state farms, covering more than 3·3 million *mow*, (220 000 ha). By 1957 this figure had grown to 710 with an area of more than 15 million *mow*. Half a million workers and 10 000 tractors (in terms of 15 h.p. units) were employed, giving a yield of 1190 *chin* of grain. It is recorded[19] that in 1960 the Ministry of State Farms and Land Reclamation had under its control 2490 state farms, employing 2·8 million workers and staff members, cultivating more than 78 million *mow* (5 million ha), using 28 000 tractors and producing over 5000 million *chin* of grain. Since then there have been no comprehensive figures published, but continued reports of new state farms and their achievements indicate that this expansion has continued, probably with increasing intensity, e.g. 36 state farms were opened in 1966 in the northeast bringing 450 000 ha of virgin black soil under the plough. Mao Tse-tung has consistently put his faith in this development and has urged the people 'fundamentally solve the problem of agricultural co-operation [that is] ... jump from small-scale farming with animal-drawn farm implements to large-scale farming with machinery – which includes state-sponsored land reclamation carried out on a large scale by settlers using machinery.'[20]

The objectives of state farms are clearly stated. They are to be the means of greatly increasing production; they are to stand as examples to cooperatives, and later to communes, and to provide them with help wherever possible; they are to be the main agents in the reclamation of the wastelands, especially in border and coastal areas, and they are to be the main means of large-scale resettlement of the people.

On the production side, the task of the state farms is 'to provide the state with marketable grain, cotton, meat and other types of farm and animal products'. Most of the state farms have the virtue that they come into production rapidly and are able to produce considerable quantities of grain in the same or following year in which they are set up. Their recorded performance to date, however, is not very spectacular, and in 1960

Plate 3   Reaping by combine on a state farm

yields were judged, on the whole, to be rather disappointing. Sinkiang state farms reported the following yields in 1960:

300 *chin* wheat per *mow* on 100 000 *mow*
960 *chin* maize per *mow* on 600 *mow*

which is low when compared with most eastern commune yields, but this is not a fair comparison since state farming is extensive and commune farming very much more intensive.

By far the greater part of the present production of agricultural machinery goes to these big farms, which, with their huge fields are better able to use the machines then the communes. It is on the state farms that the knowledge and skills in their economical use is learnt. It is the intention that this acquired knowledge shall be disseminated as quickly and as widely as possible. One advantage of China's socialized economy is that there is generally a greater willingness to share knowledge of newly-learnt techniques than there is in a competitive society.

'The majority of China's state farms have been set up on wasteland or uninhabitable land subject to drought or waterlogging, on difficult alkaline or acid soils and in areas regularly hit by sand and wind storms.'[21] These are found mainly in the northeast, northwest, far west and along the coast. It should cause no surprise that the state farms are sited in these marginal, inhospitable regions when it is remembered that all good, easily-worked land has long since been densely occupied.

Many of the earliest state farms were established by soldiers of the PLA (People's Liberation Army) in the first years of the new regime, notably in Sinkiang and the northeast. On or before demobilization they set about land reclamation and settled on it. By 1960 180 mechanized state farms, occupying 11·6 million *mow* had been established in Sinkiang on the north and south slopes of the Tienshan. Many millions of peasants in China Proper, displaced by water conservancy works and the like, together with youngsters just

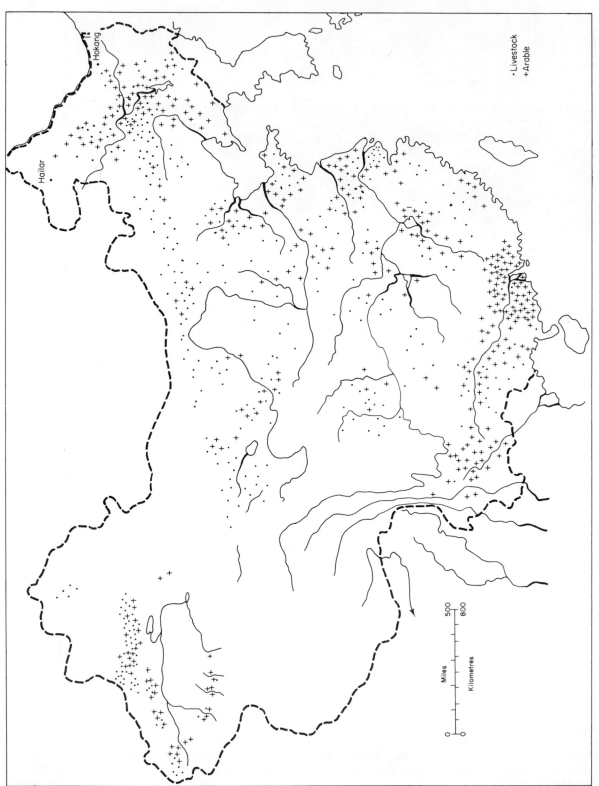

Fig. 41 State farms 1957

leaving school, have been resettled – not always successfully – on these frontier farms.

Thirty State-owned Overseas Chinese Farms were set up in Kwangtung, Kwangsi, Yunnan, Kweichow and Fukien to accommodate and settle more than 60 000 Chinese who returned from overseas. These returnees were seldom agriculturalists and were mainly former workers, small producers and small businessmen, who required training before they became productive farmers[22].

The many state farms, which are situated in regions having long and rigorous winters, as in Heilungkiang, Tsaidam and Sinkiang, are faced with the problem of adequate productive employment during the long non-growing period. In spite of the hardships of the inner Asian winter, the 'slack' period has been occupied with capital construction – drainage, irrigation, land reclamation, the building of pumping stations, together with repair work in the farm's workshops. The slogan in this connection has been 'self-reliance', i.e. avoidance of the use of state capital in these works[23]. Winter occupations in Heilungkiang have been profoundly affected since 1964 by the development of the Taching oilfield.

Experimental farms and demonstration farms

A number of farms and agricultural institutes have been established specifically for experimenting in all aspects of agriculture, from methods of planting and harvesting to farm management. It is reported that at the end of 1964 there were ten big, consolidated experimental centres and hundreds of smaller ones in the country[24]. In 1974 they were much more numerous.

Supplementary to these experimental farms are the demonstration farms, which have multiplied enormously in recent years. In 1965 it is stated that there were more than 10 000 run mainly by the communes themselves. These demonstration farms have two main functions. They test the results of the experimental farms on sample plots in local conditions and then, as their name indicates, they demonstrate their results and findings to the brigades and teams throughout the countryside in very much the same way as the TVA popularized their scientific findings among the Tennessee peasantry. This education is their most important work. Over the centuries the Chinese farmer has earned for himself a high reputation. Nevertheless, in spite of all his meticulous care and devotion to the soil, he is conservative and has been the slave to his agricultural calendar, which

he has followed religiously[25]. Professor Ts'ai Hsu of Peking Agricultural University, writing on this subject, says:

'The North China peasants hold that wheat becomes pregnant during the solar term of "summer begins" and draws ears during the solar period of "grain fills". Therefore they do not pay much attention to overwintering wheat at the time of resumption of growth [February and March] when the wheat ears begin to grow. But, if the soil is dressed and hoed at the time, the ears grow bigger. If this dressing and hoeing is done only at the jointing stage, only bigger grain results.[26]

He maintains that the dissemination of ideas such as this are the main job of the demonstration farm and the sample plot, which must be very well run. When properly demonstrated, innovations and changes are accepted by the peasants with acclaim.

Agricultural planning

We have sketched the chaotic state of the country in 1949 when the CCP came into power and the immediate steps that were taken to bring some law and order into being. The succeeding three years until 1952 were engaged in the work of rehabilitation and preparation for planned development. The general scheme of things was set out in a series of Five-year Plans of which there have been three to date: 1953–7; 1958–62 and 1966–70. Although the State Planning Commission, formed in 1952, must have formulated full, detailed blueprints of their plans, these have never been published in any comprehensive form. They have appeared as a series of yearly targets set for various sections of agriculture and industry and have therefore been subject to the handicaps of such target planning, *viz* lack of coordination and the constant danger of bottlenecks resulting in imbalance.

The First Five-year Plan stated clearly three main planning aims. First and foremost was the transformation of China from an agricultural to an industrial nation; second was the change from a capitalist to a socialist society; and third was the change from an individual peasant economy to one based on cooperation. We have followed the progress of this last change from 1953 to 1957 and also its continuance during the Second Five-year Plan (1958–62) to the establishment of the commune.

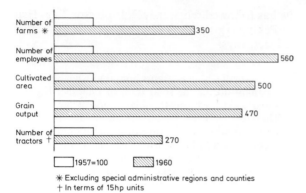

Fig. 42   Growth of State Farms, from Peking Review*, 28 April 1961*

At the Second National People's Congress of the Chinese People's Republic in April 1960, the National Agricultural Development Programme (1956–67) was approved. This programme has come to be known as the Twelve-year Plan and it attempted to give some direction over this period. Clearly it was formulated during the First Five-year Plan since it spoke only of cooperatives and not of communes, although these had already been in existence for two years at the time of its publication. Its preamble states its purpose:

> This is a programme of endeavour to increase productive capacity in agriculture rapidly, in order to reinforce socialist industrialization in our country and to raise the standard of living of the peasants, as well as all people, during the period from the First Five-year Plan to the third.[27]

The programme is in forty sections and covers the whole gamut of agricultural development from cooperative organization to moral welfare and the conversion of landlords and rich peasants. The section headings are:

1. Consolidation of the System of Agricultural Cooperatives
2. Active Increase of the Output of Food Crops and Other Agricultural Crops
3. Development of Livestock
4. Promoting Implementation of Measures for Output Increase and Adoption of Advanced Experiences: Two Fundamental Conditions for Increasing Agricultural Output
5. Building Water Conservation Works to Develop Irrigation and Prevent the Scourge of Flood and Drought
6. Vigorous Increase of Rural Manure and Chemical Fertilizers
7. Improvement of Old-style Farm Tools and Popularization of New-style Farm Tools
8. Actively Multiply and Popularize Recommended Strains and Varieties of Crops Suitable to Local Conditions
9. Expansion of Multiple Crops Acreage
10. Increasing Cultivation of High-yielding Crops
11. Actively Improve Farming Techniques, with Suitable Measures Adopted to Meet Local Needs
12. Improvement of Soil
13. Promote Water and Soil Conservation
14. Protect and Multiply Draft Animals
15. Prevention and Treatment of Plant Diseases and Insect Pests
16. Reclamation of Wasteland and Expansion of Acreage Cultivation
17. Economic Development of Mountainous Areas
18. Development of Forestry, and Afforestation, Wherever Possible, of all Wasteland and Mountains
19. Expand Output of Marine and Freshwater Fishing and Increase Cultured Aquatic Products
20. Perfect the Management of State-owned Farms
21. Improve Research in Agricultural Sciences and Technical Guidance
22. Strengthen Meteorological and Hydrological Services
23. Industrious and Frugal Management of Cooperatives and Households
24. Raise the Rate of Manpower Utilization and the Rate of Labour Productivity, and Develop Diversified Economy in the Agricultural Cooperatives
25. Food Grain Reserves
26. Improve Housing Conditions
27. Extermination of the Four Pests
28. Strive to Eliminate Diseases That Do the Most Serious Harm to the People
29. Protection of Women and Children
30. Enforce the System of 'Five Guarantees', Preferential Treatment for Family Members of Martyrs and Disabled Revolutionary Military Personnel, and Care and Respect for Parents
31. Eradication of Illiteracy, and Development of Cultural and Educational Undertakings in the Rural Areas
32. Develop Broadcast Networks in the Rural Areas
33. Develop Telephone and Postal Networks in the Rural Areas
34. Develop Communications and Transport in the Rural Areas
35. Improve the Commercial Network in the Rural Areas
36. Develop Credit Cooperatives in the Rural Areas

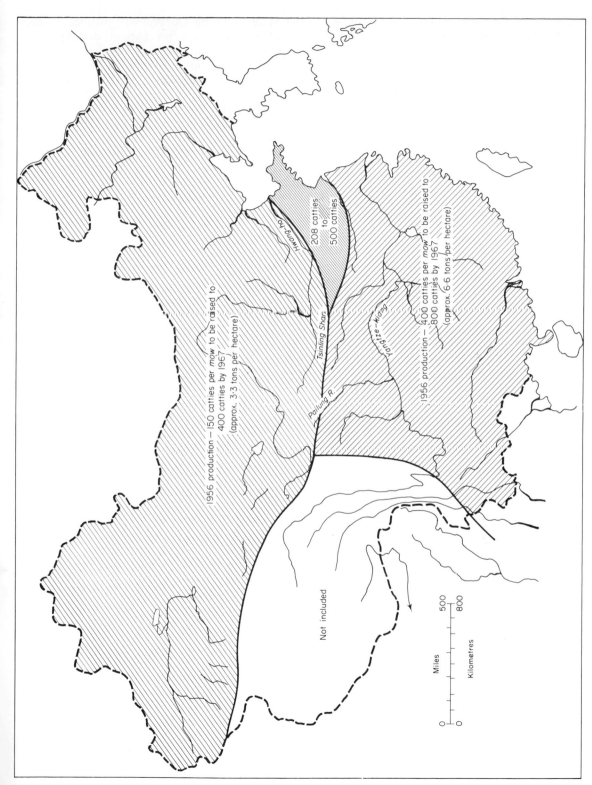

Fig. 43   Twelve-year plan grain production zone targets

37. Develop the Enthusiasm of Demobilized Soldiers for the Socialist Construction of Rural Areas
38. Raise the Socialist Enthusiasm of Youths in the Rural Areas
39. Transform the Landlords, Rich Peasants, and Counter-revolutionaries and Other Bad Elements in the Rural Areas and Safeguard the Socialist Order of Rural Areas
40. Urban Workers and Cooperative Peasants Must Help Each Other

Most of the publication is couched in general terms of direction, exhortation and encouragement but, in a few instances, definite targets are set. Section 2, which deals with the increase of output of food crops, runs:

> In the twelve years starting with 1956, in areas north of the Yellow river, the Tsinling Mountains, the river Pailung and the Yellow river in Tsinghai province, the average annual yield of grain should be raised from the 1955 figure of 150 *catties/mow* to 400 *catties*. South of the Yellow river and north of the Huai river the yield should be raised from the 1955 figure of 208 *catties* to 500 *catties*. South of the Huai river, the Tsinling Mountains and the river Pailung it should be increased from the 1955 figure of 400 *catties* to 800 *catties/mow*.

In Section 6 it demands 'that each household in the countryside raise an average of 1·5 to 2 head of hogs by 1962, and 2·5 to 3 head of hogs by 1967'.

Successful communes, brigades and production teams often report their achievements, relating their yields to these targets.

In spite of the great emphasis, which the CCP throughout has placed on the peasantry as basic to the revolution, it failed signally in the First and Second Five-year Plans to give adequate expression to this in the amount of capital investment it was prepared to assign to agriculture during this period. The planners concentrated their attention on the very rapid development of heavy industry[28]. During the First Five-year Plan the State Planning Commission planned to use 42 740 million *yuan* on capital development, assigning 24 850 million *yuan* (58·2 per cent) to industry, mining and electric power and only 3260 million *yuan* (7·6 per cent) to agriculture, forestry and water conservancy. This attempt at very rapid industrialization and the comparative neglect of agriculture was continued with greater intensity in the Second Five-year Plan, especially at its inception in the Great Leap Forward (1958–9). This and the succeeding years of bad harvests led to gross imbalance in the whole economy.

Apart from the assistance obtained from Russia between 1950 and 1954 in the form of loans (£500 million), which had been fully repaid in 1965, China has had to rely on its own resources in finding the necessary capital for development. This has had to come very largely from surplus agricultural production. Foresight, together with great economic experience and statistical information, neither of which were available to them, were required of the planners if wise utilization of capital resources was to be made. That experience was dearly bought during the hard years from late 1959 to 1962 when the series of bad harvests and economic disorganization forced the planners to review the whole position. The period 1959 to 1963 was one of retrenchment and reorientation in the industrial field. A new order of priorities was instituted in which the needs of agriculture took first place, followed by light industry and heavy industry. Industry was called on to serve agricultural development and to give priority to agricultural equipment, particularly fertilizer plant, all kinds of agricultural tools, from tractors to hoes, and irrigation and drainage machinery. This was the pattern of planning until the start of the Third Five-year Plan in 1966. Since the Cultural Revolution (1966–9) renewed emphasis has been placed on industrial development.

References

1 T. J. Hughes and D. E. T. Luard, 'Land reform', *The Economic Development of Communist China, 1949–58* (London, 1959).

2 Jan Myrdal, *Report from a Chinese Village* (London, 1965).

3 Solomon Adler, *The Chinese Economy* (London, 1957), chapter 6.

4 *Cooperative Village, Kao Pei Tien* (Peking), Appendix.

5 K. R. Walker, 'Collectivization in retrospect', China Quarterly, no. 26 (April 1966).

6 D. H. Perkins, *Market Control and Planning in Communist China* (Cambridge, Massachusetts, 1966), chapter 4.

7 Sir Richard Acland, *The Times*, 29 September 1965.

8 'Survey of a commune', *Peking Review*, no. 10 (March 1966).

9 Shu Tai-hsin, 'The function and power of production teams in production administration', *Kung-jen Jih-pao* (Peking, July 1961).

10 P. Worsley, *Inside China* (London, 1975), chapter 4.

11 'Survey of a commune', *Peking Review*, no. 13 (March 1966).

12 *Far East Trade*, October 1959.

13 Richard Hughes, *The Chinese Commune* (London, 1960).

14 *China Reconstructs*, April 1965.

15 J. Rose, 'Sinjao, a Chinese commune', *Geography*, **51**, no. 233, Part 4 (1966).

16 Gargi Dutt, 'Some problems of China's rural communes', *China Quarterly*, no. 16 (October 1963).

17 *Far Eastern Economic Review Yearbook*, 1965.

18 E. Chavannes, op. cit., chapter 29, 17th treatise.

19 Wang Chen, 'China's state farms: production bases of farm and animal products', *Peking Review*, April 1961.

20 Mao Tse-tung, *The Question of Agricultural Cooperation* (Peking, 1959), pp. 22–3.

21 New China News Agency (NCNA), Peking, May 1966.

22 NCNA, Peking, September 1964.

23 See A. Donnithorne, *China's Economic System* (London, 1967), chapter 4 for a fuller treatment of state farms.

24 *Jen-min Jih-pao*, Peking, October 1964.

25 Fei Hsiao-tung, op. cit., pp. 144–53.

26 Ts'ai Hsu, 'Sample plots in agricultural production', *K'o-houch Ta-chung*, no. 9 (September 1964).

27 *National Agricultural Development Programme (1956–67)*, Peking, April 1960.

28 K. R. Walker, 'A Chinese discussion on planning for balanced growth: a summary of the views of Ma Yin-Ch'u and his critics', in C. D. Cowan (ed.), *The Economic Development of China and Japan* (London, 1964).

5   Agricultural Production

Production, production and ever more production is one of China's most urgent needs if a rapidly growing population is to maintain and increase its intake and if the aim of industrialization is to be achieved. There are two roads which lead to this desirable end and both must be followed simultaneously. On the one hand, every effort must be made to bring more land under cultivation, and on the other, better use must be made of the land already under cultivation.

EXPANSION OF THE AREA UNDER CULTIVATION

Opportunities for the extension of cultivation within China Proper, i.e. the eighteen Provinces* of old China, are limited. This is the region which has been densely settled throughout the centuries and in which more than 80 per cent of the population lives. In the present state of knowledge, very little land suitable for cultivation has been left undeveloped. In fact development in some areas has been pushed beyond rightful limits; forests have been cleared where they should have been left standing, notably in south and central China; hilly grasslands have been ploughed where they should have been left for grazing, as in the dry lands of the northwest. Much of this marginal land, in the past, has been cultivated only intermittently, coming under the plough during periods of population pressure and reverting to waste when numbers have been decimated as, for example, by the recurrent famines of Shensi, Shansi and the North China Plain or by political unrest and civil war as in the Taiping Rebellion

(1850–64) when, it is estimated, some 20 million people were killed. The turmoil of the first half of the present century has not been conducive to agricultural expansion.

With the peace which followed 1949 and the development of the cooperatives, there has been considerable inducement to extend cultivation. In the upsurge of enthusiasm in 1954 large areas of hill-land in south and central China were brought under the plough, often unwisely since ploughing in many instances was up and down the slope instead of following the contours, leading to immediate soil erosion and endangering the paddy fields below. More successful has been the extension of the terracing in the loess regions of the northwest, which has been possible under the advanced cooperatives and even more under the communes. The work of terracing requires overall planning of the whole hill slope or ravine, the coordination of a considerable labour force and the constant supervision and repair of all retaining walls. This was not generally feasible under individual ownership.

'There was one well-to-do peasant here called Li Kuo-tung. He and his family tried to terrace the side of one small ravine. That family worked on that job for fifty years and failed. The trouble was that such a project has to be treated as a whole; the whole ravine

---

* Kansu, Shensi, Shansi, Hopei, Honan, Shantung, Szechwan, Hupeh, Hunan, Anhwei, Kaingsu, Chekiang, Kiangsi, Fukien, Kweichow, Yunan, Kwantung, Kwangsi.

must be terraced, otherwise . . . say you built terraces here' and he indicated a spot towards the mouth of a ravine, 'but the farmer higher up fails to terrace his fields, then your terraces will be either undermined or destroyed by soil and water coming down on top of them from above.'

'When we formed elementary and advanced farm co-ops there seemed to be a better chance of success. They had more manpower to deploy their mutual-aid teams and controlled a larger area, but still the job couldn't be done satisfactorily . . . but the communes planned the whole job here and coordinated its plans with the neighbouring communes. Naturally it consulted and took advice from the teams and brigades because they know their own lands better than anyone else. It unified the work of the brigades. So step by step we terraced the slopes and ravines. It was a lot of work. We built 170 kilometres of earth embankments. That meant moving 328 000 cubic metres of earth. We also rationalized the arrangements of plots by filling in and levelling up fields. We started with 15 000 small plots and ended with 9000 larger ones.'

It is hard to overestimate the importance of terracing. In this part of Chuwo *Hsien* there is no river water readily available for irrigation. Except for rain, snow and a small spring or two, water comes from underground cisterns where rainwater is collected, and from wells, some of them over 70 metres deep, from which water is drawn by windlass. So the main effort has been put into terracing as a means of soil conservation and of preserving every drop of water that falls from the skies, and meticulous cultivation of the terraces so as to retard evaporation[1].

This work of terracing has been extended also in the wetter plateau land of the southwest (Yunnan and Kweichow).

The 'raised field' system, another method of bringing new land within China Proper into cultivation, has come into use in recent years. It is stated that in and around the region of the North China Plain (Hopei, Shantung, Honan, North Kiangsu and Anhwei) there are areas of low-lying, swampy, saline and sandy land, which together comprise an area larger than the whole of France. The raised fields are created by digging drainage ditches on two sides of rectangular plots of land. The earth removed from the ditches is used to raise the level of the fields by anything from a few centimetres to over a metre. This not only prevents waterlogging, but also helps to lower the water table and so avert salinization. The method is used for bringing new swampy land into cultivation and also for improving the yield of fields subject to waterlogging and salinization. The work, which is arduous, demands a high degree of cooperation since it usually involves the construction of large drainage canals. Communes of northern Anhwei on the plain north of the Hwai-ho, claim that half a million of their members created 'raised fields' on 160 000 hectares of low-lying land in the winter and spring of 1965–6[2].

In recent years a considerable amount of land has been reclaimed along the coasts north of the Yangtze mouth. This is land which has been built up by the silt brought down by the Hwang-ho, Hwai-ho and Yangtze-kiang and has been enclosed by dykes in recent years. It extends far to the east of the old dyke, the Fan Kung Ti, built in the seventh century AD. This newly-acquired land is occupied mainly by state farms. The land nearest the seaboard is utilized for salt production and that further inland, which is less saline, is devoted to cotton growing.

A further source of increased acreage in China Proper has been the incorporation of graves into the arable lands. It has been estimated[3] that nearly 2 per cent of the farmland of the country was occupied by family burials. Graves, sometimes measuring as much as 4 metres in diameter, were often sited in the middle of the best land, either as a mark of filial piety and/or by the decision of the geomancer. The communist requirement that all graves occupying valuable arable land be moved to wasteland has apparently been carried out almost universally and with little resistance. Confucianism, and with it ancestral veneration, had been on the wane for many decades and perhaps it was never as single-minded as was sometimes thought, as Han Su-yin indicates:

> Third Uncle, so prone to the past, addicted to tradition, ancestral veneration, the preservation of rites, must have found it a searing time. But later, in his autobiography, he wrote that he knew the burial grounds were profitable fields, that ancestral sanctuaries were selected for investment purposes and ways of consolidating the property system and that this business of veneration, selecting propitious spots in accordance with the wind and water diviner, was actually a functional way of acquiring land and of evading the more onerous agrarian and house taxes.[4]

Virgin lands

When we look outside China Proper to discover new lands that can be brought into cultivation, it is the Northeast and eastern Inner Mongolia that immediately holds our attention. Here and here alone in the whole of China are vast steppelands of rolling fertile black earth. They are very sparsely populated and are capable of rapid development without preliminary costly reclamation expenditure. All three provinces of the Northeast (Liaoning, Kirin and Heilungkiang) have, during the last twenty years, greatly extended their arable areas, but it is in Heilungkiang that the most spectacular gains have been made. Between 1952 and 1957 more than $1\frac{1}{2}$ million hectares were reclaimed, amounting to about 27 per cent of the reclaimed land of the whole nation. Since then the movement has been greatly extended. Unfortunately there are no supporting statistics for this period. In 1957 there were already 36 state farms in Heilungkiang alone, farming 630 000 hectares, 36 public security farms and 13 military farms[5].

Partly for historical reasons, these virgin steppelands have remained untouched in the past. This was the land of the Manchus and was devoted mainly to nomadic animal husbandry. It was forbidden to the Chinese until the latter half of the nineteenth century. Its emptiness is also due to the long and severe winters, which, until the advent of modern farming techniques, made arable farming in this area precarious.

It is a region which requires careful husbandry since it could easily become another of the world's dust bowls. The strong, cold, dry northwest winter winds are a real menace. Great care will have to be taken to see that adequate wind screens are grown. According to all reports, the communes of the Northeast are alive to this danger.

Wastelands
In addition to the virgin lands, which, generally speaking, can be brought under the plough with little or no preliminary capital expenditure, there are many outlying regions in Sinkiang, Tsinghai, Inner Mongolia and southeast Tibet, which are capable of development and which, in fact, in many instances are rapidly being developed. From an agricultural point of view they are all inhospitable and marginal and for the same reason, viz lack of water. Given adequate irrigation facilities and agricultural know-how, most of them can be made to blossom as the rose in spite of the short growing period and hard, bitter winter, which are common to them all. Many hundreds of thousands of hectares of new arable land have been developed in the last twenty years in Sinkiang and Inner Mongolia and more recently in southeast Tibet. The numerous state farms in Tsaidam basin have opened up 20 000 hectares of wasteland since 1954. 'Tsaidam' means salt marshes[6]. More intensive animal husbandry has been fostered in Tsinghai and Inner Mongolia with the drilling of

thousands of wells in the steppelands. These are considered more fully when dealing with Agricultural Regions, chapter 6.

BETTER USE OF LANDS ALREADY UNDER CULTIVATION

Water conservancy
Flood prevention – A great deal of China's arable land has, throughout the centuries, been subject to flooding, which has reduced its productive capacity to a very considerable degree. The problem of flood prevention rested heavily on the shoulders of China's earliest emperors and throughout China's history the 'Son of Heaven's' madate has resided partly in his ability to deal with floods[7]. 'If now I cannot overcome the floods, how can I meet the people's expectations?' In legendary times Emperor Yao (2357 BC) ordered his minister Yu to bring the unruly waters of the lower Hwang-ho under control. Yu's devotion to the task laid on him is remembered to this day and is held up as an example to Communist youth. (See Historical Geography, p. 37).

There are records of floods going back over 2000 years, but unfortunately these are not of great value as there is no objective standard for what constitutes a flood. Officials, reporting to emperors, or to their superiors, have been influenced by all sorts of considerations such as tax relief in time of calamity. Also, provincial records are not of comparable duration, some being over the whole 2000 years and others only a few hundred years. Nevertheless, the records do give a clear picture of a country constantly menaced by inundation – a menace which has continued unabated into the present century.

The measures to meet it have had but very indifferent success. The almost universal method used for attempting to contain the rivers of China has been that of building higher and higher dykes, although Yu, even in the legendary years, was aware of the dangers of the method and knew the value of 'divide and rule'. He divided the lower Hwang-ho (now the notorious Hai-ho and its tributaries) into nine channels, reuniting them at their outlet into the Po-hai. This example was followed by Li Ping (255–206 BC) and his son Li Erh-lang in taming the Min-kiang in west Szechwan (see p. 55). The magnitude of the task of controlling the rivers, the lack of technical know-how and wherewithal, conservative and often decadent and corrupt government combined to deter any determined attack on the problem on a nationwide or regional scale. Dykes were built, piecemeal fashion, when and where the danger threatened and more often than not were ineffective. Flood disasters remained endemic.

Only since 1949 has any comprehensive system of flood control and water conservation been undertaken. It is no matter of surprise to find *shui*, water conservation heading the 'Eight-Point Charter', the list of directives issued in the late 1950s for agricultural advice and direction:

> *shui* – water conservation
> *fei* – fertilization
> *t'u* – soil conservation
> *chung* – seed selection
> *nai* – dense planting
> *pao* – plant protection
> *kung* – tool improvement
> *kuan* – field management

During the years succeeding Liberation the great river basins have been harnessed   first the Hwai-ho and then the Hwang-ho as being the more menacing. The Yangtze, although having experienced serious floods in 1931, has not yet received as much attention as the other two. Detailed description of the great engineering works that have been carried out – the dams, the reservoirs, the retention basins, the dyke building, the dredging and the afforestation – is reserved for treatment in their respective geographical regions. While these works have not yet entirely eliminated the spectre of flood, it is no longer the threat to life and crops it was in former years. Of the many revolutionary changes effected since 1949, flood control and water conservancy are probably the most basic to Chinese agricultural productivity. In the past tens of thousands of square kilometres have gone unharvested due either to inundation or lack of water. These have now been salvaged.

Irrigation

Irrigation and drainage – While flood control is the primary objective of all the great water conservancy schemes, they invariably serve many other ends, the chief of which are irrigation, power generation and river control for navigation.

After the dam has been built and the reservoir filled, a great deal of auxiliary work in the form of canals, channels, sluicegates, etc. has to be done. In the early years this side of development was often neglected. Many reports from planners, especially before the formation of communes,

complained that only 20–30 per cent of the water made available by the reservoirs was actually being used. Bigger local organizing units were necessary if this auxiliary work were to be done successfully, especially in view of the general lack of mechanical digging aids and the reliance which has to be put on the manpower. That things were not altogether satisfactory in this respect, in 1965, is shown by the report of the National Conference on Water Conservancy held in September 1965:

> The Conference was of the opinion that, for some time to come, emphasis should be laid persistently on building small water conservancy projects, while the big and medium sized ones should be built according to necessity and possibility, in a planned manner, step by step, and to the point.
>
> Our country has vast territories. The natural conditions in one place may differ entirely from those of another and may change every year. When designing and building water conservancy projects, therefore, these differences and changes must be taken into close consideration.[7]

Irrigation has become the focal point in agricultural development and production since 1959. It figures prominently in the Eight-point Charter. Irrigation works, with which drainage must be included in many instances on the plains, have a dual purpose. On the one hand, they are an insurance against far too prevalent crop failure and, on the other, a means of greatly increasing agricultural acreage and output, enabling two or more crops to be taken annually where only one is possible in dry farming.

Clearly it is impossible and undesirable to attempt to record all the work that is being done in this field all over China's vast territories. Reports are continually coming in from all localities of achievements, many of considerable size and extent. All that can be done is to quote typical examples, illustrating the different methods that are being used or tried in differing geographical environments. With this in mind, we have classified them generally under three headings: arid regions, hilly lands and plains, although it is not always possible to draw a clear line of demarcation between them.

Irrigation in arid regions – For many centuries there have been pockets of population in the oases around the Takla Makan desert in the Tarim Basin. These communities rely on the melt water from the snowfields and glaciers of the Kunlun and Tien Shan. Their continued existence through history has depended on how climatic changes and political security have allowed them to make use of these water resources[8]. The oases mark the lines of ancient imperial trade routes, notably the Silk Road, and are the sites of towns which have existed for more than two millennia. Others have been overcome by desert sands and have decayed. The irrigation works of the extant oases communities have been greatly expanded since 1949 and some of the derelict sites have been revived by the construction of new works, new canals, channels and sluices. A major disability of the region has always been the loss of water in the channels through seepage. This has largely been overcome by lining the beds of the channels with cobbles. Since the formation of the communes, the former irregular plots, together with the newly developed land have been reorganized into precisely arranged rectangular plots of 6–12 hectares, surrounded by intersecting channels, which allow an even and controlled distribution of water. The plots are lined by shelter belts of trees, two, three or four rows deep. The many state farms of this region, started largely by the PLA, are irrigated in the same way and have the same appearance. It is stated that, between 1949 and 1964, the irrigated area of this region has been increased nearly three-fold[9] and large increases continue to be reported annually.

The farmers of the Turfan depression obtain their irrigation water mainly by wells from ground water. In the lowest lying parts of the depression they have developed the Persian and Afghanistan method of *karez* irrigation, i.e. by cutting long, horizontal tunnels into the hillsides, thus tapping the water table and leading the water out by gravitation.

Medium-size dams with sluices are being built on many rivers descending the northern slopes of the Tien Shan and irrigated farmland is being developed there. But the main interest in Dzungaria is centred on the extension of well boring to serve animal husbandry on the steppeland.

Two distinct types of water conservancy have been developed in Inner Mongolia and the northern tip of Ningsia Hui Autonomous Region. Along the great bend of the Hwang-ho the standard canal–channel–sluice-gate type of irrigation has developed. Irrigation works of the Ningsia area date back to the Ch'in dynasty (221 BC). Since the construction of the Tsingtung reservoir they are being extended and are now known as the 'Yellow River Irrigation System'. In addition to the 200 000 hectares of farmland fed by gravitational irrigation here, more than 12 000 hectares of arid upland have recently been brought into cultivation by pumping. The water is lifted between 5 and 15 m above the level of the supply canals. Previously well-digging had been tried and had failed because the high saline content of the underground water made it unsuitable for irrigation[10].

Another area on the Hwang-ho, developed mainly by the China International Famine Relief Commission in 1929, lies between Paotow, Saratsi and Hokowchen. This also is being greatly extended. Care has to be taken in all these areas that adequate water is available to prevent alkalization of the soil. There are some swampy parts where drainage, rather than irrigation, has to be undertaken.

Once away from the river and surface water, particularly on the northern slopes of the Hara Narin Ula and the Ying Shan, the type of water conservancy changes to well-digging and boring, which was carried on in a rather haphazard fashion until the late 1950s. Since the formation of the communes this well-digging has been more rational. In 1963 a team from Nanking University – the base from which Lossing Buck conducted his research in the early 1930s – consisting of several hundred geologists, geographers, biologists and meteorologists carried out a comprehensive survey of the Inner Mongolian grasslands. They found and tapped abundant water on the lava plateau, which will make possible the opening up of 200 000 sq km of arid grassland for stock-breeding[11]. Water conservancy of Inner Mongolia north of the highland rim is rightly being directed to the development of animal husbandry, which in many parts is losing its nomadic character.

Another fairly arid region where modern well-digging has been developed is in the loess of the Wei basin, Shensi. Here it is reported that 23 000 pump-operated wells, each capable of irrigating 100 *mow* (4 ha), have been opened on the plains and 160 deep wells in the hills. As a result 171 000 hectares are now under irrigation, representing 20 per cent of the cropland of the province[12].

Irrigation in hilly lands – The time-honoured method of irrigation, which has served the rice growers in the hills over the centuries, has been to build a retaining pond at the head of the valley and to lead the water down from terraced field to terraced field or to rely simply on a sufficiency

Plate 4   *Locally built Tungshen hydro-electric power-station, South China*
The quotations are from Mao Tse-tung's sayings. They read (horizontally):
We advocate regeneration through our own efforts.
We hope that there will be foreign aid, but we cannot count on it:
We rely on our own efforts, on the creative power of the army and the people.
(vertically):
To sail on the oceans one relies on the helmsman:
To make revolution one relies on Mao Tse-tung's thought.

of rain at the right time. This still remains true for very many parts, but the problem is now being attacked in two new ways.

The first method, and the one which is being used in most upland districts up to the present, has been possible only since communes have enabled the coordination of big, local labour teams. It is either to build a reservoir or tap the river high up in its course and to build a large main canal of considerable length. This canal is led around the contours of the hills and by aqueducts over valleys, disturbing water to the countryside en route. It is a method demanding both engineering skill and capital.

Two outstanding examples of this method may be quoted. The Red Flag Canal of Shansi[13] has received much publicity as an example of self-reliance. It is, in fact, a network of canals, based on the upper reaches of the Chang-ho. By means of three main canals of over 100 km in length it leads water through the mountainous region of the Tai-hang Shan and irrigates 22 000 hectares of dry upland. It has involved much tunnelling and bridging with innumerable aqueducts and culverts. Stone from the mountains has been used in preference to concrete in construction because it is cheaper and nearly all the work was done with human labour and simple tools. The total cost was 13 million yuan of which only 4·3 million was borne by the central authorities, the rest being found by the communes[14]. It was started in 1960 and completed in 1969.

The second example is that of the Shaoshan Irrigation System, built in Hunan in the region of Mao Tse-tung's childhood. This, again, is a hilly region subject to drought. Its main canal, which is 174 km long and some 30 m wide, has three large aqueducts, the longest of which is 530 m, and seven tunnels with a total length of 2·8 km. It is navigable for boats of 30 ton, serves for fish breeding, power generation and irrigates 66 000 hectares. It was built in 10 months and, like the Red Flag Canal, mainly manpower and small tools were used in its construction[15].

Recent experience in Szechwan has caused its engineers to turn away from these schemes of large canals. Up to 1955 reliance was placed on building nearly 10 000 small or medium ponds on the flat land and in the hills, but they proved unsatisfactory. Being small, they dried up quickly and water was not available when most needed. Moreover, they tended to occupy valuable arable land. Between 1955 and 1962 it was the policy to

build large reservoirs having good storage but this, in its turn, also proved unsatisfactory for it was found that the distribution of the water from the reservoirs was too difficult. Fields are widely scattered and the undulating land necessitates long canals. This led the Szechwanese to the conclusion that gravitational irrigation in hilly land was not viable. Therefore, in 1963, they turned to a third experiment which, it is claimed, is proving a success. The essence of the scheme is to build large numbers of small stone dams in rivulets and streams, holding back small reservoirs, larger and lower than the previous ponds. Water is then lifted by pumps from these reservoirs as required, the power being supplied by small hydro-electric stations, which abound in Szechwan. This method is styled 'the integration of pumping and storage ... with chief emphasis on electro–mechanical irrigation.'[16]

It is claimed that the small stone dams have the added advantages of controlling the flow of streams, thus serving the big hydro-electric plants. Moreover, they occupy stream beds rather than arable land as did the ponds. Finally the supporters of the experiment claim that it is much cheaper than canal irrigation even at its best: 'The average construction costs in terms of per *mow* of irrigated acreage, for the different kinds of principal water conservation installations are: reservoirs ¥. 51·70; ponds in hills and on plains ¥. 10·30; stone dams ¥. 8·50. For every 100 yuan of investment, the effective irrigated acreage is 1·93 *mow* in the case of reservoirs, 9·7 *mow* in the case of ponds, and 11·76 *mow* in the case of stone dams.'[16]

However, this experiment will have to be tried out for a much longer period before any useful generalization can be made, for Szechwan's topography and climate differ markedly from the rest of the country.

Irrigation on the plains – The method of watering the fields of the North China Plain, used over the centuries, has been that of well irrigation. Water has been raised from shallow brick or stone-lined wells by man or donkey power or by windmill and distributed by hand over the fields or through small channels, using 'dragon-backbone' treadles. All these are still widely used but are steadily being replaced by deeper wells, using asbestos, iron or cement pipes for lining. Over 1 million small tubewells of an average depth of 30–40 metres and of $1\frac{1}{2}$–2 cusec capacity have been dug on the North China Plain in the years since

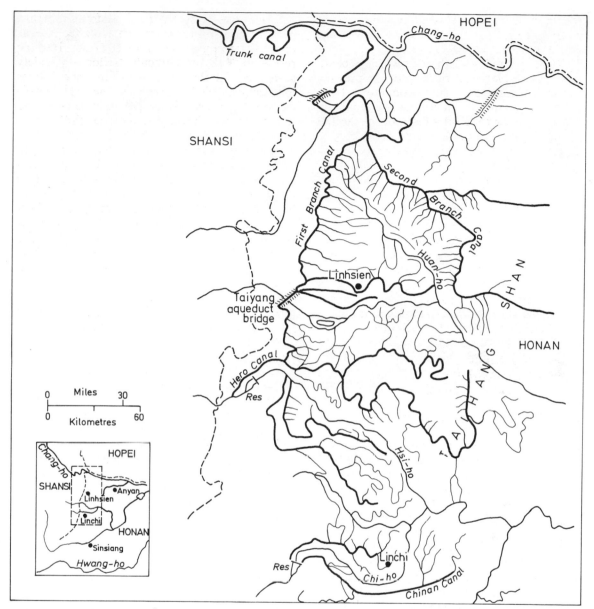

Fig. 44   The water conservation carried out in the Red Flag Canal scheme, Tailhang Shan, Hunan

1968[17]. More and more of the slow, hard manual work is being done, and done more efficiently, by small diesel or coal gas pumps.

An interesting experiment is being carried out along the lower reaches of the Hwang-ho where twenty syphon irrigation systems have been installed, introducing paddy-rice cultivation to the area for the first time. Taking advantage of the elevated level of the river bed, syphon pipes lift water from the river over the dykes to the surrounding fields. Irrigation and drainage here must be carefully coordinated if alkalization is to be avoided. Water, after use for irrigation, must be given an outlet otherwise the underground water level rises, leading to alkalization of the soil. Properly used, the syphoned water dilutes the

Plate 5   A typical small chemical fertilizer plant now common in most hsien throughout China

alkalis and frequent changes of water in the fields help to carry off the harmful salts. In the dry season when the water in the river is low, the system is reinforced by diesel or electrically-powered pumps. In the first large-scale attempt at rice growing in this way, 13 000 ha have been irrigated. This method has the advantage of being cheap and easy to install and requires no motive power to operate. It is thus well within the financial means of any production brigade[18].

Extensive areas of China's vast plains lie at such low levels that, during the rainy season, the water table is at the surface and liable to flood, while during the dry season growth may stop for lack of water. These areas, which comprise some of the most fertile land, need drainage and irrigation facilities if they are to produce to their fullest capacity.

The region, where these conditions are most clearly seen, is the Pearl river delta, a low-lying area subject to both flood and drought. Flooding occurs when the three rivers West, North and East are abnormally full in summer, and the situation

becomes really serious when this coincides with especially high tides in the estuary, occasioned, may be, by the presence or proximity of a typhoon. In the past, embankments and dykes have been built to meet these dangers. In the four years 1959–63 a big conservancy campaign was carried out. It included extensive dyke strengthening, the building of retention reservoirs and sluices, and the installation of 2600 electric pumping stations, generating 246 000 h.p., part of the duties of these being to keep the low-lying land drained during the five summer months when 80 per cent of the rain falls. This region lies within the tropics and has a twelve-month growing season provided adequate water is available. During the seven dry months the function of the pumping stations is reversed and irrigation is the order of the day[19]. The years 1963 and 1964 provided very severe tests of this new system. It stood up well first to the prolonged drought of 1963, when Hong Kong's water shortage was such that its inhabitants were rationed to four hours' water on each fourth day only. Then, in 1964, when Kwangtung ex-

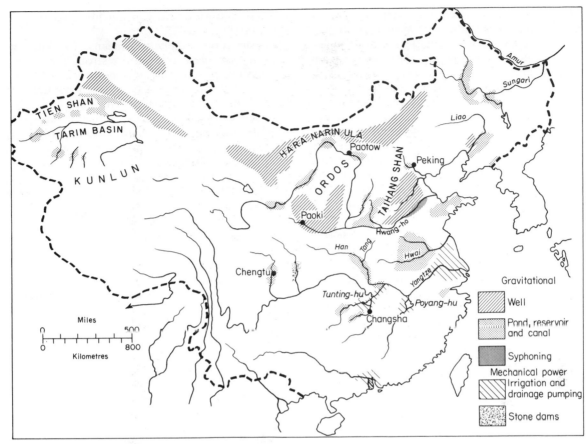

Fig. 45   Location of irrigation schemes cited in text

perienced its heaviest recorded rainfall, most of the fields were saved from disastrous flooding. It is estimated that 70 per cent of the 3·3 million hectares of rice-growing farmland in the area now have guaranteed irrigation and drainage facilities[20].

The Pearl river delta provides the best example of a powered irrigation and drainage network, but it is by no means the only area that has developed such a network. Kiangsu and Anhwei in the Yangtze delta provide very similar topographical conditions, as also do wide stretches of lowland around the Tungting-hu and Poyang-hu in Hunan, Hupeh and Kiangsi. In all these, extensive dyking has been reinforced by the ever-increasing reliance placed on either diesel or electrically-powered pumping. A great deal of use is being made of the small 8 h.p. diesel motor, which can easily be moved to the desired spot by manpower or by boat along the irrigation and drainage

channels. Hupeh farmers sing this song in praise of their 8 h.p. diesel motor:

> Four men carry our motor,
> To run it only one is needed.
> On the hillside or the plains,
> High or low our fields are watered.

Fertilizer (fei)

A great deal of land in China which is being farmed today has been under cultivation for some 2000 years. By great industry and careful adherence to traditional methods, fertility has been maintained fairly well over all these centuries. Admittedly the standard of return in terms of effort expended has been low and has tended to decrease during the last century as population and land hunger have increased.

Fertility has been maintained almost entirely by the application of organic matter, of which night soil, i.e. human excreta, has formed – and still forms – the preponderating part. Other in-gredients have been animal manure, mainly pig, composting of all waste matter, ashes, bones, feathers, mud from ponds and some green manure. The latter has not been widely used, especially in the densely-populated areas, as it entailed the use of land urgently and immediately needed to produce food.

Night soil, to be an effective manure, must be carefully maturized. Every village, every hamlet, virtually every household in the country had its *kang*, a huge earthenware container, let into the ground, for this purpose. Every morning from every town and city there emerged a long train of coolies carrying buckets of night soil into the country, an unpleasant, laborious and inefficient business as Giuseppe Regis points out. 'Given the very low average active fertilizer content of material used, viz from 15 to 45 times less than that of chemical fertilizer in the more common com-pounds, the labour involved in the collection, preparation, transport and spreading of these natural materials is enormous.'[20] Conversely, it must be remembered that the heavy summer rains lead to leaching. There is, therefore, some virtue in the repeated top dressing of night soil through-out the season as compared with the single annual dressing, much of which may be quickly leached into the subsoil. Moreover, this universally ac-cepted method of fertilization came under con-demnation as a great breeder of disease, causing greater loss than gain. Nevertheless, while com-munes are giving greater attention to more hy-gienic use of night soil, it remains the chief source of fertilizer. In a recent Peking article it was stated that 'if all night soil is fully utilized its fertilizing power will be equal to more than 10 million tons of ammonium sulphate'[21]. A recent nationwide soil survey reported that 80–96 per cent of the land was deficient in nitrogen, 40–55 per cent in phosphorus and 15–24 per cent in potash.

All the big Chinese cities are now developing modern sewage facilities but, as might be expected, only in conjunction with the use of the effluent on the land. This is a new field for Chinese scientists and therefore one fraught with some danger to health. In most instances, at present only the first step in the biological treatment of the sewage is done at the sewage plant, the effluent then being channelled direct to the rice fields instead of to ponds for oxidation. Industrial waste water, the disposal of which is assuming growing impor-tance, is required to undergo the necessary treat-ment in factories before being liberated for ir-rigation[22].

Pig breeding, largely as a means of producing manure, has been urged most strongly on pro-duction teams and individual peasants.

The value and importance of green manure has been stressed in recent years and now, with the development of the larger production units of brigades and teams, it is more possible of rational implementation. Milk vetch and cow vetch appear to be the most widely sown. They produce a very heavy crop of up to 70 ton/hectare in the south. They are especially effective when ploughed into acid, saline and sandy soils, giving much-needed organic matter. In north China sweet clover is sown in spring between rows of winter wheat and ploughed under after the summer wheat harvest. Sesbania, grown in parts of the Hwang-ho basin, serves as basic fertilizer for cotton. Throughout China there has been a spectacular increase in green manure crops, the area rising by 660 000 hectares in 1964 and 1·3 million hectares in 1965. In rice-growing Chekiang and Kiangsu, there is now on average 1 hectare of green manure crop to every 2 hectares of paddy fields, which, if supplemented with some chemical fertilizer and farmyard manure, provides sufficient basic fer-tilizer[23].

Production and use of chemical fertilizer re-ceived little attention before 1949[24]. With few exceptions, it was beyond the means and the know-how of the peasants. Before liberation, peak production was 230 000 tons in 1941. In 1949 only two chemical works at Nanking and Talien were functioning, producing some 20 000 tons of am-monium sulphate between them. By 1952 pro-duction had recovered nearly to the 1941 peak level. Under the First Five-year Plan (1952–7) three big plants were built at Kirin, Taiyuan and Lanchow, mainly with foreign equipment. The first and largest of these was at Kirin, which drew on the trained personnel throughout the country, proceeded to train its own workers, and thereafter to train for the rest of the country. It is reported that between 1958 and 1963 Kirin Chemical Company trained 23 000 skilled workers for a score or more chemical plants. Four more large factories at Shanghai, Kaifeng, Canton, and Chienchiang in Kweichow were added in 1963–4, bringing the total to seven large nitrogenous plants each with an annual capacity of over 100 000 tons. In the first half of 1965 a further dozen large or medium (10 000 tons p.a. capacity) factories were built, but these proved quite inadequate to meet the growing demand. In consequence, there was a countrywide building of small and medium-size plants. By 1964 they numbered over 150 and accounted for about 30 per cent of the total output of which about one-third was nitrogeneous and the rest phosphates[25]. The small plants range between 2000 and 5000 tons p.a. capacity, concentrating mainly on liquid ammonia production[26]. These small concerns came under criticism on account of their high production cost per unit. A synthetic ammonia plant with an annual output of 800 tons, enough to meet the needs of 13 000 hectares, can be built by a commune in 4–6 months, but its subsequent production costs amount to $163 per ton as compared with $74–$82 in large plants[27]. However, against this must be placed the saving in distribution and the relief to China's hard-pressed railway and road transport. With the big development of oil in the north, the emphasis there is now placed on large-scale plant, while the south and southwest still favour small plant production.

Plant at Tanyang, Kiangsu was built in 1965 for the specific purpose of making, by a new process, ammonium bicarbonate, which is claimed to be nearly as effective as ammonium sulphate and cheaper. Its virtues are that it does not acidify or harden the soil; its shortcomings that it evaporates and disintegrates quickly. Therefore it is not a satisfactory product for large-scale production at a big plant since it would require storage and long transport haulage. It is, however, eminently suitable for a small plant, which supplies local needs and is especially acceptable in south China for double-cropping paddy, where it is used as soon as manufactured[25].

China is now successfully producing urea. Shanghai has succeeded in making the quality of steel necessary to resist the high corrosion and pressures occasioned by the process. The first urea factory, the Wuching Chemical Works, Shanghai has a 36 m high tower for recovering carbon dioxide and has a big compressor. Its production is estimated at 350 000 tons p.a.

The production of chemical fertilizers is proving to be one of China's most successful industries and, possibly for this reason, quite good statistics and data are available. Production rose from 6·9 million tons in 1964 to 25 million tons in 1973 of which 11·5 million tons came from large plant and 13·5 million from small. Of these totals 4·9 million tons and 2 million tons were of nitrogen and phosphate respectively in 1964 and 14·61 and

10·39 million tons in 1973. The total rose to 30 million tons in 1974 and it is estimated that it will be 75 million tons in 1980.[28] Only a very small quantity of potassium is produced at present. So great is the present demand for fertilizer that, in spite of the massive increase in home production, imports continue to rise. In 1964–5 China imported 410 000 tons; since 1967 the figure annually has been over 4 million tons. Moreover, in 1973–4 contracts were made with foreign firms to build complete plant to the value of nearly $500 million.

Seed selection (chung)

Better seed selection is one of the most promising fields for the increase of agricultural production. The steadily decreasing yields per *mow*, which have been marked over the last century, have, in no small measure, been due to the poor strains from which the crops have been grown. This is not to say that the peasant has not been conscious of the advantages accruing to good seed. A common rural saying is 'One grain of superior seed, one thousand grains of good food', but, far more often than not, he has had Hobson's choice. He has had to take his seed from his own previous crop and seldom has he been able to hold back the best for next year's sowing. Moreover, opportunities for proper storage of seed have rarely been available. Prior to 1949 there had been some research and experimenting at a few centres, notably at the Agricultural College, University of Nanking, but in comparison with the size and needs of the country, these were entirely inadequate.

After 1949 the Chinese Academy of Agricultural Science and the Agricultural Scientific Research Institute were formed. The former now has branches in every province and from them has spread a network of some 1700 centres of seed breeding and seed propagation at *hsien*, commune, production brigade and even production team levels. As a result, it is claimed that new and rejuvenated strains have replaced the old over more than half the sown land of China.

Naturally the main work has been concerned with the five main grain crops, rice, wheat, maize, kaoliang and millet, together with soya beans and cotton. More recently it has extended to root crops and oil-bearing seeds. Experimenting in this field has been country-wide, often effectively at brigade and team level. A few examples will have to suffice to give some idea of the work that is being done. Reports seldom, if ever, are of controlled experiments and contain no record of the

Plate 6   The all-service light tractor, the production of which is now growing rapidly

accompanying degree of irrigation, amount of fertilizer, etc., but rather of the results after a new strain has been used and tested under normal conditions over a wide area.

Rice has probably received more attention than any other cereal. What is looked for is a high-yielding plant with low stalks, which are not easily bent by wind or rain, and one which tillers early for it is on this tillering that increase in the number of spikes or ears depends. Late tillering is worse than useless since it increases foliage without producing concomitant grain and merely restricts light. Different qualities are required for early and late crops in double-cropping, and again for late single-crop rice in the Yangtze valley, where it is in rotation with winter wheat or barley. A strain which has received great acclaim in Central China is known as 'Nung k'en 58', or by the farmers as 'three-eights' because of the claim that it yields 800 *catties/mow* (approx. 6·6 tons/hectare), 800 *catties* of straw/*mow* and 80 per cent greater yield than other strains[29]. It has a high tillering rate, resists lodging and withering, ripens five days earlier than its rival, 'Lao Lai Ching', and has the further virtues of being white and tasty and of greater volume when cooked. This is just one of dozens of strains being produced to meet the very varied climatic and soil conditions in which rice is now being grown.

Wheat is receiving only slightly less attention than rice. The main demands here are for seed which ripens quickly and is more resistant to disease. Two new and favoured strains are 'Neihsiang 5' and 'Heihsiang 36', named from the *hsien* in Honan in which they were developed. They have a high disease resistance and high yield, averaging 400 *catties/mow* (3 tons/hectare), which is the target set for north China in the Twelve-year Plan for Agriculture (see p. 104). Another strain, 'Taitzu No. 30', produced after several years of testing for farmers in Tsinghai, which is 2000 to 3000 m above sea level and has only 120 frostless days. This is a cross between the local, early ripening hardy strain and a later ripening, bigger yielding strain. It ripens in 104 days and thus commends itself to western regions, which have a short growing period.

Millet and kaoliang are both hardy crops, resistant to drought and disease. The main aim of the seed grower, therefore, is to increase the yield. Old strains, for the most part, produced only one ear per stalk. The new sorghum, 'Hsiung Yueh 253', it is claimed, is many-headed and yields 1000 *catties/mow* (approximately 8·2 tons/hectare).

Vigorous efforts to introduce hybrid maize throughout the country have so far met with only limited success. Although hybrid strains yield up to 30 per cent higher than ordinary maize, they do not breed true. It is necessary to produce double-cross seeds each year as the strain loses its hybrid vigour after the second year. U.S. hybrid seed has been tried but does not adapt well to Chinese conditions[30].

Mechanization (kung)

If the Chinese peasant of the 1940s could have been transported back 2000 years in time to the Han dynasty, he would have found his counterpart using much the same tools as himself. The hoe, the sickle and the iron-tipped plough were, and still are, the main instruments used on the land and of these the hoe figures most prominently. Further, apart from the fact that the hoe is made of iron instead of stone, it differs little from the main tool of his neolithic forebears. It is only since 1949 that a real revolution in agricultural tools in China has begun to take place.

Mechanization and the widespread use of better agricultural tools forms an essential part of the communist plan of socialist industrialization, as the following quotation from Mao shows:

> Only when socialist transformation of the social–economic system is complete and when, in the technical field, all branches of production and places wherein work can be done by machinery are using it, will the social and economic appearance of China be radically changed.... If, in a period of roughly three five-year plans, we cannot fundamentally solve the problem of agricultural cooperation, if we cannot jump from small-scale farming with animal-drawn farm implements to large-scale farming machinery... we shall fail to resolve the contradiction between the ever-increasing demand for marketable grain and industrial raw materials and the present generally poor yield of staple crops. In that case our socialist industrialization will run into formidable difficulties; we shall not be able to complete socialist industrialization.[31]

Later the CCP called for mechanization of agriculture in these rather cryptic terms: 'work for a minor solution within four years, get an intermediate solution within seven years and achieve a major solution within ten years'. These early calls for such rapid mechanization in agriculture were later muted.

It is possible to discern fairly well-marked steps in such progress as has been made towards mechanization since the People's Government came into being. The period from 1949 to 1952 was one of rehabilitation in which production was concentrated on small and traditional tools. Peasants had to make the best use they could of their old tools. During the First Five-year Plan (1952–7), when industrialization was getting under way and new factories were coming into production, 'walking on two legs' was the order of the day. Nearly all the new agricultural machinery produced went to the newly-formed state farms, while the developing cooperatives had to be content with semi-mechanization, the use of more and better hand and animal-drawn tools produced largely in the local hsien and coop. workshops. It was only after the farmers had pooled their land in the cooperatives that mechanization began to become viable. Then followed the Great Leap Forward (1958–9) during which there was a considerable increase in production of tractors, etc., only to be succeeded by two years of confusion or 'consolidation' in the industrial sphere. Between 1963 and 1970 industry was directed largely in the service of agriculture. Consequently all kinds of equipment from ploughs and carts to tractors, combines, bulldozers and irrigation pumps have become increasingly available, although in no way approaching satisfaction of the total needs of the countryside.

It is not surprising that it is in the northeast, northwest and on the North China Plain that mechanization has progressed most rapidly and most intensively for these are the regions which lend themselves best to large-scale farming and where the majority of state farms and larger combines are to be found. Farms in these regions have received priority as tractors and farming machinery have begun to come off the lines of the growing number of factories. No. 1 Tractor Works, Loyang was the first to come into production in 1958. Since then large tractor centres have been developed at Tientsin, Nanchang, Anshan, Shenyang, Hangchow and Wuhan[32].

In a country the size and complexity of China, a great variety of machines is necessary if the needs of the various parts are to be met. During the First Five-year Plan many models, mainly of the heavier type, were imported from the Soviet Union, Czechoslovakia, Hungary and Roumania. Since 1960, these imports have fallen steeply and China now looks almost entirely to its own factories for supply. In early years production was greatly handicapped by lack of the vast variety of different qualities of steel which go to the making of a tractor[33]. In consequence, the quality

of early models was not up to standard. The great efforts made in recent years in the steel industry to produce high-quality steel of all grades has resulted in marked improvement. There are now 13 different types of tractor in production in China, ranging from big 100 h.p. bulldozers down to small hand-pushed cultivators. Of these eight are specifically for agricultural use. The 'Hung Ch'i' (Red Flag) and 'Tungfanghung' (East is Red) are the most popular of the caterpillar type and are mass-produced. The 'Hung Ch'i' (100 h.p.) is the heaviest and is made in Anshan. It is used for the roughest work and is specially adapted for opening up virgin land in the Northeast. The 'Tungfanghung' (54 h.p.) is manufactured at No. 1 Tractor Plant, Loyang and is used for general, heavy farm work – ploughing, harrowing and combine harvesting. Three out of four of the four-wheel tractors are in mass production. They are the 'T'ieh Niu' (Iron Ox), 45 h.p., made in Tientsin; the versatile 28 h.p. 'Tungfanghung' (East is Red), which can be adapted for cotton and maize cultivation, is made at No. 1 Tractor Plant, Loyang and the 'Fengshou' (Bumper Harvest), 35 h.p., made at Hangchow. The fourth, 'Leap Forward', 20 h.p., is still in the experimental stage. Wuhan specializes in the production of a hand tractor, the 'Worker–Peasant' of 7 h.p., which is light and easy to operate. Because it is so manoeuvrable, it is especially suitable for terraced paddy fields and small plots. Canton has developed the 'Kweifeng 10', a 10 h.p. hand tractor, which is specifically built to deal with the hard-clay ricefields. With it the farmer can plough 1 hectare in 8 hours, at least five times as much as he can do with a water buffalo[34]. Shenyang is now producing a hand cultivator of 3 h.p.

In the Northeast, land of large-scale farming and state farms in 1966 it is claimed that one-third of the land was being ploughed by tractors and that the resulting produce per farmhand is many times greater than the communes still using traditional methods[35]. State farms accounted for 32 per cent of total tractors, 50 per cent mechanical farm tools, 82·5 per cent combines and 68 per cent motor cars for heavy-duty agricultural purposes[36]. In 1949 there were only 401 tractors in the whole country and these were all imported. In 1958 the figure was 45 330 and in 1966 it probably stood at over 200 000 with more than 2200 state tractor stations. However, in spite of this spectacular rise, it is a very long way from satisfying the country's needs. In a report in 1963 it was

Plate 7   Planting rice seedlings, Hainan, Kwangtung
The invention of this machine has eliminated much back-aching hand transplanting

estimated that there were 1300 million *mow* (approx. 87 million hectares) of land that could be worked by machines and that an annual output of 200 000 tractors (15 h.p. units) would be necessary to meet this need. It is hoped to achieve this output in 20–25 years[37]. In 1962 less than 10 per cent of China's ploughland was being worked by mechanical methods in the modern sense of the term. Only in recent years has sufficient attention been paid to the provision of machine spare parts, to the establishment of adequate repair shops and to the training of sufficient skilled personnel – an error common to nearly every country in the early stages of its industrial development.

For the most part, Chinese farmers have, to date, had to be content with what is termed semi-mechanization, which includes anything from rubber-tyred carts and barrows to animal-drawn drills, threshers and rice transplanters. From the point of view of total produce and numbers employed, of China's two agricultural 'legs', this semi-mechanized one is still far more important than the fully mechanized. A great deal of skill and ingenuity has gone into the invention and production of innumerable small agricultural implements. It is difficult to appreciate, without actually experiencing it, the advance achieved by so simple an innovation as the introduction of rubber tyres replacing the iron rims of the carts in the north, and the ball-bearing bicycle wheels, replacing the old wooden, squeaking wheels of the barrows of the south. Not only are they much more efficient, being so much easier to move, but also they do not furrow or rut the dirt paths and roads to the same extent. The old iron-tipped wooden plough has now largely been replaced by the modern plough, the share of which turns a deeper and better furrow than the old. In the Northeast, where crops are grown on ridges, which allow more earth to be exposed to the warmth of the sun, the new ploughs are modelled on the share and mould board of the British plough[38]. Man and animal-drawn five-row seeders or drills for flat land and three-row for hilly land, double-row wheat and cotton cultivators, hand threshing machines replacing old flailing methods, hand-pumped sprayers and fertilizer dressers are now being widely used and are being produced almost entirely at local *hsien* or commune workshops.

One of the most important of these semi-mechanical inventions has been the rice transplanter, which should, in time, eliminate the back-breaking toil of hand-transplanting of rice seedlings. The first of these machines, the 'Liling No. 2, Hunan', appeared in 1956. It is simple and can be made by any skilled carpenter. It has been succeeded by the 'Nan 105B, Nanking', which is more complicated, factory-made and animal-drawn. It is estimated that, by hand, one man can transplant half a *mow* with 15 000 clusters of seedlings in a day. Using the 'Liling' one man can transplant 3–4 *mow* and, using the 'Nan 105B' one man and one animal can transplant 30 *mow*. The first big rice-transplanter factory has now come into production. It makes the new 'Kwangsi-65' type, which thrusts five clusters of rice seedlings into the mud at a time and is adjustable[39]. A further advantage of these machines is that they speed up the work. Transplanting of rice from seed bed to paddy field should be done in a 10-day period. Delay leads to low yields, hence the tremendous pressure of work at these times[40].

In spite of all this activity, a vast amount of agricultural work is still being done with old, antiquated tools and complaints are heard that even these in some parts are in such short supply that some members of production teams are unable to earn the labour points of which they are capable through lack of these simple tools[41].

Plant production (pao)

It is quite impossible to estimate with any degree of accuracy the loss of production in China through pest and plant disease ravages but, throughout the centuries, it assuredly has been very great. In some locust-infested areas, for example, it has, at times, amounted to virtually the whole crop. At long last concerted efforts are being made to stop this breach in the production dyke. Scientific research and widespread education of the peasant are being brought to bear. Attack on the problem is being made on three main fronts: better methods of cultivation, which help to destroy the pests; increasing use of insecticides and fungicides; and the production of more disease-resistant strains.

The locust menace, which has so often ravaged the provinces of the north, is now being tackled with some vigour. The increasing availability of insecticides and the collectivization of the economy combine to make the attack more effective. Peasants in every commune in the most badly affected province, Honan, have had special training in locust control and every production team has the responsibility of reporting immediately any sign of infestation. The whole commune can then go promptly into action, dusting insecticides over large areas to kill nymphs and young locusts before they put on wings. Efforts are also being made to control the sandy, alkaline areas beside the Hwang-ho, where the locust winters[42].

Similarly, in the lower Yangtze provinces there has been a successful campaign against the water snail, but with this difference, that this is protection for the human beings and animals, who produce the food rather than protection of the plants themselves. The water snail is the host of the blood fluke, which causes schistosomiasis (snail fever), a debilitating disease. Where the fever has been eliminated, a big increase in agricultural produce and livestock breeding follows[43].

China, herself, is now producing a wide range of chemical insecticides and fungicides. Naturally, the greatest attention has been focused on the needs of the great staple crops and mention of two or three of these must serve to give some idea of the work being done.

The rice borer, which on average causes 15–20 per cent damage to the rice crop, is the main enemy in the Yangzte paddy lands. It has been found that thorough winter ploughing and weed clearing is effective, especially if this is reinforced by later spraying and the use of special lamps at night to attract the borer moths. The use of phosphorus fertilizer, promoting early maturity of the plant, helps to repel the borer[44].

Two new fungicides, *p*-amino benzene sulphonic acid and sodium *p*-amino benzene sulphonate, have been found effective in combating wheat rust in the north. These are both harmless to man and beast[45]. Nevertheless, the most effective remedy lies in the promotion of resistant strains.

Cotton throughout China is troubled by the red spider, which has developed a resistance to the phosphoric insecticides used until recently. Now tedion is being successfully used instead[46].

The red ant (tetramorium quineense falreijus), which is a natural predator on the sugar-cane borer, is now being systematically introduced in the southern cane-growing areas. It is also being introduced to combat maize, rice and sweet potato borers[47].

Another pest which causes much damage is the army worm, so called because the larvae assemble and migrate from field to field. It is also known among the southern farmers as the 'night thief' because of its night activities. The old peasant method of finding and destroying the eggs was not effective and has been replaced by dusting with 5 per cent DDT and 1 per cent powder[48].

These are but a few of the many instances of the growing interest in and use of modern methods of pest control. It will be many years yet, however, before supplies of insecticides are sufficient to meet the needs of the country or knowledge of their best use has spread universally.

Close planting and deep ploughing

The 'Eight-point' Charter calls for close planting and deep ploughing as a means of achieving greater output per *mow*. During the First Five-year Plan much experimenting was done in this field, the results of which led, for a time, to fanatical optimism, for the very high yields which could be obtained under laboratory conditions were given universal validity. For example, 5000 *chin* of winter wheat per *mow* were raised in North China by intensive, experimental methods on a few small plots. In the wild enthusiasm then obtaining, some planners jumped to the conclusion that this order of production could immediately be achieved throughout the country. Any idea of 'diminishing returns in agriculture' was ridiculed and 'the productive capacity of the land is unlimited' was affirmed[49]. On this basis the 'three-three' system of agriculture was proposed whereby the crop-growing area was actually to be reduced. One third of the land was to be under crops, one third to be afforested and one third to be left to lie fallow.

> If more than 10 per cent of the winter wheat fields planted this year will produce 5000 *chin/mow*, the sowing area of wheat may be duly reduced next year. If the per *mow* yield of grain crops can be universally raised to a level ranging between 3000 and 5000 *chin/mow*, the sowing area for grain can be reduced from 1800 million *mow* in the country to less than 600 *mow*.[49]

Note the disparity between this estimate and the targets of the Twelve-year Plan (p. 104). Happily more realistic and prudent councils quickly prevailed.

Close planting and inter-row planting were advocated, but its success clearly depends largely on the amount of fertilizer available and the quality of ploughing. The old Chinese plough seldom turned the earth to more than a depth of 100 mm. The new ploughs, provided adequate power is available, can turn a 200–250 mm furrow. Unfortunately, the too-quick and too-wide adoption of the Russian-type plough has not been a great success. Experience in south China has shown that light yellow oxen are not strong enough for this work. The Agricultural Development Programme called for deep ploughing to a depth of 250–600 mm, depending on the nature of the soil, to be carried out at intervals of 3 years. It was claimed that, by the end of 1958, 53 million ha had been so treated. However, Philips and Kuo[27], writing in 1961, stated: 'There are recent indications that the policy may be changing since it seems to be recognized that these techniques aid agricultural production only under certain conditions and that their over-emphasis may produce negative results.' Deep ploughing may be valuable in some instances in the south, where some plant food, lost through leaching, may be recovered. On the other hand, deep ploughing in the paddy lands may be disastrous if the iron pan, the thin impervious layer, which retains the water, is broken. Little is heard of deep ploughing today.

Field management (kuan)

Under this heading comparatively little has been written specifically of the 'Eight Points', possibly because it could be made to embrace nearly the whole gamut of agricultural production. Most of what should be included, such as the rotation of crops and the techniques of cultivation, receives some treatment in chapter 6 which deals with agricultural regions.

We have touched briefly on the efforts being made to wean the peasant from his reliance on the old Agricultural Calendar (see Fei Hsiao-tung, *'Peasant Life in China'*, pp. 146–8). Closely associated with this is the peasant's reluctance to abandon his cherished customs, festivals and superstitious beliefs, which, in the eyes of the planners, are obstacles to modern agricultural practice and must be eliminated as quickly as possible – a task that is proving by no means easy.

Under this heading there is a call for constant and greater frugality. 'Attention should be paid to acclaiming exemplary cases of being high cost conscious, of leading a frugal life, and of increasing savings and family accumulation of wealth.... All wedding and funeral ceremonies and other social parties should be held in the simplest manner in rural areas. An effort should be made to change all irrational customs and habits.'[50]

The 'ever-filled' granary in old China was a concept and a sign of good government. Today all communes and brigades are urged to have up to one-and-a-half years' reserve of grain for emergency use. A great difficulty in this connection is adequate storage. In the north, the grain is stored in great piles under matting. This is sufficient cover during the dry winter, but not in summer, nor does it give protection against the ravages of rodents, grain moth, mites and weevils which do great damage. Better granaries are being built and a new, aluminium phosphide fumigating agent is being widely used[51].

Partly as an application of communist educational theory of combining study with practice, partly to increase agricultural production, partly to meet the problem of shortage of schools and teachers, and partly to meet the demand for more qualified clerical personnel in the communes, there has been a great extension in rural areas of the work-study school, whereby boys and girls in middle schools divide their time between academic subjects and work in the fields. After the formation of the communes there was often a lack of clerical staff to carry out all the accountancy entailed in their complex activities. This is still, to some extent, a factor contributing to inadequate statistics. From below there was for some time constant complaint and criticism of bureaucratic demands for the completion of endless and needless forms.[52]

Forestry

Figure 19 shows most of China Proper and the Northeast with woodland cover. A line drawn from Yunnan to Heilungkiang effectively divides the country into two natural regions, the dry, treeless west and the wet, forested east. Even the cultivated plains of the east would largely be covered with trees if the land had no human occupation. But the map, useful in giving a reminder of natural conditions, gives quite a false picture of the forestry situation as it exists today.

When the Chinese began their expansion southwards from the largely treeless loess region in Ch'in (221–206 BC) and Han (206 BC–AD 220) times, they encountered the densely forested areas of the Chu and Yueh peoples in the lower Yangtze, described by Ssu-ma Ch'ien as 'a large territory, sparsely populated, where people eat rice and drink fish soup, where the land is tilled with fire [i.e. ladang cultivation] and hoed with water; where people collect fruits and shellfish for food'. These were lands where the arduous work of forest clearance had to be done before traditional cultivation could begin and these were the conditions which faced the colonists everywhere in their southward movement. Thus the forest was regarded as an enemy and this has coloured the Chinese farmer's attitude to woodland right down to the twentieth century. As population increased, so destruction of the wooded lands continued far beyond the needs of clearance for cultivation. The uplands have furnished him with fuel, first with wood from the trees and then with grass, which has replaced them, for, in spite of the widespread abundance of coal, these are the only fuels which will serve his brick cooking stoves. It is interesting to speculate on what the effects would have been had an acceptable coal-burning stove been introduced at some time in China's history. The farmer also burns off his hillsides in winter for the ash, which, in theory, is washed down to the cultivated fields below by the summer rains. The burning also provides better young fodder for his animals. Another reason advanced for the clearance of the hillsides, at least in the southern half of China, is that it deprives robbers and wild animals of cover; the latter certainly still do considerable damage to crops[53]. But these have been poor returns compared with the disastrous soil erosion which forest clearance has engendered.

The result of this deforestation over the centuries is that, instead of the 30 per cent tree cover, which, in the opinion of Soviet experts, is necessary for adequate climate and soil regulation, China has a mere 5 per cent. Su Ming[54] estimated that in 1950, of a total of 933 million hectares only 50 million hectares were forest land, or just over 5 per cent. Philip and Kuo placed it at 8 per cent and compared it with U.S.S.R. 33·9 per cent, U.S. 32·6 and India 21·6 per cent. Moreover, this remnant of forest is, for the most part, remote and inaccessible.

Afforestation

Since 1949 there have been serious and sustained efforts to promote afforestation in all parts of the country. It was realized that, if success were to be achieved in this field, the masses of peasants must be educated to appreciate the value of forests, that well-forested hills, by retaining water after heavy rain, prevent violent spate and so regulate the flow of the rivers, thus curbing flood, drought and soil erosion. In the drier west the value of the shelter belt in controlling wind and shifting sand had to be demonstrated.

Throughout the twentieth century realization of the importance of afforestation had been growing in informed circles. 'Arbor Day' was instituted and the value of trees taught in some schools. Once a year schoolchildren proceeded from school to the countryside, carrying young saplings, which they planted on the hillsides. Equally regularly each winter women, armed with their little bill-hooks, would emerge and strip the hills not only of their saplings but also grass and even roots in their search for fuel, thus vitiating any good that might have been done. Even if seedlings or saplings escaped this treatment, their chances of survival were minimal, since seldom was any after-care expended on them. With this experience in mind afforestation authorities have attempted mass education on the techniques of tree planting and after-care.

The division of the ownership of land into small plots is inimical to good forestry, which usually flourishes under large ownership. Prior to 1949, uncultivated areas adjacent to villages were regarded as belonging to the village generally, although there was no legal ownership. Consequently there was rarely much sense of responsibility. Chances of successful afforestation have been greatly enhanced by the joint ownership of land, which has come with the cooperatives and the communes. However, the following extract shows that the problem of ownership and care still demands attention:

> Party committees of all levels should correctly solve concrete problems peculiar to different localities according to Party policies and local conditions, and more properly arouse the enthusiasm of various quarters for afforestation. The main concern should be the correct handling of the problem of ownership in the collective economy. Today, there still exist some wasteland, sandland, grassland, and morasses between *hsien*, communes, and brigades whose ownership remains to be determined, with the result that, when afforestation is carried out, these areas are often unattended. In these types of areas, ownership should be promptly determined so as to insure rational benefits from afforestation. In the people's commune, too, decision should be taken as to what belongs to the communes, brigades, or production teams. In the meantime, commune members should be encouraged to plant trees in front and in the rear of their houses. A clear announcement should be made to the effect that whoever plants the trees will own them. In this way, the problem of firewood for commune members can be partially solved, the need for a small quantity of timber for the use of the family can be met, and the economic income of the commune members can be increased. The determination of forest ownership is an important problem in forest development.[55]

Afforestation planning presents a further example of 'walking on two legs'. On the one hand, great shelter belts of 1000 km and more in length have been grown in the north, at the instigation of the central authorities. On the other hand, 'round-the-village forest belts' have been urged on all localities. To carry out this work thousands of seed nurseries have been established throughout the country and every spring concerted drives, involving hundreds of thousands of mainly young persons, have resulted in the planting of vast areas with trees. The altruistic and patriotic element in this work has made a considerable appeal to the youth of the country. In this way it is estimated that 3·7 million ha were planted between 1949 and 1957 and it was planned that 2·6 times this amount would be added between 1957 and 1967[27]. Between 1954 and 1958 nearly 40 million ha were surveyed for forestry purposes, about half by ground methods and half by aerial survey. In spite of all the work done to date, it had raised the forest cover to only about 10 per cent of the whole by 1966, and forestry is still regarded as a weak link in the national economy[56].

The main areas in which afforestation has been effective are:

1. *The Northeast.* Since 1953 a reported 946 000 hectares have been afforested in this region, mainly in the Ta Hingan and Siao Hingan, along which line a shelter belt of poplar, willow and sugar maple, known as a 'Great Green Wall'; 1600 km was completed by 1958. Along these mountain slopes 300 nurseries, raising mainly Korean pine, Scots pine, hardy poplar and Manchurian ash, have been established. The long, cold winter restricts the planting period to only one month from mid-April. More than 60 per cent of China's felled timber comes from this region. The industry, which is now well mechanized, employs 40 000 full-time forestry workers, who felled and replanted 133 000 hectares in 1965[57].

2. *North China Plain.* A great deal of planting has been done along the dykes of the Hwang-ho, helping to strengthen them, and over the sandy wastes left by earlier flooding, helping to bind the shifting sands and reclaim the land for cultivation. Here the shelter belts are generally grown in a rectangular, criss-cross pattern.

3. *Loess Region.* In this region of natural grass and scrub, efforts are being made to grow Chinese fir, poplar and Himalayan cedar. Trees here need careful planting and early attention, but once established they thrive. In the neighbouring Yinchwan region of Ningsia Autonomous Region, which is known as the 'silvery land' on account of the alkali salts which form a glittering layer, 15 afforestation centres have been opened and considerable progress made, particularly in the towns, where streets are now tree-lined with aspen, weeping willow and Chinese wax trees, and in the irrigated areas, where spruce, golden larch, fast-growing oleaster, elms and poplars are grown.

4. *Inner Mongolia and Sinkiang.* Here state farms are stated to have planted 14 700 hectares between 1950 and 1964. The belts, 3–5 trees deep, skirt the farms and fields, line the sand dunes, irrigation canals and roads. The trees are now 12–15 m high and observers report a reduction of wind velocity of 27–40 per cent, evaporation reduction of 20–25 per cent, and effective protection of crops within a distance of 250–300 m[58]. Similar work is being done by the communes which occupy the oases around the Takla Makan desert and the northern slopes of the T'ien Shan.

5. *Szechwan.* The Red Basin, whose natural cover is rich and very varied forest, suffered severe deforestation during the Sino–Japanese War (1937–45). This has now, to some extent, been remedied. Reports state that around Chengtu and Penki, 10 million mulberry trees have been planted along the roads, rivers, canals and fields. With the building of the Chengtu–Paoki railway and the improvement of road communications, the vast and formerly inaccessible forests of north Szechwan have been opened for development. The forests here are of great variety, providing timber for many industries such as shipbuilding, musical instruments, sports equipment, fine furniture, etc. The new timber industry is being mechanized with funicular railways, cranes, and powered saws[59].

6. *Central China.* The forests of Hunan, Hupeh and Kiangsi received particularly rough treatment during the long troubled years of revolution, civil war and Japanese invasion during the first half of the twentieth century. The forests of west Hunan and west Hupeh, chief source of timber for the lower Yangtze basin, were severely exploited with comparatively little re-afforestation after felling. This, to some degree, has been remedied since 'Liberation'.

7. *South China.* On the hills, which form so large a part of south China, there has been much planting of tung oil, tea oil, Chinese chestnut, together with bamboo and many kinds of fruit. Along the sandy coast, coconut palms have been raised to help in anchoring the dunes. There has been some experimenting in the aerial sowing of pine seeds both here and in Kweichow[60].

Some indication of the progress in afforestation, which has been made in this region, is the emphasis which is now being made on the necessity for making fire lanes and taking fire precautions.

References

1 'In Yangtan People's Commune', *Peking Review*, no. 10 (March 1966).
2 NCNA, Hofei, 3 May 1966.
3 I. Lossing Buck, *Land Utilization in China* (Shanghai, 1937).
4 Han Su-yin, op. cit., pp. 34–5.
5 Sun Ching-chih (ed.), *Economic Geography of Northeast China* (Peking, 1959).
6 NCNA, Sining, 26 April 1966.
7 *Peking Jen-min Jih-pao*, 9 September 1965.
8 O. Lattimore, *Geographical Journal*, **110**, nos 4–6 (1947), p. 180.
9 NCNA, Urumchi, 31 October 1964.
10 NCNA, Yinchuan, 1 September 1965.
11 NCNA, Nanking, 14 June 1965.
12 NCNA, Sian, 10 September 1965.
13 *Red Flag Canal* (Peking, 1975).
14 *Peking Jen-min Jih-pao*, 21 April 1966.
15 *China Reconstructs*, August 1966; *NCNA*, Changsha, 5 August 1966.
16 Kuo Te-tsun, 'An investigation into the construction of small stone dams in Tzuehung Hsien', *Ching-chi Yen-chiu* [*Economic Research*], no. 7 (July 1965).
17 D. H. Perkins, 'A conference on agriculture', *China Quarterly*, no. 67 (July 1976).
18 *Peking Review*, no. 27 (2 July 1965).
19 Su Tsung-sung, 'Irrigation renews the land', *China Reconstructs*, November 1964.
20 NCNA, Canton, 17 October 1964.
21 Giuseppe Regis, 'Developments in Chinese agriculture', *Far Eastern Trade*, January 1962; *Peking Jen-min Jih-pao*, 5 November 1965.
22 *K'o-hsueh Ting-pao* [*Science Journal*], no. 2 (17 February 1965).
23 NCNA, Peking, 5 June 1965.
24 *Liu Jung-chao*, 'Fertilizer application in Communist China', *China Quarterly*, no. 24 (October 1965).
25 Kao Kuang-chien, 'Great strides forward in fertilizers', *China Reconstructs*, February 1965.
26 Colina MacDougall, 'Industrial upsurge', *Far Eastern Economic Review*, 30 September 1965.
27 R. W. Philip and L. T. C. Kuo, 'Agricultural science and its application', *China Quarterly*, no. 6 (April 1961).
28 Kang Chao, 'The production and application of chemical fertilizers in China', *China Quarterly*, no. 64 (October 1975).
29 Li Mei-sen and Yeh Ch'ao-lin, 'Superior strains', *Chung Kuo Ching-nein* [*China Youth*], no. 8 (April 1965).
30 NCNA, Chengtu, 27 November 1965.
31 Mao Tse-tung, *The Question of Agricultural Co-operation* (Peking, 1956), p. 34.
32 *Far East Trade*, **21**, no. 1 (July 1966).
33 L. T. C. Kuo, 'Agricultural mechanization in China', *China Quarterly*, no. 17 (January 1964).
34 NCNA, Canton, 1 June 1966.
35 NCNA, Peking, 31 January 1966.
36 Shang Chih-ling and Mu Ching-p'o, 'Fifteen years of agricultural mechanization of state farms', *Technology and Agricultural Machinery*, no. 11 (Peking 1964).
37 Chun Wen, 'China's farm machine-building industry', *Peking Review*, no. 26 (July 1963).
38 Ching Tan, 'Machinery especially for Chinese farms', *China Reconstructs*, August 1964.
39 NCNA, Nanning, 14 November 1965.
40 Yang Min, 'Mechanizing rice planting', *Peking Review*, 5 July 1963.
41 *Lung-ts'an Chin-jung* [*Rural Finance*], no. 10 (21 May 1965).
42 NCNA, Chengchow, 23 October 1965.
43 NCNA, Nanchang, 20 October 1965.
44 NCNA, Changsha, 16 May 1965.
45 NCNA, Peking, 20 October 1965.
46 NCNA, Wuhan, 20 October 1965.
47 NCNA, Foochow, 20 July 1965.
48 *China Reconstructs*, 18 May 1965.
49 *Peking Review*, no. 42 (1958), pp. 12–13.
50 *National Agricultural Development Programme* (1956–67).
51 NCNA, Shenyang, 7 June 1965.
52 P'an Ling, 'What should we do with too many reports and forms?' *Nan-fang Jih-pao*, 5 June 1964.
53 G. Fenzel, op. cit.
54 Su Ming, 'Forestry in New China', *Jen-min Tsung-pao*, 16 November 1950.
55 'Make an early preparation for Developing the afforestation movement', editorial, *People's Daily*, Peking, 15 December 1964.
56 *People's Daily*, Peking, 6 February 1966.
57 NCNA, Harbin, 10 June 1965.
58 NCNA, Urumchi, 21 January 1965.
59 NCNA, Peking, 18 December 1965.
60 NCNA, Kweiyang, 29 May 1965.

6   Agricultural Regions

Differences of altitude and rainfall combine to divide China into two parts which are not far from equal in area. To the north and west lie the great plateau lands of Tibet, Inner Mongolia and Sinkiang, the eastern boundary of which roughly marks the 375 mm isohyet. Lands to the west become progressively drier and lands to the east progressively wetter. This isohyet also approximates quite closely with the Great Wall which divided 'China Proper' of the eighteen provinces from the outlying imperial lands; the China of the *Han Jen*, the Men of the Han or true Chinese from the barbarians of the outer regions. When Ch'in Shih Hwang Ti (221–206 BC) built this wall, his object was not only to check the entry of the barbarians into China, but also to dissuade the Chinese frontiersmen from moving outside, for this meant passing from a settled, agricultural economy into a nomadic, pastoral way of life. Thus, our first big division is one which stretches across the entire land from southwest to northeast, separating pastoral from arable farming.

The arable region itself can be divided into two almost equal parts by a line running from west to east from the Nan Shan in Kansu, through the Tsinling Shan and Funiu Shan to the sea. This is a line of great geographical significance. It divides the geologically older north from the younger south; climatically the north is drier and colder than the south; northern soils are alkaline in contrast to the acid soils of the south; dry farming, with comparatively little irrigation, producing wheat and millet, contrasts strongly with the wet rice paddy which is general in the south. Even the people show different characteristics. Generally speaking, the Han Jen of the north are taller, slower and more phlegmatic than the shorter, volatile T'ang Jen of the south.

The further subdivision of these arable lands has followed quite closely those made by Lossing Buck in his *Land Utilization in China* on the basis of the outstanding crop or crops of the area, which will serve as a focal point for detailed discussion of all the agricultural activities of the district. Most of these areas are larger than the British Isles and consequently have considerable variety within their borders.

PASTORAL FARMING

The grasslands of the northwest, which support the pastoral activities, occupy about two-fifths of China's territory. Big differences of altitude, climate and topography are responsible for great variations in type and productivity. These grasslands stretch from eastern Inner Mongolia to the Pamirs in west Sinkiang and from the U.S.S.R. border at Altai to the Indian border at Lhasa. Large areas, such as the Takla Makan, are pure desert and are without population, but the greater part of the region is steppeland, and can be divided into four zones, which, although they have a common grassland denominator, vary considerably in character[1].

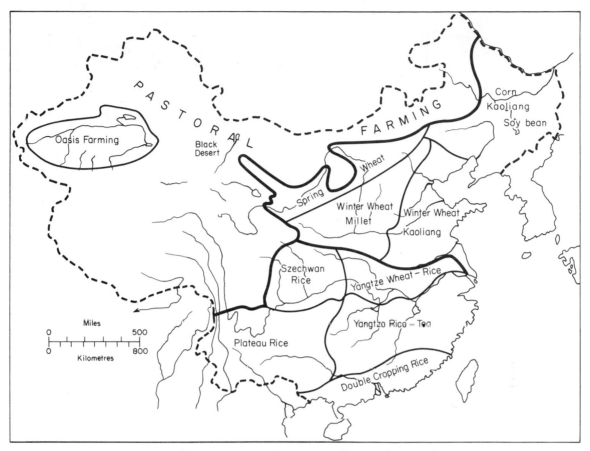

Fig. 46   Agricultural regions (After Lossing Buck)

1. Easter Inner Mongolia and Heilungkiang on the east-facing slopes of the Ta Hingan Shan. These are the most luxuriant of the pastures, lying on the wetter, eastern-facing slopes of the mountains and receiving some effect of the summer southeast monsoon.

2. The Inner Mongolian high plain, lying north of the Yin Shan, Hara Narin Ula and the Kansu Corridor. This land is undulating; its winters are longer and colder and it is more arid than eastern Inner Mongolia. It is estimated to contain 860 000 sq km of grassland, of which less than half is used on account of aridity. It becomes progressively less productive from east to west.

3. Sinkiang contains a considerable proportion of true desert, notably the Takla Makan and parts of central Dzungaria. Over 60 per cent is, in fact, virtually uninhabited. The best grasslands lie on the mountain sides of the Kunlun and Tien Shan

above the ring of oases, which surround the Tarim basin, in the Ili valley and around the Dzungarian basin, especially on the northern slopes of the Tien Shan and Altai Shan.

4. The Tibetan Plateau as a whole is too frigid and too arid to bear much good grass. There is some good pasture in the eastern part of Tsinghai, but it becomes progressively poorer as the country becomes higher, rockier, drier and more desolate in the west. Pasture is also good in southeast Tibet around Lhasa.

From earliest times the mode of life in these grasslands has been basically nomadic. It has varied largely in response to the quality of grass and the availability of water. Generally speaking, the more arid the land the greater has been the movement, the group or tribe sometimes moving 10–20 times in a year over distances of 150–200 km. As might be expected, the nearer the approach

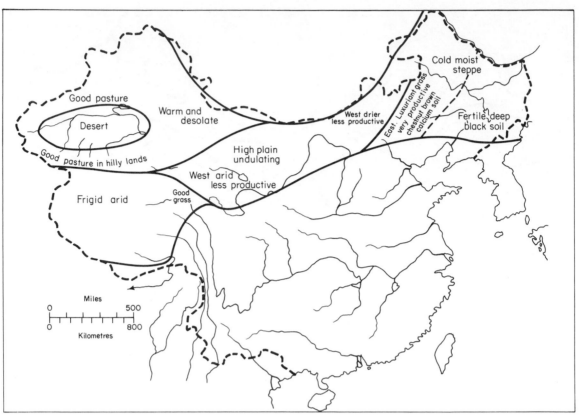

Fig. 47   Grasslands of the north

to settled communities, as, for example, along the elongated oases of the northern bend of the Hwang-ho, the less nomadic has been the way of life and a traditional zone of semi-pastoralist, semi-arable farmer is to be found.

Until recently most of these lands have been occupied by leagues and 'banners' (or companies) owning only tribal allegiance. Law and order and the rule of a central government have been lacking. There was considerable banditry and cattle rustling[2]. In consequence, the use of the pasture has generally been wanton and competitive leading to overgrazing and deterioration. Both winter feed and winter shelter have been inadequate, resulting in disease and the ravages of predators, notably wolves. Animal husbandry has been primitive, conservative and backward. Thus annual losses have always been very great and population of men and animals has tended to remain stationary.

With 'Liberation' in 1949, some measure of central control over these vast outlying areas began to be possible. Old tribal sovereignty has been abolished. Boundaries of territory have been established and the rights of use of land have been fixed with a view to eliminating unplanned and reckless grazing, and the reduction of friction. Old league and banner organizations have been retained alongside the coming of cooperatives and communes. These reforms were a necessary first step towards achieving, as in the U.S.S.R., the general aim of a planned and settled pastoralism instead of nomadism, and also the promotion of much greater animal productivity. Even so, the idea that the pastures are very wide and that it does not matter whether their use is fixed or not, dies hard.

To open up the grasslands properly and scientifically, comprehensive surveys must be carried out in the hydrographic, geological, ecological and pedological fields. Already much work has been carried out over wide areas. A large research centre, covering all aspects of pastoral life and including the Chinese Grassland Research Institute of Zoology and the Institute of Botany, has been established in Inner Mongolia and is doing valuable work[3]. During the years 1950–65 much effort has been expended on convincing the pastoralists of the value of careful grazing. Seasonal and rotational grazing has been used in a rough way by herdsmen for a long time. It now needs mapping and planning so that pastures may be closed and the grasses properly nursed, to allow them to tiller and seed. The Icechao League of Inner Mongolia now closes specified parts of its pastureland regularly between May and August[1].

Great attention has naturally been focused on increasing water supply. Surveys have revealed wide areas, particularly in Inner Mongolia, that have abundant underground water, which is being increasingly tapped by the sinking of thousands of wells. Between 1949 and 1963 it was reported that more than 20 000 wells were sunk in Inner Mongolia alone. These include 100, some 100 m deep, equipped with power pumping machinery[4]. Drinking water for human beings and herds is now much more plentiful; in many areas water is available for the irrigation of fodder crops (clover), for green manure and for the afforestation of dunes by growing artemisia and other drought-resisting plants and trees, so regenerating failing pastures[5]. The Ala Shan Left Banner, occupying a notoriously dry area with no rivers, reports that it has sunk 2200 new wells and tapped 380 springs, thus converting 8900 sq km of dry grassland into good pasture and enabling the communes to grow fodder crops of clover.

Much of the best pasture in Sinkiang is high up in the mountains of the Kunlun, Tien Shan and Altai. In the Kunlun rich grasses lie above the loess-covered moraines of the lower slopes. Here and on the north and south slopes of the Tien Shan the pastures are fed by the melting snows from above. In Dzungaria the influence of Siberia is greater than in the Tarim; snowfall is greater and rainfall increases with altitude. In the Altai a belt of steppe lies above an expanse of desert and semi-desert. Above the grasslands is a belt of forest, composed largely of Siberian larch and white birch, whose bark is useful in souring milk. This is a great hunting area (wolf, fox, sable, ermine, bears and wolverines). Above the forests are the alpine meadows on which the famous Altai horses are bred. The Ulyungui Nor and the Irtish river abound in fish and waterfowl. With the improvement in communications these are beginning to be exploited commercially.

Sheep and goats, roughly in equal proportions, are by far the most important, the most ubiquitous and most numerous animals reared on the grasslands. Cattle, horses and camels follow in that order, and these are more specialized territorially. In addition to the Altai horses mentioned above, the Ili valley is famous for its fine breed of 'San-ho' horses, which are very hardy and strong and are reputed to be able to travel 30–40 km/day for days on end. Bactrian camels are reared in large numbers in the Kansu Corridor, a region which grows an abundance of shrubs and wild plants relished by camels. It is reported that there are now more than 40 000 camels in this area[6].

There is a sharp differentiation of numbers, kinds and distribution of animals between the true pastoral zone and the semi-pastoral, semi-arable zones. Pastoral regions rear only sheep, goats, cattle, horses and camels. Semi-pastoral, semi-arable regions have a much smaller proportion of sheep and a considerable number of pigs, together with some donkeys and mules.

There are no comprehensive figures of animal population for the whole of the pastoral region, but there can be no doubt that, over the last twenty years, numbers have increased enormously, so much so that warnings against blindly doing so have been issued. In 1946 it was estimated that there were 8 million head of livestock in Inner Mongolia. In 1962 the figure stood at 32 million[8]. In 1965 it was reported that 11·26 million head of young animals had been added during the breeding season, bringing the estimated total to 40 million head. Tibet was estimated to hold 10 million head, an increase of 600 000 over 1964. This figure probably includes the 3·6 million lambs reported to have been born in 1965 in Tsinghai[9].

There are several reasons for this rapid increase

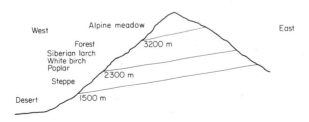

Fig. 48   Section of Dzungaria and Altai Shan

of stock. Apart from the great improvement in water facilities and the increased storage of winter forage, far greater care is now being expended on the animals themselves. Paddocks and sheds, giving shelter against winter blizzards – the great killer – are now widespread. The dipping of animals and injections are cutting down the incidence of disease. Many women have been trained to serve with the mobile veterinary units, which move over the steppeland, fulfilling a valuable educational function in animal husbandry.

The experimenting in and introduction of new breeds is having a profound effect on the life, not only of the pastoral people, but also on those of the settled regions of Sinkiang and Inner Mongolia. In Sinkiang, the development of the first fine-wool breed of sheep, the *gungnais*, was started in 1954, producing a large animal giving delicious mutton, a high propagation rate, adaptability to differing natural conditions and a high-grade wool. This latter quality is forming the basis of a rapidly developing indigenous woollen industry. The introduction of Romney Marsh and Lincoln

Distribution of Livestock, Inner Mongolia[7]

	Sheep & goats	Cattle	Horses	Camels	Pigs	Donkeys	Mules
	%	%	%	%	%	%	%
Pastoral zone	81·1	13·8	4·1	1·0	—	—	—
Agric. & agric./ pastoral zone	58·9	19·4	2·8	0·1	13·3	5·0	0·5

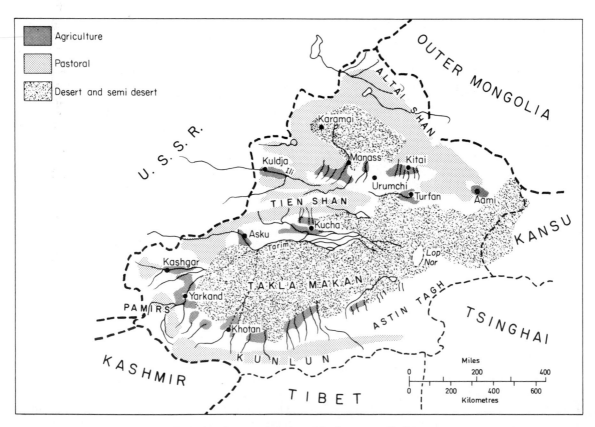

Fig 49   Pastoral and arable farming. Sinkiang.

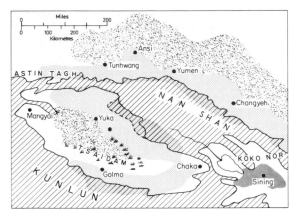

Fig. 50   Pastoral and arable farming, Tsinghai

Long-wool pedigree sheep into Inner Mongolia, has, among other things, resulted in the increase of the yield of wool per sheep to 3 kg, about five times the previous yield. There are now several million head of this breed[10].

Similarly, in the sphere of cattle breeding, the crossing of short-horned bulls with local cows through artificial insemination has resulted in a big increase in beef and a threefold increase in milk yield. Crossing Heilungkiang cows with Puichow bulls has achieved a rise in average milk yield from 553·5 kg during the period of lactation to 2705·5 kg in the fourth generation. By 1965 in Inner Mongolia, 2500 women had been trained in animal artificial insemination[10]. In Tsinghai experimental farms have been established, attempting the domestication of wild animals, including deer, whose antlers are the source of drugs used in traditional Chinese medicine. The cross-breeding of the domesticated Tibetan sheep with the hardy, wild breed (*ovis ammon dotvina*) and the domesticated yak with the wild yak are two experiments which are proving successful[11].

As a result of the big increase in milk, reports state that Inner Mongolia now has 17 major milk-processing factories, producing powdered and condensed milk, butter, lactose and cheese, and an increasing number of meat-canning factories[12].

Mechanization in the pastoral areas is still in its initial stages. Pumps for wells, and shearing machines are steadily being introduced. Horse-drawn forage harvesters and rakes are now widely used in the better pastures and in large communes; where the supply of water is such that extensive forage crops are grown, tractors are in use[13].

Nevertheless, the National Livestock Breeding Conference, 1965, while reporting an increase of 10 million head of improved breeds, stated that 'compared with farming of the land . . . the breeding of large animals is still a weak link in agriculture'[14]. Draught animals are in short supply and are still urgently needed throughout China.

Within this vast region of pastoralism or emptiness lie a few pockets of settlement, most of which have been in existence for twenty centuries or more. They are, with few exceptions, oases situated in the more arid parts of the area.

Most notable is the ring of oases in the Tarim Basin, which surround the Takla Makan. They lie at the foot of the Kunlun, Astin Tagh and Tien Shan, which enfold the basin. Each oasis is sited on a river descending from the snow and ice fields above and at a point below the piedmont gravel, which the river has deposited as it fanned out onto the plain. Thence the river continues for varying distances until it is lost in the desert. Such are the sites of Charchan, Keriya, Khotan, Yarkand, Kashgar, Aksu and Kucha, cities through which the Imperial Silk Route and Imperial Highway passed in the days of the Han dynasty (206 BC–AD 220) ascendancy. They existed then, as they still do today, solely by virtue of the water supply from the snow-capped mountains above and are surrounded by inhospitable desert. Farther north, on the northern slopes of the Tien Shan and Bogdo Ula, there were small settlements on the steppeland at Urumchi, Kitai and Manass, ports of call on the caravan route to the Dzungarian Gate.

It is these settled centres and the regions immediately around them that have undergone so great a change since 1949. The census of 1953 showed Sinkiang as having a population of 4·874 million, of which 4·918 million were Turkic and only 300 000 Han Chinese. Of the Turkic people, 3·64 million were Uighurs and 475 000 Kazakhs. There are smaller numbers of Kirghiz, Mongols and Huis. In 1964 the Uighur population was given as 4 million. The Han population was stated to have risen to 2·6 million, an average increase of 255 000 a year, due largely to immigration[15].

This enormous influx of Chinese is located largely in Dzungaria in and near the old settlements and new towns along the northern slopes of the Tien Shan and Bogdo Ula. This immigration is the result of a set government policy, which has two main aims. One aim is to sinicize this outlying

Plate 8   Pastoral farming in Naitung valley, southeast Tibet

region, which is essentially Moslem in religion
and culture, and so make more secure a weak
frontier. The other aim is the opening of a
promising outlet for China's ever-growing population. Given modern engineering and technological resources, this is a region which is capable
of great development in spite of its aridity and
extremes of climate. Schomberg in 1932 estimated
that from one-third to one-half of Sinkiang's
water ran to waste and that, with proper conservation, it could irrigate up to 8 million hectares of
barren land.

When the civil war came to an end in 1949, the
large contingents of the People's Liberation Army
(PLA), stationed in Sinkiang and deeply steeped
in revolutionary ideas, were converted into a
Production and Construction Corps. Ever since, it
has devoted its energies and skills to all kinds of
reclamation and construction work, including big

projects of water conservation, reclamation of
saline lands, the establishment of state farms and
communes, afforestation and the building of railways and highways. As the projects have been
completed, large numbers of the Corps have been
demobilized and have settled on the farms or in
the new towns and factories, which they have
built. Their places have been taken by a constant
flow of recruits to the PLA and school leavers
(15–22 years) from China Proper who volunteer
for 3 years' service in the area[16]. It is claimed that
this Corps alone has reclaimed more than 10
million *mow* of virgin land, has established over
100 state farms and built many complete systems
of industry[17]. It is difficult to arrive at an accurate
assessment of what has been accomplished in the
settled areas in the years since 1949 as reports are
often confused and confusing, but there can be no
doubt that a great deal has been achieved and

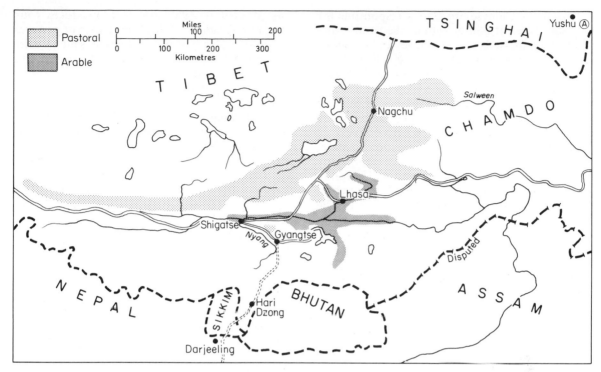

Fig. 51   Pastoral and arable land, southeast Tibet

revolutionary changes have taken place in the agricultural and industrial fields.

Because of the preponderant Turkic composition of the people of Sinkiang and the independent nature of the Uighur people, the formation of cooperatives and communes has been introduced with some circumspection. Great care was taken to reassure the pastoralists that their means of subsistence, i.e. yurts, personal belongings such as utensils, rugs, saddles and trappings for horses, together with a sufficient number of horses for transport, would remain in their private ownership[16]. Whether this reassurance will ultimately carry conviction and achieve conversion of the Uighurs to the new way of life, time alone will tell. Nevertheless, communes now appear to be the universal pattern of rural organization. Roughly a twofold development can be distinguished: the extension of old, existing oases in the periphery of the Tarim Basin in which the Uighurs predominate and the establishment of new towns and villages on the northern slopes of the Tien Shan where the people are mainly Chinese.

By utilizing the waters from the many rivers from the Kunlun, by building reservoirs and constructing thousands of kilometres of canals, the old oases of Keriya, Khotan, Yarkand and Kashgar have been expanded beyond recognition. They have pushed northward into the desert and extended laterally east and west, filling much of the empty desert space which formerly separated them. Along this southern edge of the Tarim Basin 42 new oases have been established, opening up 53 000 hectares (approx. 800 000 *mow*) to new cultivation. Around Khotan alone 40 new villages have been set up by 45 communes[15]. The old towns have developed modern industries and now have the amenities of modern cities. Kashgar, which had a population of 30 000 in 1949, is now a city of over 100 000. Freeberne[15] quotes the following description of the growth of a new town, north of Kashgar:

Atushi, capital of the Kezlesu Khalkhas Autonomous *Chou* in western Sinkiang, has emerged with several other towns on the stretch of wilderness ringed by towering mountains on the edge of the Great Gobi Desert [Takla Makan]. Today it has a population of tens of thousands, with all the amenities of a modern township – office buildings, factories, hospital, cinema, department store, bank, post office and schools.

Immigrant Chinese are mainly responsible for the establishment and growth of the rural settlements, the hundreds of new villages and the many new towns, e.g. Shihhotzu, along the northern slopes of the Tien Shan. It is here that a great number of the state arable and state stock-breeding farms have been carved out of the arid land. The state farms, with their large 20–30 hectare fields, ringed with shelter belts of trees, are highly mechanized. There were in 1966 76 state-owned tractor stations in the area, controlling nearly 5000 tractors (15 h.p. units). The grain crops consist of winter and spring wheat, hybrid maize, millet and kaoliang with some rice. The claim is made that Sinkiang is now self-sufficient in grain. Commercial crops are cotton and sugar-beet. Cotton-growing is centred in the newly developed area of the Manass river and its production is six times greater than it was in 1949. Sericulture is also increasing both here and in the Tarim oases.

The north and northwest of Tibet, known as Chang Tang, is an arid, frigid and barren plateau, the greater part of which is over 5000 metres high. It is virtually unpopulated. Levels descend towards the southeast and east to an average of about 3600 metres and it is here that the main grasslands are found.

The main stockbreeding area is around Nag-chuhu, about 200 km northeast of Lhasa. This region supports 6½ million head of stock out of a Tibetan total of 16 million and is highly regarded on account of its high survival rate. In 1964, 1·23 million lambs survived out of 1·4 million born[13]. This has been due largely to the rapid extension of veterinary services in the outlying regions and to the introduction of a new vaccine, which is said to be most successful in combating 'nyker', an infectious sheep disease most virulent in the bitter winter. The Tibetans are now organized into stock-breeding cooperatives.

Arable farming is confined to the lower, warmer valleys in the southeast in the Lhasa, Shigatse, Gyangtse area. The cultivation of barley and wheat is reported to have been widely extended since 1951 under the influence of better tools, water supply and cooperation. *Tsamba*, made from barley, has become the staple diet. Tea, which formerly was transported from Szechwan in brick form by coolie labour, now enters in larger quantities by the motor highway. This trade has not yet been ousted by local production which is increasing. The first plantation of 10 000 shrubs was planted in 1952 and now produces four acceptable grades[19]. A lively exchange of pastoral and arable plus consumer goods is said to exist now between the stockbreeders of the north and the agriculturalists of the south.

In 1952 Tsinghai's farming activities were almost entirely concerned with pasture. The only arable farming possible was in the extreme east of the province in the lower-lying area around Sining. Fine-fleeced and coarse Tibetan and Mongolian sheep were reared on the slopes of the Astin Tagh and Nan Shan, producing 19 000 tons of fleece per annum. Yaks were reared around Koko Nor. These, the best mountain pack animals, are capable of carrying 150 kg loads for distances of 30–40 km/day. They give rich milk and produce good meat. Tsinghai's big, hardy South Tibetan horses are well known. Bactrian camels are bred in considerable numbers around the Tsaidam[20].

Since 1952 all these activities have continued and increased, but the region has undergone radical change. The discovery of oil and coal have led to the rapid development of roads. Between 1949 and 1964, 15 000 km of motor road have been built, cutting transport time to one-tenth and cost to one-fifth. This has had considerable effect on pastoral and arable farming and has produced much the same results as we have noted in Sinkiang and Inner Mongolia, i.e. the establishment of communes, the extension of irrigation, the reduction of nomadism, the growth of settled arable farming and the establishment of industries associated with farming.

Arable farming around Sining, which is now a modern city of 210 000 inhabitants, has been greatly extended. A new early-ripening spring wheat, 'Chinchun No. 1', has been evolved to cope with the short growing period of not more than 120 days, and yields of 6 ton/hectare are now obtained on the irrigated land on the Tsaidam plateau[21].

The revolutionary changes we have noted in agriculture in these vast pastoral lands of Sinkiang, Inner Mongolia and Tibet have impinged on and revolutionized every aspect of life. The rapid advance of irrigation and the growth of forage crops is steadily reducing nomadism and the herdsman is deserting his *yurt* for a house, a settled life and all that it entails. Even if he is still nomadic, the old *yurt* is giving place to a new plastic type, which retains all the features of the traditional doomed tent, made of felt with its collapsible lattice framework. The plastic has many advantages over the felt type. Its outer covering is of artificial leather, lined with foamed plastic. The lattice is made of plastic tubing and the rigging of caprone ropes. The windows are of organic glass and the floor is covered with plastic sheeting. It has greater resistance to insects and moisture, is lighter, more durable and has better insulation and ventilation[22].

The herdsman's sheepskin clothing is giving way, at least in summer, to textiles of wool and cotton. His diet is now more varied than formerly and his stock of consumer goods, which often includes a radio set, is greater. A considerable amount of education has been introduced, mainly through travelling schools and 'part study–part work' schools in which study time is varied according to the pressures of agricultural work. The subjects taught, in addition to political ideology, are reading, writing, simple arithmetic and farming, according to the particular circumstances. Travelling libraries are making their appearance. Finally, mobile clinics, concentrating on preventative medicine, are raising health standards.

ARABLE FARMING

Spring Wheat Region

Now moving to China Proper and the regions of arable farming; these are classified and labelled according to the most characteristic crop or crops of the area and serve as a basis for discussion of all the agricultural activities.

It is appropriate to start with an analysis of the Spring Wheat Region as it marks the zone of contention between pastoral and arable farming. As already remarked (p. 44), the boundary between these two ways of life coincides closely with both the 375 mm isohyet and the line of the Great Wall. Throughout the centuries the Chinese farmer has tried to push northward and northwestward and there to establish his fields and farms. Time and time again he has been pushed back, not so much by the hostility of the 'barbarians', the lawless nomadic tribesmen, although their resistance and predatory raids have been by

no means negligible, but rather by the unyielding climatic barrier, which makes arable farming bitterly hard and precarious. It remains to be seen how successful modern technology will be in overcoming the natural hazards. This is a region of great extremes of temperature, with a growing period of about 6 months, a low rainfall of 375 mm or less, which, in addition, is most unreliable. Between two-thirds and three-quarters of its precipitation falls in the 3 summer months, June to August, and is liable to fail approximately one year in three.

Pierre Teilhard de Chardin, travelling on one of his many palaeontological excursions along the Hwang-ho between Paotow and Ningsia (Yinchwan) in 1923, laments the encroachment of the farmer into this area in these words:

> We are in Mongolia, a country whose true landowners – shepherds living in their yourts – are gradually being ousted (all along the river) by Chinese settlers, who scratch the ground and spoil the country far more than they enhance its value (because by recklessly destroying the age-old soil of the steppes and by cutting down the few trees that still remain, they loosen the sand, cause the formation of dunes and generally accelerate the terrifying erosion of these parts).[23]

In the early days of rehabilitation and socialization between 1949 and 1952, the People's Government sought to reassure the pastoralists against the inroads of the agriculturalists by proclaiming a policy of 'protect pasturage, prohibit reclamation'[2]. Since then, with the development of co-operatives and communes and the sinking of thousands of new wells in the pasturelands, this policy has been discarded to some extent and encroachment has gone on apace, most markedly to the north of Huhehot and in the Ala Shan region.

The main intensive arable farming is concentrated in the three oases in the northward bend of the Hwang-ho, two of which are of ancient origin, dating back to Han times (206 BC–AD 220) and all of which have undergone renovation and great extension since 1956. The oases around Wuwei

	Jan	Feb	Mar	Apr	May	Jun	Jul	Aug	Sep	Oct	Nov	Dec
Saratsi (933 m)												
Temp °C	−15·2	−9·5	0·0	8·3	17·8	20·6	22·8	21·1	13·9	6·7	−4·5	−15·2
Rainfall mm	3	5	8	8	23	46	99	74	51	15	3	3
Lanchow (1555 m)												
Temp °C	−6·6	−4·5	5·9	11·7	16·1	21·1	22·8	16·7	9·4	9·4	2·8	−3·3
Rainfall mm	2·5	2·5	2·5	5·2	30·5	27·9	101·6	149·9	66·0	5·2	0	2·5

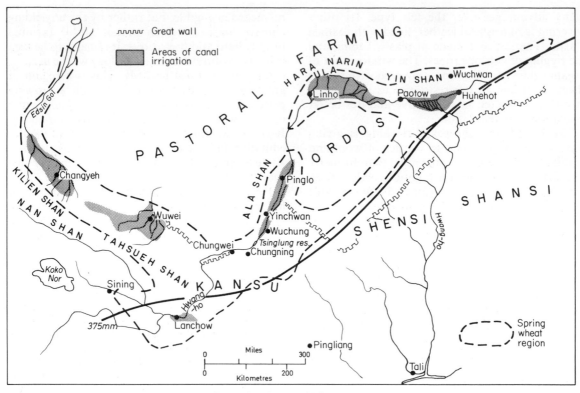

Fig. 52   Spring Wheat Region

and in the Edsin Gol have also been developed. Utilizing the snowfields of the Kilien and Tahsueh Shan, the irrigated area of these oases was increased from 120 000 hectares in 1949 to 410 000 hectares in 1964 and the total farmland in the Kansu Corridor has risen to 710 000 hectares[24]. All these areas rely almost entirely on irrigation. In a wide area around Lanchow, where dry-field farming has been the norm hitherto and where little irrigation has been practised, modern water conservancy is revolutionizing crop yield and a new strain of spring wheat, 'Taitzu 30', has been evolved. It is a cross between the local Lanchow–Sining hardy, early ripening, small-eared variety with a later ripening, big-eared variety. It ripens in 104 days and is hardy. It is therefore suitable for use in Tsinghai, around Sining and is coming into general use[25]. Wheat yields vary from 40 to 200 *catties/mow* according to the availability of water.

The main food crops are spring wheat, millet, barley, rice and legumes. Potatoes are grown in the drier parts. In 1952 it was estimated that 88.3 per cent of the cultivated land was devoted to food crops[2]. Spring wheat is the staple food of the people. It is sown towards the end of March and harvested in the middle or towards the end of July. Together with all the wheats of the north, it is a hard wheat, good for bread and noodles. Wheats tend to become softer the farther south they are grown. There is quite a quick transition from the spring wheat to the winter wheat zone. Yinchwan grows 99 per cent spring wheat and Pingliang 99 per cent winter wheat; the yield per *mow* is much the same for both types[2]. Millet is an insurance crop – insurance against the uncertain rainfall – for it is hardier than wheat, withstands drought better and will flourish on poorer soils. Sown at the beginning of May, it is reaped early in September. It is the staple cereal of the herdsmen. Barley grown here has a shorter growing period than spring wheat by about ten days. The production of rice in this region is determined by irrigation facilities and flourishes most in the Ningsia plain. Until recently most of the rice was planted direct, thus avoiding the back-aching

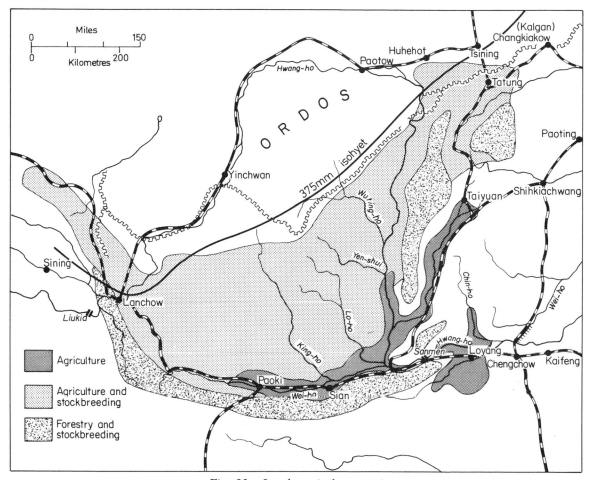

Fig. 53   Land use in loess region

labour of hand transplanting but achieving a lower yield. With the introduction of transplanting machines (p. 100) techniques are changing and direct sowing is disappearing. Rice, which here is 95 per cent non-glutinous, is classified locally into 'big' and 'little'. The 'little' predominates because the 'big' is much more exacting in all aspects of its cultivation, requiring earlier sowing, better irrigation and green manuring. However, it does give a greater yield. Soyabeans, string beans, green beans and cow peas are the main legumes grown and form an important part of human diet. Black beans and peas are grown for fodder. This is a good fruit-growing region. Apples, pears, apricots, peaches and grapes all flourish and melons from Ningsia and Lanchow are well known. Trees grown in the region around Chungning bear fruit

which produces *Lycium Chinense*, used exclusively for pharmaceutical purposes.

The main cash crops are cotton, sesame, hemp, sugar-beet and local tobacco. Cotton growing has had a chequered history over the last fifty years. It suffered heavily during the Sino–Japanese War, but in recent years has prospered. It is grown mainly in central Kansu, on the Ningsia plain and in the newly irrigated areas in the Kansu Corridor. Hemp has a similar distribution to cotton. Because it is deep-rooted and is resistant to wind and sand, sesame is widely grown. The seed produces a high yield of edible oil; 1 *catty* of oil is obtained from 3 *catties* of seed. The fibre is used for making sacking, coarse cloth, sandals and paper. It is also used as fuel. Sugar-beet has a promising future. Since the introduction of a Russian variety from

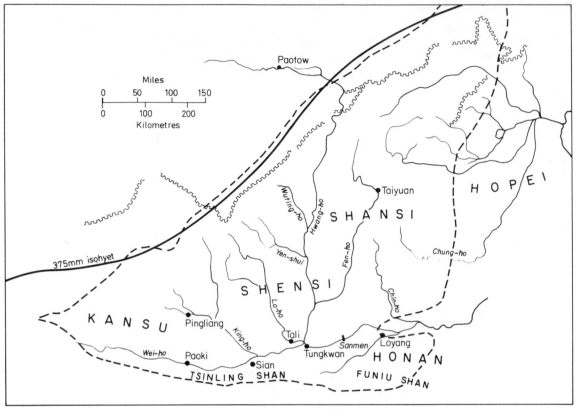

Fig. 54   Winter Wheat-Millet Region

Sinkiang during the Sino–Japanese War, it has grown to be third in importance as a beet producer in China. It is yielding 4000 *catties/mow* with a 11–16 per cent sugar content[26].

Within the arable farming areas of the spring wheat region there is a considerable amount of animal husbandry. We have already noted the differences in kind and numbers of animals raised in the pastoral and semi-arable, semi-pastoral regions. The more intensive the arable farming the greater these differences become. For religious reasons, the Moslem farmers, who are numerous in this region, concentrate more on rearing sheep, while the Chinese (Han) farmers are the hog raisers. Formerly one-tenth of the sheep and goats were slaughtered for their skins alone[2]. With the development of meat canning, a fuller use is being made of the animals. The main livestock regions are I-meng, the land bordering the Ordos desert and Wu-meng, the lands bordering, and to the north of, the Hara Narin Ula and the Yin Shan. Wu Ch'uan-chun and his colleagues estimated the I-meng as 7 per cent cultivation, 20 per cent

shifting sand and semi-shifting sand dunes, 30 per cent stationary dunes, 33 per cent steppe, 10 per cent mountains[2]. It is here that Chinese farmers, in recent decades in their extension of arable farming, have encroached on the steppe and in places have created a 'dust-bowl'. Wu-meng has been the scene of the greatest development of well digging and pastoral settlement.

Winter Wheat-Millet Region

Lying southeast of the Spring Wheat Region is the Winter Wheat–Millet Region. Its boundaries are the 375 mm isohyet on the northwest, the Tsinling Shan and Funiu Shan on the south and the Taihang Shan and Wutai Shan, on the east, marking the steep descent on to the North China Plain. The whole area is a deeply dissected plateau, but its old topography is masked by a layer of loess, which is coincident with nearly the whole region and which, in places, is more than 75 m thick. It is the presence of this loess which has determined the pattern of life of the area throughout the centuries. As already seen (p. 41), the ease with which the loess can be worked was one of the main reasons for the early development of agriculture and the birth of Chinese civilization in this region. Since then it has been a leading factor in shaping agricultural activities, settlement, communications and housing, and is in no small way responsible for the precariousness of life here.

The Winter Wheat–Millet Region is notorious as the worst famine area in China. By far the greater part of its agriculture is dry-field farming, and this has to rely on rainfall, which, at best is not plentiful. It shares with the Spring Wheat Region the handicap of unreliable and very variable seasonal rainfall; but, except in the limited irrigated parts, does not share the insurance which irrigation provides. Thus it has been periodically devastated by famines, so vividly described by Mallory, in which millions have died[27]. It is to be hoped that the recent widespread water conservancy measures, together with the great improvement in communications, enabling the rapid transport of relief, have now made such disasters a thing of the past.

Writing in 1951, Shen[28] reported that this region had a total area of 380 730 sq km of which only 82 880 sq km, or about 22 per cent, was cultivated. One-third of the cultivated land was terraced and only one-tenth irrigated. These proportions have now changed, although to what extent it is not possible to say accurately. The ancient irrigation works of the Wei and King valleys around Sian, and in the Fen valley, which had fallen into disrepair and were renovated by the China International Famine Relief Commission after the famine of 1932, have now been greatly extended. However, they still constitute only a small proportion of the cultivated land.

Winter wheat and millet are the two chief crops grown in the dry fields, whether in the valleys or on the terraced hills. Winter wheat is grown to some extent over most of the region but is densely cultivated in the Wei valley from Paoki to its confluence with the Hwang-ho and in the Fen valley. Wheaten flour, from which northern bread (*mien pao*) is made, is the staple food. Proso-millet

has a similar distribution, with the difference that there is no dense production in the Fen valley. Some kaoliang is grown in the upper Wei and upper Fen valleys and in the extreme north of the region. Also the extreme north is the most important oat-growing area of China, where it is an important fodder crop. Some rice is grown under irrigation in the middle Wei valley and in the Lo valley around Loyang. Rape is widely and thinly distributed with some concentration in the middle Wei. Cotton is the outstanding economic crop. It is centred in the Wei valley around Sian, Sienyang, Sanyuan, Tali and in Honan in the Lo valley. The frost-free period is only 180–190 days, therefore the earlier maturing Chinese varieties are preferred to the longer staple American Upland varieties.

Winter Wheat-Kaoliang Region
This region embraces the whole of the North China Plain. Its western boundary is the steep edge of the Shansi plateau and its eastern boundary the Po-hai and the Hwang-hai (Yellow Sea). Its southern border has no clear physical feature to mark it. The course of the Hwai-ho is taken as an arbitrary line, indicating the transitional zone between the wheat-growing north and the rice-growing south.

The vast, flat or gentle undulating plain is built of immense alluvial deposits, together with loessial airborne material, each of which continues to make its annual contributions, the former through flooding rivers and the latter by dust storms, which plague the north. The flatness of the plain, which is virtually treeless, is interrupted only by the Shantung mountains.

This is one of China's densely populated regions, peopled almost entirely by Han Jen, 80 per cent of whom are engaged in agriculture. They are settled in innumerable hamlets and villages, large and small – a shape of settlement, which has not been fundamentally altered by the changes to commune organization in the last twenty years. In other respects, however, land reform and the coming of cooperatives and communes have been

	Jan	Feb	Mar	Apr	May	Jun	Jul	Aug	Sep	Oct	Nov	Dec
Sian (334 m)												
Temp °C	0·6	3·9	10·0	17·2	23·9	27·8	30·0	27·8	22·2	17·2	6·7	1·7
Rainfall mm	10	8	15	43	51	71	84	127	41	41	8	10
Taiyuan (788 m)												
Temp °C	− 8·4	− 3·3	3·9	12·2	18·3	22·8	25·0	22·8	17·2	10·6	2·2	− 5·7
Rainfall mm	8	0	10	8	15	43	125	86	41	15	0	3

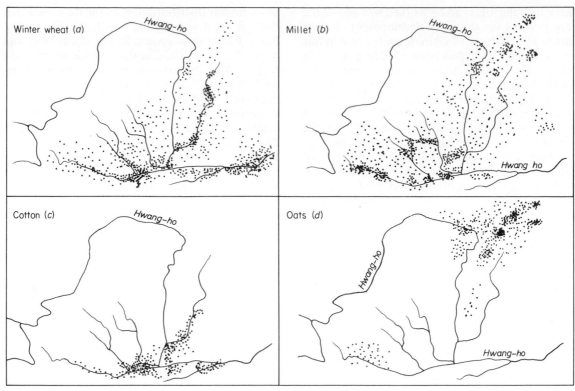

Fig. 55   Crops, Winter Wheat – Millet Region

revolutionary. Communal ownership of the land has resulted in a great increase in the size of fields, which, previously under individual ownership or tenancy, had usually been $\frac{1}{5}-\frac{1}{2}$ hectare. This, in its turn, has materially affected much of farming techniques. For example, this increase in the size of field has made mechanization or semi-mechanization of farming possible and this possibility has been further enhanced by the widespread construction of high-tension lines, carrying power to irrigation, etc. Nevertheless, apart from state and demonstration farms of the region, such development is still only in its initial stages in many parts.

The farmer of the North China Plain has two main enemies, flood and drought. Flooding stems mainly from the Hwang-ho, Hwai-ho and Hai-ho. Measures to meet this danger have been dealt with under 'Water Conservancy'. Drought, while not so devastating as in the Winter Wheat–Millet Region, is, nevertheless, a constant anxiety and danger. The time-honoured method of meeting this menace has been the sinking of wells and

raising water either by manpower or animal-power (usually donkey). When drought has been severe, wells have often proved inadequate to permit the sowing of crops or their maintenance, and famine has ensued. Only about 10 per cent of the land was irrigated and there was little terracing. This would still appear to be the general pattern if the following report from Jenhsien *hsien* in 1966 can be taken as typical of the North China Plain, although it reveals that more coordinated effort than formerly can be brought to bear to meet drought when it does occur.

Rainfall was inadequate in Jenhsien *hsien*, Southern Hopei Province, all through sowing to harvesting. When the time for sowing came, the fields were covered with a thick layer of dry earth. 10 000 out of 14 000 hectares of wheat fields had no irrigation facilities to fall back on. . . . The Jenhsien *hsien* Committee of the Communist Party organized study of what Chairman Mao said about conquering difficulties. . . . The anti-drought battle went ahead with revolutionary determination. Members of the Yung-

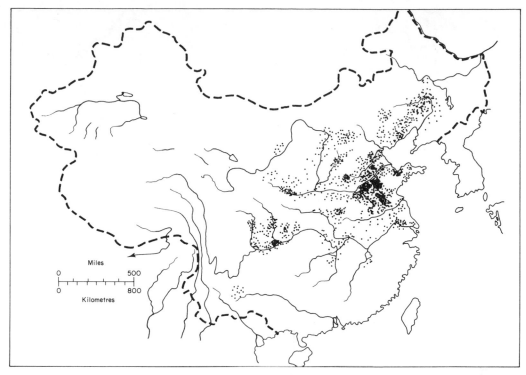

Fig. 56   Wheat

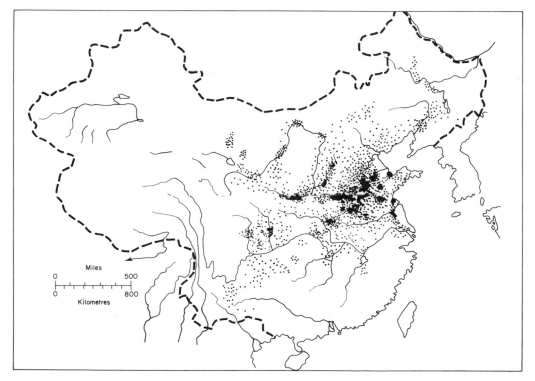

Fig. 57   Kaoliang

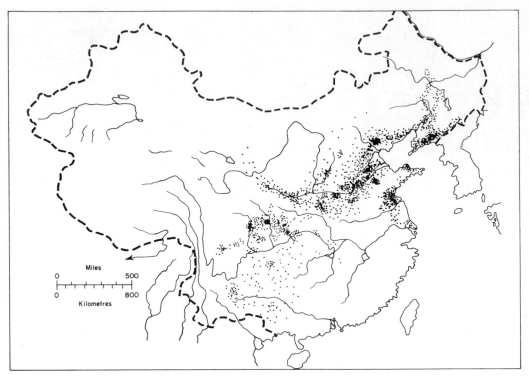

Fig. 58   Corn

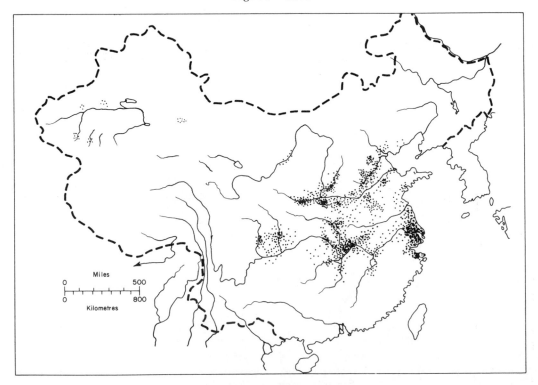

Fig. 59   Cotton

Plate 9   Bumper corn crop, Ta Chai production brigade, Shansi
Ta Chai is constantly held up as a model for the rest of the country

fuchuang commune dug wells and sowed wheat in time. Within a few months, the communes in the *hsien* had built 27 000 new wells, renovated 6500 old wells and dug 95 ponds. 10 000 hectares of arid farmland was brought under irrigation. Thus the people have not only won the battle against drought this year but have created conditions for stable harvests in the future[29].

The main food crops are winter wheat, kaoliang, foxtail millet, barley, corn, soyabeans and sweet potatoes. This region is the great wheat granary of China and more than 150 million people living in the area depend upon wheat as their staple food. It is sown in September as soon as possible after reaping the summer harvest of soyabeans, kaoliang or millet. Traditionally it was harvested at the Tuan Wu Festival, on the fifth day of the fifth month of the Chinese calendar,

i.e. towards the end of May. Adherence to the old agricultural calendar, to a large extent, no longer obtains. Gone, too, are many of the old techniques such as pulling the grain instead of reaping but, owing to differences of knowledge, techniques, management and soils, there are very great differences in output of wheat per *mow* as between different communes, brigades and teams, sometimes amounting to more than 10 times. High output production brigades are those which achieve a yield of over 300 *catties/mow*. However, a good deal of experimenting is going on and these standards appear to be undergoing a change. New strains, such as the 'Shan Nung 205', 'Peking 8', 'A Fu' and 'P'ing Yuan', suiting different local conditions, have been evolved. More attention is being given to the right time of planting so that full advantage can be taken of the autumn sun and temperature, thus promoting tillering before the winter onset. Because soil temperature on salt and alkali soils is some 2°C lower than in the case of ordinary soil, sowing must take place 10 days earlier; this entails more careful pest control. In view of the emphasis, which, in China, during recent years has been placed on the importance of chemical fertilizer, the following extract from the report on wheat-growing by the Crop Culture and Cultivation Research Institute, Chinese Academy of Agricultural Science in November 1965 is instructive:

> In areas comparatively lacking in fertilizer resources, stress is laid on the application of basic fertilizer and seed fertilizer.... Where the soil has a low degree of fertility and is lacking in effective phosphorus, application of phosphorus fertilizer as basic fertilizer has a marked effect of causing seedlings to grow strong, promoting branching before winter, and raising output.
>
> In districts where fertilizer is more abundant, some areas had in recent years applied chemical fertilizer to the exclusion of peasant household manure. This led to increasing hardening of the soil. Though the quantity of fertilizer applied increased with the years, yet the output of the land did not rise. In view of this, the practice of depending solely on chemical fertilizer was overcome. Peasant household manure began to be used as the main fertilizer, and it was used in combination with chemical fertilizer.
>
> This is a matter of direction concerning the application of fertilizer.... But peasant household manure has a low content of effective nutrients, and it produces its effect slowly, unable to meet promptly the maximum demand of wheat plants for nutrition. By applying peasant household manure in rational combination with chemical fertilizer, it is possible both to raise output per *mow* rapidly and to nurse soil fertility continuously.[30]

Rust is the chief wheat disease in the north and, to date, no really satisfactory rust-resisting strain has been bred. Red mold, which causes severe damage in years of higher temperature and greater humidity, is a much greater menace to wheat in the Yangtze valley than in the north.

A notable social change has occurred with regard to women's labour. Formerly, wheat threshing was the first outdoor women's work of the year in the north[31]. Today, women work in the fields at all times.

Kaoliang (Chinese sorghum) ranks second in importance to wheat. This plant, which grows to a height of 2–3 m, carries a closely bunched head of several hundred grain, each grain being about the size of a sweet pea. It is well suited to the area because, like millet, it can withstand severe drought and is not easily destroyed by flood. It is a coarser food than wheat, but it forms a very important item in the people's diet and gives a heavy yield per *mow*. Its tall, strong stalk is valuable for wattle and daub building, fencing and roofing. It is also used extensively for fuel. New hybrid kaoliang has been grown on demonstration plots in Honan, yielding 4·27 tons/hectare. The same strain grown in an area waterlogged for one month yielded 2·25 tons/hectare, a 60 per cent improvement on local strains[32]. Kaoliang is often planted between widely spaced rows of wheat in order to obviate the problem that kaoliang needs to be planted before the harvesting of wheat, if a satisfactory crop is to be obtained. In like manner cotton also competes with wheat. Sweet potatoes are a heavy crop and also form an important item in the peasants' diet. They are included in official records as grain on a ratio of four parts potato equal one of grain.

With the expansion of irrigation there is a noticeable tendency to grow rice rather than wheat, especially in the Hwai valley and southern Shantung, where it is reported that 'low-lying lands formerly suitable only for sorghum, sweet potatoes and other dry crops, are now growing rice with an average yield of 3 tons/ hectare'[33] Saline, waterlogged land, which has been drained in the Linyi district north of Tsinan, has been turned into paddy. This preference for rice is not surprising since the average rice yield per hectare is 6 tons as compared with 2½ tons of wheat. However, it must be remembered that rice requires a great deal more care in its cultivation.

Other food crops are corn, soyabeans and peanuts. A great variety of vegetables is grown, including cabbage, spinach, turnip, onion, cucumbers, melons, squashes, beans and peas. These are grown principally on the peasants' private plots.

Cotton is by far the most important economic crop of the region. The main producing areas are western Shantung, southern Hopei and Honan. Most of the cotton grown is of short staple, Chinese varieties of less than 25 mm staple, but these have a high lint yield. In spite of all efforts to encourage the increase of quality and quantity, the output of cotton still lags behind the constantly increasing demand. There is a persistent 'contradiction', i.e. competition, between cotton and grain for growing space[34]. Saline lands bordering the Po-hai have been brought into cotton cultiva-

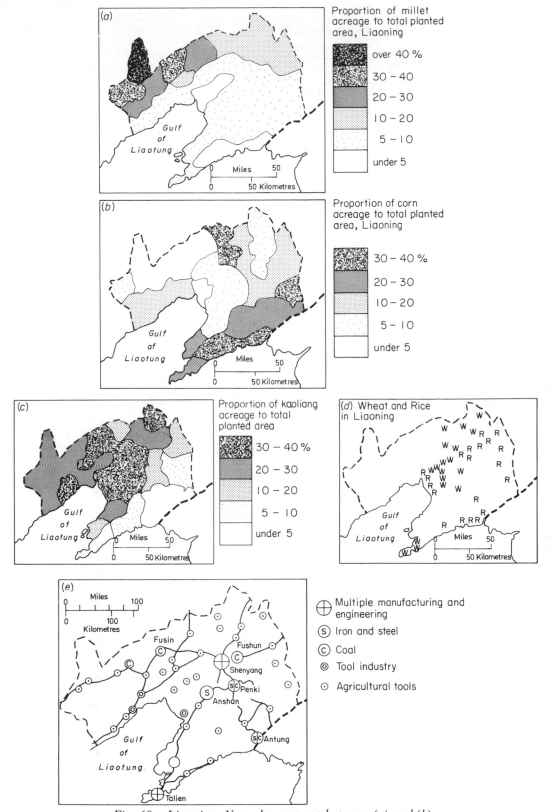

Fig. 60   Liaoning. Note the contrast between (a) and (b)

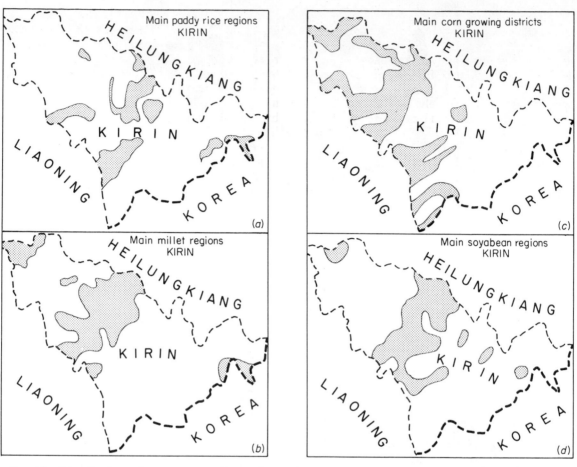

Fig. 61   Distribution of rice, corn, millet and soya bean growing in Kirin. Note Kaoliang distribution almost identical with millet

tion. By careful cultivation and the addition of fertilizer and pond and riverbed mud, soils containing as much as 3·17 per cent salt have increased their yield from 10 *catties* ginned cotton per *mow* to 80 *catties* or more[37].

Corn–Soyabean–Millet Region

The terminus of the Great Wall is at Shanhaikwan on the Po-hai. This marks the narrowest point of the coastal plain, which leads from the North China Plain to the Northeast, as the former province of Manchuria is now called, and which is divided into three provinces, Liaoning, Kirin and Heilungkiang. This corridor leads from the flat, alluvial plains of the Hwai, Hwang and Hai into a vast country of undulating steppeland, bordered on the west by the Ta Hingan Shan and

on the east by the densely forested East Manchurian Mountains. The steppeland is covered, for the most part, by a rich chernozem soil. It is open to the influence of the southeast monsoon and, in consequence, has a summer maximum of rainfall, most places receiving an annual precipitation of between 500 and 650 mm, with a considerably heavier fall in the east than in the west. Winters are long and bitter as a result of the northwest winds from the Siberian high pressure zone. The region stretches about 1500 km from north to south and thus there is a considerable difference in temperature between north Heilungkiang and south Liaoning. There is a growing period of 120–150 days according to latitude, but the long summer days, with 14–16 h of sunshine, compensate this to some degree.

A general pattern of grain crop distribution can be discerned. Millet and kaoliang tend to be grown in the somewhat higher and drier western parts, whilst rice is grown mainly in the southeast and in the coastal areas. Some winter wheat is grown in central Liaoning, but it is not a popular crop owing to its comparatively low unit yield. Its production has been urged on communes because it provides year-round work. The growth of spring wheat is increasing in Heilungkiang.

Millet and kaoliang still constitute the principal food of the farming population, but the steady growth in the standard of living is shown in the increasing demand for rice and wheat. Experiments by Professor Kung Chi-tao have led to the evolution of a new strain of kaoliang, bearing several clusters in place of the usual single cluster, which all mature at the same time and give a yield of 3·7 tons/hectare. This is an increase of 50–100 per cent over other good strains[36]. Another new strain, the 'Hsiung Yueh 253', ripens in 130–140 days, which is an improvement, although it compares unfavourably with that of the North China Plain, which ripens in 120 days.

Corn, which has now superseded kaoliang in importance, has a longer growing season than millet or kaoliang and is therefore grown in the lowlands. The most important producing area is a belt stretching from the plain of Liaoning northward into the lowland of Kirin and Heilungkiang. This is an extension of the corn belt, which stretches from Szechwan right across the North China Plain. Some idea of the importance of this crop can be gained from the table below.

Table 1   Percentages of Sown Area

	Kirin (1957)	Heilungkiang (1957)	Liaoning (1958)
Rice	6·2	3·1	7·5
Corn	19·7	20·7	31·5
Kaoliang	15·5	10·4	9·0
Millet	18·3	16·3	10·6
Wheat	1·1	12·8	0·8
Soyabeans	20·0	20·9	15·0
Cotton	—	—	4·2
Peanuts	—	—	3·4

Compiled from *Economic Geography of Northeast China*

In spite of its northerly situation, rice has been grown in the Northeast for a long time. Its main region is along the southeastern Korean border from the Liaotung peninsula to the Yenki district in Kirin. It is closely associated with the Korean people, who are regarded as experts in a method of rice-growing peculiar to the region. Great claims have been made for recent experiments in rice-growing made by Korean farmers in Kirin, which have raised the yield from 2·2 to 3 tons/hectare by old methods, to a new average of 4·9 tons/hectare[37]. This has been achieved partly by nursing early rice seedlings under plastic sheeting and so avoiding frost, and partly by irrigating rice paddies only at night, using water warmed by the sun during the day and so maintaining a higher night temperature. But these experiments, which have been carried out over 3300 hectares, have not been controlled for they have been accompanied by better manuring, better seed selection and close planting. Therefore it is not possible to measure how much of the increased yield is attributable to the 'Korean Method'.

Rice-growing has been extended north right into the Sungari and Nun river valleys where the crop is being cultivated by more extensive farming methods than in the south. This is due, in some degree, to the Shenyang production of the 3 h.p. or 7 h.p. walking tractor, suitable for paddy fields. Here in the north there is an abundance of farmland and a shortage of labour. Rice is planted in rows more than 300 mm apart – the conventional method farther south is to plant rows 150 mm apart – thus enabling weeding to be done by animal or walking tractor. It also has the advantage of giving better ventilation and admitting more sunshine[38].

The soyabean, which shares first place with corn and millet, is grown in every province in China but is more important here than anywhere else. It is a very important part of Chinese diet. Bean curd (*tu fu*) in some shape or form is served at most Chinese meals. *Tu-chiang*, a fluid expressed from soyabeans, has, for centuries, formed a valuable baby and invalid food. The oil, obtained by crushing, is used universally as a cooking oil. The residue, in the form of large round cakes, is a valuable cattle food.

When the Northeast was under Japanese rule, the export of soyabeans from that region was of great importance, especially during the First World War, when it was in great demand for making explosives. Manchurian export of soyabeans at that time stood at over 4 million tons p.a. Since the Second World War, the United States has undertaken production and this export trade has fallen, but Chinese production has been main-

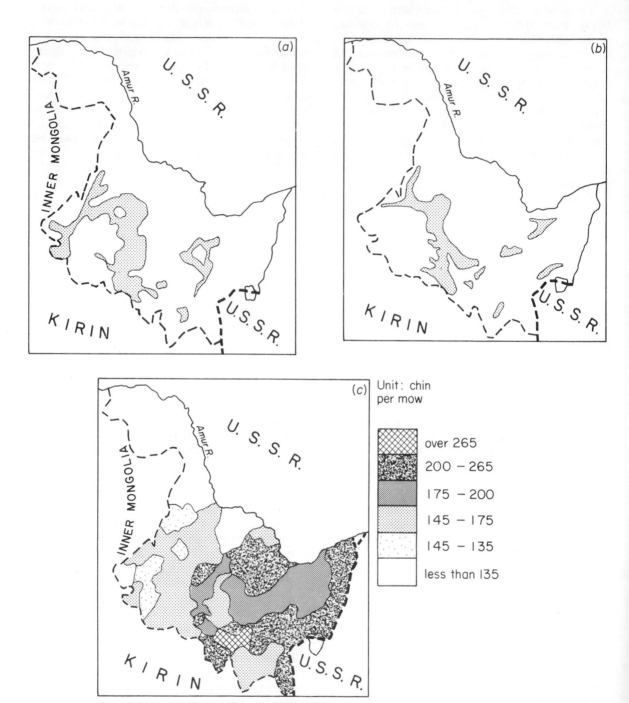

Fig. 62   Heilungkiang: (a) distribution of sugar-beet and flax; (b) distribution of soya beans; (c) average
unit yield for grain during first five-year period

	Jan	Feb	Mar	Apr	May	Jun	Jul	Aug	Sep	Oct	Nov	Dec
Luta (Talien) (10 m)												
Temp °C	− 3·9	− 3·9	2·2	8·9	15·0	20·0	22·8	24·4	20·6	14·4	6·1	− 1·1
Rainfall mm	13	8	18	23	43	46	163	130	102	28	25	13
Shenyang (34 m)												
Temp °C	− 12·8	− 10·6	− 2·2	7·8	15·6	21·1	24·4	23·3	16·7	8·9	− 1·7	− 10·0
Rainfall mm	5	5	20	28	50	86	160	155	84	41	28	5
Harbin (159 m)												
Temp °C	− 19·4	− 15.2	− 4·5	5·6	13·3	18·9	22·2	20·6	10·6	4·4	− 6·2	− 16·4
Rainfall mm	5	5	10	23	43	104	147	107	56	31	10	5

tained and absorbed for home use. The Northeast is still the most important producing region, and one-fifth of the planted area of Kirin and Liaoning is devoted to it. It is usually grown in a three-crop rotation with kaoliang and millet and is sometimes interplanted with corn. The extension of rice-growing tends to push the cultivation of soyabeans into the rolling hills of the west. In spite of the importance of the crop in the past, cultivation methods have been poor and unit yield low. Application of chemical fertilizer and the introduction of better seed in recent years have helped to raise the standard in the Northeast. A new strain, 'Feng Shou 4', has a higher yield, but like so many higher bearing strains is more prone to disease, although it is more resistant to drought and pests.

Peanuts (groundnuts), grown mainly in south Liaoning and the lower Liao valley, are second only to soyabeans as a source of edible oil. Like soyabeans, their cultivation has been backward but shows a similar recent improvement.

Of the economic crops of the Northeast, cotton and sugar-beet now vie with each other in importance. The main cotton-growing area is in the Liaoning plain, along the Liao river itself, in the Luta peninsular and in the southwest around Chinchow. It has the comparatively high yield of 132 *chin* of ginned cotton per *mow* and an average staple of 23–4 mm. It faces problems of spring drought and high precipitation in late summer during the ripening season. Sugar-beet is grown mainly in Kirin on the Sungari plain where it is the most important economic crop. In 1958 it still occupied only 1 per cent of the planted area, but since then this has been greatly increased together with local sugar refineries. In 1959–60 output was reported as 250 000 tons, which represented 3·5 per cent of the national output, placing it seventh in the national scale. Flax is grown in quantity in the Sungari valley. Liaoning is one of the chief producers of flue-cured tobacco, producing 6·3 per cent of the national total in 1958. Tussore silk, which is produced from silkworms reared on chestnut-leaved oak, mainly in east Liaoning, suffered a near eclipse in 1948 when prewar peak production of 200 000 *tan* of dried cocoon fell to 10 000 *tan*. Its production in 1957 was reported to be approximately 1 million *tan*.

Fruit-growing is becoming an important agricultural activity, especially in Liaoning, where apple-growing is increasing very rapidly. It is stated that it now produces 80 per cent of the whole of China's output. The humid oceanic influences, significant diurnal temperature changes and sufficient sunlight combine to produce apples of fine quality. Pears are second in importance. Good grapes are grown in Luta peninsula.

Heilungkiang is the province in which the greatest number of state farms has been established and the greatest degree of mechanization has taken place. In 1966, 36 such farms were in existence and 453 000 hectares of virgin land had been brought into cultivation. Nearly all these were started by veteran soldiers of the PLA, who have later been joined by younger people. It is reported that all have been set up 'in accordance with the Nanniwan revolutionary spirit of self-reliance', i.e. following the pattern of the brigade of the 8th Army in the early 1940s, which was sent to Nanniwan, near Yenan to open up wasteland[39].

Reports on the Chiayin State Farm set up in March 1964 in the north of Heilungkiang state that it has now 740 workers.

They made conscious efforts to break away from the pattern borrowed from abroad for the running of state farms. They decided, for instance, not to build modern residential quarters like those of the cities and thus risk becoming divorced from the masses of the peasants.... At first all the leading functionaries

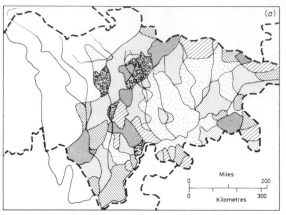

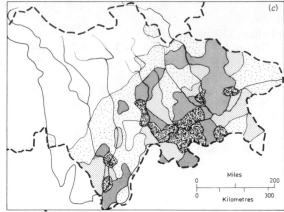

Percentage of corn to total crop acreage

Percentage of rice acreage to all crops in Szechwan

- 50 – 65 %
- 40 – 50
- 30 – 40
- 20 – 30
- 10 – 20
- 5 – 10

- Over 40 %
- 30 – 40
- 20 – 30
- 10 – 20

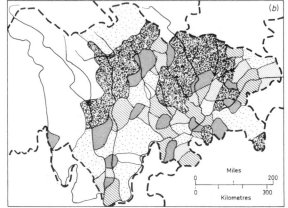

Percentage of wheat to total crop acreage

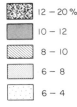

- 12 – 20 %
- 10 – 12
- 8 – 10
- 6 – 8
- 6 – 4

Fig. 63   Szechwan: corn, wheat and rice

and the workers lived in tents. They began reclamation work while still building dwellings and roads. They made no special arrangements with any building department but erected all the dwellings and other buildings themselves. Now everyone on the farm lives in simple housing similar to that of the nearby villages. They all lead a frugal life.[40]

Thus these northern state farms present a different appearance from many of the southern ones. 'Thousands of settlements now make a patchwork of this former desolate area and every farm has its own schools, clinics, shops, clubs and other services.'

The main crops grown on the State farms, which are highly mechanized, include spring wheat, soyabeans and corn. There are some state farms engaged in animal husbandry, which has been, and still is, the livelihood of the Mongolians, who occupy the western foothills of the Ta Hingan Shan. Estimates credit Heilungkiang alone with 5·9 million hectares of pasture and 1·65 million hectares of wasteland suitable for grazing. The main animal breeding region is in the Nun valley, where horses are most important. This contrasts strongly with Liaoning where more than 80 per cent of the large animals are yellow oxen and donkeys needed for draught purposes.

Table 2   *Principal Crops of Liaoning*
(in 100 billion chin)

	1949	1952	1957	1958
Rice	3·40	5·99	13·03	20·08
Corn	17·04	25·16	34·58	83·04
Kaoliang	29·66	38·64	39·93	16·80
Tubers	2·99	4·19	7·79	11·15
Soyabeans	8·13	11·07	15·34	19·71
Cotton	0·82	5·50	2·24	4·07
Tobacco	0·03	0·45	0·38	0·50
Apples	1·00	1·70	3·33	4·34
Tussore Silk	0·41	1·06	0·66	0·88

Compiled from *Economic Geography of Northeast China*, p. 86

Szechwan Rice Region

We now move south of the Tsinling–Funiu Shan line which, until recently, divided the wheat-growing north from the rice-growing south. We have seen that, as irrigation facilities develop, there is an increasing urge and ability to grow rice farther north. There is no corresponding tendency to extend wheat-growing farther south. All five of the remaining agricultural regions have rice as their staple crop, the differentiating factor or factors being either the manner or amount of the rice grown or the nature of subsidiary products.

It is interesting to note that the production of rice had risen considerably in 1949, whereas figures of production for nearly every commodity in the country for that year were at their lowest ebb. The reason for this is that from 1936 and throughout the Sino–Japanese war there was a continual migration from the east in Szechwan resulting in a great increase in demand and production of rice. It is now the country's greatest producer.

Rice is grown under irrigation in the hills and on the plains. The efficiency of irrigation varies very considerably in different areas. We have seen something of the ancient irrigation system of the Chengtu plain. It is here and in the Yangtze valley around Chung-king that the highest yields per hectare are obtained. This is achieved by taking an early rice crop, a late autumn rice crop and a spring catch crop, usually of vegetables. Some account has been given of the experiments in irrigation that are being made in the hilly lands where water conservancy is most backward. It is reported that, in 1958, 11 per cent of the paddy land was still relying on storing water in the fields themselves, a most precarious method. The Red Basin grows more rice than it needs for local consumption and therefore exports a fair amount to the north by the new railway to Paoki and by boat down the Yangtze. The accompanying maps of rice, wheat and corn acreage show an interesting localization of distribution, intensive rice-growing being concentrated in the lowlands to the south and southeast, and wheat and corn in the uplands of the north and west.

The important food crops of the dry farmland area are wheat, corn and sweet potato. The drive during the last fifteen years has been to bring these dry fields under irrigation. Insofar as this has been achieved, yields have been for the most part doubled. About three-quarters of the wheat grown is winter wheat. Almost the entire crop of wheat and corn is consumed within Szechwan itself.

Szechwan is one of the country's major corn-producing areas. Recently the communes have undertaken the mass production of double-cross maize, which has a 30–40 per cent higher yield per hectare than local strains, but requires a yearly production of double-cross seed otherwise it loses its hybrid vigour[41]. In common with so much of the poorer land of China, sweet potatoes form the staple food of the peasants of the dry upland farming areas.

Szechwan's main economic crops are oil seeds, cotton, sugar, tobacco and fibres[42]. Of the oil producers rapeseed is by far the most important, occupying more than one-third of the economic crop acreage. Rape is a winter crop on paddies and in the dry corn fields and thus is very widely distributed throughout the Red Basin. Peanuts and sesame are also grown alternatively with corn and produce a large amount of vegetable oil. The acreage under cotton increased considerably to 2·3 million *mow* during the Sino–Japanese War. This trend has continued; the acreage had more than doubled by 1958 and now occupies about one-third of the land devoted to economic crops. Its growth is concentrated in the Chengtu plain and in the northwest. Attention has recently been given to developing a strain which matures early in order to avoid the unfavourable autumn rains, thus raising former low yields to 37 *catties/mow*[43]. Sugar-cane production ranks second to Kwang-tung or third if Taiwan is included. Introduced from Fukien in AD 1670, it prospered until the beginning of the twentieth century, since when it has had a chequered history. It has now recovered. Although natural conditions are not as favourable as those of Kwangtung, heavy crops are reaped.

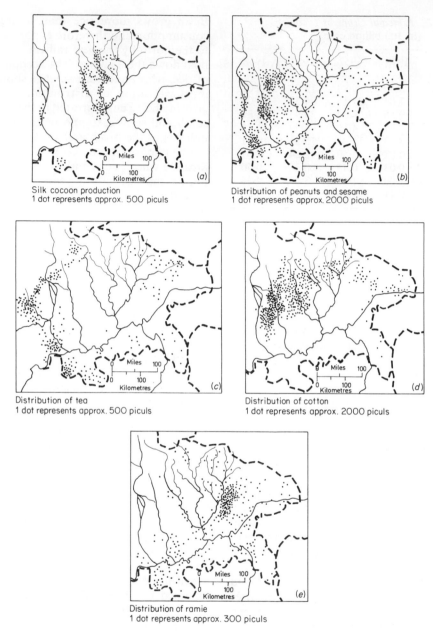

Fig. 64   *Szechwan: silk, peanuts and sesame, tea, cotton, and ramie*

Planting takes place in February and March and the crop is harvested between November and April. In recent years sugar-beet has been successfully introduced. In 1964, 8 big or medium-sized (300–500 tons/day capacity) and 112 small (15–30 tons/day capacity) refineries were either built or improved, doubling the refining capacity of the province[42]. Tobacco is grown on some 700 000 *mow* of which about one-third is in the Chengtu plain. It is virtually all sun-dried and finds a ready market throughout the rest of China. Ramie (*ssu ma* – silky flax) and hemp (*ho ma*) are the two chief fibres, the production of which stands second only to Hupeh. Ramie is grown mainly east of the Kialing Kiang. Tea production is concentrated in the foothills of the Tibetan plateau. Although green tea and a small amount of black tea are produced, by far the most important is the 'border' or brick tea, a coarse, rough mixture of leaves and stems grown mainly for export to Tibet and Mongolia. It is pressed into slabs or tiles about 130–50 mm square and 12 mm thick, making it suitable for transport, formerly on the backs of coolies but, happily, today largely by lorries. The production of green (unfermented) and black (fermented) tea is increasing rapidly to meet the needs of the province.

Sericulture in Szechwan is said to date back to the Ch'in dynasty (221–206 BC), made famous in the Shu brocades and Pa satins. In addition to the mulberry trees, which flourish in the Szechwan climate and on which the silk industry is based, the province is rich in oak trees. Experiments are going on in the use of the oak leaf as feed for silkworms. A record production in 1925 of 700 000 *piculs* (1 *picul* = 60 kg) of dried cocoons gave 70 000 *piculs* of reeled silk. Due to Japanese competition and internal disorder, production fell to 100 000 *piculs* of cocoons in 1949. By 1958 a partial recovery had been made, 250 000 *piculs* being produced, representing 15–20 per cent of the national output[43].

The province has a great variety of fruit, ranging from tropical to temperate. Bananas, pineapples, oranges, tangerines, dragon eyes, and lichee are grown in the lower, warmer valleys of the south, while apples, peaches, pears and plums are grown mainly in the higher, cooler northwest, the southward-flowing rivers providing the main means of transport.

It is estimated that about 18 per cent of Szechwan is forested. The main stands are in the west and in the upper reaches of the Min, Tatu and Fow rivers. The forests here range from evergreen broadleafed and deciduous trees below 2500 m, to spruce and fir up to 3500 m. Above this height there is alpine meadow and little tree growth[43].

The forests of the Mitsang Shan and Ta Pa Shan in the north and east are composed mainly of Huashan pine, green kang, chestnut oak and cypress. On the lower slopes, below 100 m, there is a variety of oil-bearing trees, wood oil (*tung yu*), tea oil and tallow. Of these wood oil is by far the most important commercially. It forms the basis of paints and varnish and has figured prominently in the export trade, especially to U.K., throughout the twentieth century. It also has many domestic uses, including waterproofing oiled cloth (*yu pu*) and the preserving of all river craft. In recent years the cultivation of wood oil has re-

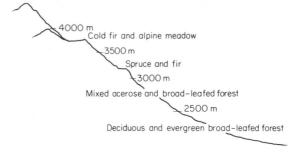

Fig. 65   Forest in Western Szechwan

ceived more careful attention, resulting in marked improvement in output. It is grown almost exclusively in the eastern half of the Red Basin, east of the Kialing-kiang.

Szechwan is reputed to have the highest cattle population of all the provinces of China. In the Red Basin the cattle are almost exclusively draught animals, chiefly yellow oxen and water buffaloes. These have been greatly increased since 1949, together with pigs, which are reared for their meat and also as a source of manure. On the broad, natural grasslands of the highlands of the northwest, there is pastoral farming, including the raising of horses and yaks.

Table 3   Szechwan Livestock (10 000 head)

	Hogs	Oxen*	Buffaloes
1936 estimate	900	140	200
1949 ,,	1019	392	236
1952 ,,	1378	471	219
1957 ,,	2500	482	237

*Includes yaks and milch cows

Yangtze Rice–Wheat Region

The fertile lower Yangtze basin, drained by the main river and its great tributaries, the Han, Siang and Kan, contains six important provinces, Kiangsu, Anhwei, Hupeh, Hunan, Kiangsi and Chekiang, which together have a population of about 180 million people or nearly one-quarter of the whole of China.

Although the area has many common geographical and agricultural features, we have divided it into two regions largely to emphasize the

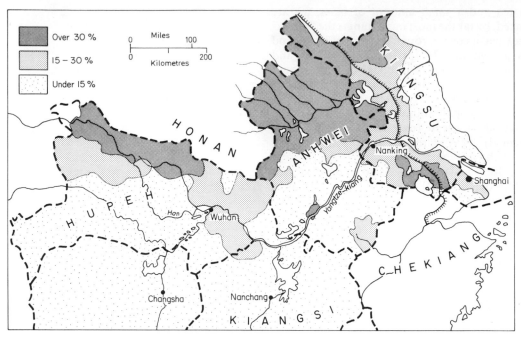

Fig. 66   Percentage of cultivated land under wheat (compiled from Economic Geography of Central China 1960 *and* Economic Geography of Eastern China 1961, *Institute of Geography, Chinese Academy of Sciences)*

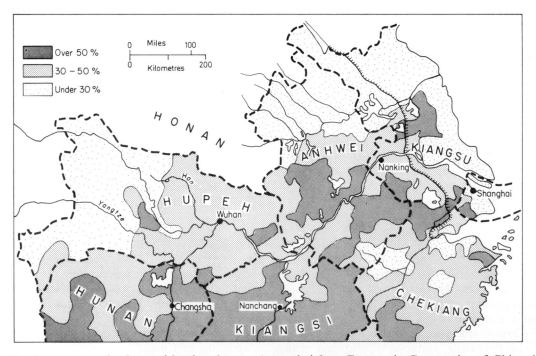

Fig. 67   Percentage of cultivated land under rice (compiled from Economic Geography of China 1960 *and* Economic Geography of Eastern China 1961, *Institute of Geography, Chinese Academy of Sciences)*

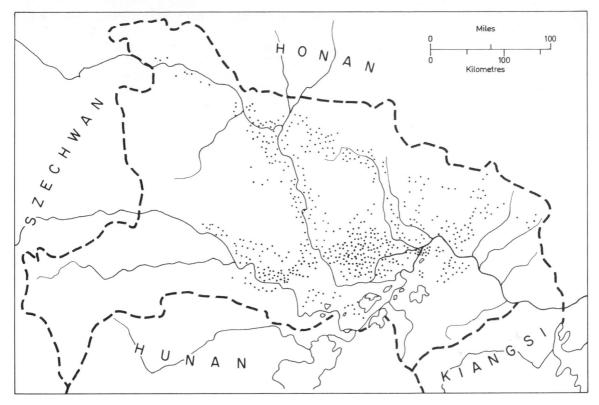

Fig. 68   Hupeh cotton production distribution (from Economic Geography of Central China, *Institute of Geography, Chinese Academy of Sciences)*

virtual disappearance of wheat production south of the Yangtze. Throughout the entire area rice is by far the most important food crop grown. North of the Yangtze in Kiangsu, Anhwei and Hupeh approximately 33 per cent of the food-crop acreage is devoted to rice, 28 per cent to wheat, 10 per cent to barley, 9 per cent to corn and 6 per cent to sweet potatoes. South of the river in Hunan, Kiangsi and Chekiang, the proportions are approximately 70 per cent devoted to rice, 7 per cent to wheat, 5 per cent to barley, 3 per cent to corn and 4 per cent to sweet potatoes. When actual grain outputs are compared, the contrasts are even more arresting[44]. The three northern provinces which form the Rice–Wheat Region produced, in 1957, 407 million *tan* (1 *tan* = 50 kg) of rice and 95·9 million *tan* of wheat, which respectively represented 60 per cent and 14 per cent of the grain output, while the three southern provinces of the Rice–Tea Region produced 438 million *tan* of rice and only 9·2 million *tan* of

wheat, which respectively represented 85 per cent and 1·8 per cent of the grain output.

The main summer crops of the Rice–Wheat Region are rice, sweet potatoes, peanuts, sesame, cotton, fibres and tobacco. The winter crops are winter wheat, barley, peas, beans and green fertilizer. Nearly all the agricultural land of the region is double-cropped. When grown in succession to rice, barley has a slight advantage over winter wheat in that it matures somewhat earlier, thus giving more time for ploughing and puddling the paddy in preparation for transplanting the rice seedlings. Barley is used for human consumption much more readily in central China than in Europe. While the acreage under corn in this region is not nearly as great as rice or wheat, the introduction of new hybrid strains has resulted in greatly increased output.

When it is remembered that the Yangtze valley has been the main source of agricultural raw materials for export during the last 70–80 years, it is surprising to learn that only about 7 per cent of the total cultivated land in this region is devoted to economic crops, i.e. crops other than food grain. Of the economic crops cotton is by far the most important, occupying about half the acreage. The main growing areas are Kiangsu and Hupeh. Hupeh was one of the chief cotton producers before 1936 and led the country in 1928 with an output of 4·2 million *tan* of lint. This fell to less than 1 million *tan* in 1949, but subsequently recovered and in 1957 Hupeh was again producing 4·5 million *tan* with an average yield of 100 *chin/ mow*. The main growing areas are in the Yangtze–Han plain between Ichang and Wuhan and along the lower valley of the Han. Because cotton must be planted in April and wheat is not harvested until May, it is a common practice in Hupeh to interplant cotton and wheat. However, because of their earlier maturity, barley or oats is preferred in rotation with cotton. The average length of staple is 18–20 mm. Most of the cotton is processed in Hupeh. No. 1 Cotton Mill, Wuchang was established with the latest Lancashire machinery at the turn of the century. No. 2 Cotton Mill has been built recently and has all the most modern equipment. Kiangsu's main cotton-producing areas are in the Yangtze delta between Shanghai, Wusih and Nantung and along the coast. The coastal strip is largely land reclaimed from the sea over many centuries; its soil is saline. Cotton, being a plant which is more tolerant to salt than most others, has therefore been developed in this area, the former large private farms now being taken over by state and commune. Yields from saline lands have been very small in the past. However, by meticulous cultivation, which has included thorough draining of the saline land which is usually very subject to waterlogging, by ploughing in winter and collecting the accumulated surface salt after the thaw in the spring, by constant harrowing, weeding and fertilizing and, finally, by expert seed selection, production from soil containing as much as 3·17 per cent salt has been raised from 10 *catties* of ginned cotton to 84 *catties/mow*[34]. Cotton processing is centred in Shanghai.

The main fibres produced in the Rice–Wheat Region are ramie, hemp and jute. Southeast Hupeh is China's leading producer of ramie (*ssu ma*) with an output of 350 000 *tan* in 1957, which comprised about one-third of the country's total production. This is still 40 000 *tan* less than the prewar peak. Ramie is the Chinese equivalent of linen and provides a very acceptable cloth for wear in hot, humid, summer days in Central China. There are three harvests a year in May, July and October. Better cultivation and processing is necessary to meet the rising demand. Many areas in the Yangtze delta are admirably suited to the growth of jute on account of the high summer water-table. Production has increased greatly in the last decade to meet the rapidly rising demand.

Vegetable oils produced from rapeseed, sesame and peanuts form a large proportion of the economic crops of the region. Of these rapeseed is clearly the most important and has a very wide distribution. Rape, which is a winter crop, matures earlier than wheat or barley and thus gives more time for rice preparation. Its production, therefore, tends to increase with the extension of rice production. Peanuts usually are grown on dry lands and on newly rehabilitated sandy wastelands, and do not compete with grain crops. Sesame is a summer crop, which alternates with wheat, barley, beans and peas. It has a poor resistance to heavy rainfall and therefore its production tends to decrease southward[44]. Some 250 000 *tan* of good quality wood oil (*tung yu*) is produced annually in west Hupeh from trees grown round homesteads, around fields and along roads.

The area around T'ai Hu in Kiangsu and extending into south and west Anhwei has for long been one of the most important sericulture regions in China[45]. Between 1929 and 1932 it enjoyed a period of great prosperity when more than 1 million *mow* were under mulberry orchard. Thereafter it encountered difficulties. During the Sino–Japanese War sericulture was discouraged and silkworm strains, in consequence, were weakened. This, together with the increasing competition of synthetic fibres, had resulted by 1949 in a fall of production by at least 50 per cent. Since 1949 there have been big efforts to revive the occupation, but there is keen competition from food crops for the low-lying plains in this densely populated area. Efforts are therefore being made to establish sericulture in the somewhat higher land around Nanking and Chinkiang, and also to develop the tussore wild silkworm on the scrub-oak woodland of that area[46]. Six schools of sericulture have been started on the slopes of the Tapiehshan in an endeavour to introduce the most modern techniques[47].

A small amount of tea is grown in the uplands along the southern border of Kiangsu and south

	Jan	Feb	Mar	Apr	May	Jun	Jul	Aug	Sep	Oct	Nov	Dec
Shanghai (10 m)												
Temp °C	3·3	3·9	7·8	13·3	18·3	22·8	26·7	26·7	22·8	17·2	11·1	5·6
Rainfall mm	51	57	86	94	91	188	150	145	119	79	51	33
Hankow (36 m)												
Temp °C	4·4	6·1	10·0	16·7	21·7	26·7	29·4	29·4	25·0	19·4	12·8	7·2
Rainfall mm	48	48	97	152	165	244	180	97	71	81	48	28

Anhwei. It is of excellent quality, known as 'Po-lo-chun', which is one of China's six famous teas. A large new state plantation has recently been opened for the development of black tea for export.

Since 1949, the amount of land devoted to tobacco growing in Anhwei has been extended from 60 000 to 300 000 *mow* (1957). The yield is reported to have been raised from 50 to 100 *chin/mow*. It is planted after the wheat harvest in late May and harvested between late August and late September.

Of the large livestock in the Rice–Wheat Region approximately 85 per cent are oxen and water buffaloes. Horses and mules decrease in numbers towards the southern borders of the region. Although numbers of oxen and buffaloes are large, estimated at more than 7 million in 1957, they are still inadequate for draught work on the farms. Hogs are ubiquitous and, following the national drive in recent years, have greatly increased in numbers. Some sheep are reared in north Anhwei and north Hupeh. In Kiangsu the breeding of angora rabbits as a secondary village occupation has developed rapidly recently. The wool is sent to Shanghai mills for manufacture into jerseys and scarfs for export to the U.S.S.R. and East Europe.

Rice–Tea Region
The Rice–Tea Region contains within its borders three fertile alluvial basins, the floodplains of the Siang and Yuan around the Tungting-hu in Hunan, that of the Kan-kiang around the Poyang-hu in Kiangsi and that of the Sinan around Hang-chow Wan in Chekiang. The climate begins to assume a subtropical character, especially in the southernmost parts, and as a consequence the growing season is lengthened.

A glance at the food crop statistics is sufficient to emphasize the all-important position that rice occupies in the sustenance of the people south of the Yangtze. About 70 per cent of the cultivated land is devoted to rice and this forms 85 per cent of the total food output for the three provinces, Hunan, Kiangsi and Chekiang, which make up this region. In rice production, Hunan ranks second only to Szechwan, which is nearly three times bigger and has nearly twice the population. In 1957 Hunan produced 193 million *tan* of rice. Thus, it is able to produce more than it needs and exports considerable quantities eastward down the Yangtze.

We have seen something of the efforts that are being made to modernize and extend irrigation, especially around the Tungting and Poyang lakes (see p. 110). Nevertheless much of the paddy, particularly in south and west Hunan, is still irrigated by old 'mountain pool' and 'flat pool' methods. These pools vary in size, but none are really large and few are adequate. The 'flat pools' are usually shallow and entail lifting water to the fields. This is done painstakingly and rather inefficiently by the old methods. It will be many years yet before the lifting is everywhere replaced by diesel or electric pumps. In Hunan rice is the summer crop, followed usually by a later autumn crop of beans, buckwheat or sweet potatoes. In favourable conditions a third crop of rapeseed or

	Jan	Feb	Mar	Apr	May	Jun	Jul	Aug	Sep	Oct	Nov	Dec
Changsha (92 m)												
Temp °C	6·1	7·8	10·6	17·2	21·7	26·1	30·0	30·0	25·0	18·9	12·8	7·2
Rainfall mm	46	97	147	155	198	224	121	132	86	91	79	46
Wenchow (3 m)												
Temp °C	8·3	8·3	11·7	16·1	20·6	25·0	28·3	28·3	25·0	20·6	17·8	10·6
Rainfall mm	47	86	124	140	178	251	190	239	203	81	53	41

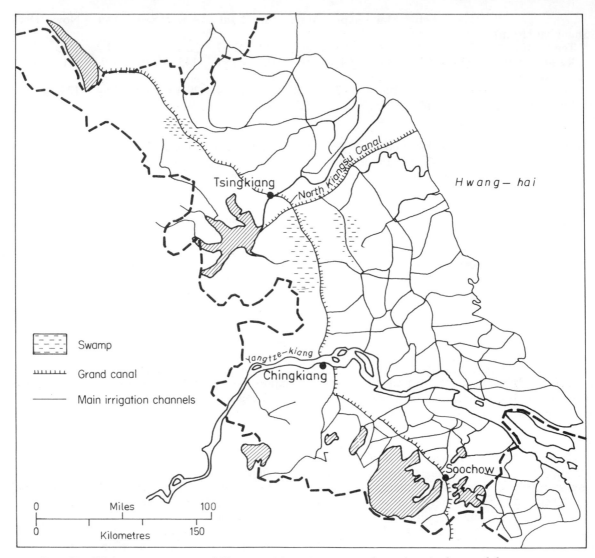

Fig. 69   Water conservancy of Kiangsu. Many irrigation channels are also used for transport

green fertilizer is reaped. Recently there has been an increase in the double-cropping of rice in the Ningpo and Wenchow districts of Chekiang. It is maintained that, given adequate irrigation and labour facilities, climatic conditions in Chekiang are everywhere suitable for double-cropping, followed by a green fertilizer crop (*astragalus sinicus*)[46].

Tea, which has been the national beverage since at least the eighth century, is the outstanding economic crop of the three provinces. Chekiang ranks first and Hunan second in national pro-

duction, raising 466 000 *tan* (one-fifth of the national output) and 370 000 *tan* respectively in 1957. The tea export trade suffered a shattering blow in the 1880s, when Indian and Ceylon teas, grown on large plantations and processed under careful supervision, swept the western market – a blow from which China's tea trade has never properly recovered. However, such is the importance of the domestic market and demand that the loss of the export trade was a comparatively minor matter. The natural conditions of the three provinces are well suited to tea production. They

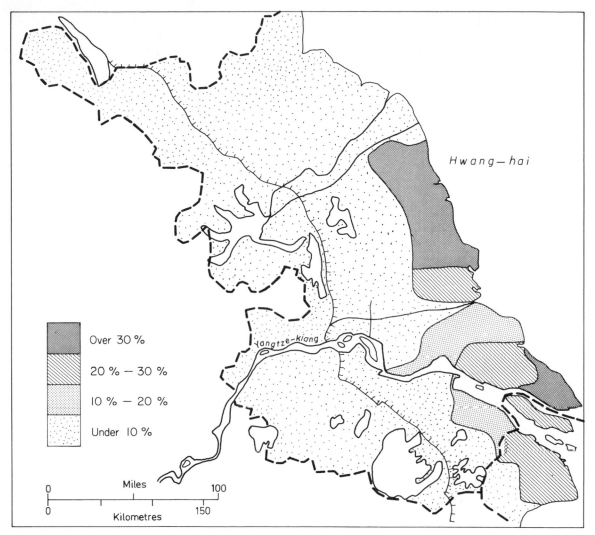

Fig. 70   Percentage of cultivated land under cotton in Kiangsu. Note 30 per cent category saline and sparsely populated (compiled from Economic Geography of East China, Hua Tung Ching Chi Ti Li, *ed. Sun Ching-chih)*

all enjoy a long frost-free period. High summer temperatures, abundant summer rain and high humidity and deep soil on well-drained hills ensure rapid leaf growth. Both green and black teas are grown, much of which has been of poor quality, due to the fact that production has been in the hands of individual small peasant farmers to whom tea-growing has been a secondary occupation. Larger plantations and specialization, consequent on the formation of cooperatives and communes, should bring improvement in quality and quantity. Some of Hunan's coarser qualities are made into brick tea for transport to Tibet, Mongolia and the U.S.S.R. Kiangsi produces 'Ning Hung' and 'Fou Hung' red tea in the Siu-shui valley.

The great activity in sericulture in southern Kiangsu, noted above, is extended southward with even greater intensity into Chekiang, which has always been China's greatest silk producer. As in Kiangsu, sericulture is one of the chief secondary occupations of the villages.

Silkworm production in this province is divided into four periods – spring, summer, autumn and late autumn. Of these the period for the spring silkworm

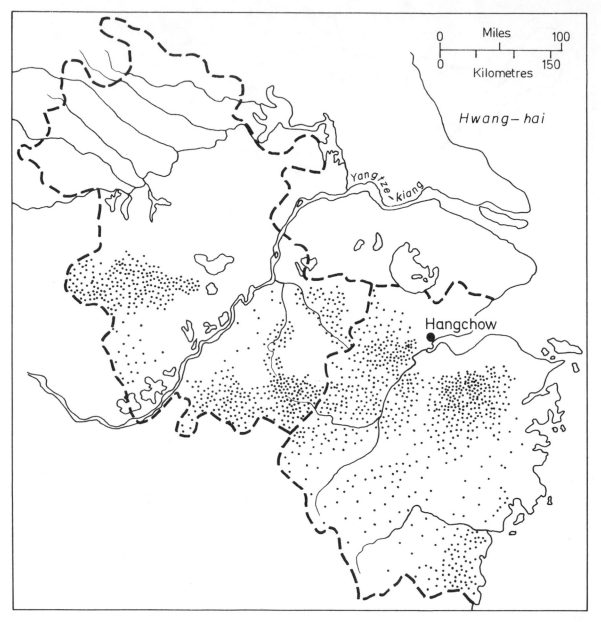

Fig. 71   Distribution of tea in Anhwei and Chekiang (from Economic Geography of East China, *Hua Tung Ching Chi, ed. Sun Ching-chih)*

is the most important, as more than 75 per cent of the year's cocoons are produced during this time. In spring the mulberry leaves are particularly juicy and tender, and the climatic factors, such as temperature and humidity, are also ideal for silkworm culture. Furthermore, manpower use for spring silkworm culture does not conflict with farming activities.[46]

Like Kiangsu, sericulture in Chekiang has suffered the same setbacks of suppression during the Sino–Japanese War and the competition of synthetic fibres, and production has not yet reached the prewar peak. In 1957 there were 1·73 million *mow* of mulberry orchards in the province and

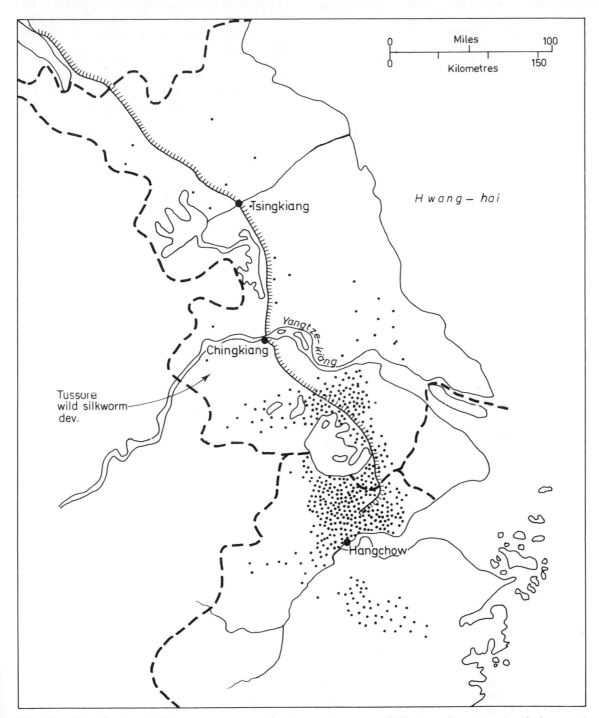

Fig. 72   Distribution of silkworm cocoon production in Kiangsu and Chetiang Provinces (each dot equals 1000 shi tan (*from* Economic Geography of East China, *Hua Tung Ching Chi, ed. Sun Ching-chih*)

490 000 *tan* of cocoons were produced. Increasing care is being given to silkworm egg selection and to the improvement of mulberry orchards.

Cotton production is of less importance south of the Yangtze than north. In Chekiang the main growth is on the plain to the north and south of Hangchow Wan. Here the usual rotation is two years of rice and one of cotton, the pattern of which is: first year, wheat, barley, rape or other winter crop, followed by cotton; second year, winter green fertilizer crop, followed by late-maturing rice; third year, further green fertilizer crop, followed by double-cropping rice[44]. The cotton crop is sent mainly to Shanghai for manufacture, but some spinning and weaving is done in Hangchow. Of the fibres, ramie and hemp are produced in Hunan and Kiangsi, while jute is more important in Chekiang.

Nearly 60 per cent of the economic crop acreage is devoted to the growth of vegetable oils. Rape-seed, as usual, is by far the most important and is widely distributed over the whole of the region. A good deal of sesame is grown in Kiangsi.

Much of the natural forest has been cleared from the uplands of the region, but considerable reserves still remain in the remoter parts. The densest forests are in west Hunan in the middle and upper reaches of the Yuan-kiang and the southeastern side of the Siang-kiang, producing fine stands of 'Ch'en' cedar and 'Yao' cedar and 'Ma-wei' pine, which is in much demand for mining and railway ties. In 1957 1·8 million cu m were cut, of which about two-thirds was cedar and one-third pine. A great deal of this was exported down the river to Hupeh and east China. Hunan also produces excellent rapid-growing bamboo, which, in addition to its thousand and one uses in handicrafts, papermaking, umbrellas and many kinds of household utensils, is also finding an extended use in building construction[46]. The character of the forested uplands changes gradually eastward through Kiangsi to Chekiang. Cedar gives place to pine (*pinus massoniana*), fir, chestnut, camphor and pseudo-sassafras. Bamboo, on the lower slopes, continues to be of great importance industrially. Chekiang is one of the richer forest provinces with an estimated 57 million *mow* of woodland in 1958, which represents about 37 per cent of the land area. Considerable care and attention is being given throughout the whole region to afforestation of the uplands; in Chekiang 780 000 *mow* are reported to be planted with wood oil (*Aleurites cordata*).

Fruit production has received remarkable impetus during the last two decades. The growing of citrus fruits (oranges, tangerines and grapefruit), peaches and pears figures largely in the west in Hunan and Kiangsi, especially around the lakes. In Chekiang, fruit production extends to loquats, apricots, strawberries, walnuts, dates and chestnuts as well. Some sugar-cane is also grown.

Throughout the whole of the Rice–Wheat and Rice–Tea Regions freshwater fishing makes an important contribution to food production. This is dealt with in a later section.

Southwest Rice Region

Yunnan and Kweichow, which together comprise the Southwest Rice Region, form the most remote part of China Proper. For the most part it is a plateau of a general height of some 1200 m, but higher in the west and deeply incised with steep valleys. It was into this land that the many and varied tribes, who occupied the middle Yangtze valley, were pressed by the Chinese *Han Jen* of the north as they expanded southward between 200 BC and AD 900. Consequently, of the 36 million people who today occupy these lands, nearly one-third are what are termed 'minorities'. Of these the chief is the Puyi, numbering about 1·25 million at the 1953 census, followed by the Pai, Tai, Hani, Tung, Miao, Ka-wa, Hai, Na-hsi, La-yu, Chingpo, Yao and many others. They have had little contact with the Chinese until recently and, for livelihood, have followed generally 'slash and burn' agriculture and hunting. Population becomes increasingly rural (more than 90 per cent and decreasingly dense (less than 40/ sq km) westward.

It is surprising that there has not been more intensive Chinese occupation of the region, for in many parts it has a most attractive and equable climate. Yunnan, meaning 'South of the Clouds', is noted for its warm, dry, winter days with its clear sunny skies. In summer it has ample rain, particularly in east and west. The centre has something of a rain shadow.

From October to April, tropical continental air masses move southward. The Yunnan Plateau is controlled by west-bound currents that are warm and dry. The whole plateau enters into its dry season. After April the tropical continental air masses move northward. Southwesterly wind currents from India and southeasterly seasonal winds from the Pacific Ocean separately control the east and west areas of the plateau, bringing rich rains.[43]

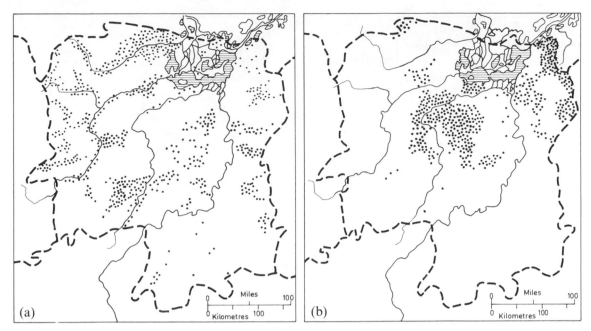

Fig. 73 (*a*) *Rapeseed production in Hunan* (*each dot equals* 1000 tan) *note main production along river valleys;* (*b*) *Tea production in Hunan* (*each dot equals* 500 tan) *note main production in uplands.*

East Kweichow is lower, cloudier and colder in winter and has a more equable distribution of rainfall than Yunnan. The whole region enjoys a long growing period but, owing to its mountainous character, is handicapped by the small proportion of cultivable land as is shown on figures 74(a) and 74(b).

In spite of its favourable climate, this southwest region has the unenviable reputation of being the most backward agriculturally in China Proper. This undoubtedly is due, to some extent, to its remoteness and isolation, to the poverty of soil and to the limited amount of cultivable soil, but it is equally certain that it is also the result of human factors. It has been noted above that an appreciable proportion of the population is tribal,

which, until recently, has had little impact on agriculture. Since 1949, the People's Government has been assiduous in its attempts to integrate these people into the body politic and economic. This has been done by granting local self-government to the tribal *chou*, by sending well-qualified cadres to assist in development* and by forming

* Fei Hsio-tung, an eminent sociologist, has done much to assist in the development of these people and was their representative in Peking for many years.

'Institutes of Minorities' in many large cities, the largest being in Peking. To these institutes, the local leaders are sent for training in administration and in modern agricultural and industrial practice. In this way the establishment of cooperatives and communes in these backward areas has been

	Jan	Feb	Mar	Apr	May	Jun	July	Aug	Sep	Oct	Nov	Dec
Kunming (1805 m)												
Temp °C	8·9	10·6	15·6	18·9	21·1	22·2	21·1	21·1	18·9	17·2	13·3	9·4
Rainfall mm	13	13	15	18	96	155	249	208	137	91	43	15
Kweiyang (1390 m)												
Temp °C	2·2	5·6	11·7	17·2	21·7	22·2	24·4	25·0	20·0	13·9	11·7	8·3
Rainfall mm	25	28	23	74	178	209	229	104	138	107	51	15

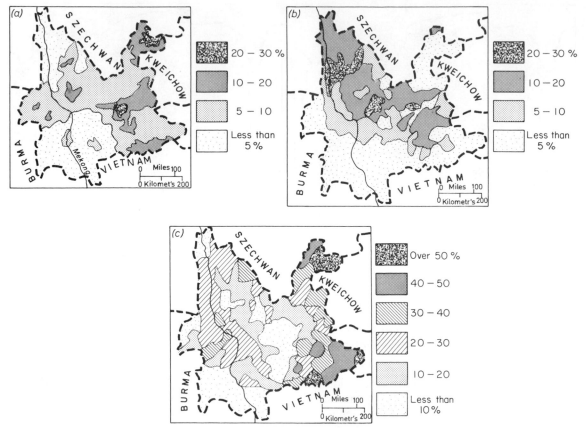

Fig. 74 (a) *Percentage of cultivated land in Yunnan note small percentage in deep valleys and high ridges of southwest, and high percentage on central plateau and Yangtze valley;* (b) *percentage of wheat to cultivated land in Yunnan;* (c) *percentage of corn to cultivated land in Yunnan* (*compiled from* Economic Geography of Southwest China, *Peking, 1960*)

quicker and more successful than might reasonably have been expected. Another reason for the backwardness of agriculture has been the degenerate social state of the Chinese population itself. Absentee landlordism, uncharacteristic laziness and love of ease, exploitation of women's labour and general addiction to poppy growing and opium smoking have all been contributary causes[48]. Land reform, the prohibition of poppy-growing and opium smoking and the emancipation of women have gone a long way towards social regeneration and the establishment of higher agricultural standards.

Rice is the most important grain crop grown. Although the acreage devoted to corn rivals it, the yield per *mow* from rice was more than twice as great in 1957. Rice-growing is concentrated in the south and southeast of the region, where 92 per cent of the production is paddy and 8 per cent

upland rice. There are big differences in unit yield as between districts, depending on cultivation methods, many of which were reported as being poor and slipshod in 1957, average yield being only 150–200 *chin/mow*. Where water supply is adequate, rice is followed by a winter crop of wheat, barley, rape or beans, but too often fields have, unnecessarily, been left fallow during the winter. Reports since 1957 indicate that, with the extension of irrigation, the situation has changed materially. A network of 180 electric pumping stations has been built round the Tien Chih lake, Kunming since 1958, serving 13 000 hectares and guaranteeing them against drought, which is the main hazard in central Yunnan. A new rice strain, 'Wannung No. 1', developed at Kweiyang on an experimental farm, bids to raise production per *mow* to over 500 *chin*[49]. One other example must suffice to indicate the change taking place in the

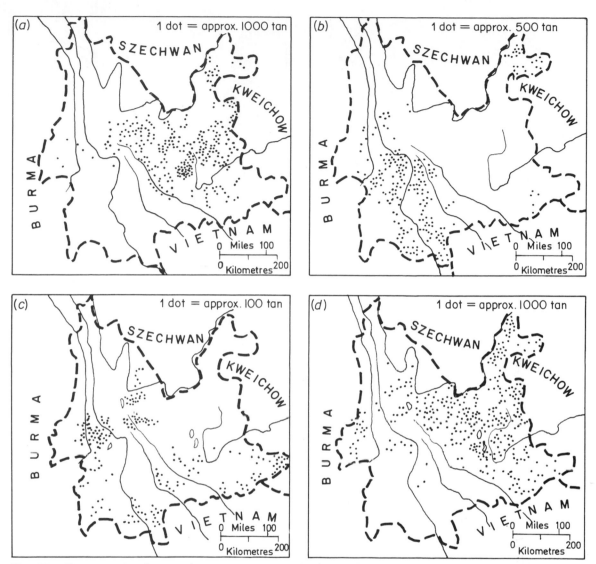

Fig. 75   Yunnan: (a) tobacco; (b) tea; (c) cotton; (d) rapeseed. Kweichow; (a) percentage of cultivated land; (b) percentage of paddy to total cultivated area; (c) percentage of corn crop to total cultivated area (compiled from Economic Geography of Southwest China, *Peking 1960)*

remoter tribal regions. Reports from Te-Hung Tai and Chingpo Autonomous *Chou,* which has a population of 400 000 composed of Tai, Chingpo, Pengling, Lisu and Achong nationalities, claim that 54 per cent of its farmland is now fully irrigated, served by more than 60 electric power stations. Hillsides have been terraced and a diversified economy developed, which includes summer rice and winter wheat, the growing of pineapples, bananas, papaya and citrus fruit, tea and coffee-growing and the rearing of pigs[50].

Figures 77 and 78, show a clear zoning of the three main grain crops, rice in the southeast, corn on the central plateau and wheat in the northwest. Rapeseed, grown in winter and heavily cropped on the central plateau, is the most important of the oil seeds. Soyabeans also are widely grown and are usually planted between the rows of corn on the uplands. They are grown here mainly as a food and not for oil extraction.

Both provinces have an excellent climate for tobacco, the main production of which is concentrated on the central plateau. Tobacco stock is good and recent improvement in methods has

Karst country, Kwangtung

Liukia gorges, Hwang-ho

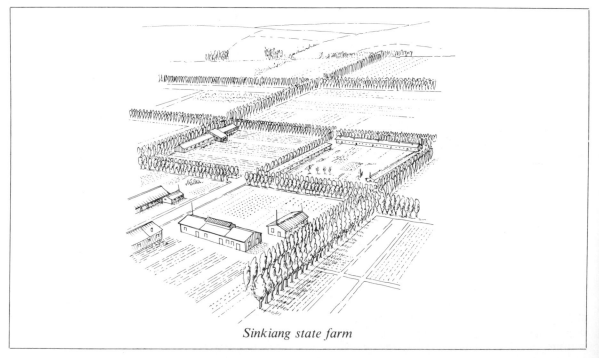

Sinkiang state farm

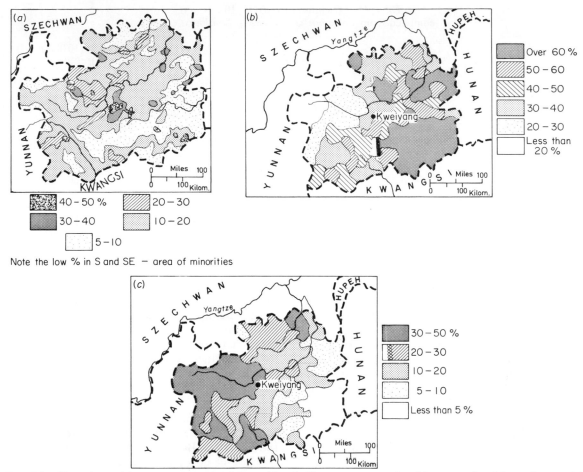

Fig. 76   Kweichow: (a) percentage of cultivated land; (b) percentage of paddy to total cultivated area; (c) percentage of corn crop to total cultivated area. (Compiled from Economic Geography of Southwest China, *Peking 1960)*

raised the yield to 245 *chin/mow*. Some indication of the importance placed locally on this crop can be gleaned from the fact that a special middle school has been opened in Kweiyang and offers two courses, one for tobacco cultivation and the other for food crops.

Cotton, which in the past was not extensively grown and was of poor quality, is now being rapidly developed. A successful long-staple strain has been bred, which, if sown in November instead of March, flowers before the heavy rainy season. Formerly much of the crop was spoiled by the June rains, which harmed pollination and promoted excessive vegetational growth to the detriment of the boll. Yields of 1500 kg/hectare (about 80 *chin/mow*) are reported[51].

Tea is grown in Yunnan and Kweichow. The main producing areas are the district west and south of Erh-hai and in the hills south of the Yangtze in the extreme northeast. Green tea forms the bulk of the output, but black and brick tea are also grown. Yunnan's production, 180 000–190 000 *tan* in 1958, is about double that of Kweichow. A little sericulture is practised, the silkworms being raised mainly on oak leaf. The production of sugar-cane, which has suffered in the past from the long winter-spring aridity, is getting a new lease of life as irrigation develops.

Like Szechwan, this region received large numbers of migrants, fleeing westward before the Japanese forces between 1936 and 1945. As a consequence, agriculture and industry were advanced. Progress over the twenty-one years between 1936 and 1957 is shown in the following tables:

Table 4   Agricultural Products (10 000 *tan*)
(compiled from *Economic Geography of Southwest China*)

	Rice	Wheat	Cotton	Tobacco	Peanut	Rape	Sugar-cane	Livestock (10 000 head)		
								Cattle	Buffalo	Hog
Yunnan										
1936	3498	613	4	—	24	107	—	49	54	276
1949	4439	322	1	4	13	46	508	185	95	—
1952	5132	392	5	11	17	42	609	208	108	371
1957	7124	617	7	61	61	90	1509	303	139	652
Kweichow					*Corn*					
1936	3177	120	5	22	1587	—	—	57	60	142
1949	4221	66	3	26	1201	49	—	154	70	288
1952	4748	102	5	32	1480	73	—	170	76	360
1957	6720	405	5	99	2231	165	—	250	92	615

Double-cropping Rice Region

This region covers roughly the provinces of Fukien, Kwangtung and Kwangsi. Geologically it consists mainly of igneous and metamorphosed formations in the east from which overlying sedimentaries have been largely eroded and extensive limestone formations in the west, giving rise to fantastic karst scenery. For the most part the region is hilly and even mountainous, the only areas at all comparable to the wide, alluvial plains of the Yangtze and Hwang-ho being the floodplain of the lower Si-kiang.

The whole region enjoys tropical or subtropical temperatures, which, given adequate water, ensure a growing season of 12 months. There is a marked and heavy summer maximum of rainfall.

While the population of Fukien and Kwangtung is predominantly Chinese, it is distinguished from the Han Jen of north China. The people of the south refer to themselves as T'ang Jen or Men of T'ang, the dynasty (AD 618–907) during which the south was firmly and extensively settled. The people have their own distinctive dialects of Cantonese and Fukienese, although, of course, they have the same written language as the north. In the west, however, only 11·4 million out of a total of 19·4 million are Chinese, the remainder being minorities, who, as in Kweichow and Yunnan, were pushed into the hills by the advancing Chinese. By far the largest of these people is the Chuang, who number over 7 million. For this reason, the People's Government has established here the Kwangsi Chuang Autonomous Region. Other important tribes are the Yao (484 000), Miao (219 840), T'ung (148 424) and Yao-lao (44 666). In addition there are considerable numbers of 'boat people', living on the water in the river estuaries and along the rugged coast. Most of the Chinese emigration to Malaysia, Indonesia and Borneo in times past has been from this double-cropping rice region, and it is from these emigrants that remittances are still received.

As its title indicates, the characteristic crop is rice, to which 68 per cent of the planted area is devoted. Most of the lower-lying land, having adequate water facilities, grows an early and a late crop of rice, followed by an over-wintering crop of wheat, peanuts, beans or green manure. To do this the late crop must follow the early in quick succession. There is a local saying 'In the morning, yellow; in the evening, green', indicating that the standing ripe rice is reaped in the morning and that, by evening, the same fields should be green with the transplanted seedlings of the new crop.

	Jan	Feb	Mar	Apr	May	Jun	Jul	Aug	Sep	Oct	Nov	Dec
Canton (15 m)												
Temp °C	13·3	13·9	17·2	21·7	26·7	27·2	28·3	28·3	26·7	23·9	19·4	15·6
Rainfall mm	23	48	107	173	269	269	205	219	165	86	31	23
Foochow (20·4 m)												
Temp °C	11·7	11·1	13·3	17·8	22·2	26·7	28·9	28·9	24·4	19·4	15·0	10·0
Rainfall mm	46	96	114	122	150	207	160	183	213	51	41	48

Table 5 Southwest Rice Region Grain Crops, 1957
(compiled from *Economic Geography of Southwest China*)

	Acreage planted		Yield mow	Total output	% of total
	10 000 *mow*	% of total		10 000 *tan*	
Rice					
Yunnan	1593	27·3	447	7124	57·0
Kweichow	1342	26·6	501	6720	63·9
Wheat					
Yunnan	501	8·6	123	617	4·9
Kweichow	405	8·6	100	405	3·9
Corn					
Yunnan	1388	23·8	193	2672	21·4
Kweichow	1131	24·1	197	2231	21·2
Barley					
Yunnan	312	5·4	92	283	2·3
Kweichow	161	3·4	96	155	1·5
Sweet potatoes					
Yunnan*	227	2·4	245	682	2·7
Kweichow†	221	2·3	286	637	3·0
Beans and peas					
Yunnan	542	4·6	112	656	2·7
Kweichow	118	1·3	77	91	0·4
		Economic Crops, 1957			
Rapeseed					
Yunnan	276	4·7	54	94	
Kweichow	378	8·1	44	165	
Peanut					
Yunnan	54	0·9	113	61	
Kweichow	13	0·3	143	19	
Tobacco					
Yunnan	91	0·8	85	73	
Kweichow	92	0·9	108	99	
Cotton					
Yunnan	38	0·7	18	7	
Kweichow	37	0·4	17	6	
Fibres					
Yunnan‡	14	0·3	62	9	
Kweichow§	11	0·2	56	6	
Sugar-cane					
Yunnan	30	0·5	5078	1500	
Kweichow	5	0·1	3801	176	

* Potatoes and yams   † Sweet and Irish potatoes   ‡ Mainly hemp   § Mainly ramie

This is an exaggeration, but it serves to emphasize the need for getting the second crop in as quickly as possible. Late planting means a poor yield, hence the need for the rational use and economy of labour, especially at peak times in rice cultivation. Officials are called away from their offices and students from their desks at such times, but such help as they can give is probably small when compared with the increasing mechanization in the rice fields that is taking place in the form of transplanting machines and tractors for reaping and ploughing. The new powered rice trans-planter, which is a great improvement on the machines of 1958, transplants 12 *mow* of seedlings in a day. The new rotary tiller, drawn by a 35 h.p. tractor, works well in muddy paddy fields and it is claimed that the new, long-distance spray, having a 15 m jet, keeps the rice borer infestation down to 1 per cent and is considered revolutionary. It is to the production of this kind of agricultural machinery that industry has been directed since 1960, but there is no clear report of how widely it is now in use.

The great efforts that have been expended in

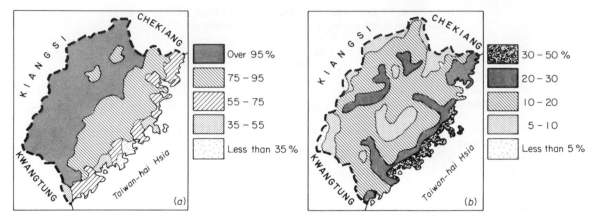

Fig. 77   Double cropping rice: (a) *percentage of total crop area planted in rice in Fukien: note almost exclusive rice cultivation in uplands;* (b) *percentage of cultivated land to total land area (from* Economic Geography of South China, *ed. Sun Ching-chih)*

extending irrigation and drainage in this region have been directed primarily to furthering rice production. Under a long-range plan, reservoirs have been built on the Tung(East)-kiang, most unruly of the three rivers (Si, Tung and Peh), thereby relieving the strain on the plains below during typhoons and heavy rains. In the low-lying Pearl river delta, 1200 electric pumping stations guarantee 460 000 hectares of farmland against flood and drought[52]. Of Kwangtung's 30 million *mow* of farmland 24 million *mow* are now said to be well irrigated. Similar claims are made for the more restricted arable areas of Fukien and Kwangsi. The latter, owing to its limestone formations, is more prone to drought. Thousands of wells are being sunk, tapping the abundant underground supplies of water[53]. Since 1958 20 000 hectares of land have been reclaimed from the sea in the Pearl river delta area by means of building massive dykes, and much of this land is already harvesting double-cropped rice[54]. The work and capital throughout is attributed almost entirely to the communes.

Much attention has also been focused on the development of a short-stalked variety of rice which will stand up to the heavy downpours and the high winds experienced in the south. High-tillering varieties, developing many spikes to each plant, have recently been bred and yields of $7-7\frac{1}{2}$ tons/hectare are now generally being achieved. Cultivation has been further aided by extensive building of chemical fertilizer plant. Kwangtung alone now has thirty-two large and small plants, which produced more than 500 000 tons of ferti-

lizer in 1964[55]. American expert opinion considers that China's rice yields compare favourably with those of the better parts elsewhere in the world and that increase will be difficult even with more fertilizer and better seed-breeding.[56]

Wet rice is often rotated with dry crops – wheat, beans, taro – to allow the surface of the rice fields to be baked by the sun, which, it is held, improves soil fertility. Taro is an important crop in this connection. It has a long growing period and is therefore interplanted with fast-growing vegetables such as beans, cucumbers, pai tsai (cabbage), followed by jute seedlings and potatoes when the taro leaves wither. In this way as many as five or six crops can be harvested in a year.

Wheat plays a small part in the remaining grain crops. Corn is produced in appreciable amount only in Kwangsi. Tubers, mainly sweet potatoes, are an important part of the general diet.

Oil seeds occupy more than half the area devoted to economic crops. Peanuts are by far the most important, followed by sesame. Rapeseed has, only recently, come into prominence. The tropical character of the region is emphasized by the fact that coconut and palm oil, tea oil, cassia, citronella oil and aniseed oil are all produced there. Kwangsi is an important producer of wood oil and tea oil, ranking second respectively to Szechwan and Kwangtung in the national scale.

The cultivation of sugar-cane is rapidly increasing. Natural conditions throughout the region, and particularly in Hainan, are very favourable. Kwangtung, which is the biggest producer, raised its output over the previous year

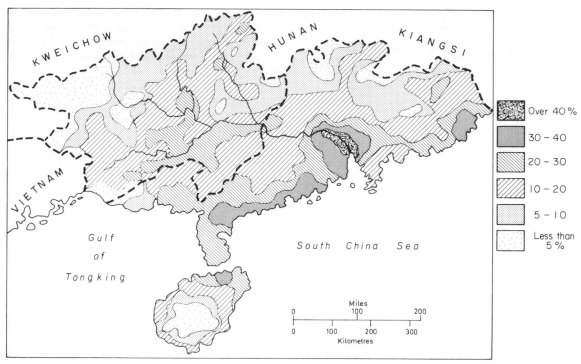

Fig. 78   Double cropping rice: percentage of cultivated land to total land area Kwangtung and Kwangsi
(*from* Economic Geography of South China, *ed. Sung Ching-Chi*)

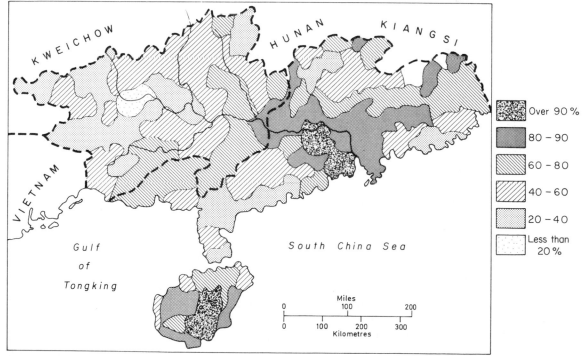

Fig. 79   Double cropping rice: percentage of total crop area planted in rice Kwangtung and Kwangsi
(*from* Economic Geography of South China, *ed. Sung Ching-Chi*)

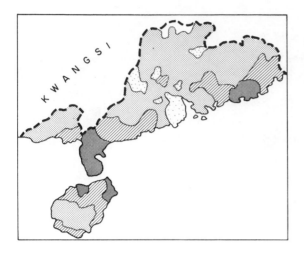

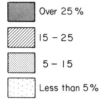

■ Over 25 %

▨ 15 – 25

▨ 5 – 15

□ Less than 5%

Fig. 80   Double cropping rice: ratio of sweet potatoes to cultivated land area in Kwangtung (from Economic Geography of South China, *ed. Sung Ching-Chi)*

by 100 000 ton in 1964–5. The cane yielded 11·1 per cent sugar of which 77 per cent was number 1 grade. Cane yield in Fukien is reported as 75 tons/hectare. The most important producing areas are the Chu-kiang (Pearl river), Han-kiang around Swatow, the coastal region between Foochow and Amoy and northern Hainan, where the two most important varieties are 'East Java 3016' early ripening and 'Formosa 134' late ripening. It has been found that interplanting in alternate rows of sugar-cane and peanuts raises the yield of both and this is now practised on a wide scale. The peanut tubercles are able to assimilate nitrogen from the air and so enrich the soil. After the pods are gathered the vines and leaves are ploughed in. The peanut plants also reduce evaporation and so conserve water for the canes[57]. A great increase in sugar refining has accompanied the rise in cane production. In 1965, Kwangtung alone had 7 large and 28 medium refineries with an annual total sugar output of 40 000 ton[58].

Although lying outside the Rice–Tea Region, Fukien enjoys national fame as a tea producer on account of its 'Wu-yi' and 'T'ieh-kwan-yin'

varieties. As might be expected, the main tea gardens are in the northeast, contiguous to the Chekiang gardens. The climate gives a long growing period, permitting picking during 10 months of the year. Although tea culture methods have made marked advances recently they are still somewhat primitive[58]. There has been an increase in coffee-growing in recent years, but the amount is still very small.

Sword hemp (*Bryophyllum Houghtonii*) and sisal are both grown in Kwangtung. The former is a tough fibre, resistant to sea water and is

Table 6

	1949–52 Planted area		1957 Planted area	
	10 000 *mow*	%	10 000 *mow*	%
Food Crops				
Rice				
Kwangtung	7030	83·9	7271	72·4
Kwangsi	—	—	3391	60·4
Fukien	215	76·9	221	71·4
Wheat				
Kwangtung	110	1·3	359	7·6
Kwangsi	—	—	391	5·2
Fukien	15	5·6	24	7·9
Corn				
Kwangsi	—	—	833	14·8
Tubers				
Kwangtung	1085	13·0	1863	18·6
Kwangsi	—	—	627	11·2
Fukien	40	14·5	45	14·6
Economic Crops				
Sugar-cane				
Kwangtung			176	24·1
Kwangsi			56	13·2
Fukien			37	17·1
Peanuts				
Kwangtung			378	51·9
Kwangsi			236	55·4
Fukien			111	50·9
Rapeseed				
Kwangtung			—	—
Kwangsi			35	8·2
Fukien			45	20·8
Fibres				
Kwangtung (hemp and ramie)			34	5·8
Kwangsi (jute and ramie)			12	2·9
Fukien (jute and ramie)			10	4·3
Tobacco				
Kwangtung			37	5·1
Kwangsi			15	8·4
Fukien			10	4·3

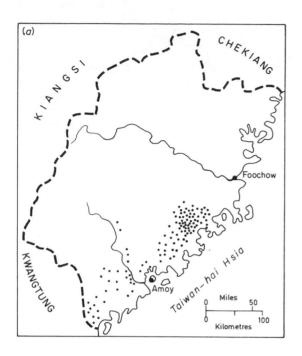
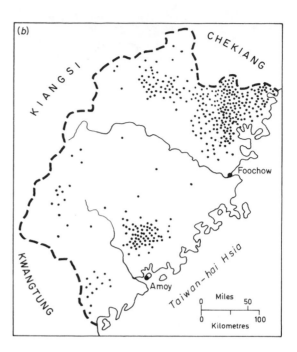
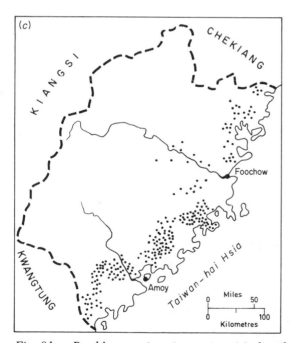
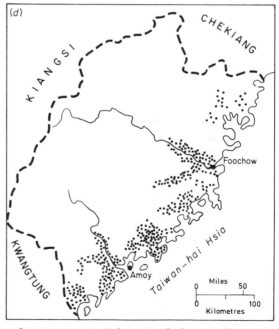

Fig. 81   Double-cropping rice region: (a) distribution of sugar-cane in Fukien (each dot equals approx. 100 000 tan); (b) distribution of tea in Fukien (each dot equals approx. 200 tan); (c) distribution of jute in Fukien (each dot equals approx. 500 tan); (d) distribution of fruit in Fukien (each dot equals approx. 3000 tan).

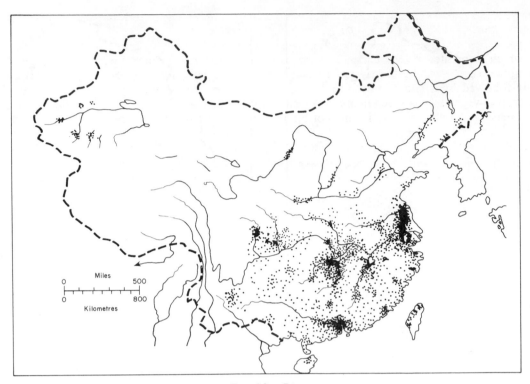

Fig. 82   Rice

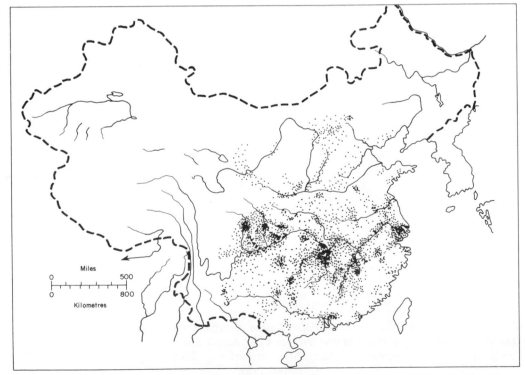

Fig. 83   Rapeseed

therefore good material for fishing nets. It is also valuable industrially for the manufacture of motor tyres, conveyor belts, etc.[60]. Some ramie is grown. Jute, which is planted in March and reaped in September, is grown along the river banks. It is usually followed by a late rice crop and then a catch crop of vegetables or green manure. A small but increasing amount of Sea Island cotton is grown in the south.

Sericulture is practised mainly in the lower Si-kiang basin and the Pearl river delta. Fast-growing white mulberry enables seven to eight pickings to be made in the year, with a result that Kwangtung produces one-eighth of the entire country's cocoons. Many varieties of wild silkworm are raised in west Kwangtung and Kwangsi on oak and camphor leaves[60].

The variety of fruit grown in this region reveals its tropical and subtropical nature. In addition to the vast quantities of citrus fruits (oranges, tangerines, pomelo and grapefruit) that are grown and exported, melons, longans, lichees and olives are produced in the river valleys and alluvial plains. Papaya, bananas, mango, pomegranates and betel nut are grown in the south and in Hainan. Pineapple, which demands little from the soil and can be successfully cultivated on quite steep hillsides, is now being extensively cultivated. Transportation and storage of fruit is improving and the canning industry is increasing very rapidly.

Virtually all the large livestock of this region are used for draught purposes. As might be expected in so intensive a rice-growing area, water buffalo form a larger proportion (nearly 50 per cent) than farther north. The national campaign to increase hog raising has been most intensive in the Double-Cropping Rice Region since its emphasis is so much on the production of manure. It is reckoned that one hog produces between 2000 and 3000 *chin* of manure annually, which may be instrumental in producing an additional 200 to 300 *chin/mow* of rice. Since the formation of cooperatives and communes, peasants have been urged to raise pigs collectively. That there has been some struggle and resistance to propaganda in this field is shown by the fact that by 1964 only about 30 per cent of the hogs in this region were raised collectively, the rest being raised on private plots either indirectly for the collective or for individual households. In the latter case manure would not find its way to the paddy fields. Clearly there is a strong temptation to breed pigs privately. 'Some rich peasants, seriously affected by the spontaneous tendency towards capitalism, tried their utmost to play down the role of collective hog-breeding[61].'

Table 7 Crop Production (million ton)

Year Peak	Total grain	Rice	Wheat	Misc. grain	Potatoes (4:1)	Soya-beans	Cotton lint	Rapeseed	Peanuts	Sugar-cane
pre 1949	150	52·5	23	—	—	9·84	0·84	1·75	2·76	3·25
1949	113	38·3	13	36	10	4·24	0·44	0·73	1·27	2·64
1950	132	50	15	—	—	—	0·71	—	—	—
1951	145	59	16·8	—	—	—	1·04	—	—	—
1952	164	68·4	18·1	52	16	7·9	1·30	0·93	2·32	7·12
1953	167	70·4	18·1	51	17	8·03	1·18	0·88	2·1	7·21
1954	170	69·7	23·2	49	17	7·5	1·06	0·88	2·77	8·59
1955	183	75	—	55	19	7·6	1·50	0·97	2·92	8·11
1956	199	82	—	53	20	8·5	—	0·94	3·33	8·67
1957	193	81·7	23·7	54	21	8·4	1·63	1·00	2·34	13·18
1958	220	—	—	—	—	8·7	—	—	2·78	—
1959	250	—	—	—	—	9·6	—	—	—	—
1960	—	—	—	—	—	—	—	—	—	—
1961	—	—	—	—	—	—	—	—	—	—
1962*	178	80·6	20·8	54	24	—	—	—	—	—
1963*	179	78·4	21·8	55	24	7·8	1·0	0·5	1·9	—

* Unofficial estimates (probably on the conservative side) (from *F.E.E.R. Year Book 1965* and *F.E.E.R*, No. 186, 21 July 1966).
† *Current Science*, Vol. VI (1968) no. 12.
‡ T. A. Close, *F.E.E.R.*, 5 January 1967.
§ Anna Louise Strong, estimate in *Letter from China*, Foreign Language Press, Peking, 15 January 1968.

Agricultural Production (thousands metric tons)

	1964	*1965*	*1966*	*1967*	*1968*	*1969*	*1970*	*1971*	*1972*	*1973*	*1974*
Rice	81 943	92 076	91 117	95 162	94 299	98 041	105 228	109 031	105 197	111 954	115 213
Barley	15 501	16 501	16 501	17 001	17 001	17 001	19 001	19 801	19 001	20 001	20 501
Wheat	25 520	20 022	25 729	28 024	27 017	28 510	31 004	32 502	34 502	36 004	37 002
Oats	1 759	1 800	1 900	1 909	2 000	2 100	2 500	2 709	2 500	2 700	2 756
Maize	23 842	25 541	25 552	26 064	26 051	27 245	29 254	30 057	28 571	30 384	31 085
Potatoes	28 019	30 016	29 616	30 423	30 422	31 228	34 824	36 030	32 027	36 027	38 027
Sweet Potatoes	87 348	93 131	92 860	94 120	93 845	95 302	106 641	111 391	102 928	111 204	113 100
Soybeans	11 238	11 036	11 033	11 175	11 743	10 987	11 645	11 741	11 240	11 761	11 860
Groundnuts	2 407	2 426	2 475	2 437	2 256	2 451	2 572	2 679	2 494	2 698	2 700
Tea	177	180	180	188	191	195	199	260	291	309	318
Sugar cane	27 005	32 229	32 670	31 502	34 547	34 742	35 746	38 631	38 869	30 664	40 000
Sugar beet	3 803	4 000	4 400	4 500	4 650	5 025	5 200	5 500	6 000	6 100	6 200
Rape seed	1 147	1 143	1 128	1 125	1 074	942	992	1 052	1 152	1 202	1 252
Sesame seed	372	368	367	368	368	368	367	368	361	367	367
Jute & Allied fibres	403	443	471	490	506	513	508	239	231	301	310
Cotton seed	2 994	3 298	3 687	3 861	3 601	3 713	3 992	4 163	3 557	4 295	4 295
Cotton Lint	1 389	1 540	1 671	1 801	1 671	1 605	1 692	1 649	1 778	2 147	2 147
Tung oil	100	105	105	95	85	70	70	76	76	76	76

Figures from *Statistical Year Book for Asia and the Pacific*, U.N. 1975.

Table 8   Food Crops

	10 000 *mow* units	Planted area		Total output	
		% Total crop acreage	% Food crop acreage	10 000 *tan*	% Food crop
Rice					
Rice–Wheat Region					
Kiangsu	3269	22·5	30·6	13422	57·0
Anhwei	3372	22·4	28·2	12190	53·1
Hupeh	3253	29·6	40·5	15111	68·9
Rice–Tea Region					
Hunan	5669	55·2	69·8	19333	86·1
Kiangsi	4414	53·9	80·5	12474	91·3
Chekiang	2443	39·2	59·7	11945	76·5
Wheat					
Rice–Wheat Region					
Kiangsu	3164	19·6	26·6	3148	13·4
Anhwei	4021	26·1	33·7	4010	17·5
Hupeh	1734	15·8	21·6	2438	11·1
Rice–Tea Region					
Hunan	500	4·9	6·2	301	1·3
Kiangsi	226	2·8	4·1	114	0·8
Chekiang	468	7·5	11·4	513	3·3
Barley					
Rice–Wheat Region					
Kiangsu	1102	6·8	9·3	1341	5·7
Anhwei	—	—	—	—	—
Hupeh	873	7·9	10·9	894	4·1
Rice–Tea Region					
Hunan	221	2·2	2·7	137	0·6
Kiangsi	106	1·3	1·9	71	0·5
Chekiang	304	4·7	7·4	377	2·4
Corn					
Rice–Wheat Region					
Kiangsu	938	5·8	8·9	1751	7·4
Anhwei	—	—	—	—	—
Hupeh	692	6·3	8·6	1194	5·4
Rice–Tea Region					
Hunan	249	2·4	3·1	276	1·2
Kiangsi	26	0·3	0·5	35	0·3
Chekiang	239	3·8	5·8	514	3·3
Sweet potatoes					
Rice–Wheat Region					
Kiangsu	532	3·3	4·5	1034	4·4
Anhwei	1132	7·5	9·5	323	14·1
Hupeh	285	2·6	3·5	895	4·1
Rice–Tea Region					
Hunan	40	0·4	0·5	67	0·3
Kiangsi*	296	3·6	5·4	729	5·3
Chekiang	266	4·3	6·5	1650	10·6

* Tuber, 90 per cent sweet potatoes.

Table 9   Economic Crops, 1957

	Planted area			Total production
	10 000 *mow* units	% All crops	% Econ. crops	10 000 *tan*
Cotton				
Rice–Wheat Region				
Kaingsu	1084	6·7	66·7	400
Anhwei	300	—	28·8	—
Hupeh	875	8·0	53·7	454
Rice–Tea Region				
Hunan	121	1·2	21·2	43
Kiangsi	109	1·3	12·5	52
Chekiang	113	1·8	21·5	—
Ramie				
Rice%–Wheat Region				
Kiangsu*	45	0·3	2·8	—
Anhwei*	51	--	4·9	—
Hupeh	33	0·3	2·0	35
Rice–Tea Region				
Hunan	25	0·2	4·4	18
Kiangsi†	29	0·4	3·3	65
Chekiang‡	77	1·2	14·7	—
Rapeseed				
Rice–Wheat Region				
Kiangsu	210	1·3	12·9	—
Anhwei§	645	—	61·7	—
Hupeh	264	2·4	16·2	106
Rice–Tea Region				
Hunan	294	2·9	51·6	111
Kiangsi	515	6·3	59·1	103
Chekiang	246	3·9	46·9	—
Sesame				
Rice–Wheat Region				
Kiangsu	—	—	—	—
Anhwei	—	—	—	—
Hupeh	309	2·8	19·0	210
Rice–Tea Region				
Hunan	22	0·2	3·8	11
Kiangsi	135	1·6	15·5	59
Chekiang	—	—	—	—
Peanuts				
Rice–Wheat Region				
Kiangsu	251	1·6	15·4	—
Anhwei	—	—	—	—
Hupeh	111	1·0	6·8	276
Rice–Tea Region				
Hunan	50	0·5	8·8	76
Kiangsi	68	0·8	7·8	115
Chekiang	25	0·4	4·8	—
Tobacco				
Rice–Wheat Region				
Kiangsu	—	—	—	—
Anhwei	41	—	3·9	—
Hupeh	—	—	—	—
Rice–Tea Region				
Hunan	16	0·2	2·8	16
Kiangsi	—	—	—	—
Chekiang	—	—	—	—

* All fibres, including jute, hemp and bast.   † Ramie and jute.
‡ Jute.   § Vegetable oil crops, including peanuts and sesame.

References

1 Chia Shun-hsui, 'Grass plains', *K'o-hsuch Ta-chung* [*Popular Science*], no. 9 (September 1964).

2 Wu Ch'uan-chin et al., *Economic Geography of the Western Region of the Middle Yellow River* (Peking, 1956).

3 NCNA, Huhehot, 28 July 1965.

4 NCNA, Huhehot, 27 November 1964.

5 NCNA, Huhehot, 15 March 1966.

6 NCNA, Lanchow, 22 August 1965.

7 *Economic Geography of Inner Mongolian Autonomous Region* (Peking, 1957).

8 T'ang Yi-jen, 'Animal husbandry's place in the national economy', *Hsin Chien-she* [*New Construction*], no. 12 (December 1964).

9 NCNA, Peking, 8 June 1966.

10 NCNA, Huhehot, 5 February 1965.

11 NCNA, Sining, 11 February 1965.

12 NCNA, Huhehot, 8 September 1965.

13 NCNA, Huhehot, 2 August 1965.

14 *People's Daily*, Peking, 10 July 1965.

15 Michael Freeberne, 'Demographic and economic changes in the Sinkiang Uighur Autonomous Region', *Population Studies*, **20**, no. 1 (1966).

16 NCNA, Peking, 28 January 1965.

17 *Far Eastern Economic Review*, 16 November 1965.

18 NCNA, Lhasa, 3 September 1965.

19 NCNA, Lhasa, 22 February 1965.

20 V. G. Kahmykova and L. Kh. Ovdiyento, *Geographical Survey of Northwest China* (Moscow, 1957).

21 NCNA, Sining, 6 June 1966.

22 NCNA, Huhehot, 2 June 1965.

23 P. Teilhard de Chardin, *Letters from a Traveller* (London, 1957), p. 81.

24 NCNA, Lanchow, 14 December 1964.

25 NCNA, Sining, 4 May 1965.

26 NCNA, Huhehot, 10 November 1964.

27 W. H. Mallory, *China, Land of Famine* (New York, 1926).

28 T. H. Shen, *Agricultural Resources of China* (Ithaca, New York, 1951).

29 NCNA, Paoting, 17 July 1966.

30 *Preliminary Scientific and Technical Summing-up of Bumper Wheat Harvests in 1965*, Crop Culture and Cultivation Research Institute, Chinese Academy of Agricultural Science; *Peking Kuang-min Jih-pao*, 16 November 1965.

31 M. C. Yang, *A Chinese Village – Taitou, Shantung* (London, 1946).

32 NCNA, Peking, 26 June 1965.

33 NCNA, Tsinan, 17 June 1966.

34 *Chung-huo Nung-yeh K'o hsueh* [*Chinese Agricultural Science*], no. 3 (15 March 1965).

35 *People's Daily*, Peking, 9 February 1965.

36 NCNA, Shenyang, 8 April 1965.

37 NCNA, Shenyang, 1 April 1965.

38 NCNA, Shenyang, 25 November 1964.

39 NCNA, Harbin, 13 January 1966.

40 NCNA, Harbin, 14 September 1966.

41 NCNA, Chengtu, 27 November 1965.

42 NCNA, Chengtu, 22 July 1965.

43 Sun Ching-chih (ed.), *Si-nan Ti Ch'u Ching-chi-Ti-li* (*Economic Geography of Southwest China*) (Peking, 1960).

44 Sun Ching-chih (ed.), *Economic Geography of Central China* (Peking, 1960).

45 Fei Hsiao-tung, op. cit.

46 Sun Ching-chih (ed.), *Economic Geography of East China Region* (Peking, 1961).

47 NCNA, Hofei, 17 November 1965.

48 Fei Hsiao-tung and Chang-chih-i, *Earthbound China: A Study of Rural Economy in Yunnan* (Chicago, 1945).

49 NCNA, Kweiyang, 31 January 1966.

50 NCNA, Kunming, 13 December 1965.

51 NCNA, Kunming, 26 November 1965.

52 NCNA, Canton, 23 October 1964.

53 NCNA, Nanning, 21 April 1965.

54 NCNA, Canton, 7 August 1965.

55 D. A. Perkins, op. cit.

56 NCNA, Canton, 28 December 1964.

57 NCNA, Canton, 8 September 1965.

58 NCNA, Canton, 14 March 1965.

59 Sun Ching-chih (ed.), *Economic Geography of South China* (Peking, 1959).

60 Liang Jen-ts'ai, 'Economic geography of Kwangtung', *Academia Sinica*, 1958.

61 *Nung-lin Kung-tso T'ung-hsu* [*Agricultural and Forestry Work Bulletin*], no. 6 (6 June 1964).

7   Communications and Transport

Before embarking on an analysis and description of recent developments in communications in China, it will be as well to be reminded of some of the underlying geographical factors in this field. The mere distances involved are enormous. As the crow flies, it is about 3000 km from Canton to Tsitsihar in Heilungkiang; about the same distance from Peking to Kashgar in western Sinkiang; some 2800 km from Peking to Lhasa, and 2500 km to Kunming. Relief or climate makes access to some parts very difficult. This is particularly true of the Tibetan plateau, whose great height and the innumerable ridges, which have to be crossed, make travel most arduous and hazardous. The intervening deserts between China Proper and Sinkiang tend to isolate the outlying west. Long winters and frozen rivers have, until recent years, made access to the remote Northeast difficult for a larger part of the year. Within China Proper there are some districts in which difficulty of movement is notorious. The loess region of Shensi, with its deep, steep-sided valleys enforcing long and arduous detours, is a case in point. Another example is the rugged land which separated Szechwan from Yunnan. Until the construction of the Burma road and the new railway, it was quicker and easier to journey from Chengtu to Kunming by going down the Yangtze to Shanghai, then by sea to Haiphong, thence by rail to Kunming rather than attempt the perilous direct route.

In spite of the immense distances and difficulties, vigorous and efficient emperors in the past have been successful in holding the huge Chinese empire together over long periods. This could be done only by the establishment and maintenance of adequate communications, thus enabling administrative contact with the outlying parts to be sustained. The Han (206 BC–AD 220), T'ang (AD 618–907), Yuan (1279–1369) and Ch'ing (1644–1911) were all successful in doing this, at least in their earlier years. Marco Polo, writing when the Yuan (Mongol) dynasty was at the height of its power, gives a glowing description of the efficiency of post houses and posting, stating that, in emergency, messages could be carried 200 km in a day[1]. As soon as the emperor and court became effete and communications were allowed to deteriorate, the empire began to fall apart and break up.

Much of the trade was in the form of tribute to the emperor and travelled along the imperial routes to the capital of the time. Most notable of these was the Imperial Silk Route through Kansu and Sinkiang, which was also the main road followed by Chinese pilgrims to India and by which Buddhism entered China.

Throughout the centuries there has been a marked contrast in the means of transport used in north China and those used in the south. In the drier, less wooded north, carts drawn by horses, mules, donkeys and camels, have been the main method of moving goods, most rivers being unnavigable. Dr Needham has pointed out the early advances made by the Chinese in the use of equine tractive power by such inventions as the stirrup, breast-strap and collar harness[2]. For movement over desert and semi-desert regions Bactrian camel caravans have been the main means used. Farther south in the wetter, forested regions, reliance has been placed almost exclusively on man's shoulders and legs by means of the carrying pole, wheelbarrow and sedan chair, wherever water transport could not be used. Roads, for the most part, were mere paths, occasionally paved with stone slabs but, more generally, were mere earth tracks, which became deeply rutted by the wheel barrows in wet weather.

With the expansion southward during the T'ang dynasty and the consequent shift of the economic heart of the country into the Yangtze basin, the movement of bulky tribute grain over long distances to the northern capitals presented an increasing problem. This grain was essential to the life of government, court and army. The problem gave rise to an era of canal building, which produced the New Pien Canal from the Yangtze near Nanking to Kaifeng and so to Ch'ang-an (Sian), the then T'ang capital, and later, in the Yuan dynasty, the Grand Canal from the Yangtze to Peking.

MODERN DEVELOPMENT
Railways
Lines of communication and means of transport remained essentially unchanged for 2000 years. from the Han dynasty until the latter half of the nineteenth century when western intrusion was beginning to make itself felt.

The first railway to be built in China was a short, narrow-gauge (750 mm) line between Woosung and Shanghai. It was built with foreign capital and with foreign enterprise and opened in 1876. It met with official and local peasant opposition and, in 1877, its rails were torn up and shipped to Taiwan. Official opposition sprang from the deep-seated conservatism of the Imperial Court and the intense hatred and fear of foreign aggressiveness; while peasant opposition stemmed from the widespread necromantic belief in *feng shui*, the spirits of wind and water which were believed to reside in the land, especially in high places. These spirits were disturbed at one's peril and the well-being of the whole countryside might thereby be endangered. *Feng shui* was a factor which developers of railways, telegraph and mines found they had to reckon with seriously since it could easily be evoked by anyone whose interest it was to hinder development. The author remembers how, in the early part of the twentieth century the building of a mission hospital at Anlu had to be re-sited on a less socially favourable spot because the buildings on the chosen site would have overtopped the pagoda and so upset the *feng shui*. Apart from one or two small mining lines in Honan and Hopeh, no further attempt at railway construction was made until the closing years of the nineteenth century.

The defeat of China by Japan in 1894 and the general belief that China was on the verge of disintegration was the occasion of a campaign of intrigue, known as 'the battle of concessions' in which most of the great powers of the day scrambled and schemed to obtain concessions and spheres of influence in which they might operate in China. It was the jealousies between these powers that helped to keep the tottering Ch'ing dynasty from falling until 1911. Russia (and later Japan) obtained preponderating influence in Manchuria; Germany in Shantung around Tsingtao; France in Yunnan next to her colonial territory in Indo-China; Great Britain around Tientsin and Shanghai and in the Yangtze valley.

Then followed a spate of railway building between 1900 and 1920 as the table below shows. More than 9600 km of track were built during those years, very largely with foreign capital. Belgium secured building concessions out of proportion to its size partly because, being small, the Chinese Government considered it less menacing than the rest[3]. By skilful negotiation the Chinese secured that ownership and administration rested with their government.

Main Railway Lines (1900–23)

	Opened	km
Peking–Mukden (Shenyang)	1903	840
Peking–Hankow	1905	1208
Tientsin–Pukow	1912	1016
Peking–Kalgan–Tatung–Paotow	1909	749
	1915	
	1923	
Shangai–Nanking	1908	309
Shanghai–Hangchow	1908	283
Lunghai (Suchow–Tungkwan)	1916	824
Canton Kowloon	1911	179
Taiyuan–Shihchiachuang	1907	242
Tsingtao–Tsinan	1904	410
Yunnanfu (Kunming)–Laokai	1910	462
Manchuria		
Chinese Eastern (1·5 m gauge)	1903	1729
South Manchurian	1903	830

Apart from the Peking–Mukden line, which was built largely with British capital, all Manchurian railways were the work of Russia and Japan during this period. The Russians short-circuited their Siberian railway by a line running from Chita, via Mancholi, Tsitsihar and Harbin, to Vladivostok and built up a network in the north, which was known as the Chinese Eastern Railway. This, and a system Russia developed in the south, the Southern Manchurian Railway, were of 1·5 m gauge. When Japan defeated Russia in 1904, she took over this southern network and, in 1907, converted it into standard gauge. When she annexed Manchukuo in 1931–2, Japan took over the entire system. Between 1916 and 1928 the country was divided and in the hands of warlords. Although some railway building continued, this disturbed period is notable rather for the deterioration of track and rolling stock. There was another burst of building under the Kuomintang between 1928 and 1936, bringing the total length of track (including Manchukuo) to over 19 000 km. Unhappily this was followed by ten years (1936–46) of war with Japan and then three years of bitter civil war between Kuomintang and Communists, which left communications throughout the country in a parlous state, further accentuated by the destruction of bridges, culverts, rolling stock and permanent way as the KMT retreated. Of this meagre existing length (19 242), '6000 km were lost through the Japanese invasion of Manchuria in 1931 and 10 000 km were lost or destroyed during the first five-and-a-half years of the Sino–Japanese War'[4].

Railway development in Communist China

Sun Yat Sen, in his later years, was very conscious of the part that railways must play in the modernization of his country. During the First World War he sketched a building programme, which envisaged 160 000 km of track. He returned to the subject in his *San-min Chu-ih*.

When they came into power in 1949, the Communists had clear ideas as to the position of the railways in their policy of creating a modern, industrialized state. The railways were to serve in the wide dispersal of industry. Founded originally largely on foreign capital and initiative, nearly three-quarters of the country's industry was located in the coastal regions and thus was, in some degree, a symbol of erstwhile imperialist dominance. Moreover, from a strategic point of view, dispersal of industry would render the

country less vulnerable in time of war. Railway development was also essential to national integration, to the drawing together of the outlying, underdeveloped regions and to the assurance of unified political control. Finally, railway development was imperative if the vast reserves of raw materials, which these regions contained, were to be opened up and made accessible.

Some idea of the importance attached to railway development can be gathered from the fact that, in 1953, under the First Five-year Plan, 17·1 per cent of the total state investment capital was allocated to communications, 13·3 per cent going to railways and the remaining 3·8 per cent to all other forms of transport. The actual planning and construction of new lines after 1949 follows closely the ambitious plans of Chang Kia-ngau, Nationalist Minister of Communications in 1942 for railway expansion at the end of the Sino–Japanese War. He envisaged the building of some 23 000 km of track, but unfortunately was never able to implement his plans[4].

Between 1952 and 1960 the following new main lines were opened:

North and Northwest – The Lunghai Railway, which had been carried to Tienshui, west of Paoki before 1949, was extended to Lanchow, which was rapidly becoming a large industrial centre. From this base at Lanchow, a new line of over 1100 km, known as the Sinkiang Friendship Line, has been constructed across the intervening steppeland and desert into the Tarim Basin and Dzungaria to the Sinkiang capital, Urumchi. This railway has clear economic and political purposes. Until complete pipelines are laid, the railway is the only economical method of delivering the oil from the Karamai field of Dzungaria to the east. It also provides an outlet for the increasing raw materials and finished products of the region. Its political raison d'être is to bring the Uighur, Kazakh and Kirghiz population consciously within the national fold and to enable the central government's writ to run. It was also intended to be a link with its communist neighbour and it was planned to join with the Soviet Kazakhstan line from Ayagur, through the Dzungarian Gate. Unhappily discord between the two countries brought building to a stop and the Chinese line ends at Manass.

A line has been built from Lanchow to Sining. This is to be extended into the Tsaidam to tap the oil and other mineral resources, which have

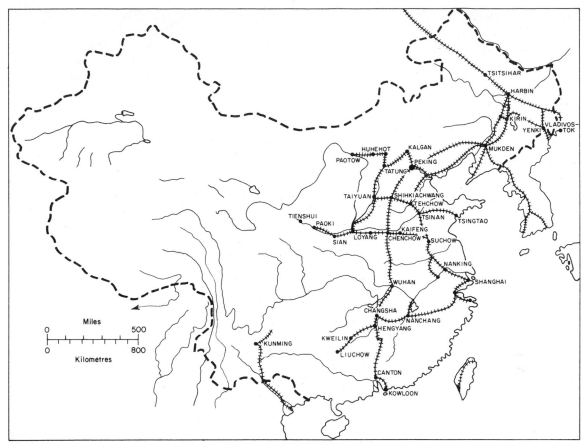

Fig. 84   Railways, 1949

recently been discovered. A railway from Tsining northward to Erhlien links with the Outer Mongolian line to Ulan Bator and so to the Siberian railway, thus providing a direct route from Siberia to China Proper. A further important extension is that from Paotow to Lanchow, following the course of the Hwang-ho and opening up the growing oases of the region.

West – The two big cities of Szechwan, Chengtu and Chungking have been joined by a rail running through Neikiang. However, it was the completion of the line from Chengtu to Paoki, thus linking Szechwan with the Lunghai Railway and the north, that excited national enthusiasm. This line had been planned and partly surveyed by the Nationalist government, but credit for its final achievement rests with the People's Government. It proved a difficult engineering undertaking, involving an immense amount of tunnelling

and bridging through the Tsinling Shan, which divides Szechwan from Shensi.

Two further lines have been built from Chungking. One links it with Kweiyang, capital of Kweichow and the other runs via Neikiang to Ipin. Both these lines will eventually be continued to Kunming.

South – The Henyang–Kweilin line was quickly extended for 420 km from Liuchow to the Vietnam border at Pingsiang, thus giving rail communication with Hanoi. This was opened in October 1951. In 1955 a branch from this line at Litang was built to Chankiang, which is rapidly becoming an important southern port.

Southeast – Both Foochow and Amoy are now linked by rail to the Yangtze valley. Following their respective river valleys of the Min and Kiuling, their tracks join at Shakikow and meet the Nanchang–Hangchow line at Yintang. Built

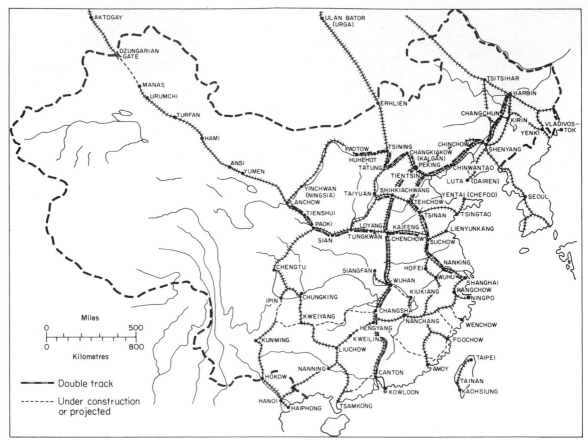

Fig. 85   Railways, 1960

rapidly for military purposes to meet possible menace from Taiwan, these railways, nevertheless, have considerable economic usefulness.

It is significant to note that, apart from the short line built from Wuhan to the steel works at Hwangshih – a line to be continued eventually to Kiukiang – and the projected line from Kingtihchen to Wuhu, no railway construction has been undertaken in the lower Yangtze valley in spite of its great economic importance. This is an eloquent comment on the value of this great river as a line of communication and transport. A railway line has now been built from Wuhan up the Han-ho via Huang-fan to Huang-hua. It is planned to extend this rail to the upper reaches of the Han, thence across the Ta Pa Shan and descend into Szechwan down the Chou-ho via Ta hsien and Ch'u hsien to Chungking.

Very few new main lines have been opened in

the northeast since 1949. The region was already served by a more complete network than existed anywhere else in China. Some 400 km of lumber lines have been built in the extreme north in the Ta Hingan and Siao Hingan mountains. The main development in the northeast has been the double-tracking of the main line from Harbin to Shenyang. Similarly, all the main lines of the south, the Peking–Hankow–Canton, the Tientsin–Pukow, Peking–Paotow and the Lunghai from Suchow to Lanchow have been double-tracked, thus rendering them far more capable of carrying the heavy load they have been called upon to bear. Even so, serious bottlenecks have not been avoided.

The railway building programme sketched above has been carried through with great speed, urgency and energy. The initiative and enthusiasm shown have not always been accompanied by adequate surveying and engineering. This has resulted in mistakes involving considerable renovation work. The planners clearly had intended the pace of railway construction to be continued throughout the Second Five-year Plan, for 20·9 per cent of national capital investment was allocated to communications of which three-quarters was to be devoted to railways. In fact, the railway building programme slowed down after the Great Leap Forward (1958); emphasis since has been laid on improvement and upkeep of existing lines. Even during the First Five-year Plan, one-third of the capital allocated to the railways was ear-marked for renovation and one-fifth for rolling stock[4].

In 1971 it is estimated that there were more than 40 000 km of railway in the country. Every province, except Tibet, is served by at least one main line. It has 11 international rail connections, 5 with Korea, 2 with the U.S.S.R., 2 with Vietnam, 1 with Hong Kong and 1 with Mongolia.

A marked change in railway construction took place during and after the Great Leap Forward,

a change which provides an outstanding example of 'walking on two legs', i.e. the support of central schemes by local effort. The need for some form of transport of raw materials to the hundreds of thousands of local 'backyard' blast furnaces led to the construction of all sorts of local 'rail-roads' of greatly varying efficiency and ingenuity, ranging from Emmett-like contraptions of wooden or cast-iron rails and converted lorries as locomotives, to trackless trains on pneumatic wheels. Most of these faded out with the collapse of the ill-fated Great Leap, but many also formed the basis for subsequent feeder lines, sponsored by communes and of much greater value and efficiency. Richard Hughes, writing of these, says 'Cast-iron rails used in Anhwei province withstand a pressure of up to 50 tons/metre and the commune-made locomotives can run on them at a speed of 35 km/h.'[5] Although they have now been largely replaced by road transport, they have served a useful purpose, particularly as their construction formed no charge on the national investment fund.

Table 21   Length of Railway Tracks Laid (from Ten Great Years, *Peking, 1960)*

		Track and branch lines (km)					
		Total	New lines	Restored lines	New double-track lines	Restored double-track lines	Special purpose lines
Period of Rehabilitation of National Economy							
	Total	12090	7513	1749	1833	995	4451
	1950	808	97	427	—	284	172
	1951	1021	743	138	—	140	185
	1952	1233	480	605	—	148	236
	Total	3062	1320	1170	—	572	593
First Five-Year Plan							
	1953	706	587	—	14	105	494
	1954	1132	831	—	49	252	283
	1955	1406	1222	39	87	58	458
	1956	2242	1747	285	206	4	866
	1957	1166	474	150	538	4	569
	Total	6652	4861	474	894	423	2670
Second Five-Year Plan							
	1958	2376	1332	105	939	—	1188

Note: In addition to the above figures, 4400 km of narrow-gauge tracks for forest railways were laid between 1950 and 1958

Table 22   Rapid Increase in Volume of Goods Carried by Modern Means of Transport
(thousand tons) (*from* Ten Great Years, *Peking, 1960*)

	Total goods carried	Carried by railways	Carried by motor vehicles	Carried by ships and barges
Pre-1949				
Peak	—	136 650	8 190	12 640
1949	67 130	55 890	5 790	5 430
1950	115 690	99 830	9 210	6 650
1951	135 060	110 830	14 120	10 110
1952	168 590	132 170	22 100	14 320
1953	212 270	161 310	30 940	20 010
1954	264 670	192 880	43 030	28 750
1955	278 430	193 760	48 960	35 700
1956	372 150	246 050	79 130	46 960
1957	411 710	274 200	83 730	53 770
1958	633 760	381 090	176 300	76 360

The prewar peak of railway freight is quoted[6] as being 40 400 million ton-km. This figure fell to 18 400 million in 1949 and then rose steadily and rapidly year by year to 185 520 million ton-km in 1958. No figures have been published since that date. Although it is certain that this rate of increase in freight carried has not been maintained, the absolute amount of goods carried has continued to rise. Railways are still by far the greatest transporters.

Ever since 1949 the railways have been called upon to do more work than that for which they are technically fitted. The most difficult period was during the Great Leap Forward when transport demands were increased almost overnight. Since then, the big development of road transport, and the emphasis which has been laid on regional development by communes, has relieved pressure. Undoubtedly the Cultural Revolution activities and free transport accorded to the Red Guards between July 1966 and January 1967, when millions of young people were transported, again placed considerable strain on the railways. Owing to continued Cultural Revolution factionalism, China's railways were placed under military (PLA) control in September 1967.

Table 23   Freight Turnover by Modern Means of transport (million ton-km)
(*from* Ten Great Years, *Peking, 1960*)

	Total	Railways	Motor vehicles	Ships and barges
Pre-1949				
peak	—	40 400	460	12 830
1949	22 980	18 400	250	4 310
1950	42 690	39 410	380	2 900
1951	59 340	51 560	570	7 210
1952	71 540	60 160	770	10 610
1953	93 010	78 140	1 300	13 570
1954	113 830	93 240	1 240	18 640
1955	125 120	98 150	2 520	24 440
1956	152 060	120 350	3 490	28 210
1957	172 930	134 590	3 940	34 390
1958	236 400	185 520	6 960	43 910

Plate 10   Roadbuilding in the north Kweichow plateau

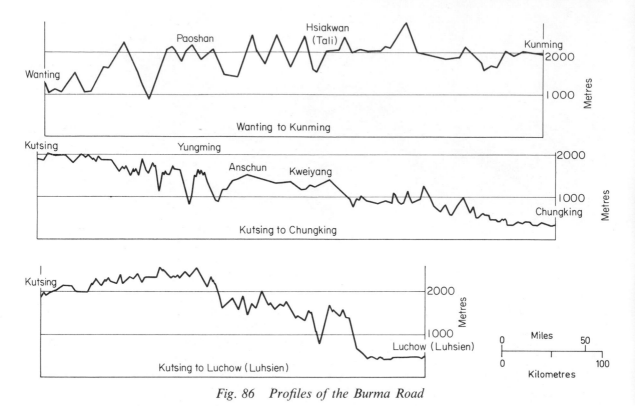

Fig. 86   Profiles of the Burma Road

Roads

There was comparatively little change either in routes used or the vehicles passing over them during the 2000 years from the Early Han dynasty to the beginning of the twentieth century. The roads for wheeled traffic in the north were mere dirt tracks to which no attention to upkeep was given. In the south, the narrow paths, which served as roads for wheelbarrows and pedestrians, were occasionally paved – usually the work of some rich landowner or virtuous widow 'earning merit' – but there was no attempt throughout the country at either maintenance or systemization except for short periods as, for example, under the Yuan dynasty, and even then the emphasis was on courier service rather than transport. All movement was slow and expensive. A journey of 30 km a day by land was as much as could ordinarily be accomplished and it was arduous. A strong coolie, using a carrying pole, could carry a *tan* (100 *catties*) about 30 km in a day. The normal method of payment was to provide the coolie's food plus a mere pittance of a wage. Nevertheless, it was a most expensive method of transport as Sun Yat Sen, in his *San-min Chu-ih* was at pains to point out with more fervour than accuracy, remarking that it took 10 days for 10 000 coolies to move 10 000 ton over 500 *li* (275 km) while the same work could be done by train requiring only 8 hp and the services of 10 men. A ton-kilometre per day could be regarded as the average work of a coolie carrier. 'Today in level and hilly areas engaged in subsidiary food production the amount of labour used for transport in the field represents about 35 per cent of the total labour force. In mountainous areas it is about 60 per cent.'[4]

Automobiles began to be introduced into China during the second decade of this century. Their use was confined to the metalled roads within the concessions and the short, mainly dirt, roads a few kilometres around the cities. Between 1930 and 1936, the Nationalist government carried out extensive roadbuilding, which was continued in

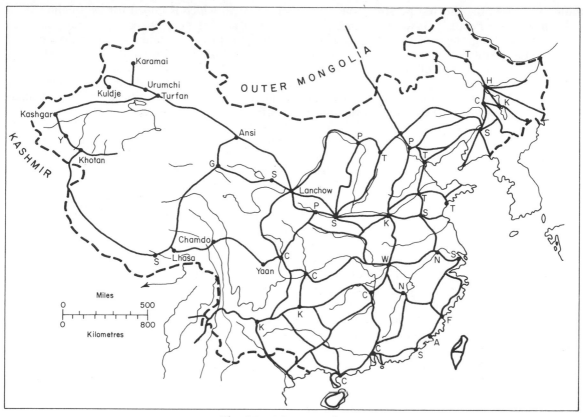

Fig. 87   Motor roads, 1959

west China during the Sino–Japanese War and included the spectacular Burma Road over the many north–south longitudinal high ranges and deep valleys, which divide Burma from Yunnan. After reaching Kunming from the Burmese border, this road forks, one branch running north to Neikiang and Chengtu and the other, via Kweiyang, to Chungking. With the end of hostilities, the section between Myitkyina and Paoshan lost much of its raison d'être, but the remaining sections have served as the foundation of a road network for the southwest. The above profiles of the roads give some idea of the difficult terrain of these sections.

The years of civil war and chaos between 1946 and 1949 resulted in sad depreciation of existing roads. One report estimated that, in 1949, there were only 75 000 km of roads, most of which were barely usable for motor traffic[7]. Certainly, those of Central China over which the author travelled at that time were calculated to ruin any

Table 24   Length of New and Improved Highways (km) (*from* Ten Great Years, *Peking, 1960*)

	Total	New Highways
Period of rehabilitation of National Economy		
1950	15 463	450
1951	19 545	1 366
1952	11 168	1 940
First Five-year Plan		
1953	9 654	2 598
1954	7 164	3 824
1955	8 138	3 578
1956	89 717	55 930
1957	38 168	17 472
Second Five-year Plan		
1958	210 000	150 000
Total	409 017	237 249

Note: Figures for 1956 and after include lower grade highways. highways.

motor vehicle in the shortest possible time.

From 1950 the People's Government embarked on a strenuous programme of roadbuilding, which has continued in intensity. Unfortunately there are no comprehensive figures of achievement in this field after 1958.

As with railways, so with roads. The Central Government has undertaken the construction of the great arterial highways and has left the local roads to the initiative of the communes. The following are the great motor roads to outlying provinces and remote regions, which have been built since 1949:

(a) The Kansu–Sinkiang Highway follows the same route as the Sinkiang Friendship railway. From Lanchow it passes along the northern slopes of the Nan Shan through Wuwei, Changteh and the oil refineries of Yumen to Ansi. Here a branch swings south through Tunhwang, famous for its Buddhist caves and carvings, over the Tangching Pass at the western end of the Nan Shan, and so into the Tsaidam. From Ansi the road continues through the desert to Hami and the Turfan Depression. At Turfan the road divides, going north and south of the Tien Shan. The northern route passes through Urumchi and Manass and on to Ebi Nor. As it approaches the U.S.S.R. frontier it turns south to Kuldja, the heart of the Ili valley. The southern branch runs through Kucha and Aksu and all the oases of the northern rim of the Takla Makan desert to Kashgar; then it turns south to Yarkand and Khotan. The intention is to complete the circuit of the Tarim Basin through Charchan and Charkhlik, but it may be some time before this is done. This south-eastern corner of the basin is the least important economically and this, combined with the engineering difficulties of shifting sand, wind and the crossing of torrential rivers descending from the Kunlun, is likely to postpone action.

(b) The Khotan–Lhasa route leaves Khotan to cross the Kunlun by the Karakoram Pass. Following the northern slopes of the Karakoram mountains, it passes through the disputed territory of northeastern Kashmir and along the Tsangpo or Brahmaputra, via Gartok and Shigatse to Lhasa. Most of this road is through very high and bleak country. The mountains, the rarefied air and low temperatures, often below $-20°C$, make roadbuilding hazardous and most arduous. Difficult tasks, such as building this road and the road along the southern edge of the Tarim Basin are undertaken by the PLA Engineer-

ing Corps, which is famed for its toughness[8].

(c) Lhasa is now linked by motor road with Chengtu through some of the most difficult country. Like the Burma Road, it has to cross large numbers of north–south ranges and valleys, but it has to contend with much greater heights and attendant constructional and maintenance difficulties occasioned by snow and rock falls. Between Chamdo and Kinsha–Kiang (Yangtze) most of the road runs at a height of between 3000 and 4500 m. Its highest pass is 4889 m. As it descends from the Tibetan Plateau it crosses the Tatu river by a new steel bridge, which has been built close to the chain bridge, rendered famous by its dramatic capture during the Long March. It is now possible to travel by bus from Chengtu to Lhasa, taking about 2 weeks on the journey instead of at least 6 months before the road was constructed. The purpose of the road is primarily political, bringing southeast Tibet and the many indigenous tribes of western Szechwan within Central Government control. However, the increasing flow of goods is proving that the road has economic value. It also makes possible the fuller survey of a region of great potential mineral wealth.

(d) Leaving Lhasa, the Lhasa–Sining Highway traverses the desolate and sparsely populated Tibetan–Tsinghai plateau until it descends into the Tsaidam. This section of the road, although very high (3000–4000 m) does not have to negotiate deep, longitudinal valleys and ranges as does the Lhasa–Chengtu Highway. The road turns eastward at Golmo and, skirting the Chinghai (Koko Nor), runs to Sining and Lanchow. Again, this is a road the purpose of which is primarily political. Nevertheless, the building of a road network based on the highway has done much to develop the industrial potential of Tsinghai especially its oil and coal. It is reported that in 1949 there were only 472 km of rough road near to Sining. In 1964 there were 15 447 km of motor road, which have cut transport time to one-tenth and cost to one-fifth[9].

(e) Linking with Sining and Lanchow is the recently constructed motor road from Lanchow, via Ahpa, to Chengtu. It follows a route through 142 km of high mountains and gorges, the line which constituted the Red Army's severest ordeal on its Long March. The road forms part of the highway network, which is being built in west Szechwan and Tibet in order to make close contact with the minorities.

Apart from the great trunk roads, which have been the responsibility of the Central Government, a great deal of road development has been carried through in all the provinces by local authorities. The pattern of development has been much the same throughout. The commune, often with some technical and material help from the State has constructed a main motor road through its territory, linking with similar roads by its neighbours. Production brigades have then been responsible for building 'country roads' leading to the villages and hamlets. These roads, which usually have little metalling, are fit for trucks in fine, i.e. dry weather. There can be no doubt that, in this way, local markets have been greatly widened and stimulated[10]. At present there are few tarred or concreted roads except near to big industrial conurbations.

Bridges

Closely associated with the modern development of railways and roads has been a great upsurge in bridgebuilding. It is strange that, although China in the past has figured so little in road-building, yet its engineers have pioneered in bridgebuilding. Joseph Needham describes how Li Ch'un built the first segmental arch bridge across the river at Chaohsien, Hopeh in AD 610. This is a beautiful structure, which is still standing and, since its recent repair, is in full use. China also was 1000 years ahead of Europe in the building of suspension bridges. In the Sui dynasty (AD 581–818) bamboo cables were used for this purpose, but in succeeding centuries these were replaced by iron chains[2].

Modern bridgebuilding received its initial impetus from railway development at the beginning of the century. The Hwang-ho was bridged just north of Chengchow in 1905 to carry the Peking–Hankow railway and at Tsinan to carry the Tientsin–Pukow railway. Apart from these two, no other outstanding bridge was built before 1949, although, of course, a great many smaller structures were constructed as the railways developed.

Bridges were a major casualty in the Sino–Japanese War and in the subsequent civil war, particularly during the final defeat and withdrawal of the Nationalist forces. The broken bridges were repaired or rebuilt at great speed during the years of rehabilitation (1950–2). Thereafter an ambitious programme of new building was undertaken. The most outstanding achievement to date has been the construction of the Yangtze Bridge at Wuhan, providing at the time of building the only dry crossing of the river from west Szechwan to its mouth. The Yangtze, 1500 m at this point, seriously interrupted railway communication between the Peking–Hankow and the Wuchang–Canton lines. For more than thirty years plans for connecting the two by bridge had been discussed and surveys of the river made, but no action was taken. With the aid of Soviet engineers and technicians the work was undertaken. A two-decker bridge, carrying a double-track railway below and a six-lane road above, was completed in 1956 – no mean engineering feat when one remembers the width of the river and the 14 m change in water level between summer and winter. The Yangtze was again bridged at Chungking and an even more ambitious bridging plan was completed at Nanking in September 1968.

The following is a list of major new bridges built between 1950 and 1958[6]:

Name	Province	Length (m)
Wuhan: Yangtze river bridge	Hupeh	1670
Tungkwan: Yellow river bridge (temporary structure)	Shensi	1070
Hunan–Kweichow Railway: Hsiangkiang bridge	Hunan	844
Shenyang–Shanhaikwan Railway: Talingho bridge	Liaoning	830
Fentai–Shacheng Railway: Yungtingho No. 1 bridge	Hopeh	722
Lunghai Railway: Hsinyiho bridge	Kiangsu	700
Paotow–Lanchow Railway: Sanshengkung Yellow river bridge	Inner Mongolia	683
Peking–Paotow Railway: Kweishui bridge	Hopeh	663
Hunan–Kwangsi Railway: Liukiang bridge	Kwangsi	616
Peking–Canton Railway: Changho bridge	Hopeh	569
Fengtai–Shacheng Railway: Yungtingho No. 8 bridge	Hopeh	526

Plate 11   Nanking Bridge, completed in 1968, is six and a half kilometres long
In spite of China's ancient skill in bridge-building, virtually no modern construction was undertaken before 1949

Since 1958 many more bridges have been constructed, including the first modern highway bridge in Tibet over the Tsangpo at Lhasa. This is a reinforced concrete structure, 730 m long and having 19 arches[11]. A big conference on bridge construction in the Northwest was held in 1965, attended by representatives from Tibet, Sinkiang, Tsinghai, Kansu Ninghsia, Inner Mongolia and Shensi. These are the regions in which bridge and culvert building is especially difficult on account of high altitudes, low but concentrated rainfall leading to dangerous freshets, wide, shallow river beds and unstable river courses, encumbered with large loads of silt and stones.

Water transport
In primitive economic conditions movement by water is the easiest and cheapest form of transport. Where roads and adequate wheeled transport are absent it is often also the most comfortable. Consequently, in central and south China, where rivers are navigable for small craft over most of their length, this method of movement of goods and people has had great prominence. In deltaic regions, such as obtain in the lower Yangtze and Si-kiang, water transport has been by far the most important[12]. In north China, where rivers are less navigable, more wheeled transport is used, but even here rivers are used wherever possible, for example by inflated hide rafts on the middle Hwang-ho, which are floated down, deflated and returned overland to source in much the same fashion as on the Tigris in Babylonian times.

Canals
Relying as they did on the transport of tribute grain to support the court and army at the capital, emperors from a very early date recognized the importance of water communications and engaged in canal building accordingly. As Chinese domination extended further south and as greater and greater reliance was placed on the grain of

the south, which became the economic heart of the country, so the need for water transport became more pressing. In consequence, the Sui emperor, Sui Yang-ti (AD 605) caused, at shocking loss of life, the New Pien Canal to be cut from the Yangtze to Kaifeng and so to his capital at Ch'ang-an (Sian).

When the Mongol (Yuan) dynasty was established (1279) and Kublai Khan moved the Imperial capital to Peking, the need for easy and quick transport of supplies from the south was even more pressing. Kublai Khan therefore ordered, in 1283, the cutting of the Grand Canal, linking Hangchow with Peking. This was the extension of a small, old canal, cut by a prince of the State of Wu (506 BC) between Tai-hu and Hangchow. The Grand Canal measures 1700 km and links, from south to north, five rivers, the Chientang, Yangtze, Hwai, Hwang and Hai. For many years it formed a main artery of communications from north to south, but constant maintenance was necessary because it cuts right across the floodplains of the Hwai and Hwang-ho and thus is subject to silting from their repeated inundations. The Grand Canal finally fell into disuse, except for local transport over short stretches, when the Tientsin–Pukow railway was opened in 1912. Canals are early victims of internal disorder. It was surprising, therefore, to find the Grand Canal virtually useless in 1949.

With the development of the Hwang-ho conservancy schemes from 1950 onward, the Grand Canal naturally came under discussion and was incorporated as an integral part of the plans for flood control and drainage. Work began in 1958 on its renovation. It has been straightened, widened and deepened and a new course of 70 km has been cut. New modern locks and lock-gates have been constructed throughout its length. Formerly 50-ton barges were the largest that could be used; now 200–500-ton barges can sail on all sections; when complete, 2000-ton craft will be accommodated. Its main use at present, apart from local traffic, is the conveyance of coal from north to south and grain in the reverse direction, although it is reported that, with the increasing productivity of the North China Plan, there is less need now for the transport of southern grain[13].

River development and shipping

Of China's great rivers, the Yangtze-kiang, with its tributaries the Han, Siang and Kan, ranks far above all others as a line of transport, both from the point of view of the area served and the amount of traffic carried. Second is the Sungari and then the Si-kiang. Neither the Hwang-ho nor the Hwai-ho figures high on the list, largely on account of the flooding which occurred so frequently in their lower reaches. With modern conservation, which has been and still is being undertaken, these two rivers are now increasing in value as lines of communication.

Something of the regime and the size of the Yangtze has already been seen (pp. 282–9). For many centuries it has been a busy artery for sailing junks, large and small, which, even in the winter when the river is at its lowest level, are able to ply from its mouth to Ichang. Here most river craft stopped, blocked by the series of gorges between Nanto and Wanhsien. The Chinese have a saying, 'The Way to Szechwan is as difficult as the way to Heaven', to describe the passage of these gorges, which could be undertaken by haulage by tracker teams along paths hewn out of the cliff sides – a perilous and arduous endeavour for tracker and boatman. The current through the gorges is terrifyingly fast and the channel beset with rocks and shoals. At the notorious Goat Horn Reef the river falls 7 m in 2·5 km and at one point the channel was only 30 m wide[14]. A graphic description of a passage of these 160 km and more is given by Han Su-yin[3]. By the second decade of the twentieth century, powerful small steamers were able to make the precarious journey unaided by trackers, but their numbers were few and their impact not very significant.

A great deal of money and energy has been expended since 1950 in rendering this most difficult section of the river safer for navigation. 12·6 million yuan has been spent on dredging and clearing. More than 200 shoals have been cleared, innumerable rocks have been blasted and removed. The narrow channels have been widened and marked by buoys, and bank signals now make passage through the gorges possible by night as well as by day. By 1959 it was possible to make the return trip from Wuhan to Chungking and back in less than a week. Freight charges have been reduced many times with the introduction of tug and barge trains, which can now navigate the improved channels[15].

The nature of shipping on the Yangtze underwent a revolutionary change after 1860 through the establishment of treaty ports along the river and the opening of the river to international trade and foreign bottoms. Two British companies,

Butterfield and Swire, and Jardine, Matheson began to operate along the river in 1872 and 1873 respectively and were closely followed by the newly-formed, indigenous China Merchants' Steam Navigation Coy, an important happening as it was the first instance of Chinese officials entering into commercial competition with foreigners[16]. Commenting on the special regulations governing shipping on the Yangtze, the *China Year Book*, 1925 stated 'In most countries inland navigation is reserved to the natives of the country. In China, however, the inland waterways are open to foreign navigation'.[17] This was an obvious cause of offence and complaint by the Chinese against foreign imperialism in spite of the very considerable increase in trade that it occasioned. Checked after the 1927 revolution, foreign shipping thereafter was prohibited up the Yangtze beyond Shanghai.

In summer when the river is in spate, ocean-going vessels of 10 000 to 15 000 tons, drawing more than 9 m, can reach Wuhan, 1000 km inland. Navigation, however, must be carefully timed as a sudden drop in water level in late summer could leave such ships stranded with no chance of exit until the rise of water the following year. Regular steamships, plying up and down the river as far as Wuhan throughout the year, must be specially constructed to draw not more than 2 m, such is the change in level between summer and winter. Clever designing during this century has enabled passenger-freight vessels of 5000 tons to be built fulfilling these conditions.

Cheap labour conditions have militated against the introduction of modern wharfage equipment at the river ports. Loading and unloading of goods, has, without exception, been manpower and carrying pole, a slow, hard job, especially in winter when the water is low and long ramps up the steep banks from the hulks, which serve as wharves, have to be climbed. Since 1950 these conditions have steadily been changed. Now all the major river ports are largely mechanized. Wuhan now has 40 modern wharves, served mainly by conveyor belts for loading and unloading. The change is especially noticeable and welcome at Chungkiang, which stands on cliffs above the river. Cable cars, chutes and overhead cables have now replaced much of the man-handling up steps and ramps.[18]

For many years the marking of channels by buoys and lightships, from Shanghai to Wuhan, was well maintained. It deteriorated badly during the Sino–Japanese War and civil war and thus stood in urgent need of rehabilitation in 1949. Since then this work has been taken seriously in hand. It is reported that night navigation is now possible from Shanghai through the gorges to Ipin, the channel being marked by 2800 buoys and bank signals based on the Soviet chain-signal system from Shanghai to Chungkiang. In 1959 the system was electrified[19].

The development of modern shipping and equipment on the Yangtze has been discussed above, but it should be remembered that the greater part of the goods moved up and down the river is still carried by native Chinese craft – small *hwatzu*, junks and rafts propelled by wind or manpower. These are undergoing rapid change. It is stated that between 1960 and 1961 no less than 10 000 junks on the river were mechanized, 150 000 h.p. having been installed.

While the planners have expended a great deal of energy and money on the development of the Yangtze, it has by no means received exclusive attention. The navigability of the Sungari and Liao in the northeast and the Si-kiang in Kwangtung and Kwangsi have been greatly improved in the last fifteen years. The numerous multi-purpose dams built in their courses have had increased navigability as one of their objectives. Moreover, many of the smaller rivers have been improved by the combined efforts of local communes. A case in point is the lower Wu-kiang as it descends from Kweichow to the Yangtze below Chungking. The channel has been dredged and shoals removed so that, it is claimed, there is ten times as much traffic on the river as in 1949[20].

Coastal shipping

China has some 14 000 km of coastline, which is strikingly different north and south of the mouth of the Yangtze-kiang. The south and southeast coasts are rugged and replete with deep, natural harbours. Mountains come down to the sea in most places and the few coastal plains are narrow. Consequently the hinterlands of ports along this stretch of coast tend to be restricted. Navigational hazards spring from sudden storms and typhoons and, in the past, from piracy rendered easy by virtue of many convenient hide-outs. Towns have tended to be comparatively small and the population traditionally has looked outwards to the sea for a livelihood. It is mainly from Fukien and Kwangtung that China's seamen have come and

Plate 12   The launching of a 25 000-ton freighter at Shanghai
Shipbuilding, although still in its infancy, is increasing rapidly

from Fukien that the bulk of overseas Chinese derive.

Sharply contrasted is the coastline north of Shanghai, which, apart from that of the Shantung peninsula, is smooth and devoid of natural harbours. Any ports here are essentially man-made. This is particularly true around the Po-hai into which the Hwang-ho, Hai-ho and Liao-ho pour their loads of silt. It is significant that there is no coastal town of any size between the Shantung peninsula and Tientsin. Shipping in the Po-hai and Lioatung Wan is handicapped by the shallow waters and also by the offshore dust storms, which can make navigation dangerous.

Coastal trading has flourished in the south from early days, but was much less active in the north. It received some impetus during the Yuan dynasty when Kublai Khan, employing a couple of ex-pirates as directors, organized regular sailings carrying grain from the Yangtze mouth to Taiku (Tientsin) to reinforce grain movement on the Grand Canal.

The opening of the Treaty Ports after 1840 was the signal for a big increase in coastal traffic in which British and Japanese shipping firms became particularly active. This growth continued for a whole century until the outbreak of the Sino–Japanese War in 1936, when all Chinese and many foreign vessels fell into Japanese hands and coastal shipping came to a standstill. At the end of the war China was virtually without modern river or ocean-going ships, and it was not until after 1950 that some recovery was made.

China was not without some experience in shipbuilding. Prior to the Sino–Japanese War most of the river steamers and a fair proportion of the coastal vessels were built in the yards at Talien (Dairen), the Kiangnan Shipyard, Shanghai and in the Hong Kong shipyards. In the early decades of this century the work was mainly under British supervision, but after 1930 Chinese engineers were increasingly responsible. Nearly all the material used in construction came from abroad.

In order to meet imperative needs immediately

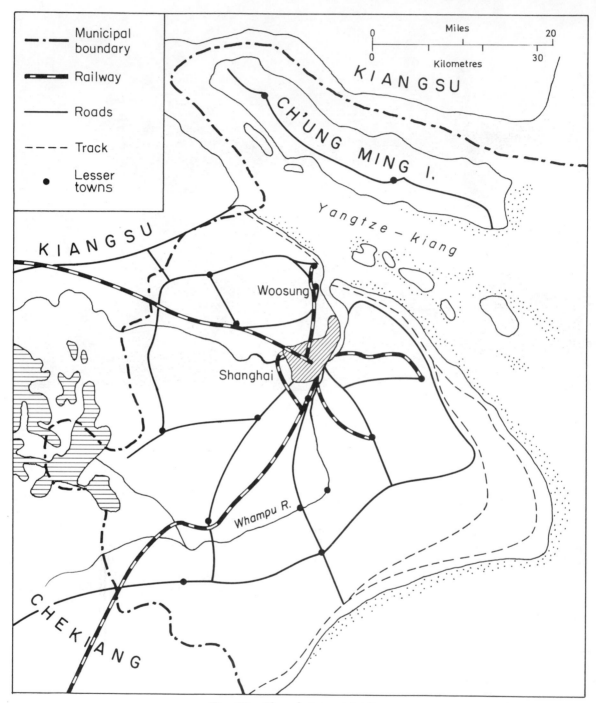

Fig. 88   Shanghai municipality

Plate 13   Extension of harbour work at Tangku, port for Tientsin at the mouth of the Hai-ho, making berths for 10 000-ton vessels in the shallow northern waters

after 1949, it was necessary to buy some vessels from abroad and to rely on foreign shipping for coastal trading. However, the People's Government quickly rehabilitated the former shipyards and brought them into production, concentrating at first on the building of river craft and coastal vessels. A Ship Research and Designing Institute has been established at Wuhan, specializing in passenger and cargo ships and tugs for the Yangtze. In 1965 the first small oil tanker of 3000 tons for coastal service was launched. The shipyards at Shanghai are now building ocean-going ships up to 13 000 tons for which they have designed and produced successfully an 8820 h.p. low-speed marine diesel engine, the largest yet in China[21]. It is claimed that all sea-going ships have now been fitted with radar equipment, wireless direction finders and sound-echoing detectors. These are very modest achievements by comparison with Japan's present massive production, but a start has been made on what appears to be sound lines. Needless to say, all Chinese passenger and cargo ships are state owned and controlled. Official overseas operations began in 1961[22].

Ports

Prior to 1949, Shanghai was by far the most important port of China and ranked sixth in world trade. The only others of real significance were Tientsin with its outport at Taku, Whampoa, the port for Canton, and Dairen.

Growth of merchant shipping fleets
(thousands gross reproduced tons)

1968	1969	1970	1971	1972
766	792	868	1022	1182
1973	1974	1975	1976	1977
1479	1871	2828	3589	4245

Figures from *Statistical Year Book*, U.N. 1977.

Shanghai's strength as a modern port lies in its great hinterland of the Yangtze basin. Its growth has been very rapid. In northern Sung times (1074) it appears in the records as a fishing village with a shipping officer to manage the taxation of Yangtze shipping. Later, in Ming times, it acquired a wall and fortification to meet the ravages of Japanese pirates, but it was still only a very small town in 1840, when, at the end of the Opium war, it was chosen as the site for a British concession, which was expanded into the International Settlement in 1863, from which its rapid development dates. It is interesting to note that its first factory, built in 1862, was a shipyard. Population soared. By 1865 it already was 690 000; in 1936 3·74 million and in 1948 5·2 million. Shanghai today is a municipality, answerable directly to Peking. It has an area of 5910 sq. km and a population of some 10 million, of which more than 6 million are within the city boundary[23].

After Liberation in 1949, there was an initial attempt to reduce and disperse some of Shanghai's population in accordance with the general policy of dispersal of the country's industry, but economic momentum and the natural positional advantages proved too strong and the policy was quickly reversed. Since then there has been a very rapid growth of industry, especially in heavy engineering, shipbuilding, chemicals and textiles, and the port has renewed its earlier activity.

Shanghai, from its earliest days as a modern port, has always had to face severe difficulties of silting, resulting from the Yangtze's heavy load, which persistently threatens to block the mouth of the small tributary, the Hwangpu, on which Shanghai stands. Only constant and efficient dredging can keep its outlet into the Yangtze at Woosung clear. For a big international port handling huge quantities of raw materials, Shanghai was singularly deficient in modern loading and unloading equipment before 1949. The reason for this was the abundance and cheapness of labour. Since then there has been a great deal of up-to-date equipment introduced and, consequently, a quickening turn-round of ships in the port.

Shanghai has retained its pre-eminence as the first port of the country, but other ports, old and new, have their place in the progress that has been made. All the major ports have taken on a new look and all now have modern, mechanized loading equipment, better wharfage and road and rail communications.

Tientsin now has a new outport at Tangku.

Formerly only vessels of less than 3000 tons could enter the Tai-ho. The rest had to anchor at the bar at Taku, which, as a port, has now been virtually discarded in favour of the new harbour at Tangku on the left bank of the Hai-ho. Its construction was started by the Japanese during the 1936–45 war, but it was left unfinished with only two wharves capable of accommodating 3000-ton ships. It is now complete with wharves large enough to take 10 000-ton vessels, warehouses, modern loading equipment, including coal conveyor belts, the latest dredging equipment and good railways. Tangku is thus more capable of serving the rapidly growing commercial and industrial needs of Peking and Tientsin and of handling the bulk of north China's import and export trade. Similarly, facilities have been improved at Lushun (Port Arthur), Talien (Dairen), Hulutao, Chinwantao and Yingtow. Canton was formally opened to foreign ships for the first time in November 1965. The river has been dredged and new warehouses and wharves, capable of handling ships up to 4000 tons have been built. Formerly all Canton's shipping was handled at Whampoa, 37 km down stream.

An entirely new port has been constructed at Tsamkong (Chankiang) in Kwangtung, opposite Hainan. Formerly it had one small wharf for sailing and small passenger boats. It is now a modern harbour with wharves accommodating ships up to 10 000 tons.

Air

The Sino–Japanese War (1936–45) severely interrupted the development of civil air transport, which had begun early in the 1930s. There was some acceleration and progress between 1946 and 1949, but on the defeat and retreat of the Nationalist forces in 1949, the meagre fleet of civil planes was withdrawn to Hong Kong where it was impounded. A long legal battle over ownership then ensued. Thus the Communist Government found itself virtually without civil aircraft and with only primitive airfields.

Between 1950 and 1958 rapid progress was made, but air services, of necessity, were restricted to only the most pressing priorities. These consisted mainly of the transport of important political and economic personnel, such as leading cadres, engineers and technicians; topographical and geological teams and their equipment; aerial

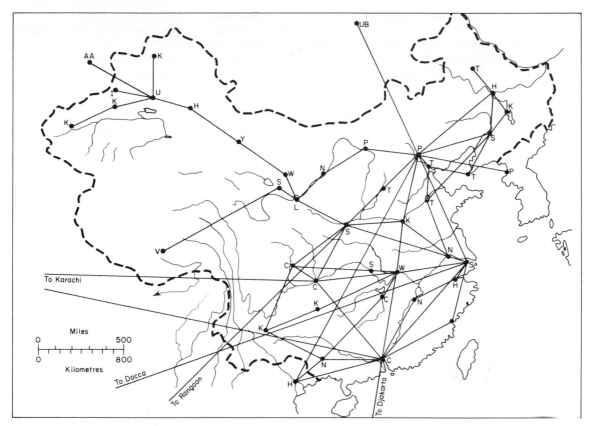

Fig. 89   Main air routes of China, 1966.

Progress in Civil Aviation
(*from* Ten Great Years, *Peking, 1960*)

Year	Freight turnover (*thousand ton-km*)	Passenger turnover (*thousand passenger km*)	Total flight hours for industrial and agric. purposes (h)
1950	820	9 780	
1952	2 430	24 090	959
1957	8 250	79 870	9 168
1958	13 310	108 990	17 845

photography; the transport of fragile instruments, spare parts and urgently required machinery. Towards the end of this period, the needs of agriculture, such as the distribution of chemical fertilizer, pest spraying, the rapid transport of fish fry and the control of forest fires began to receive some attention. By 1958 most of the main cities had some air communication and a considerable increase in air traffic had been achieved.

However, it has been since 1959 that the main progress in development, coordination and organization of regular flights has taken place. Peking and Shanghai are the two great hubs from which routes to more than 70 Chinese cities radiate. These domestic routes cover over 34 000 km[24]. Newly established through-routes from Shenyang to Sian via Peking and Taiyuan, and from Shenyang to Chengtu, are reported to take $7\frac{1}{2}$ h and $8\frac{1}{4}$ h respectively. Slow as this may appear by comparison with western standards, it is, nevertheless, a great advance in communication.

China now possesses three international airports, Peking, Shanghai and Canton, each fully provided with the necessary standard equipment for 24-hour flying service. The routes operating in 1967 were to the U.S.S.R., Mongolia, Korea, Vietnam, Burma and Pakistan[25]. Although China today designs and produces its own planes, these are not yet in sufficient supply. Aero engines from Rolls-Royce are imported and contracts for their production in China are in hand.

Broadcasting

The constant propagation of Leninist–Maoist ideology lies at the very heart of Chinese Communist policy. It is not surprising, therefore, to find that adequate provision has been made for this essential modern means of communication of ideas. Every corner of China is penetrated. Every commune, every village, has its public receiver set and television set. Chinese-designed and produced transistors are now widely available at a price which is within the means of a thrifty worker.

References

1 Marco Polo, *The Travels of Marco Polo, the Venetian*, Book II, chapter 20.
2 J. Needham, 'Science and China's influence in the world', in R. Dawson (ed.), *Legacy of China* (Oxford, 1964), p. 271.
3 Han Su-yin, op. cit.
4 V. Lippit, 'Development of transportation in Communist China', *China Quarterly*, **27** (July 1966), quoting Chang Kia-ngau, *China's Struggle for Railroad Development* (New York, 1943).
5 Richard Hughes, op. cit.
6 *Ten Great Years* (Peking, 1960).
7 *Kung-lu* [*Highway*], **10** (1964).
8 *Min-tzu T'uan-chieh* [*National Unity*], **10** (1964).
9 NCNA, Sining, 11 October 1964.
10 NCNA, Foochow, 28 June 1965.
11 NCNA, Lhasa, 20 October 1965.
12 Fei Hsiao-tung, op. cit.
13 *China Reconstructs*, July 1963.
14 *China Reconstructs*, January 1965.
15 *Far Eastern Trade*, December 1961.
16 Lin Kwang-chin, 'British–Chinese Steamships' rivalry in China, 1873–85', in C. D. Cowan (ed.), op. cit.
17 *China Year Book*, 1925, p. 1039.
18 *Peking Review*, **17** (1966).
19 NCNA, Chungking, 30 July 1965.
20 NCNA, Kweiyang, 20 June 1965.
21 NCNA, Shanghai, 13 December 1965.
22 *Far Eastern Trade*, November 1961.
23 China Reconstructs, March 1962.
24 Ling Shang, 'Rapid development of civil aviation', *Shih-shih Shou-ts'e* [*Current Events*], **9** (1964).
25 *Ta-kung Pao*, Peking, 4 October 1964.

8   Population and Power

POPULATION

The discussion and analysis of China's population is deliberately included under the heading of Power in order to emphasize how big and important an element it has been, and still is, in China. In agriculture and transport, man, together with animals, has been virtually the only source of power. In fields throughout the centuries, he has worked individually or in small clan groups. On occasion, he has been mobilized into great labour armies to carry out some big national work, such as building the Great Wall under Ch'in Shih Hwang Ti, or the New Pien Canal in the Sui dynasty or the Grand Canal under Kublai Khan. The mobilization of such large numbers was possible only after the break-up of the feudal system at the end of the Chou dynasty (221 BC). It was nearly always compulsory, the exceptions being on occasions of emergency dyke repairs. These mobilizations in the past have been accompanied by great hardship, cruelty and loss of life, and consequently are looked back on with loathing and hatred by the common people.

The Chinese peasant is sturdy and tough, patient and persistent and, within wide limits, amenable to organization. When inspired and willing, he is capable of great endurance, as we have seen during the Great Leap Forward. Chinese Communist intention is to achieve a modern, industrialized, Socialist state as quickly as possible, which involves mechanization in all its manifestations and breaking free from this reliance on manpower. This has been achieved to some extent in the modernization of transport, the building of integrated steel plant, the equipping of mines and ports, and in the mechanization of state farms but, viewed in the setting of the country's vast needs, only a beginning has been made. Most of the great reconstruction work so far carried out has, of necessity, had to be handled by human muscles and by the mobilization of vast numbers. Even the building of the big dams, such as San Men, has been largely the work of hoe, basket and carrying pole. The rapid construction of the Shasi and Tachiatai retention basins in the Yangtze were achieved by the mobilization of more than half a million workers, men and women from the localities, working with simple tools. Patriotic fervour, socialist propaganda and considerable care for the welfare of these armies appear to have made such mobilizations possible without arousing the deep-seated hatreds, which have accompanied all such previous mobilizations.

China's manpower has been notably increased by the emancipation of women, which has steadily been taking place throughout the twentieth century and which has gained great momentum since 1949. An important aspect of rural and urban communes has been the freeing of large numbers of women from household ties and chores onto the labour market. Women's equality of status with men in China carries with it the obligation to tackle even the same physical work

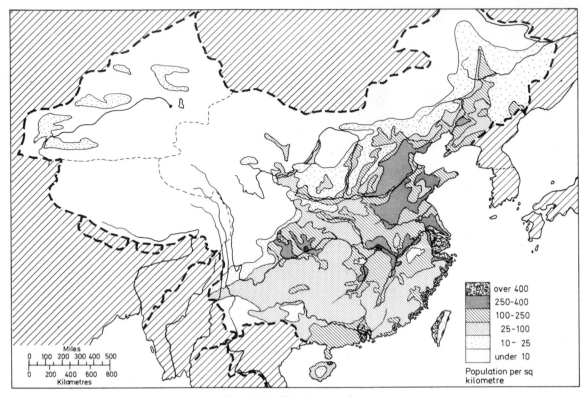

Fig. 90   China's population

as men and to carry the same responsibilities, from judges to tractor drivers. This has met with an amazing positive response and has increased the labour force enormously.

Numbers
In 1953, for the first time since the Han dynasty, a census of the people was carried out. Previously all figures of population were estimates based on the number of households or on food consumption or salt consumption and, more recently, on postal material. The results of these estimates showed great variation and very little reliability. The necessity for reliable information on numbers in a modern state, especially in a planned communist society as compared with one of free enterprise, is obvious. Equally obvious are the difficulties of taking a census in a country so vast and of such variety as China. It is not surprising, therefore, to find that, in this first counting of heads, the Government used a very simple schedule of five questions[1] – too simple according to some experts. No attempt was made

to carry through the census on any one single day, or to attempt a *de facto* numbering, i.e. the persons actually present at a particular place at a certain time. Instead the *de jure* method was used, i.e. recording those persons habitually present. When the census was published in 1954 and the total population for Mainland China was given as 582 603 417, nearly 100 million higher than the highest pre-1949 estimate (that by the Post Office in 1929), some outside observers were very sceptical as to its honesty and reliability[2]. There appears to be little reason for questioning the honesty of the figures although they have not the same accuracy as similar Western demographic statistics. In some outlying border regions, occupied by national minorities, the normal registration could not be undertaken and estimates had to be made. Other unusual elements of the 1953 census were the inclusion of the population of Taiwan, which, although at present politically separate, is regarded by both the Communist and the Nationalist governments as an integral part of China. Also included were the Overseas

Plate 14   Women in China today enjoy equal status with men and are engaged in every kind of work

Chinese, i.e. Chinese settlers in foreign lands and students studying abroad.

These figures, published by the Statistical Bureau in November 1954 differ slightly from those of the Government Report in June 1954. From 1953 to 1957 records were kept of changes in population and these were published by the Statistical Bureau. Since then they have ceased. It was the announced intention to conduct a second census in 1963, but this did not materialize. There have been many subsequent estimates of China's total population, one of which is that by

Edgar Snow reporting a conversation with the Premier when Chou En-lai estimated it to be not quite 800 million (January 1971).

Direct census registration of the Mainland	574 205 940
Borderland National Minorities estimate	8 397 477
Taiwan (1951 figures)	7 591 298
Overseas Chinese	11 743 320
Total	601 938 035

Table 10 *Population Distribution of Mainland China by Provinces* (in thousands)
(*from* Ten Great Years, *Peking, 1960*)

Province	1953	1957	1965**		1976¶
Szechwan	62 304	72 160	72 000		80 000
Shantung	48 876	54 030	57 000		68 000
Honan	44 214	48 670	50 000		60 000
Kiangsu	41 252	45 230	47 000		55 000
Hopei	35 984	44 720	43 000		43 000
Kwangtung	34 770	37 960	43 000		42 000
Hunan	33 227	36 220	38 000		38 000
Anhwei	30 343	33 560	35 000		45 000
Hupeh	27 789	30 790	34 000		40 000
Chekiang	22 865	25 280	31 000		35 000
Kwangsi Chuang Aut. Region	19 560	19 360	24 000		24 000
Yunnan	17 472	19 100	23 000		28 000
Kiangsi	16 772	18 610	25 000		24 000
Shensi	15 881	18 130	21 000		26 000
Kweichow	15 037	16 890	20 000		24 000
Shansi	14 314	15 960	20 000		26 000
Fukien	13 142	14 650	20 000		20 000
Kansu	12 928	12 800§	13 000		8 000
Ningsia Hui Aut. Region	—	1 810	2 200 (1970 est)		3 000
Northeast					
Liaoning	18 545	24 090	29 000		33 000
Jehol	5 160	— *		incorporating parts	
Heilungkiang	11 897	14 860	25 000	of Inner Mongolia	32 000
Kirin	11 290	12 550	20 000		23 000
Inner Mongolian Aut. Region	6 100	9 200	7 000		8 000
Sinkiang Uighur Aut. Region	4 873	5 640			10 000
Sikang	3 381	— †			
Chinghai	1 676	2 050			3 000
Tibet	1 274	1 270			1 400
Muncipalities					
Shanghai	6 204	6 900	11 500 (wider municipality)		
Peking	2 768	4 010			
Tientsin	2 693	— ‡			
Total	582 603	646 530			835 000

* Jehol incorporated in Liaoning   § Ningsia withdrawn from Kansu
† Sikang incorporated in Szechwan   **est. by Cheng-siang Chen
‡ Tientsin incorporated in Hopei   ¶ est. by Colina MacDougall, 'The Chinese Economy in 1976', *Ch. Q.*, *70* (1977).

The distribution of the population is best appreciated by an examination of the accompanying population map and the provincial table (p. 208). The concentration in the east, in the North China Plain, in the Yangtze basin and along the southeast and southern coasts is most marked. The report states that 505 346 135 or 86·74 per cent of the total population is rural, that is, living in hamlets, villages and small towns of 2000 or less inhabitants. This proportion, as between rural and urban, has changed somewhat in favour of urban in the last twenty years, but it is still true to say that more than four-fifths of China's population is rural. There are great contrasts in density of population; in some rural regions the density is very great indeed, for example, in the irrigated areas of the Chengtu plain in Szechwan densities of 750 to 1200 persons/sq. km are not uncommon. Kiangsu, with an area of 107 300 sq. km, has a population of 41 252 192 giving an overall density of 384 persons/sq. km, but in the rural river valleys there is a density of over 1000 sq. km^3. On the other hand, many parts of the Tibetan plateau and in the Takla Makan are virtually uninhabited.

Since 1949 there has been a big and rapid increase in urban population. Some indication of this growth is given by the report that in the five

Table 11. Population of Cities having over 500 000 inhabitants.
(Year-end of 1957 in thousands) (*from* Ten Great Years, *Peking*)

City	Population	City	Population
Municipalities directly under		Kiangsu	
central authority		Nanking	1419
Peking	4010	Suchow	676
Shanghai	6900	Soochow	633
		Wusih	613
Hopei			
Tientsin	3200	Chekiang	
Tangshan	800	Hangchow	784
Shihkiachuang	598		
		Fukien	
Shansi		Foochow	616
Taiyuan	1020		
		Honan	
Liaoning		Chengchow	766
Shenyang	2411		
Lushum–Talien	1508	Hupeh	
Fushun	985	Wuhan	2146
Anshan	805		
		Hunan	
Kirin		Changsha	703
Changchun	975		
Kirin	568	Kiangsi	
		Nanchang	508
Heilungkiang			
Harbin	1552	Kwangtung	
Tsitsihar	668	Canton	1840
Shensi		Szechwan	
Sian	1310	Chungking	2121
		Chengtu	1107
Kansu			
Lanchow	699	Kweichow	
		Kweiyang	504
Shangtung			
Tsinan	862	Yunnan	
Tsingtao	1121	Kunming	880
Tzepo	806		

years between 1953 and 1958 the number of cities having more than 1 million inhabitants has grown from 8 to 15; those having 500 000 to 1 million from 16 to 20, and those having 100 000 to 500 000 from 73 to 80[4]. The most striking growth has been in the new economic centres of the northeast and the north where there was a large absolute and relative increase. Table 11 lists the cities of more than 500 000 in 1957. Since then no comparable figures have been published. Ever since 1949 it has been the Government's policy to curb the growth of urban population as far as consistency with industrial development will permit. Nevertheless the city has its attractions in China as elsewhere, and there has been a big increase in numbers

POPULATION

Growth in Number of Big and Medium-sized Cities

Population	No. of cities		
	1952	*1957*	*1970*
Over 5 million	1	1	2
3 to 5 million	—	2	4
1 to 3 million	8	11	15
0·5 to 1 million	15	20	22
100 000 to 500 000	81	90	142
Under 100 000	54	52	185
Total	159	176	370

The 1953 official census classified the people into ethnic groups or 'nationalities'. Of these the 'Han' (Chinese) form the prepondering group,

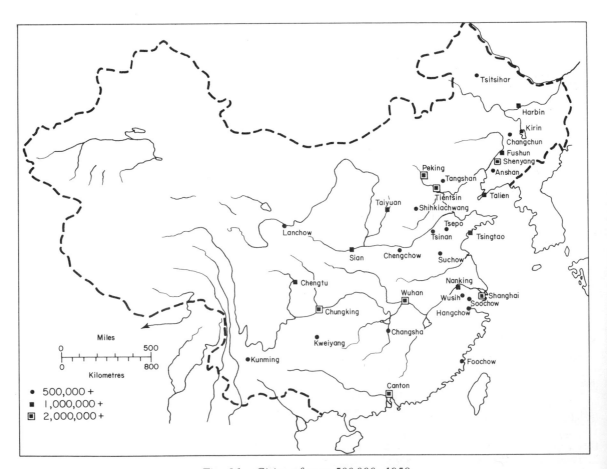

Fig. 91   Cities of over 500 000, 1958

numbering 547 283 057 or 93·4 per cent of the whole. The report makes no attempt to differentiate between the northerners (Han Jen) and southerners (T'ang Jen) on whom we have already commented. Within their common culture, there are still marked differences of stature, spoken language, facial characteristics and temperament between north and south, of which one is very conscious when journeying between the two regions. The northerners are generally taller, slower and more phlegmatic than their more volatile compatriots of the south whence revolutions have more commonly emanated. Moreover, the northern Chinese are more homogeneous than those of the south, where the main admixture of other nationalities occurs.

These 'national minorities' number in all 35 320 360 or 6·6 per cent of the whole. No fewer than 51 of them are listed in *Ten Great Years*. Where these nationalities are found in large numbers, they have been given some semblance of autonomy and self-government. The main examples are the Kwangsi Chuang Autonomous Region, where the Chuang people numbered 6 611 455 in 1953; the Sinkiang Uighur Autonomous Region, where the Uighurs numbered 3 640 125 and the Inner Mongolian Autonomous Region, where the Hui or Chinese Moslems and the Mongols respectively form the majority of the population. Other important minorities are the Tibetans (2 775 622); the Yi (3 254 269) in the Szechwan–Yunnan borders; the Miao (2 511 339) in Kweichow and west Hunan; the Pu-yi (1 247 883) in southwest Kweichow; the Koreans (1 120 405) in the Yenpien Korean Autonomous *chou* in Kirin. The Manchus, who at the census numbered 2 419 931, now have no region of concentration and have become integrated throughout the country. It is instructive to note that, in addition to the Yi, Pu-yi and Miao, the majority of the smaller tribes or nationalities are found in the southwest in western Szechwan, Kweichow, Yunnan and west Kwangsi. The People's Government takes great credit for its treatment of these minorities, in its care for their economic well-being, the raising of their living standards, in educating them in local government, in raising the standard of literacy and in inventing a written language in those cases where none has existed previously. Institutes of National Minorities with this educative end in view are a feature of many large cities, notably Peking and Wuhan.

In common with some Asian countries, but contrary to Western experience, men in China outnumber women. In view of the importance placed, in the past, on male succession and the performance of correct ceremonies in ancestral worship by the male head of the family, it is not surprising that more value was placed on boys than on girls and more care was lavished on them. In times of famine, it was common practice among the poor people to abandon female babies and to sell their young girls to wealthier people. With the decline of Confucianism and the growth of Western standards, the status of women has risen during the last 50–60 years and with it, the chances of survival of female babies has improved, especially since 1949. The change, however, had not, by 1957, become apparent in the total figures of sex composition[5]:

Year	Total Population	Male	Female (*thousands*)
1949	548 770	285 140	263 630
1953	595 550	308 850	286 700
1957	656 630	340 140	316 490

Chinese living in Hong Kong, Macau and abroad are not included.

However, Professor Chandrasekhar quotes the following figures and, commenting, says 'The cultural modes favoured the male infant. These have now changed, and the change is reflected in the sex ratio of infants under three years. That the sex ratio becomes increasingly unfavourable to the female in the higher age groups is noteworthy'[1].

Sex Ratio at Various Age Groups	
Age groups	*Sex ratio* *Number of males per 100 females*
0	104·9
1—2	106·2
3—6	110·0
7—13	115·8
14—17	113·7
18—35	111·5
36—55	106·8
56 and over	86·7

The age composition of a society or country has very considerable influence on its economic well-being. Other things being equal, the greater the proportion of its people who are of working age, the greater will be its productive capacity. Exactly what constitutes 'working age' is difficult to determine and differs from country to country and also within the same country. In China, children are brought into productive employment at an early age in rural areas. Moreover, Communist politicians and educators lay much emphasis on practical experience and very many schools – particularly middle schools – are run on a part-time study, part-time work basis. During the summer months an appreciable amount of work in the fields is done by boys and girls. It is therefore difficult to make clear-cut divisions between productive and non-productive ages, such as school-leaving at one end of the scale and retirement at the other. At the time of the 1953 census the age composition of China's population was[1]:

Age group (years)	Distribution %
0—4	15·6
5—9	11·0
10—17	14·5
0—17	41·1
18—49	45·4
50 and over	13·5

Comparable figures for U.K. in 1959 were

0–14	23·2
15–64*	62·3
65 and over†	14·7

* Men only 60–64 years.
† Women of 60 years and over included

These figures emphasize the youthfulness of China in 1953 with 86·5 per cent of its people under 50 years of age. Although no statistics are yet available, the proportion of those over 50 today is considerably greater, due largely to much improved public hygiene and medical care.

Population growth
China's population, until the seventeenth century, had remained fairly constant at a figure somewhere between 100 million and 200 million, held steady by the Malthusian checks of war, famine and pestilence. During the long peaceful reigns of the two great Manchu emperors, K'ang Hsi and Ch'ien Lung, the population grew rapidly to an estimated 300 million by 1850. It should be noted that during this period there was no concomitant increase in the amount of cultivable land. Hence,

from this time on land hunger began to be felt and, as population continued to increase, it became acute in the twentieth century.

The 1953 census revealed that there were 582 million people living in the country; returns in 1957 showed this to have risen to 656 million, an annual increase of nearly 15 million. The figure estimated in 1971 was 800 million and, if the trend continues, there will be over 1000 million well before the turn of the century. The reasons for this explosion of numbers are not far to seek. To a very large extent the Malthusian checks have been removed. Since 1949 China has enjoyed a peace and political unity unknown in the previous one hundred years. Threatened famine and its death toll have been averted by rationing of supplies and a more even and equitable distribution of food, made possible by the development of modern communications. Even more important has been the rapid extension of public hygiene and the cult of cleanliness throughout the country. During the early years after 1949, the authorities concentrated attention on preventive medicine. Training for doctors, during these years, was reduced from 6 to 3 years in order that this preventive side should be implemented. The result has been that, while the number of births has remained fairly constant, the death rate, estimated at about 27 per 1000 in the early decades of the twentieth century and 18 per 1000 in 1952, had fallen to 11 per 1000 in 1957 and is still falling.

Table 12 Crude Birth and Death Rates in Mainland China. (from S. Chandrasekhar[1], by courtesy of Hong Kong University Press)
(per 1000 population)

Year	Birth rate	Death rate	Natural increases
1952	37	18	19
1953	37	17	20
1954	38	13	24
1955	35	12·4	22·6
1956	32	11·4	20·6
1957	34	11	23

The fall in infant mortality rates is even more striking. There are no reliable figures for these rates before 1949, but some estimates place infant deaths at nearly 200 per 1000 population per annum. In rural areas alone the rate stood at

138 per 1000 in 1954. It had fallen to 109 in 1956. The infant mortality rate for the whole country, including the urban population, was down to 34·1 in 1957[1]. Figures for cities alone show a remarkable fall. For example, infant death rates in Peking, Shanghai and Canton in 1952 stood at 65·7, 81·2 and 47·7 per thousand. By 1956 these had fallen to 35·1, 31·1 and 25·1 respectively[1].

Such population changes pose the Government with problems. Orthodox Chinese communism is inflexibly opposed to the Malthusian theory of population, holding that China is well able to feed any increase in numbers that may occur and that increasing numbers, far from being a weakness, constitute the strength of the nation. Mao Tse-tung, with his faith pinned firmly on the masses and their support, has emphatically affirmed his belief in large numbers. 'I hope that these people will take a wider view and really recognize the fact that we have a population of six hundred millions, that is an objective fact and that this is our asset. It is a good thing.'[7]

This optimistic and confident view continued until 1954 when some questioning began to arise since production was not increasing as rapidly as had been anticipated. A rather vacillating policy has since ensued. The first official suggestions of the desirability of some birth control came at the National People's Congress in 1954 when Shao Li-tze stated 'It is a good thing to have a large population but, in an environment beset with difficulties, it appears that a limit should be set'. He urged the advertisement of birth control by contraceptive methods. However, it was not until March 1957 that Madam Li Teh-chuan, Minister of Health, launched a full-blooded birth control campaign. Throughout the year great publicity was given everywhere to the use of contraception.

It was at this time that Ma Yin-ch'u, one of China's leading economists, published his paper, 'The New Principle of Population', in which, while stressing his opposition to the Malthusian theory, attacked the orthodox communist attitude to population questions. He contended that a high population and a high growth in numbers slows down economic development and that curbing of population growth was necessary in order to produce a higher quality of people. He advocated limitation by family planning and contraception on the one hand and much greater capital expenditure on the mechanization of agriculture, water conservancy and irrigation, mainly on small-scale works, in order to raise living standards. He argued that, with mechanization and automation, a big population was not necessary. In spite of his declared opposition to Malthusian ideas, he was denounced as Malthusian, his critics contending that, in China, there was a labour shortage and not the reverse, and meeting Ma's arguments with the doctrinaire statement 'Everyone knows – according to the viewpoint of Marxism and Leninism on the population question – that unemployment and surplus population are the production of capitalists, privately owning the means of production'.[8]

The Great Leap Forward followed shortly after in 1958–9. In the universal enthusiasm and confidence of these years control of numbers was lost sight of. It was the near-famine years of 1960 and 1961 which again focused attention on the question. Once again contraception was advised, stressing the need for family planning, the proper spacing of childbirth and the care of the mother's health, rather than the curbing of numbers. From 1962 onwards emphasis has been placed on late marriages. 'Planned childbirth and late marriage is the established policy of our country during the socialist construction period.'[9] While the legal age is 18, the ages of marriage recommended are 23–27 for women and 25–29 for men. Earlier marriages are condemned on the basis that they are physically and mentally harmful to the health of parents and children and that they distract youth from study and productive work[10]. But the main reasons given are: to strengthen women's education, to increase their revolutionary spirit, to use their productive labour for 6–10 years before marriage and to promote their independence of former mother-in-law dominance. Undoubtedly one aid in the population containment programme has been the implementation of the Five Guarantees (*wu pao tien*) for the old – guarantees of food, clothing, shelter, medical care and decent burial – thus removing the urge for children for support in old age. Abortion is now legalized but resorted to reluctantly. The advocacy of late marriage and smaller families has been vigorously preached throughout the country. A three-child family is regarded as the ideal. As might be expected, these measures appear to be having greater success among the urban than the rural population.

COAL

Reserves

During the Middle and Late Ordovician era, the great Cathaysian geosyncline, which at that time stretched from the northeast to Indo-China, was divided by the raising of the Chin Ling axis from east to west. This axis has remained a permanent geographical factor ever since, dividing the country geologically, climatically, vegetationally, economically and even politically. At that time, land to the north of the axis was raised, while that to the south was deeply submerged. During the Carboniferous and Permian, great areas in the north were alternately submerged in shallow seas and continental shelves and raised above sea level. This is the period of the formation of the great coalfields of Shensi, Shansi, Hopei, Honan and the Northeast. From the Permian onward, north China has not been deeply submerged. Comparatively small basins were below sealevel in Tertiary times, when the immensely thick coal beds of Fushun and Fusin were laid down in the Northeast.

Most of the coal of central and southern China is of secondary formation. There were some Carbo–Permian deposits along the northern periphery of the deep southern sea, but the great

Table 13   Coal Reserves and Production (from N. Dickerman[11], by courtesy of U.S. Bureau of Mines

Province	Reserves 1934–45 (figures in million metric tons)				Production 1944 (thousand metric tons)
	Anthracite	Bituminous	Lignite	Total	
N.W.					
Shansi	36471	87985	2671	127127	6250
Shensi	750	71200		71950	650
Kansu	59	997		1056	110
Ningsia	173	284		457	140
N.E.					
Heilungkiang		5000	3980	8908	3047
Kirin		5581	478	6059	6117
Liaoning	36	2606		2642	10940
Jehol		4714		4714	5359
Chahar	17	487		504	9300
N. China Plain					
Shangtung	26	1613		1639	10300
Hopei	975	2088	2	3965	12000
Honan	4455	3309		7764	300
Central China					
Hupeh	45	309		345	40
Hunan	741	552		1293	550
Anhwei	60	300		360	1250
Kiangsi	271	420	9	700	120
Kiangsu	25	192		217	1100
Red Basin					
Szechwan	293	3540		3833	2700
S.W.					
Yunnan	77	1539	694	2310	260
Kweichow	822	1696		2518	250
Kwangsi	45	1111	1	1157	200
S. and S.E.					
Chekiang	22	78		100	2
Fukien	147	6		153	30
Kwangtung	59	274		333	100
W.					
Tsinghai	240	584		824	—
Sinkiang		31980		31980	180

Plate 15   Hwainan coalmine, near Pengpu, Anhwei

coalfields of Szechwan and the widely scattered fields of Hunan, Hupeh, Yunnan, Kweichow and Kwangtung are of Rhaetic origin, when the whole of southern China had been uplifted.

There has been no publication of overall coal reserves since 1949, but the subsequent extensive geological surveys that have been carried out have doubtless raised considerably the figures published by Nelson Dickerman in 1948, which showed total reserves of over 283 billion metric tons of which nearly 230 billion were bituminous. China is well served with reserves of some 45 870 million tons of anthracite and has comparatively little lignite. The 1934–45 estimated reserves serve to give a fair general picure of coal distribution.

By far the most extensive reserves lie in the northwest of China Proper in the provinces of Shensi, Shansi, Kansu and Ningsia Autonomous Region. Much of the coal is hidden beneath sandstone and loess deposits, but lies exposed in large areas along axes running from north to south along both sides of the Hwang-ho, also to the north of Paotow and in some places in Ningsia. Huge reserves of good quality anthracite lie mainly to the east in Shansi, while the bituminous is mainly to the west. Happily there has been comparatively little tectonic movement in the region and, consequently, the coal seams are generally horizontal, thereby facilitating mining. Although the seams here cannot compare with the great thicknesses of the exposed beds in the Northeast, they are, nevertheless, ample, varying from 3 to 13 m.

The Northeast ranks second in reserves, but has only about one-eighth of those of the northwest. Bituminous is distributed widely throughout the three provinces and lies exposed on the eastern and western edges of the Cathaysian geosyncline. Anthracite is virtually absent, but there are considerable deposits of lignite in Heilunkiang. Two Tertiary coal basins are located in Liaotung, at Fushun and Fusin, each having exposed coal seams of up to 120 m thickness.

The reserves of the North China Plain (Shantung, Hopei and Honan) are also found along the west and east edges of the Cathaysian geosyncline, i.e. along the faulted edges of the Wutai and Taihang Shan, on the one hand, and the western scarps of the Shantung peninsula on the other. It is highly probable that there are rich coal deposits lying below the deep alluvium of the plain. Honan is the only province of the North China Plain which has large reserves of anthracite. These are a continuation of the Shansi beds.

The statistical table of reserves reveals the great difference in wealth of coal that exists between north and south China immediately the Tsinling Shan is crossed southward. The Rheatic beds of the Red Basin of Szechwan alone carry reserves which can bear comparison with those of the north. Szechwan's coal lies buried in the centre of the basin under Cretaceous red sandstone, but outcrops mainly on the periphery, particularly in the south and southeast, along the crests of the anticlines. The provinces of the southwest plateau (Yunnan, Kweichow and Kwangsi) have fair bituminous reserves quite widely distributed. Kweichow has fairly extensive deposits of anthracite. Eastward and southward the reserves become progressively poorer, especially around Fukien and Chekiang.

No figures of coal reserves for Inner Mongolia are available. The 1934–45 estimates for Sinkiang were 31 980 million tons and for Tsinghai 240 million tons of anthracite and 584 million tons of bituminous. Since then extensive geological surveys have been made in both these regions and there is reason to believe that these figures should be considerably increased. Sinkiang's main coalfields extend along the northern slopes of the Bogdo Ula from Manass to Kitai and in the Ili Valley, centred on Kuldja. There are abundant peat beds in Inner Mongolia.

Production

Coal has been in general use in China for cooking and smelting since the Sung dynasty (960–1279) when it was replacing charcoal[12]. Marco Polo reported with wonder the use of coal in these words: 'Throughout this province there is found a sort of black stone, which they dig out of the mountains, where it runs in veins. When lighted, it burns like charcoal, and retains the fire much better than wood; inasmuch that it may be preserved during the night, and in the morning be found still burning. These stones do not flame, excepting a little when first lighted, but during their ignition give out considerable heat.'[13] Mine shafts over 30 m deep were sunk and galleries were fitted with bamboo pipes for drainage and for pumping fresh air and evacuating gases.

Theoretically all soil and therefore all coal and minerals belonged to the State. However, some private exploitation in mining was permitted and during the Ming dynasty (1368–1644) there was steady growth of private enterprise. Nevertheless, it was always kept under close control by the scholar–administrator class. Towards the end of the dynasty, Emperor Wan-li clamped down on private mining in an edict which declared: 'It is no longer permitted to open private mines without authorization: the important thing is not to disturb the bowels of the earth.'[12]

The extraction of coal by modern methods did not take place until the beginning of the twentieth century. Mining corporations and companies, often combined Chinese and foreign ventures, obtained concessions from the Government and began operations. Most notable of these were the Japanese South Manchurian Railway Company's Fushun Collieries in 1907, the Peking Syndicate (1905) operating in Honan and the Kailan Mining Administration (1912), whose concessions lay in the region behind Chingwangtao[14]. Their development was part cause and part effect of the railway development of that period. For example, the Peking–Mukden Railway served and was served by the Kailan mines. The Peking–Hankow Railway followed closely the scarp slopes of the Wutai and Taihang Shan, pushing branchlines into the Shansi plateau to tap and develop the exposed anthracite of the edge. Coal exploitation was conditioned by communications and therefore was confined to the east. Shansi's great coalfields remained virtually untouched, except for shallow local mines, until the post-1949 development of railways in the region.

Methods of coal extraction have varied enormously, ranging from fairly advanced mechanization to an entire reliance on manpower. All mining has been influenced by the abundance and cheapness of human labour, which has militated against the introduction of machinery. Some large collieries were well mechanized and installed reasonable safety precautions, but in very many the conditions below ground were unspeakable, as described by George Cressey and as experienced by the author in Shihhweiyao, Hupeh, where the galleries were low and unpropped and were the beds of rushing streams, and where ventilation was practically non-existent. Since 1949 much attention and energy has been focused on improving all safety measures in mines[15].

Coal production rose gradually and somewhat unsteadily throughout the first half of the twentieth century:

Year	Tons (*thousands*)	
1912	13 000	
1923	22 000	
1930	16 839	
1944	71 263	
1949	32 430	
1958	270 000	
1959	335 000	(planned)
1966	240 000	(estimated)
1967	190 000	(*Current Scene*, Vol. VI, no. 12 [1968] 6)
1973	300 000	(estimated)

The phenomenal rise in output since 1949 reflects the great effort that has been put into industrial development. The dispersion of industry has had the effect of stimulating modern coal mining in many regions where previously it had been conducted on a primitive local scale. By 1958 it was reported that new pits, with a total annual output of 150 million tons had been opened since 1949. These included big developments at Kweisui, north of Paotow, Tatung and Taiyuan: also the rapid expansion in Sinkiang,

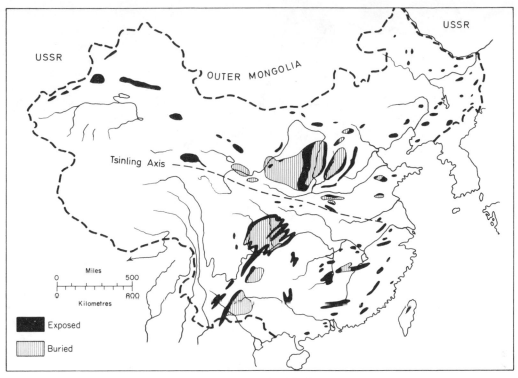

Fig. 92   Coalfields

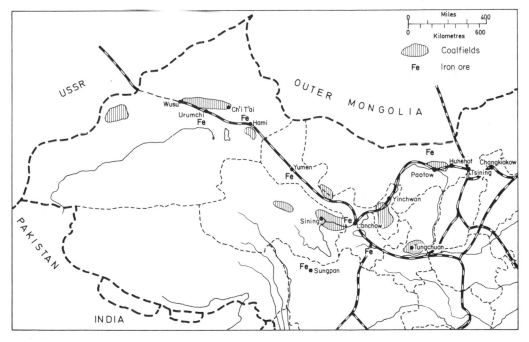

Fig. 93   Coalfields of the Northwest

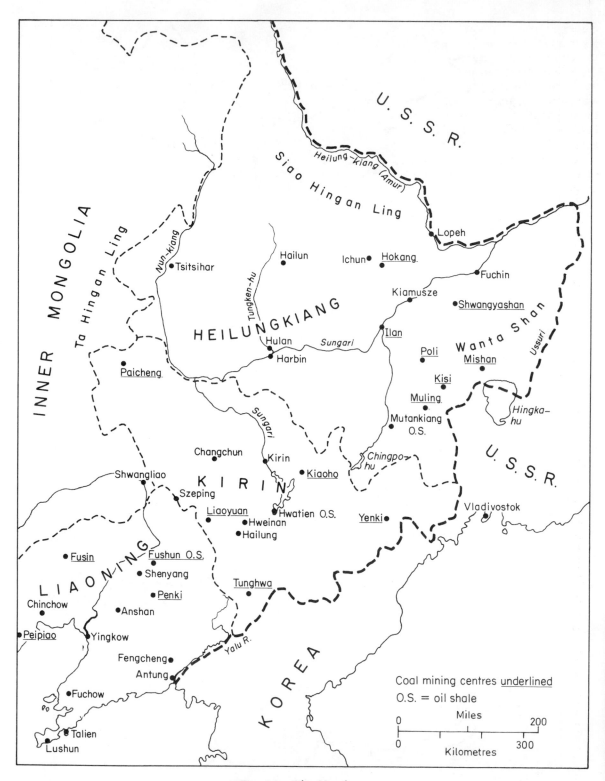

Fig. 94   The Northeast

east and west of Urumchi, to serve growing industrialization there. However, the same report voiced the complaint that too great a proportion of capital investment allocated to coal development was still going into the well-established north and Northeast and so maintaining an imbalance in the distribution of industry[16]. While no comprehensive account of the coal industry has been published, the constant reports in newspapers and magazines of the opening of new pits and their capacities give some indication of the scope of development. For example, a new mine shaft, designed and constructed by Chinese engineers and having an annual capacity of 1·8 million tons, was recently completed in the Kailan mining area[17]. Three new mines with capacities of 900 000, 1·2 million and 1·5 million tons p.a. were opened between 1958 and 1964 at Pingtingshan, south Honan, exploiting seams of coking coal up to 17 m thick. All three mines are mechanized and serve the needs of the Wuhan Iron and Steel Works[18].

The Northeast remains China's main coal-producing area, which is not surprising in view of the ease with which much of it can be mined. Not only at Fushun and Fusin in Liaoning, but also at Hokang in Heilungkiang there are open-cast mines with coal seams of immense thickness. Fushun, which was first developed by the Japanese and has now been extended, is reported to be producing over 20 million tons annually. Here the coal seam, which varies between 35 and 110 m in thickness, is overlain by layers of oil shale and green shale, which are used respectively for oil distillation and soapmaking or water softening. The oil refinery, built by the Japanese, is sited immediately above the cut, which is some 7 km long and 1400 m wide. The Fusin mines, which are similar in formation, are beginning to rival Fushun in output. Both are highly mechanized. Penki and Peipiao, also in Liaotung, in 1957 produced respectively 5 million and 2·8 million tons of good

coking coal. Hokang's open-cast seams total 40 m in thickness and produced 4·9 million tons in 1957. Other large Heilungkiang mines are sited at Kisi and Shwangyashan, which produced 5·8 million and 2·3 million tons respectively in 1957[19]. Smaller workings are at Mishan, Poli, Ilan and Muling. Kirin's most important mines are at Liaoyuan, which produced 3 million tons of good industrial coal in 1957, and at Tunghwa where good coking coal is obtained.

Chinese claims have been made recently of the discovery of new cokemaking methods by blending weakly-coking coals and so producing coke of greater strength and lower ash content than conventially made coke. If these claims are substantiated, the discovery will be of great importance as China's supplies of good coking coal are limited in amount and distribution.

The following estimate by Tatsu Kambara[20] shows the prominent position held by coal.

OIL

The first recorded use of oil and natural gas in China comes from the Eastern Han dynasty (AD 25–220) when 'fire wells' were drilled at Ch'unglai *hsien* in Szechwan and the natural gas was used for the processing of salt. Towards the end of the Ming dynasty (1368–1644) wells at Chienwei, Szechwan, several hundred metres deep were being drilled[21]. Apart from this, however, no other development of oil resources appears to have taken place during the succeeding centuries.

Although the presence of oil in north Shensi at Yench'ang and at Yumen in west Kansu was known in the early twentieth century, little was done to develop it. Domestic lighting at that time was by oil lamps throughout the land. The fuel for these came almost entirely from American, British and Dutch companies. This rich market may have influenced American assessments of China's

An Estimate of Primary Energy Consumption in China (1973)

	Actual	Coal Equivalent in million metric tons	%
Coal	300 million tons	300	80
Oil and Shale Oil	40 " "	57·2	15
Natural Gas	10 billion cu. metres	12·7	4
Hydro Electricity	3 billion kilowatts	4·2	1
	Total	374·1	100

potential oil reserves in such statements as 'both the types of rocks and their genetic age in the greater part of China preclude the possibility of there being any petrol deposits worthy of exploitation'[22] and 'There is almost no possibility of petroleum deposit in the greater part of China.'[23] Almost complete reliance on foreign imports of oil continued until 1949. China's peak output before this was in 1943 when 320 000 tons were produced, as against 1·95 million tons imported.

Since 1949, in concurrence with the general policy of industrial development, the attaining of national self-sufficiency in oil production has been a constant aim, borne out by the large amount of capital which has been invested in this field. Extensive geological surveys and prospecting have been – and still are being – carried out. During the first 10 years after 1949, this work was greatly assisted by the U.S.S.R., which supplied many technologists, introduced advanced skills and survey techniques, and much oil-drilling machinery. This help was withdrawn abruptly in July 1960 since when the Chinese have relied on their own resources to a large extent.

As a result of this prospecting, the oil situation has changed radically; many new fields have been discovered and old fields extended. Exact information is not available but estimates of reserves stand between 1·2 and 1·8 billion metric tons of which 90 per cent is located in northeast and northwest China, the largest being at Taching and Tsaidam at 400 and 250 million metric tons respectively.[20]

Karamai field

The presence of oil in Sinkiang was known at the turn of the century but very little was done towards its development. Only a small amount was obtained from a few shallow wells – not enough even for the supply of local lamps. Between 1953 and 1957 the Russians played a big part in surveying and opening up a most fruitful field in the semi-desert of Dzungaria in the vicinity of Karamai, where reserves are estimated at 100 million tons. Production of oil from here rose rapidly from 330 000 tons in 1958 to 780 000 tons in 1959, and from an estimated 1·5 million tons in 1963 to 5 million metric tons in 1973. Until 1959, oil from Karamai was transported by truck to the railhead. A pipeline of 150 km now links the field to Tushantzu where a refinery has been built. There are also smaller fields in the Tarim basin, along the southern slopes of the Tien Shan at Kashgar, Aksu and Kucha and also in the Turfan Depression[24].

Yumen field

Oil was discovered in the Yumen area in 1937, but it was not until after 1950 that its exploitation was energetically pursued[25]. Careful prospecting revealed an estimated reserve of 100 million metric tons. Extensive drilling has been carried out, resulting in greatly increased production. It is estimated that, in 1973, the output of the Yumen field was 3 million tons. Yumen has its own refinery with an annual capacity of 400 000 tons and is now linked by pipeline with the Lanchow refinery, which has a capacity of 1 million tons p.a.[26].

Tsaidam field

A great deal of prospecting and experimental boring in the Tsaidam has revealed a most promising field of good quality oil. Production is increasing annually and a refinery with a capacity of 300 000 tons p.a., has been built at Leng-hu, just south of the Tangching Pass over the Nan Shan. Estimated production of crude oil in 1973 was 2 million metric tons.

Szechwan field

The early knowledge and use of natural gas in Szechwan indicated that this should be a profitable source of supply. Nevertheless extensive earlier prospecting proved fruitless. It was not until 1958 that efforts were rewarded in the discovery of good oil over a wide field in the Lower Jurassic and Triassic strata in the vicinity of Nanchung and Penglai, central Szechwan. This field is now being energetically worked; its output remains relatively small: an estimated 1 million metric tons of crude oil in 1973.

Taching (Great Joy) field

Prospecting for oil in the Northeast commenced in 1955 but it was not until 1958 that the first strike was made at Taching on the Sungari plain about halfway between Harbin and Tsitsihar. From that date on great efforts were made to develop the field, involving working throughout the bitter winters in temperatures sometimes − 20° to − 25°C. Production facilities were completed in 1964 and since then output has increased by leaps and bounds, far exceeding other fields, reaching 20 million tons out of a national total of 37 million tons of crude oil. The Taching field is proving

Plate 16   Taching oilfield, Heilungkiang, in the bleak Northeast
China's most recent and biggest oil producer. The country is now producing more than its present need and is exporting oil

Plate 17   Tushantzu refinery for the Karamai oilfield in the heart of the semi-desert

much more extensive than original surveys suggested.[20] The work here has been carried out entirely by the Chinese and is held up as the great example in the industrial field as is Tachai in the agricultural field. It now has the largest refinery in China with a distillation capacity in 1975 of 5 million tons. The remainder of its crude oil is transported to the Fushun and Dairen refineries by the newly constructed pipeline 1152 km in length.

Shengli and Takang fields

Two new fields, both southeast of Peking came into production in 1973. Shengli, the earlier, has an annual estimated production at present of 5 million tons and Takang of 1–1·5 million tons.

Production has risen dramatically from 320 000 metric tons in 1943 (peak year before 1949) to 1·4 million in 1957, 7·5 million in 1962, 12·4 million in 1968 (when self-sufficiency was achieved), and 68 million tons in 1975, when China became an exporter of oil, perhaps only temporarily while her own requirements are relatively small.[20] Until 1961 the greater part of the oil imports came from the U.S.S.R. Since then there has been a marked decrease from that source and a corresponding increase in supplies from Roumania[24].

The main difficulties China has had to face in developing its oil supplies lie first in the position of the oilfields themselves, which, for the most part, lie in the remote west and north. Transport of oil by road and rail is expensive and is still the main means. Some progress has been made in laying pipelines: between Karamai and the rail head; Yumen and Lanchow; a recently opened line of 1152 km from Taching to Dairen (Talien) and Hopei. Domestic-built tankers of 24 000 tons now ply between Dairen and Shanghai and Nanking. In the early stages of development there was acute shortage of all kinds of surveying and drilling equipment and of technical know-how. Russian aid in both these respects was invaluable, especially in training of oil engineers and technicians. Since the withdrawal of Russian aid, the Chinese claim that they are now well able to cope by themselves, Yumen and Lanchow both now producing the necessary equipment and precision instruments[27]. Early difficulties concerned with inadequate refining plant have now been overcome. Crude oil production in 1966, estimated at between 9 and 10 million tons was more than its refineries could deal with[28]. In recent years, complete refining plant has been urgently imported from Italy and West Germany. At the same time Chinese engineers are continually experimenting, evolving and adapting techniques germaine to local needs. They claim to have built a 'platforming' unit to obtain a large range of highly purified benzenes through the use of a catalyst containing platinum[29].

China's reserves of oil shale are estimated to be 21 billion tons and production of shale oil is considerable. Out of a total of 40 million metric tons of crude oil in 1973, 3 million came from shale. In 1963, 1·8 million tons of oil was obtained from Fushun alone. Other centres in the Northeast are at Mutankiang and Hwalien. An open-cast mine yielding 1·5 million tons of shale annually has been opened at Mowming, south Kwangtung, which has a small refinery turning out gasoline, diesel oil and kerosene. The main oil shale deposits are found in the northwest and southern Szechwan but, as their location largely coincides with liquid oil, they are not likely to be exploited to any great extent at present. Production in 1973 was estimated at 3 million metric tons. The main producer of natural gas is still Szechwan. Total national production in 1973 was estimated at 10 billion cu. metres.

With the rapid development in road building, an ever-growing production of cars and tractors and an increasing use of diesel locomotives, the demand for oil is also increasing rapidly. In 1965 the annual consumption per head of its 700 million people was only 18 to 22 litres as compared with Japan's 580, U.S.S.R.'s 900 and U.S.A.'s 4000 litres per head[24].

ELECTRIC POWER

Because of the ease of its distribution and its adaptability to the needs of industry and agriculture, the planners are relying mainly on the development and use of electrical power. In industry, it can be transformed to meet the needs of many kinds of production such as the special needs of aluminium manufacture and the new steel electrical furnaces. In irrigation and drainage work, electrical power is proving more convenient and dependable than the internal combustion engine. In the Pearl river delta more than 2500 electric power stations for irrigation and drainage had been installed by 1965; 60 per cent of the farm land of the Yangtze delta is irrigated and

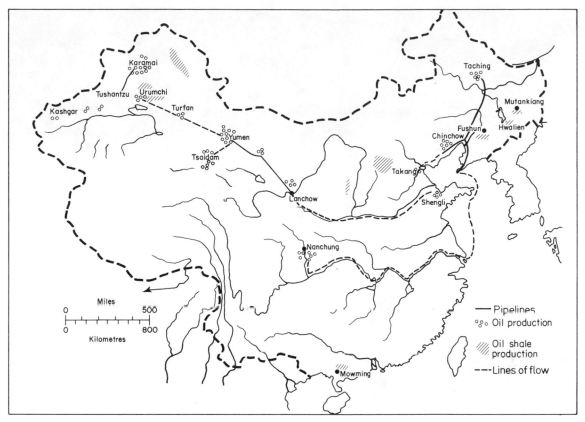

Fig. 95   Oil

drained by electric power and the well water of the North China Plain is now lifted largely by the same means. To this end China is attempting to follow the pattern of all modern industrial countries in building a number of power networks, based on a coordination of thermal and hydro-electric generation.

Growth of Electric Energy

	1949*	1952*	1955*	1959*
Production		(million kWh)		
Total	4 310	7 260	12 280	27 530
Hydro	—	—	—	—

	1964†	1967†	1970†	1974†
Production		(million kWh)		
Total	65 000	60 000	77 000	118 000
Hydro	20 000	25 000	27 000	35 000

As might be expected in a country so vast and diverse, this development is uneven. The construction of grids, based on already established industrial and mining areas with large cities as centres, has gone ahead rapidly. Less developed areas are relying on medium and small plants, using local resources such as minor water power, small collieries and shallow deposits of natural gas, with a view to eventual linking. It is claimed that electricity is now available to most of the villages in over 1200 of China's 2126 *hsien* and that rural consumption of electricity is 25 times greater than it was in 1957[31].

Realizing that the generation of electric power is more quickly achieved and the plant cheaper to erect by the use of coal rather than water power, attention has been concentrated on the building of thermal plant. Even in the Northeast, where hydro-electric power was more developed than elsewhere in China, it was estimated in 1959 that 60 per cent of the electric power was thermally generated[19].

China's potential water power is enormous, one recent estimate placed it at 500 million kW[32]. Although great effort has been put into the development of this power since 1949, most of the water conservancy schemes have had flood

Plate 18   The dam of the fourth staircase of the Kutienhsi hydro-power station, Fukien

control, irrigation and drainage as their primary objectives. The only hydro-electric power developed in China before 1949 was by the Japanese in the Northeast, where two big dams were built. One at Fengmen, near Kirin at the head of the Sungari reservoir, had a capacity of 850 000 kW when it was built, but the plant was partly destroyed and the dam damaged and neglected during the Sino–Japanese War. It was subsequently repaired and now has a capacity of 567 000 kW. The other dam was built at Supung on the Yalu river, and had a capacity of 600 000 kW. Since 1949 the Chinese have built three further dams in the Northeast, each developing power: Kumotsin on the Nun-kiang, above Tsitsihar, developing 209 000 kW; Mutan-kiang, developing 383 000 kW; Tahoufang, near Fushun, which has a storage capacity of 1970 million cu. m but for which no kilowatt capacity is available.

In China Proper the outstanding development has been on the Hwang-ho. Two great multi-purpose dams have been built, one at Liuchia,

above Lanchow and the other at Sanmen, below Tungkwan Gorge. Each has a capacity of 1 million kW. The completion of the generating plant of the latter suffered a severe setback by the withdrawal of Russian technicians in 1960. A further dam at the Lungyan Gorge, above Liuchia, is planned to serve the Tsaidam. A large dam at Kwantung on the Yungtung-ho serves Peking and district, but the actual output is not available. Among the many water conservancy projects in the Hwai-ho basin, the main achievement from a hydro-electric point of view is the dam at Futzeling, built in 1954, which develops 11 000 kW. All the above were built with Russian assistance.

Great publicity has been given to the completion in 1965 of the Sinan (Hsinan) Dam in Chekiang. It is 105 m high and has been built entirely to Chinese design and by Chinese workmen. It already has four 72 500 kW generators and can accommodate a further five, giving a total of 652 500 kW. It serves the power grid linking Hangchow, Shanghai and Nanking and also the farming population of the delta area[33]. Far-reaching plans for the Yangtze-kiang development have been mentioned but these projects have not yet been started.

NUCLEAR POWER

China's nuclear research and activities are centred at Lop Nor in the Takla Makan Desert, Sinkiang.

She exploded her first H-bomb in June 1967 and has since tested six more thermo-nuclear devices in the megaton class. It is reported that she has made great progress in the development of thermo-nuclear warheads, so reducing them in size as to make them compact enough for missile delivery.

Production of Energy (thousands of metric tons of coal equivalent)

	1964	*1966*	*1968*	*1970*	*1972*	*1974*
Total Primary Energy	306 001	351 019	326 517	417 962	451 968	548 351
Coal	290 000	327 000	300 000	382 380	401 000	444 500
Crude Petroleum	12 495	19 110	22 050	29 547	43 512	95 550
Hydro + Nuclear						
Electricity	1 046	1 219	1 392	2 264	3 397	3 996

Figures from *Statistical Year Book for Asia and the Pacific*, U.N. 1975

References

1 S. Chandrasekhar, *China's Population* (Hong Kong, 1959).

2 Lin Nai-jui, 'Population problems in China', *Contemporary China*, Vol. I, 1956–7 (Hong Kong, 1958).

3 Hu Huan-yung, *Wen Hui Pao*, 21 March 1957.

4 Wu Yuan-li, 'Principal industrial cities in Communist China', *Contemporary China*, Vol. V (Hong Kong, 1961–2).

5 *Ten Great Years* (Peking, 1960).

6 S. Chandrasekhar, *Communist China Today* (Bombay, 1962).

7 Mao Tse-tung, *On the Correct Handling of Contradictions among the People* (Peking, 1957).

8 C. D. Cowan, 'Ma Yin-Chi on population' in C. D. Cowan (ed.), op. cit.

9 *Nan-fang Jih-pao*, Canton, 14 April 1965.

10 Michael Freeberne, 'Birth control in China', *Population Studies*, **18**, no. 1 (1964).

11 N. Dickerman, 'Mineral resources of China', *Foreign Mineral Survey*, U.S. Bureau of Mines.

12 E. Balazs, op. cit.

13 Marco Polo, op. cit., Book II, chapter 23.

14 *China Year Book*, 1925.

15 *Peking Review*, no. 17 (22 April 1966).

16 NCNA, Peking, 27 December 1958.

17 NCNA, Peking 22 October 1964.

18 Chi Cheng-ju, 'Opening a vast coalfield', *China Reconstructs*, October 1964.

19 Sun Ching-chih (ed.), *Economic Geography of Northeast China* (Peking, 1959).

20 Tatsu Kambara, 'The petroleum industry in China', *China Quarterly*, **60** (October 1964).

21 'From dependence on "foreign oil" to basic self-sufficiency in petroleum', *Shih-shih Shou-tse* [*Current Events*], no. 8 (1964).

22 F. G. Clapp, *Petroleum Science*, **1** (1938), p. 139.

23 W. S. S. Rogers, *History of Industrial Development in U.S.* (1941).

24 B. Heenan, 'Chinese petroleum industry', *Far Eastern Economic Review*, nos 5, 13 & 16 (1965).

25 Yen Erh-wen, 'Oil to dominate old China', *China Reconstructs*, April 1966.

26 Chang Kuei-sheng, 'Geographical bases for industrial development in Northwest China', *Economic Geography*, **39** (1963), pp. 341–50.

27 NCNA, Lanchow, 24 April 1965.

28 Colina MacDougall, 'Production reports', *Far Eastern Economic Review*, 29 September 1966.

29 NCNA, Peking, 1 September 1966.

30 Pao Kuo-pao, 'The role of electric power in the national economy', *Hsin Chien-she* [*New Construction*], no. 4 (20 April 1965).

31 NCNA, Peking, 16 September 1965.

32 *Far Eastern Trade*, January 1966.

33 *Peking Review*, 15 October 1965.

9   Industrial Development

DEVELOPMENT OF MODERN INDUSTRY

At the beginning of the twentieth century modern industry in China was still in its infancy. By far the larger proportion of man-made articles in use by people throughout the land were produced by hand in small local workshops: agricultural tools, such as hoes and ploughshare tips, and domestic utensils in local foundries and blacksmiths' shops; cloth by hand loom in cottages or small workshops; food processing and flour milling either in the home or local mill.

Such modern industry as there was, was distributed near the coast or along the banks of the Lower Yangtze, notably in the Treaty Ports at Shanghai, Tientsin, Wuhan, Hangchow and Wusih, and was involved mainly in mining and smelting, textiles, the processing of foodstuffs, and public utilities (water and electricity supplies). Between 1895 and 1913 there were 136 foreign-owned firms and 549 Chinese-owned firms, which might be termed modern and which were engaged in these activities. The former contributed about 45 per cent, of which nearly 50 per cent was British and 25 per cent Japanese, and the latter 55 per cent of the total capital employed. The total capital involved amounted to between £30 and £35 million. Foreign interests were centred mainly on mining and smelting, followed by foodstuffs, textiles and public utilities. Chinese firms concentrated more on textile manufacture, than on mining and smelting, public utilities and foodstuffs[1].

Western European demand during the First World War gave considerable impetus to Chinese industry. From that time on, until the outbreak of the Sino–Japanese War in 1936, industrial expansion was continuous, albeit fitful owing to political circumstances. Its location in China Proper remained along the littoral and along the Yangtze as formerly. From 1927 onwards, following the Northern Expedition, there was growing hostility towards foreign firms, all of which were regarded as products of imperialism, and industry fell increasingly into the hands of Chinese capitalists and entrepreneurs. The years 1945–9 following the war were marked by civil war, political corruption and financial chaos due to inflation (see Rise of Communism, pp. 83–92. Industry was brought to its lowest ebb for two decades. Such was the inheritance the Communists entered into and out of which they have since attempted to build a modern industrialized, socialist state.

We have already examined at some length the steps taken to this end in the agricultural field. In the industrial and commercial sphere, six periods are clearly discernible between 1949 and 1967:

1. 1949–52 was a time of recovery and rehabilitation in every aspect of national life. In industry it meant the immediate halting of inflation, the taking of the first steps of government penetration into control of industry, the control of banks and the establishment of government trading companies, which took over the entire wholesale trade. Prices and wages were success-

fully pinned to an index based on five commodities: rice, flour, oil, coal and cotton[2] and have remained stable ever since. Central control was firmly established and opposition, particularly that of manufacturers and traders, was met by two campaigns, known as the 'three anti' and the 'five anti'. Recovery during this period was not assisted by the floods and poor harvests of 1949 or by participation in the Korean War, 1950. It was during these three years that the bases for the First Five-year Plan were worked out.

2. 1952–6. During this period, which largely coincides with that of the First Five-year Plan (1952–7), a great deal of socialization of industry took place. By 1956, private enterprise in China had virtually ceased to exist except for a few small traders, having been taken under state-owned or joint State–private management[3]. Of the gross industrial output in 1956, 54·6 per cent was produced by state-owned enterprises, 27·1 per cent by joint State–private ownership, 17·1 per cent by cooperative industry and only 1·3 per cent by individual and private capitalists[4]. Nearly all produce from mine and factory was sold at the state or cooperative stores, which undertook distribution to the consumer. The individual handicraftsman or peasant was not allowed to sell his produce privately in a free market. This was a period of increasing bureaucratic control.

After 'Liberation' in 1949, it was the intention of the Central Government to carry out economic development of the country along the Russian pattern in a series of five-year Plans. Accordingly, in 1952, the finance and Economic Affairs Committee instituted the State Planning Commission, under the chairmanship of Li Fu-ch'un, which then formulated the First Five-year Plan[5]. Although the plan was launched and work started in 1953, it was not officially inaugurated until July 1955, when Li Fu-ch'un made a speech to the First National People's Congress. Many reports of progress and achievement were issued, but no comprehensive outline of the plan was made public.

Some idea of the importance and emphasis placed on industrial development, as distinct from agricultural, social and cultural, can best be obtained from the proportions of capital allocated for investment in these fields between 1953 and 1957: Industry 58·2 per cent, Communications 19·2 per cent, Agriculture, including water conservancy, 7·6 per cent, Education and Public Health 7·2 per cent.

Industries were grouped and placed under the control and direction of ministries of the Central Government: Electrical Power, Coal, Petroleum, Metallurgical, Chemical, Building Materials, Machine Building, Electrical Equipment, Timber, Textiles, Food Industry and Light Industry.

The total capital to be invested in all fields was 42 billion yuan or approximately £6000 million. Of industry's share, 88·8 per cent was destined for new construction and modernization in heavy industry – an indication of how small consideration was given to consumer goods and needs during the period.

The main objectives were the building of 694 important large factories and mines, of which 156 were to receive help from the U.S.S.R. and were to form the backbone of the whole industrial reconstruction. The 156 concerns covered all branches of industry. They included the extension of the already very large Anshan Iron and Steel Works, the building of new, integrated steel plant at Wuhan and Paotow and 17 other smaller plants, 15 electric power stations each with more than 50 000 kW capacity, 31 coal mines with more than 1 million tons p.a. capacity, a dozen or more machine, tractor and car factories, 23 new cotton mills, leading to an increase by 1·5 million spindles, and 6 sugar refineries each with an annual capacity of 50 000 tons. The reason given for small investment in light industry were that many existing works, such as cigarette factories, were working far below capacity and that such factories were dependent on raw materials, the increase in production of which would, of necessity, be slow*.

Planning of production was based on the fixing of annual targets for factories and works within each industry, a method fraught with many pitfalls. All planning requires close coordination between all branches of industry and must be backed by adequate information and a highly qualified and incorruptible civil service. Happily, during this period accurate information became increasingly available as the new State Statistical Bureau grew and developed a good professional standard. A highly qualified civil service was not immediately available and had to be developed by hard experience. In view of the corruption which ran through KMT administration, the rapid achievement of a high standard of honesty

---

* Information from notes at an interview with Hsueh Po-ch'ao in Peking, December 1955.

was remarkable. Remarkable, also, was the quickly rising standard of technical efficiency, which was greatly helped by Russian aid and which resulted in the lowering of production costs, particularly in the iron and steel, and mining industries.

3. 1956–8. There was considerable murmuring in agriculture and industry against so much central bureaucratic control. Consequently there was some relaxation and some free markets were reintroduced. In March 1957, Mao Tse-tung made his famous 'Let a Hundred Flowers Bloom' speech to intellectuals, inviting freer criticism. This criticism came with greater force and volume than was anticipated. In spite of the undoubted achievements in production under the First Five-year Plan, the planners came under heavy criticism from CCP academic economists, notably from Ma Yin-ch'u. Ma attacked the entire basis of target planning as being too crude and giving too little consideration to what was the optimum in each field, that over-centralization and bureaucracy led to loss of flexibility, and that departmentalism led to lack of coordination and the formation of watertight compartments. He wanted more care and research and less haste before embarking on new schemes and new machines. He criticized the too rapid movement of industry away from the littoral into the interior as being wasteful of capital and skilled labour and advocated the greater use of price increases as an incentive to production – now known in China as 'economism'[6]. For his pains Ma Yin-ch'u was demoted and disgraced, and criticism suppressed. This period of relaxation of central control was short-lived, brought to an end by the Great Leap Forward and the sudden birth of the communes.

4. 1958–60. The Second Five-year Plan started in 1958 and, as with the First Plan, was accompanied by no overall or detailed blueprint of targets for the five years. The general aim was to increase the tempo of production; a slight change in favour of agriculture was indicated. 'In that year [1958], the Chinese Communist Party's Central Committee and Comrade Mao Tse-tung, having summed up the experience gained in the First Five-year Plan, put forward the general line of going all out, aiming high and achieving greater, faster, better and more economical results in building socialism. That general line inspired the whole Chinese people with still greater keenness and determination to rely on their own efforts

and work energetically to make their country strong and prosperous.... In the years 1958–60, investment in capital construction was greatly increased and far exceeded that in the whole First Five-year Plan'[7]. This was the mood which led to the fantastic and fanatical outburst of energy and enthusiasm, known as the Great Leap Forward. These upsurges of effort are an essential part of Mao's philosophy of struggle as the essence of life[8]. Its manifestation on the agricultural side was the creation of the communes. On the industrial side it took the form of the self-imposition of higher and ever-higher targets of production. Emulation was the keynote. Peasants turned from their fields to iron smelting; Great Britain's steel production was to be surpassed by 1972, and so on. The movement had as its object 'communism in our time'. It was largely spontaneous and apparently no carefully organized planning preceded it. Near economic anarchy resulted. Although there was a great increase in production – the Second Five-year Plan was said to have been fulfilled by 1960 – it was uncoordinated, and resulted in many casualties. Not least of these was the collapse of the Statistical Bureau, crushed under the weight of an inflow of over-optimistic and often quite unrealistic returns. Since this collapse, few firm figures of production for the whole country have been published, but only percentage increases.

5. 1960–3. The Great Leap Forward came to a sudden end and was succeeded by a policy of 'readjustment, consolidation, filling-out and raising standards'. It was admitted that 'during that period [1958–60] some new problems cropped up in our economic development. First, for three successive years, 1959–61, China was struck by exceptionally severe natural calamities – mainly prolonged droughts and serious floods and waterlogging.... Second, while all branches of industry registered increases in productive capacity during 1958–60, the rate of increase was not even. This caused certain discrepancies between industries producing raw and other materials and processing industries.... Third, in July 1960, the Soviet Government unexpectedly withdrew all the 1390 Soviet experts working in China, tore up 343 contracts and supplementary contracts on the employment of experts, and cancelled 257 items of scientific and technical cooperation ... It was against that background and in view of the above-mentioned considerations that the policy of "readjustment, consolidation, filling out and raising

standards" was formulated.'[7] Apart from the factors listed above by Fang Chung, the withdrawal of labour from agriculture during the 'Great Leap' was a significant contributor to the disorganization that followed. In addition to the acute food shortage, industry, especially light industry, suffered from lack of agricultural raw materials. Attention was therefore turned to the re-establishment of agriculture, which became a first charge on industry. As we have seen, industry was required to concentrate on the production of agricultural machinery, fertilizer and irrigation and drainage equipment. The proportion of capital investment going to agriculture and essential raw materials was considerably increased. Heavy industry was also directed to make strenuous efforts to strengthen its extractive side, and industry as a whole was required to increase the variety and raise the quality of its products. Finally, the policy looked to a better integration and coordination of the whole industrial system.

6. 1966–9. Successive good harvests and annually increasing agricultural production after 1964 caused attention once again to turn to the production of heavy iron and steel goods and the formulation of a Third Five-year Plan. Before this materialized, however, another upsurge, the Great Poletarian Cultural Revolution (GPCR) took place in 1966 and lasted until 1969. This upheaval had its roots in the growing contention between two opposing schools of thought, epitomized by Mao Tse-tung and Liu Shao-chih. Mao has always placed his faith in the strength and sense of the masses; in egalitarianism and the elimination of classes; in developing throughout society the ideal of 'serve the masses' as the incentive to work before individual material reward – i.e. 'put politics first'. Liu Shao-chih, on the other hand, intent on rapid industrial development, relied more and more on graduated rewards for industrial endeavour, which resulted in 'elitism and growing class consciousness'. The resulting struggle disrupted Chinese society for three years and was finally resolved by the triumph of Mao's approach.

The repercussions of this clash were felt more severely in industry than in agriculture and it was only after 1969 that it got back onto an even keel. In spite of fluctuating policy as between agricultural and industrial investment, industry has made a phenomenal advance in the years from 1949 to 1971 as the following figures for gross value of industrial output (in million yuan in 1952 constant prices) show: 1949, 14 020; 1952, 34 330; 1958, 78 390; 1971, 294 420.[9]

Before turning to a detailed examination of the main industries, a brief glance at some of the economic and social handicaps suffered and advantages enjoyed by China in its present industrial development will be useful.

One of the great handicaps since 1949 has been the securing of adequate capital for its vast planned expansion. Apart from loans received from Soviet Russia in the early years, China has had to rely on her own resources. Russian help, £100 million in 1950 and £400 million in 1954, was only a small proportion of the £6000 million budgeted for the First Five-year Plan. Nevertheless it was very valuable as the loans were supplied largely in the form of complete plant, enabling individual industries to start production quickly. For the rest, the Central Government has had to rely on internal saving derived from taxation, from domestic borrowing in the form of loans and bond issues and from profits of government enterprises. In 1957 taxation accounted for just over half the revenue and state enterprises just under half. Loans, etc., amounted to a mere one-thirtieth. U.S.S.R. loans were short-termed and were repaid mainly in grain and agricultural raw materials. Since the strained relations between the two countries in 1960, China has had no outside assistance in capital, which accounts for the persistent propaganda on the need for 'self-reliance'.

It was only after the Boxer Indemnity money was utilized for overseas education that Chinese students went abroad in significant numbers. Even so, comparatively few received education in industry or technology during the first half of the twentieth century. Consequently, China was ill-equipped with trained technicians, engineers and managerial personnel to undertake the tasks before it in 1949. Hence great effort has been put into the development of large technical colleges and institutes throughout the country. The natural industriousness and application of the Chinese has gone a long way already to offset this disadvantage and the initial shortage of trained personnel is rapidly being overcome.

The Chinese have long been an inventive people. This ability they have turned to good account in meeting many industrial handicaps, which have confronted them through their lack of modern equipment. They have also made wide use of the advantage which socialized industry has over private enterprise in the freer sharing of new ideas and inventions. In agriculture and in industry, when a new method is evolved or a new machine or process invented, there is an eagerness to make it available as generally as possible.

Leading Industrial Centres

Anshan	Leading integrated iron and steel centre (rolled steel, seamless tubing, angle steel, rails, cables). Coal. Large Chemical Works. Cement
Canton (Hwangchow)	Textiles. Machinery. Chemicals. Cement. Many new small works
Changchun	Machine tools. China's biggest motor vehicle plant, making Liberator and Red Flag trucks, limousines
Chengtu	Oil refinery with capacity of over 1 million tons p.a. Chemicals. Machinery. Textiles
Chungking	Integrated iron and steel plant (steel ingots, rolled steel, low-alloy steel). Agricultural machinery. Lorries, vans and 40-seater coaches. Chemical fertilizers
Fushun	Coal. Steel. Chemicals. Oil refinery (shale)
Fusin	Coal
Hangchow	Textiles (silk and cotton). Chemicals
Harbin	One of the major machine-building centres (hydro-turbines). Textiles, oil refinery
Hofei	New small iron and steel works. Textiles
Huhehot (Hu-ho-hao-te)	Woollens. New small steel works
Hwainan	Major colliery. Chemicals
Kirin	Chemical fertilizer. Steel. Oil refinery
Kunming	Small iron and steel works. Milling and boring machines. Textiles. Chemicals
Kweiyang	Coal. Iron and Steel. Textiles. Chemicals
Lanchow	Large oil refinery. Oil equipment. Coal. Chemicals. Textiles (wool)
Lhasa	Small pharmaceutical factory. Turbine pumps. Fertilizer
Loyang	Large car and tractor plant. Large ballbearing plant. Oil refinery. Textiles (cotton)
Luta (Talien and Lushun)	Chemicals. Machinery. Shipbuilding. Textiles. Diesel locomotives
Maanshan	Coal. Iron and steel (rolled steel)
Nanking	Large motor vehicle plant. Machinery (gears, precision instruments, optical, transistors, medical). Chemical fertilizer and insecticides. Cotton cloth and yarn. Oil refinery
Nanning	Rice transplanter factory
Paotow	Integrated iron and steel plant
Peking	Many medium and small factories. Textiles and synthetic fibres. Precision instruments. Chemicals
Shanghai	Seamless steel tubing. Rolled steel. Tractors. Shipbuilding. Machinery. Precision instruments. Textiles. Synthetic fibres. Chemicals and fertilizers. Food processing
Shenyang	Major heavy and light machine making (lathes of all kinds). Transformers. Big textile centre. Cement. Chemicals

Sian	Steel. Machinery. Textiles. Chemicals
Taiyuan	Integrated heavy iron and steel works. Chemicals. Machinery (casings). Textiles
Tangshan	Steel and machine works. Textiles. Cement. Oil refinery
Tatung	Steam and diesel locomotives. Coal
Tientsin	Steel and rolling mills. Machine tools. Chemical fertilizer machinery. Textiles (spinning). Pharmaceutical products. Electrical instruments. Tobacco
Tsingtao	Steel. Machinery. Textiles. Chemicals
Urumchi (Tihwa)	Iron and steel. Cement. Agricultural machinery. Textiles. Nitrogenous fertilizer plant
Wuhan	Integrated iron and steel works. Machine tools. Walking tractors. Agricultural pumps. Shipbuilding plate. Textiles. Tobacco

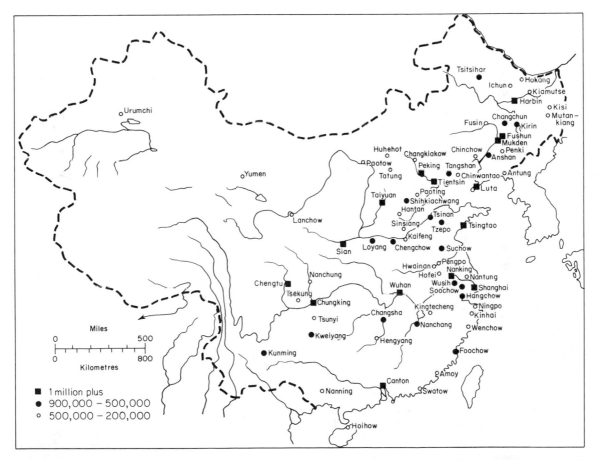

Fig. 96 Principal industrial cities in China. Note very rapid growth of cities of 500–200 000 in the far Northeast. Absence of cities of over 200 000 in the West. (Compiled from Yuan-li Wu, Contemporary China, *Vol. v, 1961–2)*

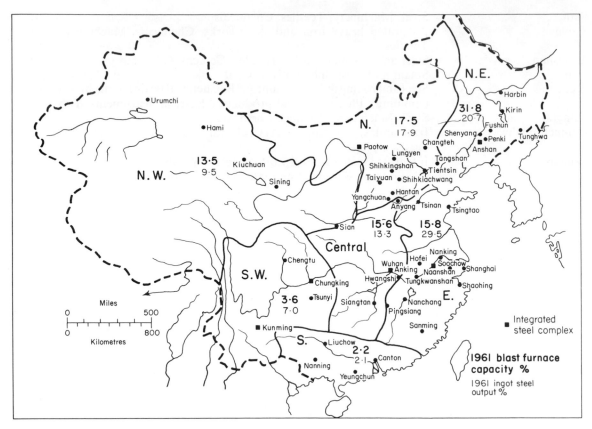

Fig. 97   Steel centres, 1964 (compiled from R. Hsia, Changes on the location of China's steel industry,
China Quarterly *No. 17, 1964)*

IRON AND STEEL INDUSTRY

Iron ore resources

After his extensive travels and survey in China
between 1870 and 1872, Baron von Richthofen
was of the opinion that there were extensive iron
ore deposits in the country. This opinion ran
counter to the generally held view, that the quality
and quantity of iron resources was poor in China,
and was discredited. The seven reports on the
Chinese Mining Industry, which were published
between 1921 and 1948, each showed progressive
increase in estimate iron ore reserves, rising
from 677 899 000 tons in 1921 to 5 432 934 000
tons in 1948[10]. In spite of these figures, the
opinion persisted that China was poverty stricken
as far as iron resources were concerned. J. S. Lee
declared 'It is quite clear that China can never be
an iron-producing country of any importance.'[11]

George B. Cressey, even as recently as 1955, could
write 'There is enough to care for present needs but
it is clear that China cannot equal the industrial
countries.'[12] These low assessments may have
been influenced by the fact that by far the
largest reserves, i.e. those of Liaoning (387·5
million tons in 1921), are of a low iron content,
which, at that time, was considered very near the
economic margin. The deposits in the rest of the
country, although less in quantity, were of good
quality. The first proper survey of outlying regions
of the northwest, and southwest were not undertaken until 1945.

*Iron Ore Deposits and Iron Content, 1921. (Re-
printed from* Yuan-li Wu[10] The Steel Industry in
Communist China, *by permission of* The Hoover
Institution on War, Revolution and Peace, Stanford University. © 1966 by the Board of Trustees
of the Leland Stanford Junior University.

(thousand metric tons)

	Total iron ore deposits	Total iron content	Percentage
Liaoning	387 580	105 205	27·1
Chahar	69 200	36 200	52·3
Hupeh	52 666	29 780	56·6
Anhwei	50 000	25 125	50·3
Kiangsu	35 000	17 500	50·0
Shantung	29 920	14 138	47·3
Hopeh	22 279	9 234	41·4
Kiangsi	18 060	8 671	48·0
Fukien	7 500	3 650	48·7
Honan	3 400	1 640	48·2
Chekiang	2 300	1 050	45·7

The situation has altered materially since 1949. Extensive surveys have been carried out and new fields discovered. Although no official statistics have been published, it is certain that iron reserves now stand at a much higher figure than formerly. The old prognostics of a country destined to confine its industrial activities to light industry alone have been discarded and China has joined the ranks of heavy industry.

Geological prospecting between 1949 and 1957 is stated to have disclosed iron resources at 5600 million tons and estimated reserves at between 12 000 million and 15 000 million tons, of which three-fifths have an iron content of 30–50 per cent[13]. Recently, large iron ore reserves have been reported from east Szechwan, west Kweichow and in northwest Kansu and the Ho-hsi corridor.

Iron and steel manufacture

China's first essay into modern iron and steel production was carried out by a progressive viceroy, Chang Chih-tung, who, on his transfer from Canton to Wuchang, Hupeh, bought modern machinery (two blast furnaces and two converters) from Europe and founded the Hanyang Iron Works in 1894, two years before Japan built its first iron and steel works at Yawata. The main purpose of the works was the production of steel rails for the Peking–Hankow Railway. Excellent iron ore was available at Tayeh, halfway between Hankow and Kiukiang. Chang's venture was beset with difficulties from the start, the chief of which were lack of adequate capital, poor management, unsatisfactory supply of coking coal and inefficient transport, which consisted of junks. The concern was taken over by Sheng Hsuen-huai, who formed it into a private company, the Hanyehping Coal and Iron Co. Ltd in 1908. Although Sheng discovered good coking coal at Pinghsiang in Hunan, the capital cost of developing adequate transport to Hanyang was crippling[1]. Throughout its activities, the lack of capital forced the company to borrow heavily. Between 1902 and 1913 no less than sixteen loans were obtained from Japanese banks on the guarantee of continuing shipments of iron ore and pig iron. Thus the Japanese steadily gained control of the Hanyehping Co. Their interest was in the Company's iron ore, which was wanted for the development of their own works at Yawata – an interest they maintained until their defeat in 1945. When the author visited Shihhweiyao in 1948, millions of tons of Tayeh iron ore still lined the river bank, stacked awaiting shipment to Japan, which never materialized owing to U.S. submarine activity towards the end of the war. The world demand for iron and steel during the First World War kept production at the Hanyehping works alive until 1919; thereafter it rapidly declined and virtually all smelting had ceased by 1925. Shanghai, during this period, developed a very active engineering and shipbuilding industry, which had very little impact on the indigenous iron and steel industry since practically all the steel used was imported from overseas.

Development of the vast resources of the Northeast began soon after the Japanese acquired control of the South Manchurian Railway from the Russians in 1904. The first iron and steel works were built at Penki in 1910; by 1918 30 000–40 000 tons of pig iron were produced. The building of these works at Penki was followed by the foundation of the Anshan Iron and Steel Works in 1919, which have since grown to such great proportions. The industry here was – and still is – well supplied with ample coal and raw materials. Most rapid development occurred after the Japanese annexation of Manchuria in 1931 and particularly after 1936 when the Manchurian Industrial Development Plan was inaugurated[14]. During the twelve years of occupation capacity and production were raised:

Year	Pig iron (tons)	Plant capacity (tons)	Steel production (tons)
1932	368 181	637 750	—
1936	633 393	637 750	344 000
1938	900 000	1 879 760	622 000
1943	1 726 700	2 500 250	837 000

By 1943, which was the peak year of production, there were nine modern blast furnaces in operation. There followed a rapid decline as the Allies gained increasing victory over the Japanese during the Second World War. By 1945 work had ceased completely. While Russia was in control of the region (1945–8), she dismantled and removed a great deal of the plant, estimated at 70–80 per cent and valued at U.S. $131 million[10].

As a result of the Sino–Japanese War all iron and steel-producing works in eastern China fell into Japanese hands. The KMT Government and many industrialists retreated west into Szechwan and the southwest, carrying with them what equipment they could. With this and what could be brought in by the Burma Road, some iron and steel industry was developed, but it did not attain any great dimension.

Post-1949 development of iron and steel

We have mentioned the great emphasis that was placed on the development of heavy industry in the First Five-year Plan (p. 104). This is reflected clearly in the statistics, which show the rapid and steady growth of output between 1950 and 1957. The figures also reveal the effect which the Great Leap Forward had on the industry. Disregarding the output of 'backyard furnaces', production of iron and steel was nearly doubled in 1958–9 by stupendous efforts on the part of workers. During the 'Great Leap' it is reported that some 2 million – the figure includes large numbers of rebuilds and replacements – blast furnaces, the majority of which were not more than 3 m high, were built of mud brick and erected on any piece of waste land available, hence their name 'backyard furnaces'. Lack of adequate blast, reasonable ore and technical knowledge led to the production of about 3 million tons of metal, the vast bulk of which was useless except for the manufacture of simple agricultural tools, such as hoes. The fever, which sprang from the nationwide desire to achieve industrialization immediately, died and in the confusion which followed, the furnaces were discarded. The better-built, medium-sized plant, which was built during this period, has survived and is performing a useful function.

In 1958 the CCP Central Committee divided the country into seven economic regions. The iron and steel industry has played a major part since 1949 in this new locational pattern for industry as a whole. The extent and nature of the change is

demonstrated in the following statistics given by Ronald Hsia[15]

Location of China's Steel Industry

Regional Distribution of Blast Furnace Capacity

Economic Region	1945*	1953	1957	1961
	%	%	%	%
N.E.	67·8	59·1	79·6	31·8
N.	19·7	25·1	14·4	17·5
E.	7·6	5·7	4·0	15·8
Central	0·3	0·8	0·5	15·6
S.W.	4·6	9·3	1·5	3·6
S.	—	—	—	2·2
N.W.	—	—	—	13·5

Regional Distribution of Ingot Steel Output

Economic Region	1945*	1953	1957	1961
N.E.	65·3	65·9	67·8	20·7
N.	30·5	24·4	10·7	17·9
E.	1·7	5·5	14·7	29·5
Central	0·6	2·1	4·1	13·3
S.W.	1·9	1·1	2·7	7·0
S.	—	—	—	2·1
N.W.	—	—	—	9·5

* Before Russian dismantling

Northeast – The first steps taken after 1949 towards the rehabilitation of industry were centred in the Northeast. New, fully automated iron and steel plant was imported from Russia to replace the plant removed in 1945. This was erected by Soviet experts at Anshan, and has become by far the greatest integrated steel complex in China, comparable in size and efficiency to great Western complexes, such as Port Talbot, South Wales. It contains ten large blast furnaces. No. 10, the last to be built, has a capacity of 1513 cu. m, includes smelting rolling and finishing mills, and turns out a full range of products from heavy steel girders, rails and steel plates to seamless tubing of all sizes and for all purposes. During the First Five-year Plan it was virtually the only source of materials for the construction of other steel bases[16]

In the early years 1950–7, a great deal of the country's available capital and skilled personnel was concentrated on the development of this

Mineral Production (000's metric tons)

	1964	1966	1968	1970	1972	1974
Coal	296 000	327 000	325 000	391 900	428 000	462 000
Iron ore	20 350	22 000	21 000	24 000	30 500	34 500
Antimony	75	15	12	12	12	12
Bauxite	400	400	380	500	580	600
Copper ore	90	90	90	100	100	100
Mercury	900	900	690	690	900	900
Tin concentrates	27	25	21	22	22	23
Tungsten concentrates	12·1	10·1	10·1	7·6	9·4	10·7
Salt		13 000	15 000	15 600	18 000	25 000
Crude Petroleum	2 000	2 400	2 650	2 900	3 150	3 900
Cement	—	8 000	9 000	10 000	4 000	25 000

Figures from *Statistical Year Book*, U.N. 1975

Production of Pig Iron, Ingot Steel and Finished Steel (thousands of metric tons)

Year	Pig Iron	Ingot Steel	Finished Steel
1961	15 000	9 500	8 000
1962	15 000	10 000	9 000
1963	17 000	12 000	10 000
1964	18 000	14 000	11 000
1965	19 000	15 000	12 000
1966	20 000	16 000	13 000
1967	14 000	11 000	9 000
1968	19 000	15 000	12 000
1969	20 000	16 000	13 000

All from K. P. Wang *China: A Handbook* (Ed. Yuan-li Wu), David Chambers 1973.

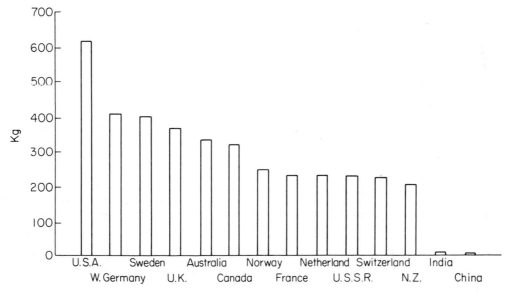

Fig. 98   Per capita world consumption of steel 1955

centre. Skilled workers from other parts of the country, notably Shanghai, were transferred here in the initial stages and much training was done by the Soviet experts. The withdrawal of Soviet technicians in 1960 was a setback which has been overcome. Anshan remains the main training and steel research centre of the country.

Closely associated with Anshan are the steel works at Penki and Fushun. By 1957 the three centres together had annual capacity of 5·67 million tons of pig iron – more than double the Japanese peak capacity in 1943. In 1960, Anshan's capacity was 4·17 million tons of pig iron and 5·57 million tons of ingot steel. Other large steel centres in the Northeast are at Kirin and Tunghwa.

Before 1960, attention was focused mainly on increasing quantity without due regard for the diverse needs of modern industry. Since then emphasis has been increasingly on quality, and Anshan's boast now is that it can meet the most exacting steel requirements and is making steel to thousands of specifications. Although the Northeast steel production has continued to increase, its relative position has declined as the other economic regions have progressed.

North China – The Northern Economic Region includes Hopei, Shansi and Inner Mongolia. As the statistics show, it is an important area, producing nearly one-fifth of the country's ingot steel and having nearly one-fifth of its blast-furnace capacity.

Its biggest works are at Paotow, the new complex, completed in 1961. This is based on good coking coal from Ta Ching Shan, iron ore from the rich fields to the north at Pai-yun-o-po and local limestone. Owing to the late start in building this complex and to the fact that it came into production just at the time when production throughout the country was being curtailed, its output has not yet been outstanding. The provinces of Hopei and Shansi, however, have many other recently developed iron and steel centres, outstanding among which are the Iron and Steel Corporations of Taiyuan and Lungyen, which together had a blast furnace capacity of 2550 cu. m in 1961. Here, and particularly in the Eastern Economic Region, there has been a rapid development of converter steel, contrasting with Anshan's predominantly open-hearth steel. Writing of this, R. Hsia says: 'The speedy rise in the importance of converter steel originates from the campaign for small-scale production, which more than the introduction of overall planning has hastened the locational dispersion of China's steel industry.'[15]

East China – Shanghai, which was the only large steel centre in China which was really functioning in 1949, was scheduled under the dispersion of industry plan for reduction in size. As already seen, some of its trained personnel were transferred to the Northeast, but this policy was soon reversed. Since then, Shanghai has continued to function and grow as a leading steel manufacturer. It does not rank high as a producer of pig iron. In 1959 No. 1 Iron and Steel Plant built two new furnaces of 255 cu. m capacity, but between 1952 and 1957 it increased its ingot steel output from 75 000 tons to 480 000 tons. Whereas before 1949 it drew its raw materials and semi-raw materials from overseas, it now gets them mainly by water transport down the Yangtze. Much of its iron and steel making, which previously had been unco-ordinated, has now been integrated and it is producing high-quality alloy steels, steel plates of all grades, silicon sheet steel, zinc and tin plate, seamed and seamless tubes[17].

East China, which before 1949 had little iron and steel significance apart from Shanghai, has developed very rapidly since 1957. The main growth has been at Maanshan, Tungkwanshan and Hofei in Anhwei, Nanking in Kiangsu, and Tsinan and Tsingtao in Shantung, but there has also been development in a number of other smaller places. During the Sino–Japanese War the Japanese built a small iron smelting plant at Maanshan, based on the rich iron ore of the district. This has now been developed into a medium-size integrated iron and steel complex with a blast furnace capacity of 8000 cu. m.

East China is now the leading region in the production of ingot steel. Overall planners are experiencing difficulty in achieving and maintaining a balance between the production of pig iron, ingot steel and finished steel. At present, ingot steel capacity is in excess of the other two[10].

Central China – Iron and Steel production in this area, which had ebbed so low as to be virtually non-existent by 1949, has since revived to the extent that, in 1961, it possessed 15·6 per cent of the country's blast furnace capacity and produced 13·3 per cent of its ingot steel output. The revival has been due mainly to the establishment of the Wuhan Iron and Steel Corporation. This great new complex started production in 1958 and was completed in 1961. It is situated about 8 km down-stream from Wuchang on the right bank of the river. Its plant comprises the largest blast furnace in southeast Asia, very modern open-hearth ovens, rolling mills and refractory material plant, and has an annual capacity of 3 million tons of steel. Its main and subsidiary workshops cover 10 sq km. The Tayeh mines, which are the main supply of high grade iron ore (50–60 per cent) have been extended and four new mines opened. The ore dressing plant has been modernized, froth flotation and magnetic separation methods for the separation of copper and iron have been in-stalled and the railway has been electrified. Tayeh itself is a considerable ingot steel producer, having four open-hearth and four electric furnaces. Coking coal is obtained from the mines at Pin-hsiang, Hunan; Siangtan, Hunan and Hwainan, Anhwei. A new field at Puchi, South Hupeh, which will reduce transportation costs consider-ably, has recently been discovered. Iron and steel works have been built at Pingsiang, which, in 1960, had a total blast furnace capacity of 982 cu. m. Two new combines have also been established at Siangtan, Hunan and Anyang, Honan.

Southwest – The development of the iron and steel industry in southwest China, which took place as a result of the Sino–Japanese War, has continued. The Chungking Iron and Steel Cor-poration, whose original plant came from Wuhan in 1938, considerably expanded its blast furnace capacity during the first two Five-year Plans. The industry here is based on good haematite ore from mines at Kikiang, south of Chungking, and at Kiangyu on the Chengtu–Paoki railway. There is good coking coal around Chungking at Kiangpei, Pahsien, Pishun and Hochwan. The mining is still largely from small pits and awaits fuller develop-ment[18].

The most notable expansion has been in Yunnan where the Kunming Iron and Steel Cor-poration, between 1958 and 1961, built four fairly large blast furnaces, the output of which has begun to rival that of Chungking. Kunming works are served by iron ore from Wuting, 40 km north-west of the city, and from Hwang-chia-tan, also by coal from I-ping-lang. It is intended that the Chungking and Kunming works be developed into fully integrated plant. Kweichow's iron and steel industry is centred at Tsunyi, north of Kwei-yang. Throughout the southwest region a fair amount of wrought iron is still produced by in-digenous methods.

Although the pig iron output of the southwest is very small compared with that of the rest of the country, its ingot steel output is quite appreciable. However, the importance of the iron and steel industry of this region should not be measured so much by comparison of output with the northern and eastern regions as by the needs which it serves in this remote area and the saving of transport thus achieved.

South – The southern economic region consists of two provinces, Kwangtung and Kwangsi. It did not figure in iron and steel returns until 1961, when it had 2·2 per cent of the country's blast-furnace capacity and furnished 2·1 per cent of its ingot steel output. Its main development is at Liuchow, Kiangsi, where a medium-size iron and steel complex has been built[19]. There is good grade iron ore to the south in the Hung Shui valley. The only supply of good coking coal comes from Fuchung, some 100 km to the east of the city. There is also an iron ore field at Shihlu on the west coast of Hainan, which is reported to have a reserve of 200 million tons of high-grade ore (54–67 per cent), easily worked and containing only a very small admixture of phosphate, sulphur and copper. This was opened up by the Japanese during the Sino–Japanese War and then produced 1·5 million ton p.a. If good coking coal can be found, this may well prove to be an important iron and steel centre in the near future.

Northwest – The North West Economic Region consists of Sinkiang, Kansu, Shensi and Tsinghai. Like the south, its development has been very recent, but unlike the south, its growth has been very rapid indeed. The reason for this lies in the discovery of rich and extensive iron ore deposits in west Kansu at Chingtiehshan, on the basis of which a large integration iron and steel complex has been built at Kiuchuan (Suchow), some 80 km east of Yumenshih. The Kiuchuan Iron and Steel Corporation is comparable in capacity and output to Paotow. Other centres of lesser importance but by no means insignificant have been established at Sian, Lanchow, Hami, Sining and Urumchi. In 1960 pig iron and ingot steel capacities, in thou-sand metric tons, were: Sian (500/450); Sining (400/300); Hami (800/600); Urumchi (800/600)[10]. This development bids to have profound influence on the life and character of the whole northwest region.

NON-FERROUS MINERALS

Recent systematic surveys are proving that China has large resources of non-ferrous minerals, and her potential reserves of tungsten, antimony, tin and molybdenum are now reckoned to be the richest in the world[20]. Great deposits of graphite, manganese, tin, lead, magnetite, gold and antimony were reported to have been discovered in 1957 in the Northeast in the Heilungkiang valley. Certain minerals, such as mercury (mercuric sulphide or cinnabar), which is the source of Chinese vermillion paint and red seal-ink, have been known and worked for many centuries, but any exploitation of non-ferrous minerals has been – and for the most part still is – by small-scale indigenous methods.

The research arm of the Geology Department in Nanking University claims to have established a relationship between granite formations and minerals in China, the Caledonian period having an association with gold, the Indo-China and Yenshan periods with tin and the Yenshan period with tungsten[21].

Antimony

Stibnite, the source of antimony, is found in all the provinces of the southwest. The richest deposits are in Hunan and the biggest mine is at Hsikwanshan, west of Changsha. Antimony is a valuable alloy in the manufacture of pewter and of white metal, the much-favoured material for ornaments, trays and urns. It is important in casting printers' type because of its property of expanding at the moment of solidification, and in making bearing metal.

Formerly China was the world's largest producer. Pre-1949 peak production was in 1916, during the First World War when 42 800 tons were produced. China's closest competitors at that time were Mexico and Bolivia. The main processing was centred in Hankow. Internal disorders led to decreasing production and finally, as a result of the Sino–Japanese War, China disappeared from the world market, which turned to the Americas for supplies. However, there has been a rapid recovery since 1949. In 1951, antimony exports were again 20 000 tons; the Hsikwanshan mines producing 12 000 tons. With the growing industrialization of the country, internal requirements will probably absorb the greater part of production.

Bauxite

Bauxite is fairly widely distributed throughout the country. Because the manufacture of aluminium is dependent on the supply of cheap and ample electric power, the exploitation of bauxite resources has been very limited in the past. Some development, based on cheap thermal power, occurred under Japanese rule at Penki and Anshan. The building of big multi-purpose dams, generating cheap hydro-electric power may lead to the growth of aluminium production, but the demands of power for irrigation and drainage are likely to have precedence for some time to come. Recently, good deposits of bauxite have been discovered in Kweichow. Their exploitation awaits the development of the Wukiang hydro-electric station.

Copper

In spite of the fact that the Shang and Chou dynasties are famous for their bronzes and that China for millennia used copper coinage, the annual production of copper during most of that period amounted to a few hundred tons. Records show that the average annual production between AD 847 and 859 was 290 tons. New copper mines were opened in Yunnan by the Mongols during the Yuan dynasty (AD 1279–1368). These mines were greatly extended during the Ming dynasty (1368–1644) and by 1727 output had risen to 3 million *catties* (approx. 1600 tons). The mines were worked by private enterprise under government supervision through official yardmasters[22]. Production was not maintained. In the 1930s it had fallen to less than 500 tons p.a.

While it was realized that copper deposits were quite widespread, it was generally held that these were limited. The best ores (3–10 per cent) are found in northeast Yunnan at Hwetseh (Tungchwan), in northwest Kweichow at Weining and in west Szechwan. In the Northeast the biggest deposits are at Tienpaoshan, near Yenki, Kirin where the ores have a content of 1·7 per cent copper, 6 per cent zinc and 5 per cent lead. Recent surveys have revealed that copper resources are much greater than previous estimates. Discoveries of copper sulphide in the Lanchow area are said to disclose reserves equal to those of Yunnan, and further reserves have been discovered in Ningsia. Total reserves are now reckoned to equal those of Chile.

Gold

Placer gold is reported to be widespread through China, the best deposits being in Heilungkiang, Kirin and Sinkiang. Any production is by indigenous methods and consequently is of negligible quantity.

Manganese

It is now estimated that reserves of manganese ore, which formerly were regarded as being very meagre indeed, are ample for China's needs and, moreover, are well located near the iron and steel centres, an important factor, as an average of 6 kg of manganese is required for every ton of steel[23]. Manganese is distributed widely over southern China and in the Northeast. Recently, further deposits, estimated at 700 million tons, have been discovered in Kwangsi[24].

The main producing centres in the south are at Siangton, near Changsha, Loping near Tayeh, and Mosun and Kweiping in east Kwangsi. The large deposits near Chinchow, southwest Liaoning, were heavily worked by the Japanese, and produced about 10 million tons annually.

Marble

Throughout the centuries fine marble of many varieties has been in great demand for the building of palaces and temples. Examples are the 'white jade' marble so much in evidence in the bridges, steps and balustrades of the Imperial Palace and Altar of Heaven in Peking. The fine and beautifully marked marble of Tali, Yunnan is renowned throughout the country and now figures in foreign trade, Egypt being a keen buyer since 1949.

Mercury

The presence of mercury has been known in China for over 2000 years and its working is one of China's oldest industries. During the nineteenth century more than 1000 metric tons were produced annually from a belt of land some 95 km wide and stretching from southeast Szechwan across Kweichow to western Hunan[25]. Production fell to between 130 and 470 tons p.a. in the early part of the twentieth century and continued to fall during the Sino–Japanese War. No production figures for the post-1949 period are available. The use of mercury in the past has been in the manufacture of vermillion paint and red seal-ink, China's colour for denoting felicity and happiness.

Nickel

Formerly Sinkiang was the only known Chinese source of nickel. This was of a very low grade and of little importance. The first deposits in China Proper were recently discovered in west Szechwan in conjunction with rich sources of mica and asbestos. Szechwan is proving to be one of the richest areas of non-ferrous minerals.

Salt

Salt has always been in short supply throughout the centuries, partly owing to transport difficulties and partly to its production being a government monopoly and therefore regarded as a revenue-raising medium. Today, in addition to increasing domestic demand, the requirements of modern chemical industry are emphasizing its importance and improved communications are making its transport from remote parts possible.

There are three main sources of supply. The coastal evaporation saltfields are sited in Hopei, Shantung, Kiangsu and Liaoning. Changlu, Hopei is the most important centre, producing 93.7 per cent sodium chloride. The brine wells of Szechwan form a second source. Deep drilling in this region dates from the Earlier Han dynasty (206 BC–AD 24) and has continued to this day. A third and increasingly important source is the huge deposits from the dried lakes in the northwest, notably in Ningsia Autonomous Region and in the Tsaidam of Tsinghai. 'Tsaidam' is the Mongolian word for 'Salt Marshes'. Here it is estimated that there are reserves of 26 billion tons. Writing of this, K. S. Chang says, 'Part of the 350 km highway across the region has been built on a bed of salt and even the mile posts are made of salt chunks'[26]. There are vast quantities of potash at Ta-erh-lan and boron at Tatsaidam. Chinese geologists claim to have discovered in this salt lake four previously unknown borate minerals, viz hungtsaoite (named after the geologist Chang Hung-tsao), carborite, hydrochlorborite and trigonomagneborite[27]. Borate minerals are increasingly important ingredients in high-energy fuels and in the metallurgical and chemical industries.

Tin

China's tin reserves lie in association with the Malayan tin belt. The biggest reserves are found in Kwangsi and extend into southern Yunnan and southern Hunan. The tin veins are associated with granite, which disintegrates and the tin is washed

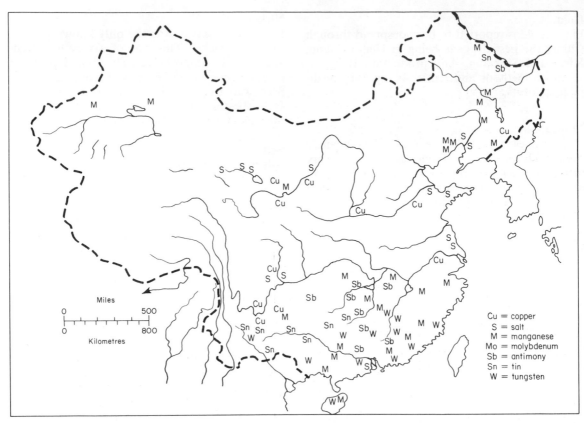

Fig. 99   Non-ferrous minerals (while the South and Northeast show a wealth of non-ferrous minerals, the blank areas do not necessarily denote a dearth, but only a lack of information)

down into the limestone, where, in places, it forms a rich storage of high quality. Being, with copper, an alloy in the making of bronze, it has been worked from very early times. Much the same indigenous methods then used have continued to the present day. Only during the last two decades or so have more modern methods begun to be used.

The main mining areas are at Kokiu, near Mengtsz, Yunnan and around Kweilin. During the twentieth century production has varied between 6000 and 15000 tons p.a. due to fluctuating world prices of tin and to the political state of the country. Peak production was achieved in 1938 when 15540 tons were mined. During the 1930s exports at times exceeded 10000 tons. No separate figures are available for tin exports since 1949, but appreciable amounts of tin, mercury and antimony have gone to U.S.S.R. annually since that date.

Tungsten (wolfram)

High-grade wolframite ores were first discovered in south Kiangsi in 1915[25]. By the 1930s China had become the world's largest producer. Production between 1934 and 1944 varied between 5000 and 18000 tons of 60 per cent oxide concentrates and represented between 30 and 60 per cent of the world's production.

The ore appears in two main belts, the more northerly of which stretches through south Hunan, north Kwangtung and south Kwangsi. The southern belt runs from Fukien along the coast to Hainan. The most important deposits are at Tayu, south Kwangsi.

Tungsten has proved a valuable earner of foreign currency but, with the growth of national industry and the need for tungsten in the manufacture of all kinds of high-grade steel, China's own market is likely to absorb an increasing proportion of its production.

Plate 19   125 000 kw turbo-generating unit built and installed in Shanghai

ENGINEERING INDUSTRY

Probably the present engineering industry reflects more clearly than any other branch of industry its close links with the heritage of the past and also its break from it. Modern Chinese engineering is revealing so much of that inventiveness which was so fertile in earlier centuries – the knowledge of magnetism, astronomy, explosive chemistry and the use of many forms of power[28]. However, the Chinese in times past made comparatively little practical use of their inventions. Herein lies the difference between past and present, for today no effort is being spared to exploit to the full every new idea from whatever source.

The long period of quiescence and conservatism in China, during which the West underwent its industrial, commercial and technological revolutions, left the Chinese with a great leeway in all engineering departments, not least the shortage of engineering designers. One method of offsetting this shortage, used effectively since 1949, has been to secure the free interchange of technical and scientific information between factories, colleges and scientific institutes and 'to bring the wisdom of the masses into play', i.e. workers on the factory floor are invited to participate. All are urged 'to compare with, learn from and catch up with the advanced and help those who lag'. A national network coordinating research departments in all major factories throughout the country, has been set up.

In the early 1950s it was big national news when a Chinese-built factory started manufacturing so simple a tool as a pneumatic drill for drilling blast holes in mines. In 1967, the fact that China is making, in plant of her own designing and building, everything from pins to electronic computers is some indication of the advance and sophistication achieved in these years. The speed with which this has been accomplished has been fraught with dangers and mistakes, particularly in the heavy machine making and motor industries. Since 1960 much greater care has been given to trial testing before going into mass production.

The aim in industry is to achieve basic self-sufficiency. At the end of the First Five-year Plan it was claimed that 60 per cent of the nation's industrial needs were being met internally and that by 1963 this figure had risen to 80 per cent. As standards of living and industrial needs rise, this percentage will require ever-increasing effort to maintain and increase.

Machine making

China's first plant for producing machinery was erected in Peking in 1883, but it never functioned. Between that date and the inception of the First Five-year Plan, machine building throughout China Proper was confined almost entirely to the assembly of imported parts. During their occupation of Manchukuo, the Japanese developed some machine and tool making in Shenyang, but even this did not attain any great proportions.

Heavy engineering – It was during the First and Second Five-year Plans that the most striking advances in heavy machine building were made. The work has continued since 1960 but at a slower rate and, as already seen, with the emphasis transferred to agricultural needs. Plant for building the heaviest machinery has naturally been erected either where the raw material is produced or in those places to which it can be transported easily. Thus the greatest centres have grown at Shenyang and Shanghai with Wuhan developing later. Both Shenyang and Shanghai deal with the construction of complete installations such as large hydro-electric power plants, oil refineries, blast furnaces, rolling machines, heavy cranes and steel presses, steam-generating equipment and all kinds of mining equipment, including shafts, cutters, loaders, hoists and drills. The Shenyang Heavy Machinery Plant, founded in 1953, mass-produces all grades of lathes and has built a big verical lathe, capable of processing parts up to 1·25 m, and a horizontal 12-ton lathe, 8 m long[29]. It also specializes in turbine rotors. Up to 1965 its turbine rotor casting team, had produced nearly 100 rotors of different and increasing sizes; in 1953 a

10 000 kW rotor for Kwanting Reservoir Hydro-electric Station near Peking; in 1958 a 72 500 kW hydro-electric turbine for Hsinanching Station, Shekiang, and in 1964 it succeeded in casting a 100 000 kW water turbine of first-rate quality in exactness and smoothness[30]. Shanghai engages in similar heavy machine building. The Shanghai Hydraulic Machinery Plant recently built the biggest radial crane and much equipment for hydro-electric power stations. The Kiangnan Shipyard, Shanghai, which built the first 10 000-ton ocean-going freighter, successfully built a 12 000-ton hydraulic, free-forging press, 23 m high with a bed plate of 260 tons and capable of forging 200–300-ton ingots. The significance of this achievement lies not so much in the size of the press, although that is considerable, but in the engineering ingenuity required, since China had no factory equipped to handle such huge parts. Since 1959 Wuhan has rapidly developed its heavy machine building industry and recently produced a vertical boring and turning mill with a diameter of 6·3 m. Tatung is the main centre for building steam and diesel locomotives. Other iron and steel centres, notably Paotow, Harbin, Tientsin and Chungking are now entering the field of heavy machine building.

High precision machinery – At the other end of the engineering scale, China has developed her ability and capacity for making high-precision machinery with startling rapidity. She is now making highly sophisticated instruments in virtually all fields. These include such items as capillary spectro-scopes, a large microscope with a resolution of X200 000, an electrostatic electronic accelerator with a voltage of several million electron volts, a microbalance accurate to one-millionth of a gram, automatic plasma-cutting equipment for refractory metals, and gear-grinding machines for making ballbearing rings. Tientsin recently produced a hot rolling machine for rapid high-precision production of fluted twist drills, using one of the very latest industrial techniques in the world[31]. While the main centres of this high-precision work are at Shanghai, Tientsin, Nanking and Shenyang, its distribution is now becoming quite widespread.

MOTOR INDUSTRY

No motor vehicles were produced in China before 1949. In 1957 a few *kaifang* or 'liberation' trucks

Plate 20   Tungfanghung tractor plant, Loyang

Loyang	Leading tractor plant, specializing in 75 h.p. *Tungfanghung*, 54 and 40 h.p. tractors and 160 h.p. bulldozers
Changchun, Kirin	No. 1 Motor Vehicle Plant producing 'liberator' lorries and, recently, 6-seater saloons
Tientsin	45 h.p. *Tieh Niu*, i.e. 'Iron Ox' tractor, light lorry and cross-country van – 9-seater coaches
Shenyang	Tractors and spare parts
Nanchang	Tractors and spare parts
Nanking	New cross-country truck for negotiating southern muddy roads
Tsinan	8-ton heavy duty 'Yellow River' truck – 10-ton two-way tip lorry
Taiyuan	Taiyuan heavy machine plant – 4 cu. m bucket excavator
Anshan	100 h.p. *Hung Chi*, i.e. 'Red Flag' tractor
Wuhan	7 h.p. 'Worker–Peasant' hand tractor
Canton	10 h.p. hand tractor, 3½-ton 'Red Guard' lorries
Peking	Diesel-electric trucks and mounted cranes
Huhehot	Diesel engines
Chungking	25-ton dumping lorry, vans and 40-seater coaches

were trial-produced at Loyang but, until 1958, reliance was placed on imports from the U.S.S.R. In that year the Loyang Tractor Plant was opened and production began in earnest. The aim, as in the rest of industry, is to attain self-sufficiency and this, it is claimed, is nearly achieved in all fields of the motor industry, with the exception of saloon cars, a large proportion of which still come from eastern Europe. Attention has naturally been focused on the production of commercial vehicles and, since 1960, particularly on tractor building (see p. 122).

Loyang has developed into the greatest centre of industry, but many other major plants, all of which are now geared for mass production to serve the 2200 state tractor systems, have been built throughout the country. These are listed below giving their main specializations.
Diesel engines, ranging from 50 to 300 h.p. are in mass production and are reported to be coming off the production line in sufficient numbers to meet current agricultural and industrial needs. Three types of high-power, low super-charged diesel engines, ranging from 450 to 1000 h.p. are being built[32].

CHEMICAL INDUSTRY

It is stated that in 1949 only 100 or so chemical products were being made in China. In 1952 the figure stood at 300; in 1957 at 2000 and in 1962 at 8000 and included products in every branch of the chemical industry. In October 1965 an article in *Far East Trade* declared that 'the industry stood on the threshold of mass or experimental production of everything modern chemistry can make'. This is true, but what proportion is still experimental and what is in mass production is, at present, impossible to ascertain.

The emphasis that has been placed on the production of chemical fertilizer and its widespread manufacture in small plant has been shown on pp. 117–19. In 1949 ammonium sulphate alone and in small quantities was being produced. In 1963 chemical products included ammonium nitrate, ammonium bicarbonate, ammonium chloride, calcium cyanide (lime nitrogen), urea, calcium superphosphate, calcium magnesium phosphate and potassium sulphate.

On the pharmaceutical side there has been a very rapid growth. Chinese chemists are now not merely reproducing Western drugs but are producing new ones flowing from their own research. In China, the production of penicillin, aureomycin and syntomycin was developed in the First Five-year Plan and streptomycin, chloromycin and neomycin during the Second Five-year Plan. Chinese chemists are claiming the production by a new technology of streptomycin that produces neither pain reaction nor post-injection fever. In

the field of insecticides, antibiotics for the treatment of fruit and animal diseases, especially in relation to virus pneumonia in pigs, are being produced. Many of these pharmaceutical products are made in the chemistry laboratories by scientists and laboratory technicians and await mass production.

The manufacture of plastics has developed only since 1958, progressing very rapidly from celluloid and bakelite to a wide range of polythene and cellulose products. In 1965, 26 000 tons of plastics for farming and industrial use were produced – five times the 1964 output. Of these 12 000 tons were for farm use, particularly polythene sheeting for the protection of rice seedlings. The use of plastics in this way claims to bring 10 per cent increase in rice yield.

The largest chemical centres are at Kirin, Shanghai, Tientsin, Taiyuan and Lanchow.

BUILDING INDUSTRY

While China is justly famous for the beauty of its architecture, it is remarkable how comparatively little of its ancient buildings has survived the passing of the years. This low survival quotient is undoubtedly due, in part, to the ravages of war and internal unrest, but it is also due to the nature of the material used. Traditionally, the framework of buildings has been of timber, stone or brick being merely the infilling material. It is true that there are many stone monuments such as the beautiful Altar of Heaven in Peking and the An-chi Bridge at Chao-hsien, Hopei, but the greater proportion are timber structures as in the Imperial Palace and the Temple of Heaven. This is also true of humbler dwellings, which, in south and Central China are almost exclusively constructed of wood frame and baked or mud brick, *sha-mu* (Cunninghamia sinensis) which is resistant to white ant, generally being used for the wooden structure.

The amount of building construction which has taken place in China since 1949 is breathtaking, although not surprising since it is essential and complementary to the industrial and agricultural revolution. Writing of this, Kang Chao says, 'China in the first decade of the Communist rule had put out houses, buildings, roads, dams, reservoirs, etc. at a higher rate than industrial and agricultural goods'[33]. In the early years of this decade the question of style and quality of building was hotly debated – whether emphasis should be laid on high quality and beauty in the Chinese tradition or whether speed, cheapness and utilitarian needs should be the criterion. So far as dwellings and most industrial plant are concerned the latter has been the guide. Houses and workers' tenement blocks are usually built of drab grey brick. It is reported that over 90 per cent of the walls in China at present are made of small, heavy solid clay bricks, which have poor heat and sound insulating properties[34]. Attention is now being given to this problem and new types of composition brick of cinder, coal ash, fly ash, oil shale or blast furnace slag mixed with aerated concrete are being used.

For the bigger industrial works, public buildings, sports arenas and halls reinforced concrete is used. In consequence there has been a vast expansion of the cement industry. In the 1920s demand for cement was small and was met largely by imports from Germany and Japan, and from the Green Island Cement Works in Hong Kong. In China only eight cement works existed and some of these were very small; the largest was the Chee Hsin Works at Tongshan, Hopei. After the Sino–Japanese War there was some development, and a large new cement works was built at Shih-hweiyao, near Tayeh, Hupeh and opened in 1948. This was reputed at the time to be the biggest works in Southeast Asia, having a capacity of 2000 tons/day. It was well sited, being based on local coal and excellent local limestone.

Since 1949 cement production has leapt ahead, rising from less than 1 million tons p.a. to 7 million tons in 1963, and 9 million tons in 1964 and has continued to rise. In 1964 there were 12 plants, each producing between 700 000 and 200 000 tons p.a., and some 80 smaller works producing less than 100 000 tons p.a.[35]. In 1963 the first large cement works entirely designed and built by the Chinese was opened in Sitsun, Canton. This plant has an output of 400 000 tons p.a. and a rotary kiln of 125 m. Recently, however, the emphasis has been on building small shaft kilns of about 20 000 tons p.a. capacity on the grounds that these entail less capital outlay, are quick to build, are economical in fuel and transport, and serve local needs. The boast now is that every province, municipality and autonomous region has its own cement plants. Attention has turned to the grading of cement. There are now twenty varieties in production, including high grades for bridges, reservoirs, dams and the oil industry.

No figures are available showing the amount of timber cut since 1949 to meet constructional demands, but the increase must be very great indeed. Forestry authorities affirm that afforestation is taking place at an even greater rate than timber cutting.

The following* shows the increase in timber used 1964 to 1974

Cut Timber (thousand cubic metres)

1964	1966	1968
150 560	156 615	163 755

1970	1972	1974
170 915	178 935	188 310

* *Statistical Year Book for Asia and the Pacific*, U.N. 1975.

LIGHT INDUSTRIES

Textile manufacture

Silk – The beginnings of sericulture are sunk in the depths of Chinese mythology when, some 4000 years ago, Hsu Lung-she is reputed to have discovered the art of reeling and weaving silk. Legend, which has the backing of Stein in his *Ancient Khotan*, has it that the Chinese guarded their secret of silk rearing and making until AD 419, when a Chinese princess, who was given in marriage to the King of Khotan, smuggled silkworm eggs and mulberry seeds in her baggage. Until then China had been the sole producer of silk and had enjoyed a lucrative trade with the West along the famous 'Silk Route' through Sinkiang. Despite the loss of her monopoly and the development of sericulture in the West, China continued to be the main supplier to foreign countries and was still responsible for half the silk trade of the world at the turn of this century. In 1915 she exported 66 115 kg of white, yellow, re-reeled and steam filature silk, 20 605 kg of wild silk, 20 715 kg cocoons and 77 180 kg of waste silk. Wild silk at that time commanded a good market as it was considered the best material for aeroplane wings. From this date on until the middle of the 1950s, with the exception of a short prosperous period 1929–32, the market rapidly declined[36]. This was due largely to Japanese competition and the development of synthetic fibres, but it was also due to poor

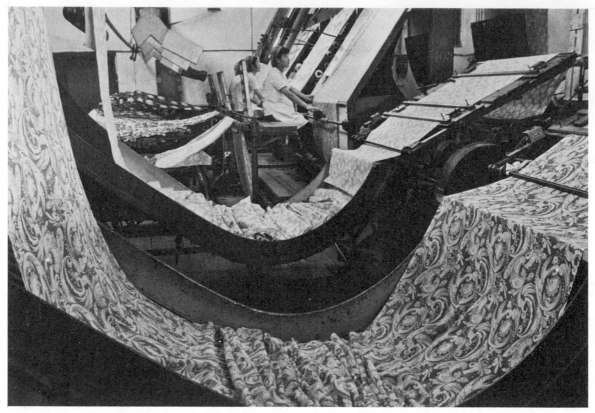

Plate 21   Producing dacron fabrics

organization, antiquated machinery, and carelessness and ignorance. Some effort was made to
resuscitate the industry between 1932 and 1936,
but the Sino–Japanese War brought the industry
to a very low ebb.[37]

The main silk reeling and weaving areas are
sited in the cocoon-raising areas. White silk, the
chief producing areas of which are in the Wusih
district of Kiangsu and Shaohsing district of
Chekiang, is processed mainly in Shanghai, which
also carries out 90 per cent of the printing and
dyeing. Other centres are at Hangchow, Huchow
and Hankow. A considerable amount of white
silk is also produced in Kwangtung and is
processed mainly in Canton. Yellow silk from
Szechwan, Yunnan and Shantung, and wild silk,
the product of silkworms fed on oak leaves,
from the northeast and Shantung, is less well
organized. The industry, although now under
commune direction and somewhat better managed, is still largely a cottage industry. The
machinery used is generally obsolete and the

methods still primitive. Efforts are being made,
especially in Chekiang, 'the home of silk', and
Kiangsu to raise standards and to create new pat-
terns, fabrics and motifs, but the silk industry
everywhere faces severe competition, not only
from new textiles, but also from the demand for
land for food crops. It is a very uphill task.

Cotton – It comes as a surprise even to people
familiar with China to learn that the ubiquitous
indigo-blue cloth, worn by the masses of Chinese
peasantry, is a comparatively recent innovation.
Although the cotton seed was introduced into
China as early as the eleventh century, its cultivation was little developed, possibly due to the
opposition of the sericulturalists whose interests
it would have challenged. The clothing of the
common people was made from natural fibres,
such as hemp and rami and from wild and waste
silk. Cotton clothing remained a luxury of the
rich until the latter part of the nineteenth century
when foreign cotton cloth began to be imported
in quantity and American varieties of cotton seed

were introduced.

In the early 1920s cotton-growing was greatly extended in two belts, one along the Yangtze valley with main concentration in Kiangsu and Hupeh, and one in the Hwang-ho basin mainly in Honan and in the Wei-Fen valley. At this time all indigenous varieties were short staple of 17 mm or less, but had the advantage of a high lint yield and relative freedom from pests to which the longer staple, imported American varieties were prone. By the 1930s Chinese production of cotton lint was averaging some 800 000 tons p.a. In spite of the development of modern textile mills in Shanghai, Tientsin and Wuhan, the demand for cotton cloth greatly exceeded national output and large amounts of cotton cloth and raw cotton were imported. A good deal of spinning and weaving of locally grown cotton was done by the peasantry in their own homes.

Since 1949 a great deal has been done to extend the cultivation and the manufacture of cotton. Research into methods of cultivation and new varieties has not only increased output in the established and high-yieling areas of Kiangsu, Hupeh, Honan and Shensi, but has opened up new or previously little-developed regions. New varieties have enabled Liaoning, which has only 150–160 frostless days, to produce successfully long-staple cotton. Kunming, by means of new cultivation methods, is now also successfully growing long-staple cotton. Irrigation has greatly extended the growing area and output of Sinkiang and the northwest. As a result, production of raw cotton rose from a pre-war peak of 840 000 tons to 1·3 million tons in 1952, 1·65 million tons in 1957 and 2·4 million tons (planned) in 1962. Although no firm figures have been published since, reports from all districts since 1963 indicate that this upwards trend has been maintained.

The spinning and weaving industry, which was concentrated so much in the eastern provinces, most notably in Shanghai and Tientsin, has been greatly extended. New mills have been built in every cotton-producing area and many old mills have been renovated. The output of cotton yarn rose from 1·8 million bales in 1949 to 6·1 million bales in 1958 and cotton cloth from 1890 million metres in 1949 to 5700 million metres in 1958. Since 1963 it is claimed that production has increased by 15–17 per cent p.a. In 1965, 46 new textile mills (37 cotton, 6 printing and dyeing, and 3 silk weaving) were opened in provinces as far apart as Sinkiang and Kwangsi, adding in all 1·4 million spindles, capable of producing enough yarn for 1230 million metres of cloth. The cotton mills built in 1965 included one of 150 000 spindles and 2400 looms[38] in Wuhan (the largest in the city) and one of 50 000 spindles and 2000 looms at Lanchow, the latter having an annual capacity of 46 500 bales of yarn and 56 million metres of cloth. This Lanchow mill, designed and built entirely in China, serves the newly developed Kansu cotton fields, which are growing good, long-staple cotton[39]. The new cotton-growing areas in the northwest in the Turfan, Urumchi, Manass and south Sinkiang regions have each developed their own cotton industries. Recently there has been a big development in the Wei valley at Sian where the 4th State Cotton Combine of Shensi has built a mill having 100 000 spindles and 4000 automatic looms with an annual capacity of 66 million metres of cloth.

In 1964 cotton manufacturers were directed to give more attention to and cater more directly for peasant needs, in consequence of which it is reported that 1200 million metres of coarse cloth, drills, corduroys, cotton serge and venetians were produced in the first 6 months of 1966. In spite of the very great increase in production which has been achieved, cotton cloth is still in short supply and is still rationed.

Natural fibres – As mentioned above, the common people of China in times past have relied largely on natural fibres for their clothing. Of these fibres hemp (*ma*) is the most important. It is grown in all provinces, but more intensely in the north and northeast than in the south. In addition to its use as a coarse summer cloth, it is used for all kinds of cordage. Ramie (*ssu-ma* or silk hemp) is, as its name implies, a finer fibre than hemp and weaves into a cloth very similar to linen, which is very acceptable in the hot summer months because its ventilation properties are superior to those of cotton. It differs from hemp in that it is a perennial plant, producing three or four crops a year over a period of about twenty years. Its main production area is in the middle Yangtze basin in the provinces of Szechwan, Hunan, Hupeh, and Kiangsi. It makes fine cordage and canvas. On account of its resistance to water it has been much used for fishing nets, but is now being supplanted by synthetic fibres for this purpose. Hemp and ramie are retted and sun dried to extract the fibre from the stems. Manufacture of both fibres is, for the most part, confined to the regions of production and is carried out in small local mills.

Since 1949 there has been a considerable increase of jute-growing in the Yangtze delta region of Kiangsu and Chekiang and around the shores of the Tungting and Poyang lakes, in the lake-studded lands of Hupeh and also in the delta flats of the Pearl river. Yields of between 3·75 and 5 tons/hectare are being achieved[40]. The main jute mills are in Shanghai, Hangchow and Canton. The new mill, on the Soochow Canal near Hangchow has 10 596 spindles and 630 looms, making yarn, gunny bags and jute cloth.

Synthetic fibres – This is an entirely new industry in China and of very recent and very rapid development. In November 1964, it was reported that there were already more than 60 textile, knitwear, dyeing and printing mills producing chemical fibre products in polyester, vinylon and chinlon[41]. The main centres are in Shanghai, Peking and Shenyang, but many provinces are now producing significant quantities of polyvinyl chloride fibres, woven in mixtures and made into filter cloth, fishing nets and ropes. These new fibres are more resistant to abrasion, acid and alkalis than natural fibres and are steadily replacing them. A new mill has been opened in Sining, Tsinghai, an area rich in coal, salt and limestone, the raw materials for the manufacture of polyvinyl chloride fibre[42]. By 1965 China's synthetic fibre mills had an annual capacity of between 300–400 million metres, said to be equivalent to the production of 6 million *mow* devoted to cotton and mulberry[43].

Woollens – Apart from the spinning and weaving of local wool in cottages or small works in the north and west, modern manufacture of woollen goods was concentrated in Shanghai, the raw material coming mainly from Australia. With the recent development of new breeds of sheep, producing much finer wool in the Inner Mongolian and Sinkiang steppelands, there has been a rapid growth of the woollen industry in the northwest. By 1957 new factories had been built at T'ienshui, Sian, Yulin, Yinchwan, Sining and Urumchi. More recently, a large mill was opened at Huhehot, employing 100 technicians and 2000 workers, partly recruited from local herdsmen.

Footwear

In the early decades of this century the usual footwear of the common people was similar to that which had been worn for many previous centuries. There was rarely a household without its board onto which every piece of scrap cloth and rag was pasted until it attained a thickness of 5–8 mm. This was then cut into the shape of shoe soles, industriously sewn through and through to give added strength and stiffness and then attached to a cloth upper. This was essentially women's work and, at least in the countryside, done within each household. Amongst the peasantry this still remains one of the most important forms of footwear. For work in the fields straw sandals or clogs were, and still are, worn, otherwise the peasant went barefoot. The more wealthy wore cloth or felt shoes or boots with a thick felt sole.

As the century has advanced rubber-soled shoes with canvas or felt uppers have become increasingly popular, until today they are almost universally worn by the younger generations and are regular wear for the army. Hundreds of millions of pairs are being manufactured annually. These shoes and boots have the virtue of being cheap and fairly durable. In the cities, leather footwear is also quite common, the leather coming increasingly from the grasslands of the north and northwest. Black cloth shoes with felt soles are still often used for formal indoor wear.

Production of Rubber Footwear
(1000 pairs)

1949	28 900
1953	76 360
1958	182 360

Food processing

Apart from specialties, such as Peking Duck, special teas, ginger and dried fruits, which were sent to all parts of the country, food processing formerly was done locally for local consumption. It has been only in the last 60–70 years that it has been carried out on anything approaching a large scale in modern factories.

The modern flour-milling industry was started by the Russians in Harbin and spread rapidly in the northeast and along the east coast provinces. In 1925 there were 123 modern flour mills, situated as follows[36]

Manchuria	50	Shansi	1
Kiangsu	44	Honan	1
Hupeh	9	Anhwei	1
Shangtung	6	Hunan	1
Chihli (Hopei)	5	Kiangsi	1
Szechwan	3	Yunnan	1

Plate 22   Camera manufacture, Chinkwang instrument plant, southwest Szechwan
Light industry is very widely spread throughout China. The Chinese are very adept at all
kinds of fine work. The chief camera production centres are Harbin, Shanghai, Tientsin
and Tantung

Tientsin and Shanghai mills relied to some extent on Canadian and U.S. wheat and all mills were handicapped by the irregular supplies of native wheat caused by unsettled conditions and interruption in transport. During succeeding years the milling industry developed, but continued to be handicapped for the same reasons. With the more settled political state of the country since 1949, modern flour mills have sprung up everywhere, particularly in the inland provinces of the north.

The egg products industry before 1949 was organized mainly for export. It was centred mainly in Hankow, which processed (froze, preserved or dried) over 2 million eggs a day at the peak of its production in the late 1920s. There has been no report of the progress of this industry since 1949.

The fact that land used for arable farming is much more productive of food calories per hectare than if used for cattle-raising or dairy farming is the main reason why so little milk has been produced in China Proper. Whether a distaste for milk and milk products, particularly in south and central China, has also been a cause of this lack of dairy farming, or whether it has been simply an effect due to unfamiliarity, is an open question. Soyabean milk (*tu chiang*) is used as a substitute, especially for weaning babies. There has, however, been a marked change in habit and taste during the past 20–30 years and the demand for milk has risen rapidly. More dairy farming is being done in south China and many milk-processing factories have been built in the grasslands of the north and northwest where irrigation is resulting in much better pasture. Inner Mongolia alone had 17 major milk-processing factories producing powdered milk, condensed milk, butter, lactose and cheese[44].

The development of fruit and meat canning has also made great progress in recent years. The temperate fruits of the north – pears, plums and peaches – and the subtropical and tropical fruits of the south – lichee, tangerine, pineapple, mangoes and peanuts – are now being tinned for both the home and export markets. Beef and mutton are now being canned in increasing quantities in the northern and northwestern provinces. Pigs are ubiquitous in China and little canning is done. However, special dried pork from Szechwan is distributed to other provinces.

Cigarettes

Tobacco is said to have been introduced into China from the Philippines during the early part of the sixteenth century and to have spread gradually over the country. By the beginning of the twentieth century nearly every province was growing the tobacco plant. It was used at first mainly medicinally and for snuff, and later for smoking in long thin-stemmed pipes or water pipes which had very small bowls and used only a pinch of tobacco at each filling. This filling occupied almost as much time as the actual smoking. On social occasions, when the men were gathered together, the pipe would be passed round the circle. Thus comparatively little tobacco was used and home supplies were sufficient to meet demand.

In 1913 the British-American Tobacco Co. started a factory in Shantung and began to promote the growing of American leaf. Cigarette smoking quickly became popular and there was a very rapid development of the trade. In the 1930s there were many large factories in Shanghai, Tientsin, Harbin, Mukden, Hankow and Canton.

Cigarettes (*thousand crates*)			Tobacco (*tons*)
1949	1600	1964	790 000
1953	3552	1965	797 000
1958	4750	1966	800 000
Later figures		1967	866 000
not available		1968	869 000
		1969	796 000
		1970	806 000
		1971	802 000
		1972	856 000
		1973	968 000
		1974	982 000

From *Statistical Year Book for Asia and the Pacific*, U.N. 1975.

The cigarette-smoking habit has continued to grow and today is widespread – one of the few vices in this puritanical land. Some idea of the recent growth of cigarette manufacture can be gained from the following figures:

Consumer goods

For the first two decades after Liberation emphasis was consistently on the production of capital goods. Propaganda has continually appealed to the people's patriotism and social conscience to work hard, live sparingly and eschew waste. Nevertheless, incentive to effort in the form of increased consumer goods has not been entirely ignored. For the great mass of people there undoubtedly has been some rise in living standards. Evidence of this rise is seen in the continually increasing number of bank deposit accounts of the masses. It is reported that there were 160 000 new fixed deposit accounts opened in Peking in the first six months of 1965[45]. More concrete evidence of this rise in living standards is seen in the increasing quantity and variety of goods in the stores and shops – goods almost entirely of Chinese manufacture, such as sewing machines, wrist watches, clocks, vacuum flasks, electric torches, cameras, glassware, transistor radios and cosmetics. Soaps and detergents are in greater supply. Matches, which formerly were of very poor quality have vastly improved. It used to be said, facetiously, that when one match from a boxful would ignite, then one might as well throw the rest of the box away. Bicycles are now more plentiful and are an important means of transport in the cities and country. In 1949 the annual production of bicycles was only 14 000. It had risen to 165 000 in 1953 and to 1·174 million in 1958. No later figures are available. Big as these increased figures may appear, they must always be measured in relation to the needs of the 800 million people who have to be served.

Porcelain

The former world-famous Chinese porcelain fell on evil days after the fall of the Ch'ing dynasty (1911). Even the celebrated kilns at Kingtechen, Kiangsi were turning out very little porcelain of even medium quality. Liling, 30 km west of Pingsiang, was reduced to one factory, and by 1925 Canton had ceased production. Most of the old glazing secrets were lost in this decline.

Since 1949 there has been a very considerable

revival. Some thirty new kinds of glaze have been introduced. Kingtechen has again sprung into activity and new kilns cover a large area. Although some high-quality porcelain for presentation purposes is being turned out, production is being concentrated on meeting the needs of the masses. It is reported that 85 million pieces of glazed ware were produced in 1965[46]. While some of the ware is taken by road, the bulk is transported by river and canal. The kilns at Liling have also been revived and once again are producing underglazed blue and white porcelain of good quality, which is much in evidence in public utilities such as the railway service. Canton's old-established large works are also in full production, as also are many others scattered through the provinces.

HANDICRAFTS

Handicrafts, which have been the basis of industrial production through the centuries in China, have posed a problem for the planners of a socialist society. Blacksmiths, carpenters, bamboo and coir artisans, stone cutters, embroidery workers and a host of others have worked mainly as independent individualistic units. The economy has been based on the family or household, generally of low productivity and standing low in the social scale.

With the development of the cooperatives and then the communes, attempts have been made to draw these handicraftsmen into the new organization, recognizing that the 'rural handicraft industry is an important component of the collective economy of the people's commune and that it is also "the vanguard" of the handicrafts that give direct aid and support to agriculture'. In 1965 it was estimated that there were about 10 million of these workers in the whole country. That this movement of incorporation has not been easy is evidenced by the following quotation from the *People's Daily*:

> The production teams find it rather difficult to control them. The handicraftsmen themselves are small producers and are spontaneously inclined towards capitalism. They always look for work which pays higher wages and, as a result, the farm implements of some production teams cannot be prepared in good time.[47]

It has been thought necessary to go slowly and carefully in persuading them to adopt collective ownership and factory organization.

Handicraftsmen in our country have rich experience in production. They are nimble-minded and clever and dexterous in using their hands and are both resourceful and full of inventive spirit. Since the handicraft industry deals mostly with small products, the scale of handicraft enterprise should not be too large and the degree of centralization should not be too high. Attention should therefore be paid to preserving its small and flexible features.[48]

Some success has been achieved in developing training centres for apprentices as in Soochow, the home of art and embroidery work, where a part-work, part-study handicraft art centre has been established to teach designing, decoration, restoration and copying of old paintings. More than 1000 apprentices had passed through the school by 1958[49].

FISHING INDUSTRY

China's shallow coastal waters and many great rivers have proved for many centuries fine fishing grounds. Fish have figured as an important item in the diet of the rich and middle-class Chinese. Like pork, however, fish appeared on the table of the peasant only at infrequent intervals, in spite of the fact that most hamlets and villages in central and south China had their ponds in which some fish were bred. Since 1949 it is claimed that fish appears much oftener on the tables of the masses. There can be no doubt that there has been a very big increase in the amount of fish taken since that date, although some reserve must be placed on the last published figures for 1958, the year of the Great Leap[50].

		Million tons
1949	about	0·5
1952		1·66
1957		3·12
1958		6·03

Sea fishing

China has a coastline of some 14 000 km, the greater part of which looks out on a wide continental shelf over which the warm Kuro–Siwo current from the south mingles with the cold Kamchatka current flowing soutward along the Siberian and Korean coasts. These shallow seas, like the Grand Banks of Newfoundland, are fine fish breeding grounds. Although these grounds have been fished for many centuries, it is only with the introduction of mechanization within the twentieth century that they have begun seriously to be exploited. The Japanese for some decades have fished the region intensively with trawlers and drifters. Only since 1949 has China entered into competition. Most of China's fishing until then was concentrated on inshore or fairly close offshore work.

The kinds of fish caught vary somewhat from south to north. The croaker, in one form or another, and the cuttlefish, are found all along the coast. Between the Gulf of Tonking and the mouth of the Yangtze the most typical is the large yellow croaker, a fish of 350 mm or more in length and having few small bones. Farther north the small yellow croaker is found in large shoals in the Pohai, Yellow and East China Seas. It is the staple food of the fisher folk along the coast. Horsetails, rich in protein and fat, are deep-sea fish, which in late summer swim into the shallow seas to spawn. Prawns abound in the Po-hai and Yellow Seas. A great deal of these catches is preserved. Most of the large yellow croaker is either sun-dried or canned, although some is frozen. The small yellow croaker is usually salted.

In recent years there has been a big increase in shellfish breeding. In Liaoning the area of inshore shoals for this purpose has been extended to 13 000 hectares; 50 species are reared, including oyster, corbicula, hard clam ark shell for which the region is famous, abalone and sea scallop[51]. Large amounts of shellfish are also raised in the sheltered bays of the southeast coast. Fukien rears razor clam, surf clam, oysters and ark shell. 10 000 tons of oysters are harvested in Santu Bay alone[52]. The artificial culture of kelp (*laminaria japonica*) together with red laver and agar is also being energetically pursued. This edible seaweed, which is the source of iodine and other industrial materials, was formerly raised only in the colder waters of the north.

Since 1949 mechanization has gone on apace. The main fishing all along the coast is now done by motorized junks. Although China now has shipyards specializing in the construction of trawlers, drifters and seine fishing boats, the main concentration during these years has been on the conversion of junks. A trawler costs 500 000 *yuan* to build and requires a highly skilled crew to work it, whereas a junk can be mechanized for 50 000 *yuan* and, apart from the need of a trained mechanic, already has its trained crew. These mechanized junks can fish over a wider range and for a longer season than the sailing junk. Nevertheless, quite recently modern trawler and drifter

fleets have been built up, having Shanghai, Talien and Tsingtao as their bases, which ports also have processing plants and icemaking and cold storage facilities. In 1963 Shanghai shipyards built China's first whaler, which has been operating in the Yellow and East China Seas[53].

Fishermen, operating individually or in small groups as they generally do, and dealing in a very perishable commodity, are especially vulnerable to exploitation by the middleman and need protection. As in Hong Kong, where the Government has initiated and built up a strong fishing cooperative, so in China the well-being of the fishing community has been fostered. Sea-fishing cooperatives and communes have been established all along the coast, giving a security formerly lacking and resulting in a correspondingly increased output. They have been encouraged to make their homes on land rather than on their boats and to develop subsidiary occupations in agriculture and animal husbandry. Fishing communes in the Chusan Islands, one of China's leading fishing grounds, are reported to have sold 87 000 tons of fish to the State in May 1967[54].

The only notable fish import into China is shark's fin, the necessary ingredient for the famous soup, which appears on the menu of most Chinese feasts.

Fish thousands metric tons

	1970	1971	1972	1973	1974
Total	6255	6880	6880	6880	6880
Fresh Water	4153	4568	4568	4568	4568
Marine	2102	2312	2312	2312	2312

Figures from *Statistical Year Book for Asia and the Pacific*, U.N. 1975

Freshwater fishing

Freshwater fishing in China can be divided into two categories, the fish taken from its many rivers and natural lakes, and those taken from artificial ponds.

All China's great rivers, notably the Yangtze, the Sikiang and the Sungari, abound in fish, but not to the same extent as the middle Yangtze, its lakes, the Tungting and Poyang, and the lakes in the plain of Hupeh. Here the main catches are grass carp, snail carp, silver carp, big head (the delicious mandarin fish), anchovy, anadromous reeves and also the famous small ice fish, which is only a few centimetres long.

Of the inland lakes, Ulyungur Nor, North Dzungaria, is famous for its fish, which, with the development of communications, are beginning to find an easier market. Koko Nor (lake Tsinghai), China's largest lake, has a unique scaleless species of edible carp. Neither the Mongolians nor the Tibetans living along its shores have been fish eaters and only recently has fishing been developed.

All the big new reservoirs resulting from dam-building are being stocked. Sinankiang reservoir, Chekiang, China's biggest man-made lake, has been stocked with 35 million fish fry of 60 different species. There are now eight breeding grounds around the reservoir, three fishing fleets, a tool and repair factory, a fishing research centre and cold storage with a capacity of 20 000 tons.

The main fishing methods are with net, using

Increase in the Output of Major Products

	Steel (thousand tons)	Pig iron (thousand tons)	Coal (thousand tons)	Electric power (million kWh)	Crude petroleum (thousand tons)
1949	158	252	32 430	4 310	121
1950	606	978	42 920	4 550	200
1951	896	1 448	53 090	5 750	305
1952	1 349	1 929	66 490	7 260	436
1953	1 774	2 234	69 680	9 200	622
1954	2 225	3 114	83 660	11 000	789
1955	2 853	3 872	98 300	12 280	966
1956	4 465	4 826	110 360	16 590	1 163
1957	5 350	5 936	130 000	19 340	1 458
1958	11 080 (8 000)	13 690 (9 530)	270 000	27 530	2 264

Note. The figures for the output of steel and pig iron in 1958 include steel and iron produced by indigenous methods. The figures within parentheses do not include steel and iron produced by indigenous methods.

	Cement (thousand tons)	Timber (thousand cu. m)	Sulphuric acid (thousand tons)	Soda-ash (thousand tons)	Caustic soda (thousand tons)
1949	660	5 670	40	88	15
1950	1 410	6 640	49	160	23
1951	2 490	7 640	149	185	48
1952	2 860	11 200	190	192	79
1953	3 880	17 530	260	223	88
1954	4 600	22 210	344	309	115
1955	4 500	20 930	375	405	137
1956	6 390	30 840	517	476	156
1957	6 860	27 870	632	506	198
1958	9 300	35 000	740	640	270

	Chemical fertilizers (thousand tons)	Penicillin (kg)	Metal-cutting machine tools (number)	Power machinery (thousand h.p.)	Electric motors (thousand kW)
1949	27	—	1 582	10	61
1950	70	—	3 312	11	199
1951	129	—	5 853	26	225
1952	181	46	13 734	35	639
1953	226	593	20 502	144	918
1954	298	2 189	15 901	172	957
1955	332	7 829	13 708	247	607
1956	523	14 037	25 928	657	1 069
1957	631	18 266	28 000	690	1 455
1958	811	72 607	50 000	2 000	6 052

lights at night, with trap, sometimes using otters to drive the fish, and with cormorants.

Fish breeding in artificial ponds has been practised for very many years. Most Chinese villages, particularly those in the centre and south, follow a common pattern of lay-out. Those in the plains are usually built on slightly higher ground above their fields, often with a small grove of trees above them, thus ensuring the proper *feng shui*. Immediately below the village is the pond, which receives garbage and sewage. This pond is generally stocked with fish, which are given the most rudimentary care.

Distinct from this rough fish breeding, the output from which is not very great, is the pisciculture in ponds made exclusively for the purpose and carried out carefully and intensively. This manner of fish culture, although practised before 1949, has grown with considerable rapidity everywhere since the formation of cooperatives and communes, especially in the Yangtze and Si-kiang basins. In some communes in Kwangtung the ponds cover several hundred hectares. The ponds must be well constructed and about $1\frac{1}{4}$ m deep to guard against loss during the summer heat. Usually they are dug deeper at one end; this

	Power-generating equipment (thousand kW)	Locomotives	Motor vehicles	Merchant vessels (thousand dwt. tons)	Tractors	Combine harvesters
1952	—	20	—	16	—	—
1953	—	10	—	35	—	—
1954	—	52	—	62	—	—
1955	—	98	—	120	—	3
1956	—	184	1 654	104	—	22
1957	198	167	7 500	54	—	124
1958	800	350	16 000	90	957	545

	Cotton yarn (thousand bales)	Cotton cloth (million m)	Paper (thousand tons)	Rubber footwear (thousand pairs)	Bicycles (thousand units)
1949	1 800	1 890	228	28 900	14
1950	2 410	2 520	380	45 670	21
1951	2 680	3 060	492	65 060	44
1952	3 620	3 830	539	61 690	80
1953	4 100	4 690	667	76 360	165
1954	4 600	5 230	842	85 840	298
1955	3 970	4 360	839	97 450	335
1956	5 250	5 770	998	103 480	640
1957	4 650	5 050	1 221	128 850	806
1958	6 100	5 700	1 630	182 360	1 174

	Cigarettes (thousand crates)*	Edible vegetable oil (thousand tons)	Sugar (thousand tons)	Salt (thousand tons)	Aquatic products (thousand tons)
1949	1 600	444	199	2 985	448
1950	1 848	607	242	2 464	912
1951	2 002	731	300	4 346	1 332
1952	2 650	983	451	4 945	1 666
1953	3 552	1 009	638	3 569	1 900
1954	3 728	1 066	693	4 886	2 293
1955	3 567	1 165	717	7 535	2 518
1956	3 907	1 076	807	4 940	2 648
1957	4 456	1 100	864	8 277	3 120
1958	4 750	1 250	900	10 400	4 060

* One crate contains 50 000 cigarettes

Ten Great Years, compiled by the State Statistical Bureau, Foreign Language Press, Peking, 1960

assists in harvesting and also provides a haven for the fish in the event of drought. The strips of land between the ponds are often planted with mulberry in the southern provinces.

One of the difficulties facing this pond form of pisciculture has been the securing of adequate supplies of fish fry. Until 1958 it was not possible to rear fish fry in captivity. Supplies had come exclusively from the middle Yangtze and the Pearl river; this fish fry was exported in recent years by air to all parts of Southeast Asia. Experiments have been going on since 1921, but it was not until 1958 that the Aquatic Research Unit claimed success in breeding fish fry in captivity. This has been achieved by injecting hormones into female fish. The experiments claim that 70 per cent of the females spawn and that 80 per cent of the eggs hatch[55]. The cost is only a fraction of that for fish fry caught in the Pearl river or the Yangtze. The results are being popularized in other provinces.

The feed for the pond fish varies from province to province. Pig, cow and poultry dung, together with some night soil and bean cake is general. In Kwangtung silkworm pupae and sugar-cane leaves are used. The fertile silt from the pond bottom makes top-grade manure for rice, sugar-cane and mulberry growing.

Income from pond fisheries, when properly managed, is high. In the wheat–kaoliang lands of Shantung the income from each *mow* of water surface is roughly five times greater than from cropland[56]. In the double-cropping rice region of Kwangtung the proportion is not as high, but even in the New Territories of Hong Kong it is reckoned that one *mow* of pond is worth two of paddy. The output from Kwangtung's ponds was reported as 72 000 tons in 1964, a 40 per cent rise over 1962.

References

1 A. Feuerwerker, 'China's nineteeth-century industrialization', in C. D. Cowan (ed.), *The Economic Development of China* (London, 1964).
2 T. J. Hughes and D. E. T. Luard, op. cit.
3 D. H. Perkins, *Market Control and Planning in Communist China* (Cambridge, Massachusetts, 1966).
4 *Communiqué on Fulfilment of the National Economic Plan in 1956*, Peking, 1 August 1957.
5 A. Donnithorne, 'China's economic planning and industry', *China Quarterly*, **17** (January 1964).
6 K. R. Walker, op. cit.
7 Fang Chung, 'An economic policy that wins', *Peking Review*, **11** (1964).
8 Mao Tse-tung, *On Contradiction* (Peking, 1960).
9 R. M. Field, N. R. Lardy, J. P. Emerson, Industrial output by province in China 1949–73', *China Quarterly*, **63** (July 1975).
10 Y. L. Wu, *The Steel Industry in Communist China* (Stanford, Califormia, 1965).
11 J. S. Lee, op. cit.
12 G. B. Cressey, *Land of the 500 Million* (New York, 1955).
13 B. Crozier, 'China and her race for steel production', *British Iron and Steel Federation Quarterly Steel Review*, July 1959.
14 A. Rogers, 'Manchurian iron and steel industry', *Geographical Review*, **41** (1948).

15 R. Hsia, 'Changes in location of China's steel industry', *China Quarterly*, **17** (January 1964).
16 Colina MacDougall, 'City of steel', *Far Eastern Economic Review*, 11 November 1965.
17 Sun Ching-chih (ed.), *Economic Geography of East China Region* (Peking, 1961).
18 Sun Ching-chih (ed.), *Economic Geography of Southwest China* (Peking, 1960).
19 Sun Ching-chih (ed.), *Economic Geography of South China* (Peking, 1959).
20 *Far Eastern Trade*, April 1958.
21 NCNA, Nanking, 2 August 1965.
22 E. Balazs, op. cit.
23 M. Erselcuk, 'Iron and steel industry in China', *Economic Geography*, **32** (1956).
24 *People's Daily*, 5 March 1958.
25 K. P. Wang, 'Mineral resources of China with special reference to the non-ferrous metals', Geographical Review, **34** (1944).
26 Chang Kuei-sheng, op. cit.
27 NCNA, Peking, 4 June 1965.
28 J. Needham, 'Science and China's influence on the world', in R. Dawson (ed.), *The Legacy of China* (Oxford, 1964).
29 An Shih, 'Catch up with the world's advanced technical level', *Sheh-sheh Sou-ts'e* [*Current Events*], 6 March 1965.
30 *China Reconstructs*, November 1965.

31 Colina MacDougall, 'Production reports', *Far Eastern Economic Review*, 29 September 1966.
32 NCNA, Peking, 19 February 1966.
33 Kang Chao, 'Growth of the construction industry in Communist China', *China Quarterly*, **22** (1965).
34 NCNA, Peking, 21 February 1966.
35 NCNA, Peking, 31 March 1964.
36 *China Yearbook*, 1925.
37 Fei Hsiao-tung, op. cit.
38 NCNA, Wuhan, 27 September 1965.
39 NCNA, Lanchow, 4 July 1965.
40 NCNA, Peking, 24 May 1966.
41 NCNA, Shanghai, 21 November 1964.
42 NCNA, Sining, 7 October 1965.
43 *Peking Review*, **25** (1965).
44 NCNA, Huhehot, 8 September 1965.
45 NCNA, Peking, 22 July 1965.
46 NCNA, Nanchang, 4 December 1965.
47 *Ta-kung Pao*, Peking, 15 February 1965.
48 T'ien Ping, 'Tremendous changes in the handicraft industry in the past fifteen years', *Ta-kung Pao*, Peking, 9 October 1964.
49 NCNA, Nanking, 5 June 1965.
50 *Peking Review*, 17 March 1959.
51 NCNA, Shenyang, 22 May 1966.
52 NCNA, Foochow, 13 February 1966.
53 *China Reconstructs*, March 1965.
54 NCNA, Hangchow, 7 June 1967.
55 Tu Hsueh-hao, 'Breeding freshwater fish', *China Reconstructs*, June 1966.
56 *Peking Review*, **46** (1965).

10   Foreign Trade

With the exception of the period from 1840 to 1930, during which the Western Powers imposed an 'open door' policy on China, the Chinese Government has consistently had a controlling voice in its country's foreign trade.

Earliest trade was by caravan over the landward routes of the steppe, semi-desert and desert through the Jade Gate at Yumen. Goods carried by pack animal (camel, mule, horse, sheep and ass) were, of necessity, small in bulk and high in value. Exports from China during the Han dynasty (206 BC–AD 220) were almost entirely silk, destined for Roman consumption, while imports were mainly gold, silver, glass, amber and precious stones. During the T'ang dynasty (AD 618–907) there was considerable expansion of overseas trade with Japan, Korea and the Near East, centred at Yangchow on the lower Yangtze. Much of this trade was carried by Arab and Persian traders, who must have been quite numerous since it is recorded that several thousand Arab and Persian traders were killed in a riot in Yangchow in AD 760[1]. By the eleventh century the commodities handled were much more varied. Exports included textiles (mainly silk), porcelain, tea, copper and precious metals; imports included incense, perfumes, spices, pearls, ivory, coral, amber, agates and crystals[2].

Western interest in China was aroused during the thirteenth and fourteenth centuries by the reports of returning travellers from the Far East, notable among whom were Marco Polo and Ibn Battuta. This interest was further stimulated by the voyages of discovery of Diaz and Vasco da Gama, opening a new route to India and the Far East. The Portuguese were the first westerners to establish any kind of a trade footing in China. In 1557, they were allowed by the Chinese emperor to erect 'factories' on the peninsula of Macau. These 'factories' were actually small enclosures or compounds in which they built living quarters and warehouses. Close on the heels of the Portuguese came British, Dutch and French traders all eager to start business.

At much the same time, i.e. from the fall of Kazan (1552) until the death of Peter the Great (1725), the Russians carried through a vast colonial expansion in Siberia, bringing Russia into trading communication with China on its northern borders. By the Treaties of Nerchinsk (1689) and Kiakhta (1727) strict rules of trade between the two countries were laid down, permitting 200 Russian traders to enter Chinese territory at Kiakhta once every three years for a period of 80 days. The main commodities exchanged were furs and later woollen broadcloth from Russia, and silk, porcelain and brick tea from China.

A similar strict governmental control was exercised over trade with westerners in the south. Trade here was conducted from Canton and Canton alone. Here, in 1702, a foreign trade monopoly was set up, supervised by a Chinese minister, called the Hoppo, through whose hands all foreign trade had to pass. This organization was superseded in 1720 by a guild of thirteen Chinese merchants, the *co-hong* appointed by the

Chinese Government. Each foreign merchant was assigned to one of the Chinese merchants through whom he had to conduct all his business. Most of the trade was in British hands, conducted by the East India Company. The main goods handled were opium, woollen broadcloth and some furs in exchange for Chinese silk, porcelain and tea, which, unlike the brick tea supplied to the Russians, was of high quality[3].

Western merchants, full of energy and initiative, found this method of trading was restricting and frustrating, but the Chinese Court and Government was really not interested in foreign trade. Some idea of its attitude to traders and its condescending attitude to all barbarians can be gained from the following extract from Emperor Ch'ien Lung's edict in dismissing the British Government's mission under Lord Macartney in 1793[4]:

> The Celestial Empire, ruling all within the four seas, simply concentrates on carrying out the affairs of Government properly, and does not value rare and precious things. Now you, O King, have presented various objects to the throne, and mindful of your loyalty in presenting offerings from afar, we have specially ordered the Yamen to receive them. In fact, the virtue and power of the Celestial Dynasty has penetrated afar to the myriad kingdoms, which have come to render homage, and so all kinds of precious things from 'over mountain and sea' have been collected here, things which your chief envoy and others have seen for themselves. Nevertheless we have never valued ingenious articles, nor do we have the slightest need of your country's manufactures.

This attitude and the restrictions led to much ill-feeling and a great deal of corruption and smuggling. In the early decades of the nineteenth century the opium trade grew to vast proportions, so much so that it was causing a drain of silver from China. When, in 1840, Chinese officials, on orders from Peking, clamped down on the opium trade and confiscated and destroyed 20 000 chests of opium in Canton, war broke out between China and Great Britain. In this war, known as 'The Opium War', China was defeated. Peace was concluded by the Treaty of Nanking in 1842 and marks the beginning of the breakdown of Chinese isolationism and a revolutionary change in foreign trade organization.

The terms of this treaty, although concluded with Great Britain, basically affected all foreign countries. It forced China to open five of her ports, Shanghai, Amoy, Canton, Foochow and Ningpo to foreign trade. 'Most favoured nation' treatment on the basis of the 'open door', was accorded to all. Under the so-called Tientsin Treaties of 1858, after the 'Arrow' war, China was forced to open the Yangtze to steam navigation of ships flying foreign flags, and 'concessions', i.e. areas of land leased to foreign nations in which their own government and laws were administered, were granted. Along the Yangtze these concessions were at Hankow, Changsha, Chungkian, Kiukiang, Wuhu, Nanking and Chinkiang and along the east coast at Suchow, Hangchow, Newchwang, Tientsin, Tsinan and Weihsien. Michie, writing in 1864, comments on the contrasting ways between the north and south by which trade with China was furthered[4]:

> The Russians have won their way into China by quiet and peaceful means, while we have always been running our head against a stone wall and never could get over it without breaking it down. The Russian meets the Chinese as Greek meets Greek; craft is encountered with craft; politeness with politeness and patience with patience. They understand each other's character thoroughly because they are so closely alike.

With the opening of the treaty ports foreign trade increased very rapidly in volume and in variety. The Yangtze ports fed Shanghai with the vast resources of raw material of the basin and contributed to Shanghai's rise from an insignificant town in 1840 to the sixth port of the world in the early twentieth century. The main items in China's overseas trade in 1923 were:

Foreign Trade 1923

Main imports	HK Taels* (thousands)
Cotton goods (excl. yarn)	131 886
Rice	98 199
Kerosene oil	58 292
Raw cotton	53 816
Sugar	51 998
Metal and minerals	44 938
Cotton yarn	41 634
Cigarettes	28 273
Flour	27 233
Machinery	26 678

* The Haikwan or Customs Tael equalled 583·3 grains of silver 1000 fine. It was entirely a money of account and had no coin representing it. In 1923 it was the equivalent of Mex. $1·50 or about 17½p.

Main exports	HK Taels (thousands)
Raw silk cocoons, etc.	154 351
Beans and products	127 338
Raw cotton	32 605
Skins, hides, furs	25 982
Silk piecegoods	24 542
Tea	22 905
Timber	21 301
Coal	20 545
Ground nuts	18 617
Wood oil	17 477

Although opium does not appear in the above figures, its use was considerable and its cultivation widespread at this time, when the country was divided and warlords were dominant. Poppy growing was often made compulsory by the local warlord, it being a profitable taxable commodity. Large quantities were also imported from Japan and Indo-China. Much of Yunnan's opium production was exported to Tongking and re-entered the country at ports along the east coast.

Foreign Trade Distribution 1923
HK Taels (millions)

	Imports into China	Exports from China	Total
Hong Kong	248	176	424
Japan	211	198	409
U.S.A.	154	127	281
Gt. Britain	120	43	163
India	55	12	67
France	7	40	47
Germany	32	12	44
Russia	10	33	43
Korea	12	30	42

While the volume of foreign trade fluctuated violently during the first half of the twentieth century, its composition remained fairly constant. Exports were almost entirely raw or semi-raw materials, and imports were largely manufactured articles. After the establishment of the Kuomintang regime in 1927 there was a marked rise in the number of Chinese commercial firms engaged in foreign trade at the expense of foreign business houses, a trend which continued until 1949.

The establishment of the People's Government in 1949 brought with it radical changes in the organization, direction and composition of China's foreign trade. Steps were taken immediately to eradicate the 'semi-colonial' and private capitalist bases of the trade. Both Chinese and foreign private traders were quickly eliminated, although foreign firms were compelled to keep their doors open and maintain their staffs for several unhappy years. All overseas commercial dealings were placed in the hands of the Minister of Foreign Trade under whom fourteen corporations now operate†. All these corporations have their headquarters in Peking, branches at the main ports and representatives abroad. In western Europe only two trade centres have been established, one in London and the other in Berne. China maintains a big trading organization in Hong Kong. As a consequence of this method of administering trade there is little or no contact between the ultimate buyer and seller. Contracts give inadequate security to the foreign exporter. The present terms give maximum protection to the Chinese side. 'There is a striking difference between the wording of their [the Chinese] contracts of purchase and of sale. The former binds the foreign seller very tightly, whilst the latter is in effect little more than a statement of intent.'[5] Nevertheless, because of the Chinese reputation of trading integrity and because the Chinese market holds such great potentials, trading with western capitalist nations persists and increases.

*Foreign Exchange Rate of Yuan**

Currency	Unit	Price in Yuan	
		Buying	Selling
£	100	430·42	432·58
U.S. $	100	183·51	184·43
French franc	100	41·30	41·50

* People's Bank of China, 31 December 1974.

The total volume of China's foreign trade was 2½ times greater in 1973 than in 1965.

The direction of China's foreign trade changed very rapidly between 1949 and 1951. Ever since Great Britain forced open the Chinese doors in 1840, Chinese trade had been orientated seaward and was mainly with Japan, U.S.A. and western

†Trade Corporations: Animal Byproducts; Cereals, Oils and Fats; Silk; Tea; Foodstuffs; Imports and Exports; Machinery; Metals; Minerals; Native Produce; Sundries; Transport Machinery; Technical Projects; Transport (forwarding, insurance, etc.).

Europe. After 1949 China once again turned her eyes landward through the Jade Gate. Her reasons for doing this were political and economic. She naturally turned to countries of like communist ideology from whom she could obtain long-term credit if necessary and who were willing and able to supply her with urgently needed capital equipment and complete industrial plant. Although trade with capitalist countries continued until the outbreak of the Korean War, 1950, it virtually ceased when the United Nations embargo was placed on most goods going into China. Trade with U.S.A. stopped completely and was not resumed until quite recently[6]. By October 1951, 77·9 per cent of China's exports were going to the U.S.S.R. and 70 per cent of her imports were coming from that country. Sino–Soviet trade was assisted and enhanced by U.S.S.R. loans and credits which were forthcoming until 1957. It should be noted that these loans were quickly repaid after 1960 and that from 1956 on China has contrived a constant favourable balance of trade even with the U.S.S.R.

The development and content of China's foreign trade can best be seen in the statistics which follow but it well to remember that foreign trade comprises only about four per cent of the gross national product. The decline in trade with countries of the Communist Bloc after the political rift with U.S.S.R. in 1960 is most marked, imports and exports falling to about one-third of their value between 1960 and 1965. Cuba alone among the members of this group showed any increase in trade. During the same period, trade with countries outside the Communist Bloc showed considerable increase. Agricultural raw materials continue to form the great bulk of Chinese exports, although the proportion is now less. This is due to the increase in made-up textiles and light industrial goods, such as enamel ware, leather goods, bicycles, sewing machines and light industrial plant.

Table 14   China's Foreign Trade 1960–74. Imports. (from F.E.E.R. Yearbooks)
(million U.S. $)

	1960	1961	1963	1965	1967	1970*	1974*
Communist Bloc							
U.S.S.R.	817·0	369·4	187·04	189·00	50·20	—	120
Cuba	32·0	95·6	72·74	97·30	—	—	—
E. Germany	87·4	49·6	10·03	—	—	—	—
Poland	50·1	26·6	19·32	—	28·55	—	—
Rumania	—	—	13·72	—	39·40	—	—
Czechoslovakia	—	—	9·31	—	19·00	—	—
Non-communist Bloc							
Japan	2·7	16·6	62·42	245·04	288·32	600	2085
Australia	23·5	161·5	202·06	167·76	200·50	140†	385†
Canada	9·0	120·9	97·20	97·50	85·56	—	154
W. Germany	5·4	30·5	15·40	78·96	206·00	200	482
U.K.	89·8	36·5	37·40	72·34	108·00	143	193
France	52·8	36·4	58·39	60·09	93·22	97	183
Italy	39·7	29·7	9·31	56·42	73·58	76	121
Hong Kong	21·0	1·4	12·24	12·56	8·37	5	20
Argentina	1·4	4·2	3·09	83·73	6·45	—	—
Pakistan	14·8	10·0	12·90	43·35	34·97	—	—
Egypt (U.A.R)	46·9	14·6	16·38	45·13	18·95	—	—
Ceylon	25·3	17·4	21·13	36·12	31·53	—	—
Indonesia	35·4	36·4	34·00	—	—	—	—
Malaya	—	3·8	5·40	—	21·9	50	—
Singapore	—	—	—	—	31·32	—	—
U.S.A.	—	—	—	—	—	—	967

* U.S. Congress Joint Economic Committee: China: Assessment of the economy Washington, 1975
† Includes N.Z.

hang Shan, Funiu Shan and Shantung, which are better drained and are the sites of early civilization on the plain. The less well drained regions nearer the coast are often marshy and saline.

After it emerges from its gorges between Tung-kwan and Sanmen and reaches the plain, the Hwang-ho becomes a slow-flowing, meandering river, which fills only a small part of its wide, shallow bed during the dry winter, but with the summer rains is transformed into a fast-moving leviathan, full of menace. Some idea of this change in regime can be gleaned from the figures of discharge, which record a maximum flow of 25 000 cu metres per sec and a minimum of only 245 cu metres p.s.[9] Such variation in volume between summer and winter has led to constant inundation, which in fact has built up the plain over which it flows. Chinese history records more than 1500 inundations in the last 3000 years and 26 changes in course, 9 of which were of a major nature. Up to 602 BC the Hwang-ho flowed north and found an outlet near to present Tientsin. It then made a drastic change and flowed out to the Yellow Sea south of the Shantung Peninsula and there it remained until AD 70 when it took up a course much along its present bed. Between AD 1048 and 1324 the Hwang-ho moved back to its earlier lines and flowed out again near Tientsin, after which it again found its outlet south of Shantung. In 1851 the Hwang-ho turned north and flowed into the Po-hai. In 1938, when the Japanese invaded the heart of China, the Kuomintang Government deliberately cut the southern banks of the river in the hope of checking the enemy advance. About 54 000 sq km of land in the northern Hwai basin were flooded, resulting in the death of nearly 900 000 people. The river was thus turned south of Shantung once again. It was returned to its former northern course in 1947 as a result of United Nations action.

Endeavours to control this unruly river have been an important function of Chinese government all through the centuries. Unhappily Li Ping's advice, 'Keep low the dykes, keep deep the channels' has not been followed here, and reliance has been placed exclusively on dyke building. These dykes have not been built as one concerted scheme but piece-meal, locality by locality. Generally their constructors have favoured building the dykes 8–12 km apart, thus allowing the river plenty of room with the idea that when it was in spate it would be accommodated. The trouble has been that, even if this has been achieved without the

dykes breaking, the river is very slow and consequently deposits much of its load of silt on the bed. As time has gone on the bed has been continually raised in this way and this, in its turn, has necessitated constant raising of the dykes, with a result

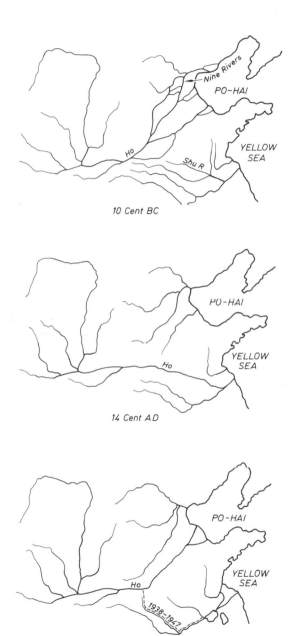

Fig. 103   Some changes in the course of the Hwang-ho

that today the bed of the river stands higher than the surrounding country. As one approaches the river, it looks like an endless, uniform range of low hills. The dangers of such a situation are not hard to see. If, through laziness on the part of the local farming community or through political unrest, the dykes are allowed to fall into disrepair or there is an exceptional summer spate and a breach is made, then the ensuing flood is doubly serious. The country around is inundated to a greater or lesser degree and the season's crops destroyed, but worse, when the spate is over and the level of the river falls, the flood waters cannot return to the old bed. They have to find a new line of drainage; and hence the river may make one of its periodic changes of course. It is significant that, because of the raised bed, the Hwang-ho receives no tributaries below Kaifeng, the point below which most changes of course have taken place. The cost in human loss of life and suffering through the centuries has been enormous. The cost in material loss each year – loss of harvest, ruined fields, and so on – is staggering. Flood spells famine and disease. The river richly deserves the stigma attaching to its name 'China's Sorrow'.

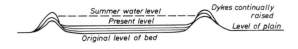

This building up of the river's bed above the surrounding plain can better be appreciated when the summer load of the river is examined. It is no exaggeration to say that it leaves the gorges at Sanmen like a thick, yellow soup. The Chinese have a saying that 'If you fall into the Hwang-ho you never get clean again'. The average silt concentration per cubic metre is 34 kg as compared

with 10 kg in the Colorado, 4 kg in the Amu Darya and 1 kg in the Nile. It is estimated that the load carried annually is 415 billion cu. m and that 40 per cent of this is deposited in the river bed, while 60 per cent reaches the seaboard. Nearly 90 per cent of this silt comes from the loess region and enters the main river between Hokow and Shanhsien, figures which give some idea of the seriousness of soil erosion in Shansi and Shensi, where an average of 3700 tons of soil is carried away annually from every square kilometre of land. This is 27 times greater than the world average. The reaches above Hokow contribute only 10·9 per cent of the total load.

The problem of conservation of the Hwang-ho is further complicated by the nature of its rainfall. At least four-fifths of the precipitation over its middle and lower basins fall in the four summer months, resulting in a great change in the river's summer and winter levels. The rain often falls in torrents, which accentuates its erosive power, particularly in the loess region. To add a further complication, this is the area with the greatest annual variability of rainfall, giving it its notoriety as the most famine-prone part of China.

It was with such factors as these in mind that the State Council commissioned the Hwang-ho Conservancy Committee to examine and report on the control of the river. With the help of considerable Soviet technical assistance, it carried out a very extensive geological and geographical survey and presented its report to the First National People's Congress on 18 July 1955 under the title 'Report on the Multi-purpose Plan for Permanently Controlling the Yellow River and Exploiting its Water Resources'.

The scheme, as its title implies, has several purposes in view. The main objective is the control of the Hwang-ho's flow, thereby stopping flooding; it also aims at providing ample irrigation water and thus greatly increasing agricultural production throughout the basin. The generation of

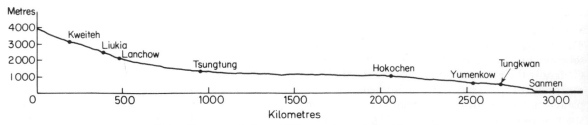

Fig. 104   Section of the middle reaches of the Hwang-ho

hydro-electric power is intended to assist irriga-tion works and also provide industrial power wherever large dams are built. Finally, it is pro-posed eventually to make the river navigable for vessels of 500 tons from its mouth to Lanchow. The planners have concentrated attention on the middle reaches of the river lying between Kweiteh in eastern Tsinghai and Sanmen in Honan. The whole plan is expected to take 50 years to complete.

The main feature of the comprehensive plan is, in the words of the report, 'what we call the Staircase Plan for the Yellow River. By this we mean a plan to build a series of dams on the main river so that the levels form a sort of staircase. This plan divides the middle reaches of the river – from the Lungyang Gorge above Kweiteh in Tsinghai to Taohwayu at Chengkao in Honan – into four sections and utilizes each of them in keeping with its special characteristics.'

The top step or level of the staircase is from the Lungyang Gorge to Tsungtung, near Wuchung; the second from Tsungtung to Hokochen; the third from Hokochen to Yumenkow; the fourth from Yumenkow to Taohwayu. In other words, it is utilizing the four natural divisions we have noted above. Within these sectors, the planners envisage constructing four great multi-purpose projects, to be built by the central government. These are to be supported by forty-four secondary dams, under-taken by the central and local authorities together, and these, in their turn, are to be supplemented by thousands of minor dams and works, which are the responsibility of the *hsiens* and communes alone. Two further secondary dams on the plain below Taohwayu are planned.

When the plan is completed there will be two great multi-purpose dams in the top level, one in the Lungyang Gorge at Kweiteh and the other at Liukia. That at Kweiteh is intended to serve Sinang and eastern Tsinghai and that at Liukia, Lanchow and district. The dam at Liukia has already been completed, forming a reservoir of 4900 millin cu. m. It is capable of reducing the maximum flow of the river from 8330 cu. m/sec to 5000 cu. m/sec. It has a 107 m high head of water and a hydro-electric capacity of 1 million kW and an annual average output of 6600 million kWh. Because it is sited in a sparsely populated area the formation of the reservoir has necessitated the resettlement of only 27 000 people.

The dam at Tsungtung and the secondary dams between it and Hokochen – the section with a very gentle gradient – are intended to serve mainly irrigation and drainage works and to improve navigation.

It should be noted that no large multi-purpose project is planned in the third, i.e. loess sector from Hokochen to Yumenkow. The engineers and geologists have decided that 'for geological and geographical reasons the building here of large dams and reservoirs is impracticable'.[10] Below Yumenkow the river valley becomes much broader, but at the confluence of the Wei and the Hwang at Tungkwan the course turns sharply east and again enters gorges. At the eastern end of these is the Sanmen Gorge, which was chosen as the site for the biggest and most important of the multi-purpose projects. At this point two rocky islets stand in the middle of the river, dividing it into three gateways, known as 'The Gate of Man', 'The Gate of the Gods' and 'The Gate of Ghosts'. These three passages have been closed by a dam 90 m high. The resulting reservoir, when full, will have a head of water 350 m above sea-level and will have a capacity of 36 000 million cu. m, second only in size to the Kuibyshev reservoir. The lake extends as far north as Lintsin on the Hwang-ho and to the west of Tali on the Wei-ho. This is a very densely populated region. When the reservoir is full it will necessitate the resettlement of 600 000 people, but during the first phase only half that number has had to be moved.

The Sanmen Dam is clearly the most important contributor to the whole conservancy scheme. Its most important function is the control of the summer flood waters as they issue onto the plain. It is estimated that the reservoir itself can reduce the heaviest imaginable flow from 37 000 cu. m/sec to 8000 cu. m/sec. 'If ever extraordinary floods occur at Sanmen Gorge and in the Yi-ho, South Lo-ho and Chin-ho, tributaries of the Yellow river east of the Sanmen Gorge, the locks at Sanmen Gorge can be closed to hold back all flood waters from above the gorge for four days.'[10] The reservoir is also called upon to step up the flow of water to the North China Plain during the winter months, thus raising the level for irrigation and maintaining an adequate level for navigation.

The Sanmen was planned to have a hydro-electric capacity of 1 million kW with an average annual output of 9800 million kWh, providing power for the industries of Loyang, Chengchow, Sian and Kaifeng. The plans and machinery were to be provided by U.S.S.R. Most unfortunately, disagreements and tensions between Soviet Russia and China arose before the installation of this machinery was completed, with a result that

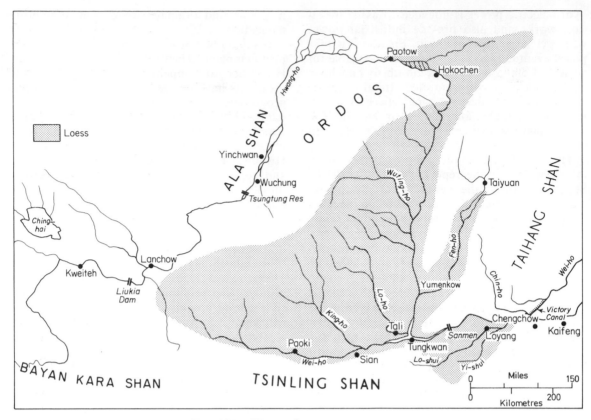

Fig. 105   Hwang-ho water conservancy

Russian plans and technicians were withdrawn and this side of the project has not yet been finished, a great disappointment and handicap and not the least of the reasons for the continuing ill-feeling between the two countries.

Several of the 44 secondary projects have been completed. It is difficult to ascertain the precise number. Notable dams have been built on the Wei-ho at Paoki Gorge, where 113 000 hectares are now irrigated with the help of the power developed at the dam. There is another on the Wutung-ho, right-bank tributary of the Hwang-ho in the heart of the loess. A big dam has been built on the King-ho, left-bank tributary of the Wei, forming the Tafowszu reservoir, which has a storage capacity of 1500 million cu. m, generates 20 000 kW and irrigates 216 000 hectares.

However, attention has been focused less on these secondary dams, which are built as joint projects of central and local authorities, than on

the small efforts, which rely entirely, or almost entirely, on commune manpower, capital and initiative. The Report called for the construction of '215 000 works to protect the heads of gullies, 638 000 check dams, 79 000 silt-precipitation dams and small irrigation projects to water 4·76 million *mow* of farmland, build 300 earth dams across gullies and repair 4300 km of roads in gully areas.'[10] It is this local work that has been pursued so energetically in the loess region during the autumn and winter months by commune, brigade and production teams. Emphasis has been placed on soil retention. Small dams are built and small reservoirs formed, which, when filled with silt, as they quickly are, are turned over to cultivation and other dams built. Such is the immense silt load which descends each year that, until the supporting projects of afforestation, grassing, terracing and irrigation have become widespread and firmly established, the life of even the large reservoirs is likely to be short, as the Report admits:

> The Sanmen Gorge reservoir will last 50 to 70 years – perhaps even longer – thanks to its large storage capacity, the silt-detaining dams on the tributaries of the river and, above all, to the work on water and soil conservation in the middle reaches. By that time, as a result of a series of other measures, the disasters brought by the Yellow river will have been greatly reduced. As for the difficulties that may arise in power generating, irrigation and navigation as a result of silting up of the reservoir, they will be comparatively easy to deal with.[11]

The cost of the first phase of the whole project up stream from Sanmen was scheduled at £780 million.

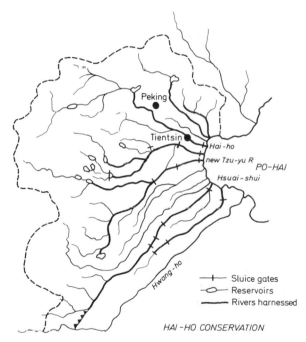

Fig. 106   The 'nine courses of Yu' (see Peking Review, *no. 39, 27 September 1974)*

Flood-prevention measures below the Sanmen dam consist of control of the Lo shui and Yi shui, right-bank tributaries and the Chin-ho, left-bank tributary of the Hwang-ho. This control is in the form of dams, reservoirs and quite extensive irrigation works in their upper reaches. It should be noted that these three rivers are the last to join the Hwang-ho, which, for the next 1000 km, meanders across the plain to empty into the shallow and rapidly filling Po-hai.

In the middle 1950s the Victory Canal was cut, linking the Hwang-ho to the Wei-ho (not to be confused with the Wei-ho of Shensi and Kansu). The Wei-ho is a tributary of the Nanyun-ho, whose lower reaches, below Lintsing, have been canalized and form the final stretch of the Grand Canal. By means of the Victory Canal some water can be diverted into the Wei in time of need.

Since 1949 a great deal of work has been devoted to building, repairing and strengthening the dykes along the banks of the Hwang-ho. At particular danger spots, the dykes have been raised and faced with stone. Care has also been given to the extermination of burrowing animals, such as foxes, which have done much to weaken the dykes in times past.

The group of nine rivers in the northern half of the North China Plain, which the legendary Yu is reported to have subdued more than 3000 years ago, has been giving trouble continually over the last 600 years during which it is reported to have flooded no less than 383 times. In 1939 Tientsin was under water for a whole month. Virtually the entire river system of Hopeh drains eastward from the Taihang Shan and Wutai Shan and unites with the Hai-ho in a single outlet, through Tientsin, to the sea at Tangku. These rivers, so prone to flood in summer, often run nearly dry in spring, just when water is most needed for seedlings.

A good deal of work to rectify matters was carried out between 1949 and 1963 and new concerted schemes have been going on since 1964 under the name of the 'Heilungkiang' project. Scores of reservoirs have been built in the upper reaches of the rivers, extensive river-dredging operations have been carried out and a new outlet for Paiyangtien Hu has been cut. It is reported that 400 000 commune members were engaged on this work in the slack winter season of 1965–66[11]. The accompanying map shows the progress made by 1974.

Flood control of this plain has been greatly helped by the construction of the Kwantung Dam in the Western Hills on the Yungting-ho to the northwest of Peking. The Yungting joins the Hai-ho a few kilometres above Tientsin and, until this big earth dam was built, contributed its unwelcome summer quota. The dam is 45 m high and has a capacity of nearly 3000 million cu. m. In addition to flood prevention, it provides drinking water and hydro-electric power for Peking, and irrigation water for 1·3 million hectares[12]. Flood control has been further assisted by the construction of a conduit from the Miyun reservoir, 65 km northeast of Peking[13].

Any project involving the formation of large reservoirs and the inundation of large tracks of land on the North China Plain will also involve problems of human resettlement, for here is the greatest congregation of farming communities in the world. The North China Plain, which is almost identical in extent with Lossing Buck's winter wheat–kaoliang area, covers about 388 500 sq km of which some 70 per cent or 272 000 sq km are cultivated. The population of the plain is over 100 million, of which approximately 80 per cent are engaged in agriculture. In many rural districts there are some 400 persons per square kilometre of cultivated land but considerably less in the saline areas near the coast. The population is very widely dispersed throughout the plain in hamlets and villages. Here and there are larger market towns, usually walled. These walls are now largely being pulled down and the material used for road making and building. The people are almost entirely Han Jen with a few Manchus, now indistinguishable from the rest, scattered amongst them. The northerner is a taller, slower, more stolid person than his T'ang countryman in the south.

Even before 1949 this was a region of larger fields and larger farms than farther south, although not so large as those of the loess region. The average size of fields in the North China Plain was $\frac{1}{2}$ hectare as compared with 0·07 ha in the rice–tea area south of the Yangtze and 0·05 ha in the double-cropping rice area of Kwangtung. Farms, too, were larger, averaging 2 ha and were very much larger than this in the poorly drained and saline areas. Farm ownership here was much more general than in the south. Standards of production and of living were generally higher here than in other areas north of the rice-growing line. Although the basis of production has changed from individual ownership and enterprise to communes and a socialist economy and, although in most villages communal kitchens and schools, etc., have been built, the general appearance of the villages has not changed appreciably. Villagers continue to live in the same simple, mud-brick houses with their brick stove beds and their walled courts or yards.

The main crops cultivated are winter wheat, millet, kaoliang, barley, soy-bean, corn, sweet potatoes, peanuts, and a large variety of vegetables, including cabbage, turnip, onions, garlic, radishes, cucumbers, spinach, string beans, peas, melons and squashes. Until recently about 39 per cent of the cultivated land was double-cropped. The main summer crops are sweet potatoes, peanuts and soy-beans, which occupy about 60 per cent of the land, millet 30 per cent and vegetables 10 per cent. Winter wheat and barley are grown from November to June, or the land may be left fallow through lack of fertilizer since farms are lightly stocked and farmyard manure is scarce. Generally speaking, before 1949 the poorer the family the more sweet potatoes were grown and the less wheat.

Wheat is a good cash crop but is harder to grow and requires more cultivation and more manure than sweet potatoes. The land is ploughed and fed in late August and September as soon as the summer crop of soy-beans, millet or sweet potatoes has been harvested. By the end of November the shoots are strong. If at this time there is a heavy snowfall there is great rejoicing, especially at Chinese New Year, for the snow provides a protective cover for the crop during the bitter cold of January and February. Harvesting is done at about the June festival of Tuan Wu (Double Fifth), i.e. 5th day of the 5th month.

Foxtail millet and kaoliang are the main summer cereals and together with sweet potatoes they provide the staple food of the country folk. All three crop heavily, and as all three stand up to drought conditions well, they give some security against the failure of the winter wheat. Peanuts, which are an alternative crop to sweet potatoes, are sown in May. They need a sandy soil and dry weather. Harvesting takes place in October when the plant is deeply hoed, and the vines are lifted as a whole with the shells still clinging.

Marketing facilities on the North China Plain have been better than in other parts of China. The dirt-mud roads or tracks over the flat land have made communication easier than in the hilly or mountainous west and south. Moreover, railway communications had their earliest development over the Plain.

While the land and climate, the hardworking, tough peasantry and, to a large extent also, their crops have remained the same, big changes have taken place in organization and farming technique since 1949. The flat or undulating plain lends itself readily to the kind of amalgamation that has taken place under the cooperatives, collectives and communes. Fields, the average size of which was about half a hectare, are now often 20 hectares and more. This increase in the size of fields makes possible the economic use of farm machinery. It is here on the North China Plain that mechanization is being given priority.

Irrigation, which was practised on not more than 10 per cent of the Plain, has now been greatly extended largely by sinking thousands of wells and by the construction of local earth dams. The emphasis which is now laid on the greater use of chemical fertilizer is resulting in much less land being left fallow. The problem of graves has been tackled vigorously in the north. Lossing Buck estimated that at least 2 per cent of good arable land was devoted to ancestral graves. Often these graves were in the middle of the field, which was not only a waste of valuable land occupied by the grave itself but also rendered ploughing much more difficult. Now most of the graves have been removed to cemeteries on waste land. Another change is the greater use of women's labour in the fields. In many places on the North China Plain formerly it was customary that women's work in the fields should not begin until threshing of the winter wheat or barley. Since the formation of the communes, women have been working continuously throughout the year alongside the men.

The North China Plain is rich in imperial capitals. It includes within its borders the most ancient Chinese capital and three cities that, in their time, have been imperial capitals. The Great City Yin, the Shang capital, near Anyang, stood on the Hwang-ho when it flowed north, close to the Taihang edge, and found an outlet in the 'Nine Rivers' near presentday Tientsin. Loyang, now capital of the province of Honan, stands at the eastern end of the east–west gate of Tungkwan and was the imperial city of the Later Han emperors (AD 25–196). Today it has developed into an important industrial centre, specializing in car and tractor manufacture. Between AD 960 and 1127 Kaifeng was the imperial capital of the Northern Sung and was then called Pienking. We have seen that it was sited at the point from which most of the changes of course of the Hwang-ho have occurred. In consequence it is a point of some strategical importance. Movement along a north–south line east of Kaifeng is more difficult than to the west and therefore there is something of a bottleneck between Kaifeng and the Funiu Shan.

The third imperial seat of the plain, Peking, is a comparatively new city. It was first built by the Liao emperors (AD 937–1123) and named Yenching. When the Chin Tartars (Golden Horde) ousted the Liaos they adopted Yenching and renamed it Chung-tu. However, Peking did not attain true imperial status until the Chin in their turn were driven out by the Mongols in AD 1234 and the Yuan dynasty was founded. Kublai Khan began to build the city of Cambaluc, which means the Khan's City, near the old site. With a vast empire stretching right across Asia to Europe and the whole of China to the south, the importance of Peking as the governmental centre is abundantly clear. All subsequent governments, Ming and Ch'ing, Republic and People's Republic, have recognized this, and Peking has retained its status ever since, except for one short break between 1927 and 1949.

Peking is now the hub of a vast governmental and administrative machine whose controls reach out to all corners of the realm – to Tibet, Chinghai, Sinkiang, Heilung-kiang and to farthest Yunnan – with an intimacy and effectiveness never known before in China. Since its foundation it has always been one of the chief centres of education. Christian missions in the first half of this century played a prominent part in the promotion of western learning here by the creation of the PUMC (Peking Union Medical College) and Yenching University, which is now the campus of the National University of Peking. Since 1949 Peking has been the site of feverish new development in higher education, especially on the technical side. No fewer than 17 colleges and technical institutes, usually catering for about 5000 students each, have sprung up in the city's environs. The people of Peking have regained an acute consciousness of, and pride in, their historical heritage. All the architectural gems which have escaped the ravages and neglect of the last 40–50 years – notably the Forbidden City, the Summer and Winter Palaces, and the Temple and Altar of Heaven – have been renovated and are now museums, open to the public, which throngs to see them. Like most modern capital cities, Peking is rapidly developing as an industrial centre, having coalfields near at hand and now hydro-electric power from Kuanting.

Tientsin, which served as port for Peking and is now itself served by Ta-ku, has developed into a big industrial as well as a commercial centre.

1f. The Hwai Basin

The Hwai river, which is about 1100 km long, flows over a vast alluvial, lake-studded plain and

Plate 23   *The Temple of Heaven, Peking*
This, like the Forbidden City, is now in an excellent state of preservation and is open to the public

drains 174 000 sq km, more than two-thirds of which is under cultivation. There is no appreciable watershed between the Hwai and Hwang-ho on the north nor between the Hwai and the Yangtze in its lower delta reaches. There are, however, distinct differences between the Hwai and the Hwang-ho. We have seen that the latter receives no tributaries in its course across the plain. The Hwai receives a large number of long left-bank tributaries, rising in the Funiu Shan, all of which follow roughly a NW–SE direction and a lesser number of shorter right-bank tributaries in its upper reaches from the Ta Pieh Shan. The tributaries and the main river all drain into the Hungtze-hu, whence the waters have often found an indeterminate route to the Yellow Sea, and have even on occasion flowed south into the Yangtze. The Hwai is not so burdened with silt as the Hwang-ho since the Funiu Shan and Ta Pieh Shan from which it derives most of its water have comparatively little loess covering.

The Hwai Basin being farther south, the climate

is more equable than that of the North China Plain: winters are shorter, the growing period longer and the summer rains heavier. Nevertheless, the crops grown are more closely akin to those of the northern plain than of the Yangtze Basin. Winter wheat, millet and kaoliang are more characteristic than rice, and for this reason, if for no other, the Hwai and the lower Hwang-ho basins should be classed as one region.

The fact that two-thirds of the land is under crops proclaims how fertile a plain this is but, like the North China Plain, it is very subject to flood. The Hwai has not built up its bed above the surrounding level of the land as the Hwang-ho has done, yet most of the country is so low-lying that great stretches of the river have been dyked. In consequence, the same difficulty is experienced, although in a lesser degree than with the Hwang-ho, of returning the waters to the river bed after flooding.

Because of the devastation caused by the cutting of the Hwang-ho's banks in 1938 and its deflection

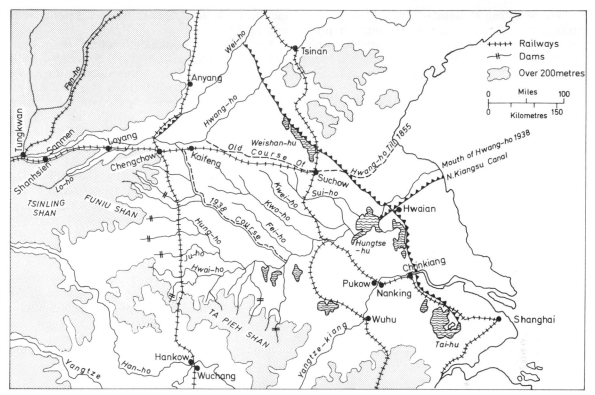

Fig. 107   The Hwai Basin

into the Hwai, the present government has given priority to water conservancy in this basin, even over the Hwang-ho.

Control of the upper reaches of the Hwai and its many tributaries came under comprehensive planning. In all, 27 reservoirs high up in the hills are contemplated. Between 1951 and 1957 seven of these were completed: at Paisha on the Hun river, Pankiao on the Nanhung, Shihmantan on the Peihung, Paishan on the Ju, Tapoling and Nanwan on the Hwai. These are all in the northwest or west and their dams are comparatively low, being between 30 and 35 metres high. Since 1957 three much larger dams on the southern tributaries have been built at Lungshan, Meishan and Futseling. The dam at Meishan is 85 metres high, has a storage capacity of 2000 million cu. m and irrigates 230 000 hectares[15]; that at Futseling is 70 metres high. All these works are multi-purpose and generate hydro-electric power to a greater or lesser extent.

Recently, further dams have been constructed on the southern right-bank tributaries and the whole coordinated into one of China's biggest water conservancy schemes, known as the Pi–Shih–Tang Irrigation system. This coordination was begun in 1958. By it, in 1959, 60 000 hectares were irrigated; by 1966 this figure had reached 306 000 hectares which were served by 2000 km of canals, together with countless auxiliaries. 80 000 hectares were added in the autumn and winter of 1965/66[16], and the work is continually being extended. As a result of these conservation works, the vast arable lands of the Hwai basin are much more secure from flood and drought than formerly[17]. Nevertheless, exceptional summer rains and typhoon visitation still can give rise to great anxiety.

The plain is crossed from north to south by the Peking–Tsinan–Suchow–Nanking–Shanghai railway line and the Peking–Chengchow–Hankow railway line. The Grand Canal, built by Kublai Kahn, fell into disrepair under the later Manchus and is now being dredged and largely rebuilt.

1g. The Shantung Peninsula

Although Shantung (Eastern Mountains) province physiographically belongs rather to the Liaotung peninsula and North Korea, it is convenient to deal with it in conjunction with the Hwang-ho as it is so intimately integrated with Chinese history and philosophy. It was here that early cultures flourished; here that the early emperors sacrificed to Shang-ti, Lord of Heaven; here that Chinese philosophy found its home; and here that Confucius was born and later buried. Here also was the home of the Kung dukes and it still is the home of their direct descendants. A further reason for including the Shantung Peninsula in the Hwang-ho basin is that it divides the North China Plain from the Hwai plain and is the bastion against which the Hwang-ho has shifted its course, now north, now south through the centuries.

The province consists of the denuded remains of an ancient mass of Archaean rocks, having a northeast–southwest trend. It is the southern extension of the East Manchurian Mountains of Liaotung, and is divided into two halves by a depression which runs from north to south. The eastern portion is made up mainly of Archaean schists and gneiss with some crystalline limestone. The western half, which is higher, is largely of carboniferous limestone and contains the main coal measures. It has been uplifted and very heavily faulted. W. Smith describes western Shantung as a shattered horst.[18] From the coalfields along its western border more than 10 million tons of bituminous coal were produced in 1944. Considerably more than this amount is now being mined. The country as a whole has a landscape of gentle upland. Its highest peak, Tai Shan, rises to a little over 1500 m and is one of China's five sacred mountains. Its slopes are covered with temples and monasteries. The thousands of pilgrims who visit it each year approach it from the city of Tai-an in the west.

The coast of the peninsula is precipitous, rocky and beautiful, but it is dangerous to shipping on account of the frequency of fogs. It has a number of excellent natural harbours which unfortunately have no extensive hinterland. Being so much enwrapped by the sea, its climate is rather more temperate and equable than that of the North China Plain.

Generally the soils on the hills are poor and thin, with the result that severe soil erosion has followed persistent deforestation. This has been met on the lower slopes by extensive stone-faced terracing.

The main population, which numbered 48 876 548 in the census of 1953, is second only to that of Szechwan. It is concentrated in the fertile valleys in a density which rivals that of Chengtu. The land is most intensively cultivated but yet is unable to sustain the numbers. Consequently this has been the region from which Manchuria has drawn its seasonal labour and, in more recent years, its main supply of colonists. Crops are similar to those of the North China Plain. In addition, sericulture has been important. Shantung silk is produced from worms whose food is largely oak leaves rather than mulberry.

Tsinan, the capital of the province, lies on the North China Plain to the west of the Tai Shan and near the banks of the Hwang-ho. Sited as it is in the coalfield, it is rapidly increasing in industrial importance. It is also a railway junction on the Peking–Shanghai railway line. A branch runs west to Wenhsien, thence southeast through the depression to Tsingtao on Kiaochow Bay.

In 1897 the murder of two German missionaries in Kiaochow was made the justification by Germany for the seizure of the region around the Bay. A treaty was signed handing over the land on a ninety-nine year lease. The area was then developed with great energy. A great deal of German capital was sunk in the construction of the port of Tsingtao, in afforestation which changed the landscape, and in building the branch railway mentioned above. Kiaochow Bay, which is 30 km long by 24 km broad, is not very deep and required a good deal of dredging. The Japanese took the port in 1914 at the beginning of the First World War after which time trade began to decline. The port was restored to China in 1922.

The main port on the north coast is Chefoo. This was opened to foreign shipping in 1862 after the signing of the 1858 treaty with Great Britain.

2. THE YANGTZE-KIANG BASIN

The Chinese words *ho* and *kiang* are both used for rivers of major proportions. When used without a prefixing word, *Ho* is taken to mean the Hwang-ho and *Kiang*, the Yangtze-Kiang. In fact the Hwang-ho in all early writings is referred to simply as *Ho*. As is often the case with great rivers, the Yangtze has different names for different reaches. The 1600 km or so from mouth to the gorges at

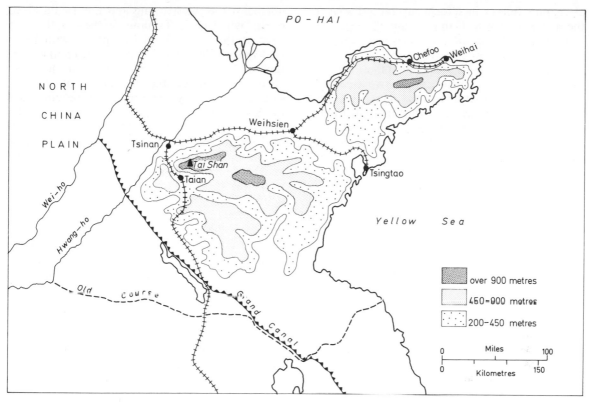

Fig. 108   Shantung

Ichang are known as the *Ch'ang-kiang* or Long River. From Ichang to Sui-fu it is called *Ch'uan-ho* and above this, in the torrential mountain course, the *Kin-sha-kiang* or the River of Golden Sand. It is 5590 km long and has a catchment basin of 1·85 million sq km, more than twice that of the Hwang-ho. It flows entirely south of the Tsinling line and consequently its basin contrasts strongly with that of the Hwang-ho. Both rivers have upper reaches in the Tibetan plateau, but once descended from there the Hwang-ho flows through desert and loess and a natural vegetation mainly consisting of prairie grass, while the Yangtze cuts its way through basin after basin of what was formerly dense temperate and subtropical forest.

The river can be divided conveniently and clearly into four main regions: the torrent course of the Tibetan highlands; the Red Basin of Szechwan; the huge middle basin of Hukwang, which embraces the entire area of Hupeh, Hunan and Kiangsi; and finally the deltaic region of Anhwei and Kiangsu.

2a. The upper reaches

It will be noted that the Kinsha-kiang, the Mekong (Lantsang in China) and the Salween (Nu-kiang in China) follow closely parallel north–south courses through the length of their passage in the mountainous eastern edge of Si-Kang. At one point only 50 km separates their beds. They cut deep narrow valleys or gorges of 600 m–1200 m deep. As often as not the rivers themselves alone fill the valley bottom. Their steep sides are heavily forested and the valley bottoms are hot, damp and malarious. The rivers are rapid and quite unnavigable.

Four different explanations of this parallelism have been advanced by reputable geologists and geomorphologists. Lee suggests that it is the result of parallel, consequent drainage following sag-lines on a fluted surface of warping; Heims, that it is the Himalayan revolution in Alpine folding; and Credner suggests that channels have developed along parallel belts of weak rock on a peneplain. A final suggestion is that of rifting along fault lines, which form natural spillways for the melt water of Si-Kang glaciers.[19]

These parallel mountain ranges and deep river beds form the borderland between Burma and China, and account for the fact that there has been so little intercourse between the two countries. China has made several attempts at the invasion of Burma in the course of its history but, even if successful, the conquest has been short-lived. Communication between the two countries is too difficult to maintain. Kublai Khan sent an expedition half a million strong to subdue Burma. He lost half his army by disease and exhaustion in crossing these malarious, forested parallel ranges of the border, Wise rulers, if they have concerned themselves at all with Burma, have been content with nominal submission and token tribute.

At approximately 27° N the Yangtze suddenly reverses its course to NNE and thenceforward zigzags its way in a series of transverse and longitudinal valleys in a general easterly direction for about 800 km, still flowing in gorges of a thousand metres or more deep, until it emerges into the Red Basin. In this section it receives a number of large left-bank tributaries which conform to the general north–south drainage pattern, but there are no tributaries of note coming in on the right bank. As a result of uplift in the west in the Middle Pliocene, the headwaters of a river (later to be known as the Yangtze) draining into the Red Basin cut back and captured the upper courses of the Red River and part of those of the Mekong[19] (see fig. 109). The effects of this dramatic river capture, bringing as it does a considerable additional flow to the Yangtze from the melting snowfields and glaciers of Si-Kang, are great, both geographically and economically.

Population in this region is very sparse. Hsi-fan hill tribes occupy the wider parts of river valleys in the Si-Kang mountains. Above Suifu (Ipin), in northwest Kweichow, the main concentration of the Lolo, earlier occupiers of Szechwan, is found.

2b. The Red Basin of Szechwan
The Yangtze emerges at Sui-fu from this rugged mountainous region which constitutes the western half of the huge province of Szechwan into the hilly, butte country, which characterizes the eastern part of Szechwan and which forms the Red Basin, so named by Richthofen. This basin has well-defined margins of fold mountains, raised at the end of the Cretaceous. On the north and northeast are the Mitsang and the Ta Pa Shan, behind which lie the Tsinling. To the west the steep edge of the Azure Wall Mountains with many peaks rising 5000 m and some to well over 6000 m, such as Minya Konka (7590 m) form the rather abrupt border of the Si-Kang plateau. The southern boundary is marked by the mountains of the Kweichow plateau.

From late Cretaceous times until probably the Middle Pliocene this basin formed a lake in which deep deposits of red sandstone were laid down on heavily folded limestone in which the Rhaetic coal measures lie. The red sandstone has since remained largely undisturbed by folding. The uplift in the west in the Middle Pliocene led to considerable rejuvenation and cutting back of the rivers, the capture of the headwaters of the Red river and to a big increase of inflow into the lake. It was probably at this time that the lake found its outlet to the east into the Middle Yangtze depression and so was drained.

The Basin itself slopes generally from about 1000 m in the north to 500 m in the south. The rivers, which conform to this slope, cut deeply into the soft red sandstone, often exposing the harder limestone and the coal measures. The Chinese characters for Szechwan are 四川, meaning Four Rivers, which are usually taken to be the Min, the Lu, the Fu and the Kialing. They all rise in the mountains of the north, and are fast-flowing and unnavigable except for junks and small river craft. Three rivers – the Fu, Kialing and Chu (Pai) – each have broader valleys of 30 km to 50 km width in their middle reaches, but the valley becomes much more constricted after the junction at Hochuan and remains so until their confluence with the Yangtze. The main river hugs the high ground to the south of the basin and flows fast in a deep-cut trench with many short gorges. The river is barely 100 m wide at Chungking, where a difference in level of 20 m is experienced between summer and winter. Navigation is difficult between Chungking and Fong Kieh (Kweichow), but comparatively easy as compared with the reach between Kweichow and Ichang, which constitutes the famous Yangtze Gorges.

Between Kweichow and Ichang the river cuts through lofty limestone mountains with precipitous sides, in a series of magnificent gorges which cut right across the rock structures. Earlier physiographic explanation of their causation was that the river had sought out lines of weakness and had cut down along them, but Barbour finds this un-

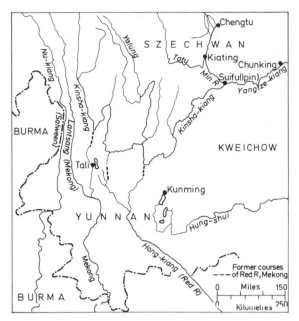

Fig. 109 River capture by the Yangtze-kiang

acceptable.[20] He suggests two possible explanations, either that the drainage is antecedent or superimposed. He rejects the former in favour of the latter, pointing out that it is probable that the mountains through which the river cuts were folded long before the present drainage system and, moreover, that the Taling-ho, a tributary of the Yangtze in this stretch, has cut down through five anticlines of strata identical with those of the Gorges without being thrown off course. He supports a theory of superposition from a thinly veneered peneplain on the grounds that the folds are sufficiently ancient (probably Yenshan) and that 'maximum summit levels show a consistency of skyline across truncated structures'.

The Red Basin is strongly mountain-bound and the Gorges provide the only direct line of entry from the east. The current is very powerful, running at 4 to 6 knots, and in a few constricted and very dangerous stretches it reaches as much as 10 knots. Navigation is therefore notoriously difficult. For a thousand years and more junks have made the passage, hauled up against the stream by tracker teams, sometimes 100 strong, straining in their harness along the specially cut narrow paths high up on the cliff face. The passage is dangerous both for crews and teams and demands a high degree of cooperation, mutual reliance, courage and endurance. Carelessness or faint-heartedness can easily lead to crew or team or both being swept away. In this century specially designed high-powered river steamers have been constructed to contend with this current but, at least until recently, their share of the total river traffic over this reach of the river has been very small.

To meet this difficulty of navigability and also to control floods in the lower basins, there is a great project, still in the survey stage, of building a 120 m dam at Sanhsia, near Patung, at the lower end of the Wushan Gorge. If and when this dam is built, it will create a lake reaching back nearly to Chungking. It will generate 15 million kW and will make the river navigable for 10 000-ton vessels up to Chungking. Two further dams are planned, one at Chungking and the other at Suifu (Ipin).

The climate of Szechwan is startling and unexpected.[21] Here in the heart of a great landmass, where one might expect to find considerable extremes of temperature, it is equable. Chengtu, which is 1600 km inland and 475 m above sealevel, has an average January temperature of 7° C as compared with Shanghai, which is 10 m above sea-level and on the coast and has an average January temperature of 3° C. Average July temperatures are high, being 26° C. Even so they are 2° less than Shanghai. Very seldom is there snow or frost except on the mountains. The basin enjoys a growing season of eleven months. H. L. Richardson says of it: 'to come to Szechwan in the winter time from the adjoining province of Shensi is to experience a dramatic contrast between the frozen yellowish land of the Wei valley and the lush green growth of the Red Basin'.[22] The reason for the equable nature of the climate lies in the fact that the basin is land-locked by high mountains, particularly on the west and north. Thus the bitter winter winds from the Mongolian high are deflected father east to the middle and lower basins of the Yangtze.

The average annual rainfall for most of the province is 1000 mm. Winter precipitation is sparse but its meagreness is compensated to some extent by high humidity and cloudiness, which prevents much loss by evaporation. There is a Szechwan proverb which runs: 'When the sun shines the dogs bark'. South of Szechwan lies the province of Yunnan, the meaning of which is 'South of the Clouds'. The heavy summer maximum of rainfall results in a big rise in river levels.

While the natural vegetation for the whole area is forest, the nature of the forest varies consider-

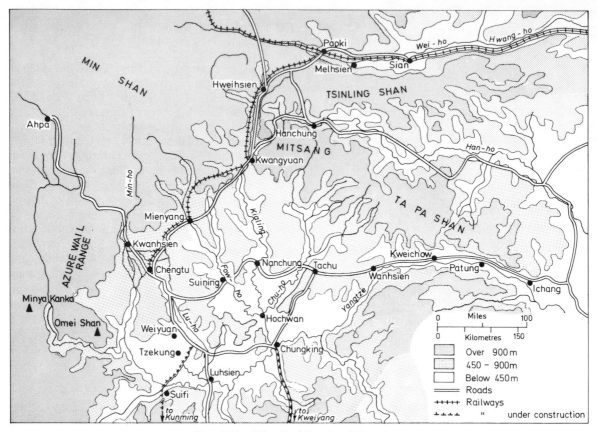

Fig. 110   The Red Basin of Szechwan

ably with altitude. Much of the valleys and lower hillsides has been cleared and terraced for cultivation. Where left untouched, evergreen broadleafed forest abounds. As is almost universal in China, around each temple and near each village there is a grove of trees, intimately connected with *feng shui*. In Szechwan these groves are composed largely of cypress, golden chestnut and bamboo. Above 600 m the evergreen forest begins to give way to deciduous broadleafed forest and *Cunninghamia*. At 1800 m little deciduous vegetation remains, coniferous forest, rhododendrons and shrubs and flowers taking its place. Szechwan has achieved botanical fame in that a species of conifer, *Metasequoia*, believed to be extinct, has been found to be growing here. Above 2700 m there are alpine pastures. Purple–brown forest soil and mountain podzolized yellow soils are general.

Because of the long growing period, more than two-thirds of the cultivated land is double-cropped. There is a great amount of terracing and

about three-quarters of the land is irrigated. The incidence of crop failure is very much less than in the lower basins of the Yangtze. This is due partly to there being less liability to flooding.

It is said that anything grown anywhere in China can and is grown in Szechwan. With the exception of the truly tropical produce of Hainan and south Kwangtung, this is virtually true. Rice is the summer cereal and wheat the winter variety. In addition corn, rapeseed, sesame, kaoliang, soybeans, sweet potatoes and tea are all grown extensively. Szechwan corn is famous, that produced in the hills being especially good. Opium (now prohibited) was formerly a very important cash crop. Many kinds of fruit are grown, including peach, apricot, persimmon, pear and citrus of many varieties. Sugar-cane, introduced from Fukien, is grown in large quantities in the river valleys of the southwest and forms an important cash crop. Tea is grown mainly in the north and northwest where winters are warmer and soils good. It is of special

	Jan	Feb	Mar	Apr	May	Jun	July	Aug	Sep	Oct	Nov	Dec
Chengtu (475 m)												
Temp °C	6·7	7·8	12·8	17·2	21·1	20·4	25·6	25·6	21·7	17·8	13·3	7·8
Rainfall mm	5	10	15	43	71	104	148	246	104	46	10	3
Chungking (230 m)												
Temp °C	8·3	10·0	14·4	19·4	23·3	26·1	27·8	28·9	24·4	19·4	15·0	10·0
Rainfall mm	15	20	36	102	140	180	142	129	147	117	51	23

quality, the long, round, thick leaf being good for brick tea, which is exported mainly to Tibet. The province stands third to Chekiang and Kwangtung in sericulture. Wanhsien in the east and Loshan in the south are the main producing centres, while the silk trade is centred in Chungking. The *tung yu* (wood oil) tree abounds in the eastern part of the Red Basin, especially in the Gorges and neighbouring areas. There are two main species: *Aleurites fordii* and *Aleurites montana*. The trees flourish on the hillsides up to about 600 m. Szechwan has a wealth of medicinal herbs both wild and cultivated, which have a nationwide reputation. The main pharmaceutical centres are Kwanhsien, Suifu (Ipin) and Hochuan.[23] Szechwan has a pig population estimated at nearly 16 million in 1952 and stands first in China as a producer of hog bristles. In 1936 16 000 *piculs* (1 *picul* = 60 kg) were produced, the trade being centred in Chungking and Wanhsien.

It was estimated that in 1957–8 some 13·5 per cent of the total area of the province or 114·99 million *mow* was arable land. Of this 83·1 per cent was devoted to grain production, 55·38 million *mow* or just under half was paddy, and 59·61 million *mow* was under dry crops[24]. Some idea of the relative importance of the main crops can be gleaned from Table 25.

Szechwan's mineral resources lie in coal, salt and oil, and to some extent in iron. Her coal reserves are estimated at 293 million tons of anthracite and 3540 million tons of bituminous coal, a considerable amount, although meagre as

compared with Shansi and Shensi. The main reserves lie in the east and centre but there are outcrops all round the margin of the Basin. Anthracite deposits lie in the west along the lower Min river. Rivers have cut deeply into the red sandstone and have exposed the underlying coal seams, which are often mined by adits. Production which in 1930 was 90 000 tons of anthracite and 2 462 159 tons of bituminous coal, is now many times greater.

It was thought that Szechwan's iron resources were sufficient to support only light industry but recent surveys have revealed considerable iron-ore reserves. Chungking now has large integrated iron and steel plant.

The existence of oil and natural gas in Szechwan has been known for well over 1000 years. It is not surprising, therefore, that Szechwan has been regarded in this century as one of China's most hopeful fields. Nevertheless it has remained largely unsurveyed until recently. The National Geology Survey of China placed reserves at nearly 400 million barrels, but production before the Second World War was a mere 92 000 *catties* (1 *catty* = 595 gm) from natural wells. There was a low-temperature coal distillation plant in west Szechwan, which produced diesel oil and petrol substitute with a high octane number and therefore good for aviation, but production was very small. Postwar oil survey reports in Szechwan remained disappointing until 1958, when dramatic discoveries were made in the Nanchung region of the Kialing river valley. Reports from the Szech-

Table 25   Szechwan Crop Output (10 000 *piculs*)[24]

Date Prewar	Rice	Wheat	Corn	Sweet potato	Cotton	Rape-seed	Sugarcane
(1936 Estimate)	15631	3685	2954	5654	38	—	2500
1949	18464	1990	3003	3460	30	307	1121
1952	21007	1795	2950	4059	83	379	2518
1957	27374	3276	4269	6365	140	553	3445

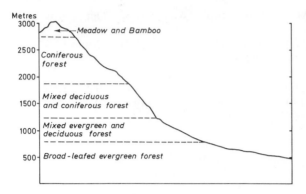

*Fig. 111   Natural vegetation at Omeishan,
Szechwan*

wan Petroleum Survey Bureau state that oil in quantity over a wide field has been found in the Lower Jurassic (300–450 m) and Triassic (1800 m). The oil is of good quality, having high condensability and low viscosity. This field has been energetically developed and produced an estimated 1 million tons in 1973.

Salt production, which is an old industry, is centred mainly in Tzeliutsing, which lies between the Min and Lu rivers, although other districts are also engaged in the trade. Brine is raised from deep wells by means of bamboo pipes and is evaporated. Half a million tons of salt are produced annually.

Szechwan has the highest population of all the provinces with 74 million persons, and a density of 645 per sq km in the crop area.[25] This is in spite of the fact that the population was decimated in a great uprising four centuries ago. The unoccupied land was quickly repeopled by migrants from neighbouring provinces.

Communications in the Red Basin are difficult. The many rivers have cut deeply into the soft red sandstone, rendering cross-country travel difficult. The rivers themselves are fast-flowing and navigable only for small craft for the most part. In the past very little wheeled transport has been used, for the 'roads' have been mere flagstone paths. One such road is worthy of mention. In the Later Han (AD 25–220) an official route ran from Chengtu via Mienyang and Kwangyuan, thence over the Ta Pa Shan and Tsinling Shan to Paoki in the Wei valley and so to Ch'ang-an (Sian). This very difficult route was the more remarkable because nearly one third of its length was built on trestles in the precipitous mountain slopes or along stream beds.[26] Along this same route a rail-

way has now been constructed – a really remarkable engineering feat. By means of this line Chungking is now linked to Paoki via Chengtu and to the Lunghwa east–west line along the Wei valley. A second line is planned to link Wuhan with Chungking via Huang-hua on the upper Han-ho, across the Ta Pa Shan and down the Chou-ho to Chungking.

The Sino–Japanese War (1937–45) had considerable influence on road communication in the province. The Government (Kuomintang) retreated before the Japanese advance and took refuge behind the mountain walls of Szechwan. During these years a sizeable network of motor roads – much of indifferent surface – was built. This has been further developed since 1949.

There is one region of the Red Basin which deserves special mention, and that is the Chengtu Plain. The Min river emerges from the Azure Wall Mountains onto the plain at Kwanhsien, where its flow is checked. The Min is a considerable river, even in winter, being 45 m wide and 2 m deep. In summer it is a torrent nearly a kilometre wide. In earlier times it fanned out over a wide area, causing a stone waste in the north and marshlands in the south. We have seen (p. 110) how Li Ping in the Ch'in dynasty (221–206 BC) controlled this flood and converted the area into one of the most fertile lands. The rice crop from the Chengtu plain is reckoned at about 10–12½ tons per ha, nearly twice the average elsewhere. It is now the most densely populated agricultural region in the world. Perhaps what is even more remarkable than this transformation from waste to productivity is the fact that for more than 2000 years the great network of channels and sluicegates has been maintained through all vicissitudes. Nowhere else in history is there such an example of material and organizational continuity. Engineers of the People's Republic are now modernizing the works by the substitution of control dams and lock gates for the old fish snouts. There are now more than 1100 km of channels.

2c. The Middle Basin
When the Yangtze emerges from the Gorges at Ichang it descends onto a series of three plains, which, since they lead into one another and are of much the same geographical nature, we have grouped under the heading Middle Basin. These plains are the successors to former depressions or old lake basins, which have since been largely filled

Plate 24   Paoki–Chengtu railway
Typical of the difficult terrain through which this line has been built

with eroded red sandstone from Szechwan. In many parts there are thick 'red beds' lying unconformably on limestones, micaceous sandstones, quartzites and conglomerates. The process of infilling these depressions is not yet complete. Much of the land is lake-studded along the Yangtze borders and along the Han near its confluence with the mainstream. The flat or gently undulating plain is often suddenly interrupted by isolated hills or ranges of hills rising abruptly. Characteristic are the well known Lushan Hills, near Kiukiang which are 13 by 25 km, springing from the plain to over 1500 m.

In its course through the Middle Basin, the Yangtze or Ch'ang-kiang, as it should be called in these lower reaches, receives its biggest tributaries. Its great left-bank tributary, the Han, rises in the Tsinling Shan and flows for nearly 480 km in an easterly direction between the Tsinling and the Ta Pa Shan. On entering Hupeh it turns south in a much broader valley or floodplain and widens its

bed, which varies between 1 and 1½ km in width over much of this reach. It turns abruptly east again and threads its way through a maze of lakes as it approaches its confluence with the Yangtze at Hankow (Mouth of the Han). Two large right-bank tributaries, the Yuan and Siang, and many smaller rivers empty into the Tungting lake before it, itself, enters the main river. The Han and these right-bank rivers constitute the catchment area of the first of the three plains and are known collectively as Hukwang, i.e. Hupeh and Hunan, which names mean North of the Lakes and South of the Lakes, respectively.

About 110 km below Wuhan spurs of the Ta Pieh Shan on the north and the Wan Fu Shan on the south approach the Yangtze at a point known as Split Hill. Here the river narrows to less than a kilometre in width. Split Hill marks the point of entry into the second of the plains of the Middle Basin, the catchment basin of which constitutes practically the whole of the province of Kiangsi.

Plate 25   The recently opened trunk line between Chengtu, Szechwan and Kunming, Yunnan
In earlier times it was quicker and less hazardous to travel down the Yangtze to Shanghai,
go by sea to Hanoi and up the Red river to Kunming

This plain is drained by the river Kan, which empties into the Poyang lake, thence into the main river.

Near the port of Anyang the Ta Pieh Shan approach the river, which again becomes more constricted. The place of narrowing is known as 'Hen Point' and leads into the third of the Middle Basin plains, which occupies most of central and southern Anhwei. Its boundaries are lower and less well defined than the two to the west. The eastern limit is marked by a further narrowing of the river at 'The Pillars'. From this point to the sea the land assumes a true deltaic character.

The river bed at Ichang is only 40 m above sea-level and is 1500 km from the sea. In winter it flows slowly in a channel sometimes barely 2 m deep at Hankow. At this time of year a trip from Hankow to Shanghai, even on the large river steamers, is dull, since one sees merely the high brown mud banks, except where the hills come down to the river. In summer the scene is entirely changed: the river comes down as a mighty flood. At Hankow, where the Yangtze is $1\frac{1}{2}$ km wide, the average difference between summer and winter levels is 14 m. In times of exceptional flood, as in 1931 and 1954, the flow reaches astronomical figures. In 1954 the flow was measured at more than 70 750 cu. m per second (cf. the Thames, 66 cu. m p.s.).

Throughout the length of the plains of the Middle Basin there is a network of dykes which serve to keep normal summer flood waters from wide tracts of arable land, but over large areas flooding is a usual annual occurrence. The many lakes which cover the land adjoining the river are thereby linked up. Marco Polo and Abbé Huc were amazed at the size of the river. Both reported it as being more than 15 km wide and both were discredited on that account. But both saw it in the summer when river and lake combine and when it is, in fact, that width in some places.

This variation in regime constitutes a difficulty to navigation at the height of both winter and summer seasons. In winter the shallow water and shifting sandbars make the passage up to Wuhan in craft drawing more than 2 m most difficult, necessitating almost constant sounding. In summer, vessels of 10 000 to 15 000 tons can reach Wuhan. Navigation dangers at this season consist mainly in keeping to the river channel and in not wandering off over the countryside as smaller craft are liable to do. If grounded and the river level falls suddenly, as it often does, such craft may be left high and dry for a whole year. For many decades the river course up to Wuhan has been marked by lightships and light buoys in the summer.

While not as subject to flood as the Hwang-ho, the Yangtze nevertheless experiences at times serious inundations in the Middle Basin. The load of silt brought down is heavy: it is estimated that 140 million cu. m of solid material passes Hankow every year. However, the flow and scour is sufficient to carry the greater part of this down to the sea. Thus the bed of the river has not been built up above the level of the surrounding land. But the Middle Basin is a large region of heavy summer rainfall and the normal inflow from the large tributaries is very great. The two great lakes Tungting and Poyang, which in the past have acted as reservoirs and so helped to regulate the flow, are now shallow and less effective for this purpose. Much of the rainfall comes from cyclones which pass down the Yangtze valley. When, as happened in July 1931, a series of seven cyclones passed in quick succession, the flood waters rose to record heights. Then 16·15 m was recorded at Hankow, topping the Bund by 2 m. Nearly 40 000 sq km, much of which was under crops, were flooded.

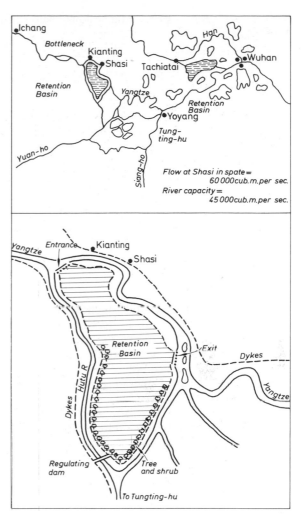

Fig. 112   Yangtze water conservancy: Shasi and Tachiatai retention basins

Another similar, even greater, rise was recorded in 1954. While big cities like Wuhan were saved by raising the local dykes, serious floods again covered the countryside.

The long-term scheme to meet this menace, as we have seen, is to build great dams higher up the river in the Gorges and at Chungking and Suifu and so control the flow. Immediate measures have taken the form of constructing two large artificial retention basins, one at Shasi between the Yangtze and the Tungting lake, and the other at Tachiatai between the Yangtze and the Han, the latter being for relief of the Han's flood waters. Dykes have been raised to form a reservoir or basin into which the waters can be deflected and held when the river

	Jan	Feb	Mar	Apr	May	Jun	July	Aug	Sep	Oct	Nov	Dec	Total
Average Temp °C	4·4	6·1	10·0	16·7	21·7	26·7	29·4	29·4	25·0	19·4	12·8	7·2	
Rainfall (mm)	48	48	97	152	165	244	180	97	71	81	48	28	1259

is in spate and is threatening to burst its banks. The Shasi basin is 920 sq km in area and has 5350 million cu. m capacity. It was built in 1954 in 75 days, using very little machinery and an army of 300 000 workers. It is used for cultivation in the winter months but held in readiness during the summer.

Winters in the Middle Basin are short and cold. About 640 km separates north Hupeh from south Hunan and consequently a considerable difference in temperature is experienced. Average conditions are reflected in the climatic statistics of Hankow:

Winters are wetter than on the North China Plain. Occasional medium falls of snow occur and rarer, beautiful but rather destructive glazed frosts. Summers are hot. The summer rains and the vast flooded paddy fields produce a very high relative humidity, which is most enervating. The hot damp nights with temperatures over 27° C and a relative humidity of over 85 per cent unrelieved by the slightest breeze have to be experienced to be appreciated. Rainfall has a better seasonal distribution than north of the Tsinling Shan. The growing season varies from nine months in the north to ten months in the south.

Soils in northern districts tend to be neutral. Acidity increases quite appreciably in the south.

The dense mixed forests of broad-leafed trees and *Cunninghamia*, which covered these plains 2000 years ago, have long since been cleared as have also the hills lying in their vicinity. The wilder and more mountainous borders in west Hupeh and southwest and south Hunan are still heavily forested, although cutting has been very heavy during this century. It is from these regions that the huge timber rafts of pine, fir, bamboo, locust, maple and camphor are floated down to Wuhan and beyond to the cities of the lower Yangtze. Afforestation here, as elsewhere, is being pushed energetically.

The Middle Basin is one of the most productive regions of the country. Wherever possible rice is grown as the summer cereal and it is certainly the most important crop. The region around the Tungting lake and in the lower Yuan and Siang is renowned and is in fact the most important rice

area in China. The Kan plain and the lower Han are also heavy producers. So keen is the desire to grow rice that farmers in the upper Han persist in its cultivation when wheat would be the more reliable crop and sometimes they meet with disaster. Cotton is also a very important summer crop, followed by corn and soy-beans.

The chief winter crops are barley, wheat, rapeseed and sesamum seed, and broad beans. Barley is preferred to winter wheat as it matures and ripens early enough for the rice crop to be planted. About two-thirds of the cultivated area is doublecropped and irrigated. Much of the irrigation is by gravity from ponds at the heads of valleys. Where water has to be raised, reliance formerly was placed on wooden paddle pumps operated by human power. Much of this work is now done by diesel pumps.

Tung yu (wood oil) is an important product. The trees are grown mainly in west Hupeh and in the upper Han and Yuan river valleys. The oil is expressed locally by crushing and it is sent down to Hankow in bamboo crates lined with oiled paper.

Tea is grown mainly on the sides of the rolling hills south of the Tungting and Poyang lakes in Hunan and Kiangsi. While its place in international trade has waned since the 1880s, when Indian and Ceylon teas became popular in Europe, it is still a very important crop today. Tea remains the universal drink of the Chinese people.

Cotton is an important Hupeh crop in the middle and lower Han basin. It is mainly short staple of less than 25 mm. Wuhan is a very active textile manufacturing centre. No. 1 Cotton Mill at Wuchang was established at the turn of the century. New mills equipped with the latest modern machinery have recently been established in Hanyang.

Of the fibres grown in the Middle Basin, ramie, from which grass cloth or Chinese linen is made, is outstanding. It is a perennial plant which grows on the hillsides. A fair amount of hemp is harvested and some jute is grown south of the river at Wuchang.

The mineral wealth of this region consists

Plate 26   Shaoshan village, Hunan, Mao Tse-tung's birthplace
A typical Yangtze valley village with grove above, paddy fields around and fish pond below

mainly of the high-grade iron ores of the Tayeh district of Hupeh, the coking coals of the P'ingh-siang district of Hunan and the rich, newly discovered Onan field at Puchi. The development of these resources at the turn of the century has been described in the section dealing with economic development before 1949. Since 1949 new deposits near to Tayeh have been found and four new mines opened at Cheng Chiao, Lin Hsiang, Jin Shan Tien and Lung Liu Shan. Modern mining equipment and an ore-dressing plant, using froth flotation and magnetic separation methods to separate iron and copper have been installed. The railroad from Tayeh to Shih Hui Yao, river port for shipping the ore to Hankow, has been electrified and there is now rail connection between Tayeh and Wuchang. Shih Hui Yao itself has local coal and some of the purest limestone in the land. It has developed some smelting, but the bulk of the raw material goes upstream to the great works at Wuhan. Based on the fine supply of limestone and easily available coal, the biggest cement works in this part of Asia were opened at Shih Hui Yao in 1949.[27]

In company with Paotow, Wuhan was selected by the economic planners of 1952 as one of the two new centres for the development of heavy iron and steel industry. The old site of the iron and steel works at Hanyang, chosen by Viceroy Chang Chih-tung, has been abandoned to modern textile works and vast new development has taken place at Wukang 8 km below Hankow. Here the Wuhan Iron and Steel Corporation has built a fully integrated plant, including ore-dressing and ore-sintering plant, blast furnaces, open-hearth ovens, rolling mills, refractory materials plant, etc. In all there are 18 main and 31 subsidiary workshops, covering 10 sq. km. The blast furnaces are the largest in this part of Asia and are entirely automatically controlled. They have an annual output of 3 million tons of steel. One blast furnace has an output of 2000 tons of pig-iron per 24 hours. The blooming mill can roll 7 and 15–ton steel ingots and is moreover entirely automatic.

Wuhan, which is the collective name given to the three cities of Hankow, Hanyang and Wu-chang at the confluence of the Yangtze and the Han rivers, lies in the heart of the Middle Basin. It provides a classic example of nodality. The Yangtze itself forms a great east–west highway from the Red Basin of Szechwan to the fertile plain of Kiangsu. The Han river communicates with the northwest over the Tsinling Shan to the Wei valley

and Lanchow. The Yuan and Siang link Wuhan with Kweichow in the southwest and Kwangtung in the south. Furthermore, Kwangtung is linked with Wuhan via the Mei Lung Pass, thence by the Kan river and Poyang lake. This, incidentally, was part of the imperial route between Canton and the capital.

In the course of its 1700 years of history, Wuhan has been sacked many times but has always risen, phoenix-like, from its ashes thanks not only to its nodality but to the fact that the whole region is so productive. The twentieth century has accentu-ated its centrality by the building of the Pei-Han Wuchang–Canton railway. Until 1957 this railway suffered the severe handicap that all north–south through traffic had to be ferried across the river at Hankow – a difficult task in winter because water was so low and no easier in summer because of the strength of the current. Ever since 1913 there were projects for building a bridge but these never progressed beyond the survey stage until 1955, when construction actually began. With the help of Russian engineers the river has been bridged between Tortoise Hill in Hanyang and Serpent Hill in Wuchang at its narrowest point; albeit the bridge is 1651 m long, of which 1142 m are actually over the river. The bridge carries a lower double-rail track and an upper six-stream highway and is high enough to allow the passage of 10 000-ton ships during summer high water. It is an engineer-ing feat of which the Chinese are justly proud. Since then the Yangtze has been bridged at Chungking and at Nanking.

Wuchang, the provincial capital, has been the administrative and educational centre. It was a walled city until 1928 when, after the Kuomintang victory, the walls were pulled down and a ring road constructed. Expansion to the east of the city for administrative, educational and industrial pur-poses since 1952 has been very great indeed. Han-yang, also walled, was favoured as a place of retirement for officials and gentry. Outside its walls at the confluence of the Han and Yangtze, the Hanyang Iron and Steel Works were built.

Hankow has always been the commercial centre but it entered into international trade only in 1861 when a British concession was granted. In the closing years of the century further concessions were given to France, Germany, Russia and Japan. The nature and rise of Hankow's trade are shown by the figures below, which serve also to shed some light on production and trade in the Yangtze Basin, particularly in Hupeh and Hunan.

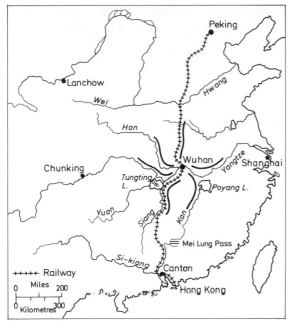

Fig. 113   The nodality of Wuhan

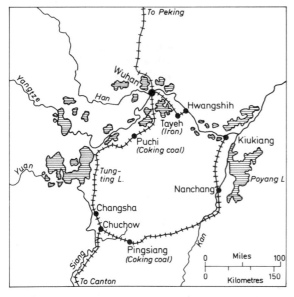

Fig. 114   Wuhan's iron and coking coal supplies

The figures are in Haikwan *taels*, a customs unit of 583 grains of silver, a stable measure which is no longer used. Hankow's part in foreign trade rose rapidly, if unsteadily, from 1861 to 1928. Especially in the first quarter of this century political events were clearly reflected in the volume of trade as the accompanying graph shows.

All ports on the Yangtze suffered a series of heavy blows after the Kuomintang revolution of 1927 from which they have not yet recovered. The loss of foreign concessions, the closing of the Yangtze to foreign bottoms, the world slump of 1932, the Sino–Japanese War, during which Hankow suffered particularly heavy bombing by first Japanese and then American aircraft, and finally the stagnation of trade between 1946 and 1949 – all served to bring international trade on the Yangtze to a standstill. No foreign vessels now ply on the river.

Hankow's progress in international trade has been traced in some detail since it reflects in some degree the experience of the other, lesser important, ports in the Middle Basin – Wuhu, Kiukiang, Shasi, Ichang and Changsha.

Shipping on the Yangtze may be divided into three categories. Ocean-going ships of 10 000 to 15 000 tons can navigate to Hankow in the summer months and smaller ocean craft can reach Ichang. Specially constructed river boats of 5000 tons, drawing less than 2 m, together with large numbers of smaller launches, are used the year round for both passengers and goods, and for long and short journeys. Lastly there are innumerable junks, large and small, which ply up and down the rivers and along the southeast coast, each flying its distinctive flag indicating the nature of its cargo, and each providing a home for one or more families.

Owing to the big change in river level between summer and winter, wharfage at the big river ports is impossible. Landing is made at hulks connected to the shore by pontoon bridges, which can be adjusted in length according to the needs of the season. Loading and unloading up and down the steep river banks was done entirely by human labour in the past. Today much of this is done by recently installed mechanical belts. The smaller towns along the river have to rely on carrying their passengers and freight out in small junks to the passing river steamer in midstream.

2d. The Yangtze Delta

At a point, known as 'The Pillars', about halfway between Wuhu and Nanking, the Yangtze emerges onto a flat, deltaic plain. Apart from the hills which persist for some way along the left bank, the delta is unrelieved by uplands of any height and is reminiscent of the Fenlands of England and the polders of Holland. Much of it is the same level as the river and some parts are below. It is a mass of intersecting canals, many of which serve the

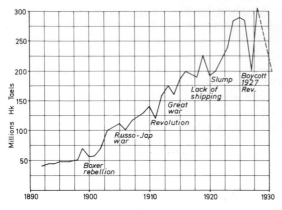

Fig. 115   Hankow's trade

treble purpose of drainage, irrigation and communication. From Nanking to the sea there is no clear physical divide between the Hwai and the Yangtze. The former has, on occasion, emptied into the East China Sea through the northernmost of the Yangtze's outlets when that river had three mouths. The southern limits of the delta are marked by rolling hill-land which rises on the Chekiang northern borders into the Pai Chi Shan. The delta extends as far south as the borders of the Hangchow Bay and is covered by innumerable lakes, the greatest and most famous of which is the Tai-hu, which simply means 'Big Lake'.

The Yangtze carries a very heavy load of silt. It is estimated that more than 140 million cu. m

of solid material passes Hankow each year, but owing to its greater volume and greater velocity than the Hwang-ho, a much larger proportion of this load reaches the sea. Some subsidence is taking place in the delta area, but deposition is occurring at a greater rate and the coastline is being pushed seaward quite rapidly. Much of the silt is carried southward by the East China Cold Current, which flows south along the coast with the result that the Chusan Archipelago is filling up and Hangchow Bay becoming shallower. As the silting in the delta takes place, reclamation dykes are built in which there are sluice gates, which allow an inflow during the flow of the tide, bringing further silt, which settles, and also fish, which are netted at the gates as the tide ebbs. The Yangtze is tidal as far as 'The Pillars'.

Contrary to expectation, approach to the seaboard brings no increase in equability of climate. Winters in the delta, although short, are severe. The average January temperature of Shanghai is 3·3° C as compared with Hankow's 4·4° C. The region is open to the cold north winds which sweep down from the North China Plain and the Hwai Basin. Summers are hot, damp and very enervating. Rainfall is better distributed than in the north with an average of 33 mm in December and 188 mm in June. Rainfall variability is much less here than in the northern wheat area. Lossing Buck records 11 calamities between 1904 and 1929 as compared with 24 in the north.

The combination of rich alluvium, a hot, wet

Hankow Trade Figures*

Foreign Exports 1872		Foreign Exports 1928	
Haikwan Taels		Haikwan Taels	
Tea	12 356 541	Tea	17 002 282
Wood oil	1 384 149	Wood oil	9 615 538
Silk	1 281 884	Sesamum seed	6 053 570
Vegetable tallow	606 763	Cotton seed	1 552 747
		Vegetable tallow	1 815 319
		Vegetable oils (total)	19 037 174
		Egg products	12 174 570
		Tobacco	5 469 875
		Fibres	3 455 656
		Cotton	2 834 777
		Beans	2 800 000
		Flour	2 328 851
		Timber	2 151 396
		Bristles	1 586 665
		Silk (cocoons)	1 007 290

* from Chinese Maritime Customs Reports.

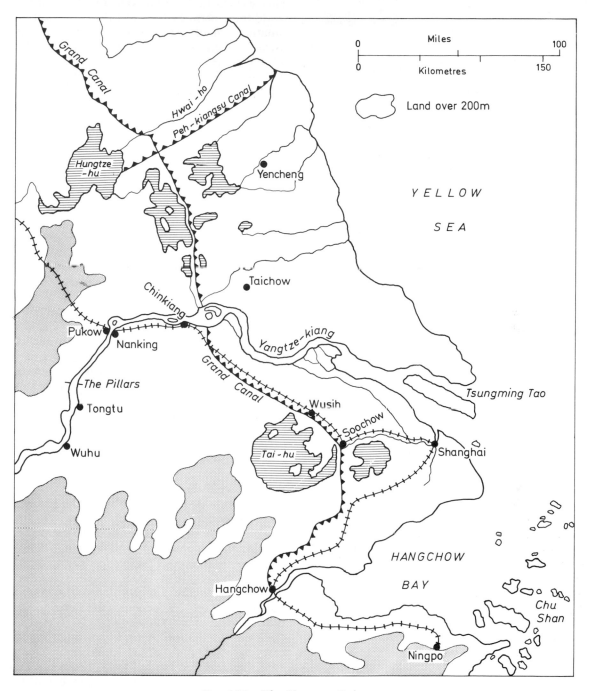

Fig. 116   The Yangtze Delta

Fig. 117   The Yangtze Delta cotton and salt region

and ignorance of sound methods of sericulture. This was further accentuated by the slump in world trade between 1929 and 1933. To meet this situation schools were opened to improve silkworm rearing in all its stages. Cooperative societies were formed and for a while the industry flourished. Subsequent war and the development of synthetic products, such as rayon and nylon, have dealt a severe blow. Mulberry trees line the dykes and holdings, and mulberry groves dot the whole countryside.

Cotton growing, which is now more important than silk, is concentrated largely in the coastland strip between the mouth of the Hwai and the Yangtze. In the seventh century a long dyke or sea wall, known as the Fan Kung Ti, was built against the inroads of the sea. Since then there has been a steady seaward extension of the land through deposition from the Hwai and the Hwang-ho. A further dyke has more recently been built along the coast. The land nearest the seaboard is devoted to salt production by evaporation in shallow pans, the ground water being highly saline. Farther inland and as the land loses its salinity, cotton replaces salt production. Cotton is more tolerant of salt than most other crops and good yields can be grown on ground where the salinity is not more than 0·16 per cent. The region lent itself to plantation development in the hands of large companies, a few of which had as much as 40 000 ha. These, since the revolution of 1949, have been converted into state farms or absorbed into the communes. This low-lying coast is rather vulnerable to flooding, especially during the high winds of the late typhoons.

Population is very dense in the delta. Kiangsu, with an area of 277 900 km, the coastal strip of which as we have seen is saline and not densely peopled, has a population of 47 million. The crop area has an average of 545 people per sq. km.

The delta region is better served by railways than the rest of the Yangtze Basin. The Peking–Tientsin–Tsinan line divides at Pengpu, one branch going to the Yangtze opposite Wuhu and the other to Pukow. A 6½ km two-tier bridge, carrying both rail and road traffic, completed in 1968, has replaced the rail ferry. From Nanking the railway runs to Soochow and Shanghai, thence to Hangchow and Ningpo.

The Grand Canal, keeping to the eastern edge of the Hungtze-hu and Kaoyu-hu, cuts right across the delta to Chinkiang. It is continued through Nanking to Hangchow via Wusih and Soochow.

summer and a very shallow water table, giving adequate water supply, leads to heavy cropping. Rice is by far the most important summer cereal and stands second in production only to Hunan in the Middle Basin. Other summer crops are cotton, soy-beans and corn. Rice is grown in rotation with winter wheat to some extent, but barley is generally preferred because of its earlier ripening. Rapeseed and broad beans are also winter crops. More than two-thirds of the delta is double-cropped. Between 1949 and 1957 Kiangsu increased food grain production from 6·6 to 11·8 million metric tons, Anhwei from 4·5 to 11·5 and Chechiang from 4·2 5o 7·8 million metric tons. These production figures have been raised very considerably since that date.

Before the Sino–Japanese war of 1937, silk was the most important cash crop produced in the delta region. During the early part of the century it had fallen on bad times owing largely to neglect

During the first half of this century it fell into disrepair, so that through traffic was not possible. Recently it has been resuscitated and is again in operation. Local communication and transport are very largely by water, using the vast network of irrigation and drainage canals.

The lower Yangtze is rich in towns of note. At the head of Hangchow Bay is Hangchow itself, a city of bridges and canals, held to be one of the most beautiful in the world. Marco Polo visited it about AD 1290 and was ecstatic over its charms. It was the capital of China under the Sung between AD 1127 and 1278. Soochow, east of the Tai-hu, vies with it in beauty. The Chinese have a saying 'Heaven is above but Soochow and Hangchow are below'. Hangchow Bay is so shallow as to permit no port along its shores. It is subject to very rapid tides; at spring tide a bore of 2·5 m or more sweeps up to its head. Across its mouth lie the islands of the Chusan Archipelago, mountainous and about one hundred in number. The largest, which measures about 32 by 16 km and gives its name to the group, is a great Buddhist centre.

Nanking, the 'Southern Capital', has a long history as the capital of various kingships from AD 229 onward, but it was not until 1368 that it became, under the Ming, an imperial capital and then only for 34 years. It was famous for its magnificent buildings until the delta region suffered so severely during the Taiping Rebellion. Nanking was taken by the rebels and its monuments were entirely destroyed. Between 1927 and 1949 it was adopted by the Kuomintang as the national capital. Sun Yat Sen was buried there in 1925. Its population in 1957 was recorded as 1 419 000.

Shanghai overshadows all other cities of the delta both in size and in economic importance. It stands at the mouth of the Yangtze and has for its hinterland the whole of the vast Yangtze Basin from which flows the produce of one tenth of the world's population. Its siting, however, is by no means as impressive as its situation. It stands on the left bank of the Hwangpoo or Woosung creek, about 19 km above its confluence with the Yangtze. The Hwangpoo is the main channel draining the system of lakes to the west. As it approaches the Yangtze it widens to about 640 m at its mouth. It is strongly tidal and has a good tidal scour. Below the confluence the Yangtze itself requires constant dredging and most careful conservancy in order to maintain a satisfactory navigation channel. More than 1500 million cu. m

of mud must be dredged annually, thus enabling ocean-going ships to reach the heart of the city at high tide.

In the eleventh century Shanghai was a mere customs post at the mouth of the Yangtze. By the thirteenth century it had developed to become the county town of Kiangsu, a walled city fortified against Japanese pirates. In 1843, after the Treaty of Nanking, Sir George Balfour chose a site alongside this walled city for a British concession, which in 1863 became the International Settlement. In spite of the ravages of the Taiping, who sacked the native city, trade grew rapidly and by 1895 its population was 411 573, of which 286 753 was in the foreign settlements. It grew to over 1 million by 1910 and 6 million in 1954. Before the Second World War Shanghai stood as the eighth largest port of the world. For a short while after 1949, the planners, in accordance with the policy of a wider distribution of industry, tried to disperse some of this population and divert its industry elsewhere but this attempt was quickly given up and trade and industry resumed their normal trend. Today Shanghai is a municipality (*shih*) i.e. it has provincial status and is responsible directly to the central government at Peking. Its boundaries embrace the city itself, 9 counties (*hsien*) and some 30 offshore islands. Its estimated population is 11·5 million of which about 6 million live in the city.

Shanghai is pre-eminent as industrial, commercial and financial centre. Its industries range from shipbuilding, heavy iron and steel, machinery, cement works, chemicals (paint, dyes, pharmaceutical products, fertilizer), textiles (cotton and fibre), silk filaturing, to high-precision products and consumer goods of all kinds. A great deal of China's foreign and coastal trade flows from Shanghai. In consequence it is a leading banking centre, housing China's two major banks, the People's Construction Bank and the Bank of Communications; also two British banks, the Hong Kong and Shanghai Bank and the Chartered Bank, which underwrite foreign transactions. There are two airports, one catering for the international lines and the other catering for local traffic.

To deal with the previous appalling overcrowding a great deal of town planning has been undertaken since 1949. Industrial, commercial, residential and agricultural zones have been developed resulting in a much better organized city than formerly.

3. THE SI-KIANG BASIN

The Si-kiang Basin is divided from the Yangtze Basin by a broad mountain mass, descending in height from the Kweichow plateau and extending eastward in Kwangsi in a general east–west trend in the ranges of the Nan Ling. These ranges veer to a NE–SW direction in Kwangtung and continue this trend right through Fukien to Hangchow Bay. Pressure from the northwest in Palaeozoic 'Sinic' times, accompanied by extensive folding, determined this NE–SW axis.

The inland ranges on the borders of Kwangtung, Kwangsi, Hunan and Kiangsi are mainly pre-Carboniferous, sedimentary formations, comprising slates, sandstones and schists, with intercalated beds of shales and clays which have been intensely folded and metamorphosed. The ranges generally have sharp crests and are steep-sided, making rice production difficult. It is for this reason that this inland region is comparatively sparsely populated. To the west there are extensive limestone formations, giving rise to a karst topography, which is every bit as fantastic in its grotesque shapes as Chinese art depicts it. Spires and pinnacles crowned with temples rise abruptly from the plain. Caves, caverns, sink-holes, underground streams, intermittent streams – all the phenomena of karst country are to be found here in profusion.

Nearer the coast and along the littoral a great granitic batholith extends from Hangchow Bay to Vietnam. Most of the older overlying sedimentaries, which are the only fossil-bearing strata in this area yet discovered, have been eroded. Large outpourings of igneous rock are characteristic of the coastal areas, which have been folded and faulted. Deep submerging, probably in Pliocene and Pleistocene times, has resulted in a rugged ria coast, rich in good harbours along its whole extent. High humidity and high temperatures together produce rapid and deep disintegration of the granite, which is then very prone to gully erosion, producing a poor, infertile soil with lateritic qualities. Farther inland derived soils are sandy with a good admixture of clay and are therefore more fertile.

Kwangtung and Kwangsi are drained by three main rivers which unite in one deltaic mouth, the Pearl or Chu river. These three are the Si (West) river itself, the Pei (North) and the Tung (East), of which the first is the most important.

The Si-kiang is much smaller than the Yangtze, being only 2340 km long as compared with the Yangtze's 5580 km. Nevertheless it is a considerable river both in width and volume. It is a kilometre wide at Wuchow where it is joined by the left-bank tributary, the Kwei-kiang, and in times of great flood it has a volume of over 56 000 cu. m per second. Because it flows for the most part through narrow and confined valleys, variations in river level as between summer and winter are also very great. At Wuchow they measure between 20 and 25 m. There is no vast floodplain as there is in both the Hwang-ho and Yangtze. Only when the river issues onto the alluvium of the delta just above Shamshui is there any considerable expanse of flat land. Even this is broken especially near the coast, by islands of hills which rise abruptly from the silt.

The Si-kiang Basin embraces most of the two former provinces of Kwangtung and Kwangsi, which were known collectively as Liangkwang – the Two Kwangs – and were governed by one viceroy until the downfall of the Manchus in 1911. Kwangsi is now known as Kwangsi Chuang Autonomous Region. The intention of these Autonomous Regions, of which there are four today in China, is to give some special assistance to and protection of, the rights of the aboriginal or minority peoples in the area. Here in Kwangsi, which has a total population of $19\frac{1}{2}$ million, there are 6·6 million Chuang, 2·6 million Miao and about 9·6 million Yao. The total population of Liangkwang is just over 54 million. Thus the vast majority are Han Jen, or more correctly T'ang Jen, speaking the difficult Cantonese dialect with its ten tones. The Cantonese claim that theirs is nearer the original pure Chinese than Mandarin, the official language and the speech of the north. Mandarin, it is alleged, has been modified and corrupted by repeated invasions of barbarians from the north. Be that as it may, the language officially adopted and being popularized today throughout China is called *putonghua* (common speech). It is based on the northern dialect with Peking pronunciation as the standard. It should be noted that the People's Government regards China as a unitary government. The Autonomous Regions are not federated states as in the U.S.S.R. but are integral parts of a united whole.

The delta, which measures about 110 km from north to south and 90 km from east to west, consists of a network of distributaries on the west

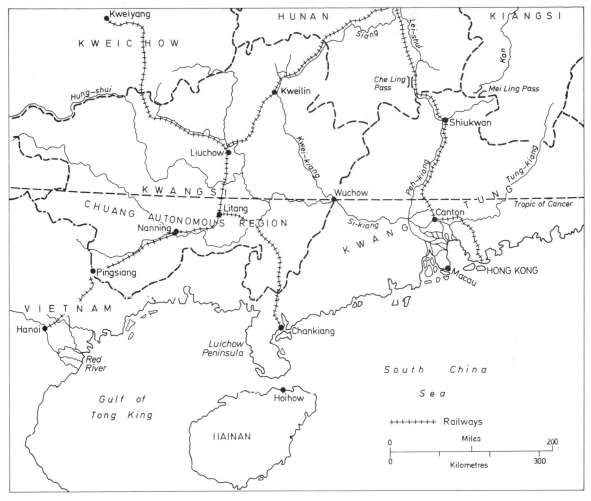

Fig. 118   The Si-kiang Basin

and north and a wide main channel, the Pearl river of the east, which empties into the South China Sea between the islands of Portuguese Macau on the west and the islands of British Hong Kong and the New Territories on the east.

The channels and canals of this maze, measuring about 2400 km are constantly changing course: old channels are abandoned and new ones developed. Through the centuries man has worked continuously to maintain the channels from silting until now it is estimated that there are two to three times as many man-made canals as there are natural distributaries. The farmlands reclaimed here are protected against flooding by dykes lined with trees, in much the same manner as those of the Yangtze Delta, and it is here that so

much irrigation and drainage has been carried out in the past two decades.

The Tropic of Cancer passes just north of Canton, cutting the Si-kiang Basin into two more or less equal parts. The northern half, because of its general higher elevation and its more northerly position, is subtropical, while the southern half is essentially tropical, especially along the southwest coast and on the island of Hainan. The region experiences three quite clearly marked seasons. From mid-October to mid-January is a delightful time with clear skies, warm and dry. From mid-January to mid-March, around the time of Chinese New Year, is the coldest period when damp, dull weather is experienced. Only on the higher ground is frost experienced. This is

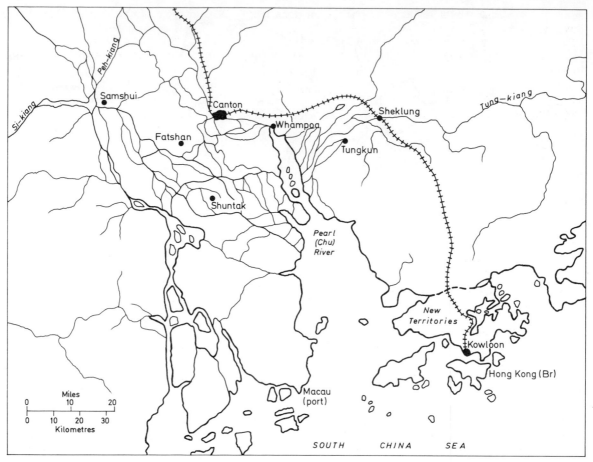

Fig. 119   The Si-kiang Delta

followed by a long, wet, enervating summer when both temperature and relative humidity are high. Walls stream with condensation and shoes grow mould overnight. Annual rainfall ranges between 1520 mm and 2000 mm, three-quarters of which falls in the long hot summer. Temperatures throughout the year are high enough in the entire area to give a twelve-month growing period.

Such a climate should ensure a vast covering of luxurious tropical and subtropical forest, especially in the more mountainous regions. In fact the whole area has suffered severe deforestation. Even in the remoter, steeper parts of Kwangtung, which are sparsely populated (an average of 25 persons per sq. km), the natural vegetation has been destroyed and replaced by scrub and grasslands. Fenzel[28] attributes this spoliation of the natural cover to three main causes. The Chinese farmer, as he moved southward in the early centuries, encountered forest as an enemy, as an obstacle to be cleared, and he has maintained this attitude ever since. Chinese literati have lacked that appreciation of forests which was present in the hard-hunting feudal lords of medieval Europe. Last, and probably most important, the ownership of the land was by small plots, but forests flourish best under large ownership. It may well be that, with common ownership of the land, the present ambitious afforestation projects for this area will come to fruition. In recent years strenuous efforts have been made to educate the peasantry in the value and care of forests, and large areas have been afforested. Pine, fir and eucalyptus, together with bamboo, are the main trees planted. These are fast growing and are fit for cutting in ten years. The following lines are

	Jan	Feb	Mar	Apr	May	Jun	July	Aug	Sep	Oct	Nov	Dec	Total
Kwellin													
Temp °C	9·0	6·8	9·6	12·3	18·2	22·1	26·8	28·5	27·6	25·9	22·3	15·5	
Rainfall mm	41	102	109	239	358	417	203	178	76	66	53	41	1883
Canton													
Temp °C	13·3	13·9	17·2	21·7	26·7	27·2	28·3	26·7	23·9	19·4	15·6		
Rainfall mm	23	48	107	173	269	269	205	219	165	86	31	23	1618

an example of the custom now so much in vogue in China of turning to song and verse to mark any achievement:

The forest in Chieh Shou is green and luxuriant.

The mountains are covered with verdant bamboo and trees.

To protect the forest well,

We hasten to open fire lanes[29].

Since 1949, there has been a rapid increase in the development of rubber plantations, especially in Hainan.

Temperature and rainfall combine to give Liangkwang a twelve-month growing period. Rice is by far the most important crop. Nearly all the rice grown is freshwater paddy and is double-cropped. A first harvest is taken in late June or early July and a second between mid-October and mid-November. The early crop is a different variety from the late. A little brackish water paddy is grown in the newly reclaimed lands along the sea-board and some upland (dry) rice is grown on the hills inland. Both brackish paddy and upland rice take longer to mature than freshwater paddy and only one crop a year can be secured. Good fresh-water paddy farming can usually secure a catch crop of vegetables or roots between the November harvest and the spring planting. Other important crops are sweet potato, corn, sugar-cane, ground-nuts, tea and many kinds of vegetables. Fruit grows in profusion in this tropical climate. Prominent are the pineapple, citrus fruits (tan-gerine, mandarine and pomelo), lychee, longan, papaya, guava, banana and persimmon. Kwang-tung's silk production is still considerable and ranks third to Szechwan and Kiangsu. Some indigo is also produced. Soils are acid and need constant liming, and rapid leaching of the soil due to heavy summer rains necessitates heavy fertiliza-tion.

Farms in the south are fairly well stocked with water buffaloes for draught work in the paddy fields. The work in the paddy fields of ploughing, puddling, planting and reaping is steadily being mechanized by use of the walking tractor. Large numbers of hogs are raised, many of which are exported daily down the Pearl river from Canton to Hong Kong. Poultry and duck farming is also important, particularly in the delta area.

Fishing, both inshore and deep sea, is a con-siderable industry all along the indented coast and in the shallow waters of the Pearl river estuary. Chinese junk-trawlers, drifters and long liners fish the South China Sea. Inshore waters have been badly overfished in most parts, but farther south they still provide a rich harvest in spite of inroads by Japanese fishing fleets, which until recently were highly mechanized and better equipped than the Chinese. During the last two decades mechan-ization of Chinese boats has made great strides, making a big extension of deep-sea fishing pos-sible. The main catches are yellow croaker, golden thread, white herring, mackerel and pomfret. Freshwater fish-farming in artificial ponds, parti-cularly in the delta region is an important and growing side of the fishing industry. The upper Pearl river is particularly important as a breeding ground for fish fry, which is exported to all parts of Southeast Asia.

The Si-kiang Basin is scheduled for develop-ment as a light industry area. The reason for this is that there is a deficiency of coal in this region. It is possible that this decision will be changed at a later date if the very high hydro-electric potential of the many fast-flowing rivers is properly de-veloped, for there are good reserves of iron ore in both the valley of the Han (Mei) river and in northern Hainan. Manganese is found in quantity in the southwest and in the Liuchow peninsula, and there are rich deposits of tungsten in northern Kwangtung on the Kiangsi border. At present practically all the light industry of Kwangtung is concentrated in the delta area. In addition to the many very small local refineries, large centres dealing with the rapidly increasing sugar-cane production have developed at Shunteh and Tung-kun. The main silk filature and weaving centres are at Canton, Shunteh and Fatshan.

The island of Hainan, which is only slightly smaller than Taiwan, is capable of much development. The southern part of the island is very mountainous, the Wuchih (Five Fingers) Mountains, with their five radiating ranges, reaching a height of over 1800 m. There are wide plains in the north bordering the narrow Chungchow Straits, which separate Hainan from the peninsula of Liuchow.

Much of the island, especially in the south, is occupied by tribes of Miao and Lu, who were, until recently, still practising *milpa* or *ladung* migratory agriculture. Standards of life were low and the people prone to the debilitating diseases of the tropics, notably malaria and hookworm. Amongst these tribes settled agriculture is becoming the order of the day and preventive medicine is conquering the diseases. T'ang Jen and Hakka from the mainland are the main occupants of the northern plains. Here, because the climate is more truly tropical than the rest of China, coconut and rubber are being developed in addition to rice cultivation and tropical fruit growing. There are big deposits of high-grade iron ore in the northwest, which are being developed.

For communication, reliance is still placed on water transport. The rivers, although fast-flowing, are navigable for junk and launch and these carry a great deal of the inland traffic. The Kwei-kiang, a left-bank tributary of the Si-kiang, is connected by a short canal with the headwaters of the Siang river and thus provides a continuous, albeit small, waterway to the Yangtze Basin. The new railway to Vietnam follows these same headwaters to Kweilin, thence to Liuchow, Nanning (capital of the Autonomous Region) and Munankwan at the border. One branch line runs from Litang to the coast at Chankiang and another runs from Liuchow up onto the Kweichow plateau to Kwei-yang. Both the road and the Canton–Hankow railway follow the valley of the Pei-kiang and cross the Nan Ling by the Che Ling Pass down into the Lei-shui valley and so to Hengyang and Changsha. The road forks at Shuichow in the Pei-kiang valley, one arm running over the Mei Ling Pass to the headwaters of the Kan-kiang and so into Kiangsi. This is the route of the former famous imperial road to Peking.

Canton is the only really large city of South China: it has now a population of 3 100 000. As we

Plate 27   *Li and Miao members of Hungtao commune, Kwangsi*

have seen, it figured prominently in the events which led to the First Opium War, 1841–2, when it was the gate of entry for foreign goods. The river was then adequate for ocean-going vessels but now is to shallow to permit large ships to reach it. Whampoa, lower down the river, can take vessels of 10 000 tons and is now Canton's outport.

Canton has been the home of revolutionary movements in this century. The abortive revolt, led by Sun Yat Sen, which was the prelude to the Revolution of 1911, occurred here and is commemorated by a monument which is remarkable for the many stones in its make-up contributed by Chinese in the U.S.A. It was from Canton that Chiang Kai-shek led his victorious army northward in 1926 and it was here that the Communist Canton Commune was set up for a few days in 1927.

Since 1949 great development has taken place. The city planning, started by Sun Yat Sen in the 1920s, has been continued; the streets widened and cleaned up, with parks and avenues of trees, as in so many of China's cities today, so that Canton now is indeed beautiful. Its industry has undergone considerable expansion, and now includes heavy iron and steel, machinery, chemical and cement works and some shipbuilding. Light industry includes food-processing, glass and porcelain ware, textiles and machinery (bicycles, clocks and watches, sewing machines and the like). Traditional handicrafts flourish.

Haikow on the north coast of Hainan is a small but active port. Chan-chiang is rapidly developing as the port for Kwangsi.

4. THE SOUTHEAST COAST

The southeast coastal region is that area which lies between Ningpo and Swatow, a land of mountains and steep-sided valleys cut deep into the granites, granodiorites, porphyries and igneous rocks, which are the main geological constituents. The western border of the region is marked by the crests of the Wuyi Shan, which are also known as the Bohea Mountains and from which the Bohea congou tea derives its name. The southeast border is the deeply indented, precipitous ria coast, strewn with islands. It is similar to the Kwangtung coast in formation but is more rugged and it differs from the Kwangtung coast in that the excellent harbours have little or no hinterland comparable with the Si-kiang. A series of short, fast-flowing rivers cut their way down to the sea from the mountainous interior. None of them is of use for communication, except for small junks and sampans, which have to be hauled up-stream by trackers.

Of the hundreds of streams emptying into the Taiwan Straits four are worthy of note, each of which has a town and port of some size at its mouth. In the north, in southern Chekiang, Wenchow stands at the mouth of the Wu-kiang. Farther south is the largest of the Fukien rivers, the Min, which has one left-bank and one right-bank tributary which are comparatively large. The Min cuts a deep valley and enters the sea at Foochow without forming a floodplain. About 220 km to the south is Amoy at the mouth of the Kiulung-kiang, which, while much smaller than the Min, has gentler gradients and a plain 25 sq. km above its entry into the sea. Amoy stands on an island and has an excellent harbour. Sixteen kilometres to the east and still in the mouth of the bay, Hsia-men Wan, is the island of Quemoy – *Chin Men* in Mandarin and meaning 'Golden Gate' – fortified and held at present by the Kuomintang forces of Taiwan. Forty-eight kilometres to the northeast is the modern village of Chuanchow, which stands on the site of old Zayton, the great medieval Chinese port for India, Java and Japan, and much

visited by Arab merchants. Last of the four southeastern rivers is the Han-kiang, which flows within the borders of Kwangtung province and has Swatow at its mouth. All four of the cities mentioned are ports which figured prominently in the 1870s when the China tea trade was in its heyday. At these ports the famous tea clippers gathered during the summer and set out on their race to London.

The climate of this southeastern area is essentially subtropical. The Tropic of Cancer passes right through Swatow Bay. Thus the whole of Fukien and the southern half of Chekiang, which together form the region, lie outside the tropics. The broad belt of mountainous country along the whole northwest border affords protection against the cold north winds in winter. Winter temperatures seldom fall below freezing at sea-level in the south but are considerably lower in the north. Summers everywhere are hot. This is a region of heavy rainfall with a marked summer maximum, usually more than two-thirds of the total precipitation occurring in the five summer months, May to September. This, too, is the Chinese coast most affected by typhoons, which may be expected any time between May and October, although their main incidence is in August and September. They originate in the Pacific to the east of the Philippines and Taiwan and usually move west and northwest, many striking the Kwangtung and Fukien coasts. Typhoons bring with them torrential rains and hurricane winds of 150 k.p.h. and more. Barometric pressure may fall 40–50 mm in a few hours; the sea-level rises alarmingly and with disastrous results to shipping and property bordering the sea. It is fortunate that these typhoons die out quickly as they penetrate inland.

The many and high ranges of the Wuyi Mountains have served to isolate the southeast from the rest of China to a considerable degree. The original inhabitants, the Min Yueh, remained independent of Chinese rule until nearly the end of the Later Han dynasty. Subsequent pressures from the north have resulted in many infiltrations of people, notably the Hakka or 'Guest Folk' during the ninth and tenth centuries when Mongol (Khitan) pressure was at its height. The mountainous nature of the country with its isolated valleys has resulted in many local and widely differing dialects which virtually constitute a different spoken language from Mandarin, although it must always be remembered that the

	Jan	Feb	Mar	Apr	May	Jun	July	Aug	Sep	Oct	Nov	Dec	Total
Foochow (20 m)													
Temp °C	11·7	11·1	13·3	17·8	22·2	26·7	28·9	28·9	24·4	19·4	15·0	16·0	
Rainfall mm	46	96	114	122	150	207	160	183	213	51	41	48	1431
Swatow (40 m)													
Temp °C	15·0	13·9	16·7	21·1	25·0	27·8	28·9	28·3	27·8	24·4	20·0	16·7	
Rainfall mm	36	63	79	145	229	267	198	213	142	71	41	38	1522

written language throughout China is the same. The people are ruggedly independent and are reputed to have less polished manners than their compatriots of the north and south.

Geography has influenced livelihood in the southeast to much the same extent and in much the same way as it has done in Norway. Topography is the ruling factor. The mountainous character of the area and the deep, narrow valleys limit farmland to about 8 per cent of the whole. Although, like Kwangtung, the soil is acid and not very fertile, this small proportion is farmed most intensively. Rice, as elsewhere, is the main crop and grown wherever possible. The growing period is long enough to enable two crops per annum to be taken. Other important food crops are sweet potatoes, vegetable oils (rapeseed and sesamum-seed), beans, groundnuts and vegetables. Sub-tropical fruits – citrus, peaches, persimmon – and sugar-cane are produced in quantity.

This is the most famous tea-growing area of China, especially in the centre and north, around and behind Foochow and Wenchow, whence come the Bohea teas. Every summer during the 1870s and 1880s the tea clippers used to gather at the ports to await the tea harvest. On their outward passage in early summer they sailed southwest on the Northeast Trades until the South American coast was reached; then, with the Southeast Trades on their port side the clippers hugged the Brazilian coast until the Roaring Forties were encountered. Turning due east the sailing ships used these westerlies until they had nearly reached Australia, when again the Southeast Trades were used to carry them northwestward. After the clippers had passed through the Sunda Straits and crossed the Equator, the SW monsoon carried them to the Southeast China coast. The return passage in the autumn made similar use of the prevailing winds by following quite a different course. By the time that the tea had been harvested, processed and packed, the SW mon-

soon had given place to the NE monsoon. These following winds were used right across the Indian Ocean to Madagascar. With the SE Trades on their port the sailing vessels maintained their southwesterly course and, by hugging the South African coast, the Cape was rounded with the least possible encountering of the headwinds of the Roaring Forties, which at this season are much farther south. Thereafter the SE Trades carried the clippers across the South Atlantic to Cape São Roque. Rather than turn directly homeward from here and face headwinds from the NE Trades, the clippers continued to the Bahamas with the NE Trades on their starboard side and then turned for home across the North Atlantic on the westerly Anti-trades. The first clipper home with its tea cargo secured not only the best price but gained considerable prestige in shipping circles. An exciting account of one of these races is given by John Masefield in his novel *Bird of Dawning*.

The other resources that this mountainous southeast coast region offers comes from its forests. Heavy rainfall and subtropical temperatures ensure the production of a good forest cover of conifers (*Cunninghamia* and pine), camphor and bamboo. The last provides material for innumerable purposes from pens to scaffold poles, and from chopsticks to tables. Timber cutting has been heavy and there has been some deforestation, especially in the more accessible regions along the lower reaches of the rivers, but it has not reached the serious dimensions of the north and centre.

Restricted agriculture has turned the faces of the people seaward to look for a living. The many good natural harbours and the plentiful timber supplies for shipbuilding have combined to develop here the fisherfolk of China. The thousands of bays and inlets afford good grounds for inshore purse seine fishing and oyster culture. Many of the larger junks, which form the deep-sea fishing fleets operating from Ningpo,

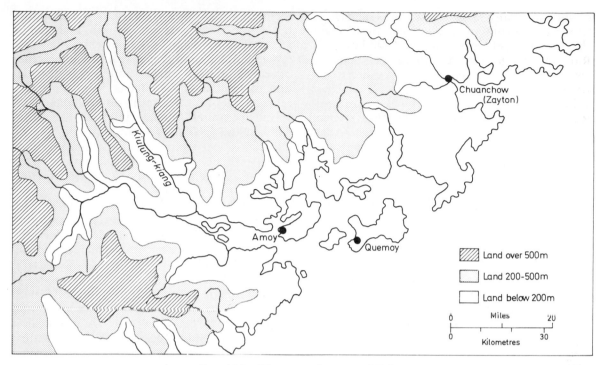

Fig. 120   The rugged coast of Fukien

Wenchow, Foochow and Amoy, have been mechanized. These ports also supply a large proportion of the merchantile fleet of junks which carries the very considerable coastal trade extending not only as far north as Tientsin but inland up the Yangtze as far as Ichang. As with Devon in England, so Fukien in China has become the region from which its sailors have been recruited. Fukien sailors supply most of the admirable crews which man so many of the western steamship lines.

In spite of the intensive use of its limited agricultural land and the full exploitation of its timber and fishing resources, Fukien has been unable to meet the pressure of its increasing population. This pressure, which was intensified in the last two decades of the nineteenth century by the failure of the tea trade through Indian competition, has been relieved during the last century by emigration mainly to Malaya, Borneo and Indonesia.

5. THE YUNNAN–KWEICHOW PLATEAU

This plateau region is a southwestern extension of the Tibetan Plateau and is composed generally of rough mountainous land, having a general level of 1800–2100 m above sea-level in the west, with many snow-capped peaks rising to over 4500 m. The plateau descends eastward, many parts of Kweichow having a general level of less than 900 m, the mountains being less rugged and the valleys wider.

Western Yunnan is characterized by north–south ranges, between which the Mekong, Salween and Irrawaddy flow and which have constituted so great a barrier between China and Burma in the past. Deep, steep-sided and heavily wooded valleys with fast-flowing, unnavigable and often unfordable rivers make communication in these parts extraordinarily difficult. Many of these valleys are 1500 m deep and perhaps only 750 m wide at that height and within hailing distance. Yet it may demand a whole day's strenuous journey to get from one side to the other. Occasional swaying bamboo rope bridges, slung 150 m above the rocky chasm, help the traveller across. It was in these malarial infected valleys that Kublai Khan lost nearly half his forces when invading Burma. Farther south these ranges are lower, less precipitous and more easily crossed. This western region has been heavily folded and is still unstable and subject to earthquakes. A severe one in 1925 resulted in great loss of life and had long-lasting effects on agriculture. The comparatively slight changes in level caused by earthquakes spell disaster to paddy farmers, whose fields must of necessity be absolutely level if they are to be flooded.

The character of the plateau changes eastward. Central and south Kweichow and south Yunnan are composed largely of Devonian limestone and have developed the same fantastic karst landscape which we noted in West Kiangsi. In the western part of the plateau the erosion cycle has not advanced as far as it has in the east and much of the drainage system is underground. A feature of the karst region is the large number of small isolated valleys, known locally as *patze*, which are reminiscent of the *polje* of Yugoslavia. They are deep and often oval in shape, giving them the appearance of arenas, especially as their sides are lined with the irregular terraced fields which follow the contours of the steep valley slopes.

The Kinsha (Upper Yangtze) cuts a deep trench along the north side of the plateau from which it receives many short right-bank tributaries in the west and the much larger Wu-kiang in the east. The latter drains the greater part of northern Kweichow, which is lower and a gentler topography than the rest. Thus the Yangtze drains the northern regions of the plateau; the Mekong, Salween and Irrawaddy drain the west; and the Red river and Si-kiang the south and southeast.

The climate of this plateau is the most equable in the whole of China. Cressey says of it, 'The province of Yunnan is an island, not of land amid an ocean, but of moderate temperature and clear skies, surrounded on three sides by hot, humid lowlands'.[31] In spite of the height of the plateau, winters are mild and summers are cool by comparison with the plains to the east and south. Those who, during the Sino–Japanese War (1939–1945), were forced to trek from Central China to these regions, expatiate on the bright, clear winters and the delectable summers of Yunnan,

the meaning of which is 'South of the Clouds' – the clouds being those of Szechwan. It should be added that Kweichow does not enjoy the same reputation. It is a province with a high incidence of cloud and a much more even distribution of rainfall than Yunnan. Kunming has a range of only 13° C between average January and July temperatures. Annual rainfall ranges between 800 mm and 1000 mm for most low-lying places, although slopes exposed to moisture-laden winds have a much heavier fall. Most places are free from frost for at least ten months of the year; there is thus a long growing period.

Second only to Szechwan, this Southwest Rice Region is one of the richest forest areas of China Proper, the remoter the district, the finer the forest. In the northwest, *cryptomeria*, Lohan pine, red and white birch predominate. On the central plateau the main stands are pine, fir, cypress and oak, while in the lower south and southeast broad-leafed trees of oak, maple and poplar, and bamboo groves, mark the valleys. A great deal of the natural forest has been destroyed in the settled districts. For this reason, afforestation is being urged on all communes. In addition to quick-growing fir, wood-oil trees are being extensively planted. Mountain steppe of tall grasses is common and the whole region is renowned for its wealth of flowers – its azaleas and rhododendrons.

The main types of soil are mountain red-earths and mountain yellow podzolic earths, which occur nowhere else in China.[32] Neither results in good agricultural soil. The red-earths are badly eroded and leached. The yellow-earths, developed under mixed forest of deciduous, coniferous and ever-green broadleafed trees in which deciduous predominate, are acid. The only good agricultural soil is the purple–brown forest soil and this, unfortunately, is very limited in extent.

Favourable climate, giving a long growing season, which should lead to heavy agricultural production, is offset by the limited area of cultivable land and the poor soils. Only about

	Jan	Feb	Mar	Apr	May	Jun	July	Aug	Sep	Oct	Nov	Dec	Total
Kwayang (1390 m)													
Temp° C	2·8	5·6	11·7	17·2	21·7	22·2	24·4	25·0	20·0	13·9	11·7	8·3	
Rainfall mm	25	28	23	74	178	209	229	104	138	107	51	15	1181
Kunming (1805 m)													
Temp °C	8·9	10·6	15·6	18·9	21·1	22·2	21·1	21·1	18·9	17·2	13·3	9·4	
Rainfall mm	13	13	15	18	96	155	249	208	137	91	43	15	1053

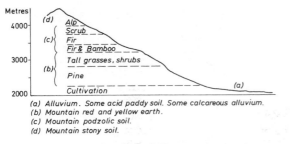

(a) *Alluvium. Some acid paddy soil. Some calcareous alluvium.*
(b) *Mountain red and yellow earth.*
(c) *Mountain podzolic soil.*
(d) *Mountain stony soil.*

Fig. 121   Profile of Yunnan vegetation

5 per cent of the total area is actually cultivated, although Buck estimated in 1937 that about 63 per cent of the uncultivated land could be put to some productive use. Production is confined to the *patze*, where rice is the main summer crop. In south Yunnan there is a little double-cropping of rice. Other summer crops are corn, barley and millet, sweet potatoes, tobacco, vegetables and some tea of high quality. Corn and sweet potatoes have formed the main staple food of the poorer peasants. The main winter crops today are oil seeds, beans and vegetables. In the past a great deal of opium was grown on account of its high cash value and the ease of its transport.[33] This was harvested just before the planting of the rice in spring and afforded an income larger than any other winter crop. Its cultivation is now forbidden.

More than half the population of the plateau is composed of the many aboriginal peoples and tribes who, in the course of preceding centuries, have been forced back into the mountains by the Chinese as they pressed south and west, rather as the Britons were forced back into the Welsh highlands by Saxon and Dane. They number about 6 million. These mountain folk tend to keep to their own modes, customs, dialects and dress. Until the 1949 Revolution they carried on trade with the Chinese of the lower lands. Usually they specialized in and marketed only one product, e.g. the Black Lolo sold fuel; the White Lolo, corn; the Miao-tzu, corn; the Pei I, fruit.[34] Since 1949 most of these people have come under local administration, known as Autonomous Chou (8) or Districts (15) designed to prevent their exploitation and assist their development.

The Chinese or Han part of the population forms the farming community of the lower lands and is engaged mainly in rice cultivation. This has been one of the most conservative and reactionary areas of China – easy-going and lacking in energy

and initiative. Before the land reform measures of 1949 there was considerable absentee landlordism. The main objective of owner and tenant alike appears to have been to find contentment, and by contentment was meant the avoidance of painful labour as far as possible. This led to much exploitation of women as labourers; a daughter-in-law was thought of in terms of a cheap, long-term labourer.[35] The lack of energy in the past can be attributed to the very widespread habit of opium smoking.

There has always been hostility and suspicion between the indigenous tribes and the settled Chinese. This has resulted in unrest and turbulence, which has been further accentuated by the presence of a body of some half a million Moslems who have come south from Kansu. In 1873 a great Moslem rebellion broke out and it was not finally quelled until the nineties.

The conservatism referred to above is due in no small measure to the isolation resulting from poor communications. The rugged topography makes all travel and transport extremely difficult. Until recently practically all transport was by way of coolie pole along paths at best paved with slabs of stone. There was an old trade route, which ran from Suifu (Ipin) south to Yunnan-fu (Kunming). Here it divided. One branch ran westward to Tali and Tengyueh and so to Bhamo in Burma. The other turned south to Mengtze and Tongking. It was along this latter route that the first railway penetration into Yunnan was made. The railway was built with French capital and its completion in 1908 was no small engineering feat, especially in the Chinese section where literally hundreds of tunnels were bored and thousands of bridges and culverts had to be built. Such was the state of the mountain paths in the north that it was quicker and cheaper to travel from Chungking to Kunming by going down the Yangtze to Shanghai, thence to Hanoi and so by rail to Kunming than by taking the overland route.

The influence of the Hanoi–Kunming railway in breaking down the isolation of the plateau was small as compared with that of the Second World War, when the Japanese invasion of the Yangtze and Si-kiang Basins drove millions of Chinese of all classes into the Szechwan Basin and up onto the Kweichow and Yunnan plateau. Schools, colleges, universities, industrialists, manufacturers and merchants alike moved in, bringing with them ideas and techniques which inevitably have shaken the old conservatism. The war also

Plate 28   A local water conservancy project in the Tai Autonomous Chou, Yunnan

led to the construction of the Burma Road from Lashio via Kunming to Chungking and Chengtu. (See Communications and Transport.)

Since 1949, under the first two Five-year Plans, railways were projected to connect Chengtu with Kunming and between Chungking and Kunming via Kweiyang and Yungfeng. This network is now completed and has helped considerably in opening up the region. Road building has also progressed very rapidly.

Fairly widespread deposits of coal and some good-quality iron, mainly near Mengtze are adequate for the development since 1949 of a rapidly expanding iron and steel industry. This is concentrated in and around Kunming, the provincial capital and only city of over 1 million inhabitants. The city also produces machinery, chemicals and cement as well as consumer goods. Much of Yunnan's wealth lies in its deposits of tin, copper, zinc and phosphorus. Tin is mined at

Ko-chiu, Shih-ping and Meng-tzu. In 1964 more than 90 per cent of China's total output of 30 000 tons was produced here. Very little of this now finds its way onto the world market on account of home demand. Copper mining, located mainly near Hui-tzu, has been worked for many centuries. It has been suggested that the bronze (tin and copper) of the Yin or Shang dynasty came from here. Tali marble is sought after throughout China for decorative building material on account of its striking and beautiful markings.

6. THE NORTHEAST (MANCHURIA)

The Northeast, or Manchuria as it is more generally known to Westerners, has been associated with China Proper since very early times in varying degrees of intimacy. Under the Earlier and Later Han (206 BC–AD 220) the lower Liao river

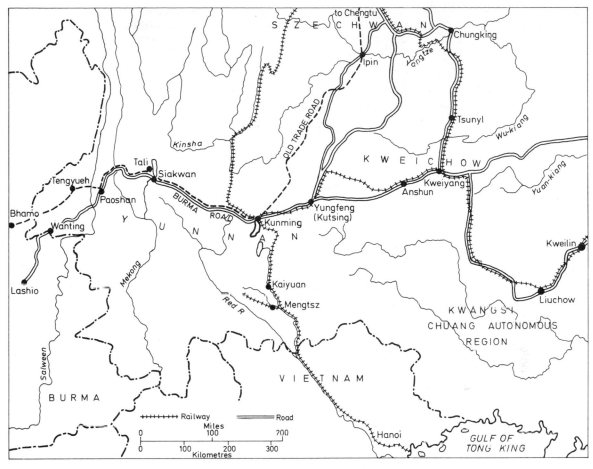

Fig. 122   Yunnan-Kweichow

region, the East Manchurian Uplands and North Korea owned Chinese sovereignty but reverted to nomadic tribal leadership on the fall of the dynasty. In T'ang times (AD 618–906) a large area, reaching well to the north of the Liao Basin, formed a kind of Chinese protectorate, while under the Chin Empire (AD 1125–1206) Chinese territory extended as far as the Amur river and had a long seacoast on the Sea of Japan. This, and a great deal more, was incorporated in the great Mongol Yuan Empire under Kublai Khan and remained under the nominal sovereignty to China under the early Ming in 1415.

Far-flung though these periodic extensions of territory may have been, that there was no real expansion to the northeast intended – or to the northwest for that matter – is demonstrated by the fact that part of the Great Wall was built here and

the purpose of this wall was to bar entry and to some extent to prevent exit. The wall was extended in a wide semi-circle to enclose the lower Liao and it thus formed a kind of Chinese Pale. Thus the coast route via Shanhaikwan into China, which was used for trade, was covered but the more difficult upper Liao route, which was more usually used by invading forces, was not defended. Owen Lattimore, at pains to emphasize the restrictive nature of the Wall, says 'A positive expansion does not build limiting walls. There are no Great Wall systems in the South'.[36]

Profiting by internal disorders due to civil war and endless court intrigues of a decadent Ming dynasty, Nurhachu, a Manchurian nomad chief, first conquered the surrounding East Mongolian tribes and gained their support, rather as Jenghis Khan had done before him. He then proceeded to

Volume of immigration and emigration from Manchuria

Year	Volume of Immigration	Volume of Emigration	Residuum	% residuum to Immigration
1923	342 038	240 565	101 473	30
1924	376 613	200 046	176 567	47
1925	491 948	239 433	252 512	51
1926	572 648	323 566	249 082	43
1927	1 016 723	338 082	678 641	67
1928	938 472	394 247	544 225	58
1929	1 046 291	621 897	424 394	41

build up a professional army of eight corps or 'banners', which owed no nomadic tribal or territorial allegiance and which were prepared to serve anywhere with a promise of a share in the fruits of victory. With this army Nurhachu overran the Chinese Pale in 1626. Although he died in that year the invasion continued and Peking fell in 1644. The militarily powerful but administratively inexperienced Manchus made peace with, and secured the cooperation of, the Chinese gentry, who had been direly persecuted in the last years of the Ming. The Manchus were thus able to establish governmental control over the whole country.[37]

The first great Ch'ing dynasty emperor, K'ang Hsi, embarked on a policy of keeping the Northeast as a closed preserve for Manchurian bannermen, who became a privileged class both here and throughout China, receiving a subsidy from the wealth of China. In 1668 K'ang Hsi closed Manchuria to the Chinese, although, up to 1644, the country was underpopulated. The Manchurians are reported to have captured and brought to the Northeast more than one million Chinese during the many sporadic raids they made on China during the declining years of the Ming Empire. A willow palisade and moat were constructed encircling and isolating the Manchurian preserve, but the prohibition was never very strictly observed. On the one hand, whenever famine occurred in north China, especially in Shantung, there was an influx of refugees into Manchuria which would have been very difficult to control. On the other hand, the bannermen, never great agriculturalists, became demoralized through being subsidized and came to rely more and more on imported Chinese labour. By 1779 it is estimated that there were more than 6 million Chinese peasants working in each of the provinces of Kirin and Fengtien (modern Liaotung). The need of the great landowners was for workers rather than tenants. Thus began the seasonal migration of labour, mainly from Shantung, which was maintained up to the outbreak of the Second World War. As might be expected there was always a residue which remained behind, but generally speaking the objective of the migrant was to make his money and to return to his ancestral home.

During the latter half of the nineteenth century Russia's penetration eastward in Siberia and along the banks of the Amur river caused grave concern to the Ch'ing government. The wide open spaces of Heilungkiang, which is the Chinese name for the Amur river and means 'the Black Dragon river', needed populating. In order to encourage colonists, the whole of this northern region was thrown open to Chinese immigrants. It is reported that more than 100 000 households had moved in by 1870. Part of this colonization in the extreme north, however, was by 'garrisons' of yeoman stock having some military tradition, whose services could be called on if necessary.[39]

In 1907 all legal obstacles to immigration were removed. Between 1920 and 1930, owing to revolution, civil war and widespread famine in north China, there was a continual and increasing migration into Manchuria. This took the form mainly of seasonal labour movement, but every year there was a residuum of between 40 and 60 per cent which did not return home. This colonization was of the refugee type. The colonist left his home with regret and with an eye to eventual return in contrast to the backwoodsman of North America of the last century, who set out in high adventure to carve a new world for himself. Immigrants before 1931 were mainly agriculturalists. Thereafter their composition changed, until by 1938 they were mainly industrial workers and miners.

Population rose very rapidly. In 1904 Sir Alexander Hosie estimated it at about 17 million. The Research Bureau of the South Manchurian

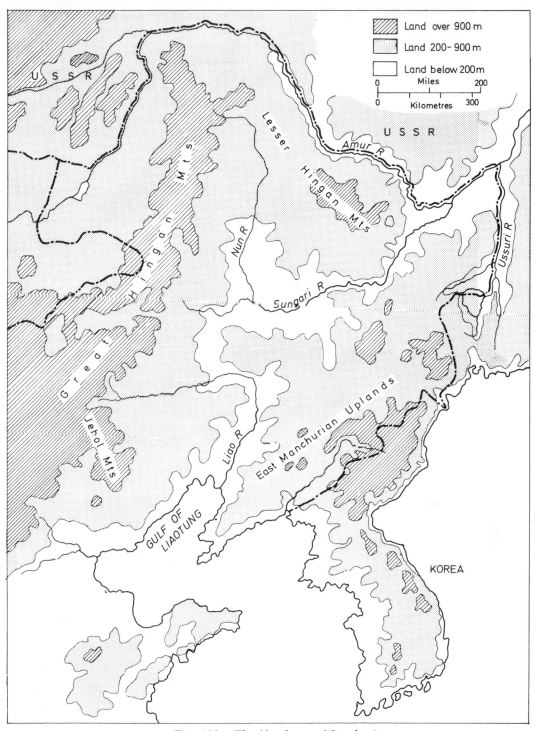

Fig. 123   The Northeast: Manchuria

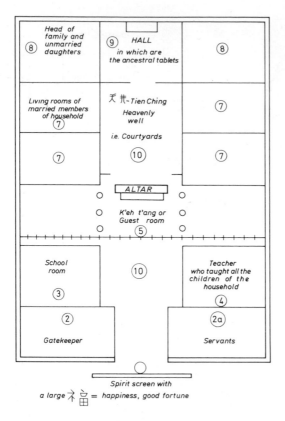

Fig. 124   Plan of a house of a well-to-do
Chinese family pre-1949

Railway Co. placed it at 34 million in 1930. The census figures in 1957 were:

Liaoning	24 095 000
Kirin	12 550 000
Heilungkiang	14 780 000
	51 425 000

The population is overwhelmingly Han in composition. The 600 000 Manchus are mainly in the upper Sungari area in Heilungkiang, the region from which they originally moved to conquer Ming China. There are 220 000 Koreans, skilled rice-growers, concentrated in southeast Kirin around Yenki. Some 38 000 Mongolians occupy the grassland slopes of the Ta Hingan Shan in the west and are engaged in animal husbandry, and 45 000 Mongolians are mainly urban dwellers, engaged in commerce and industry. In spite of the great

increase during the last twenty years, the country remains underpopulated in face of the ever-increasing demand for manpower in industry and agriculture.[41]

In view of its proximity to China Proper and its more temperate climate than the other two provinces, it is not surprising that Liaoning is the most densely populated and the most important agricultural part of the Northeast. In 1957 of its 24 million inhabitants, 8·5 million were urban and of these 80 per cent were concentrated in the conurbation centred in Shenyang. This exercises a considerable influence on the agricultural pattern of the Northeast. Intensity of cultivation and unit output tend to decrease northward and the size of farm to increase. Thirty-three per cent of the land in Liaoning is cultivated. No comparable figures are available for Kirin and Heilungkiang, but it is certain that the proportions are a good deal less. Irrigation and drainage works, which are being extended to all cultivable parts of the Northeast, are most advanced in Liaoning. Much of the lowland of the lower Liao and Hun, which is subject to flooding, has been brought under control. It is reported that half of the rural communes are now served with electric power and pumping stations.[42]

George B. Cressey, in his *China's Geographic Foundations* makes a felicitous comparison of the Manchurian plains to the courtyard of a Chinese house. Above is a plan of a house of a fairly well-to-do Chinese family of pre-1949 times. It will be seen how much of it reflects the physique of the country. True, there is nothing to equate with the spirit screen, nor is there any back door to match the outlet of the Sungari at its confluence with the Amur. The Liao River Basin and the Sungari correspond clearly enough with the courtyards, and the waterparting between them matches the *K'eh t'ang* or guest room. The Jehol Mountains as they come down steeply to the west shore of the Gulf of Liatung at Shanhaikwan correspond to the gatekeeper's lodge and the ancient Hills of the Liaotung peninsula on the east with the servants' quarters. The Ta Hingan (Great Khingan) Mountains with their steep scarp faces to the east and gentler dip slopes away to the Gobi, correspond to the living rooms on one side and the East Manchurian Uplands to the living rooms on the other. The Siao Hingan (Little Khingan) Mountains running east and west in the north match the hall, and so complete the picture.

The plains of the Liao and the Sungari rivers are

	Jan	Feb	Mar	Apr	May	Jun	July	Aug	Sep	Oct	Nov	Dec	Total
Harbin (159 m)													
Temp °C	−19·4	−15·2	−4·5	5·6	13·3	18·9	22·2	20·6	10·6	4·4	−6·2	−16·4	
Rainfall mm	5	5	10	23	43	104	147	107	56	31	10	65	546
Mukden (34 m)													
Temp °C	−12·8	−10·6	−2·2	7·8	15·6	21·1	24·4	23·3	16·7	8·9	−1·7	−10·0	
Rainfall	5	5	20	28	56	86	160	155	84	41	28	65	673
Dairen (10 m)													
Temp °C	−3·9	−3·9	2·2	8·9	15·0	20·0	22·8	24·4	20·6	14·4	6·1	−1·1	612
Rainfall mm	13	8	18	23	43	46	163	130	102	28	25	13	

largely erosional in contrast to the North China Plain, which is depositional. The Liao river is shallow and carries a heavy load of silt, which is encroaching on the Gulf of Liaotung at a very rapid rate. Old Newchuang, which was originally a port at the mouth of the river, today stands kilometres from the coast and now has Yingkow as its port. This silting of the Gulf makes the siting of a port there difficult and accounts in part for the importance and development of Dairen and Port Arthur on the eastern side of the peninsula. In consequence of its shallowness the Liao is of little use for navigation save for light junk traffic. In contrast, the Sungari is larger and deeper and is navigable for river craft of 1000 tons and more, which carry an important amount of both passenger and cargo traffic. The Sungari empties into the Amur or Heilungkiang, which marks the entire northern border of Manchuria and which has even greater navigability than the Sungari. With the recent agricultural and industrial development of this region both in the U.S.S.R. and in Northern Manchuria the importance of these two rivers has been greatly enhanced.

While the influence of the monsoon rhythm is still evidenced in the Northeast by the seasonal distribution of rainfall, its continentality is strongly emphasized by the big range of its temperatures which increase markedly from south to north. Clear winter skies and strong, bitterly cold winds from the Siberian high produce minimum temperatures at times as low as − 15°C at Mukden (Shenyang) and − 21°C at Harbin. Winters are long. Harbin has five months with average temperatures well below freezing. The spring and autumn seasons are short as the rapid rise and fall of temperatures in April and November respectively indicate. Summer temperatures on the plains average between 21° C and 24° C. With the rise in temperature comes the rain, about four-fifths of which fall in the four summer

months. The amount of rainfall decreases from south to north and from east to west. It is heaviest in the East Manchurian Uplands (Changpai Shan). Nearly everywhere on the plains it is adequate for wheat growing, i.e. more than 380 mm.

The natural vegetation of the plains is that of temperate zone grasslands. This, however, is rapidly disappearing as more and more of the plains are passing from nomadic pasturage to ploughland. The resultant soil is chernozem in character but is not considered light enough by some authorities to be placed firmly in that category. The mountain lands of the Ta Hingan (Great Khingan), Jehol Mountains and the East Manchurian Uplands are forested. As might be expected, the last, receiving the heaviest rainfall, are the most densely wooded with pine, larch and fir. The massive Manchurian pine is the best timber and has been cut, during the last fifty years and particularly by the Japanese during the Second World War, to an alarming extent. The eastern-facing slopes of the Ta Hingan Mountains are fairly well covered, but the forests quickly fade out on crossing their crests and descending the western dip slopes. Forest gives place to steppe and eventually to semi-desert and true desert. There are far-reaching and long-term plans to create a wide, continuous forest belt along the whole length of the eastern side of the Ta Hingan and to conserve more carefully the valuable timber of the East Manchurian Uplands. In 1945 it was estimated that standing timber covered about 22 million hectares, whilst 66 million hectares were in urgent need of re-afforestation.

Modern development of Manchuria stems out of the economic and political ambitions and rivalries of the Great Powers, most notably Russia and Japan, and is intimately related to railway construction. We have seen something of the earlier breakdown of Chinese isolationism mainly by the British earlier in the nineteenth century and the relative quiet which followed the Second Opium War in 1860. This quiescent period was broken first by the outbreak of the Sino–Japanese War (1894–5) which synchronized with growing Russian activity in eastern Siberia where she was building the Trans-Siberian Railways. This railway, if built entirely on Russian soil, would have had to follow the long loop of the Amur–Ussuri valleys to reach Vladivostok. Accordingly Russia sought and obtained a concession in 1896 to build the line across Manchuria via Tsitsihar and Harbin to Vladivostok. This agreement included not only the right to build the railway, which was called the Chinese Eastern Railway, but also the right to develop the land alongside the line and the granting of some measure of extraterritoriality to Russian subjects. This concession was further extended to permission to build the line from Harbin to Port Arthur thus giving Russia an ice-free port on the Pacific.

So broke out again the scramble among the Great Powers for zones of influence and concessions in a decadent and impotent China. Germany gained Tsingtao and its environs in 1897; Britain obtained Weihaiwei. In addition to the annexation of Korea and Formosa, Japan claimed the Liaotung peninsula as the fruit of her victory over China, but this was denied her through the strong opposition of Russia, backed by France and Great Britain. Mutual fears and fierce rivalry between Russia and Japan broke into open war in 1904, when Russia was signally defeated by Japan to the surprise of the rest of the world. As a result Japanese influence surplanted that of Russia in Liaoning. The development of Manchuria from that time on steadily became an integral part of Japanese imperialist policy for the creation of a Greater Japanese Empire, which culminated in the Sino–Japanese War (1937–45) and Japan's entry into the Second World War.

Until 1931 Manchuria remained nominally subject to the Peking Government, whether Manchu or subsequently Republican, although its writ seldom ran, but the direction of its economic development fell more and more into Japanese hands. In 1931 Japan, flaunting world condemnation through the League of Nations, virtually annexed Manchuria, forming it into the State of Manchukuo and making the ex-Manchu emperor, deposed in 1911, its puppet head. Thereafter Japanese dominance remained complete

until after her defeat at the end of the war in 1945. Then followed a race and a struggle between the Nationalist Kuomintang and the Communist Kungsantang for mastery, won eventually by the Communists.

It is with this history in mind and in this political setting that the economic geography of the Northeast must be examined, for Japan regarded the country purely as a means of supplying sinews for her power whether in the provision of foodstuffs for her home population, raw materials for her industries, or an outlet for her swarming people. To this end Japan lavished millions of pounds of capital on Manchuria in developing its many resources.

Some idea of agricultural development can be gleaned from the increase of land under cultivation. In 1915 some 6·6 million hectares were being tilled. In 1933 this had doubled at 13·3 million hectares and in 1939 it had grown to 17·5 million. During the Second World War there was probably little agricultural development due to concentration on the production of armaments and the consequent shortage of labour and the curtailment of farming machinery. However, since 1949 agricultural development has gone forward at an even greater rate. Farming in Manchuria, henceforward known as the Northeast, has been of a more extensive nature and the farms have been much larger than in China Proper. Consequently the region has lent itself more readily, after Land Reform in 1949, to collectivization. Collective farms, state farms and large communes are the normal organization today.

Soils of the central plains are largely of black-earth and constitute good fertile arable land. This is also true of the young alluvial soils bordering the Sungari and Liao rivers. The growing season is short, especially in the north, and only one crop can be secured each year. The main crops are kao-liang, corn and soy-beans.

The great demand for soy-bean oil in the First World War for the manufacture of explosives sent production soaring, and until the outbreak of the Second World War Manchuria was the main world supplier. During that war and ever since, the U.S.A. has become an important grower and the Northeast's share in world trade has fallen, partly for this reason and partly because China is absorbing more in its own growing industries. Wheat is the grain grown by the settlers, who push north into the new lands of the Sungari and Nun (Nonni) plains, whilst corn is a more popular crop in the

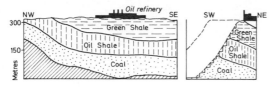

Fig. 125   Sections of Fushun coal cut

south. Millet is widely grown. Other crops are groundnuts, sweet potatoes and Irish potatoes. Sugar-beet was introduced by the Russians in 1909 and today it is an important crop, together with cotton and hemp. Some rice, mainly upland, is grown. Opium used to be a popular cash crop but it is now grown only under licence.

In 1904, when Japan took over the Russian sphere of influence in Manchuria, she formed the South Manchurian Railway Company, which was a body entrusted not only with railway building but also with the development of public utilities, industries and ports, which the railway was designed and intended to serve. By 1931, when Japan virtually annexed the country, a railway network of nearly 6000 km had been constructed and the line from Harbin to Dairen had been double-tracked. By 1943 this figure had risen to 15 000 km, which was more than the rest of China's railways put together. Up to 1945 it is estimated that the South Manchurian Railway Company had invested £350 million. Thus it was that, when the present government gained power in the region, it was not faced with the dilemma of whether to concentrate first on the development of communications or of industry: the essential network was already there.

The natural resources awaiting development were vast and widespread. Coal reserves, while not equal to those of the Shensi–Shansi field in either quality or quantity, are yet enormous and, what is more, are varied and more accessible than those of the west. The greatest reserves are sited in Liaoning at the two great open cuts at Fusin (Fushin) and Fushun, comprising 4000 million tons and 950 million tons respectively. Both are of good bituminous steam coal and have phenomenally thick seams. At Fushun the coal seam varies between 37 and 170 m in thickness and averages 73 m. It is a 'hard, smoking and asphalt' coal with the best quality at the base of the seam. The coal lies below a stratum of oil shale 73 m thick, which in its turn is covered by a layer of green shale of equal thickness. These, together with the coal, are

exposed along a cut 90 m to 140 m in width for some 6 km and can be extended for a further 7 km in a northeasterly direction. The seams are mainly horizontal, dipping from SE to NW.

The presence of coal here was known 800 years ago, but there was no large-scale working of the cut until 1914, when it began to be worked under Japanese management and capital. In 1944 about 10 million tons of coal were produced, using largely modern mechanized methods of grabs, drills, trains and funicular. After 1945 production fell: in 1949 only 2½ million tons were raised. Then followed a period of rehabilitation. By 1955 the Japanese peak production of 1944 had been nearly regained and now it is claimed that double this amount is produced annually. The Fusin (Fushin) cut is reported to have made similar advances in production.

In order to use the 180 m or so of overburden of oil shale and green shale, the Japanese built an oil refinery and distillery close to the deposits. This plant was badly neglected during the period 1945–9, i.e. between the fall of Japan and the rise of the present regime. By 1955 it had regained its former output. The Japanese experimented in the use of the green shale for soap manufacture, and it is now being used for water softening. The removal of the overburden presents an increasing problem. Not only does the amount to be moved increase as the strata dip, but sooner or later it will necessitate the removal of the oil refinery, which covers a large area and which now stands near the edge of the cut.

Associated with the coal and oil industry in this region are some of the most advanced workers' welfare and health services in modern China, including public baths, libraries, clubs, hospitals, clinics and free medical services, workers' insurance and old people's homes.

Another large coalfield in Liaoning is Hsinan to the north of Shenyang (Mukden), which has an estimated reserve of 600 million tons of good bituminous coal, Peipiao, southwest of Fuhsin, Tungpientao, near the Korean border and Penki (Penhsihu), southwest of Shenyang all produce bituminous coking coal and have reserves of 250, 236, and 220 million tons respectively. The best coking coal, however, comes from Haolichen (Haolikang) in the northeast, where there is a reserve of some 600 million tons. Also in the north is the bituminous–lignite field comprising 300 million tons at Mishan.

To match this wealth of coal there is a fair

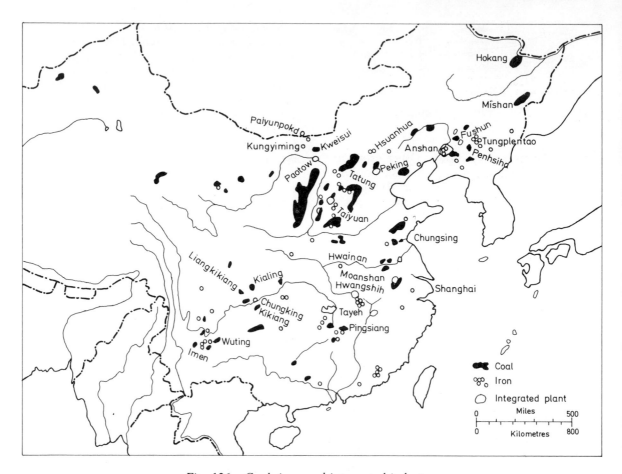

Fig. 126   Coal, iron and integrated industry

amount of iron ore, but unfortunately most of it is of lean low-grade (33–35 per cent). Japanese estimates of reserves in 1945 were 4459 million tons of low-grade and 59 million tons of high-grade (50–63 per cent), mainly haematite, the main fields being at Anshan, Penki (Penhsihu) and Tungpientao. Most of the non-ferrous minerals necessary in the production of iron and steel (limestone, dolomite and fire-clay) are found in adequate quantities in South Manchuria. There are also considerable reserves of molybdenum, copper, lead, zinc, graphite and bauxite.[43]

During their twelve years of occupation of the Northeast the Japanese were assiduous in the development of the iron and steel industry. In 1932 there was a plant capacity for the production of pig-iron of 637 500 metric tons, although only 368 181 tons were produced. No steel was made. As a result of the work done during the Five-year Plan, 1936, known as the Manchurian Industrial

Development Plan, production was at a peak in 1943 when, with a plant capacity of just over $2\frac{1}{2}$ million metric tons, there was an output of 1 726 700 tons of pig-iron and 837 000 tons of steel.[44]

The main iron and steel centre is at Anshan, south of Shenyang (Mukden) and on the main line from that city to Dairen. Here, within a radius of 130 km, all the necessary ingredients for the industry are found: coal from Fushun and Penki (Penhsihu), reasonably good, rich local iron ores and limestone from Huolienchai, only 22 km away. There were 9 blast furnaces, 59 per cent of the pig-iron from which was used for steelmaking in Anshan itself and 41 per cent sent to Japan for use in industry there. Two other centres of the iron and steel industry of less importance than Anshan are at Penhsihu and at Erhtaochiang, sited on the Tungpientao coalfield. Output in 1943 at Anshan was 3 125 000 tons; at Penki 1 125 000

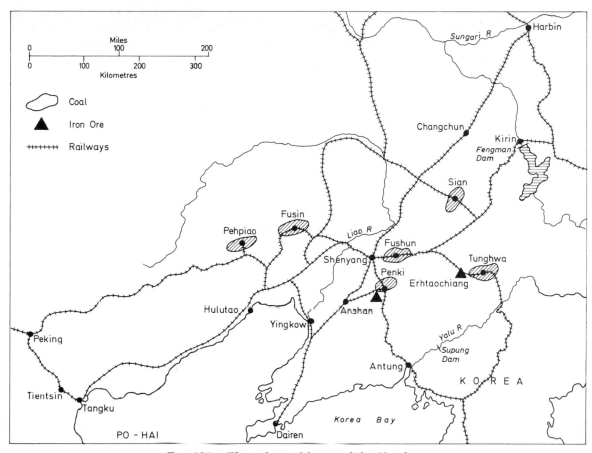

Fig. 127   The industrial heart of the Northeast

tons and at Erhtaochiang 849 933 tons.

Not till 1949 could the work of rehabilitation begin. Special emphasis and importance were laid on reconstruction in Anshan, which became the kingpin of the country's initial development as a modern industrial state. The pressing problem of skilled workers was solved partly by the help of over 2000 Russian experts and technicians, and also by bringing in 20 000 Chinese technicians and skilled men from all over the country. With the aid of Soviet experts eight blast furnaces with a capacity of 3 million tons per annum were in operation in 1955 and a further two were under construction. Heavy rolling mills, covering an area of 50 000 sq. m were completed in 16 months and had commenced the production of heavy 15 m rails (120 kg per metre), heavy structural steel girders and angle iron and steel bars for tubes. The design and the plant all came from the U.S.S.R. and the technicians were trained in the Soviet Union, but in

the subsequent extension of these works Chinese designs and Chinese experts were used. The processes, the heating of bars, rolling and shaping, cooling, storing and distributing, are almost entirely automatic. Alongside the rolling mills a seamless steel tubing mill was constructed at the same rapid rate. Here the main production is of tubes of different size and grade for use in boilers, drills, ball-bearings and water pumps. As with the rolling mills, the processes of cutting the bars, heating, boring, cooling, smoothing and finishing are to all intents and purposes entirely automatic.

In 1958 Anshan's steel output was 3·22 million tons and in 1960 over 4 million. Anshan thus became the chief supplier of structural steel for the rest of the country in its attempt to become industrialized in a couple of decades. No. 1 Tractor Plant at Loyang, the Yangtze Bridge, the new Iron and Steel Works at Paotow and at Hankow, the pipelines from Yumen and Karamai,

Fig. 128   The northeast: hydro-electric power

pumps, etc.; the manufacture of smaller farm implements such as fodder-cutters, winnowers, ploughs, harrows, etc.; and the repair of agricultural machinery and the training, within the repair shops, of mechanics for work in rural centres.

The production of chemicals has been concentrated in Kirin. The Kirin Chemical Co. is a big, integrated enterprise having three big modern plants, which deal with three main products: chemical fertilizers, insecticides, etc.; calcium carbide; dyestuffs. In and around Kirin there are many small workshops which use and re-work the waste products from big industry and which also utilize products from the surrounding forests for making turpentine, resin, pine-wood oil, etc.

Although Manchuria's water power cannot match its great wealth of power from coal, it is fairly well served. The seasonal distribution of rain and the fact that all its rivers freeze in winter are handicaps which can only be overcome by the creation of large enough reservoirs to give an even flow. A Japanese survey in 1940 estimated that, given well-sited plants, a maximum of 6 million kW could be generated. If the great frontier rivers were utilized, there was a further potential of 3 million kW awaiting development to the mutual benefit of the U.S.S.R. and China.

The largest development of hydro-electric power carried out by the Japanese was the building of the Fengman dam, 30 km above Kirin on the Sungari. This huge dam holds back a reservoir of 740 sq. km with a capacity of 10 000 million cu. m and with a maximum generating capacity of 850 000 kW. It was badly damaged and leaking at the end of the war. Repairs were completed in 1957 and new generators installed with a present capacity of 567 000 kW. It should be noted that China is now able to survey, design and build her own thermal and hydro-electric power plants.

A second hydro-electric plant has been built on the Mutan-kiang, a right-bank tributary of the Sungari at Tao Shan. It has a generating capacity of 383 000 kW. Being built under the Second Five-year Plan is a dam at Kumotsin, above Tsitsihar on the Nun (Nonni) river. This will produce 209 000 kW.

The Japanese planned an ambitious development of the Yalu river on the frontier between Korea and Manchuria, having as an ultimate output 1 133 000 kW. This was never fulfilled. Nevertheless the Supung dam alone has an output of 600 000 kW. Along this valley and associated with the Tungpientao coalfield a considerable

the heavy and light machine tool shops of Shenyang have all relied on the output of the Anshan works, which compare in size, modernity and efficiency with Port Talbot, South Wales. Anshan, like other places which have suffered a comparable amount of destruction and pillage, enjoys [*sic*] the advantage of starting afresh with all the most up-to-date equipment. Anshan has played a further very valuable part in the industrial development of the country since Liberation by the training of thousands of skilled iron and steel workers, who are now operating the many new integrated works throughout the country.

The hub of the whole industry of the Northeast is Shenyang, the modern name for Mukden. It is the capital of the province of Liaoning and is the centre of great engineering activity. A great variety of machinery and tools is produced: three types of standardized lathes are mass-produced in great quantity and distributed throughout the country.

Harbin is the main centre for the production of agricultural equipment. Here the No. 1 Machine Building Plant has three main functions: the production of heavy machinery such as turbines, generators, tractors, combine harvesters, power

industrial centre has sprung up. The discovery and rapid development of oil at Taching, Heilung-kiang in 1964 has been described above (see Power). Its effects on the economy have been profound. The population of the province rose from 14·86 million in 1957 to an estimated 25 million in 1970 (Harbin radio). This also reflects the Government's policy of settlement in this frontier region.

7. SINKIANG

As a result of a great campaign by Tso Tsung-tang, Chinese Turkestan was added to the Manchu domains in 1877. It was so called by Westerners to distinguish it from the Turkestan of the Aral–Caspian region, embracing Bokhara, Khiva and Samarkand. Its Chinese name is Sinkiang, meaning New Dominion; under the People's Government its official title is now Sinkiang Uighur Autonomous Region.

Sinkiang contains within its borders two vast basins, the Tarim and Dzungaria and a number of smaller basins, such as the Turfan and Ili, all of which, while differing widely in many respects, have (with the exception of the Ili) one feature in common, namely, that they are all basins of inland drainage. Only one out of the many rivers finds an outlet to the sea. That one is the Irtysh river, whose headwaters rise in the Altai Mountains and flow for a short distance in Chinese territory before entering their long course across Siberia to the Arctic Ocean.

7a. The Tarim Basin
More than half of Sinkiang is occupied by the Tarim River Basin, a spearhead-shaped depression, 1280 km long and 640 km broad at its widest point. Its general level is some 600 m above the sea in the east, rising to over 1800 m at the western end; it is bounded on all sides by lofty mountains. In the west are the Pamirs, a knot of mountains attaining 5400 m and more, containing high, wide valleys of glacial origin, affording in places good pasture to nomadic tribes but too high for cultivation. Through these mountains are two passes which carry routes from the upper Kashgar river, one northwestward into the Syr Darya to Ferghana and Tashkent and one southwest to the Amu Darya valley and to Bokhara and Merv, all names to conjure with in earlier trading days.

The Kunlun ranges, and behind them the Kara-koram, form a mighty and forbidding wall on the southwest. Their northern slopes are loess-covered, steep and almost unbroken in spite of their severe erosion. Their ranges rise to 5–6000 m and are most difficult to cross. Routes run from Yarkand to Afghanistan and to Kashmir, and from Khotan to Lhasa. The southern border is comprised of the Altyn Tagh, less forbidding, more broken and lower than the Kunlun but still a formidable wall, forming the northern edge of the Tibetan Plateau. From the Kunlun and Altyn Tagh innumerable small rivers and streams, whose sources lie in the snow and ice fields of the plateau, pour down onto the plain below.

Running east and northeast from the Pamirs are the many folds of the Tien Shan or Heavenly Mountains. These form the northern boundary of the Tarim Basin and divide it from both the Ili Basin and the region of Dzungaria. They are neither as high (3600 m) nor as impenetrable as the mountain ranges of the south. The lower but still difficult Karlik (Qarliq) Tagh mark the eastern limits of the basin, beyond which routes pass into Inner Mongolia.

The one long river, from which the basin derives its name, is the Tarim. It has many headwaters in the Pamirs and Kunlun which join to form the Yarkand river. This later loses its name to become the Tarim. It has only one right-bank tributary, the Khotan river. Of the many streams flowing down from the southern mountains this is the only one which does not become lost in the sands of the Takla Makan, which they all have to cross, for the Tarim itself hugs the northern borders of the basin. From the southern slopes of the Tien Shan it receives a number of comparatively large left-bank tributaries, fed by the melting snows of the mountains.

The Tarim Basin is comprised of a series of concentric belts. In the heart of the region is the Takla Makan desert, a howling wilderness, true desert for the most part utterly devoid of life and vegetation, a place of desolation of sand and rock.

Ringing this desert is a belt of piedmont gravel of varying width and thickness. This belt has been built up by the detritus brought down by the fast-running streams, which fan out on reaching the plain. It is wider and more marked on the south than the north. The streams disappear under this gravel to reappear and enter the desert in the south. These are the points at which oases are sited along the eastern end of the southern rim of the desert, notably at Keriya, Niya and Charchan (Cherchen). Here there are considerable areas of reeds, and tamarisk and wild fowl abound. In the

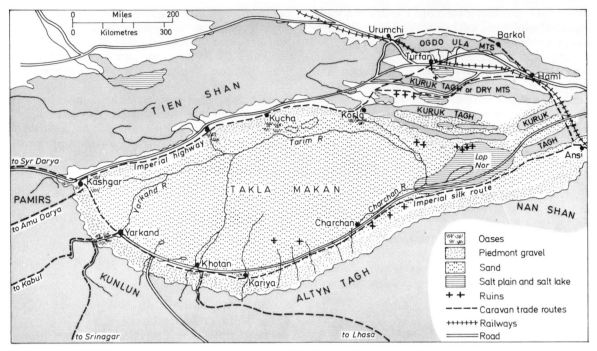

Fig. 129   The Tarim Basin

north and west the large oases, such as Aksu, Kucha, Korla (Kurla), Yarkand and Kashgar, are found above the point of entry into the gravel.

Ellsworth Huntington and Sir Aurel Stein both comment at length on the fact that, far out into the desert, some 110 to 130 km lower than the present limit of oasis settlement, ruins of large villages and towns, dating between AD 300 and 1200 are to be found. The remains of dead vegetation indicate a river flow three to four times greater at that time than today.

Above the piedmont gravel belt the Kunlun and Astin (Altyn) Tagh rise steeply. Their slopes are often marked by faults and loess-covered moraines which are barren of vegetation. The rivers descend in impassable gorges which have restricted communication between the people of the oases below and the nomad tribes which occupy the wide valleys of the well-watered plains high up on the plateau, where rich grasses grow. Above these again are higher ranges where temperature restricts vegetation to alpine tundra. Higher still are the icefields and névé, the source of all the rivers.

The Tarim, after being joined by the Kara Shahr river on the left bank and the Charchan (Cher-chen) on the right, empties into the Lop Nor, a salt lake surrounded by salt marshes and a salt-encrusted plain. This salt plain is bounded on the north by the Kuruk Tagh or Dry Mountains, on the east by the Karlik Tagh and on the south by the western extension of the Nan Shan. The piedmont gravel is so thickly deposited in the Kuruk Tagh as nearly to obliterate the crests of the ranges.

The oases which ring the Takla Makan are the links in the chain which formed the ancient imperial highways of the Han and later dynasties. These were fixed trade routes which went from oasis to oasis, divided from one another by true desert. The Imperial Highway came from the Wei valley to Ansi via Lanchow and Yumen. At Ansi it divided, one branch going north to Hami and Barkol, thence turning west and following the southern foot of the Tien Shan, passing through the large oases of Korla, Kucha and Aksu to arrive at Kashgar. The other branch, the Imperial Silk Route, passed south of the Lop Nor, through the large oases of Charchan, Khotan and Yarkand and many smaller ones to Kashgar.

It was along this southern route that Huntington gathered his early data in support of his

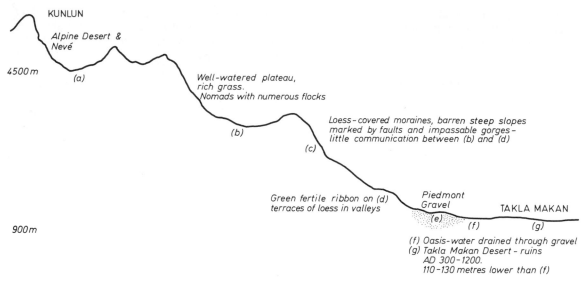

KUNLUN

*Alpine Desert &
Nevé*

4500m   (a)

*Well-watered plateau,
rich grass.
Nomads with numerous flocks*

(b)

*Loess-covered moraines, barren steep slopes
marked by faults and impassable gorges-
little communication between (b) and (d)*

(c)

*Green fertile ribbon on (d)
terraces of loess in valleys*

*Piedmont
Gravel*   TAKLA MAKAN

(e)   (f)   (g)

900m

*(f) Oasis-water drained through gravel
(g) Takla Makan Desert - ruins
AD 300-1200.
110-130 metres lower than (f)*

Fig. 130   Sinkiang: section from the Kunlun to the Takla Makan

theory of climatic cycles and of fluctuating desic-cation.[45] He deduced that there was a period of intense aridity between the third and sixth centuries AD, during which time the southern silk route was abandoned in favour of the longer northern route; that between the ninth and sixteenth centuries there was a relative abundance of moisture, when rivers and population were much larger than today; and that from the sixteenth century onwards the climate has become progressively drier. He found evidence in support of this in the fluctuations in level of Lop Nor and of desiccation in the dissected condition of the lower slopes of the Kunlun, where the loess, once grass-covered, is now dead. The regions both north and south of Lop Nor, particularly in the Kuruk Tagh, formerly the grazing grounds of nomadic tribes, are now unable to support them through lack of water and grass. From Khotan eastward there are thirteen notable rivers, some of which flowed as much as 40 km farther into the desert than they do today, where there are ruins of former prosperous communities which would today need far better systems of irrigation than existed in their heyday. The condition of dead forests in the area points to their destruction being the result of decreasing rainfall rather than the cause. Owen Lattimore comments on this evidence that, while undoubtedly climatic changes have been the cause of great displacements of population in these regions, the abandonment of oases and irrigation systems may find their explanation in human activities such as inadequate engineering knowledge at the time to deal with increasing silting or increasing salinity, or a community being reduced below survival point by war and raids.[46]

Already enough mention has been made of inland drainage, of deserts and oases for it to be clear that this is a region of very arid climate. Rainfall is both very sparse and very variable from year to year. Kashgar has the heaviest rainfall with an average of 100 mm per annum, 60 mm of which falls in April, May and June. Everywhere within the basin experiences a big range of temperature (maximum shade temperature 46°C in summer and a minimum of −7°C in winter). The diurnal range is also very great owing to rapid radiation when skies are cloudless. As with other desert climates, dust haze often hangs over the landscape and dust storms, accompanied by fierce winds, are frequent.

The Westerlies predominate throughout moderate latitudes. Those blowing across southern U.S.S.R. meet the mountain mass of which the Pamirs form a salient and are deflected northeast and southwest. The northeast stream crosses the Pamirs and Tien Shan and descends into the Tarim Basin, developing a foehn effect and a great air dryness. A surprising result is that Kashgar, in the heart of a great landmass has average winter temperatures little lower than those of Tientsin on the east coast.

Average Monthly Air Temperature
(°C)

	Nov.	Dec.	Jan.	Feb.
Kashgar	3·9	−2·2	−5·7	0
(1218 m)				
Tientsin	5	0	−2·2	0
(2 m)				

This foehn phenomenon is also experienced in the Tsaidam.

However life in the Tarim Basin does not depend on the rainfall received, but on the irrigation waters descending from the vast reservoirs of ice and snow in the mountains to the north and south. In fact a 'heavy' rainfall in the spring months is something in the nature of a misfortune, since the clouds obscure the sun and retard the melting of the snowfields for which the rainfall is no adequate substitute. Although in 1931 Khotan received a heavier rainfall than usual, it suffered from a water shortage. 80 per cent of Kashgar's water comes from snow and 20 per cent from springs. Its rainfall is regarded as of negligible importance.[47]

Throughout the centuries life in the Tarim Basin has been based on arable farming and confined to the oases. Owing to the aridity and consequent paucity of grass, there has been very little nomadic pastoralism. About 85 per cent of the fields are irrigated; the distribution of water was formerly controlled by the local elders as it was in China, but it is now in the hands of the local authorities, usually communes. The main food crops raised are, in order of importance, wheat, corn, rice, kaoliang and barley. The main commercial crop is cotton. Usually local varieties are grown, because long-staple U.S. cotton requires more water. Until recently only primitive agricultural methods and implements were used. The frost-free growing period averages 220 days.

This is one of the main regions of China chosen by the People's Government for major agricultural expansion and for the absorption of many millions of its fast-growing population. In 1932 Schomberg estimated that one third to one half of Sinkiang's water ran to waste, and that if this were utilized, some 8 million hectares could be brought into cultivation.[48] When civil war ended in 1949 the forces of the Sinkiang Military Command were formed into a Production and Construction Corps for the purpose of initiating land reclamation, which consisted mainly in building roads, reservoirs and irrigation canals, sluicegates, etc. This Corps, working in conjunction with the local peasantry, continues to function and has carried out a great deal of work of a capital nature, including the development of underground irrigation channels (karez). Claims are made that this has resulted in over 1·2 million ha of new land being brought under the plough, thus more than doubling the cultivated area in 1949. The main area of development has been along the northern side of the basin. New crops, notably sugar-beet, are being grown. Grain crops have been doubled, whilst cotton, owing to its tolerance of saline soils, has been increased eightfold. The dangers facing this rapid increase are those of former centuries, i.e. shifting sands and the development of alkaline soils. It remains to be seen whether modern techniques and know-how can adequately meet these dangers. No railway has yet been built to serve the Tarim Basin but an extensive road system is in the process of being developed.

The population of the whole of Sinkiang according to the 1953 census was 4 873 608, of which about 75 per cent live in the Tarim Basin. About 80 per cent are Uighars, who are Moslems of Turkic stock, and some 9 per cent are Kazaks, who are also Moslem, 80 per cent of whom live in the Ili valley. The remainder is made up of various nomadic tribes of Torgut, Noigut, Kirghiz, Kalmuks and Tungus, who live on the southern slopes of the Tien Shan. The Uighars form a homogeneous group of independent people. For this reason they have been given the somewhat more independent status of an autonomous region and have been treated circumspectly by the central government, which has not pressed socialization quite so hard or so rapidly as in other parts of China. Nevertheless, it is reported that from the 1 million ha land reclaimed by the Production Corps since 1958, 102 large new mechanized farms have been established. In pursuance of the Government's policy of settling the frontier lands with Chinese, the Han people of Sinkiang have increased very rapidly during the last two decades. The estimated population, as reported to Owen Lattimore when visiting in 1972, was about 8 million, consisting of slightly over 4 million

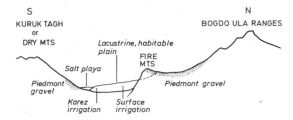

Fig. 131   Section through the Turfan depression

Uighurs, 2·8 million Han, 500 000 Kazakhs, 300 000 Hui, and 200 000 Mongols.

7b. The Turfan Depression

To the northeast of the Tarim Basin and lying between the Kuruk Tagh or Dry Mountains and the Bogdo Ula is the remarkable Turfan Depression. This is a fault trough, which descends to 154 m below sea-level. It consists of two main valleys of different height divided by a faulted range, the Fire Mountains, which, in spite of their name, are not volcanic. The wide valley to the north of the Fire Mountains is above sea-level and some 450 m higher than the valley to the south. It is covered with a thick deposit of piedmont gravel, ground water from which drains by way of canyons through the Fire Mountains into the lacustrine plain below. This valley is bounded on the north by the fault-face of the Fire Mountains, giving a range of 600 m in elevation on its southern face. A belt of piedmont gravel lines the southern border at the foot of the Dry Mountains, alongside which is also the salt playa or swamp, the remnants of the former lake which filled the depression. Today this swamp is dry in summer and wet only in winter when it freezes and when evaporation is not as great.[49]

This lower plain is the habitable part of the Turfan Basin. It has no river of any size but a large number of streams from the Fire Mountains, which provide surface irrigation on the northern side of the plain. As the plain dips to the south, surface irrigation gives place to the *karez*, the Persian and northwest Indian method of long underground tunnels, which tap the water table and lead the water to the fields.

Turfan has a climate of great extremes of temperature. Summers are intensely hot, shade temperatures rising to 51°–54° C at midday. Every house has its dug-out to which its inhabitants can retire for siesta until work is again possible. Winter temperatures fall below zero. Rain in the depression is practically unknown.

All crops are grown under irrigation. Natural conditions are particularly favourable to viticulture. High day temperatures increase the sugar content of the grapes, while cold night temperatures keep them soft and juicy. The chief vineyards are in the 'Emerald Amidst the Land of Fire' valley, where many varieties of grapes are grown, the most renowned being the white seedless grape from which the finest sun-dried raisins are produced. Other fruits are apricots, peaches, melons and nuts.[51] As in China Proper, the farmer never fails to grow peas and vetches around his grain plots and vineyards, thereby not only deriving the crop itself but adding nitrogen to the soil. Cotton and grain are other important products; 8000 hectares of wheat were reported to have been harvested in 1966, an estimated increase of 10 per cent over the previous year. Sericulture is also practised successfully.[52]

The changing order was comparatively slow in making its impact felt in the Turfan valley. Today, however, the Uighar population apparently has been successfully organized in the usual pattern of commune, brigade and production teams and is reported to have increased its vineyards by 1000 *mow*.

7c. Dzungaria

A vast basin, some 600 m lower than the Tarim, lies to the north. It is triangular in shape and is contained within the walls of the Tien Shan on the south, the Altai Mountains on the northeast and the Ala Tau on the northwest. A pass over the col between the Bogdo Ula and the Tien Shan at a height of about 3600 m leads from the Turfan Depression to Urumchi and the Dzungarian plain. The Dzungarian Gate, a rift valley in the Ala Tau, provides an outlet from the plain to Lake Balkhash and Kazakhstan. The upper waters of the Irtysh river give access to Zaisan Nor and Semipalatinsk in the U.S.S.R., while the wide valleys between the Bogdo Ula and the Altai provide a way, albeit a dreary one, in the southeast to the Mongolian Gobi.

The region has much the same pattern as the Tarim Basin but at a lower level, with the difference that it is not so arid. The central part is desert but not of the same expanse or bitterness as the Takla Makan. The two main rivers are the Manaas and Urungu. These, in company with innumerable streams, descend to the plains to be lost in the reedy marshes and in the sands. The high mountain ranges receive as much as 500–750 mm of rain, and those ranges of the north, notably the Altai, are forest-clad. Their lower slopes are wooded with willows, poplars and alders, above which come white birch, a valuable building material and one which has many uses among the nomads. Its bark contains oil which is used by the herdsmen as a lining to their pails for sour milk. Above 1800 m the Siberian larch dominates. These trees grow to over 30 m in height and form 70 per cent of the forest growth. These forests are rich in fur-bearing animals – fox, wolf, sable, ermine, bears and wolverines.

In contrast to the Tarim with its desert lands between oases, steppe and steppe–desert are the natural vegetation of the wide valleys which border the central desert-land. In consequence pastoral nomadism has been the dominant way of life in Dzungaria. Population is sparse since the pasture will not carry many sheep to the square kilometre. According to Hann a rainfall of 500 mm a year in New South Wales makes it possible to keep 250 sheep on a square kilometre of land. With a rainfall of 330 mm only 80 can be kept and with 250 mm only 4 sheep per square kilometre. Here in Dzungaria the annual rainfall is under 250 mm with the result that the pastoralist must be constantly on the move in search of fresh grass. This fact emphasizes a further contrast between the Tarim and Dzungaria. The routes in the former are fixed, going from oasis to oasis and their purpose is primarily trade. In the latter they are rather what Lattimore calls 'directions of march', broad and indeterminate ways along which the herdsman leads his flocks.[53] Trade is entirely subordinate to pasture.

Until the People's Government came into power, very little arable farming was practised. Since 1949 strenuous efforts have been made towards its development. Here, as in the Tarim Basin, the main initiators and enthusiasts have been the members of the Production and Construction Corps. Operating mainly along the foothills of the northern slopes of the Tien Shan from which the Manaas and several other smaller rivers flow, big water conservation works have been carried out and reservoirs and irrigation channels built, thus saving much of the water which formerly ran to waste. By 1956 the Corps had reclaimed over 50 000 ha, which have been organized into ten large mechanized farms. Since that date work has gone ahead at an even greater rate.

About half the reclaimed land is under cotton; the rest is under rice, wheat, corn, soy-bean, fruit and sugar-beet.

However, economic interest has centred not so much on agricultural advances, great though they are, as on the discovery in 1955 of oil in an extensive field at Karamai, 300 km northwest of Urumchi. The first attested field was 60 sq. km in area. Since 1955 six new oilfields in the area have been discovered. The proved reserve of the Karamai field in 1973 was 100 million tons. In 1959 production was 100 000 tons; in 1973 it was estimated at 5 million tons. A pipeline carries the crude oil to Manass, thence by rail to Yumen for refining. The discovery of oil quickened the building of the extension of the Lunghai railway from Lanchow, intended to link with the U.S.S.R. through the Dzungarian Gate but brought to a halt at Manass in 1960 by the rupture of Sino–Russian relations.

Following the discovery of adequate coal and iron deposits on the north side of the Tien Shan and Bogdo Ula there has been a rapid industrial development in the last two decades.

Urumchi or, to give it its Chinese name, Kihwa, stands on a desert plateau of 2750 m. It is the capital of Sinkiang Uighur Autonomous Region. In 1949 it was an old market town of 60 000. Today it is a busy modern commercial city of a quarter of a million people and centre of iron and steel, cement, agricultural machinery, ferilizer and textile production of the region. It is also the educational and cultural centre.

Lying north of the Tien Shan, but cut off from the rest of Dzungaria by the Boro Horo Ula, is the comparatively small but important valley of the Ili river, which flows westward to lake Balkhash. It lies open to U.S.S.R. Kazakhstan and to western climatic influences. It is occupied by Kazakhs and Uighurs, whose racial and cultural affinities lie westward rather than eastward. It is wetter and more fertile than the rest of Sinkiang and a large part of its population is engaged in arable farming and therefore settled. Its high production of wheat and other grain has earned for it the title of 'the granary of Sinkiang'. The pastoralists, who are mainly Kazakhs, are now becoming settled. In addition to the famous Ili 'Sanho', horses, mentioned above, they raise large numbers of sheep and goats. The valley has good deposits of coal. With this coal as its base and Kuldja, the capital, as its centre, a considerable and varied industry, which includes iron and steel, machine-building and textiles, has developed recently. It should be noted that this is one of the Disputed Areas.

8. INNER MONGOLIA

The administrative boundaries of Inner Mongolia Autonomous Region have undergone considerable changes since 1949. In the 1950s it swallowed up the former provinces of Chahar and Jehol and much of Ningsia but in 1969 its area was reduced by nearly two-thirds and it lost nearly half its population to Heilungkiang, Kirin, Liaoning, Ningsia and Kansu. The far more densely populated part of Inner Mongolia lying between the Hara Narin–Yin Shan–Tatsing Shan and the Hwang-ho has already been described.

Our Inner Mongolia natural region lies to the north of these ranges, which form the high southern rim of the Gobi depression. They have an average height of 1350–1800 metres and in many places rise to 2000–2500 metres. The land falls away towards the centre of the Gobi, which is the Mongolian name for a broad desert plain. This region of inland drainage and salt marshes is by no means uniform in character; stretches of coarse sand give place to areas of piedmont gravel and smooth rock and stone.

The deeper the Gobi is penetrated northward and westward, the drier it becomes. Rainfall is more precarious, variable and sparse. When rain does fall, too often it is in the form of a violent cloudburst. It is a region of great extremes of temperature, both seasonal and diurnal. Midday shade temperatures in summer reach 46° C and more. In winter 25°–30° of frost are experienced. These changes in temperature give rise to terrifying sandstorms and violent windstorms, which, in winter, are bitter and penetrating.

The mountains on the southern rim have some cover of woodland and scrub but vegetation for the most part is very scant. Some of the Gobi ranges are entirely barren. As the land dips away northward, in so far as it has any cover this is steppe grass, which sometimes stands 2–2·5 m high, looking like kaoliang except that it carries no heavy head of grain and is slenderer in its stalk. Like bamboo in southern China, this grass is put to a multitude of uses. The young, tender shoots are fodder for the livestock. Fully grown, it is used to make kitchen utensils, brushes, grain bins, mats for beds, curtain screens, toys, chassis for carts and fences for fixing sand dunes.[54]

The region is one of very sparse population. Over the whole area there is an average of less than one person per square kilometre. Three categories of people make up the inhabitants. There are the oasis dwellers, a settled people, the great majority of whom never move outside the limits of their small world from birth to death. Here they till their fields and gardens, the produce of which is often unique to the particular oasis, and pursue their individual handicrafts. Their products are distributed by a second class of people, the caravaneers, who move along the desert 'highways' from oasis to oasis and from water-hole to water-hole. These last are usually about 50 km apart, a distance which can be accomplished in one day. The region is still virtually untouched by modern transport and nearly all movement is done by camel, mule and mule cart, horse or on foot. The pastoralist forms the third category of inhabitants. For the most part the Mongolian pastoralist is only seminomadic. He practises transhumance, that is to say he makes seasonal movements with his flocks and herds but prefers to restrict his movements as far as possible. However, he is a *yurt* dweller and therefore can and does move as necessity dictates. The average *yurt* is circular and is from 4 to 5 m in diameter, having wooden trellis walls, usually of willow, something over 1 m high. The whole is covered by felt, the roof being upheld by long sticks of willow joined in the centre. It provides snug protection in the bitter winter. This old yurt is now giving way rapidly to one of plastic framework and covering, though retaining the conventional pattern. It is women's work both to pitch and strike camp, the packing being a comparatively simple job. The men are responsible for herding and hunting. The daily food of the pastoralist is derived directly from his flocks of sheep and goats, and herds of camels, horses and cattle. Milk, cheese and rancid butter together with mutton form his staple diet. His drink is tea, brought in brick form from Central China and usually concocted with mutton broth.

Since 1949 a widespread and determined attempt has been made to bring these seminomadic people into line with the communist pattern of the rest of the country. They were first organized into more than 2000 herdsmen co-operatives, which were later merged into 152 communes. It is clear, however, from later reports that considerable latitude and flexibility were allowed. Commune members are allowed to keep for their

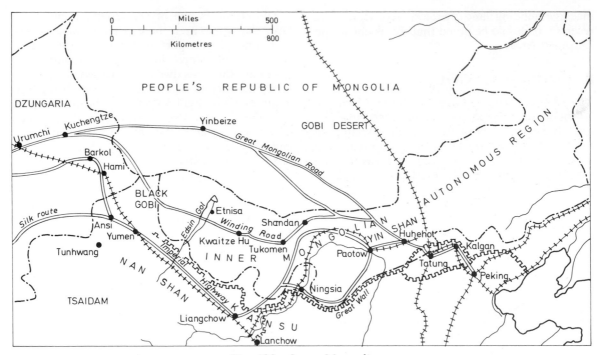

Fig. 132   Inner Mongolia

private use the necessary number of horses for personal transport and milch cows and sheep for food. Nor does the commune attempt to undertake the full supply of food needed by its members.

A clear distinction must be made between means of production and means of subsistence and different policies must be laid down for dealing with them. Members should be told clearly that they still retain, and will always continue to retain, private ownership of their means of subsistence (including houses, *yurts*, furniture, clothing, rugs, saddles and trappings for horses, etc.) as well as their deposits in the bank or in credit cooperatives, their cash and their personal ornaments made of gold and silver.[55]

The main east–west line of communication running through Inner Mongolia from Huhehot to Turfan and Urumchi is the Winding Road, described by Owen Lattimore.[56] It is of less importance today than the Great Mongolian Road to the north and the Imperial Highway to the south, along which now runs the railway line from Lanchow to Sinkiang. Its former importance is attested by the ruined remains of Etsina on Edsin Gol, a walled city inhabited in Marco Polo's day but long since deserted, and by the two big lamaseries of Shandan and Tukomen.

Monasteries were usually sited where nomads gathered for festivals. The ruins of Etsina may possibly be evidence of progressive desiccation in this region and of an Edsin Gol of considerably greater volume then than now. This river provides the only practicable north–south route across western Inner Mongolia and is the one which Jenghis Khan followed in his invasion of China in AD 1227. West of Edsin Gol the Winding Road crosses the Black Gobi, the most forbidding of all the Mongolian deserts. It is a plateau of hard, sandy clay; it is practically rainless and has no wells. The Winding Road experienced a revival of popularity in the 1920s and 1930s when use of the northern Great Mongolian Road was denied by an independent and hostile Outer Mongolia and the Imperial Highway was cut by civil war and banditry.

9. THE TIBETAN PLATEAU

The Tibetan Plateau is today divided into two large political divisions, Tibet and Chinghai (Tsinghai). Tibet extends from Kashmir in the west to the Szechwan border along the upper Yangtze and includes the Chamdo district, formerly part of Sikang. Chinghai occupies the

Plate 29   Water conservancy on the Mongolian steppe, Kansu

northeast part of the plateau. The eastern part of Sikang has been incorporated into Szechwan and is administered by the Kan-tzu Autonomous District and I-pa Autonomous District.

9a. Tibet

Tibet is a vast area of upland, having a general level of 5000 m or above, from which mountain ranges rise a further 3000 m or more. Its borders are marked by great mountain systems which stem from the Pamir Knot in the west. In the north the Kunlun and Astin (Altyn) Tagh divide it from Sinkiang below and on the south is the great Himalayan system, cutting it off from the Indo–Gangetic plain. In between these are other ranges, which run roughly parallel to the bordering ranges. The Tangla Mountains are a continuation eastward of the Karakoram, and south of the Tangla Ranges are the Trans-Himalayan Ranges.

Tibet can be subdivided into two main areas. The north and northwest, known as Chang Tang, is the highest part of the plateau and is a land of wide, barren, desolate valleys along which sweep

the bitter winds so feelingly described by Peter Fleming in his *News from Tartary*. It is a region of inland drainage. Its streams lose themselves in innumerable salt lakes, the largest of which is Tengri Nor, and in salty swamps, which lie in salt-encrusted plains. The natural vegetation of the north and northwest is alpine desert, for it is tree-less. In some parts there is a growth of scanty grass, which provides sustenance for the wild mountain sheep, asses and yaks. Human population is very sparse indeed. Not surprisingly, there are no adequate climatic records of this remote and inhospitable land. Kendrew,[58] however, makes estimates which give some idea of the rigours to be endured. At 5000 m the mean temperatures are $-24°C$ in January and $-1°C$ in July. Most of the region has less than two months with a mean temperature above freezing. In such a climate arable farming is impossible.

The Chang Tang has a general slope south and southeast down to the Trans-Himalayan ranges, south of which is a region known as Po. This is a trough lying between the Trans-Himalayan

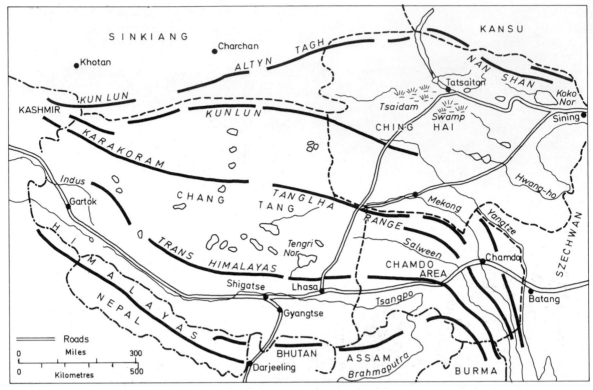

Fig. 133   Tibet

ranges and the Himalayas themselves through which the upper courses of the Indus and Brahmaputra (Tsangpo) flow. Here are deep valleys, some of which are less than 1500 m above sealevel. Temperatures are a good deal warmer than on the plateau proper, but even so are cooler than southeast China. There has always been some cultivation here but it is only since the People's Government forced its way in and ousted the regime of the Dalai Lama that there has been any large-scale development of arable farming (see Agricultural Regions). Highland barley is the staple food. Po has a wealth of forest growth denied to the rest of Tibet. There has recently been some development of light industry (clothing, footwear, woollen textiles, leather, timber) in the Lhasa area, using hydro-electric power. One of the reasons for the Chinese Government's anxiety to bring Tibet, especially Po, firmly under its jurisdiction may be the potential mineral wealth which lies hidden in this part of the plateau.

Po is the only part of Tibet that has any density of population. Three great centres of

Lamaism in Lhasa, Shigatse and Gyangtse are located in this southeast corner on which the old caravan routes and now the two new motor roads converge.

9b. Chamdo Area

The former province of Sikang has been swallowed up by the extension of Szechwan westward to the banks of the upper Yangtze or Kinsha and by the creation of a new administrative area, known as Chamdo Area. Chamdo embraces the headwaters and the upper basins of the three great rivers: the Yangtze, Mekong and Salween. It is the region where the great folds bend southeast and then south, between which the rivers flow in the same deep and forested chasms already described when dealing with the Southwest Plateau. It is still largely unexplored and is inhabited by only a few aboriginal tribes.

Travellers and surveyors returning from this area tell of its mineral wealth but its inaccessibility makes exploitation in the near future unlikely. However, it is being opened up to some extent.

The old routes from Lanchow via Sining to Lhasa, and from Chengtu via Chamdo to Lhasa have now been sufficiently built and engineered to permit motor traffic. There is now motor-road communication linking Lhasa with Sining and Lanchow; with Chengtu via Chamdo; with Yakand, Sinkiang.

9c. Chinghai (Tsinghai)

The province contains the basin known as the Tsaidam, which lies at a much lower level (2700–1800 m) than the rest of the plateau. It is bounded on the northwest by the Astin (Altyn) Tagh, on the northeast by the Nan Shan, a branch of which separates Koko Nor (Chinghai) from the Tsaidam itself. Ranges of the Kunlun mark its southern borders. Both the Tsaidam and the Koko Nor areas are regions of inland drainage.

In the centre of the western end of the Tsaidam there is some desert with a periphery of swamps and salt lakes. On the rising rolling land which surrounds them, reasonable steppe pasture is found. On the slopes of the Astin Tagh and Nan Shan the grass is really good over large areas and the higher slopes carry some forest.

Through the centuries this remote region supported a sparse population of Tibetan nomads who were an ever-present menace to the caravans following the Imperial Highway north of the Nan Shan, and sometimes a threat to imperial power. This area has suddenly sprung into a new prominence. Geological surveys during the last twelve years have revealed the presence of both oil and coal. The main oilfield lies in the extreme west, having Mangyai at its centre. A second field is sited at the heart of the region at Tatsaitan. Close by Tatsaitan, at Yuka, whose Mongolian name is Naka, meaning 'thick forest', is a coalfield with seams 38 m thick, lying near the surface. Big iron-ore deposits have recently been discovered in the Nan Shan area. In the east, near the settlement of Chaka, is a crystallized salt lake with deposits of 98 per cent sodium chloride 15 m thick over an area of 100 sq. km. This will probably be the centre of a chemical industry in the near future.

Chinghai is noted for its horse breeding. Legend has it that the horses were 'dragon-bred', piebald in colour and of phenomenal staying power, capable of doing 1000 *li* (more than 450 km) a day! We do know of their great sturdiness from accounts of the amazing surprise rides accomplished by Jenghis Khan's men and there are plenty of records today of horses trotting more than 45 km in a day. It is reported that there are now some 350 000 horses in the area.

Sining wool is famous. It is very long staple, coarse, elastic and strong, much used in rug and carpet making. Two medicinal products in big demand in China are Chinghai rhubarb and *tung-chungts'ao* (winter grass insect).

The whole province is subdivided for administrative and governmental purposes into six autonomous *chou*. The capital is Sining but Tatsaitan appears likely to become the main settlement and administrative centre in the rapidly developing western part of the province. In order to open up the region a railway has been run from Lanchow to Sining and may already have been completed as far as Tatsaitan. A motor road runs from Sining, via Chaka, Tatsaitan and Yuka, over the Tang Ching Pass between the Astin Tagh and Nan Shan to join the main route to Sinkiang through the Kansu 'panhandle' at Ansi.

Population in Chinghai had already risen to 1 676 500 in 1953, to 2·4 million in 1965, and, although statistics are not yet available, it seems reasonable to suppose that this figure has more than doubled since that date. Although the climate here is still harsh, summers are sufficiently long to permit some cultivation, given careful water conservation. The area has promising prospects for the development of pastoral farming on a large scale.

10. TAIWAN

Perched, as it were, on the brink of a submarine chasm stands the island of Taiwan. It forms a bastion in one of the great festoons of islands which fringe the western Pacific and which are part of the Alpine system of folds ringing the globe. Like Japan, it stands on the edge of the continental shelf, the sea descending to abyssal depths within a few kilometres of the eastern coast, while the depth of the Formosa Channel separating the island from the mainland is a mere 45–75 m. As a result of intense folding and faulting in both pre-Tertiary and Eocene times, the island forms a tilted block, dipping towards the mainland and having an axis of folding from NNE to SSW, extending the whole length of the land.

The island, for the most part, is very mountainous and the effect of the trend lines is to divide it into a series of five longitudinal physio-

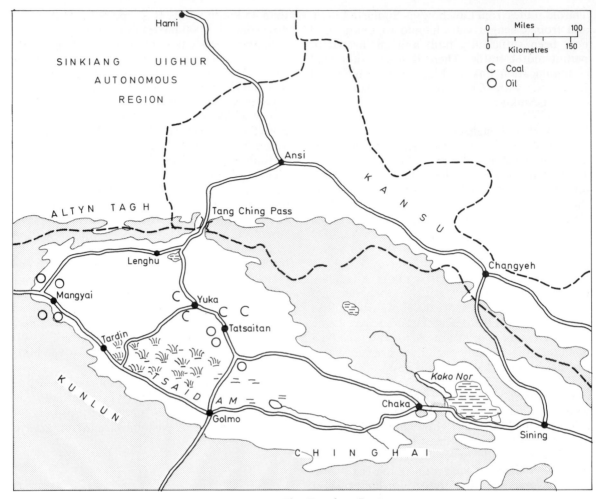

Fig. 134   The Tsaidam Basin

graphic regions.[59] On the east coast, between Hualien and Taitung, are the Taitung Mountains, rugged and so steep as to make communication along that stretch of the coast virtually impossible. These mountains are composed mainly of Miocene volcanics with some sandstones and shales. Their western edge is a precipitous scarp, which forms the eastern boundary of a rift valley, whose opposite scarp is the western edge of the Central Mountain Ranges. This valley, known as the Taitung Rift, about 150 km in length and on average 6 km in width, is filled with recent alluvial deposits. The third region, the Central Mountain Ranges, extends throughout the central length of the island. They consist of three main ranges: the Chungyang Mountains, Yushan and Alishan,

named from east to west. They are composed mainly of schists, quartz and gneiss and form a very imposing landscape, having twenty-seven notable peaks, many of which rise to over 3000 m. Much of the Alishan is faulted, giving rise to depressions, in one of which lies the beautiful Sun Moon lake. To the west of these Central Ranges lie a wide belt of hilly country whose terraces bear evidence of at least two uplifts and the rejuvenation of the river system. In the centre these hills embrace a small alluvial basin in the heart of which Taichung stands. Again west of the hills an alluvial plain runs the whole length of the island. In the centre it is 45 km wide. Across this plain flow many rivers, the four most notable of which are the Tachia, Talu, Hsilo and Tsengwen. While

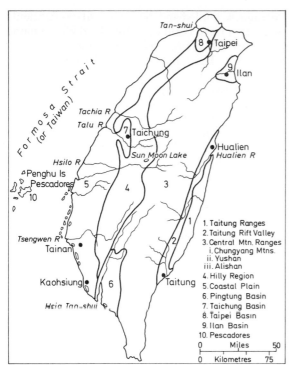

Fig. 135   Taiwan: physiographic regions

they are torrential in their upper courses, their gradients across the plain are such that they become meandering and are liable to change course, building deltas and lagoons at their mouths. There is one large river in the south, the Hsia Tan-shui, which follows a longitudinal course between the north–south folds and which has built up an alluvial plain of sands, clays and gravels in the south. This is known as the Pingtung Plain. Two smaller alluvial basins in the north, formed by the Tan-shui and Chu-shui, have Taipei and Ilan in their centres respectively.

A group of islands, known as the Pescadores or Penghu Islands, lies 34 km off the west coast in the Formosa Strait. These islands are built of a basaltic flow, 'a fragmented and dissected mesa ... composed of three flat-lying basalt flows'. There are sixty-four islands in all, many of which are fringed with coral reefs.

Taiwan has an area of about 36 000 sq. km, about the size of Holland or a little smaller than Switzerland. Its coastline is exceptionally smooth and unindented, being only 1100 km in length. It has no good natural harbours. The southern half of the west coast is shallow and full of lagoons;

the east coast is steep, smooth and without inlets.

The Tropic of Cancer passes through the middle of Taiwan, which stretches from 20° 53′ N to 25° 18′ N. It thus enjoys a climate very similar to that of Kwangtung with modifications due to its being an island 160 km off the mainland. With the exception of the north and northeast, the rest of the island has the normal monsoon pattern of summer rain and winter drought. The outflowing cold air from the Siberian high in winter passes over the East China Sea before it reaches Taiwan. In that passage it becomes warmer and picks up a good deal of moisture. It strikes the island from the northeast and brings to that part quite a heavy winter rain, while the rest of the island is in a rain shadow. Chilung, in fact, has a winter maximum of rain and a fairly even distribution throughout the year; Ilan on the northeast coast has a maximum in October. Between June and September the winds, which are generally lighter than those of winter, blow from the southwest, bringing a marked summer maximum to the south and west coastal plains. Summer, too, is the typhoon season and Taiwan, to its sorrow lies right in the most used paths of these unwelcome visitors. On an average three typhoons pass directly over some part of the island each year and many others pass nearby. They bring heavy rainfall in addition to widespread destruction to crops, buildings and shipping. Temperatures on the plains are subtropical or tropical. As in Kwangtung, summers are long, hot, humid and enervating. Midday summer temperatures are usually over 32° C and relative humidity is often between 85 and 90 per cent.

The natural vegetation of the whole island would be tropical and subtropical forest but, as with the lowlands and plains of China, most of the western coastal plain has been cleared of its tropical woodlands to make room for cultivation. Mangrove swamps occupy some of the tidal deltaic areas. Most of the more mountainous region, however, still retains its magnificent cover of forest. On the lower slopes, up to about 1500 m broadleafed evergreens flourish, including the camphor tree and oak. As elsewhere on the mainland, the camphor tree, because of its commercial value, has suffered heavy cutting, which, although curbed by the Japanese during their occupation, has resulted in bad soil erosion. Above 1500 m the broadleafed evergreens give place to conifers, pine, larch, cedar and still higher fir. It is estimated that more than half of the island is still forested.

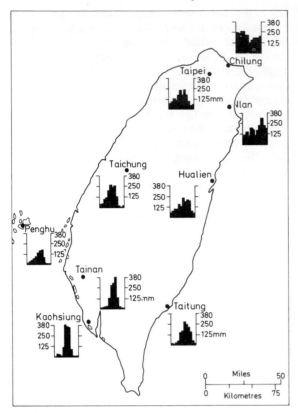

Fig. 136   Taiwan: rainfall map with graphs

Given careful forestry and conservation, this is a potential source of considerable wealth.

The resulting soils are similar to those of south China, i.e. mature, leached, acid, in need of constant fertilization and liming. On the plains there is the same tendency to laterization and on the hills to podzolization.

Although the existence of Taiwan seems to have been known to the Chinese in the seventh century, this knowledge appears to have faded from consciousness much as did the realization of the existence of North America disappear from European ken for centuries and had to be rediscovered. In 1430, not so many years before the great discoveries in the West, Admiral Cheng Ho, returning from an expedition to Thailand, was driven off course and landed on Taiwan. He returned home and gave glowing accounts of this land he had discovered. This marked the beginning of Chinese colonization of the island, which went on intermittently until interrupted for a while by Western activities. Early in the seventeenth century the

Portuguese landed and made their first settlements there. It is from them that the island got its name Formosa (Ilha Formosa, meaning 'the Island Beautiful'). The Chinese name, Taiwan, is composed of the two Chinese words *t'ai*, meaning 'look-out tower' or 'platform' and *wan* meaning 'bay'. The Portuguese were followed by the Dutch and the Spaniards, who strove to drive the Portuguese and each other out. Victory fell to the Dutch in 1642, but their triumph was short-lived.

Just at this time the Manchus were invading China and ousting the Ming dynasty. Among the many leaders and generals attempting to stem this onslaught was Cheng Cheng-kung, better known to the west as Koxinga. After fighting a losing battle against the Manchus, he shipped his army to Taiwan and there summarily defeated and drove out the Dutch (1661). After his victory many Chinese, estimated at over 2 million, who were unable to stomach Manchu domination, fled to the island. Koxinga ruled Taiwan as an independent country till his death, but in 1683 it fell to the conquering Manchus and was incorporated into China as a *fu* or district of the province of Fukien. Thereafter it continued its intermittent and undirected colonization and development, which was attended by endemic warfare with the Malayan aborigines, who were forced back into the mountains where their remnant of not more than 150 000 are still to be found.

Western and Japanese interest in Taiwan again revived in the second half of the nineteenth century as realization of its worth as a market and a source of raw material began to dawn. In order to forestall any annexation by the Great Powers, the island was again incorporated into China and given the status of a province in its own right in 1887. This precaution was, however, fruitless, for in 1895 Japan claimed the island as the fruit of victory in the Sino–Japanese War (1894–5) and for the next fifty years it was ruled by that country as part of its empire.

Those fifty years saw great development in its economy. Road and rail communications were built the length of the western coast. Water conservancy and irrigation schemes and hydroelectric works were carried out with a view, as later in Manchuria, to meeting the ever-growing needs of the homeland in Japan. It was during this period that the great hydro-electric generating station at Sun Moon lake was built. Crop land was increased and the production of all foodstuffs, particularly rice and sugar, stepped up. Un-

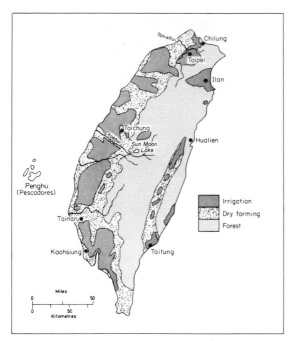

Fig. 137   Taiwan: agriculture (from C. M. Hsieh, Taiwan-ilha Farmosa *by courtesy of Butterworths, London*)

doubtedly this period of Japanese rule was one of great economic development.

With the defeat of Japan in 1945, the island fell under the rule of the Kuomintang. As many of the Taiwanese did not take kindly to their new rulers, three or four years of harsh and unsettled government ensued, culminating in 1949 in the establishment of Taiwan as the seat of the Nationalist Government under Chiang Kai-shek when ousted from the mainland. In that year and ever since there has been an influx of Chinese into Taiwan. The 1951 census placed the total population at 7 791 000 of whom more than 2 million were immigrants of the previous five years. Except for the handful of aboriginals in the mountains and some 180 000 peasants in the rift valley, practically the entire population is distributed densely along the western coastal plain and in the adjoining hilly district. It is estimated that there are 1000 persons per sq. km of cultivated land and more than 200 per sq. km for the whole country, which is a greater density than that of the mainland. This population is essentially rural. More than 90 per cent is engaged in agriculture, either directly or indirectly. Taipei, the capital, is the only town with over 500 000

inhabitants and there are only three others – Taichung, Tainan and Kaohsiung – with a population of more than 200 000.

Agriculture

As mentioned above, agriculture was fostered and developed during Japanese rule. The cultivated area rose from 660 000 ha in 1910 to 850 000 ha in 1940. In 1959 it was 860 000 ha, which constituted 24 per cent of the total area. In 1949 the Government started to undertake land reform which it had signally failed to carry out during its rule on the mainland. Here in Taiwan, however, it was not inhibited by fear of offending its landlord supporters and was further aided by having ample U.S. financial assistance. Land reform was based on Sun Yat Sen's principles and his dictum of 'Land to the Tiller' and it was no less urgently needed here than on the mainland. Tenant farmers were paying 50–60 per cent of their maincrop as rent and were responsible for all irrigation and fertilizer costs, which together swallowed 75 per cent of their income. Private and government-owned land was distributed to those actually working it. Landlords were allowed to retain 3 *chia*, i.e. 3 ha of paddy or $5\frac{1}{2}$ ha of dry farm land. They were compensated by receiving land values in 70 per cent land bonds and 30 per cent government stock. Rents were then fixed at 37·5 per cent of the main crop[60]. The result, as on the mainland initial land reform, has been the fragmentation of the land. Only 1 per cent of the land is in farms of over 10 ha; 85 per cent is in less than 3 ha and 46 per cent in less than 1 ha. The average size of farm is decreasing annually because of land inheritance customs. Apart from the facts that the landlords in Taiwan received compensation and that the redistribution of the land was carried through with comparatively little passion, this first stage in land reform was similar on mainland and island. However, there the similarity ceases since, on the mainland, it was merely a first step towards communal ownership, whereas in Taiwan private ownership was the objective.

To overcome the disadvantages of fragmentation and small individually owned farms, big efforts were made in the 1950s to develop co-operation among the farmers. Good progress was made in the initial stages, but little has been heard of it recently. There is a severe lack of farm draught animals, there being only one head of cattle (water buffalo and yellow ox) to $2\frac{1}{4}$ ha of arable land, a lower proportion than the main-

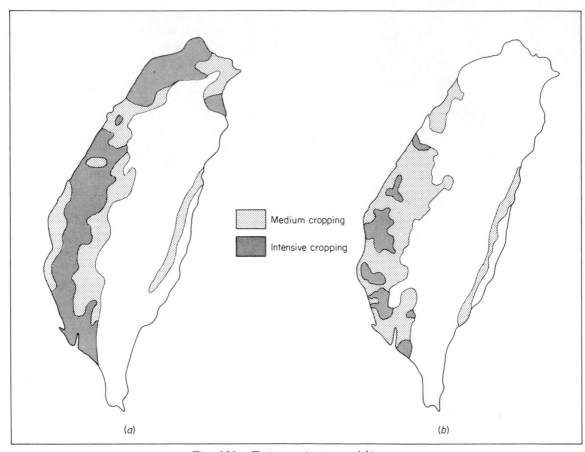

Fig. 138   Taiwan: a) rice and b) sugar

land, yet mechanization has not made headway owing to the handicaps of small farms, little capital and poor credit facilities[61].

Since 1949 new irrigation schemes have been undertaken. By far the biggest of these is known as Taiwan's TVA. In 1954 work was started on the island's most ambitious multi-purpose dam at Shihmen. The intention is eventually to provide irrigation water for the Taoyuan plateau, to regulate the flow of the Tan-shui and thus facilitate drainage and prevent flooding on the Taipei plain and to provide hydro-electric plant of 120 000 kW. Unfortunately, the big Chianan system constructed by the Japanese has deteriorated through silting and soil erosion and through failure to maintain the irrigation canals, so that what has been gained in the north has, to some extent, been lost in the south[61].

Rice is the most important crop and is grown throughout the whole length of the western coastal plain from Taipei to Kaohsiung; also intensively around Ilan and to some extent in the rift valley on the eastern side. Generally it is double-cropped with a winter catch crop as in Kwangtung. In exceptionally favourable circumstances a green summer catch crop is also taken. With improved irrigation and farming techniques output has been raised from 1·8 million tons in 1953 to 2·3 million tons in 1962. A high proportion of the crop was exported under the Japanese; today 90 per cent is consumed at home. Sweet potato is widely grown and is a staple food of the peasant population.

Sugar ranks second in the crop list. It is the main cash crop and Taiwan's main dollar earner. Like rice, it is grown widely on the western lowlands, its main concentration being in the southwest on the Chianan irrigation area. Formerly sugar-

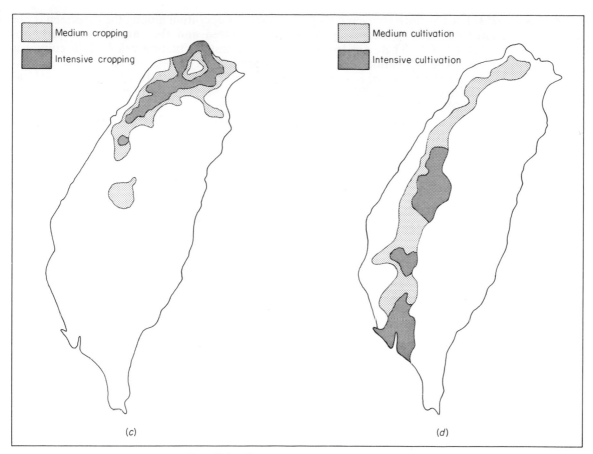

Fig. 139   Taiwan: c) tea and d) bananas

growing occupied about half of the arable area, but recently rice has been a strong contender for more land. The long growing period of 18 months and the fluctuating market prices have led to a falling off of production from 9·2 million tons in 1953 to 6·7 million tons in 1962.

Tea-growing is confined almost entirely to the hilly regions in the northern end of the island; a small amount has also been developed in the centre in the Sun Moon lake region. The reason for this is the better annual distribution of rainfall in the north, giving a long growing and picking period from April to November. The formerly popular semi-fermented oolong and paochung teas, which found a good market in U.S.A., have declined and their place has been taken by black tea. There has been a considerable extension of growing since the end of the Second World War. Production rose from 13 093 tons in 1953 to 21 728 tons in 1962.

The sudden demand for citronella oil after 1945 led to the rapid clearing of forests from the hillsides to plant citronella grass. By 1951 nearly 18 000 ha were under this crop, but the demand was short-lived and most of the cultivation stopped. The formerly wooded mountainsides have become prey to disastrous soil erosion. Many of the new, hurriedly planted tea plantations have given insufficient attention to contouring and terracing, and have added their quota to this menace of soil erosion.

Fruit has become one of the most promising agricultural products. Bananas, which in Taiwan's climate are quick-growing, are easy to cultivate and easy to transport. They also find good overseas markets. Production has risen from 105 711 tons in 1953 to 148 786 tons in 1962. Pineapples, introduced from south China in the seventeenth century, are also of some importance. Peak production in 1939 was 160 000 tons. It slumped to

75 318 tons in 1953, but has since recovered and was 101 537 tons in 1962. Most of the pineapple growing is on very small plots. There are 16 000 growers on 6270 ha[61]. The cultivation of citrus fruit (oranges, tangerines and pomelos) has more than doubled in the last decade from 32 292 tons in 1953 to 73 855 tons in 1962. Unfortunately much of Taiwan's citrus fruit is rather soft-skinned, which reduces its export value. Other fruits are papaya, mango, persimmon and peach. Most of the island's fruit and tea growing is in the hands of small farmers, whose knowledge and capital is limited. By failure to terrace and drain their hillsides properly they have contributed considerably to the recent serious soil erosion.

The eastern and central mountainous spine of the country is densely forested, much of it with hardwood. Under the Japanese the forests were carefully surveyed, registered and controlled. Much of the forest land is in private ownership but today the best conifers (hemlock, cypress, pine, spruce and fir) are in national ownership. Although of great potential value, these forests have not yet been properly exploited because of transport difficulties. The Japanese built a narrow-gauge timber railroad into the heart of the Ali-shan area and tapped the vast timber resources, but this has not been developed to any extent since their withdrawal. Magnificent camphor trees provide the raw material for the manufacture of natural camphor, which was a state monopoly under the Japanese and is now in the hands of the Taiwan Provincial Government. Taiwan's fine forest cover provides essential natural protection against flood and drought on the plains below. Careless and uncoordinated cutting of trees on the lower, more accessible western slopes is endangering irrigation works and cultivation.

Taiwan's main sea fishing grounds lie in the Taiwan (Formosa) Strait, especially around the Penghu islands. The catch is much the same as that of the southern mainland, i.e. large yellow croaker and shellfish. The western coast of Taiwan is bereft of the fine natural harbours of the rugged Fukien and Kwangtung coasts, and the industry is therefore centred mainly in ports at the northern and southern ends of the island in Chilung, Ilan and Kaohsiung and also in the Penghu islands themselves. Most of the fishing is inshore or coastal, but some deep-sea trawling and long-lining is done by mechanized vessels of 50–100 tons stationed mainly at Chilung. Although the sale of catches is now through wholesale fish markets, cooperation among the fishermen is not very advanced and they are inadequately protected against fluctuating prices. Fish culture is developed mainly along the coastal plain, particularly in the southwest. It is practised in the large irrigation reservoirs and in the farm ponds. During the two four-year plan periods (1953–60) the estimated output of the fisheries industry increased by 10 per cent.[62]

Industry

Unlike on the mainland, recent surveys have revealed little of those mineral resources necessary for the development of heavy industry. Estimated reserves of coal, which is mainly Tertiary in formation, amount to only 737 million tons of which 236·5 million tons are considered workable in the present state of technical knowledge. The main coalfield lies in the north in a belt running southwest from Chilung (Keelung). Seams are thin, being only 30–75 cm thick and are badly folded and faulted. Most of the coal can be satisfactorily coked. The present average annual production is 2·7 million tons, which is adequate for current domestic consumption. The chief mining district is in the region south of Chilung.

The possibility of oil production in appreciable quantities is remote. Severe fracturing of the anticlinal folds in the sedimentary Tertiary rocks, running nearly the length of the western foothills, has rendered successful prospecting unlikely. 'In Taiwan nearly 260 wells have been drilled. More than 100 seepages are distributed throughout western Taiwan and the eastern range. 40 or more proved anticlinal folds with oil potentialities have been discovered on the island, but only 6 fields are producing oil or gas at present.'[61] Total production between 1904 and 1951 amounted to only 187 million litres.

If Taiwan's power resources are poorly served by coal and oil, the balance is redressed by its potential and actual hydro-electric resources. At the end of the First World War, only 10 000 kW had been developed. In 1931 the Japanese began work on a big hydro-electric station. Utilizing the fine natural reservoir of the Sun Moon lake high up in the central highlands, they built a first and then a second station with a total capacity of 180 000 kW. By the early 1940s Taiwan was generating 267 000 kW of which 203 000 kW was hydroelectric. Towards the end of the Second World War all the power plant on the island suffered severe damage by U.S. bombing and it was not until 1950 that it was restored. Since that date there has been a great deal of development. The great dam at Shihmen alone has added plant of 120 000 kW capacity. By 1963 the total electrical capacity of Taiwan was 923 400 kW, three-quarters of which was generated by hydro-electric power. In all, there were 36 power stations, 10 of which were thermal (5 powered by coal and 5 by diesel oil). It is on this power that any development of industry has to rely.

Under Japanese rule, industry in Taiwan was geared strictly to the industrial needs of Japan itself. As stated previously, it was never the Japanese intention that it should in any way compete with home industry. Consequently Taiwan's production was confined largely to the provision and preliminary processing of raw and semi-raw materials. Had Taiwan possessed iron ore in exploitable quantities this would doubtless have been exported in that state to serve Japan's iron and steel industry. The dearth of iron ore has meant that there has been a meagre development of an iron and steel industry. Taiwan possesses only one blast furnace and only a few mills of moderate size.[61] Nevertheless there has been a marked increase in the output of steel from 18 000 tons in 1952 to 200 000 tons in 1960 due largely to the growth in demand from the fruit-canning industry[62]. The non-ferrous minerals are in little better case. Gold and copper are the only two found in any appreciable quantity. They are both located in the central and eastern highlands. There are three gold mines near Chilung, which work the gold-bearing quartz veins and which together produce 95 per cent of the island's gold output.[61] The only significant metal industry is aluminium which was founded by the Japanese at Kaohsiung in 1935 and is based on the ample and cheap hydro-electric power. Bauxite was imported from the Chinese mainland until 1949 and now comes mainly from Malaysia. These works were the target of U.S. bombers in the Second World War and were very badly damaged, but they have been reconditioned and are again in production.

The textile industry, involving cotton, silk, wool and ramie, is new to Taiwan and has been fostered by U.S. aid. It is still in its early stages of development. Very little cotton is grown in Taiwan, the raw material coming from the U.S.A. At present there are, in all, 200 000 spindles and 1200 looms, producing 71 million sq. m of cloth; enough, it is claimed, for the island's needs.

The real mainstay of industry, however, is sugar manufacture. It is the most mechanized and the best organized, making good use of such by-products as yeast, which goes mainly to hog feeding, and bagasse or sugar waste, which is good raw material for papermaking. Sugar export goes mainly to Japan. Closely associated with the sugar industry is jute production and the making of gunny bags. The growing of jute in Taiwan was initiated by the Japanese. Peak production under their rule in 1943 was approximately 6700 tons. By 1955 it had risen to 18 300 tons and is now sufficient to meet the present demands of the sugar manufacturers.

There is no doubt that Taiwan has made very considerable economic progress under Nationalist rule. Assessing the agricultural and industrial development since 1949 Professor Frank King says: 'Over the past five years, the increase in GNP has averaged some 8 per cent p.a., including a 4 per cent increase in agriculture. Savings in 1964 were 24 per cent of GNP and in the following year the U.S. aid programme, which had financed some 35 per cent of Taiwan's investment over a 10-year period, ceased. Prospects for the future continue bright; Taiwan has become the case of a successful aid recipient.'[62]

The geo–politics of Taiwan are involved. While neither the Communist government of the mainland nor the Nationalist Government of Taiwan is in any doubt that the island is an integral part of China, the former regards it as the last 'unliberated' part of the Fatherland still in the hands of the 'running dogs of the imperialists' and the latter regards it as the refuge from which the rightful Pretender will one day return to the mainland to re-establish a free China. Behind all this lie the power politics of the U.S.S.R. and U.S.A., the latter still regarding it – at least to some extent – as a bastion in its western Pacific fringe of defences against the communist menace. Internally the government is by no means free from problems. The majority of Taiwanese Chinese remain independently minded and critical.

11. HONG KONG AND THE NEW TERRITORIES

The bargain which Captain Elliot struck with the Chinese government at the end of the 1841 war for the cession of Hong Kong to the British in return for the Chusan Island, captured during hostilities, was regarded generally as a poor one. Palmerston,

Foreign Secretary at the time, dismissed Elliot from his post with the comment that he 'had obtained the cession of Hong Kong, a barren island with hardly a house upon it.... It seems obvious that Hong Kong will not be a mart of trade any more than Macau is.' Palmerston was right in his description of the island: it was bare, treeless and rocky with only about 2500 inhabitants; but he was quite wrong in his prognostication. In spite of many vicissitudes, epidemics and fevers, storms and typhoons, commercial crises and human blunders and a good deal of opposition both at home and on the spot, the colony has grown with great rapidity over the last one hundred and twenty years.[63]

The earliest settlement was at Victoria on the northwest of the island. This city has now spread the whole length of the northwest coast and numbers over 1 million inhabitants. In 1861 the peninsula of Kowloon on the mainland was ceded by China, thus adding a further 10 sq. km to the 83 sq. km of the island. This addition, together with Stonecutter Island, enabled the British to control adequately the magnificent natural harbour which gives 44 sq. km of deep and safe anchorage. Kowloon at that time consisted of a Chinese fort, which occupied the extreme south promontory and which had been a constant danger and annoyance to shipping in the harbour. There were also several small villages on the peninsula. Probably the population was less than 3000. Today it is a thriving, densely peopled city of $1\frac{1}{2}$ million.

In 1898 a further 932 sq. km were added to this colony of only 93 sq. km on the plea that more land was necessary for the 'proper defence and protection of the colony', but it was also urgently required for the provision of further water supply. This land was leased by the Chinese for a period of ninety-nine years and is thus due to be returned to China in twenty years' time. It is known as the New Territories as distinct from the Colony proper of Hong Kong and Kowloon. At the time of the convention granting this 1898 lease it is estimated that there were about 100 000 inhabitants in its 423 villages. Today this number has grown to about 694 000, the make-up of which still reflects the diverse linguistic grouping of southeast China. The Cantonese are the largest group and the most wealthy. They occupy the better, low-lying agricultural land and are settled in the larger villages, some of which are walled. The Hakka or 'guest people' are the second largest and occupy the higher, less valuable land in the valleys as a rule.

Both Cantonese and Hakka stem from early Yueh roots and both are essentially agriculturalists. The third and smaller group is the Hoklo, who probably occupied the land before the Cantonese. They are boat dwellers who today have also settled on the land, particularly on the islands of Cheung Chau and Ping Chau, while the fourth group, the Tanka, are essentially boat people and live their lives with their families afloat. (In recent years an increasing number of families are moving into the New Territories from Hong Kong Island and Kowloon as a result of urbanization of certain districts, notably Tsun Wan and Kwai Ching.)

From 1841 to 1941 decennial reports show a continual rise of population with marked periodic fluctuations occasioned by waves of immigration and exodus to and from China in times of political upheaval or unrest on the mainland. Once firmly established, Hong Kong has from time to time received floods of refugees seeking a temporary haven when trouble brewed across the border. An even more significant cause of these fluctuations has been the influx and exodus of labourers with each boom and recession of international trade. Since 1941, this pattern has changed. In that year, when population was estimated at about $1\frac{1}{2}$ million, Japan occupied the Colony and there followed a mass exodus, which reduced the numbers to about 600 000. The years 1945–6 saw the defeat of Japan and the quick return of the people to the pre-war level. By 1949 the population was assessed at 1 857 000, when it underwent a further large accession as hundreds of thousands of refugees fled into the Colony when the victorious Communist army swept southward. By 1963 numbers had grown to $3\frac{1}{2}$ million and in 1975 to an estimated 4·4 million. This amazing growth has several features which distinguish it from the previous pattern. The cessation of hostilities and the establishment of peace have not been attended, as heretofore, by the return of refugees to their homeland. On the contrary, a steady and illegal flow into the colony has continued over the years. In addition to this there has been a phenomenal rise in the natural increase of the population since the end of the war, as the following figures demonstrate:

	Births	*Deaths*	*Natural increase*
1949	42 500	13 000	29 000
1953	75 544	18 300	57 244
1958	106 624	21 554	85 070
1974	81 879	22 050	59 829

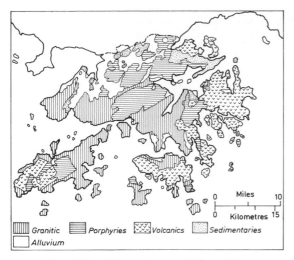

Fig. 140   The geology of Hong Kong

In 1954 the birth-rate stood at 36·6 $^{0/000}$ and the death rate at 8·5 $^{0/000}$ while only four years later the figures were 38·8 $^{0/000}$ and 7·5 $^{0/000}$ respectively. The reason for this lies very largely in the great improvement in public health and hygiene achieved in spite of the overcrowding. A further reason for population growth has been the great development of industry in the last decade. This aspect will be dealt with later in this section. More than 98 per cent of the population of Hong Kong and the New Territories is Chinese.

Hong Kong's geological history reproduces in miniature the probable geological sequence in the rest of southeast China. The oldest rocks are either Permian or early Jurassic sediments: the very few fossil remains leave some doubt as to their identity. They were folded along an ENE–WSW axis. These sedimentaries were highly metamorphosed in the Jurasside revolution when there was widespread volcanic outpouring of tuff, lava and agglomerates. A subsequent bathylith gave rise to sills and laccoliths of quartz, porphyry, granite, granite porphyry and swarms of dykes, which are the preponderating and characteristic rocks. A long period of quiescence and erosion was followed first by extensive folding, which affected the whole of southeast China and gave it its NE–SW trend and then by a further outpouring of acid lavas probably during the Miocene. Thus the great bathylith was capped by a thick covering of hard volcanics. Hong Kong granite is singularly susceptible to deep chemical weather-

ing, probably because the felspars break down easily. Where this volcanic cap is pierced by erosion and the granite core exposed, the latter weathers comparatively quickly as the accompanying section reveals.

The relief of Hong Kong and the New Territories is characterized by three broken ranges of steep and often precipitous hills. The three most notable peaks are Tai Mo Shan (953 m) in the heart of the New Territories Lantau Peak (933 m) on the large island of Lantau and the precipitous Ma On Shan (672 m) to the northeast of Kowloon, in which workable iron ore is found. The lines of these hills conform to the NE–SW trend of the geology and occupy about four-fifths of the total area. The only sizeable area of flat land is the alluvial plain in the northwest of the New Territories. The long and very indented coastline is equally rugged, with cliffs of 60–180 m in the east, where columnar volcanic formations are encountered.

From the full and accurate meteorological records which have been kept for over seventy years in Hong Kong we can get a clear and precise picture of the climate of this region. Hong Kong lies just within the tropics and on the southeastern verge of Asia. In consequence it experiences a monsoon rhythm. Easterly winds are prevalent over nine months (September to May) of the year. Only during June, July and August do the main winds come from the south and southwest. It is during these three months that, on average, the heaviest rain falls. A diagram of monthly average rainfall over sixty years gives an almost perfect picture of the monsoon rhythm, but it is false if it leaves the impression of great regularity and invariability. The truth is that considerable variation in rainfall occurs from year to year both in total amount and in monthly distribution as the three diagrams demonstrate.

It is this variability, although not as extreme as in northern China, which constitutes one of the main hazards of the farmer in south China. A failure, such as those of 1954 and 1963, probably means only a single instead of a double crop and may even jeopardize the single crop. The nature of the rainfall varies with the season. Drizzle is characteristic of February and March, damp, cold weather being often experienced at Chinese New Year (February). Summer rain occurs usually in frequent heavy downpours and sometimes in cloudbursts, which bring phenomenal and unwelcome falls. On 19 July 1926 there was a fall of 100

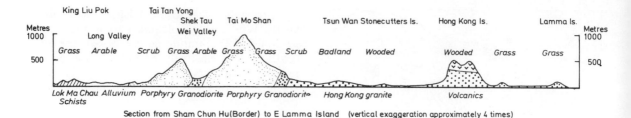

Section from Sham Chun Hu(Border) to E Lamma Island   (vertical exaggeration approximately 4 times)

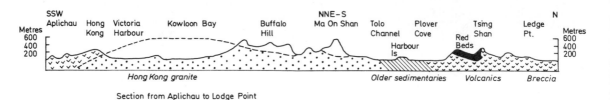

Section from Aplichau to Lodge Point

Fig. 141   Sections across Hong Kong and the New Territories

mm in one hour and over 530 mm in 24 hours. In a typhoon the downpour is accompanied by disastrously strong winds.

Hong Kong and the New Territories enjoy a full year's growing period. The fact that once and only once in seventy years has frost been recorded on the plains is sufficient comment on winter temperatures. Frost and icicles on Victoria Peak, the wealthy residential area of Hong Kong (300 to 500 m) are occasions for headlines in the papers. Although summer temperatures are not spectacularly high (36°C on 19 August 1900 is the highest recorded) they are uncomfortable on account of the dampness of the atmosphere. Average relative humidity stands between 83 and 85 per cent from April to August. October to December are delightful months with clear blue skies, warm sun and a dry atmosphere.

The natural vegetational cover of the lowlands and most of the hills before human settlement was forest and woodland. This has long since been cleared by felling and burning and now less than 4 per cent is forested. The greater part of this small amount is on Hong Kong island where closer control of cutting can be practised than in the New Territories. The most widely planted trees are the local pine (*Pinus massoniana*), eucalyptus and casuarina. Big efforts are being made at afforestation by the Forestry Department but the difficulties are great, especially in the deeply gullied and eroded granitic 'badlands'. These 'badlands' occupy just over 4 per cent of the Colony

and are for the most part entirely devoid of vegetational cover. This is a more important fact than so small a proportion of the total area would suggest, because much of this 4 per cent lies within the catchment basin of the biggest reservoir and therefore seriously affects run-off and water supplies. It is for this reason that the greatest afforestation efforts are concentrated on these lands.[64]

The original woodlands have given place mainly to coarse, tufted grass and low, woody scrub of about 30 cm in height. These cover 57 per cent of the total area. Another 16 per cent is occupied by taller scrub and bushes. The alluvial plain in the northwest is given over entirely to agriculture and is now quite devoid of natural cover. Much of the plain has been reclaimed from the sea in the last fifty years, mainly from Deep Bay into which the Shum Chun river empties its silt. Along the shallow coast here are mangrove swamps and marshes.

Climate in Hong Kong is a more important soil-forming agent than mechanical action. The combination of heavy summer rains and high temperatures brings about deep and rapid chemical weathering, particularly in the widespread granites. The resultant soils are clayey and tend to be lateritic. The heavy leaching to which they are subjected every summer results in acid soils everywhere.

There are about 275 000 persons engaged in the two primary industries of agriculture and fishing.

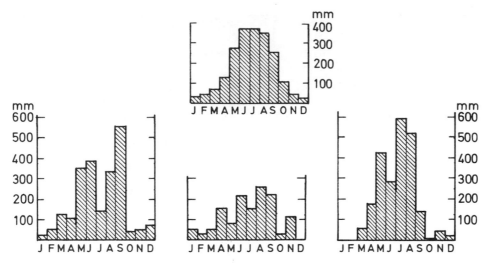

Fig. 142   Average rainfall in Hong Kong and actual rainfall 1953–5

Of these some 150 000 are dependent directly or indirectly on fishing, 60 000 actually living in boats, These are engaged in both deep-sea and inshore fishing, the latter being in grave danger of overfishing. In the last ten years great steps have been made in mechanization of the fleets to meet Japanese competition in this field. In 1958 the catch of marine fish was 44 906 tons and was worth nearly £3 million. In addition to the open sea fisheries, pond pisciculture has developed considerably in the northwest of the New Territories where one hectare of pond produces a return twice as great as that of rice paddy.

The following figures give some idea of the distribution of the agricultural land between the various crops.

	hectares
Rice land	
Two-crop paddy	8072
One-crop brackish water paddy	1160
One-crop upland paddy	98
Vegetable land	902
Orchard	380
Field crops	1392

Since rice is the staple food of the Chinese it is not surprising to find that its growth occupies more than two-thirds of the cultivated land. Although most of the paddy is double-cropped, rice production suffices to meet the needs of only a very small proportion of the Colony's population. A great deal is imported from Thailand and China.

Vegetable growing has shown great increase since the Second World War. Before that war only one-fifth of the Colony's needs were met by local growers. Today, in spite of the great growth of population, it is nearly self-sufficing. This is the most intense form of farming, some land producing as much as eight crops a year. The main vegetables grown are: white cabbage, flowering cabbage, leaf mustard cabbage, turnips, Chinese kale and Chinese lettuce. Field crops include sweet potatoes, taro, yams, sugar-cane and groundnuts.

Both the fishermen and vegetable growers have received great encouragement since the war by the establishment of the Fish Marketing Organization and the Vegetable Marketing Organization, which, although receiving help from government personnel, are non-government bodies. They are designed to organize the collection, sorting and fair marketing of the produce, eliminating private middlemen's charges, which formerly were exorbitant. In addition to marketing, the organizations have social and educational activities. Co-operative societies, assisting in buying, selling and credit are growing and flourishing in both the fishing and farming communities. Surprisingly, fruit farming in the past has received little attention. It is now increasing. Papaya, guava, Chinese lime, tangerine, lychee, *wong pei* and peach are the main fruits grown. Pineapple plantations are increasing and regaining some of their former popularity. Tea, which was grown widely on the hill slopes in the 1870s and 1880s receives no attention whatever today. Agriculture in all its

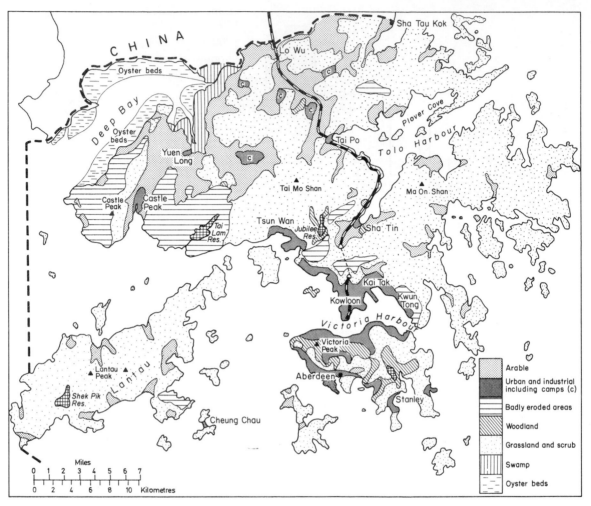

Fig. 143   Land use of Hong Kong and the new Territories (simplified from T. R. Tregear, Land Use Map of Hong Kong and the New Territories, 1957)

branches, including livestock, receives much advice, help and demonstration from an active government Agricultural, Fisheries and Forestry Department, and encouragement and financial assistance through such philanthropic bodies as the Joseph Trust Fund and the Kadoorie Agricultural Aid Association.

However, Hong Kong's interest and raison d'être has been from the outset not in agriculture but in commerce. For one hundred years, between 1841 and 1941 exactly, as a free port, having an almost complete absence of import duties, it was one of the great entrepôts of the world. Its large natural harbour was always full of ships of all nations, collecting and distributing the raw

materials of China and the manufactured articles of the Western world. Except for flourishing ship-building and ship repair works, industry was of little importance. With the Japanese occupation of the port in 1941, all international commerce was brought to an abrupt halt; until 1946 it served only Japanese war needs. Trade recovery was quick when peace returned and was broadly of the pre-war pattern. By 1951 a new peak was reached when imports were valued at £300 million and exports at £275 million. Then followed in the next four years an equally rapid and disastrous slump, when, with the outbreak and continuance of the Korean War the United Nations embargo was placed on a long list of strategic goods entering

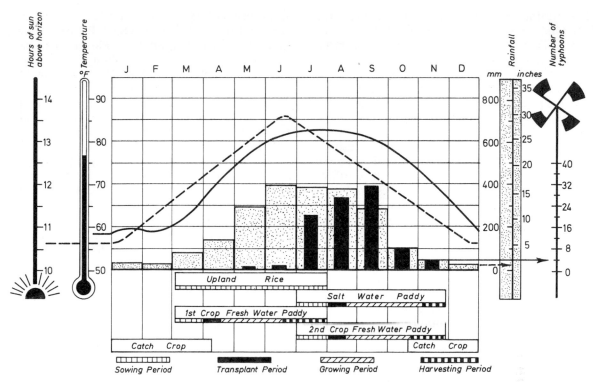

Fig. 144   Relation between Hong Kong climatic conditions and crop period of rice

China. By 1954 imports had fallen by about £80 million and exports by more than £100 million. Hong Kong's answer to this unhappy state has been revolutionary, redounding to its energy and resilience. In a matter of less than a decade it largely changed the basis of its economic life from reliance on commerce to industry. The following table conveys some idea of the magnitude of the change which has taken place.

Most of the industrial development has taken place in and around Kowloon. Many new centres have sprung up overnight. For example, Tsun Wan in 1952 was a village of about 5000, where a small camphor industry had once been carried on.

Today it is a hive of activity with a population of more than 500 000. It will be seen from the above figures that, while shipbuilding remains an important industry, it has not grown. It is in the sphere of light industry that the startling changes have taken place, particularly in textiles. The number of workers engaged in spinning, weaving and garment-making rose from 9439 in 1948 to 54 085 in 1958. Modern machinery has been installed; new skills have been quickly acquired; the quality of output is good. Many other new industries have been started. Enamel and aluminium-ware, plastic goods, electric torches and batteries, vacuum flasks, paints, boots and

Growth of Industry in Hong Kong 1948–74

Workers	1948	1958	1966	1974
Metal workers	9 914	24 342	34 265	51 410
Shipbuilding and repairs	9 729	10 049	10 307	8 733
Food Manufacture	3 308	6 921	9 201	13 625
Plastic ware	33	8 024	33 773	56 121
Rubber products	4 427	8 788	9 232	6 621
Cotton weaving	6 488	15 870	31 277	25 732
Cotton spinning	1 755	12 613	20 101	19 106
Wearing apparel	1 196	25 602	71 845	169 110

shoes, leather goods and many others figure in the list. Most of the factories are small by western standards. In addition to this more organized industry it is estimated that about 150 000 persons are engaged in traditional Chinese handicrafts, such as embroidery and drawn-thread work, brocade piece-goods, wood and ivory carving.[65]

Hong Kong's mineral wealth is not great. There are small deposits of lead, silver, wolfram and tin associated with the many dykes and intrusions. These are worked in a small way as also is some graphite on the Brothers Islands to the north of Lantau. Kaolin is worked in the west and used both in the local ceramic industry and exported. Iron-ore workings on Ma On Shan are in the hands of a Japanese concession.

From earliest days the Colony has been in trouble over water supplies. Population has constantly outrun engineering efforts as reservoir after reservoir has been built. In an endeavour to meet the needs of growing industry and the rapid rise in population during the last fifteen years, two very large dams with large catchment areas at Tai Lam Chung and Shek Pik on Lantau have been built. The whole of Plover Cove has been enclosed as a reservoir. Although this trebled the water supply, it has been found insufficient and a resort has had to be made to supplies from the mainland of China. Under agreement with the People's Government, Hong Kong receives 67 000 million litres annually from the Tung river.

Even in so short a description of Hong Kong as this, some comment on the refugee problem is called for, since it is unique. Of Hong Kong's 4 million inhabitants, between 700 000 and 800 000 have entered from the mainland in the last twelve years either for political reasons, fleeing from a government which is feared, or for economic and social reasons, or both. Some of the refugees have been wealthy but most are indigent; some are skilled but most are unskilled. They have not been herded into camps as in Europe but have mingled with, and are largely indistinguishable from, the rest of the population as the Hambro U.N. Com-

Hong Kong's Major Trading Partners
Imports into Hong Kong (millions HK$)

	1951	1956	1961	1966	1974
China	863	1038	1028	2769	5991
U.K.	619	513	757	1011	1942
Malaya	394	152	140	—	1889
Japan	392	810	864	1839	7142
U.S.A.	373	423	729	1090	4621
Thailand	156	185	256	267	—
Fed. Rep. of Germany	—	—	186	269	1193
Australia	—	—	—	—	760
Total Imports	4870	4566	5970	10097	34120

Exports from Hong Kong (million HK$)

	1951	1956	1961	1966	1974
China	1604	136	—	—	197
U.K.	215	296	589	987	2768
Malaya	741	373	267	224*	626*
Japan	193	318	107	162	1061
U.S.A.	162	117	679	2036	7422
Indonesia	245	501	173	102	—
Macau	228	58	15	—	—
Fed. Rep. of Germany	214	—	106	420	2444
Total Exports	4433	3209	2939	5730	22911

* Includes Singapore.

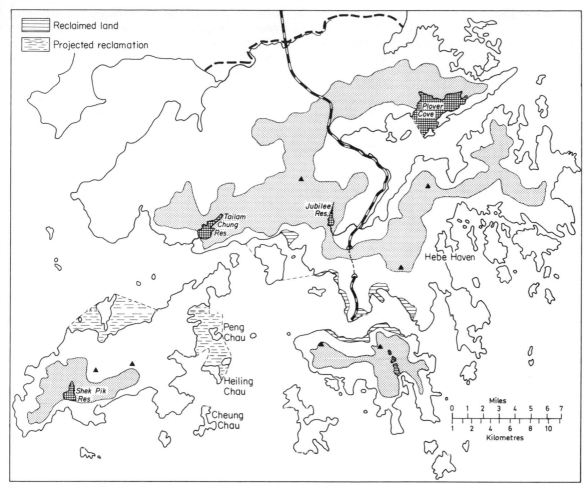

Fig. 145   Hong Kong: water supplies catchment areas

mission discovered. Many have had friends and relations in the Colony but very many more have not, and have squatted in miserable shacks on the hillsides around the two cities of Victoria and Kowloon. Such an influx has imposed enormous burdens on the authorities. Disastrous fires sweep through these squatter settlements. One alone on Christmas Eve 1954 rendered 60 000 homeless in one night. Overcrowding in some parts of the cities is very great. In Wan Chai, for example, there are as many as 5000 people to the hectare. To meet this problem the government has built large numbers of huge tenement blocks. Other problems of unemployment, underemployment, malnutri-

tion, sanitation and not least education all follow in this train. In spite of all, the Colony manages to present a gay, busy, bustling yet orderly and cleanly community, full of that *je nao* (hot noise) which most Chinese love.

In the last 10–15 years Hong Kong's profile has suffered a sea change. A city of skyscrapers, rising to 30–50 storeys, greets one on entering the harbour; land reclamation in many places has smoothed the harbour's coastline, adding about 10 sq. km of territory, and many new motor roads, supported by flyovers and a tunnel under the harbour, have relieved to some degree an ever-increasing traffic problem.

12. MACAU

Macau is a Portuguese colony situated on the right bank at the mouth of the Pearl river estuary, some 55 km WSW of Hong Kong. It consists of a small peninsula and two islands, Taipa and Coloane, having a total area of only 16 sq. km.

In 1516 the Portuguese landed on the small peninsula and there established their first trading station. It remained in their possession but under nominal Chinese control until in 1849 the Portuguese declared it to be their own territory. Although this declaration was confirmed by treaty in 1887, it has continued a matter of disputation ever since. It became the chief centre of European trade with China and so remained until the cession of Hong Kong to the British. Thereafter its importance as an entrepôt steadily and rapidly declined.

Today it is a sleepy, picturesque but decadent township in striking contrast to the bustle, noise and activity of Hong Kong.

Apart from fishing, which provides a livelihood for about a quarter of its inhabitants, and the manufacture of firecrackers, the town is given over to the tourist trade. It is a favourite week-end resort of the people of Hong Kong with which it is connected by an efficient and comfortable ferry and hydrofoil service. There are many hotels and a rather down-at-heel gambling casino. Formerly it was a notorious opium-smuggling centre. Since 1949 it has been one of the main routes through which refugees from Communist China pass in their endeavour to reach Hong Kong.

Population in 1970 numbered about 250 000 of whom some 240 000 were Chinese and 7460 Portuguese.

References

1 U.S.S.R. Academy of Sciences, op. cit., Vol. II, pp. 82–4.
2 Hung Fu, 'The geographic regions of China and their sub-divisions', *I.G.U. Proceedings*, 1952.
3 A. W. Grabau, *The Stratigraphy of China* (Peking, 1925), Part II, p. 305.
4 G. B. Cressey, 'The Ordos Desert of Inner Mongolia', *Dennison University Bulletin*, **33**, no. 8.
5 Tsui Yu-wen, 'Problems of soil-preserving vegetation in the middle reaches of the Hwang-ho', *Academia Sinica*, 1957.
6 Quoted from Dudley Buxton, *China, the Land and the People* (Oxford, 1929), p. 268.
7 J. G. Andersson, op. cit.
8 A. Little, op. cit., p. 29.
9 *Flood Control Journal*, no. 1 (September 1949), United Nations Economic Commission for Asia and the Far East.
10 Teng Tse-hui, *Report on the Multi-purpose Plan for Permanently Controlling the Yellow River*, 18 July 1955.
11 NCNA, Tientsin, 9 July 1966.
12 T. J. Lindsay, 'Water Conservancy in China', *Contemporary China* Vol. 1956–7 Hong Kong 1958.
13 Peking *Pei-Ching Jih-pao*, 22 November 1966.
14 Martin C. Yang, *A Chinese Village: Taitou* (London, 1947).
15 NCNA, Hofei, 18 March 1965.
16 NCNA, Hofei, 15 May 1966.
17 Chi Ho-teh and Chang Yen-feng, 'Carving out rivers in the hills', *China Reconstructs*, July 1965.
18 W. Smith, *Coal and Iron in China* (Liverpool, 1926).

19 G. B. Barbour, 'The physiographic history of the Yangtze', *Geographical Journal*, **87** (1936).
20 See G. B. Barbour, op. cit., for a full treatment of the subject.
21 Chang Pao-Kun, 'Climatic regions of Szechwan Province', *Meteorological Magazine*, **15**, nos 3–4 (1941).
22 H. L. Richardson, *Soils and Agriculture of Szechwan* (Chungking, 1942).
23 E. H. Wilson, *A Naturalist in Western China* (London, 1913).
24 Sun Ching-chih (ed.), *Si-nan Ti Ch'u Ching-chi-Ti-li* [*Economic Geography of Southwest China*] (Peking, 1960).
25 J. Lossing Buck, op. cit.
26 H. J. Wiens, 'The Shu Tao or Road to Szechwan', *Geographical Review*, **39** (1949).
27 T. R. Tregear, 'Shih Hui Yao – a Chinese river port with a future', *Geography*, April 1954.
28 G. Fenzel, op. cit.
29 *Nan-fang Jih-pao*, Canton, 28 October 1964.
30 G. B. Cressey, 'Land forms of Chekiang', *Annals of A.A.G.*, **28** (1938).
31 G. B. Cressey, *Land of the 500 Million* (New York, 1955), p. 227.
32 Ma Yung-chih, *General Principles of Geographical Distribution of Chinese Soils* (Peking, 1956).
33 Fei Hsiao-tung and Chang Chih-i, *Earthbound China: A Study of Rural Economy in Yunnan* (Chicago, 1945).
34 J. Lossing Buck, op. cit.
35 Fei Hsiao-tung and Chang Chih-i, op. cit.

36 Owen Lattimore, 'Chinese colonization in Manchuria', *Geographical Review*, **2** (1932).

37 W. Eberhard, *A History of China* (London, 1948), chapter 12.

38 Ho Ping-ti, *Studies on the Population of China* (Cambridge, Massachusetts, 1959).

39 Owen Lattimore, op. cit.

40 Franklin L. Po, 'Population movement to the north-eastern frontier of China', quoted from Ho Ping-ti, op. cit.

41 Sung Ching-chih (ed.), *Economic Geography in North-east China* (Peking, 1959).

42 NCNA, Shenyang, 8 April 1965.

43 A. J. Grazdanzev, 'Manchuria, 1945: an industrial survey', *Pacific Affairs*, **18**, December 1945.

44 T. T. Read, 'Economic-geographic aspects of China's iron industry', *Geographical Review*, **33** (1943); and A. Rogers, 'Manchurian iron and steel industry', *Geographical Review*, **1** (1948), p. 41.

45 See E. Huntingdon, *The Pulse of Asia* (Boston, 1910), for a full discussion of these theories.

46 Owen Lattimore, 'An Inner Asian approach to the historical geography of China', *Geographical Journal*, **110**, nos 4–6.

47 Chang Chih-yi, 'Land utilization and settlement possibilities in Sinkiang', *Geographical Review*, **39** (1949).

48 R. C. F. Schomberg, 'The habitability of Chinese Turkestan', *Geographical Journal*, **80** (1932).

49 E. Huntingdon, op. cit.

50 M. Cable and F. French, *The Gobi Desert* (London, 1946).

51 Hang Hung-wen, 'Grapes in the "Land of Fire"', *China Reconstructs*, June 1963.

52 NCNA, Urumchi, 22 June 1966.

53 Owen Lattimore, 'Caravan routes in Inner Asia', *Geographical Journal*, **72** (1928).

54 M. Cable and F. French, op. cit., p. 99.

55 *Jen-min Jih-pao*, Peking, 25 January 1959.

56 Owen Lattimore, op. cit.

57 Dick Wilson, *A Quarter of Mankind* (London, 1966).

58 W. G. Kendrew, 'Climate', in Dudley Buxton, op. cit.

59 Vei Chou Juan, *Physiography and Geology of Taiwan*. This and other pamphlets of the Chinese Culture Publishing Foundation, together with Chang Jen-hu's *Agricultural Geography of Taiwan*, have been widely drawn on for the material of this chapter.

60 *Joint Commission on Rural Reconstruction*, Taipei, December 1956.

61 C. M. Hsieh, *Taiwan – ilha Formosa* (London, 1964).

62 Frank A. A. King, *A Concise Economic History of Modern China, 1840–1961* (Bombay, 1968).

63 T. R. Tregear and L. Berry, *The Development of Hong Kong as Told in Maps* (Hong Kong, 1959).

64 T. R. Tregear, *Land Use in Hong Kong and the New Territories* (Hong Kong, 1958).

65 E. Szczepanik, *The Economic Growth of Hong Kong* (London, 1958), gives a full treatment of the subject.

12 The Unity of China

Throughout the preceding pages the vastness of China, its huge and varied population, the great differences of climate, soil, vegetation and the variety of ways of life which these occasion, have been constantly under review. Having these diversities in mind the question inevitably arises whether the country can properly be administered under a unitary government, which has been the form since the time of Ch'in Shih Hwang Ti (221 BC) or whether some form of federalism is not essential. The present government is committed firmly to the unitary form and is using every endeavour to develop the country into one conscious whole, while at the same time encouraging considerable devolution of responsibility to provinces and communes. The various autonomous regions are held to be integral parts of a unified whole and not federated units.

China Proper during the last 2000 years has been knit by clear unifying factors of which common race is the most outstanding. Even today only some 35 to 40 million out of its 800 million people belong to minorities not of Chinese origin. The remaining 94 per cent are either Han (Northern Chinese) or T'ang (Southern Chinese), who, although their many spoken dialects are vastly different, use the same written language. True, the written language has been the prerogative of the literati, a mere 10 per cent who throughout have formed the governing class. The third great unifying factor has been the common Confucian philosophy and code of behaviour, which regulated conduct and imposed standards of values in all walks of life. This code held strict sway since Han times and broke down only under the onslaught of Western intrusion in the nineteenth century. It collapsed finally in 1911 with the fall of the Ch'ing (Manchu) dynasty when China looked first to Western democratic ideas for a new philosophy. When, in 1919 at the Versailles Conference, the Allies failed to redeem pledges of ending the 'Unequal Treaties', which the Chinese reckoned had been given, disenchantment with the West followed and finally, in 1949, China embraced Communism, as interpreted by Mao Tse-tung, as its unifying faith.

Central to Mao's philosophy is the concept of 'contradiction', that within all things there are opposites, which struggle for mastery and which constitute the cause of all development. He thus repudiates any truth in determinism. Struggle, for him, is the very essence of life; its absence is synonymous with death[1]. Antagonism is essential. Writing in the midst of the Sino–Japanese War, 1936–45, when confronted by a military foe, he says: 'It is a good thing, not a bad thing, to be opposed by an enemy'. Also 'There is infinite joy in struggling against Heaven; there is infinite joy in struggling against Earth and there is infinite joy in struggling against man. Happiness is struggle.' Unhappily this concept of struggle against an enemy has carried with it a compulsion to and a cultivation of bitter and uncompromising hatred of the 'enemy' within and without China's borders. In so far as this negative principle of hatred is deliberately cultivated, it carries with it the seeds of its own destruction.

In this belief in struggle lies the key to so many

of the events and movements since 1949. The Great Leap Forward of 1958–9 was an outstanding example of the rousing and stirring of the nation to prodigious efforts to overcome production difficulties but, more deeply, the first real attempt to break with the old motivation of effort based on individual material incentives and self-interest. By Western standards the casualties of the Great Leap were so great as to be regarded as a disaster, but by Chinese revolutionaries, it is reckoned, on balance, as a success since they contend that it achieved great gains in the establishment of the communes and in the growth of social consciousness and a sense of unity.

During the years 1966–9 China underwent yet another revolution, the Cultural Revolution, which was more profound and far-reaching in its effects than any of its predecessors.[2] This movement reproduced, in its initial stages, much the same fanatical and frightening hysterical enthusiasm and over-reaction as the Great Leap and much the same disruption of production. It was also attended by many excesses. It has remained very much of an enigma to Western interpreters, who variously have seen it as a struggle for succession to Mao Tse-tung's leadership, as 'court' intrigue, as a disruption of the CCP in a struggle for supremacy between 'revisionist' and 'revolutionary' factions. There is an element of truth in each of these interpretations but, in the author's opinion, the Cultural Revolution must be regarded basically as a new ideological leap forward in an endeavour to 'secure the revolution'. It was initiated by Mao Tse-tung expressly for this purpose and reveals his hopes and his fears.

His aim, which he declared on countless occasions, was nothing less than the conversion of the whole Chinese people from their old clan and family loyalties and profit-seeking motivation to one in which the good of the whole should be the driving force. The incentive to all effort should be the satisfaction of service to the masses rather than individual material reward. In other words, the driving force should be spiritual rather than material, although Mao would hardly have used this term. His belief was that with this change of motivation comes the power to move mountains and that failure to achieve this change in men's minds would mean the failure of the revolution. This, he contended, was the *sine qua non* of all true material advancement. To this end Mao's thoughts and writings are inculcated in-season and out-of-season, before, during and

after work, to old and young and particularly to the lower-middle and poor peasantry, who comprise the vast majority, the 'masses', in whom Mao placed his faith ever since 1927[3]. It is this faith in the peasantry rather than in the industrial proletariat which constitutes the deep difference between Chinese and Russian Communism.

Mao's fears sprang from the dangers he saw in opulence and ease and the fact that the rising generations did not undergo the hardships or experience the involvement and the inspiration of the pioneers of the revolution. Hence his belief in and initiation of repeated 'leaps' or constant revolutions, which were appeals to the spirit and were intended to keep alive the element of struggle which he considered so essential. This, it would appear, was the main reason for the Red Guard movement – an endeavour to involve the entire younger generation, which was in danger of sloth and loss of revolutionary fervour. Rising standards of living and of comfort, unless accompanied by socialist indoctrination of service and the 'good of the masses', tend to feed the bourgeois appetite for self-advancement and promote the reversion to capitalism. This is the fate, Mao contended, that has overtaken Russia, which has grown rich, lost its Marxist faith, become 'revisionist' and so betrayed its leadership of Communism. This distrust of ease was further reflected in Mao's dislike of large cities and may well have been an element in the development of the communes, which, in addition to their productive and devolutionary values, have tended to stem the tide of urbanization.

The Cultural Revolution appears as foolishness to Western eyes and to the sophisticated a stumbling block. However, the author is of the opinion that it is wiser to fix attention on its aims and aspirations rather than on extravagances, excesses and mistakes. If Mao Tse-tung and those who follow him succeed in creating in one quarter of mankind this basic change of heart from Benthamite self-interest as the motivation of effort to socialist 'service before reward' it will indeed be a revolution of early Christian proportions. Succeeding generations alone will give the answer.

Good communications are always a potent factor in the promotion of unity. Their development in rail, road and air since 1949 has probably done more than any other material factor to bring the country together. The old differences and enmities between *Han Jen* of the north and *T'ang*

Jen of the south are giving way as ease of exchange of ideas and of trade have rapidly increased.

The development of communications is also playing an important part in bringing about more uniformity of speech. While the identical written language runs throughout the whole land and has been a potent factor in holding the country together, spoken Chinese in the various regions is so different as to constitute different languages. The northern Chinese are essentially Mandarin-speaking: the southerners mingle Cantonese with a vast number of dialects. Efforts are being made to develop both a common speech and a common cursive written script. The study of a form of Mandarin, having a distinct Hunan (Mao's native province) pronunciation, is compulsory in all schools, while a new romanization, *p'in yin*, has been introduced in an endeavour to provide China with an alphabet and written script. Research has also gone into the simplification of many Chinese characters (ideographs), thus reducing the time formerly spent on learning to read. Great energy is also being expended in the endeavour rapidly to make the entire people literate. The task of training an adequate teaching staff to meet all these educational demands is challenging in the extreme. Radio and television now play an ever-increasing part in the inculcation of communist Marxist–Leninist– Mao thought aimed at knitting all parts of the country into one thinking whole.

There are certain characteristics, which seem to be common to the Chinese, north, south, east and west. They are a practical, hard-working, persistent and philosophical people, capable of meeting and sustaining the bitter and exacting hardships which the present revolution towards the development of a modern, industrial, socialist state will continue to demand of them.

East, Spate and Fisher in their *The Changing Map of Asia*, writing of poverty and the population crisis in Asia say 'Yet conceivably the release of psychological energies, which normally accompanies great political revolutions, may lead to a social revolution. It is difficult to see this great and common problem can be met without one.' This would appear to be the contribution that modern China is making.

References

1 Mao Tse-tung, 'On contradiction', *Selected Works of Mao Tse-tung*, Vol. I (Peking, 1952); and *On the Correct Handling of Contradiction among the People* (Peking, 1957).
2 See Han Su-yin, *China in the Year 2001* (London, 1967), for a Chinese interpretation of Cultural Revolution.
3 Mao Tse-tung, *Report of an Investigation into the Peasant Movement in Hunan*, 1927.

Appendix

NOTES MADE AT A COOPERATIVE VILLAGE, KAO PEI TIEN, NEAR PEKING, DECEMBER 1955

1425 families; population 5855. 976 families are agricultural, cultivating 8500 *mow*.
Main products: maize, rice, wheat, cotton, potatoes.
Before Liberation poor peasants held av. 4·76 *mow*.

Land Reform, 1949.
   2260 *mow* confiscated
    260 rooms confiscated. N.B. rooms rather than houses
      6 carts
      7 draught animals
Before Liberation all fields were dry; produced 150–180 *catties/mow*.
Since Liberation, 260–400 *catties/mow* is maximum.
Increase of tools; draught animals (84–186); carts (49–150); also ploughs and harrows; 24 sprayers.
1954 started two Producer Co-ops of semi-socialistic character, consisting of 2530 *mow*, 313 families;
    1437 population of which 450 were men.
  Whole system voluntary; pooled land and divided income: 30 per cent according to land pooled; tools, carts etc. taken over at fixed price and paid in three years.

Administration
  Managing Committee
  Supervision Committee   }   all elected annually
  Chairman
  Vice-Chairman

4 Sub-committees concerned with production; Public safety; Finance; Culture and health.

5 Production teams, each with its own production area and garden team, fishing and house building.

Cultivation
  Before Liberation only one fertilization per annum; now 2 to 3; this, plus deep ploughing have given bumper harvests.

2 Kinds of maize, white and yellow:

430 *catties/mow* from white
328 *catties/mow* from yellow

No. 1 Producers Co-op. consists of 210 families; 80 per cent have increased their income in the year; many are applying for entry; at mass meeting 10 December 1955 475 additional families joined; 62 rich landlord families not eligible – may be admitted later.

No. 2 Producer Co-op. 887 families have joined; only 18 left out and 9 of these have applied. Living and cultural standards have gone up.

Education	Pre-Liberation	Now
Primary	234	918
Middle	—	830

No school fees but 4 *yuan/mow* term for heating, etc. 25 teachers.

People's Clinic and Health Centre.
Cultural House
Supply and Marketing Co-op.
Government Tax. Average of 20 *catties/mow*:
  Land – 3 grades fixed.
    (*a*) 150 *catties* and less exempt from tax
    (*b*) 210 *catties/mow*
    (*c*) 255 *catties/mow*
Wages according to working points, plus 30 per cent according to land contribution.
    Average earnings for one man: 300 *yuan* p.a.
    Family of two men and one woman (with four children): 700 *yuan* plus.
Spare Time School for Adults.

SOCIAL EXPENSES OF FARMERS IN THE NEW TERRITORIES, HONG KONG*

Funeral expenses of a farmer cultivating 2 hectares:

Item	Amount HK$	Remarks
Coffin	400	
Labourers	20	
White cloth	180	
White towels	50	
Rough fibre cloth	5	
Reporting	10	Sending messengers to friends and relatives
Good-luck presents	100	
Firecrackers	40	
Funeral feasts	675	27 tables @ HK$25·00 each
Miscellaneous	20	
	1500	

Wedding of a tenant farmer cultivating 1 hectare, five in family.

Item	Amount	Remarks
	HK$	
Ceremony money to bride's family	600	Part used as bride's dowry
Feasts	800	20 tables @ HK$40·00 each
Chinese band	50	
Sedan chair	10	
Firecrackers	30	
Raw meat for bride's family	80	Chicken, duck and pork
Gifts to bride's relatives	20	Generally to sisters and female relatives of bride
Incense and paper money (ancestor worship)	20	
Red paper scrolls	4	
Miscellaneous	40	
	1654	

The family received $300 as gifts from friends and relatives, so that the actual cost is HK$1354 (HK$16·00 = £1).

* D. Y. Lin, 'Report of 60 Families' 1955.

Select Bibliography

Adler, S., *The Chinese Economy*, Routledge & Kegan Paul, London, 1957.

Afanas'yeskiy, Y. A., *Szechwan*, Moscow, 1962.

Andersson, J. G., *Children of the Yellow Earth*, Routledge & Kegan Paul, London, 1934.

Balazs, E., *Chinese Civilization and Bureaucracy*, Yale University Press, New Haven, Connecticut, 1964.

Barbour, G. B., 'Recent observations on the loess of North China', *Geographical Journal*, 1935, nos 54–64.

'Physiographic history of the Yangtze', *Geographical Journal*, **87** (1936), p. 17.

Barnett, A. D., *China on the Eve of the Communist Takeover*, Thames & Hudson, London, 1963.

Belden, W. and Salter, M., 'Iron ore resources of China', *Economic Geography*, **2** (1935).

Bishop, C. W., 'The rise of civilization in China with reference to its geographical aspects', *Geographical Review*, **4** (1932), pp. 617–31.

'Beginnings of north and south in China', *Pacific Affairs*, **7**, no. 297 (1934).

Boone, A., 'The foreign trade of China', *China Quarterly*, no. 11 (July 1962).

Boorman, H. L., 'Mao Tse-tung: the lacquered image', *China Quarterly*, no. 16 (October 1963).

Buchanan, K., *The Transformation of the Chinese Earth*, Bell, London, 1970.

Buck, J. Lossing, *Land Utilization in China*, Commercial Press, Shanghai, 1937.

Buck, J. Lossing, Dawson, O. L. and Wu, Y. L., *Food and Agriculture in Communist China*, Hoover Institute, Praeger, New York and London, 1964.

Buxton, L. H. D. (ed.), *China, The Land and the People*, Oxford University Press, London, 1929.

Cable, M. and French, F., *The Gobi Desert*, Hodder & Stoughton, London, 1946.

Carles, W. R., 'The Yangtze-kiang', *Geographical Journal*, **12**, no. 225 (1898).

Chandrasekhar, S., *China's Population*, Hong Kong University Press, Hong Kong, 1959.

Communist China Today, Asia Publishing House, Bombay, 1962.

Chang Chih-yi, 'Land utilization and settlement possibilities in Sinkiang', *Geographical Review*, no. 39 (1949).

Chang, H. W., 'Grapes in the "Land of Fire"', *China Reconstructs*, Peking, July 1965.

Chang, J. H., 'The Chinese monsoon', *Geographical Review*, **61** (1971).

Chang, K. C., *The Archaeology of China*, Yale University Press, New Haven, Connecticut, 1963.

Chang, K. S., 'Geographical bases for industrial development in northwest China', *Economic Geography*, **39** (1963).

Chang Sun, 'The sea routes of the Yuan Dynasty, 1260–1341', *Acta Geographica Sinica*, **23** (1959).

Chavannes, E., *Les Mémoires historiques de Ssu-ma Ch'ien*, Leroux, Paris, 1898.

Chen Cheng, *Land Reform in Taiwan*, China Publishing Co., Taiwan, 1961.

Chen Cheng-siang, 'Population growth and urbanization in China, 1953–70', *Geographical Review*, **63** (1973).

Chen, Kenneth, 'Early expansion of Chinese geographical knowledge', *T'ien Hsia Monthly*, **2**, 52 (1940–1).

Chen, N. R., *Chinese Economic Statistics*, Aldine, New York, 1967.

Ch'en, J., *Mao and the Chinese Revolution*, Oxford University Press, London, 1965.

Cheng, C. Y., *Communist China's Economy, 1949–62*, Seton Hall University Press, South Grange, New Jersey, 1963.

Cheng Te Khun, 'An introduction to Chinese civilization', *Orient*, August–October 1950.

'Short history of Szechwan', *Journal of the West China Research Society*, no. 16 (1945).

Chi, C. J., 'Opening a vast coalfield', *China Reconstructs*, October 1964.

Chi, H. T. and Chang, Y. F., 'Carving out rivers in the hills', *China Reconstructs*, July 1965.

Chi, W. S., 'Water conservancy in Communist China', *China Quarterly*, no. 23 (July 1963).

Ch'i Ch'ao-ting, *Key Economic Area in Chinese History, as revealed in the Development of Public Works for Water Control*, Allen & Unwin, London, 1936.

Chiang Knoh, 'The tung region of China', *Economic Geography*, no. 418 (1943).

Chu Co-ching, 'The circulation of the atmosphere over China', *Memorandum on Meteorology*, no. 4, Nanking, China.

'The southeast monsoon and rainfall in China', *Journal of the Chinese Geographical Society*, 1, no. 1 (1934).

Chun Wen, 'China's farm machine-building industry', *Peking Review*, no. 26 (July 1963).

Collins, W. F., *Mineral Enterprise*, Probsthain, London, 1918.

Comber, E., *see* Han Su-yin.

Cornish, Vaughan, *The Great Capitals*, Methuen, London, 1922.

Cottrell, L., *The Tiger of Ch'in*, Evans, London, 1962; Pan, London, 1964.

Cowan, C. D. (ed.), *The Economic Development of China and Japan*, Allen, London, 1964.

Cranmer-Byng, J. L. (ed.), *An Embassy in China, being the Journal Kept by Lord Macartney, 1793–4*, Longmans, London, 1962.

Creel, G. H., *Studies in Early Chinese Culture*, Waverly, Baltimore, Maryland, 1937.

The Birth of China, Waverly, Baltimore, Maryland, 1937.

Cressey, G. B., *China's Geographical Foundations*, McGraw-Hill, New York, 1934.

Land of the 500 Million, McGraw-Hill, New York, 1955.

'Land forms of Chekiang', *Annals of the Association of American Geographers*, no. 259 (1938).

'The Ordos Desert of Inner Mongolia', *Denison University Bulletin*, 33, no. 8 (19).

Crook, D. and Crook, I., *Revolution in a Chinese Village*, Routledge & Kegan Paul, London, 1959.

Davies, R. M., *Yunnan, the Link between India and the Yangtze*, Cambridge University Press, Cambridge, 1909.

Davis, S. G., *Hong Kong in its Geographical Setting*, Collins, London, 1949.

The Geology of Hong Kong, Government Printer, Hong Kong, 1952.

(ed.), *Symposium on Land Use and Mineral Deposits in Hong Kong*, Hong Kong University Press, Hong Kong, 1964.

Deasy, G. F., 'Tung oil production and trade', *Economic Geography*, no. 260 (1940).

Donnithorne, A., 'China's economic planning and industry', *China Quarterly*, no. 17 (January 1964).

'Economic development in China', *World Today*, 17, no. 4 (1961).

China's Economic System, Allen & Unwin, London, 1967.

Drake, F. S., 'The Struggle for the Tarim Basin in the Later Han Dynasty', *Journal of the Royal Asiatic Society* (North China Branch), (1935).

East, W., Spate, O. and Fisher, C., *The Changing Map of Asia*, Methuen, London, 1971.

Eberhard, W., *History of China*, Routledge & Kegan Paul, London, 1947.

Endicott, G. B., *A History of Hong Kong*, Oxford University Press, London, 1958.

Erselcuk, M., 'Iron and steel industry in China', *Economic Geography*, 32 (1956).

Fei Hsiao-tung, *Peasant Life in China*, Routledge & Kegan Paul, London, 1947.

Fei Hsiao-tung and Chang, C. I., *Earthbound China: A Study of Rural Economy in Yunnan*, University of Chicago Press, Chicago, 1945.

Fenzel, G., 'On the natural conditions affecting the introduction of forestry in the Province of Kwangtung', *Lingnan Science Journal*, no. 7 (1929).

Ferguson, J. C., 'The southern migration of the Sung Dynasty', *Journal of the Royal Asiatic Society* (North China Branch), no. 55 (1924).

Feuerwerker, A., *China's Early Industrialization: Sheng Hsuan-huai and Mandarin Enterprise*, 'Harvard East Asia Studies', Harvard University Press, Cambridge, Massachusetts, 1958.

Fitzgerald, C. P., 'The Yunnan–Burma Road', *Geographical Journal*, 95, no. 161 (1940).

'The tiger's leap', *Geographical Journal*, 98, no. 147 (1941).

'The Tali District of West Yunnan', *Geographical Journal*, 99, no. 50 (1942).

The Birth of Communist China, Penguin, Harmondsworth, 1964.

Evolution of China, Cresset Press, London, 1952.

Flood Tide in China, Cresset Press, London, 1958.

The Chinese View of their Place in the World, Oxford University Press, London, 1964.

Foord, E., 'China and the destruction of the Roman Empire', *Contemporary Review*, 94, no. 207 (1908).

Fox, R., *Genghis Khan*, Lane, London, 1936.

Freeberne, M., 'Birth control in China', *Population Studies*, 18, no. 1 (1964).

'Demographic and economic changes in Sinkiang Uighur Autonomous Region', *Population Studies*, 20, no. 1 (1960).

Gamble, S. D., *Ting Hsien: a North China Rural Community*, Institute of Pacific Relations, New York, 1954.

Geil, W. E., *The Eighteen Capitals of China*, Constable, London, 1911.

The Great Wall of China, Constable, London, 1909.

Gherzi, E., *Climatological Atlas of East Asia*, Commercial Press, Shanghai, 1944.

Giles, H. A., *The Travels of Fa Hsien*, Cambridge University Press, Cambridge, 1923.

Ginsburg, N. S., 'Ch'ing-tao: development and land use', *Economic Geography*, no. 181 (1948).

'China's changing political geography', *Geographical Review*, no. 102 (1952).

Glass, S., 'Some aspects of Formosa's economic growth', *China Quarterly*, no. 15 (July 1963).

Gorbunova, M. N., 'Natural conditions and agricultural development of the Province of Szechwan', in Zaychikov, V. T. (ed.), *The Geography of Agriculture in Communist China*, U.S. Joint Publications Research Service, Moscow, 1959.

Gourou, P., *The Tropical World*, Longmans, London, 1954.

Grabau, A. W., *The Stratigraphy of China*, Peking, 1925.

Granet, M., *Chinese Civilization*, Routledge & Kegan Paul, London, 1930.

Grazdanzev, A. J., 'Manchuria, 1945: an industrial survey', *Pacific Affairs*, **18** (December 1945).

Green, A., *Asian Frontiers: Studies in a Continuing Problem*, Pall Mall, London, 1968.

Greene, F., *The Wall Has Two Sides*, Cape, London, 1961.

A Curtain of Ignorance, Cape, London, 1966.

Han Su-yin, *The Crippled Tree*, Cape, London, 1965.

A Mortal Flower, Cape, London, 1966.

China in the Year 2001, Watts, London, 1967.

Hare, F. K., *The Restless Atmosphere*, Hutchinson, London, 1953.

Heenan, B., 'Chinese petroleum industry', *Far Eastern Economic Review*, nos 5, 13 and 16 (1965).

Herrmann, A., *An Historical Atlas of China*, Edinburgh University Press, Edinburgh, 1966.

Hirst, F., 'The story of Chang Ch'ien, China's pioneer in West Africa', *Journal of the American Oriental Society*, 1917.

Ho Ping-ti, *Studies in the Population of China, 1268–1953*, Harvard University Press, Cambridge, Massachusetts, 1959.

Hong Kong: Report for the Year (annual), Government Printer, Hong Kong.

Hsia, R., *Economic Planning and Development in Communist China*, Institute of Pacific Relations, New York, 1955.

'Changes in location of China's steel industry', *China Quarterly*, no. 17 (January 1964).

Hsieh, C. M., *Taiwan – ilha Formosa*, Butterworth, London, 1964.

Hu, H. Y., 'Vegetation in China with special reference to the main soil types', *Report of the Sixth International Congress of Soil Science*, 1956.

Hu, C. Y., 'Land use in the Szechwan Basin', *Geographical Review*, **23** (1947), p. 152

Hu Huan-yung, 'A geographical sketch of Kiangsu Province', *Geographical Review*, **23** (1947), pp. 609–17.

Hudson, G. F., *Europe and China*, Arnold, London, 1931.

Hughes, E. R., *The Invasion of China by the Western World*, Black, London, 1937.

Hughes, R., *The Chinese Commune*, Bodley Head, London, 1960.

Hughes, R. H., 'Hong Kong: an urban study', *Geographical Journal*, **117**, (1951), pp. 1–31.

Hughes, T. J. and Luard, D. E. T., *The Economic Development of Communist China, 1949–58*, Royal Institute of International Affairs/Oxford University Press, London, 1959.

Hung Fu, 'The geographical regions of China and their subdivisions', *International Geographical Union Proceedings*, 1952.

Huntingdon, E., *The Pulse of Asia*, Wiley, Boston, Massachusetts, 1910.

James, H. F., 'Industrial China', *Economic Geography*, (1929), pp. 1–22.

Jen, M. N., 'Agricultural landscape of southwest China', *Economic Geography*, **24**, (1948) pp. 157–69.

Jones, F. O., 'Tunkiangyien: China's ancient irrigation system', *Geographical Review* (1954).

Kang Chao, 'Growth of the construction industry in Communist China', *China Quarterly*, no. 22 (April 1965).

'Pitfalls in the use of China's trade statistics', *China Quarterly*, no. 19 (July 1964).

Kao, K. C., 'Great Strides forward in fertilizers', *China Review*, February 1965.

Kendrew, W. G., 'Climate', in Buxton, L. H. D. (ed.), *China, The Land and the People*, Oxford University Press, London, 1929.

King, F. A. A., *A Concise Economic History of Modern China, 1840–1961*, Vora, Bombay, 1968.

King, F. H., *Farmers of Forty Centuries*, Harcourt Brace, New York, 1926.

Kingdom-Ward, F., 'Tibet as a grazing land', *Geographical Journal*, **1** (1947).

Kirby, E. S., *Introduction to the Economic History of China*, Allen & Unwin, London, 1954.

Komroff, M. (ed.), *The Journey of Friar John of Plano Carpini to the Court of Kuyak Khan, 1245–7*, Cape, London, 1929.

Kuo, L. T. C., 'Agricultural mechanization in China', *China Quarterly*, no. 17 (January 1964).

Kuo Ping-chia, *China: New Age and New Outlook*, Penguin, Harmondsworth, 1960.

Kuo Ts'ung-fei, 'Brief history of the trade routes between Burma, Indo-China and Yunnan', *T'ien Hsia Monthly*, **12** (1940–1).

Lamb, A., *Asian Frontiers*, London, 1968.

Latourette, K. S., *The Chinese: Their History and Culture*, Macmillan, New York, 1956.

Lattimore, O., 'Inner Asian approach to the historical geography of China', *Geographical Journal*, **110** (1947), pp. 180–6.

'Return to China's northern frontiers', *Geographical Journal*, **139** (1973).

'Chinese colonization in Manchuria', *Geographical Review*, **2** (1932), pp. 117–93.

Collected Papers, 1928–58, London, 1962.

Inner Asian Frontiers, Oxford University Press, London, 1940.

Lee, H. K., 'Korean migrants in Manchuria', *Geographical Review*, **22** (1932), pp. 196–204.

Lee, J. S., *The Geology of China*, Murby, London, 1939.

Legge, J., *The Chinese Classics* (5 vols), London, 1961–1972.

Li, C. M., *The Economic Development of Communist China*, University of California Press, Berkeley, California, 1959.

The Statistical System of Communist China, University of California Press, Berkeley, California, 1962.

Lin En-lau, 'The Ho-si corridor (Kansu panhandle)', *Economic Geography*, **28** (1952), pp. 51–6.

Lin, N. J., 'Population problems in China', *Contemporary China*, Vol. I: 1956–7, Hong Kong University Press, Hong Kong, 1958.

Lindsay, T. J., 'Water conservancy in China', *Contemporary China*, Vol. I: 1956–7, Hong Kong University Press, Hong Kong, 1958.

Ling Sheng, 'Rapid development of civil aviation', *Shih-shih Shou-tse* [*Current Events*], no. 9 (1964).

Lippit, V., 'Development of transportation in Communist China', *China Quarterly*, no. 27 (July 1966).

Little, A., *The Far East*, Oxford University Press, London, 1905.

Liu, J. C., 'Fertilizer application in Communist China', *China Quarterly*, no. 27 (July 1966).

Ma, Y. C., 'General principles of geographical distribution of Chinese soils', *Report of the Sixth International Congress of Soil Science*, 1956.

Macdougall, C., 'City of steel', *Far Eastern Economic Review*, 11 November 1965.

'Industrial upsurge', *Far Eastern Economic Review*, 30 September 1965.

'Production reports', *Far Eastern Economic Review*, 29 September 1966.

Mallory, W. H., *China, Land of Famine*, American Geographical Society, New York, 1926.

Mancall, M., 'The Kiakhta trade', in Cowan, C. D. (ed.), *The Economic Development of China and Japan*, Allen, London, 1964.

Mao Tse-tung, *Selected Works*, 4 vols, Foreign Language Press, Peking, 1962.

The Question of Agricultural Cooperation, Foreign Language Press, Peking, 1962.

On Contradiction, Foreign Language Press, Peking, 1960.

On Practice, Foreign Language Press, Peking, 1964.

Myrdal, J., *Report from a Chinese Village*, Heinemann, London, 1965.

Myrdal, J. and Gun, Lessle, *China: The Revolution Continued*, Pelican, Harmondsworth, 1973.

Needham, J., *Science and Civilization in China*, Vol. I, Cambridge University Press, Cambridge, 1954.

'Science and China's influence in the world', in Dawson, R. (ed.), *The Legacy of China*, Clarendon Press, Oxford, 1964.

Ovdiyenko, and Kalmykova, V. G., *Geographical Survey of Northwest China*, U.S. Joint Publications Research Service, Moscow, 1957.

Pao, K. P., 'The role of electric power in the national economy', *Hsin Chien-she* [*New Construction*], no. 4 (20 April 1965).

Payne, R., *Portrait of a Revolutionary: Mao Tse-tung*, Abelard-Schumann, New York, 1961.

Perkins, D. H., *Market Control and Planning in Communist China*, Harvard University Press, Cambridge, Massachusetts, 1966.

'A Conference on Agriculture', *China Quarterly*, no. 67, September 1976.

Philips, R. W. and Kuo, L. T. C., 'Agricultural science and its application', *China Quarterly*, no. 6 (April 1961).

Physical Geography of China, Institute of Geography, U.S.S.R. Academy of Science, Vols I & II, Praeger, New York and London, 1969.

Purcell, V., *The Chinese in Southeast Asia*, Oxford University Press, London, 1951.

Radhakrishnan, S., *India and China*, Hind Kitab, Bombay, 1947.

Ramage, C. S., 'Evapotranspiration measurements made in Hong Kong', First Report, Technical Notes no. 7, Royal Observatory, Hong Kong, 1953.

Read, T. T., 'Economic–geographic aspects of China's iron industry', *Geographical Review*, **1**, (1943), pp. 42–55.

Regis, G., 'Developments in Chinese agriculture', *Far Eastern Trade*, January 1962.

Richardon, H. L., 'Szechwan during the war', *Geographical Journal*, (1945).

Richthofen, F. von, 'On the mode of origin of the loess', *Geographical Magazine*, 1882.

Riencourt, A. de, *The Soul of China*, Cape, London, 1959.

Rogers, A., 'Manchurian iron and steel industry and its resource base', *Geographical Review*, (1948).

Rose, J., 'Sinjao, a Chinese commune', *Geography*, **51**, no. 233 (1966).

'Hong Kong's water supply problem and China's contribution to its solution', *Geographical Review*, **56**, no. 3 (1966).

Roxby, P. M., 'The distribution of population in China', *Geographical Review*, **3**, (1936), p. 506.

'The expansion of China', *Scottish Geographical Magazine*, 1930.

'China as an entity: the comparison with Europe', *Geography*, 1934.

Schoff, W. H., 'Navigation to the Far East under the Roman Empire', *Journal of the American Oriental Society*, 1917.

'Some aspects of oriental trade at the beginning of the Christian era', *Journal of the American Oriental Society*, 1915.

Schomberg, R. C. F., 'The habitability of Chinese Turkestan', *Geographical Journal*, **79** (1932), pp. 368–78.

Schram, S., *Mao Tse-tung*, Penguin, Harmondsworth, 1966.

Shabad, T., *China's Changing Map*, Methuen, London, 1972.

Shang, C. L. and Mu, C. P., 'Fifteen years of agricultural mechanization of state farms', *Technology of Agricultural Machinery*, no. 11, Peking, 1964.

Shen, T. H., *Agricultural Resources of China*, Cornell University Press, New York, 1951.

Shinkichi Eto, 'Hai-lu-feng – the first Chinese Soviet Government', *China Quarterly*, no. 8 (October 1961).

Shu, T. H., 'The function and power of production teams in production administration', *Kung-jen Jih-pao*, Peking, July 1961.

Smith, W., *Iron and Coal in China*, Liverpool University Press, Liverpool, 1926.

Snow, E., *Red Star over China*, Random House, New York, 1938.

The Side of the River, Gollancz, London, 1962.

The Long Revolution, Hutchinson, London, 1972.

Spencer, J. E., 'Salt in China', *Geographical Review*, **25** (1935), p. 162.

Stamp, L. D., *Asia*, Methuen, London, 1957.

State Statistical Bureau, *Ten Great Years*, Foreign Language Press, Peking, 1960.

Stein, Sir Aurel, *Innermost Asia*, 2 vols, Oxford University Press, London, 1928.

Stevenson, P. H., 'Note on the human geography of the Chinese–Tibetan borderland', *Geographical Review*, **20** (1952).

Stewart, J. R., 'Manchuria, the land and its economy', *Economic Geography*, **22** (1932), pp. 599–616.

Su Ming, 'Forestry in New China', *Jen-min Tsung-pao*, 16 November 1960.

Su. T. S., 'Irrigation renews the land', *China Reconstructs*, November 1964.

Sun Ching-chih, *Economic Geography of East China Region*, U.S. Joint Publications Research Service, Peking, 1961.

Economic Geography of Central China, U.S. Joint Publications Research Service, Peking, 1960.

Economic Geography of Kwangtung, U.S. Joint Publications Research Service, Peking, 1958.

Economic Geography of Southwest China, U.S. Joint Publications Research Service, Peking, 1960.

Economic Geography of Inner Mongolia, U.S. Joint Publications Research Service, Peking, 1957.

Economic Geography of Northeast China, U.S. Joint Publications Research Service, Peking, 1959.

Szczepanik, E., *The Economic Growth of Hong Kong*, Oxford University Press, London, 1958.

Tang, H. S., 'Highlights of land reform in Taiwan', *Joint Commission on Rural Reconstruction*, Taipei, 1957.

T'ang, Y. J., 'Animal husbandry's place in the national economy', *Hsin Chien-she* [*New Construction*], no. 12 (December 1964).

Tawney, R. H., *Land and Labour in China*, Allen, London, 1932.

Teggart, F. J., *Rome and China: a Study of Correlations in Historical Events*, University of California Press, Berkeley, California, 1939.

Teilhard de Chardin, P., *Letters from a Traveller*, Collins, London, 1957.

Ten Great Years, see State Statistical Bureau.

Teng Tse-hui, *Report on the Multiple-purpose Plan for Permanently Controlling the Yellow River*, Foreign Language Press, Peking, 1955.

Thompson, B. W., 'An essay on the general circulation of the atmosphere over southeast Asia', *Quarterly Journal of the Meteorological Society*, **77** (1951).

Tregear, T. R., *Land Use in Hong Kong and the New Territories*, Hong Kong University Press, Hong Kong, 1958.

Tregear, T. R. and Berry, L., *The Development of Hong Kong and Kowloon as Told in Maps*, Hong Kong University Press, Hong Kong, 1959.

Trewatha, G. T., 'Chinese cities: numbers and distribution'; 'Chinese cities: origins and functions', *Annals of the Association of American Geographers*, 1951 and 1952.

Tsai, S. L., 'The Long March', *China Reconstructs*, **14**, no. 10.

Tu Chang-wang, 'China's weather and world oscillation', *National Research Institute of Meteorology*, Vol. II, 1937.

Tu Chang-wang and Hwang Sze-sung, 'The advance and retreat of the summer monsoon in China', *Meteorology Magazine*, **18** (1944).

Tu, H. H., 'Breeding freshwater fish', *China Reconstructs*, June 1966.

U.S. Congress Joint Economic Committee, *An Economic Profile of Mainland China*, Washington, D.C., 1967.

U.S. State Department, *United States' Relations with China*, Washington, D.C., 1949.

Valkenburg, S., 'Agricultural regions of China', *Economic Geography* (1934).

Walker, K. R., 'Collectivization in retrospect', *China Quarterly*, no. 26 (April 1966).

'A Chinese discussion on planning for balanced growth – a summary of the views of Ma Yin-Ch'u and his critics', in Cowan, C. D. (ed.), *The Economic Development of China and Japan*, Allen, London, 1964.

Wang, C., 'China state farms – production bases of farm and animal products', *Peking Review*, 28 April 1961.

Wang, K. P., 'Mineral resources of China with special reference to the nonferrous metals', *Geographical Review*, **34** (1944).

Waring, H. W. A., *Steel Review*, British Iron and Steel Federation, London, 1961.

Watson, F., *The Frontiers of China*, London, 1966.

Wilson, D., *A Quarter of Mankind*, Weidenfeld & Nicolson, London, 1966.

Wilson, E. H., *A Naturalist in West China*, Methuen, London, 1913.

Wiens, H. J., *China's March towards the Tropics*, Shoe String Press, Hampden, Connecticut, 1954.

'The Shu Tao or road to Szechwan', *Geographical Review* (1949).

Wint, G., *Dragon and Sickle*, Pall Mall, London, 1958.

Wu, C. C. et al., *Economic Geography of the Western Region of the Middle Yellow River*, U.S. Joint Publications Research Service, Peking, 1956.

Wu, Y. L., *The Steel Industry in Communist China*, Hoover Institute, Stanford, California, 1965.

Economic Development and Use of Energy Resources in Communist China, Hoover Institute, Stanford, California, 1963.

Yang Min, 'Mechanizing rice planting', *Peking Review*, 5 July 1963.

Yang, M. C., *A Chinese Village – Taitou, Shantung*, Routledge & Kegan Paul, London, 1946.

Yang, P. H., 'How China conquered inflation', *People's China*, June 1960.

Yao, S. Y., 'Geographical distribution of floods and droughts in Chinese history, 206 BC–AD 1911', *Far Eastern Quarterly*, August 1934.

Yetts, W. P., 'Links between China and the West', *Geographical Review*, (1926).

Yule, Sir H., *The Book of Ser Marco Polo, the Venetian*, Murray, London, 1920.

Zaychikov, V. T. (ed.), *The Geography of Agriculture in Communist China*, U.S. Joint Publications Research Service, Moscow, 1959.

ATLASES

Gherzi, E., *Climatological Atlas of East Asia*, Shanghai, 1944.

CIA People's Republic of China Atlas, U.S. Government Printing Office, Washington, D.C., 1971.

Hsieh Chiao-minh, *Atlas of China*, McGraw-Hill, New York, 1975.

Herrmann, A., *An Historical Atlas of China*, Edinburgh University Press, Edinburgh, 1966.

Lu, A., *The Climatological Atlas of China*, Central Weather Bureau, Nanking, 1946.

The Times Atlas of the World, Vol. I (1958): World, Australasia and East Asia.

The Times Atlas of China, London, 1974.

PERIODICALS

The China Quarterly
Asia Quarterly
Journal of Asian Studies (formerly *Far Eastern Quarterly*)
Far East Trade
Far Eastern Economic Review
Pacific Affairs
Pacific Viewpoint
Current Scene
translations from China Mainland Press (New China News Agency), selections from China Mainland magazines, and current background

Peking publications:

Peking Review (weekly)
China Reconstructs (monthly)
China's Foreign Trade (bi-monthly)

Conversion Tables

li	one-third mile
mow	0·06 hectare; 0·165 acre
chin or *catty*	one and one-third lb.
picul	100 *chin*; 133 lb.
tan	100 *chin* or one man's load
tael (Haikwan)	583·3 grains silver
yuan	6·857 *yuan* equal £1 sterling
1 *kilometre*	0·621 miles
1 *sq. metre*	10·763 sq. ft.; 1·196 sq. yd.
1 *sq. yd.*	0·836 sq. metres
1 *sq. ft.*	0·093 sq. metres
1 *hectare*	2·471 acres
1 *acre*	0·405 hectares
1 *sq. mile*	2·589 sq. kilometres
1 *sq. km.*	0·386 sq. miles
1 *lb.*	0·454 kilograms
1 *kilogram*	2·205 lb.

Index